에듀윌 토익 베이직
READING RC

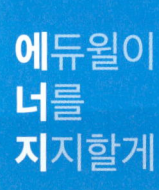

세상을 움직이려면
먼저 나 자신을 움직여야 한다.

– 소크라테스(Socrates)

머리말

영어의 플라이휠(flywheel)을 돌려라

어렸을 때 팽이를 돌려본 기억이 있나요?
손가락을 비틀어 힘껏 돌리면 핑그르르, 바라보고 있는 모든 이들을 빨아들일 것처럼 힘차게 팽이가 돌아갑니다. 그렇게 한참을 돌다가 어느 순간 마찰력에 의해 멈춰버리지요. 발명가적 기질이 있는 친구라면 한번쯤 이런 엉뚱한 생각을 해 봤을 것입니다. 멈추지 않는 팽이를 만들 수는 없을까?

누군가의 그런 엉뚱한 생각이 지금의 자동차 엔진에 쓰이는 플라이휠(flywheel)의 시초라고 볼 수 있습니다. 플라이휠은 '떠 있는 바퀴'라는 뜻으로 외부 힘에 의존하지 않고 관성만으로 회전운동을 합니다. 처음에는 상당량의 추진력을 필요로 하지만 어느 정도 가속도가 붙으면 알아서 돌아가게 되죠. 아마존의 창업자 제프 베이조스(Jeff Bezos)는 이러한 원리를 경영 전략에 도입하여 큰 성공을 거두기도 했습니다. 처음에는 막대한 인프라 투자를 필요로 하지만 일단 낮은 가격으로 소비자를 끌어 모으면 공급자가 몰려들고, 공급자가 많아지면 다시 수요가 증가하는 교차 네트워크 효과를 통해 나중에는 큰 비용을 들이지 않고도 지속적인 경쟁 우위를 유지할 수 있다는 원리였습니다.

이러한 관성의 힘은 세상의 다양한 권력이 기득권을 유지하는 원리이기도 합니다. 우리가 토익을 공부하는 이유도 이 힘에서 비롯합니다. 기업은 토익을 통해 인재 채용에 들이는 거래비용을 최소화할 수 있고, 취직을 해야 하는 학생의 입장에서도 영어 공부를 할 바에야 기업에서 요구하는 토익을 하는 게 효율적입니다. 이 단순한 이해관계가 맞물려 회전력을 얻고 나니 토익은 마침내 용빼지 않고도 오랜 기간 영어 평가 시험에서 독점적 지위를 유지할 수 있게 된 것입니다.

하지만 그러한 구조를 불평만 하고 있을 필요는 없습니다. 여러분도 영어 공부로 자신만의 플라이휠을 구축해 보시기 바랍니다. 언어야말로 어느 정도의 궤도에 오르면 축적된 실력이 쉽게 줄지 않을 뿐더러 가속도가 붙어 더 많은 표현을 더 빨리 습득할 수 있게 됩니다. 다만 그 궤도에 오르려면 처음에 적지 않은 공력을 필요로 합니다. 영어 학습에서 소위 '조금씩 꾸준히'가 먹히는 시점은 충분한 몰입과 제대로 된 공부를 통해 이 플라이휠을 얻고 난 후가 됩니다. 토익 역시 예외가 아니며, 이것이 바로 입문서가 중요한 이유이기도 합니다.

모든 시험이 그러하듯 토익 역시 요령이 필요합니다. 요령이라는 것은 오랜 경험을 통해 터득한 노하우로, 알면 시간과 노력을 줄여주고 모르면 손해를 봅니다. 하지만, 요령이 제 기능을 발휘하려면 기본기가 튼튼해야 합니다. 기본이 없는 요령은 늘 돌다리도 두드리며 건너야 하는 불안한 심리를 만듭니다. 이번에 처음 선보이는 에듀윌 토익 입문서는 요령을 홀대하지 않되, 대들보를 놓고 서까래를 얹듯 영어의 기본을 탄탄하게 하는 데 역점을 두었습니다. 그래서 처음에는 조금 더디고 힘에 부칠 수도 있습니다. 하지만 잊지 마세요. 공부 역시 플라이휠과 같은 회전력을 얻으려면 처음에 들이는 공력이 절대적이라는 걸! 그 플라이휠을 얻고 나면 여러 책과 강의실을 전전하지 않아도 됩니다. 어쩌면 토익 고득점을 얻는 것에 그치지 않고 영어를 평생 여러분의 성공 무기로 삼게 될 수도 있을 것입니다. 부디 에듀윌 토익 입문서 RC와 LC가 그 플라이휠의 든든한 두 축이 되어주길 바라 봅니다.

에듀윌 어학연구소 드림

목차

WARM-UP
- 품사의 종류 ………………………………………………………… 016
- 구와 절 ……………………………………………………………… 017
- 이야기로 익히는 문장 구조 ………………………………………… 018

PART 5·6

UNIT 01	명사 ……………………………………………………… 022
UNIT 02	대명사 …………………………………………………… 038
UNIT 03	동사 ……………………………………………………… 054
UNIT 04	수 일치 …………………………………………………… 068
UNIT 05	시제 ……………………………………………………… 082
UNIT 06	태 ………………………………………………………… 100
UNIT 07	형용사와 부사 …………………………………………… 114
UNIT 08	전치사 …………………………………………………… 130
UNIT 09	to부정사 ………………………………………………… 146
UNIT 10	동명사 …………………………………………………… 162
UNIT 11	분사 ……………………………………………………… 178
UNIT 12	등위 접속사와 부사절 접속사 …………………………… 192

UNIT 13	명사절 접속사	210
UNIT 14	가정법	224
UNIT 15	관계사	238
UNIT 16	비교 구문	254

PART 7

UNIT 17	문제 유형별 (1)	270
UNIT 18	문제 유형별 (2)	284
UNIT 19	지문 유형별 (1)	298
UNIT 20	지문 유형별 (2)	314

실전 모의고사 — 330

정답 및 해설

이 책의 구성과 특징

PART 5·6

❶ 개념 잡기

스피드 진단 테스트
간단한 토익 기출 변형 문제를 풀어 보고, 곧 학습하게 될 문법 개념을 아는지 모르는지 확인하세요. 틀린 문제가 있다면 해당 문법 개념은 더 꼼꼼하게 학습하도록 합니다.

기초 문법 개념 잡기
해당 유닛을 본격적으로 학습하기 전에 꼭 알아야 할 기초 개념을 학습하세요.

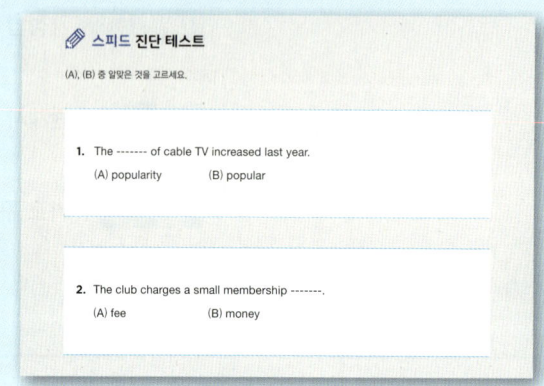

❷ 개념 다지기

간단한 예문으로 접근하는 문법 개념
구구절절한 설명은 그만! 단순한 예문으로 복잡한 문법 개념을 이해하기 쉽게 정리했습니다.

연습문제
토익 기출 변형 문제를 풀면서 학습한 내용을 실전에 적용하는 연습을 해 보세요.

❸ 빈출 유형 풀이 전략

토익에 가장 자주 출제되는 유형을 골라 단계별 풀이 과정을 보여 주었습니다. 문제를 풀 때 어디부터 어떻게 접근해야 하는지 막막했다면 풀이 전략 페이지에서 제시하는 단계를 차근차근 밟아 보세요. 토익 문제가 마냥 복잡하고 어려워 보이더라도 풀이 과정만 따라하면 입문자도 어렵지 않게 문제를 풀 수 있어요.

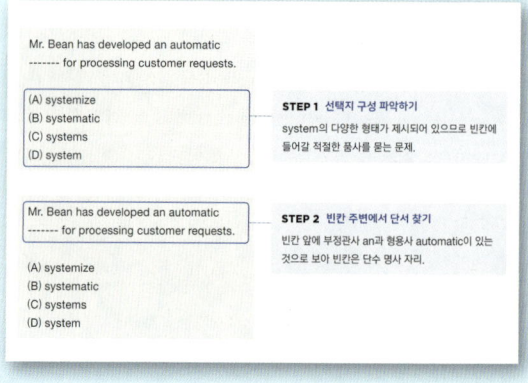

④ 빈출 어휘 학습

어휘 리스트
Part 5에서 정답이나 오답으로 출제된 어휘만 엄선하여 입문자가 학습에 부담을 느끼지 않도록 한 Unit에 16개 단어만 담았습니다. 하루에 단어를 몇십 개 이상씩 외우는 게 부담이 된다면 어휘 리스트에 있는 단어들만이라도 꼭 암기하세요.

연습문제
토익 기출 변형 문제를 풀면서 학습 내용을 확인하세요.

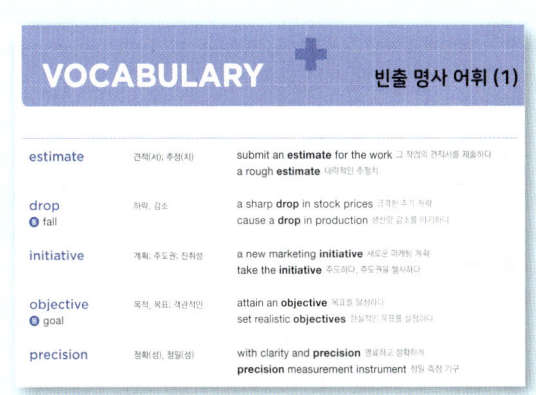

⑤ 기출 변형 문제로 실전 완벽 대비

5개년 토익 기출 문제를 완벽 분석하여 기출 경향에 맞는 문제를 출제했습니다. 앞에서 배운 문법 개념과 문제 풀이 전략을 적용하여 문제를 풀어 보세요.

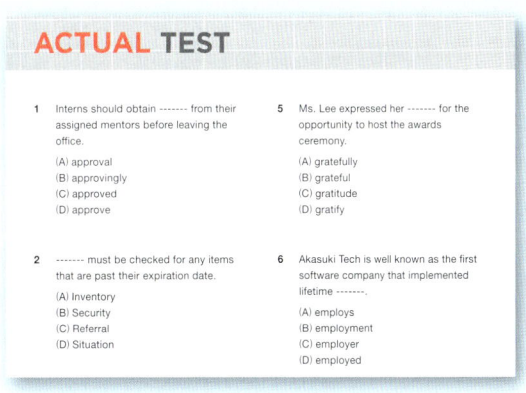

PART 7

Part 7은 문제 유형과 지문 유형으로 나누어 구성했습니다. 문제 유형 단원에서는 3단계 스텝에 따라 문제를 파악하고 지문 속 단서를 찾는 스킬을, 지문 유형 단원에서는 토익에 고정적으로 출제되는 지문 양식들의 기본 구조와 빈출 표현들을 집중적으로 학습하여 독해 시간을 대폭 단축시킬 수 있게 하였습니다.
또한 지문의 표현이 선택지에 패러프레이즈로 출제되는 Part 7의 특징을 반영하여 이를 충분히 연습할 수 있도록 패러프레이징 문제 풀이 과정을 담았으며, 미니 테스트와 ACTUAL TEST를 통해 배운 내용들을 충분히 숙지할 수 있게 하였습니다.

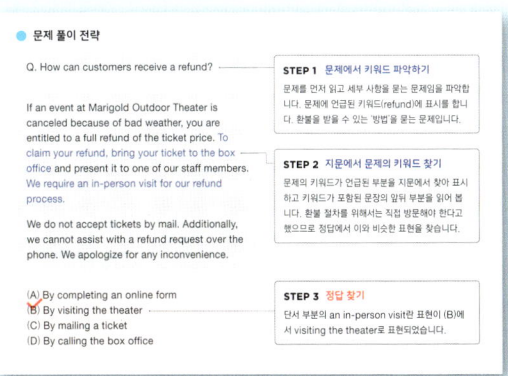

학습 일정표

2주 완성 학습 일정표

	Day 1	Day 2	Day 3	Day 4	Day 5	Day 6	Day 7
1주	Unit 01	Unit 02	Unit 03 Unit 04	Unit 05 Unit 06	Unit 07 Unit 08	Unit 09 Unit 10	Unit 11 Unit 12
	월 일	월 일	월 일	월 일	월 일	월 일	월 일

	Day 8	Day 9	Day 10	Day 11	Day 12	Day 13	Day 14
2주	Unit 13 Unit 14	Unit 15 Unit 16	Unit 17	Unit 18	Unit 19	Unit 20	실전 모의고사
	월 일	월 일	월 일	월 일	월 일	월 일	월 일

**If it doesn't challenge you,
it doesn't change you.**

도전 의식을 일으키는 일이 아니라면,
당신을 변화시키지 못한다.

4주 완성 학습 일정표

	Day 1	Day 2	Day 3	Day 4	Day 5
1주	Unit 01 월 일	Unit 02 월 일	Unit 03 월 일	Unit 04 월 일	Unit 05 월 일

	Day 6	Day 7	Day 8	Day 9	Day 10
2주	Unit 06 월 일	Unit 07 월 일	Unit 08 월 일	Unit 09 월 일	Unit 10 월 일

	Day 11	Day 12	Day 13	Day 14	Day 15
3주	Unit 11 월 일	Unit 12 월 일	Unit 13 Unit 14 월 일	Unit 15 월 일	Unit 16 월 일

	Day 16	Day 17	Day 18	Day 19	Day 20
4주	Unit 17 월 일	Unit 18 월 일	Unit 19 월 일	Unit 20 월 일	**실전 모의고사** 월 일

TOEIC 소개

🔹 토익이란?

TOEIC은 Test of English for International Communication(국제적인 의사소통을 위한 영어 시험)의 약자로, 영어가 모국어가 아닌 사람들이 비즈니스 현장 및 일상생활에서 필요한 실용 영어 능력을 갖추었는가를 평가하는 시험입니다.

● 시험 구성

구성	파트		문항 수		시간	배점
Listening Comprehension	Part 1	사진 묘사	6	100	45분	495점
	Part 2	질의 응답	25			
	Part 3	짧은 대화	39			
	Part 4	짧은 담화	30			
Reading Comprehension	Part 5	단문 빈칸 채우기	30	100	75분	495점
	Part 6	장문 빈칸 채우기	16			
	Part 7	독해 - 단일 지문	29			
		이중 지문	10			
		삼중 지문	15			
합계	7 Parts		200문항		120분	990점

● 출제 범위 및 주제

업무 및 일상생활에서 쓰이는 실용적인 주제들이 출제됩니다. 특정 문화나 특정 직업 분야에만 해당되는 주제는 출제하지 않으며, 듣기 평가의 경우 미국, 영국, 호주 등 다양한 국가의 발음이 섞여 출제됩니다.

일반 업무	계약, 협상, 영업, 홍보, 마케팅, 사업 계획
금융/재무	예산, 투자, 세금, 청구, 회계
개발	연구, 제품 개발
제조	공장 경영, 생산 조립 라인, 품질 관리
인사	채용, 승진, 퇴직, 직원 교육, 입사 지원
사무실	회의, 메모/전화/팩스/이메일, 사무 장비 및 가구
행사	학회, 연회, 회식, 시상식, 박람회, 제품 시연회
부동산	건축, 부동산 매매/임대, 기업 부지, 전기/수도/가스 설비
여행/여가	교통수단, 공항/역, 여행 일정, 호텔 및 자동차 예약/연기/취소, 영화, 전시, 공연

● 접수 방법

- 한국 TOEIC 위원회 사이트(www.toeic.co.kr)에서 인터넷 접수 기간을 확인하고 접수합니다.
- 시험 접수 시 최근 6개월 이내에 촬영한 jpg 형식의 사진 파일이 필요하므로 미리 준비합니다.
- 시험 10~12일 전부터는 특별 추가 접수 기간에 해당하여 추가 비용이 발생하므로, 접수 일정을 미리 확인하여 정기 접수 기간 내에 접수하도록 합니다.

● 시험 당일 준비물

- 신분증: 주민등록증, 운전면허증, 기간 만료 전 여권, 공무원증 등 규정 신분증만 인정
  (중 · 고등학생의 경우 학생증, 청소년증도 인정)
- 필기구: 연필, 지우개 (볼펜, 사인펜은 사용 불가)

● 시험 진행

오전 시험	오후 시험	진행 내용
09:30 – 09:45	02:30 – 02:45	답안지 작성 오리엔테이션
09:45 – 09:50	02:45 – 02:50	쉬는 시간
09:50 – 10:05	02:50 – 03:05	신분증 확인
10:05 – 10:10	03:05 – 03:10	문제지 배부 및 파본 확인
10:10 – 10:55	03:10 – 03:55	듣기 평가 (LC)
10:55 – 12:10	03:55 – 05:10	독해 평가 (RC)

● 성적 확인

- 미리 안내된 성적 발표일(시험일로부터 약 12일 후)에 한국 TOEIC 위원회 사이트(www.toeic.co.kr) 및 공식 애플리케이션을 통해 성적을 확인할 수 있습니다.
- 성적표 수령은 온라인 출력 또는 우편 수령 중에서 선택할 수 있습니다.
- 온라인 출력과 우편 수령 모두 1회 발급만 무료이며, 그 이후에는 유료로 발급됩니다.

RC 파트별 문제 유형

PART 5
단문 빈칸 채우기

파트 소개	빈칸이 포함된 하나의 문장이 주어지고, 빈칸에 알맞은 단어나 구를 4개의 선택지 중에서 고르는 파트
문항 수	30문항
문제 유형	문법 문제 (문법의 적절한 쓰임을 묻는 문제) 어휘 문제 (문맥에 어울리는 어휘를 묻는 문제)

문제지 형태

READING TEST

In the Reading test, you will read a variety of texts and answer several different types of reading comprehension questions. The entire Reading test will last 75 minutes. There are three parts, and directions are given for each part. You are encouraged to answer as many questions as possible within the time allowed.

You must mark your answers on the separate answer sheet. Do not write your answers in your test book.

PART 5

Directions: A word or phrase is missing in each of the sentences below. Four answer choices are given below each sentence. Select the best answer to complete the sentence. Then mark the letter (A), (B), (C), or (D) on your answer sheet.

101. All valuables are stored ------- in the hotel's safe.
 (A) secures
 (B) securely
 (C) security
 (D) secure

102. Following an intense -------, the Alvarado Inc. managers were able to finalize the contract's terms.
 (A) negotiate
 (B) negotiated
 (C) negotiating
 (D) negotiation

103. A reception was held to welcome Ms. Dennis and ------- team.
 (A) her
 (B) hers
 (C) she
 (D) herself

104. The human resources department ------- the compliance records required by the federal government.
 (A) maintains
 (B) cultivates
 (C) persuades
 (D) associates

105. Fairway Shipping cannot issue refunds for delays caused by circumstances ------- its control.
 (A) below
 (B) before
 (C) behind
 (D) beyond

106. ------- can be spent on repairs without the written consent of the building manager.
 (A) Nothing
 (B) Never
 (C) Somebody
 (D) Another

107. Under the new policy, salespeople are responsible for ------- their own clients.
 (A) to find
 (B) find
 (C) found
 (D) finding

108. The shuttle bus was running behind schedule due to getting ------- in rush-hour traffic.
 (A) forced
 (B) stuck
 (C) rejected
 (D) stood

PART 6
장문 빈칸 채우기

파트 소개	4개의 빈칸이 포함된 지문이 주어지고, 각각의 빈칸에 들어갈 알맞은 단어나 구, 문장을 고르는 파트
문항 수	16문항 (4개 지문 X 4문항)
문제 유형	문법 문제 (문법의 적절한 쓰임을 묻는 문제) 어휘 문제 (문맥에 어울리는 어휘를 묻는 문제) 문장 삽입 문제 (문맥에 어울리는 문장을 묻는 문제)

문제지 형태

PART 6

Directions: Read the texts that follow. A word, phrase, or sentence is missing in parts of each text. Four answer choices for each question are given below the text. Select the best answer to complete the text. Then mark the letter (A), (B), (C), or (D) on your answer sheet.

Questions 131-134 refer to the following article.

BEAUMONT, TX (April 20)—As part of the celebration of our city's history, Centennial Hall ------- an orchestra concert featuring the work of local composer Emilia Oyola. Tickets go on sale at the box office and online tomorrow. The show is set for June 3 at 7:30 P.M.
131.

While Ms. Oyola will be the conductor, some of the pieces will not be ------- . Two songs written by other local composers are also part of the lineup. ------- .
132. **133.**

The concert will mark the first performance of the Beaumont City Orchestra since the concert hall was renovated. ------- attendees to Centennial Hall will certainly notice a vast improvement in sound quality thanks to sound reflectors added to the ceiling.
134.

131. (A) host
(B) hosted
(C) will host
(D) has hosted

132. (A) hers
(B) ours
(C) theirs
(D) its

133. (A) Ms. Oyola grew up just outside of Beaumont.
(B) The orchestra is looking for new members.
(C) Ms. Oyola plays the piano and violin.
(D) It is these composers' official debut.

134. (A) Authorized
(B) Sensible
(C) Preceding
(D) Regular

RC 파트별 문제 유형

PART 7 독해

파트 소개	지문을 읽고, 지문 내용과 관련된 2~5개 문제에 대해 가장 적절한 답을 고르는 파트
지문/문항 수	단일 지문 10개 (지문당 2~4문항; 총 29문항) 이중 지문 2개 (지문당 5문항; 총 10문항) 삼중 지문 3개 (지문당 5문항; 총 15문항) → 총 15개 지문 (54문항)
지문 유형	이메일·편지, 광고, 공지·회람, 기사, 양식(웹페이지, 설문지, 청구서 등), 문자 메시지 대화문 등
문제 유형	주제·목적, 세부 사항, 사실 확인, 추론, 문장 넣기, 의도 파악, 동의어 찾기

문제지 형태 (단일 지문)

PART 7

Directions: In this part you will read a selection of texts, such as magazine and newspaper articles, e-mails, and instant messages. Each text or set of texts is followed by several questions. Select the best answer for each question and mark the letter (A), (B), (C), or (D) on your answer sheet.

Questions 147-148 refer to the following memo.

MEMO

To: Prolance Customer Service Team
From: Olivia Cronin
Re: Customer complaints
Date: September 2

The August electricity bills were calculated incorrectly, so customers received bills that were too high. We're issuing new bills this week, so please explain this to customers if needed.

Additionally, we are receiving a lot of positive feedback from customers. Therefore, starting next month, we will make printouts of what customers are saying and hang them up in the break room to help motivate the staff.

147. Why did Ms. Cronin send the message?
(A) To describe a policy
(B) To explain a problem
(C) To introduce new equipment
(D) To announce a staff change

148. When can employees start to see comments from customers?
(A) In September
(B) In October
(C) In November
(D) In December

문제지 형태 (삼중 지문)

E-Mail Message

From: Rhonda Fitch <rfitch@diazandassoc.com>
To: William Austell <waustell@diazandassoc.com>
Subject: Interview
Date: October 3

Hi William,

I would like you to cover one of the inter
I don't want to reschedule it. Please inte
invited to give a speech at a small busin
think this would be great exposure for o
discuss what you thought of the candida

Thank you so much!

Rhonda

Questions 186-190 refer to the following job posting, interview schedule, and e-mail.

Marketing Coordinator Position at Diaz&Associates

Diaz&Associates, a Seattle-based firm dedicated to providing financial planning services, is looking for a new marketing coordinator. We have been in operation for two decades, and, for the first time in our company's history, we are expanding our business into the insurance industry. Therefore, effective marketing will be crucial.

Position description: The marketing coordinator is primarily responsible for managing our social media accounts, writing articles for our online newsletter, and organizing in-person and virtual events.

Requirements: A bachelor's or master's degree in marketing, business administration, or advertising is required along with three years of project management experience. Proficiency in GoCreate design software is a plus.

Interested applicants should send a résumé to hr@diazandassoc.com.

Marketing Coordinator Interviews		
Applicant	Date & Time	Employment Details
Corina Geiger	October 8, 2:00 P.M.	Bachelor's degree in marketing; 2 years project management; proficient in GoCreate
Byoungmin Kim	October 8, 4:00 P.M.	Master's degree in business administration; 3 years project management; proficient in GoCreate
Darrell Crawford	October 9, 1:00 P.M.	Bachelor's degree in advertising; operates personal blog; 3 years project management
Sebastian Trevino	October 10, 3:30 P.M.	Master's degree in advertising; winner of Campaign Creativity Award; proficient in GoCreate
Margaret Echols	October 11, 10:00 A.M.	Master's degree in literature; 4 years project management; proficient in GoCreate

186. What is indicated about Diaz&Associates in the job posting?
  (A) It is entering a new field.
  (B) It was founded two years ago.
  (C) It will open a new branch in Seattle.
  (D) It specializes in security.

187. What is one responsibility mentioned in the job posting?
  (A) Finding new customers
  (B) Creating online content
  (C) Traveling for events
  (D) Conducting staff training

188. Who best matches the company's stated requirements and preferences?
  (A) Ms. Geiger
  (B) Mr. Kim
  (C) Mr. Trevino
  (D) Ms. Echols

품사의 종류

아래는 JR Motors라는 한 자동차 생산 업체에 대한 짤막한 소개입니다. 각 문장을 구성하는 단어들의 품사를 확인해 보면서 각 품사의 기본적인 역할을 익혀 보세요.

JR Motors **manufactures** **cars**.
　　　　　　동사　　　　　명사

JR Motors는 자동차를 생산한다.

명사
동사

동사와 명사는 문장을 만드는 데 가장 중요한 품사입니다. 동사는 우리말로 '~하다' 또는 '~이다'에 해당하는 단어로 문장에서 결코 빠질 수 없는 품사입니다. 명사는 사람이나 사물과 같은 구체적인 것을 나타내기도 하며, '생각'이나 '허가'처럼 추상적인 개념을 나타내기도 합니다.

Recently, the demand for **electric** cars has been **high**.
　　　　　　　　　　　　　형용사　　　　　　　　　　형용사

최근 전기차에 대한 수요가 높아졌다.

형용사

형용사는 명사를 꾸며주는 역할을 하거나 be동사 뒤에서 주어를 서술해 주기도 합니다.

The company will **soon** launch a line of electric cars.
　　　　　　　　　부사

그 회사는 곧 전기차를 출시할 것이다.

부사

부사는 형용사나 동사, 부사, 또는 두 번째 문장의 recently와 같이 문장 전체를 수식하며, 구체적인 시간이나 장소, 정도, 빈도, 태도 등을 나타냅니다.

It is planning to hire more employees next year.
대명사

그 회사는 내년에 더 많은 직원을 고용할 계획이다.

대명사

대명사는 명사를 대신하는 품사입니다. 위의 문장에서 주어 it는 앞 문장의 the company를 대신하는 대명사입니다.

Its factories are located **in** Detroit **and** Flint.
　　　　　　　　　　　　　전치사　　　　　　접속사

그 회사의 공장은 디트로이트와 플린트에 위치해 있다.

전치사
접속사

전치사는 명사 앞에 놓여 장소 부사구(in Detroit)나 시간 부사구 등을 만드는 역할을 합니다. 접속사는 단어와 단어, 구절과 구절, 문장과 문장 사이를 연결해 주는 다리 역할을 합니다.

구와 절

If we leave right now, we'll be at the station in time.

우리가 당장 출발하면 역에 제시간에 도착할 것이다.

두 개 이상의 단어가 모여 주어, 동사로 구성되는 하나의 문장을 만들더라도, 그것이 독립적으로 쓰이지 못할 때 '절'이라고 합니다. 두 단어 이상의 단어가 만나도 '주어+동사'의 구조를 갖추지 못하면 '구'가 됩니다.

❶ 명사구, 명사절

The chef said **using the best ingredients** is the secret to success.

그 주방장은 최고의 재료를 사용하는 것이 성공 비결이라고 말했다.

❷ 부사구, 부사절

If the bad weather continues, the construction will be delayed **until the end of November**.

악천후가 계속되면, 그 공사는 11월 말까지 지연될 것이다.

❸ 형용사구, 형용사절

The plan **to renovate the old museum** was canceled.

그 오래된 박물관을 개조하려는 계획이 취소되었다.

LA Airlines has installed kiosks **where passengers can print their own boarding passes**.

LA 항공은 승객들이 자신의 항공권을 출력할 수 있는 키오스크를 설치했다.

이야기로 익히는 문장 구조

문법을 배우다 보면 주어, 서술어, 목적어, 보어 등 문장성분을 나타내는 용어를 자주 접하게 됩니다. '품사'가 각 단어의 성격을 드러내는 용어라면 '문장성분'은 각 단어가 문장을 구성하는 데 담당하는 역할을 나타내 줍니다. 출장을 떠나는 한 남자의 이야기를 읽으며 자연스럽게 토익에서 자주 쓰이는 영어의 기본 문장 구조를 익혀 보시기 바랍니다.

주어 + 동사

The train left. 기차가 떠났다.
주어 서술어(동사)

▶ 모든 평서문은 반드시 주어와 동사를 필요로 합니다. 동사는 품사의 하나이지만 영어의 서술어는 결국 동사(일반동사와 be동사)가 담당하기에 서술어 대신 동사를 문장성분 요소로 간주하곤 합니다.

주어 + 동사 + 부사어

I ran to the bus terminal. 나는 버스 터미널로 달려갔다.
  동사 부사어(전치사구)

▶ 부사어는 동사, 목적어, 보어 또는 문장 전체를 수식하며 의미를 더하거나 한정하는 역할을 합니다. 부사어는 하나의 부사로 이루어지기도 하며, 전치사구나 to부정사구 등의 부사구가 쓰이기도 합니다.

- The bus also left 5 minutes ago. 버스도 5분 전에 떠났다.
   부사 동사   부사구

주어 + 동사 + 보어

I felt at a loss. 나는 망연자실했다.
  동사 보어(전치사구)

▶ 보어는 주어와 동사만으로는 뜻이 완전하지 못할 때, 그 불완전한 의미를 보충하는 역할을 합니다. be동사와 feel(~하게 느끼다), look(~처럼 보이다), grow(~해지다)와 같은 일부 동사 뒤에 보어가 오며, 명사와 형용사, 전치사구가 보어 역할을 합니다.

- I was late for the conference in London. 나는 런던에서 열리는 콘퍼런스에 늦었다.
   be동사 형용사   부사구

주어 + 동사 + 목적어

I had to board(=get on) the next train. 나는 다음 기차에 올라타야 했다.
        타동사   목적어

▶ 타동사 뒤에는 '~을/를'에 해당하는 목적어가 오며, board(~에 탑승하다)나 attend(~에 참석하다), affect(~에 영향을 미치다)와 같이 목적어가 '~에'로 해석되는 경우도 있습니다.

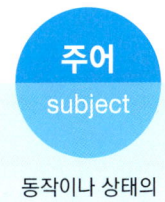  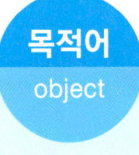  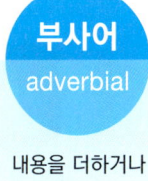

주어 subject	동사 verb	목적어 object	보어 complement	부사어 adverbial
동작이나 상태의 주체	일반동사 be동사	타동사의 대상	주어와 목적어를 보완	내용을 더하거나 한정

주어 + 동사 + 목적어 + 부사어

I met a woman named Debora on the train.
　동사　　　　목적어　　　　　　　부사어

나는 기차에서 데보라라는 이름의 한 여인을 만났다.

She took her business card out of her bag and handed it to me.
　　동사　　　　목적어　　　　　　부사어　　　　　　동　목　부

그녀는 가방에서 명함을 꺼내 내게 건네주었다.

▶ 목적어 뒤의 부사어는 굳이 없어도 말이 되는 경우가 많지만 문맥상 부사어가 꼭 필요한 경우도 있습니다.

주어 + 동사 + 목적어 + 목적격 보어

I saw her giving a presentation at the conference.
　동사 목적어　　목적격 보어

나는 그녀가 콘퍼런스에서 발표하는 것을 보았다.

I found her very attractive.
　동사　목적어　목적격 보어

나는 그녀가 매우 매력적이라고 느꼈다.

▶ 목적어 뒤에 오는 보어는 목적어를 보완해 주며, 주로 형용사, 분사 또는 명사가 쓰입니다.

주어 + 동사 + 간접목적어 + 직접목적어

Debora bought me dinner after the conference.
　　　　동사　간목　직목

데보라는 콘퍼런스가 끝난 후 나에게 저녁을 샀다.

I told her all about my business plans.
　동사 간목　　　　직목

나는 그녀에게 나의 모든 사업 계획을 말해 주었다.

She suddenly offered me a job and I accepted it.
　　　　　　동사　　간목 직목

그녀는 갑자기 나에게 일자리를 제안했고, 나는 그 제안을 받아들였다.

▶ 간접목적어는 '~에게'라는 뜻으로, 직접목적어는 '~를/을'이라는 뜻으로 해석됩니다.

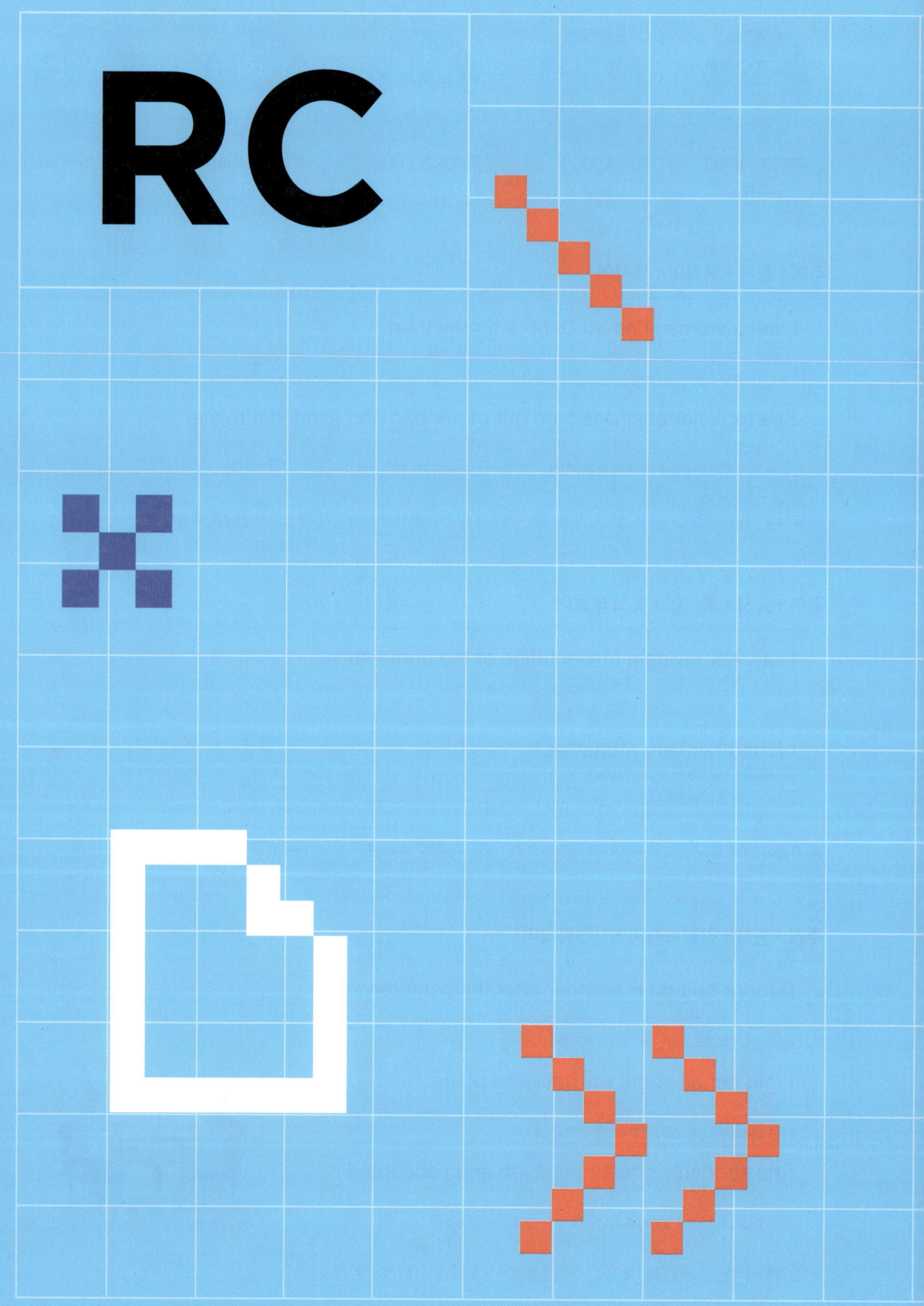

PART 5 6

UNIT

01

명사

1. 명사 자리: 관사/한정사/소유격/형용사 뒤
2. 명사 자리: 주어와 보어
3. 명사 자리: 목적어
4. 셀 수 있는 명사 vs. 셀 수 없는 명사
5. 사람 명사 vs. 추상 명사
6. 복합 명사

빈출 유형 풀이 전략
Vocabulary
Actual Test

TOEIC Grammar

약 15%

UNIT 01 명사

명사 문제는 매회 2문제 이상 꾸준히 출제됩니다. 특히 빈칸이 명사 자리임을 파악하여 알맞은 형태의 명사를 고르는 문제나 복합 명사를 묻는 문제가 자주 출제됩니다.

스피드 진단 테스트

(A), (B) 중 알맞은 것을 고르세요.

1. The ------- of cable TV increased last year.

   (A) popularity   (B) popular

2. The club charges a small membership -------.

   (A) fee   (B) money

정답 및 해석

1. (A), 작년에 케이블 티브이의 인기가 증가했다.
2. (A), 그 동호회는 약간의 회비를 받는다.

명사란?

customer(고객), store(가게, 상점)와 같이 사람이나 사물의 이름을 나타내는 말이에요.

● 셀 수 있는 명사와 셀 수 없는 명사

셀 수 있는 명사가 하나임을 나타낼 땐 명사 앞에 부정관사 a나 an을 쓰고, 여러 개라는 걸 표현할 때는 복수형으로 써야 해요. 셀 수 없는 명사는 a나 an을 쓸 수 없고 복수형도 없습니다.

셀 수 있는 명사		셀 수 없는 명사	
단수 명사	복수 명사		
an item 항목; 물품	items 항목들; 물품들	traffic 교통(량)	news 뉴스
a pass 출입증, 탑승권	passes 출입증들, 탑승권들	mail 우편(물)	paper 종이
a company 회사	companies 회사들	money 돈	clothing 의류
a shelf 선반, 진열대	shelves 선반들, 진열대들	funding 자금	knowledge 지식
a person 사람	people 사람들	equipment 장비, 용품	research 연구 조사

정관사 the는 셀 수 있는 명사와 셀 수 없는 명사 앞에 모두 쓸 수 있어요. '정관사'의 '정'은 '정하다'는 뜻이며, 이름에서 알 수 있듯 단어의 범위를 구체적으로 '한정'하는 역할을 합니다.

This new system will help you save money. 이 새로운 시스템은 당신이 돈을 절약하게 도울 것이다.
The money was raised by the charity event. 그 돈은 자선 행사에 의해 모금되었다.

● 명사의 형태

-ment, -ness, -ion, -ence/-ance, -ice, -ty 등으로 끝나는 말은 대부분 명사이며, -or, -er, -ee, -ant 등으로 끝나는 말은 대개 사람을 나타내는 명사예요.

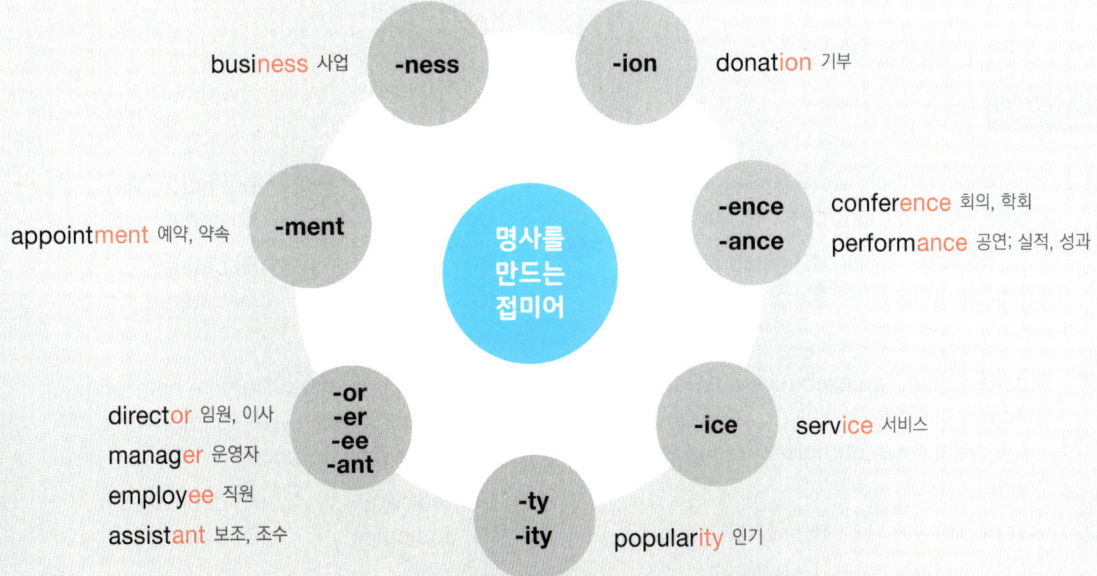

1 명사 자리: 관사/한정사/소유격/형용사 뒤

Office Monster is our main **supplier** of office equipment.
소유격 형용사 명사
supply(공급하다)+-er

오피스 몬스터는 우리의 주요 사무기기 **공급업체**이다.

명사는 관사, 한정사, 소유격, 그리고 형용사 뒤에 위치할 수 있습니다.

❶ 관사/한정사 뒤

Please complete an <u>application</u> at our Web site. 저희 웹사이트에서 **지원서**를 작성해 주세요.
부정관사 명사

The <u>process</u> for reimbursement is very simple. 환급 **절차**가 무척 간단하다.
정관사 명사

He doesn't make any <u>appointments</u> on weekends. 그는 주말에는 아무런 **약속**도 잡지 않는다.
한정사 명사
└─ some, any, no처럼 수나 양을 한정해 주는 품사를 한정사라고 합니다.

❷ 소유격 뒤

His/Brian's <u>suggestion</u> was adopted. 그의/브라이언의 **제안**이 채택되었다.
소유격 명사

❸ 형용사 뒤

He made a good <u>impression</u> on his boss. 그는 그의 상사에게 좋은 **인상**을 주었다.
형용사 명사

연습문제 정답 및 해설 p.002

1 The restaurant on Mesa Street is having a large ------- to mark its tenth anniversary.

(A) celebrate (B) celebration
(C) celebrated (D) celebrates

2 Ricardo Sosa, the executive chef at Restaurant Dove, avoids making any ------- with food journalists during peak hours.

(A) appoint (B) appointments
(C) appointed (D) appoints

3 For Dr. Saeb's retirement party, Ms. Decker hired a ------- to serve food.

(A) caters (B) caterer
(C) cater (D) catered

4 Anne Withers, the billionaire entrepreneur, is known for her ------- to improving public healthcare access.

(A) dedicate (B) dedicated
(C) dedicates (D) dedication

명사 자리: 주어와 보어

The **construction** is progressing according to schedule.
— construct(건설하다) + -ion
주어(명사)

그 **공사**는 일정대로 진행되고 있다.

명사는 주어와 보어 자리에 위치할 수 있습니다. 명사가 보어 자리에 올 경우 주격 보어는 주어와 동격이고, 목적격 보어는 목적어와 동격입니다.

① 주어

Admission is free, but **registration** is required. 입장료는 무료이지만, 등록이 요구됩니다.
주어 / 주어

This proposal is good for 30 days. 이 제안은 30일간 유효합니다.
주어

② 주격 보어: 주어 = 보어

Timing is important, but **quality** is **our priority**. 타이밍이 중요하긴 하지만, 품질이 우리의 최우선 과제입니다.
주어 / 주격 보어

The buyout has clearly been **a success**. 그 기업 인수는 분명 성공적이었다.
주어 / 주격 보어

③ 목적격 보어: 목적어 = 목적격 보어

We have appointed **the company** as **sole distributor** of our medical supplies.
목적어 / 목적격 보어

우리는 그 회사를 우리 의료용품의 **독점 판매업체**로 지정했다.

연습문제

정답 및 해설 p.003

1 The letter of ------- for the IT position was sent on August 8 by Martha Syngman.

(A) accepted (B) acceptable
(C) accepts (D) acceptance

2 The store's holiday season sales event was an unprecedented -------.

(A) success (B) successful
(C) succeed (D) successes

3 The department head called Mr. Reuben a great ------- for finishing the project ahead of schedule.

(A) leader (B) lead
(C) leadership (D) leading

4 Since the ------- of our clients is our biggest priority, we highly value your feedback.

(A) satisfied (B) satisfaction
(C) satisfy (D) satisfactory

명사 자리: 목적어

You must obtain **permission** from your supervisor first.
↳ permit(허락하다)+-ion
타동사의 목적어

당신은 먼저 당신의 상사에게 **허락**을 얻어야 합니다.

명사는 타동사의 목적어 자리에 위치할 수 있으며, 전치사 뒤에 올 수 있습니다.

❶ 동사의 목적어

We'll postpone the construction until May. 우리는 그 **공사**를 5월로 연기할 것이다.
타동사   명사 (목적어)

We need to review the implementation of the new procedure. 우리는 새로운 절차의 **시행**을 재검토할 필요가 있다.
타동사   명사 (목적어)

❷ 전치사의 목적어

전치사의 뒤에 오는 명사, 명사구, 명사절, 대명사 등을 전치사의 목적어라고 합니다.

The store is under renovation. 그 상점은 **수리** 중이다.
전치사   명사

These images may not be used without permission. 이 이미지들은 **허락** 없이 사용될 수 없습니다.
전치사   명사

Employees must submit requests for time off to Ms. Hamilton for approval.
전치사   명사
직원들은 **승인**을 받기 위해 휴가 요청서를 해밀턴 씨에게 제출해야 한다.

연습문제 정답 및 해설 p.004

1 The economic crisis has caused ------- in sales for businesses all over the country.

(A) to decrease (B) decreased
(C) decreases (D) will decrease

2 The new intern needs ------- with the copier on the third floor.

(A) help (B) helpful
(C) helpfully (D) helped

3 The mayor announced a plan for the ------- of the empty lot near the park.

(A) developing (B) development
(C) develops (D) develop

4 With just one year in -------, Cuff Motors is already turning record profits.

(A) operate (B) operated
(C) operation (D) operational

ㄴ 셀 수 있는 명사 vs. 셀 수 없는 명사

two chairs
의자 두 개

some furniture
furnitures (×)
가구 몇 개

다음과 같이 형태나 뜻이 비슷해서 셀 수 있는지 없는지 헷갈리는 단어들이 많습니다. 하지만 그렇기 때문에 토익에 빈출되니 꼭 숙지하세요.

혼동하기 쉬운 셀 수 있는 명사와 셀 수 없는 명사

셀 수 있는 명사	셀 수 없는 명사	셀 수 있는 명사	셀 수 없는 명사
a permit 허가증	permission 허가	a certificate 증명서	certification 증명
a compliment 칭찬, 찬사	admiration 감탄	a machine 기계	machinery 기계류
an account 계좌	accounting 회계	an approach 접근(법)	access 접근 (권한)

<u>Access</u> to the Web site was blocked. 그 웹 사이트의 **접근**이 차단되었다.
An access (×)

<u>A new approach</u> to training employees is required. 직원 교육을 위한 새로운 **접근법**이 요구된다.
New approach (×)

You need to get <u>a permit</u> to park here. 여기에 주차하려면 **허가증**을 받아야 합니다.
　　　　　　　허가증 (셀 수 있는 명사)

You need to get <u>permission</u> to park here. 여기에 주차하려면 **허가**를 받아야 합니다.
　　　　　　　허가 (셀 수 없는 명사)

연습문제

정답 및 해설 p.005

1 The event organizer called the management office to ask for ------- to use the event hall.

(A) permission (B) permit
(C) permitting (D) permitted

2 Every year, City Hall receives ------- on the various events of the spring festival it organizes.

(A) complimented (B) complimentary
(C) compliment (D) compliments

3 According to the job description, experience in ------- is required to work in the finance department.

(A) accountant (B) accounting
(C) account (D) accountable

4 The company is recruiting heavy machine operators with ------- in forklifts and cranes.

(A) certify (B) certifying
(C) certificate (D) certification

5 사람 명사 vs. 추상 명사

We offer 24-hour technical **assistance** by telephone.
(assistant (×))
지원 (셀 수 없는 명사)

우리는 전화로 24시간 기술 지원을 제공합니다.

사람 명사는 주로 -or, -er, -ee, -ant 등으로 끝나고, 추상 명사는 -ment, -ness, -ion, -ence/-ance, -ice, -ty 등의 접미어가 붙습니다.

혼동하기 쉬운 사람 명사와 추상 명사

		사람 명사		추상 명사
pay 납부하다; 급료	-er	pay**er** 납부자	-ment	pay**ment** 납부
employ 고용하다	-er	employ**er** 고용주	-ment	employ**ment** 고용
	-ee	employ**ee** 고용인, 직원		
produce 생산하다	-er	produc**er** 생산자, 제작자	-ion	product**ion** 생산
participate 참가하다	-ant	particip**ant** 참가자	-ion	participat**ion** 참가

🎯 출제포인트

> 선택지에 명사가 2개라면 명사의 접미어를 보고 사람 명사인지 추상 명사인지 파악한 후 문맥에 적합한 명사를 고르세요.
>
> ------- in the meeting is strongly encouraged.
> (A) Participant   ✓(B) Participation

하지만 -ion으로 끝나는 명사라고 해서 항상 추상 명사로 단정해서는 안 됩니다.
Candidates must submit **applications** by July 10. 지원자들은 7월 10일까지 **지원서**를 제출해야 합니다.
지원서 (셀 수 있는 명사)

연습문제

정답 및 해설 p.006

1. Many ------- of the museum sign the guest book after their tour.
   (A) visits   (B) visitors
   (C) visit   (D) visited

2. The hotel collects ------- when the guests check in rather than at booking.
   (A) payers   (B) payment
   (C) paid   (D) pays

3. Mesta Studios is a renowned ------- of documentaries for young adults.
   (A) producer   (B) production
   (C) produces   (D) productive

4. Ms. Nguyen will interview ------- for the manager position starting on May 14.
   (A) applied   (B) applicable
   (C) applicants   (D) application

6 복합 명사

Automoco's Copenhagen **assembly line** is
going to employ 135 people.
오토모코의 코펜하겐 공장 **조립 라인**은 135명을 고용할 예정이다.

복합 명사란 개별 뜻이 있는 두 개의 명사가 결합되어 하나의 명사로 쓰이는 것을 말합니다. 복합 명사 문제는 우리말 해석에 의존하면 틀리기 십상이기 때문에 토익에 자주 나오는 복합 명사는 통으로 외우는 것이 좋습니다.

토익 빈출 복합 명사

account number 계좌 번호	quality assurance 품질 보증
savings account 예금 계좌	warranty certificate 품질 보증서
interest rate 금리	replacement product 대체품
baggage allowance 수하물 중량 제한	expiration date 유효 기간
security policy 보안 정책	time constraints 시간 제약
employee productivity 직원 생산성	complaint form 불만 신고서
performance review/evaluation 업무 평가	customer complaints 고객 불만
job openings/vacancies 공석, 일자리	protection device 보호 장비
admission fee 입장료, 입회비	safety regulation 안전 규정
budget surplus/deficit 예산 흑자/적자	safety inspection/precautions 안전 검사/예방책
growth rate 성장률	service charge/fee 서비스 요금

Employers should follow all **safety** regulations to prevent workplace accidents.
　　　　　　　　　　　　　　safe (×)
고용주는 작업장에서 발생하는 사고를 방지하기 위해 모든 **안전** 규정을 따라야 한다.

연습문제

1. Although it has a high admission -------, the golf club has a reasonable monthly rate.
   (A) salary (B) fee
   (C) fair   (D) entry

2. Please read the data ------- policy and sign the bottom of the page.
   (A) advantage (B) initials
   (C) schedule   (D) security

3. Barsty Electronics has reported a budget ------- for the past three years.
   (A) assembly (B) account
   (C) surplus   (D) proportion

4. A small service ------- is added for orders that are less than 10 dollars.
   (A) charge   (B) provider
   (C) speed   (D) amount

빈출 유형 풀이 전략

1. 명사 자리

STEP에 따라 실제 토익 문제를 푸는 순서와 요령을 익혀 보세요.

Mr. Bean has developed an automatic ------- for processing customer requests.

(A) systemize
(B) systematic
(C) systems
(D) system

STEP 1 선택지 구성 파악하기
system의 다양한 형태가 제시되어 있으므로 빈칸에 들어갈 적절한 품사를 묻는 문제.

Mr. Bean has developed an automatic ------- for processing customer requests.

(A) systemize
(B) systematic
(C) systems
(D) system

STEP 2 빈칸 주변에서 단서 찾기
빈칸 앞에 부정관사 an과 형용사 automatic이 있는 것으로 보아 빈칸은 단수 명사 자리.

Mr. Bean has developed an automatic ------- for processing customer requests.

(A) systemize
(B) systematic
(C) systems
(D) system ✓

STEP 3 정답 찾기
선택지 중 단수 명사 (D) system이 정답.
(C) systems는 복수 명사이므로 오답.

해석 빈 씨는 고객 요청을 처리하는 자동 시스템을 개발했다.

어휘 develop 개발하다 automatic 자동의 process 처리하다; 처리 request 요청; 요청하다 systemize 체계화하다 systematic 체계적인

2. 복합 명사

STEP에 따라 실제 토익 문제를 푸는 순서와 요령을 익혀 보세요.

For the move, all office ------- will be loaded into the trucks on Rosehill Street.

(A) equips
(B) equipping
(C) equipped
(D) equipment

STEP 1 선택지 구성 파악하기

equip의 다양한 형태가 제시되어 있으므로 빈칸에 들어갈 적절한 품사를 묻는 문제.

For the move, all office ------- will be loaded into the trucks on Rosehill Street.

(A) equips
(B) equipping
(C) equipped
(D) equipment

STEP 2 빈칸 주변에서 단서 찾기

빈칸 앞에 명사 office가 있고 뒤에는 조동사 will이 있으므로 빈칸은 문장의 주어 역할을 할 수 있는 명사 자리.
또한 office와 결합하여 복합 명사를 이룰 수 있는 명사가 들어가야 함.

For the move, all office ------- will be loaded into the trucks on Rosehill Street.

(A) equips
(B) equipping
(C) equipped
(D) equipment ✓

STEP 3 정답 찾기

선택지 중 명사인 (D) equipment가 정답.

해석 이사를 위해 로즈힐 가에서 모든 사무기기가 트럭에 실릴 것이다.

어휘 move 이동, 이사; 이동하다, 이사하다   be loaded into ~에 실리다

VOCABULARY 빈출 명사 어휘 (1)

estimate	견적(서); 추정(치)	submit an **estimate** for the work 그 작업의 견적서를 제출하다 a rough **estimate** 대략적인 추정치
drop ⑧ fall	하락, 감소	a sharp **drop** in stock prices 급격한 주가 하락 cause a **drop** in production 생산량 감소를 야기하다
initiative	계획; 주도권; 진취성	a new marketing **initiative** 새로운 마케팅 계획 take the **initiative** 주도하다, 주도권을 행사하다
objective ⑧ goal	목적, 목표; 객관적인	attain an **objective** 목표를 달성하다 set realistic **objectives** 현실적인 목표를 설정하다
precision	정확(성), 정밀(성)	with clarity and **precision** 명료하고 정확하게 **precision** measurement instrument 정밀 측정 기구
supplier	공급자, 공급업체	a leading **supplier** of office equipment 사무기기의 주요 공급업체 contact the gas **supplier** 가스 공급업체에 연락하다
figures	수치	sales **figures** 판매 수치 the latest unemployment **figures** 최근의 실업률 수치
awareness	인식, 의식, 관심	raise **awareness** 인식을 높이다 convert customer **awareness** into purchases 고객의 인식을 구매로 전환시키다

연습문제

1 Ms. Selbst asked the contractor to provide an ------- for the cost of renovating her kitchen.

(A) estimate (B) attempt
(C) industry (D) objective

2 There has been a significant ------- in market shares since the CEO's resignation.

(A) supplier (B) reason
(C) collaboration (D) drop

3 It is necessary to raise ------- of the lack of access to proper healthcare in some areas.

(A) awareness (B) goals
(C) precision (D) issue

4 The new employee took the ------- in redesigning the team's workspace.

(A) documentation (B) figures
(C) initiative (D) status

capacity	용량, 수용력; 능력	a seating **capacity** of 450 450개 좌석 operate at full **capacity** 최대치로 가동하다
contribution to	~에 기부/기여	make a **contribution to** charity 자선 단체에 기부하다 result in a significant **contribution to** a department 결과적으로 부서에 큰 기여가 되다
inventory	물품 목록; 재고(품)	take **inventory** of everything in the store 그 매장에 있는 모든 물품을 목록으로 만들다 sell excess **inventory** 남는 재고품을 팔다
guidance	안내, 지도	under expert **guidance** 전문가의 지도하에 give **guidance** on company policies 회사 정책에 관해 안내하다
delivery	배송	offer free **delivery** 무료 배송 서비스를 제공하다 send the package by express **delivery** 그 소포를 속달로 보내다
confidence in	~에 대한 신뢰	have **confidence in** his abilities 그의 능력을 신뢰하다 have complete **confidence in** her 그녀를 대단히 신뢰하다
associate = colleague	(직장) 동료, 직원; 연관 짓다	a business **associate** 사업 동료 start a career as a sales **associate** 판매 직원으로 일을 시작하다
referral	위탁; 소개(서), 추천(서)	obtain a **referral** 소개서를 받다 an employee **referral** 직원 소개[추천]서

정답 및 해설 p.008

5 The city councilor's speech helped increase ------- in the town's economic future.

(A) market (B) delivery
(C) confidence (D) assembly

6 Please speak to one of our sales ------- for information about our electronics.

(A) associates (B) inventory
(C) promotion (D) features

7 On weekday nights, the restaurant rarely reaches its full -------.

(A) referral (B) cancelation
(C) capacity (D) facility

8 In her presentation, Dr. Matvey acknowledged her partner's ------- to the research study.

(A) guidance (B) venue
(C) separation (D) contribution

ACTUAL TEST

1. Interns should obtain ------- from their assigned mentors before leaving the office.

   (A) approval
   (B) approvingly
   (C) approved
   (D) approve

2. ------- must be checked for any items that are past their expiration date.

   (A) Inventory
   (B) Security
   (C) Referral
   (D) Situation

3. The majority of ------- said they preferred receiving the newsletter by e-mail.

   (A) subscribed
   (B) subscribes
   (C) subscribers
   (D) subscriptions

4. Our success in the third quarter is the ------- of an aggressive marketing campaign.

   (A) resulting
   (B) resulted
   (C) resultant
   (D) result

5. Ms. Lee expressed her ------- for the opportunity to host the awards ceremony.

   (A) gratefully
   (B) grateful
   (C) gratitude
   (D) gratify

6. Akasuki Tech is well known as the first software company that implemented lifetime -------.

   (A) employs
   (B) employment
   (C) employer
   (D) employed

7. It is a rare ------- for visitors to donate less than twenty dollars in the City Hall charity events.

   (A) except
   (B) exceptions
   (C) exception
   (D) exceptional

8. The grocery store prides itself on using only local ------- for its produce.

   (A) suppliers
   (B) clients
   (C) administrations
   (D) figures

어휘 majority of 다수의 prefer (더) 좋아하다, 선호하다 newsletter 소식지 quarter 사분기, 4분의 1 aggressive 공격적인 opportunity to do ~할 기회 host 주최하다 awards ceremony 시상식 implement 시행하다 lifetime employment (정년이 보장되는) 평생 고용, 종신 고용 rare 드문 donate 기부[기증]하다 grocery store 식료품점 pride oneself 자부심을 느끼다 local 지역 produce 농산물; 생산하다

Questions 9-12 refer to the following notice.

Notice to all FFR Employees

We are happy to announce that ---9.--- on the staff lunchroom are finally complete.

Starting Monday, the new area will be open ---10.--- from 8 A.M. until 8 P.M. We encourage everyone to use this space to eat together.

You may choose from various ---11.--- options. Menus include styles of cuisines from around the world. The cafeteria also caters to vegan diets and those with special dietary needs.

---12.--- . Microwaves and refrigerators are available for those who wish to do so.

We hope you enjoy these new facilities.

9 (A) renovate
   (B) renovations
   (C) renovated
   (D) renovates

10 (A) daily
   (B) evenly
   (C) busily
   (D) locally

11 (A) display
   (B) dining
   (C) stationery
   (D) career

12 (A) Employees may also bring food from home.
   (B) Please let us know your preference.
   (C) We expect many customers to come.
   (D) However, there are no dishwashers.

어휘 lunchroom 구내식당   option 선택(할 수 있는 것), 선택권   include 포함하다   cuisine 요리(법)   cafeteria 구내식당
       cater to ~을 충족시키다, ~의 구미에 맞추다   vegan 완전한 채식주의자; 완전한 채식주의자의   available 이용할 수 있는

UNIT 02

대명사

1. 인칭대명사
2. 소유격과 소유대명사
3. 재귀대명사
4. 지시대명사
5. 부정대명사: one, another, the other(s)
6. 수량을 나타내는 부정대명사

빈출 유형 풀이 전략
Vocabulary
Actual Test

TOEIC Grammar

약 10%

UNIT 02 대명사

대명사 문제는 매회 1문제 정도 출제됩니다. 특히 인칭대명사의 격을 구분하는 문제는 빠지지 않고 출제되며, 재귀대명사나 소유대명사 문제도 종종 나오는 편이니 꼭 숙지해야 합니다.

 스피드 진단 테스트

(A), (B) 중 알맞은 것을 고르세요.

1. Mr. Brent attended the conference with ------- manager.

(A) him (B) his

2. She reviewed the financial report by -------.

(A) her (B) herself

정답 및 해석

1. (B), 브렌트 씨는 그의 부장과 함께 학회에 참석했다.
2. (B), 그녀는 재무 보고서를 혼자서 검토했다.

대명사란?

대명사란 동일한 명사의 반복을 피하기 위해 사람이나 사물의 이름을 대신하는 말입니다.

● 인칭대명사

인칭대명사는 사람이나 사물을 가리키는 대명사로, 수와 성별, 격에 따라 형태가 달라집니다.

인칭/수		격	주격 (~은/~는/~이/~가)	목적격 (~을/~를/~에게)	소유격 (~의)	소유대명사 (~의 것)	재귀대명사 (~ 자신/~ 스스로)
1인칭	단수		I	me	my	mine	myself
	복수		we	us	our	ours	ourselves
2인칭	단수		you	you	your	yours	yourself
	복수		you	you	your	yours	yourselves
3인칭	단수		he	him	his	his	himself
			she	her	her	hers	herself
			it	it	its	-	itself
	복수		they	them	their	theirs	themselves

● 지시대명사

지시대명사는 무언가를 가리킬 때 쓰는 대명사로 가까운 것을 가리킬 때는 'this(이것)'나 'these(이것들)', 멀리 있는 것을 가리킬 때는 'that(저것)'이나 'those(저것들)'라고 합니다.

● 부정대명사

부정대명사의 부정(不定)은 '정할 수 없다'는 뜻으로, 지칭하는 대상을 구체적으로 특정할 수 없거나 수나 양을 정확히 가늠할 수 없을 때 씁니다.

one 하나; ~것	another 다른 하나	all 모두
most 대부분	some 일부	many 많은 수

This remote control is not working. I will go find another. 이 리모컨은 고장 났어요. **다른 것**을 찾아 볼게요.
Some of the workers are off today. 작업자 중 **일부**는 오늘 쉽니다.

1 인칭대명사

Ms. Burdick is out of the office.

She is on a business trip.
= Ms. Burdick
버딕 씨는 사무실에 없어요. **그녀는** 출장 중이에요.

인칭대명사는 문장에서 쓰이는 역할에 따라 주어 자리에는 주격, 목적어 자리에는 목적격이 옵니다.

❶ 주격

Some customers complained that they received the wrong items.
　　　　　　　　　　　　　　　　that절의 주어 (= some customers)
몇몇 고객들은 **그들이** 엉뚱한 물품을 받았다고 항의했다.

❷ 목적격

Mr. Lowry will order supplies tomorrow, so tell him if you need anything.
　　　　　　　　　　　　　　　　　　　　　동사 tell의 목적어 (= Mr. Lowry)
로리 씨가 내일 물품을 주문할 거니까 필요한 게 있으면 **그에게** 말하세요.

Ms. Johnson suggested seeking a new supplier, and most employees agreed with her.
　　　　　　　　　　　　　　　　　　　　　　　　　　　전치사 with의 목적어(= Ms. Johnson)
존슨 씨는 새로운 공급업체를 찾아보자고 제안했고, 직원 대부분은 **그녀에게** 동의했다.

연습문제

정답 및 해설 p.013

1 When Mr. Perkins goes to London, ------- will fly first class.

(A) he 　　　(B) him
(C) his 　　　(D) himself

2 While the branch manager is on vacation, the assistant manager is filling in for -------.

(A) herself 　(B) her
(C) she 　　　(D) hers

3 Ms. Mensch gave the clients a presentation to convince ------- to work with their new providers.

(A) theirs 　　(B) they
(C) their 　　 (D) them

4 Ms. Flitzer could not use the copier because ------- broke down weeks ago.

(A) them 　　(B) it
(C) itself 　　(D) they

2 소유격과 소유대명사

소유격		소유대명사		소유격		소유대명사
my office	=	**mine**		**his** office	=	**his**
your office	=	**yours**		**her** office	=	**hers**
				their office	=	**theirs**

소유격은 명사 앞에 위치하여 명사를 수식하는 역할을 합니다. 한편 소유대명사는 '소유격 + 명사'를 대신하는 말로 명사가 와야 할 자리에 대신 올 수 있습니다.

❶ 소유격

Workers should submit their weekly report every Friday.
= workers'
직원들은 매주 금요일에 **그들의** 주간 업무 보고서를 제출해야 한다.

❷ 소유대명사

소유대명사가 가리키는 대상이 단수냐 복수냐에 따라 소유대명사의 수도 달라집니다.

Ours is the red car parked over there. 우리 것은 저기에 주차된 빨간 차입니다.
= Our car(단수)

Theirs are the folding bicycles over there. 그들의 것은 저기에 있는 접이식 자전거들입니다.
= Their bicycles(복수)

연습문제

정답 및 해설 p.014

1 Trainees using the equipment for the first time should ask for help from ------- mentors.

(A) themselves (B) them
(C) their (D) they

2 Ms. Casey left a bag with ------- personal belongings in her hotel room.

(A) she (B) her
(C) herself (D) hers

3 All files were mixed up, so we had to check whether those were -------.

(A) our (B) we
(C) ourselves (D) ours

4 Mr. Sheffield helped me during my presentation, so I will help him during -------.

(A) him (B) his
(C) he (D) himself

3 재귀대명사

Mr. Stephen considers **himself** an expert.
주어   목적어 (= Mr. Stephen)
스티븐 씨는 **스스로를** 전문가라고 여긴다.

주어의 동작이 도로 주어로 돌아가는 관계를 나타내는 대명사로서 용법에 따라 다양하게 해석되며, -self(단수)/-selves(복수)의 형태로 쓰여요.

❶ 재귀 용법

주어와 목적어가 동일할 때 목적어 자리에 재귀대명사를 씁니다. 이때 재귀대명사는 문장의 구성 성분이므로 재귀대명사를 생략하면 문장이 성립되지 않습니다.

He devoted **himself** to studying print techniques. 그는 프린트 기술을 연구하는 것에 전념했다.
주어   목적어 (= He)

❷ 강조 용법

주어나 목적어를 단순히 강조하는 말로 재귀대명사를 쓰기도 합니다. 강조하는 말이므로 생략해도 문장이 성립합니다.

I'll speak to them (**myself**). 내가 (**직접**) 그들에게 말할게.
주어   주어 강조

❸ 재귀대명사 관용 표현

Mr. Perry carried out the research **by himself**. 페리 씨는 **혼자** 그 연구를 진행했다.
                                  = alone, on his own

Developing a world-class security program is a major undertaking **in itself**.
세계적 수준의 보안 프로그램을 개발하는 것은 **그 자체로** 엄청난 일이다.

연습문제   정답 및 해설 p.015

1 At Raya's Fashion, we make all of the clothes and accessories -------.

　(A) us　　　　　　(B) we
　(C) ourselves　　　(D) our

2 If Ms. Kiko resigns this month, Mr. Baker should be able to supervise the construction on -------.

　(A) he　　　　　　(B) his
　(C) himself　　　　(D) his own

3 The CEO planned out a crisis management system ------- to prevent for possible business threats.

　(A) she　　　　　　(B) her
　(C) herself　　　　(D) hers

4 Marge and Gerald had to set up their stall for the expo by -------.

　(A) they　　　　　(B) themselves
　(C) them　　　　　(D) theirs

4 지시대명사

This looks nicer than **that**. 이것이 저것보다 더 좋아 보인다.
단수 동사

These look nicer than **those**. 이것들이 저것들보다 더 좋아 보인다.
복수 동사

this와 that은 가리키는 대상이 단수일 때 쓰고, these와 those는 복수일 때 씁니다. 또한 명사 앞에서 명사를 수식하는 지시형용사로 쓰기도 합니다.

❶ 지시대명사

His opinion differs from that of the majority. 그의 의견은 다수의 의견과 다르다.
= opinion

Our sales figures this quarter are similar to those of our competitor.
= sales figures
이번 분기 우리 매출은 경쟁사의 매출과 비슷하다.

❷ 지시형용사

This store provides a customer-friendly environment. 이 매장은 고객 친화적 환경을 제공한다.

🔼 고난도 JUMP UP

those 뒤에 who와 함께 수식하는 말이 따라 나오면 '~하는 사람들'의 의미로 쓰입니다.

Ms. Lu will mail a copy of the annual report to those who cannot attend the meeting.
루 씨는 회의에 참석하지 못하는 사람들에게 연례 보고서 한 부를 우송할 것이다.

연습문제

정답 및 해설 p.016

1 Consumers find the Fex Electronics tablet's interfaces more stylish than ------- of their competitors.

(A) those (B) them
(C) they   (D) that

2 Ms. Tesh asked ------- who volunteered for the fundraising event to meet at noon.

(A) these (B) them
(C) those (D) themselves

3 ------- people in the conference hall are not attending the forum.

(A) This   (B) These
(C) That   (D) They

4 Our newsletter is sent out more often than ------- of other IT startups.

(A) this   (B) these
(C) their (D) that

5 부정대명사: one, another, the other(s)

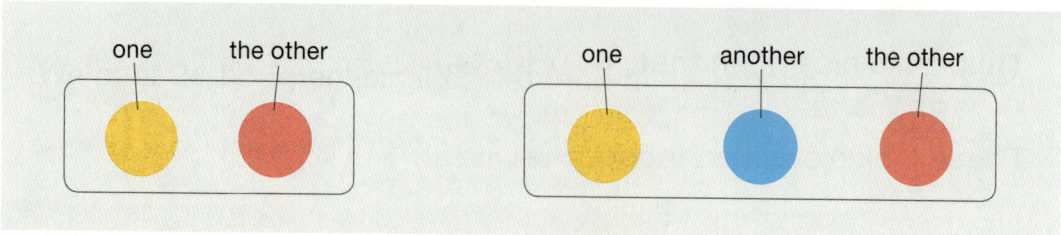

one은 숫자 1을 뜻하기도 하지만 부정대명사로 쓰이면 앞에서 언급한 사람이나 사물을 지칭하게 됩니다. 지칭하는 명사가 단수면 one, 복수면 ones를 씁니다.

❶ one - the other(s)

둘 중 하나를 가리킬 땐 one, 나머지 하나는 the other라고 합니다. 또한 셋 이상에서 하나를 가리킬 땐 one, 나머지 모두는 the others라고 합니다.

There are two elevators; one is for the residents and the other is for the visitors.
두 개의 엘리베이터가 있다. **하나는** 거주자용이고 **나머지 하나는** 방문객용이다.

❷ one - another - the others

세 개 이상의 대상을 나열할 때, 하나는 one, 다른 하나는 another, 나머지는 the others라고 합니다.

The bank has branches all over the world. One is in India, another is in China, and the others are in the U.S.
그 은행은 전 세계에 지점이 있다. **하나는** 인도에 있고, **다른 하나는** 중국에 있으며, **나머지 지점들은** 미국에 있다.

⇧ 고난도 JUMP UP

one another 서로 (= each other)

Recently, more companies are using online tools to communicate with one another.
최근 들어 더 많은 회사들이 **서로** 소통하기 위해 온라인 툴을 사용한다.

연습문제

정답 및 해설 p.017

1 Despite the low success of its first branch, Beanie Coffee has opened ------- in Paris.

(A) other (B) another
(C) any   (D) all

2 One candidate had no prior work experience while ------- was a senior accountant.

(A) other (B) the other
(C) ones   (D) either

3 All volunteers are encouraged to help ------- create a lively atmosphere in the event venue.

(A) other   (B) another
(C) each other (D) the other

4 Among the offers, the job in Springfield is the most interesting even though ------- pay more.

(A) the others (B) another
(C) each   (D) other

6 수량을 나타내는 부정대명사

Some of the buildings 건물들 중 **몇 개** | **One** of the buildings 건물들 중 **하나**

몇몇 부정대명사는 막연한 수량을 나타낼 때 쓰는데, 이때 부정대명사 뒤에 오는 명사와 동사의 수에 유의해야 합니다.

1 all, most, some

all, most, some + of the 복수 명사 + 복수 동사	all, most, some + of the 셀 수 없는 명사 + 단수 동사
all of the students 그 학생들 모두 most of the shops 그 가게들 대부분 some of the details 그 세부 사항들 일부	all of the food 그 음식 모두 most of the audience 그 청중 대부분 some of the information 그 정보의 일부

Most of the guests are familiar with the system. 손님들 **대부분**은 그 시스템에 익숙하다.
　　　　　　복수 명사　　복수 동사

Most of the audience is business owners. 청중의 **대부분**은 사업주다.
　　　　　　셀 수 없는 명사　단수 동사

2 many, both와 each, one

many, both + of the 복수 명사 + 복수 동사	each, one + of the 복수 명사 + 단수 동사
many of the houses 그 집들 중 많은 수 both of the orders 그 주문 둘 다	each of the items 그 물품들 각각 one of the concerns 그 우려들 중 하나

Both of the computers are broken. 그 컴퓨터는 두 대 모두 망가졌다.
　　　　　　복수 명사　복수 동사

One of the packages was delivered to Mr. Woods. 소포 중 **하나**는 우즈 씨에게 전달되었다.
　　　　　　복수 명사　단수 동사

연습문제

정답 및 해설 p.018

1 Before leaving the factory floor, please check that ------- of the machines are turned off.

(A) all (B) another
(C) the other (D) each

2 After the training, we expect ------- of the employees is well aware of the system.

(A) many (B) every
(C) each (D) all

3 Ms. McCarthy and Mr. Choi began working at ARFG Inc., when ------- of them were interns.

(A) one (B) both
(C) another (D) every

4 Instead of taking the bus up the mountain, ------- of our tourists like to hike it.

(A) someone (B) some
(C) other (D) each other

빈출 유형 풀이 전략

1. 주격 인칭대명사

STEP에 따라 실제 토익 문제를 푸는 순서와 요령을 익혀 보세요.

Ms. Perez will be attending the conference after all, so ------- needs accommodations.

(A) she
(B) her
(C) hers
(D) herself

STEP 1 선택지 구성 파악하기

선택지가 '그녀'를 나타내는 대명사들로 구성되어 있으므로 빈칸에 들어갈 적절한 대명사의 형태를 묻는 문제.

Ms. Perez will be attending the conference after all, so ------- needs accommodations.

(A) she
(B) her
(C) hers
(D) herself

STEP 2 빈칸 주변에서 단서 찾기

빈칸 앞에 접속사 so가 있고 뒤에는 동사 needs가 있는 것으로 보아 빈칸은 주어 자리.

Ms. Perez will be attending the conference after all, so ------- needs accommodations.

(A) she ✓
(B) her
(C) hers
(D) herself

STEP 3 정답 찾기

선택지 중 주격 대명사인 (A) she가 정답.

해석 페레즈 씨는 결국 학회에 참석할 것이므로 숙소가 필요하다.

어휘 attend 참석하다 conference 학회 after all 결국 accommodation 숙소, 숙박 시설

2. 재귀대명사

STEP에 따라 실제 토익 문제를 푸는 순서와 요령을 익혀 보세요.

Mr. Dumont gave the presentation by ------- because his partner was sick that day.

(A) him
(B) his
(C) he
(D) himself

STEP 1 선택지 구성 파악하기

선택지가 '그'를 나타내는 대명사들로 구성되어 있으므로 빈칸에 들어갈 적절한 대명사의 형태를 묻는 문제.

Mr. Dumont gave the presentation by ------- because his partner was sick that day.

(A) him
(B) his
(C) he
(D) himself

STEP 2 빈칸 주변에서 단서 찾기

빈칸 앞에 전치사 by가 있으므로 주격 대명사인 (C) he는 오답으로 소거.
또한 문맥상 파트너가 아팠기 때문에 '혼자서 발표했다'는 내용이 되는 게 자연스러움.

Mr. Dumont gave the presentation by ------- because his partner was sick that day.

(A) him
(B) his
(C) he
(D) himself ✓

STEP 3 정답 찾기

선택지 중 전치사 by와 결합하여 '혼자서, 스스로'를 의미할 수 있는 재귀대명사 (D) himself가 정답.

해석 뒤몬 씨는 그의 파트너가 그날 아팠기 때문에 혼자서 발표했다.
어휘 give a presentation 발표하다

VOCABULARY 빈출 명사 어휘 (2)

recommendation	추천; 권고	write a **recommendation** letter 추천서를 쓰다 in line with their **recommendations** 그들의 권고에 따라
compliance	준수, (명령, 요구 등에) 따름	in **compliance** with safety regulations 안전 규정에 따라 ensure **compliance** with the policy 그 정책을 확실하게 준수하다
notice	공고문, 안내문; 알림, 통지	put up a **notice** 공고문을 게시하다 give advance **notice** 사전에[미리] 통보하다
requirement	요구하는 것	meet client's **requirements** 고객이 요구하는 것을 충족하다 eligibility **requirements** 자격 요건
venue	장소	a tourist **venue** 관광지 a popular **venue** for receptions 연회장으로 인기 있는 장소
expense	비용	operating **expenses** 운영비 claim back travel **expenses** 출장비를 청구하다
concern	걱정; 관심사	raise **concerns** about online security 온라인 보안에 대해 우려를 제기하다 the company's primary **concern** 그 회사의 주된 관심사
absence	결석, 부재	**absence** from work 결근 ask for leave of **absence** 휴가[휴직]를 요청하다

연습문제

1 Marth Corp. always uses the TD Convention Center as its ------- for company events.

(A) requirement (B) ceremony
(C) venue (D) enterprise

2 To apply for the job, you must submit a recent ------- letter from a former employer.

(A) recommendation (B) concern
(C) format (D) issue

3 All documents undergo an approval process for ------- with data protection laws.

(A) compliance (B) program
(C) expense (D) participation

4 We require at least two weeks' ------- to modify an event reservation.

(A) absence (B) notice
(C) delay (D) shipment

wealth	부; 풍부, 다량	**wealth** inequality 부의 불평등 a **wealth** of expertise 풍부한 전문성
proof	증명(서), 증거	keep the receipt as **proof** of purchase 구매 증거로 영수증을 보관하다 show a **proof** of residence 거주지 증명서를 보이다
adjustment	수정, 조정; 적응	make a few **adjustments** to the poster 포스터에 몇 가지 수정을 하다 go through a period of **adjustment** 적응 기간을 거치다
enrollment	등록; 입학	complete the **enrollment** form 등록 양식을 작성하다 pay the **enrollment** fee 등록비를 내다
release	발표, 공개; 발표하다	a press **release** 보도 자료 **release** a few details 몇 가지 세부 사항을 발표하다
growth 반 decline 감소	성장, 증가	experience significant **growth** 상당한 성장을 경험하다 revenue **growth** 매출 증가
convenience 반 inconvenience 불편; 귀찮은 일	편의, 편리; 편의 시설	at your earliest **convenience** 가급적 빨리 cause considerable public **inconvenience** 상당한 대중의 불편을 야기하다
maintenance	(건물, 기계 등의) 유지	require regular **maintenance** 정기적인 유지 보수를 필요로 하다 carry out **maintenance** work 유지 보수 작업을 실시하다

정답 및 해설 p.019

5 Someone at TeK's Inc. signed a ------- of delivery of the package on February 12.

(A) wealth (B) fare
(C) closure (D) proof

6 Ms. Fuji made several ------- to the company's Web site to make it look more modern.

(A) adjustments (B) standards
(C) maintenance (D) skills

7 We have left a schedule of the cruise's events in your cabin for your -------.

(A) enrollment (B) convenience
(C) collaboration (D) accuracy

8 The housing market has benefited from recent economic ------- in Share County district.

(A) growth (B) release
(C) accounts (D) layout

ACTUAL TEST

1. Many stationery stores reported that ------- best-selling product is colored pencil set from Dendle Stationery Inc.
   (A) their
   (B) they
   (C) them
   (D) theirs

2. Contest entries will not be accepted if ------- are submitted after the deadline.
   (A) it
   (B) they
   (C) each
   (D) others

3. The first candidate demonstrated a ------- of expertise in various Paka Software programs.
   (A) wealth
   (B) term
   (C) growth
   (D) termination

4. ------- of the speakers at the conference will be staying at Diamond Hotel.
   (A) They
   (B) Some
   (C) We
   (D) Much

5. Additional chairs are available in the next room if you need -------.
   (A) us
   (B) them
   (C) you
   (D) their

6. Only ------- with valid licenses are authorized to operate heavy machinery.
   (A) them
   (B) that
   (C) this
   (D) those

7. Do not hesitate to share all your questions and ------- with our customer service department.
   (A) expenses
   (B) concerns
   (C) promotions
   (D) values

8. Of the four houses, three were in poor condition while ------- was recently renovated.
   (A) other
   (B) another
   (C) the other
   (D) each other

어휘 entry 출품작; 응모권 candidate 후보자 demonstrate 보여 주다, 입증하다 expertise 전문 지식 valid 유효한 authorize 권한을 부여하다 hesitate 망설이다 share 공유하다 poor 좋지 못한 renovate 개조하다, 보수하다

Questions 9-12 refer to the following letter.

Dear Professor Saetang,

Thank you for contacting us on the subject of organizing a field trip to the Brandywine Art Museum. We would be glad to welcome you and your students.

In addition to the standard tour, we have several special ------- that you may be interested in. Most of these are ------- activities relating to art history. There are hands-on workshops as well as seminars throughout the month of April. ------- .

Please notify ------- in advance of the date of your visit so that we may prepare.

We look forward to having you.

Regards,

Ethel Yeder

9. (A) events
   (B) treatments
   (C) venues
   (D) prices

10. (A) executive
    (B) dependent
    (C) likely
    (D) educational

11. (A) We'd like to thank you for your help.
    (B) However, I will not be available in May.
    (C) You can find the full schedule on our Web site.
    (D) Payment will be processed once you arrive.

12. (A) me
    (B) one
    (C) theirs
    (D) my

UNIT 03

동사

1. 동사의 자리와 형태
2. 동사원형 자리
3. 자동사
4. 타동사

빈출 유형 풀이 전략
Vocabulary
Actual Test

TOEIC Grammar

약 15%

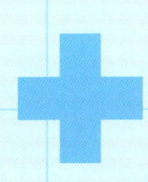

UNIT 03 동사

동사는 문장에서 서술어를 담당하는 품사로서 문장의 구조를 결정하는 데 가장 중요한 역할을 합니다. 또한 뒤에서 배울 to부정사와 동명사, 분사 등을 만들어 내고, 수 일치, 시제, 태 문제와 엮여 다양한 문법 문제로 출제되므로 이 단원을 통해 동사의 기본기를 탄탄하게 다질 필요가 있습니다.

 스피드 진단 테스트

(A), (B) 중 알맞은 것을 고르세요.

1. He ------- for a work visa.

    (A) applied   (B) application

2. The store ------- various organic products.

    (A) offering   (B) offers

정답 및 해석
1. (A), 그는 취업 비자를 신청했다.
2. (B), 그 가게는 다양한 유기농 제품을 제공한다.

💡 동사란?

모든 문장은 반드시 한 개의 서술어를 취하며, 서술어 자리를 담당하는 품사가 동사입니다. 동사는 일반동사와 be동사로 구성됩니다.

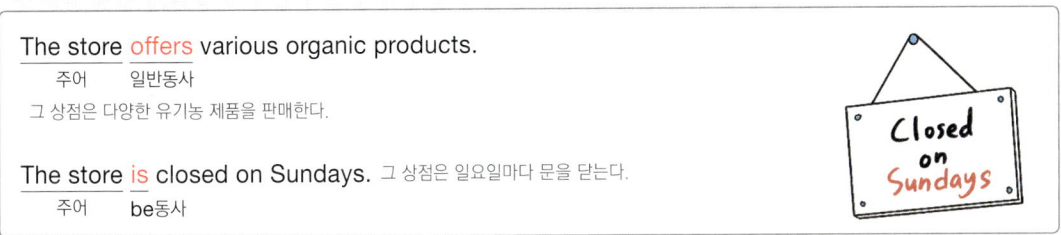

The store offers various organic products.
주어   일반동사
그 상점은 다양한 유기농 제품을 판매한다.

The store is closed on Sundays. 그 상점은 일요일마다 문을 닫는다.
주어   be동사

평서문에서 동사는 주어 바로 뒤에 옵니다. 하지만 아래와 같이 주어 뒤에 수식어구가 올 경우, 주어와 동사가 멀리 떨어져 있을 수 있습니다.

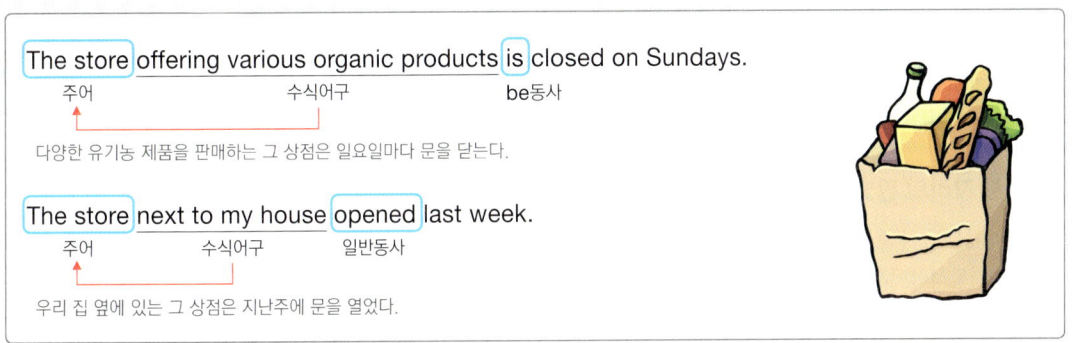

The store offering various organic products is closed on Sundays.
주어   수식어구   be동사
다양한 유기농 제품을 판매하는 그 상점은 일요일마다 문을 닫는다.

The store next to my house opened last week.
주어   수식어구   일반동사
우리 집 옆에 있는 그 상점은 지난주에 문을 열었다.

● 일반동사의 종류

동사가 자동사냐 타동사냐에 따라 뒤에 올 수 있는 문장 성분이 달라지기 때문에 동사는 문장 형식을 결정하는 가장 중심적인 역할을 한다고 볼 수 있어요.

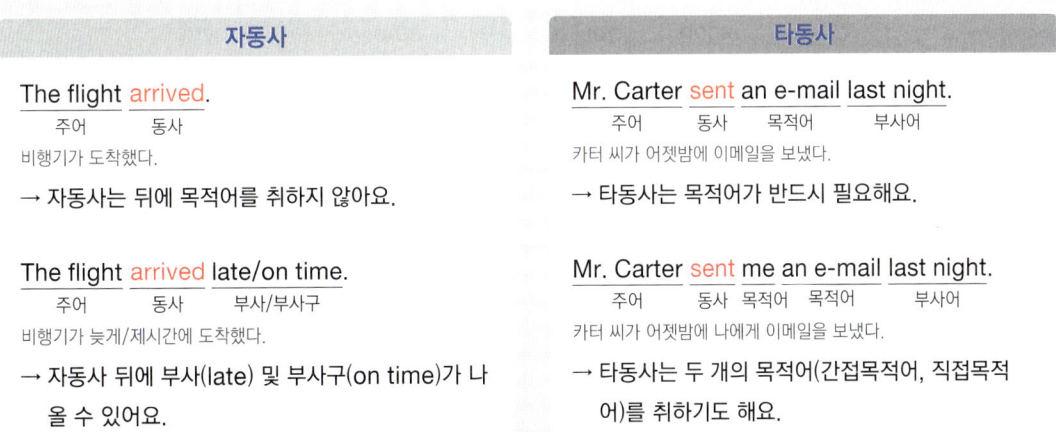

자동사	타동사
The flight arrived. 주어 동사 비행기가 도착했다. → 자동사는 뒤에 목적어를 취하지 않아요.	Mr. Carter sent an e-mail last night. 주어 동사 목적어 부사어 카터 씨가 어젯밤에 이메일을 보냈다. → 타동사는 목적어가 반드시 필요해요.
The flight arrived late/on time. 주어 동사 부사/부사구 비행기가 늦게/제시간에 도착했다. → 자동사 뒤에 부사(late) 및 부사구(on time)가 나올 수 있어요.	Mr. Carter sent me an e-mail last night. 주어 동사 목적어 목적어 부사어 카터 씨가 어젯밤에 나에게 이메일을 보냈다. → 타동사는 두 개의 목적어(간접목적어, 직접목적어)를 취하기도 해요.

1 동사의 자리와 형태

Employees **attend** a training seminar twice a year.
　　　　　　동사
직원들은 일 년에 두 번 교육에 참여합니다.

서술어 자리에는 동사 품사만 올 수 있으며, 앞에 동사를 보조하는 조동사가 붙을 수 있습니다.

❶ 동사 자리에 올 수 있는 것

All employees in marketing **attended** the meeting. 마케팅 부서의 모든 직원이 그 회의에 참석했다.
　　　　　　　　　　　　　attending (×)
　　　　　　　　　　　　　to attend (×)
　　　　　　　　　　　　　attendance (×)

Several employees **will attend** the conference. 몇몇 직원이 그 컨퍼런스에 참석할 것이다.
　　　　　　　　　조동사　동사

❷ 동사 자리의 판별

토익 문법 문제에서는 빈칸에 들어갈 품사를 고르는 문제가 자주 등장하며, 동사 자리는 앞뒤에 오는 주요 문장 성분(주어, 목적어, 보어)을 구분함으로써 판단할 수 있습니다.

Those who took online classes don't have to **attend** the training session.
　　　　주어　　　　　　　　　　조동사　　동사　　목적어
온라인 수업을 들은 사람들은 그 교육에 참석할 필요가 없습니다.

연습문제　　　　　　　　　　　　　　　　　　　　　　정답 및 해설 p.024

1 Parjak Corp. ------- a price reduction for buying out Gasny Inc.

(A) negotiating　　(B) negotiation
(C) negotiator　　(D) negotiated

2 The managing director strongly ------- the budget cuts that the company had proposed.

(A) opposition　　(B) opposed
(C) opposing　　(D) opposite

3 The cost of living ------- from town to town even within the same region.

(A) variation　　(B) various
(C) varies　　(D) to vary

4 Ms. McGee explained that changing the job requirements ------- the hiring process.

(A) to complicate
(B) be complicating
(C) would complicate
(D) be complicated

058

2 동사원형 자리

A cashier **must wear** her nametag while on duty.
　　　　　조동사　동사원형

계산원은 근무하는 동안 이름표를 착용해야 합니다.

서술어 자리에 오는 동사가 조동사 뒤에 올 때, 그리고 명령문의 문두에 올 때에는 항상 동사원형으로 쓰입니다.

❶ 조동사 + 동사원형

We will / should add staff. 우리는 직원을 증원할 것이다 / 증원해야 한다.
　　조동사　　동사원형

❷ 명령문 또는 Please 뒤

If you have any problems with the device, contact the store. 기기에 문제가 있으면 매장으로 연락 주세요.
　　　　　　　　　　　　　　　　　　　　　　　　　동사원형

Please be advised that our store will be closed on April 5. 저희 가게가 4월 5일에 휴점한다는 것을 알려드립니다.
　　　　동사원형

🔺 고난도 JUMP UP

특정 동사가 요구나 제안, 권고를 나타낼 때, 동사 뒤에 따라오는 that절에서는 〈should + 동사원형〉을 씁니다. 이때 should는 생략되는 경우가 많아요.

| ask/request/require | demand | suggest/propose | recommend/advise |
| 요청하다 | 요구하다 | 제안하다 | 권고하다 |

The landlord demanded that tenants (give, ~~gave~~) a one month notice before leaving.
집주인은 임차인이 나가기 한 달 전에 공지해 줄 것을 요구했다.

연습문제

정답 및 해설 p.025

1 On the collection day, residents must ------- their household trash from their recyclable items.

(A) separate　　(B) to separate
(C) separation　(D) separates

2 Please ------- that all of the items you have ordered are in the package.

(A) confirm　　(B) confirming
(C) to confirm　(D) confirms

3 When on the factory floor, ------- your protective gear at all times.

(A) wearing　(B) wear
(C) wears　　(D) to wear

4 Experts recommend that passwords ------- at least 12 characters long.

(A) are　(B) were
(C) be　(D) being

자동사

> He **arrived** just before the train **left**.
>   자동사   자동사
> 기차가 떠나기 직전에 그가 도착했다.

자동사는 뒤에 목적어를 필요로 하지 않는 동사이지만, 시간과 장소를 나타내는 부사구가 따라올 수 있습니다.

❶ 자동사 + 부사구

They *arrived* at the airport in time. 그들은 늦지 않게 공항에 도착했다.
  자동사   부사구 (장소) 부사구 (시간)

❷ 타동사로도 쓰이는 자동사

| end | 끝나다 (타) ~을 끝내다 | sell | 팔리다 (타) ~을 팔다 |
| open | 문을 열다 (타) ~을 열다 | close | 문을 닫다 (타) ~을 닫다 |

The library does not *open* on weekends. 그 도서관은 주말에 문을 열지 않는다. (자동사)
The company *opened* its first store in London. 그 회사는 런던에 첫 번째 매장을 열었다. (타동사)

❸ 자동사 + 전치사

어떤 자동사들은 특정 전치사와 함께 쓰여 하나의 타동사구처럼 쓰이기도 합니다.

depend/rely on	~에 의존하다	agree with[to/on]	~에 동의하다
apply for	~에 지원하다	register for/enroll in	~에 등록하다
contribute to	~에 기여하다	inquire about	~에 대해 문의하다

I would like to *inquire about* the current interest rates. 현행 금리에 대해 문의 드리고 싶습니다.

연습문제
정답 및 해설 p.026

1 The harvest festival ------- every year in the last week of October.
   (A) occurring   (B) occurrence
   (C) occurs   (D) to occur

2 A slight difference ------- between the items which sell well online and in store.
   (A) exists   (B) to exist
   (C) existing   (D) existence

3 The new headquarters building ------- on solar energy for its power.
   (A) relies   (B) deals
   (C) agrees   (D) turns

4 Ms. Vowsky contributed ------- the project by taking and organizing all of the meeting notes.
   (A) at   (B) to
   (C) on   (D) for

4 타동사

She **suggested** the Italian restaurant near the station.
　　타동사　　　　　목적어　　　　　　　부사구

그녀는 역 근처에 있는 이탈리안 식당을 추천했다.

타동사는 뒤에 목적어를 취하는 동사이며, 시간이나 장소 등을 나타내는 부사구가 뒤따를 수 있습니다.

❶ 자동사로 착각하기 쉬운 타동사

목적어가 '~을[를]'이 아닌 '~로', '~에' 등으로 해석되는 경우도 있으며, 이때 목적어 앞에 전치사를 붙이기 쉬우므로 주의해야 합니다.

discuss ~~about~~ the problem 문제에 대해 토론하다	address ~~to~~ the audience 청중에게 연설하다
reach ~~to~~ agreement 합의에 도달하다	explain ~~about~~ the situation 상황에 대해 설명하다
contact ~~to~~ the engineer 기술자에게 연락하다	approach ~~to~~ the building 빌딩에 접근하다
affect ~~to~~ the schedule 일정에 영향을 미치다	access ~~to~~ a Web site 웹사이트에 접속하다

The weather will affect (~~to~~) the project schedule. 날씨가 프로젝트 일정에 영향을 미칠 것입니다.

❷ 같은 의미를 가지는 타동사와 구동사

oppose = object to ~에 반대하다	answer = reply to, respond to ~에 답하다
attend = participate in ~에 참석하다	handle = deal with, take care of ~을 처리하다
obey = comply with ~을 준수하다	suggest = put forward ~을 제시하다

She can (~~deal~~, handle) customer complaints skillfully. 그녀는 고객 불만을 능숙하게 처리할 수 있다.

연습문제　　　　　　　　　　　　　　　　　　　　　　　　　정답 및 해설 p.027

1 You can ------- our customer service representative by phone or chat.
　(A) be reached　　(B) were reached
　(C) has reached　　(D) reach

2 The start-up's CEO ------- the people at the press conference with a lot of confidence.
　(A) addressed　　(B) spoke
　(C) handled　　　(D) dealt

3 You must ------- to this e-mail to verify your attendance at the convention.
　(A) answer　　(B) oppose
　(C) reply　　　(D) object

4 Nearly 200 employees participated ------- the team building exercise event organized by J&A Inc.
　(A) with　　(B) to
　(C) of　　　(D) in

빈출 유형 풀이 전략

1. 동사 자리 문제

STEP에 따라 실제 토익 문제를 푸는 순서와 요령을 익혀 보세요.

Ben Rawling, a professional photographer, never ------- his images because he does not want to distort them.

(A) enlarging
(B) enlarges
(C) enlargement
(D) enlargeable

STEP 1　선택지 구성 파악하기

선택지가 enlarge에서 파생된 다양한 품사로 구성됨. → 자리 문제

Ben Rawling, a professional photographer, never ------- his images because he does not want to distort them.

(A) enlarging
(B) enlarges
(C) enlargement
(D) enlargeable

STEP 2　빈칸 주변에서 단서 찾기

Ben Rawling이 주어, his images가 목적어.
→ 주어와 목적어 사이는 서술어(동사) 자리.

Ben Rawling, a professional photographer, never ------- his images because he does not want to distort them.

(A) enlarging
(B) ✓ enlarges
(C) enlargement
(D) enlargeable

STEP 3　정답 찾기

선택지 중 동사는 (B) enlarges.

해석　전문 사진작가인 벤 롤링은 자신이 찍은 이미지가 왜곡되는 것을 원하지 않기 때문에 이미지를 결코 확대하지 않는다.

어휘　professional photographer 전문 사진작가　enlarge 확대하다　distort 왜곡하다, 일그러뜨리다

2. 동사원형 자리 문제

STEP에 따라 실제 토익 문제를 푸는 순서와 요령을 익혀 보세요.

To avoid issues with your meal, please ------- the server beforehand if you have any food allergies.

(A) inform
(B) informs
(C) informing
(D) information

STEP 1 선택지 구성 파악하기

선택지가 동사 inform의 다양한 형태로 구성됨.
→ 자리 문제

To avoid issues with your meal, please ------- the server beforehand if you have any food allergies.

STEP 2 빈칸 주변에서 단서 찾기

please 뒤에 빈칸이 있음.
→ 빈칸은 동사원형 자리.

(A) inform
(B) informs
(C) informing
(D) information

To avoid issues with your meal, please ------- the server beforehand if you have any food allergies.

(A) inform ✓
(B) informs
(C) informing
(D) information

STEP 3 정답 찾기

선택지 중 동사원형은 (A) inform.

해석 식사에 문제가 없도록, 음식 알레르기가 있으시면 서빙 직원에게 미리 알려 주시기 바랍니다.
어휘 avoid 방지하다, 막다 inform ~에게 알리다 beforehand 미리, 사전에

VOCABULARY 빈출 동사 어휘 (1)

submit	제출하다	**submit** a job application 입사 지원서를 제출하다 **submit** design proposals 디자인 제안서를 제출하다
anticipate	예상하다	**anticipate** demand 수요를 예상하다 **anticipated** arrival time 예상 도착 시간
extend	연장하다; (사업, 세력 등을) 확대하다	**extend** hours during the festival 축제 동안 영업 시간을 연장하다 **extend** its operations into UK 영국으로 사업을 확대하다
discount	할인하다	**discount** bulk purchases 대량 구매에 할인을 제공하다 heavily **discount** all sale items 모든 판매 상품을 대폭 할인하다
invite	초대하다; (정식으로) 요청하다	**invite** him to a business lunch 그를 사업상 점심 식사에 초대하다 **invite** successful candidates for interview 합격한 후보들에게 면접을 요청하다
maintain	(관계, 상태, 수준 등을) 유지하다	**maintain** contact with clients 고객들과의 연락을 유지하다 **maintain** machinery properly 기계를 적절하게 유지하다
comply with	~을 지키다, ~에 따르다	**comply with** the standards 그 기준들을 지키다 **comply with** the employees' requests 직원들의 요청에 따르다
apply	신청하다, 지원하다; 적용하다	**apply** for a marketing position 마케팅 직무에 지원하다 **apply** a discount coupon 할인 쿠폰을 적용하다

연습문제

1 To lead a team project, staff must first ------- their plan to Ms. Jansen.

(A) maintain (B) submit
(C) discuss (D) afford

2 The HR manager ------- all team members to participate in the optional workshops.

(A) invited (B) grouped
(C) anticipated (D) responded

3 Each model is expected to ------- with the brand's strict safety standards.

(A) fulfill (B) comply
(C) confirm (D) extend

4 All items will be heavily ------- during tomorrow's grand opening sale.

(A) lasted (B) applied
(C) discounted (D) simplified

suspend	중단하다	**suspend** the train services 열차 운행을 중단하다 **suspend** production because of parts shortages 부품 부족으로 생산을 중단하다
obtain	얻다, 획득하다	**obtain** an official permit 공식 허가를 받다 **obtain** a refund on a purchase 구매품을 환불받다
assist	돕다, 보조하다	**assist** him to prepare the event 그가 행사를 준비하는 걸 돕다 **assist** in making the decision 결정하는 데 도움을 주다
consume	소비하다	**consume** less electricity 전기를 덜 소비하다 a time-**consuming** process 시간이 많이 걸리는 과정
charge	부과하다, 청구하다	**charge** a fee for delivery 배송 요금을 부과하다 **charge** him for the repair 그에게 수리 비용을 청구하다
donate	기부하다	**donate** 10 percent of its profits 수익의 10퍼센트를 기부하다 **donate** time and talent 시간과 재능을 기부하다
coincide with	~와 일치하다	**coincide with** the conference 그 회담과 같은 시기에 하다 **coincide with** her opinions 그녀의 의견과 일치하다
compete	경쟁하다	**compete** for the contract 그 계약을 두고 경쟁하다 **compete** with the big corporations 대기업들과 경쟁하다

정답 및 해설 p.028

5 The charity Run for Life ------- thousands of dollars for cancer research annually.

(A) suspends (B) proves
(C) donates (D) cures

6 For a leave of absence, staff members are required to ------- prior approval from their supervisor.

(A) designate (B) compete
(C) assign (D) obtain

7 For a small fee, Pet Power ------- dog owners who have trouble training their pets.

(A) charges (B) assists
(C) introduces (D) consumes

8 The completion of the restoration project is expected to ------- with the building's bicentennial.

(A) collaborate (B) uphold
(C) coincide (D) announce

ACTUAL TEST

1. Light refreshments will ------- to all guests who wish to attend a guided tour.

    (A) provides
    (B) provided
    (C) to provide
    (D) be provided

2. The Trimble Gallery ------- its twenty-fifth anniversary with a large reception last week.

    (A) celebrate
    (B) celebrated
    (C) celebrating
    (D) being celebrated

3. The airplane's equipment has to ------- with the latest safety regulations before it is used.

    (A) comply
    (B) depend
    (C) submit
    (D) adopt

4. Sales of Mako Co.'s new hybrid car already ------- the projections made by analysts.

    (A) surpassing
    (B) surpassed
    (C) being surpassed
    (D) have surpassed

5. Please ------- aware that some of the part-time jobs are as demanding as full-time ones.

    (A) to be
    (B) being
    (C) be
    (D) been

6. Association members are allowed to register ------- the conference one week before non-members.

    (A) as
    (B) from
    (C) onto
    (D) for

7. The electronics company ------- more than one million copies of its new game console.

    (A) to sell
    (B) was sold
    (C) selling
    (D) has sold

8. Mr. Timmins has asked that a taxi ------- ready for him when he arrives.

    (A) be
    (B) were
    (C) has been
    (D) being

어휘 refreshments ((항상 복수형)) 다과, 음료　attend ~에 참석하다　safety regulation 안전 규정　projection 예상
demanding 힘든　association 협회　game console 게임기

Questions 9-12 refer to the following notice.

To: Lakeland Residents
From: Lakeland City Council
Subject: Project Update
Date: March 4

The Lakeland City Council would like to provide an update on the 2nd Avenue project, as below.

A permit has been granted for the construction of a new mini shopping center on 2nd Avenue. A recent survey of citizens ------- that there is a need for more retail businesses in Lakeland. Krefton Contractors has been selected to construct the building. TC Property Management will ------- renting out the units.
9.   **10.**

The building will house more than 30 shops and restaurants. ------- supposed to be completed by next December. Other businesses in the area will remain open during the construction. ------- . However, the work crews will do their best to minimize disruptions.
                                                                      11.
12.

9   (A) indicative
    (B) indication
    (C) indicating
    (D) indicated

10 (A) point
    (B) handle
    (C) observe
    (D) deal

11 (A) It is
    (B) Yours are
    (C) Theirs are
    (D) There is

12 (A) Revenue from tourists may increase because of the change.
    (B) Safety regulations have become stricter recently.
    (C) Shoppers and workers in the area may notice an increase in noise.
    (D) Other projects are being considered to promote the area.

어휘 as below 아래와 같이 permit 허가 grant 승인하다 retail business 소매점 construct 건설하다 rent out ~을 임대하다 be supposed to do ~할 예정이다 minimize ~을 최소화하다 disruption 혼란

UNIT 04

수 일치

1. 긴 주어의 수 일치
2. 주의해야 할 주어의 수
3. 주의해야 할 수량 표현
4. 태와 시제가 결합된 수 일치

빈출 유형 풀이 전략
Vocabulary
Actual Test

TOEIC Grammar

약 15%

UNIT 04 수 일치

영어 문장의 최소 구성 요소는 주어와 동사이며 이들은 서로 긴밀한 관계를 갖기 때문에 주어의 수에 동사의 형태를 일치시키는 '수 일치'의 법칙이라는 것이 있어요. 토익에서는 동사 자리 문제와 복합적으로 출제되거나, 난이도가 높아지면 태, 시제와 결합해 출제되기도 합니다.

 스피드 진단 테스트

(A), (B) 중 알맞은 것을 고르세요.

1. Mr. Martin never ------- a deadline.

   (A) miss   (B) misses

2. A degree in a field related to economics -------.

   (A) is preferred   (B) are preferred

정답 및 해설

1. (B), 마틴 씨는 마감일을 어기는 법이 없다.
2. (A), 경제학 관련 분야의 학위가 선호된다.

수 일치란?

수 일치란 주어의 수에 동사의 형태를 맞추는 것을 말합니다. 기본 법칙은, 주어의 수가 단수이면 단수 동사 형태를, 주어의 수가 복수이면 복수 동사 형태를 쓰는 것입니다.

● be동사의 수 일치

단수 주어 + 단수 동사	복수 주어 + 복수 동사
The customer is complaining. 그 고객이 불평하고 있다.	Many customers are complaining. 많은 고객들이 불평하고 있다.
One of the customers was complaining. 고객 중 한 명이 불평하고 있었다.	Many customers were complaining. 많은 고객들이 불평하고 있었다.

● 일반동사의 수 일치

일반동사는 단수일 경우 -(e)s를 붙이며, have 동사의 경우 단수에서는 has를 사용합니다.

	단수 동사	복수 동사
일반동사	-(e)s	동사원형
have 동사	has	have

The company provides a 24-hour repair service. 그 회사는 24시간 수리 서비스를 제공한다.
　단수 주어　　단수 동사

Many companies provide a 24-hour repair service. 많은 회사들이 24시간 수리 서비스를 제공한다.
　복수 주어　　복수 동사

The company has an excellent reputation in the hotel industry. 그 회사는 호텔 업계에서 평판이 좋다.
　단수 주어　단수 동사

Both companies have an excellent reputation in the hotel industry. 두 회사 모두 호텔 업계에서 평판이 좋다.
　복수 주어　　복수 동사

1 긴 주어의 수 일치

The logo design for the athletic shoes **is** very modern.
단수 주어   수식 어구   단수 동사

그 운동화의 로고 디자인은 매우 현대적이다.

토익에서는 주어와 동사 사이에 구가 삽입되어 주어가 길어진 형태가 자주 출제됩니다. 주어가 길어진 경우, 동사 바로 앞에 오는 단어에 수를 일치시키지 않도록 주의해야 합니다.

❶ 뒤에서 수식을 받는 주어

Carl Phillip, [the chief operating officer,] has spoken to the employees about the merger.
최고 운영 책임자인 칼 필립 씨는 합병에 대해 직원들에게 말했습니다. (동격어구의 수식)

Calls [to our customer service department] are usually recorded.
저희 고객 서비스 부서로 오는 전화는 보통 녹음됩니다. (전치사구의 수식)

Cars [parked on the street] cause traffic congestion.
길에 주차된 차들이 교통 혼란을 야기한다. (분사구의 수식)

Employees [who have not yet registered for next week's seminar] are required to do so immediately.
다음 주에 있을 세미나에 등록하지 않은 직원들은 즉시 등록해야 합니다. (관계사절의 수식)

❷ 소유격의 수식을 받는 주어

The position's benefits are explained in the contract. 그 일자리의 복지 혜택은 계약서에 설명되어 있습니다.
소유격   주어   동사

연습문제
정답 및 해설 p.033

1 Logan Tech's new recruitment drive ------- already attracted five hundred applicants.

(A) has   (B) to have
(C) having   (D) have

2 Kembery, a sustainable fashion brand, ------- casual clothing for women.

(A) manufacturing   (B) are manufactured
(C) manufactures   (D) to manufacture

3 An appliance with these labels ------- to all energy-efficiency regulations.

(A) to conform   (B) conforming
(C) conform   (D) conforms

4 The article that will be published tomorrow ------- Escobar Inc.'s efforts to expand overseas.

(A) highlights   (B) highlight
(C) were highlighted   (D) to highlight

2 주의해야 할 주어의 수

JR Instruments **offers** a variety of online courses.
회사명은 단수 주어   단수 동사
JR 악기는 다양한 온라인 과정을 제공합니다.

주어로 쓰인 명사의 형태만 보고 수를 혼동할 수 있는 것들에 대해 구분해서 기억해 두세요.

❶ 주의해야 할 단수 단어: 고유명사(회사명), news

JR Logistics/Electronics/Pharmaceuticals is located in Dublin. JR 물류/전자/제약은 더블린에 위치해 있습니다.
The good news is that all lectures are free. 좋은 소식은 모든 강의가 무료라는 것이다.

❷ 복합명사는 뒤의 명사에 수 일치

benefits package 복리 후생 제도	savings account 저축 계좌
sales report 매출 보고서	sales representative 영업 사원
sports equipment 스포츠 장비	customs officer 세관 직원
human resources department 인사부	awards ceremony 시상식

The quarterly sales report indicates that the company's profits dropped dramatically.
             복합 명사 주어
분기 매출 보고서는 회사의 수익이 급격히 하락했음을 보여 주고 있다.

❸ 동명사 주어는 단수 취급

Conducting regular customer surveys helps businesses to collect data.
         동명사 주어
정기적인 고객 설문 조사를 시행하는 것은 회사가 자료를 모을 수 있도록 도와준다.

연습문제

정답 및 해설 p.034

1 By the end of this month, Samco Fashions ------- going to release a new line of swimwear.

(A) were   (B) are
(C) be   (D) is

2 The customs officer ------- the passport and other documents of people entering the country.

(A) checks   (B) checking
(C) check   (D) to check

3 The human resources department of most corporations ------- new staff members through online-based courses.

(A) train   (B) is training
(C) to train   (D) training

4 Pressing the red button on the wall ------- the alarm system for the laboratory.

(A) activating   (B) activate
(C) active   (D) activates

주의해야 할 수량 표현

Each of the budgets **was** approved.
each of the + 복수 명사 　　단수 동사
각 예산안이 승인되었다.

부정대명사 주어의 경우, 뒤에 오는 명사의 수에 따라 동사의 수가 결정되기도 하지만 그렇지 않은 경우도 있습니다.

❶ 단수 동사를 쓰는 경우

one	each	either	neither	of the + 복수 명사	단수 동사
little	a little	much		of the + 셀 수 없는 명사	단수 동사

Neither of them **was** interested in our offer. 그들 둘 다 우리 제안에 관심이 없었다.

❷ 복수 동사를 쓰는 경우

few	a few	both	several	many	of the + 복수 명사	복수 동사
a number of		a large[great] number of			+ 복수 명사	복수 동사

Both of the meetings **were** canceled. 두 회의 모두 취소되었다.

❸ 단수 동사와 복수 동사를 모두 쓰는 경우

some	any	half	most	all	of the + 복수 명사	복수 동사
					of the + 셀 수 없는 명사	단수 동사

Most of the food [you eat] **is** high in fat. 여러분이 먹는 대부분의 음식은 지방 함유량이 높습니다.

연습문제

정답 및 해설 p.035

1 Each of the Camdex-360 laptops ------- equipped with a battery that lasts for six hours.

(A) are (B) is
(C) be (D) were

2 A large number of businesses ------- a recruitment firm to find new employees.

(A) use (B) uses
(C) using (D) to use

3 The event planning team will go home early because most of the preparation ------- been completed.

(A) have (B) has
(C) to have (D) having

4 All of the clients of Parkway Accounting ------- to attend the year-end banquet.

(A) are invited (B) is invited
(C) are inviting (D) invites

4 태와 시제가 결합된 수 일치

The hiring process at large companies **involves** long screening steps.
- 주어: The hiring process
- involve (×), is involved (×)

대기업의 채용 프로세스는 긴 심사 단계를 수반한다.

수 일치 문제에 태와 시제까지 복합적으로 묻는 문제가 출제되기도 하는데, 특히 태와 결합된 문제가 자주 등장합니다. 그런 경우에는 수 일치에 어긋나는 것을 먼저 소거한 다음 태 또는 시제가 올바른 것을 찾는 것이 요령입니다. 태와 시제에 대해서는 Unit 05와 Unit 06에서 더욱 자세히 다뤄집니다.

❶ 태와 시제 복합

All of the components [you need for installation] **are included** in the package.
→ 수 일치 (복수) + 태 (수동)

설치에 필요한 모든 부품은 상자 안에 포함되어 있습니다.

> 1단계: 수 일치 → 주어는 복수 → 단수 동사 소거 → includes (×), is included (×)
> 2단계: 태 → 수동태인지 능동태인지 확인 → include (×), are included (○)

The manager **has concluded** that the marketing strategy was ineffective.
→ 수 일치 (단수) + 시제 (현재완료)

관리자는 마케팅 전략이 비효과적이었다고 결론지었다.

❷ 관계사절의 수 일치

We are looking for a staff member [who **has** extensive experience in media].
→ has의 주어: a staff member

우리는 매체에 다양한 경험이 있는 직원을 찾고 있습니다.

연습문제

정답 및 해설 p.036

1. All of the new Max cars ------- a warranty that covers three years.
   (A) providing   (B) provide
   (C) provides   (D) are provided

2. A number of keynote speakers ------- because of their expertise in product marketing.
   (A) choose   (B) is chosen
   (C) chooses   (D) are chosen

3. The report about Calvin Turner's sudden retirement ------- a great deal of interest among analysts.
   (A) has generated   (B) generate
   (C) generating   (D) was generated

4. The logistics department ------- some issues with the distribution network but can resolve them soon.
   (A) experience   (B) are experiencing
   (C) has experienced (D) to experience

빈출 유형 풀이 전략

1. 긴 주어의 수 일치 문제

STEP에 따라 실제 토익 문제를 푸는 순서와 요령을 익혀 보세요.

The sale of illegally copied music albums and films ------- in all parts of the country.

(A) prohibit
(B) is prohibited
(C) are prohibited
(D) to prohibit

STEP 1 선택지 구성 파악하기

선택지가 단수 동사, 복수 동사, 능동, 수동의 다양한 동사 형태로 구성.
→ 적절한 동사 형태를 묻는 문제.

The sale [of illegally copied music albums and films] ------- in all parts of the country.

(A) prohibit
(B) is prohibited
(C) are prohibited
(D) to prohibit

STEP 2 빈칸 주변에서 단서 찾기

주어가 길어 보이지만 The sale이 주어, of illegally ~ films는 주어를 수식하는 전치사구.
→ 단수 주어 The sale에 적절한 동사 형태를 찾아야 함.

The sale of illegally copied music albums and films ------- in all parts of the country.

(A) prohibit
(B) is prohibited ✓
(C) are prohibited
(D) to prohibit

STEP 3 정답 찾기

단수 주어에 호응하는 단수 동사는 (B) is prohibited뿐이다.

해석 불법으로 복제된 음반과 영화의 판매는 전국 각지에서 금지되어 있습니다.
어휘 illegally 불법으로 (↔ legally 합법적으로)   copy 복사하다; 복사본   prohibit 금지시키다

2. 수 일치와 태의 복합 문제

STEP에 따라 실제 토익 문제를 푸는 순서와 요령을 익혀 보세요.

Upland Instruments ------- professional-grade digital keyboards for more than twenty years.

(A) are designed
(B) to be designing
(C) was designed
(D) has been designing

STEP 1 선택지 구성 파악하기

선택지가 능동, 수동 등의 다양한 동사 형태로 구성.
→ 적절한 동사 형태를 묻는 문제.

Upland Instruments ------- professional-grade digital keyboards for more than twenty years.

(A) are designed
(B) to be designing
(C) was designed
(D) has been designing

STEP 2 빈칸 주변에서 단서 찾기

Upland Instruments(회사명)가 주어이며 단수임.
→ to부정사 (B) 소거
→ 복수 동사 (A) 소거

Upland Instruments ------- professional-grade digital keyboards for more than twenty years.

(A) are designed
(B) to be designing
(C) was designed
(D) has been designing ✓

STEP 3 태 판단

빈칸 뒤의 professional-grade digital keyboards가 목적어.
→ 능동태 (수동태 소거)

해석 업랜드 악기는 20년 이상 전문가용 디지털 키보드를 디자인해 오고 있다.

어휘 instrument 악기   professional 전문가의, 직업의

VOCABULARY  빈출 동사 어휘 (2)

lack	~가 없다, ~가 부족하다	**lack** the experience and knowledge 경험과 지식이 없다 **lack** the skills for the job 그 일에 필요한 기술이 부족하다
commit	(굳게) 약속하다; (돈, 시간을) 쓰다	**commit** more money to the project 그 프로젝트에 더 많은 돈을 약속하다 **commit** large amounts of money 많은 액수의 돈을 쓰다
reduce	줄이다; (가격을) 낮추다	**reduce** travel expenses 출장비를 줄이다 at a **reduced** price 낮은 가격으로
accept	받아들이다, 받아 주다	**accept** orders over the phone 전화로 주문을 받다 **accept** only cash 현금만 받다
implement 통 carry out	시행하다, 실시하다	**implement** changes/decisions/recommendations 변화/결정/권고를 시행하다 **implement** a recycling program 재활용 프로그램을 실시하다
allocate	(돈, 시간 등을) 할당하다	**allocate** $50,000 for online ads 온라인 광고에 5만 달러를 할당하다 **allocate** funds to hire new staff 새로운 직원을 채용하는 데 자금을 할당하다
postpone 통 put off, defer	연기하다, 미루다	**postpone** the meeting until next Monday 그 회의를 다음 주 월요일로 연기하다 **postpone** the game because of heavy rain 폭우로 그 경기를 미루다
decline	감소하다; (정중히) 거절하다	**decline** sharply/rapidly 급격하게/빠르게 감소하다 **decline** the job offer 일자리 제안을 거절하다

연습문제

1 This training program focuses on ------- innovative teaching strategies developed by leading educators.

(A) committing (B) allowing
(C) implementing (D) transporting

2 Ms. Burr's impressive educational background makes up for the fact that she ------- experience.

(A) lacks (B) borrows
(C) imposes (D) accomplishes

3 All prices will be ------- during the first hour of the store's special event.

(A) combined (B) declined
(C) attributed (D) reduced

4 Staff at Brenner's Deli don't ------- personal checks without the holder's signature.

(A) afford (B) accept
(C) refund (D) allocate

cultivate	(작물을) 재배하다; (관계를) 구축하다, 쌓다	**cultivate** mainly wheat 주로 밀을 재배하다 **cultivate** good relations with competitors 경쟁사들과 좋은 관계를 구축하다
approve	승인하다; ~을 좋게 생각하다 (~ of)	**approve** the plan 그 계획을 승인하다 **approve** of her idea 그녀의 의견을 좋게 생각하다
retain	보유하다, 유지하다	recruit and **retain** skilled staff 능력 있는 직원들을 채용하고 보유하다 **retain** 45 percent ownership of the company 그 회사의 소유권을 45% 보유하다
explore	탐구하다, 탐색하다	**explore** in more detail 더 자세히 탐구하다 **explore** the latest technologies 최신 기술을 탐색하다
arrange	(시간, 장소 등을) 정하다; 준비하다; 배열하다	**arrange** an appointment for Friday 금요일로 약속[예약]을 잡다 **arrange** the list alphabetically 그 리스트를 알파벳순으로 정리하다
convene	(회의 등을) 소집하다	**convene** a panel of experts 전문가 집단을 소집하다 **convene** an emergency board meeting 긴급 이사회를 소집하다
distribute	나누어 주다, 배부하다; (상품을) 유통시키다	**distribute** $500 bonuses to all employees 모든 직원에게 보너스로 500달러를 나누어 주다 **distribute** its products throughout Spain 스페인 전역에 그 회사의 상품을 유통시키다
accumulate	모으다, 축적하다	**accumulate** a great amount of wealth 엄청난 부를 축적하다 due to **accumulated** heavy snow 엄청나게 쌓인 눈 때문에

정답 및 해설 p.037

5 Nashville Library will offer résumé writing classes once the city council ------- its educational budget.

(A) approves (B) cuts
(C) invites   (D) convenes

6 Most people these days use their smartphone's GPS when ------- places they haven't been to before.

(A) cultivating (B) investing
(C) exploring   (D) ensuring

7 As per the employment contract, workers ------- their right to form a labor union.

(A) classify (B) accumulate
(C) retain   (D) agree

8 Orion Tech's planning committee will ------- pamphlets with details of the company's anniversary celebration to its employees.

(A) distribute (B) arrange
(C) observe   (D) register

ACTUAL TEST

1. The self-driving cars made by the Amarillo Corporation ------- a major advancement in the automotive industry.
   (A) representing
   (B) represent
   (C) represents
   (D) representation

2. Employees are encouraged to help each other with projects if the opportunity -------.
   (A) to arise
   (B) arise
   (C) arises
   (D) had arisen

3. Waldeck's newly released tablet ------- a higher-resolution screen.
   (A) to feature
   (B) feature
   (C) is featured
   (D) features

4. Burnam and Cohen Landscaping ------- an initial consultation to new customers at no charge.
   (A) provide
   (B) provides
   (C) providing
   (D) is provided

5. Some of the candidates for the position ------- a master's degree in a relevant field.
   (A) hold
   (B) holds
   (C) holding
   (D) to hold

6. Market surveys analyzing the financial sector ------- by a team of leading experts.
   (A) has been conducted
   (B) have conducted
   (C) will be conducting
   (D) have been conducted

7. Attendees at the banquet ------- by musicians who play classical music.
   (A) entertain
   (B) is entertaining
   (C) was entertained
   (D) were entertained

8. The number of video streaming platforms ------- substantially over the past few years.
   (A) are increased
   (B) have increased
   (C) has increased
   (D) increasing

어휘 self-driving car 자율 주행차   represent 대표하다, 대변하다   automotive 자동차의   feature ~을 특징으로 하다
landscaping 조경   initial 최초의, 처음의   entertain 접대하다, 즐겁게 해 주다

Questions 9-12 refer to the following article.

Operating Expenses for Small Businesses

If you are starting a new business, it is a good idea to calculate your expected operating expenses in advance. Operating expenses ------- payments for rent, utilities, and taxes.
                                  9.
------- costs are usually easy to predict, as they do not fluctuate much from month to month.
10.
Employees' wages are somewhat stable but don't forget to add additional items such as health insurance.

For companies that produce a product, the cost of the necessary raw materials ------- on the
                                                                              11.
volume of goods produced. When production levels are high, more raw materials are needed. Fortunately, for most businesses, this means sales are higher as well.

------- . Therefore, it is important to get advice from a certified accountant.
12.

9 (A) include
   (B) includes
   (C) included
   (D) had included

10 (A) Each
   (B) All
   (C) Another
   (D) Those

11 (A) depend
   (B) depends
   (C) depending
   (D) to depend

12 (A) Small businesses have a higher chance of success.
   (B) After all, many people enjoy running their own business.
   (C) There are many financial matters to consider.
   (D) The business can boost sales through online marketing.

어휘 calculate 계산하다 in advance 미리 include 포함하다 utilities 공과금 predict 예측하다 fluctuate 오르락내리락하다, 요동치다 wage 임금 stable 안정적인 raw material 원자재 depend (up)on ~에 달려 있다 financial 재정의, 금융의 certified 공인된

UNIT 05

시제

1. 기본 시제
2. 진행형
3. 현재 시제가 미래를 대신하는 경우
4. 현재완료
5. 기타 완료 시제
6. 문맥으로 판단해야 하는 시제 문제

빈출 유형 풀이 전략
Vocabulary
Actual Test

TOEIC Grammar

약 15%

UNIT 05 시제

시제는 동사의 변화를 통해 어떤 일이 일어난 때를 나타내며, 세부적으로는 12가지 시제로 구분할 수 있습니다. 토익에는 매회 2~3문항씩 자주 출제되지만 복잡한 시제보다는 현재, 과거, 미래의 단순 시제를 구별하는 유형이 비중 있게 출제됩니다. 문장 내에 쓰인 시간 부사구만 알면 정답이 가려지는 문제가 대부분이므로 부담을 내려 놓고 공략해도 좋습니다.

 스피드 진단 테스트

(A), (B) 중 알맞은 것을 고르세요.

1. Many people ------- to read e-books these days.

    (A) prefer　　　　(B) will prefer

2. The performance ------- two hours ago.

    (A) has started　　(B) started

정답 및 해설

1. (A), 요즘 많은 사람들은 전자책을 읽는 것을 선호한다.
2. (B), 그 공연은 두 시간 전에 시작했다.

시제란?

동사의 형태 변화를 통해 주어의 동작이나 상태가 과거에 일어났는지, 미래에 일어날 일인지 등의 때를 표현할 수 있는데, 이를 시제라고 합니다. 영어의 시제에는 현재, 과거, 미래의 3가지 기본 시제와 여기에 진행형과 완료형, 그리고 완료진행형을 결합시켜 만든 총 12가지의 시제가 있습니다.

	현재	과거	미래
기본 시제	V-(e)s	V-ed	will + V
진행형	am[is/are] + V-ing	was[were] + V-ing	will + be + V-ing
완료형	have[has] + p.p.	had + p.p.	will + have + p.p.
완료진행형	have[has] + been + V-ing	had + been + V-ing	will + have + been + V-ing

● 시제의 의미

시제의 종류는 12가지나 되지만 실제로 토익에서 자주 쓰이는 시제는 아래의 아홉 가지 정도입니다. 현재와 과거, 미래를 중심으로 아래의 문장이 각각 어떤 의미와 용법의 차이가 있는지 구분해 보세요.

현재	I cook dinner for her every day. 나는 매일 그녀를 위해 저녁을 요리한다.
현재 진행	I'm cooking dinner. 나는 저녁을 요리하고 있다.
현재 완료	I've just cooked dinner. 나는 방금 저녁을 요리했다.

과거	I cooked dinner an hour ago. 나는 한 시간 전에 저녁을 요리했다.
과거 진행	I was cooking dinner when she called me. 그녀가 전화했을 때 나는 저녁 요리를 하고 있었다.
과거 완료	I had cooked dinner before she arrived home. 나는 그녀가 집에 오기 전에 저녁을 요리했다.

미래	I'll cook dinner soon. 나는 곧 저녁 요리를 할 거야.
미래 진행	I'll be cooking dinner this time tomorrow. 나는 내일 이맘때면 저녁 요리를 하고 있을 거야.
미래 완료	I'll have cooked dinner by then. 나는 그때쯤이면 저녁 요리를 끝냈을 거야.

시제를 판단할 때에는 앞뒤 문맥을 잘 살피고 시간을 나타내는 부사어에 유의해야 합니다.

I cooked dinner 10 minutes ago.
나는 10분 전에 저녁 요리를 했다.

I'm doing the dishes now.
나는 지금 설거지를 하고 있다.

I'm going to read soon.
나는 곧 책을 읽을 것이다.

1 기본 시제

She **worked** / **works** / **will work** for a bank.
　　　　과거　　　　현재　　　　　미래

그녀는 은행에서 **일했다** / **일한다** / **일할 것이다**.

현재, 과거, 미래 시제는 자주 어울려 쓰이는 부사나 시간 부사구가 시제 판별의 단서가 됩니다.

❶ 현재 시제: 현재의 사실, 상태 또는 반복되는 동작이나 습관

now	currently	always	usually	regularly	every/each + 시간 명사
지금	현재	항상	보통	정기적으로	~ 때마다

The city tour bus departs every hour. 도심 관광 버스는 매시간 출발합니다.

❷ 과거 시제: 과거 특정 시점에 발생한 동작이나 상태

last + 시간 명사	시간 명사 + ago	yesterday	before/previously
지난 ~ 때에	~ 전에	어제	전에

He retired last year. 그는 작년에 은퇴했다.

❸ 미래 시제: 미래의 일에 대한 추측이나 계획

next + 시간 명사	tomorrow	soon/shortly	later	starting/beginning
다음 ~ 때에	내일	곧	나중에	~부터

We will open a new branch in Boston next month. 우리는 다음 달 보스턴에 새 지점을 열 것이다.

연습문제　　　　　　　　　　　　　　　　　정답 및 해설 p.042

1 The department head sometimes ------- team members to work in pairs.

(A) ask　　　　(B) is asked
(C) asking　　(D) asks

2 It ------- interesting to lead the workshop last month, but Mr. Norwood is not willing to do so in the future.

(A) will seem　　(B) seems
(C) seemed　　　(D) be seeming

3 Bryson Auto ------- its central office to Berlin several months ago.

(A) will relocate　(B) relocated
(C) relocates　　　(D) has relocated

4 Darren Wilson, the head of the security team, ------- our emergency procedures next Wednesday.

(A) reviewed　　　(B) reviewing
(C) has reviewed　(D) will review

진행형

He **was** / **is** / **will be** work**ing** on a paper.
과거진행 / 현재진행 / 미래진행

그는 서류 작업을 하고 있었다 / 하고 있다 / 하고 있을 것이다.

진행형은 현재, 과거, 미래의 특정 시점을 전후로 일시적으로 진행 중인 일을 강조할 때 사용되며, 일시적인 시간을 나타내는 시간 부사구가 주로 동반됩니다.

❶ 현재진행형

Jade Cosmetics **is** currently **recruiting** a marketing manager.
제이드 화장품은 **현재** 마케팅 과장을 채용 중이다.

❷ 과거진행형

She **was taking** investors on a factory tour **when the CEO called**.
대표 이사가 전화했을 때 그녀는 투자자들에게 공장 견학을 해 주던 중이었다.

❸ 미래진행형

The restaurant **will be hosting** a three-day celebration of Italian food **next week**.
그 식당은 **다음 주에** 사흘간 이탈리아 음식 축제를 개최할 것이다.

연습문제
정답 및 해설 p.043

1 At present, VC Laboratories ------- a new treatment for seasonal allergies.

(A) is developing
(B) was developing
(C) developing
(D) has been developed

2 All employees need to behave responsibly when they ------- on company business.

(A) traveled   (B) are traveling
(C) to travel   (D) has traveled

3 Triumph Gallery ------- paintings for its annual art competition until next Friday.

(A) accepting
(B) will be accepting
(C) has been accepting
(D) acceptable

4 Starting next month, employees at Richmond Co. ------- at local charities.

(A) volunteering
(B) have been volunteering
(C) will be volunteering
(D) were volunteering

현재 시제가 미래를 대신하는 경우

The meeting will begin when the organizer arrives.
　　　　　　미래　　　　　시간 부사절 (현재)

주최자가 도착하면 회의가 시작될 겁니다.

시간 부사절이나 조건 부사절에서는 미래의 일이라도 현재 시제를 씁니다.

① 시간과 조건의 부사절: when, before, after, while, until, as soon as, once, in case, if

Ms. Lewis will submit her expenses after she returns from the trip.
루이스 씨는 출장에서 돌아온 후에 비용을 제출할 겁니다.

The documents will be meticulously examined before they are sent out to clients.
그 서류들은 고객에게 발송되기 전에 꼼꼼하게 검토될 것입니다.

We will discontinue the use of color printers until the problem is fixed.
그 문제가 해결되기 전까지는 컬러 프린터의 사용을 중단할 것입니다.

Once you have placed your order, its status will be available on our Web site.
→ 시간 및 조건 부사절에서는 현재뿐만 아니라 현재완료형이 쓰일 수도 있어요.
일단 주문을 하면 웹사이트에서 상태를 확인할 수 있습니다.

② 미래를 나타내는 기본 현재와 현재진행형

가까운 미래에 일어나게끔 정해진 일에는 기본 현재 시제와 현재진행형이 미래 시제를 대신하기도 하는데, 이때는 미래를 나타내는 시간 부사구가 함께 쓰입니다.

The animal shelter is holding a fundraising event later this week.
그 동물 보호소는 이번 주 말쯤에 기금 마련 행사를 개최할 예정입니다.

The concert begins today at 7.
콘서트는 오늘 7시에 시작합니다.

연습문제

정답 및 해설 p.044

1. Ms. Mitchell will negotiate her salary when she ------- her contract on Friday.
   (A) renewing   (B) renews
   (C) had renewed   (D) to renew

2. If the landlord ------- to repair items quickly, make a formal complaint.
   (A) neglects   (B) had neglected
   (C) will be neglecting (D) neglect

3. The train ------- in about ten minutes, so passengers should get on board.
   (A) leave   (B) leaves
   (C) left   (D) leaving

4. A maintenance worker ------- new lights in the hallway later this week.
   (A) to install   (B) will be installed
   (C) installed   (D) is installing

4 현재완료

She **has worked** as a designer since 2020.
  현재완료

그녀는 2020년부터 디자이너로 일해 왔다.

완료 시제는 현재, 과거, 미래의 명확한 시점이 아닌, 두 가지의 시점에 걸쳐 일어나고 있는 일을 표현합니다. 그 중 현재완료의 출제 빈도가 가장 높고, 경험, 계속, 완료의 의미로 많이 쓰입니다.

① 경험

| ever 한 번이라도 | never 결코 ~ 않다 | before 전에 | 숫자 + times ~번 |

I **have subscribed** to a video streaming service **a few times**.
저는 동영상 스트리밍 서비스를 몇 번 구독해 본 적이 있어요.

② 계속

| since ~ 이래로 | during ~ 동안 | for[over] the last[past] + 시간 지난 ~ 동안 |

He **has worked** for himself **since** he graduated from university.
그는 대학을 졸업한 이래로 1인 기업으로 일해 왔다.

③ 완료

| just 막 | already 이미, 벌써 | recently, lately 최근에 | yet 아직 |

The video **has already broken** the record for most views. 그 동영상은 이미 가장 많은 조회 수로 기록을 깼다.

연습문제

정답 및 해설 p.045

1 Bailey Sportswear ------- its employee training program since February of last year.

(A) will improve (B) improving
(C) to improve (D) has improved

2 The holiday party is several weeks away, but the receptionist ------- the office yesterday.

(A) decorate (B) decorated
(C) to decorate (D) have decorated

3 Last month, Ms. Nelson ------- company funds to be used for an office renovation project.

(A) authorized (B) authorizing
(C) has authorized (D) will authorize

4 The number of newspaper subscribers ------- by fifteen percent over the past year.

(A) decreased (B) decreasing
(C) will decrease (D) has decreased

5 기타 완료 시제

He **will have been** at this company for 40 years
미래완료
by the end of next year.

내년 연말이면 그는 이 회사에 40년간 재직하게 되는 셈이다.

① 미래완료

미래완료는 미래 시점의 기한이 나오고 어떤 동작이나 행위가 완료될 것이라는 의미로 쓰인다.
By the end of next year, they will have completed the construction.
내년 말쯤이면 그들은 그 공사를 마무리할 것입니다.

② 과거완료

과거완료는 과거 이전에 시작된 일이 과거에 막 완료되거나 과거까지 계속되는 일을 나타내는 등 과거에 영향을 미칠 때 쓴다. 또한 과거보다 앞선 일(대과거)을 과거 시점과 구분하기 위해서도 사용한다.

| when + 과거 ~했을 때 | before + 과거 ~했기 전에 | by the time + 과거 ~했을 즈음에는 |

When Mr. Park entered the meeting room, the meeting had already finished.
박 씨가 회의실에 도착했을 때 회의는 이미 끝나 있었다.

🔼 고난도 JUMP UP

현재완료는 경험, 완료, 계속의 다양한 의미를 표현하는 반면, 현재완료진행형은 '계속'의 의미를 나타냅니다.

JK Automobiles has been providing a free annual checkup for over a decade.
JK 자동차는 10년 넘도록 무상으로 연례 자동차 점검을 제공해 오고 있다.

연습문제 정답 및 해설 p.046

1 Mr. Frost designed one of the most creative marketing campaigns the company -------.

(A) was seen   (B) sees
(C) will have seen (D) had seen

2 By the end of next year, Ferretti Electronics ------- three new retail branches.

(A) opened   (B) had opened
(C) will be opened (D) will have opened

3 McKinney Enterprises ------- the licensing agreement with GT Media by this time next week.

(A) signs   (B) has been signing
(C) had signed   (D) will have signed

4 Chavez Engineering ------- the Philadelphia area for over two decades.

(A) is serving   (B) was served
(C) to be served (D) has been serving

6 문맥으로 판단해야 하는 시제 문제

The company's stock prices **doubled** when its new product **was launched**. 신제품이 출시되자 그 회사 주가가 2배가 되었다.
(doubled - 과거, was - 과거, launched - 과거)

시간 부사구가 없는 문장은 and, but이 쓰인 등위절이나 when, because 등의 부사절에 쓰인 동사를 바탕으로 문맥에 근거하여 시제의 단서를 찾아야 합니다.

❶ 등위절

We **appreciate** your hard work **and hope** to see you again as a volunteer.
(appreciate - 현재, hope - 현재)
당신의 노고에 감사드리며 자원봉사자로 다시 뵙기를 바랍니다.

The task force team **worked** day and night, **but** they **didn't meet** the deadline.
(worked - 과거, didn't meet - 과거)
태스크 포스 팀(TFT)은 밤낮없이 일했지만 마감일을 맞추지 못했다.

❷ 부사절

They **could revise** the article before publication **because** they **had received** it on time.
(could revise - 과거, had received - 과거완료)
그들은 제시간에 기사를 받았기 때문에 출간 전에 수정할 수 있었다.

The designer **takes** measurements of the room first **when** she **arrives** at a customer's home.
(takes - 현재, arrives - 현재)
디자이너는 고객의 집에 도착하면 우선 방의 크기를 측정합니다.

연습문제 정답 및 해설 p.047

1. The work crew repainted the hallway walls and then ------- the carpet thoroughly.
   (A) cleaned
   (B) clean
   (C) cleans
   (D) cleaning

2. After Ms. Caruso ------- the furniture in the waiting area, the space looked much larger.
   (A) to rearrange
   (B) is rearranging
   (C) rearranged
   (D) having rearranged

3. Dr. Panidos ------- surgery and cannot be contacted under any circumstances.
   (A) was performing
   (B) is performing
   (C) has performed
   (D) had performed

4. Although she ------- the device carefully, Ms. Jackson was confident that it was working well.
   (A) was not examined
   (B) is not examined
   (C) had not examined
   (D) is not examining

빈출 유형 풀이 전략

1. 적절한 시제를 묻는 문제

STEP에 따라 실제 토익 문제를 푸는 순서와 요령을 익혀 보세요.

Frieda Studios ------- several popular collections for the luxury fashion market over the past five years.

(A) creates
(B) created
(C) has created
(D) will create

STEP 1 선택지 구성 파악하기
선택지가 다양한 시제로 구성됨.
→ 적절한 시제를 묻는 문제.

Frieda Studios ------- several popular collections for the luxury fashion market over the past five years.

(A) creates
(B) created
(C) has created
(D) will create

STEP 2 빈칸 주변에서 단서 찾기
시간 부사구 over the past five years
→ 기간을 나타내는 시간 부사구는 현재완료형과 주로 어울림.

Frieda Studios ------- several popular collections for the luxury fashion market over the past five years.

(A) creates
(B) created
(C) ✓ has created
(D) will create

STEP 3 정답 찾기
현재완료형은 (C) has created이다.

해석 프리다 스튜디오는 지난 5년 넘게 고급 패션 시장에서 여러 유명한 상품들을 제작해 왔다.

어휘 luxury 고급, 사치, 호화로움

2. 문맥을 통해 판단해야 하는 시제 문제

STEP에 따라 실제 토익 문제를 푸는 순서와 요령을 익혀 보세요.

The new salesperson was pleased that he ------- favorable contract terms on behalf of the company.

(A) negotiates
(B) will negotiate
(C) is negotiating
(D) negotiated

STEP 1 선택지 구성 파악하기

선택지가 다양한 시제로 구성됨.
→ 적절한 시제를 묻는 문제.

The new salesperson was pleased that he ------- favorable contract terms on behalf of the company.

(A) negotiates
(B) will negotiate
(C) is negotiating
(D) negotiated

STEP 2 빈칸 주변에서 단서 찾기

시제 문제인데 빈칸 문장에 시간 부사구가 없으므로 다른 절의 시제에 주목해야 함.
→ that절 앞의 동사가 was로 과거 시제임.

The new salesperson was pleased that he ------- favorable contract terms on behalf of the company.

(A) negotiates
(B) will negotiate
(C) is negotiating
(D) negotiated

STEP 3 정답 찾기

계약을 한 결과 만족한 것이므로 빈칸도 과거 시제가 되어야 함.
→ 정답은 (D) negotiated.

해석 새로 입사한 영업 사원은 회사를 대신해 유리한 계약 조건을 협상한 것에 만족해했다.

어휘 be pleased that[to do] ~해서 기쁘다   negotiate 협상하다   favorable 유리한, 호의적인   contract terms 계약 조건   on behalf of ~을 대신해, ~을 대표해

VOCABULARY

빈출 동사 어휘 (3)

advise	조언하다; 알리다	**advise** him to buy a ticket in advance 그에게 티켓을 미리 구입하라고 조언하다 **advise** him of transit delays 그에게 운송 지연에 대해 알리다
undergo	겪다, 경험하다	**undergo** routine maintenance 정기적인 유지 관리를 받다 **undergo** massive changes 엄청난 변화를 경험하다
import 반 export 수출하다	수입하다	**import** raw materials 원자재를 수입하다 be **imported** from Italy 이탈리아에서 수입되다
secure	확보하다, 입수하다; 안전한	**secure** a lucrative contract 돈이 되는 계약을 따 내다 **secure** funding from investors 투자자들에게서 자금을 확보하다
initiate	시작하다, 개시하다	**initiate** an online payment system 온라인 결제 시스템을 시작하다 **initiate** the new recruits 신규 채용을 시작하다
redeem	(상품권/쿠폰 등을) 현금/상품으로 바꾸다; 빚을 상환하다	**redeem** the gift certificate for cash 그 상품권을 현금으로 바꾸다 **redeem** a loan/mortgage 대출금/담보 대출금을 상환하다 **redeemable** at any of our stores 자사 어느 매장에서나 이용 가능한
vacate	(건물, 자리 등을) 비우다; (직위 등에서) 물러나다	**vacate** the room by noon 정오까지 객실을 비우다 **vacate** the position on July 10 7월 10일에 그 자리에서 물러나다
defer 동 put off, postpone	연기하다, 미루다; (의견, 결정 등을) 따르다(~ to)	**defer** making a decision until next week 결정을 다음 주로 미루다 will be **deferred** until May 5월로 연기될 것이다 **defer to** experts 전문가들의 의견[결정]을 따르다

연습문제

1 If we ------- funding from government grants, we won't need to lay off any assembly line workers.
(A) attempt (B) advise
(C) secure   (D) withdraw

2 This coupon is for full-price products only and cannot be ------- on clearance items.
(A) deferred (B) assumed
(C) redeemed (D) complied

3 The Blake Historical House will be ------- repairs after the peak visiting season.
(A) educating (B) undergoing
(C) hosting   (D) importing

4 To improve employee morale, MT Corporation has ------- a flexible working hour system.
(A) demanded (B) surveyed
(C) vacated   (D) initiated

facilitate	가능하게 하다, 수월하게 하다	**facilitate** efficient work flow 효율적인 작업 흐름을 가능하게 하다 **facilitate** communication between employees 직원 간 의사소통을 수월하게 하다
launch	시작하다, 착수하다; (상품을) 출시[출간]하다	**launch** her career as a painter 화가로 그녀의 경력을 시작하다 **launch** a new version of the software 그 소프트웨어의 새 버전을 출시하다
pledge	(공식적으로) 약속하다	**pledge** to support the project 그 프로젝트를 지원하기로 약속하다 **pledge** their cooperation 그들의 협조를 약속하다
specify	(구체적으로) 명시하다	**specify** all the details 모든 세부 사항을 명시하다 **specify** the date and time 날짜와 시간을 명시하다
waive	(권리, 요구 등을) 포기하다	**waive** registration fee 등록비를 면제해 주다 **waive** the charge for frequent customers 단골 고객들에게 요금을 면제해 주다
delegate	(일, 임무 등을) 위임하다; 대표[대리인]로 선정하다	**delegate** minor tasks to an assistant 사소한 업무들을 보조원에게 위임하다 be **delegated** to organize the meeting 그 회의를 준비하도록 선정되다
resolve	(문제 등을) 해결하다	**resolve** computer problems 컴퓨터 문제를 해결하다 **resolve** their differences 의견 차를 해결하다
proceed	진행되다	**proceed** slowly 더디게 진행되다 **proceed** with caution 신중하게 진행되다

정답 및 해설 p.048

5 The merchandising team designed a new clothing line to ------- in time for baseball's playoff season.

(A) launch (B) attract
(C) resolve (D) represent

6 Hartman's Groceries ------- to reduce its use of plastic by 50% by next year.

(A) warranted (B) inhibited
(C) reassured (D) pledged

7 If clients do not ------- the brand of materials they want, then generic ones will be used.

(A) specify (B) charge
(C) inspect (D) delegate

8 Mario's Pizzeria announced that it will ------- the charge for delivery this December.

(A) proceed (B) arrange
(C) waive (D) summarize

ACTUAL TEST

1. The water to the building will be shut off while the plumber ------- the issue.
   (A) investigated
   (B) will investigate
   (C) has investigated
   (D) is investigating

2. Before he ------- the workshop, the manager is going to summarize the aim of each session.
   (A) starts
   (B) start
   (C) will start
   (D) is starting

3. Dave Aldrich ------- the city's most recognizable architect last year.
   (A) names
   (B) is named
   (C) has named
   (D) was named

4. The building's exterior walls ------- in recent years and should be repaired soon.
   (A) deteriorating
   (B) have deteriorated
   (C) to deteriorate
   (D) deteriorated

5. The interns ------- each department in the firm by the time they complete the training program.
   (A) had assisted
   (B) are assisting
   (C) will have assisted
   (D) will assist

6. After the mechanic ------- the vehicle, he recommended replacing some worn components.
   (A) inspects
   (B) have inspected
   (C) had inspected
   (D) is inspecting

7. The director explained her reasons for promoting the least experienced employee but -------.
   (A) being criticized
   (B) is criticized
   (C) criticized
   (D) was criticized

8. Streaming Central gives customers three warnings about late payments, after which the account -------.
   (A) suspended
   (B) be suspended
   (C) had been suspended
   (D) is suspended

어휘 plumber 배관공 investigate 조사하다, 살피다 recognizable 알아볼 수 있는 deteriorate 악화되다, 더 나빠지다
mechanic 정비공 inspect 점검하다 component 부품 suspend 보류하다, 정지하다

Questions 9-12 refer to the following flyer.

TO ALL DEXTER PET STORE CUSTOMERS

Dexter Pet Store boasts the largest collection of animal-related merchandise in the region. Since 2002, our business ------- high-quality products and expert advice to keep your pets
              9.
happy and healthy. After much consideration, we decided that we want to spend more time with our family. As a result, we are planning to ------- at the end of the month. We ------- our
                                                                10.   11.
final day of business on Saturday, September 30. In the meantime, please don't hesitate to visit the store to take advantage of substantial discounts in all departments. We need to get rid of our entire inventory of stock. ------- . We appreciate your patronage through the years,
                                         12.
and we wish you and your pets all the best.

9 (A) provided
   (B) has provided
   (C) is providing
   (D) was being provided

10 (A) close
   (B) invest
   (C) acknowledge
   (D) eliminate

11 (A) are holding
   (B) had to hold
   (C) will be held
   (D) have held

12 (A) Nevertheless, the industry is growing steadily.
   (B) Some pets are easier to care for than others.
   (C) Therefore, it's a great time to stock up on supplies.
   (D) The new location will be announced soon.

어휘 boast 자랑하다, 뽐내다 merchandise (집합 명사) 상품 in the meantime 그동안에 take advantage of ~을 이용하다 substantial 상당한 inventory 재고 목록, 재고 patronage 애용

에듀윌이
너를
지지할게

ENERGY

쉼 없는 분주함은 소란스럽고,
분주함 없는 쉼은 게으릅니다.

— 조정민, 『인생은 선물이다』, 두란노

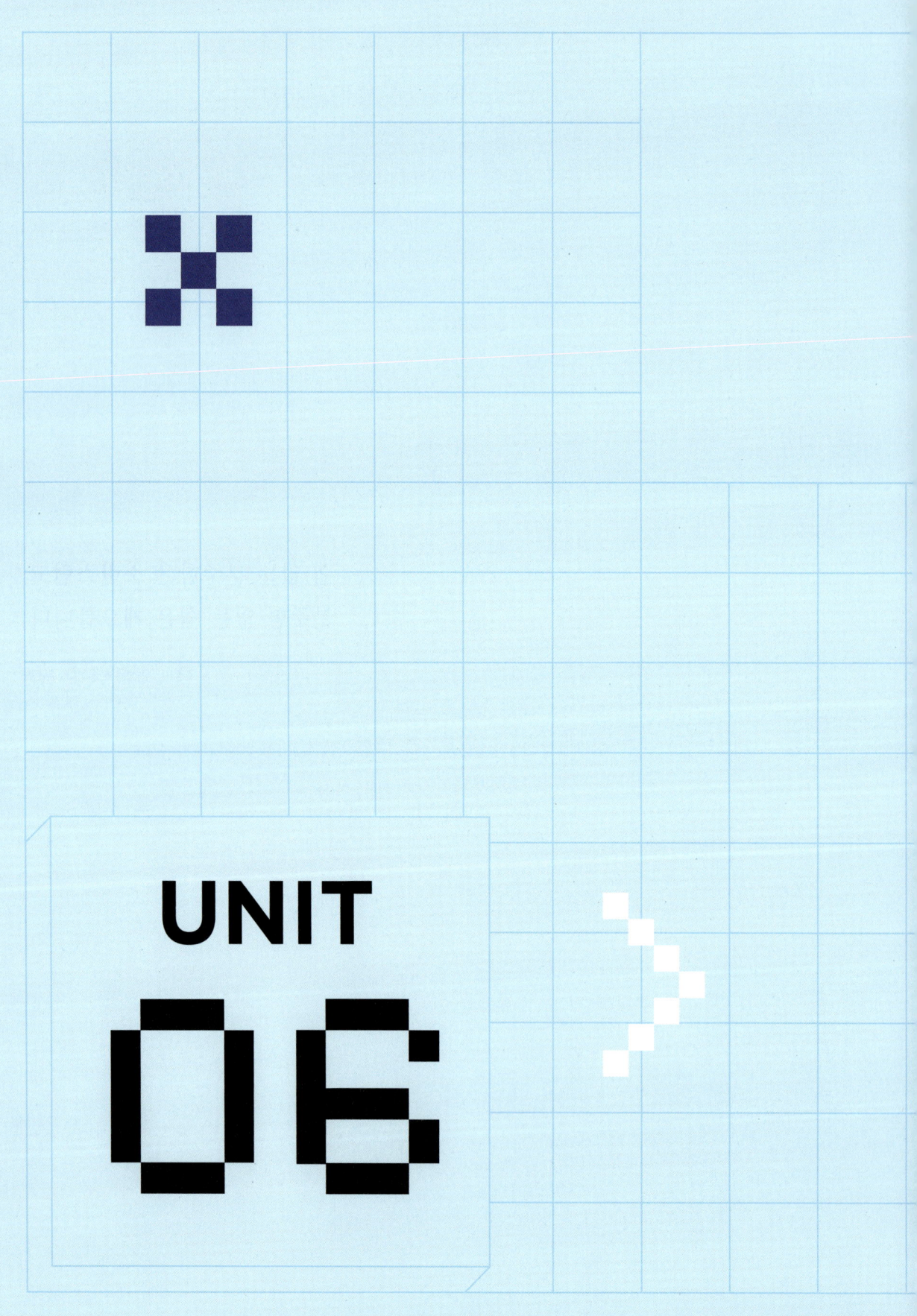

UNIT 06

태

1. 능동태
2. 수동태
3. 수동태 구문 1: be + p.p. + 전치사
4. 수동태 구문 2: be + p.p. + to do

빈출 유형 풀이 전략
Vocabulary
Actual Test

TOEIC Grammar

약 10%

UNIT 06 태

능동태와 수동태 중 적절한 태를 고르는 문제는 매회 1~2문항씩 출제됩니다. 문제 중 90% 이상은 동사 자리 뒤의 목적어 유무에 따라 정답을 판별할 수 있습니다.

스피드 진단 테스트

(A), (B) 중 알맞은 것을 고르세요.

1. The organization ------- a flea market every Sunday.

   (A) holds   (B) is held

2. The sales report was ------- to the manager.

   (A) sending   (B) sent

정답 및 해석

1. (A), 그 단체는 일요일마다 벼룩시장을 연다.
2. (B), 매출 보고서가 매니저에게 보내졌다.

태란?

'태'란 주어와 동사의 관계를 나타내는 동사 형태입니다. 주어가 행위를 하는 주체이면 능동태, 주어가 동사의 행위를 받는 대상이면 수동태를 써요. 의미는 기본적으로 같지만, 행위의 주체를 강조하느냐, 행위를 당한 대상을 강조하느냐에 따라 형태가 달라집니다.

● 능동태를 수동태로 바꾸기

The company developed a fuel-efficient car. 그 회사는 연비가 좋은 차를 개발했다.
　　　　　　　　　　　　　목적어

A fuel-efficient car was developed by the company. 연비 좋은 차가 그 회사에 의해 개발되었다.
　　　주어

● 수동태의 형태

수동태의 기본 형태는 'be동사 + 과거분사'입니다. 기본형인 'be동사 + 과거분사'가 시제와 결합하면 형태가 복잡해질 수 있으나, be[being, been] 동사 뒤에 과거분사가 오는지만 확인하면 됩니다.

	능동태	수동태
현재	offer(s)	am/are/is offered
과거	offered	was/were offered
미래	will offer	will be offered
현재진행	am/are/is offering	am/are/is being offered
과거진행	was/were offering	was/were being offered
미래진행	will be offering	will be being offered
현재완료	have/has offered	have/has been offered
과거완료	had offered	had been offered
미래완료	will have offered	will have been offered

They offered me a job.
그들은 내게 일자리를 제안했다.

I was offered a job.
나는 일자리를 제안받았다.

1 능동태

Dr. Smith **invented** a new drug last year.
　　　　　동사　　　　목적어

작년에 스미스 박사가 신약을 개발했다.

동사 자리 뒤에 목적어가 따라오면 능동태를 선택해야 하며, 자동사는 목적어 없이 항상 능동태 형태로 써야 하므로 대표적으로 출제되는 자동사를 미리 숙지해 두어야 합니다.

① 동사 자리 뒤에 목적어가 있는 경우 (타동사)

We **provide** customized services to clients. 우리는 고객들께 맞춤형 서비스를 제공합니다.
　　　　　　　　목적어

They already **hired** a replacement for the coach. 그들은 벌써 그 코치의 후임자를 채용했다.
　　　　　　　　목적어

The company **will launch** new skincare products soon. 회사가 곧 스킨케어 신제품을 출시할 것이다.
　　　　　　　　　　　목적어

② 동사가 자동사인 경우

work	happen, occur	rise, grow	exist	arrive	last	remain
일하다	발생하다	증가하다	존재하다	도착하다	지속되다	남아 있다

These days, more people **work** from home. 요즘에는 더 많은 사람들이 집에서 일합니다.

The sales of the second branch **grew** this month. 두 번째 지점의 매출이 이번 달에 증가했어요.

The parts that I ordered didn't **arrive**. 제가 주문한 부품이 도착하지 않았어요.

연습문제　　　　　　　　　　　　　　　　　　　　　　　　정답 및 해설 p.053

1 Royas, a jewelry manufacturer, ------- several store branches in the region.

　(A) operates　　　(B) is operated
　(C) operating　　(D) to operate

2 The recruiter ------- Mr. Hark to be the best candidate because of his certifications.

　(A) is considered　(B) considers
　(C) was considered　(D) considering

3 The summer sales event ------- throughout the whole month of July.

　(A) is lasted　　(B) will be lasted
　(C) will last　　(D) to last

4 Ms. Bellido ------- to her hotel room because she had forgotten her bag.

　(A) is returned　(B) were returned
　(C) returned　　(D) returning

2 수동태

A new antiviral drug **was invented** last year.
동사 (be+p.p.)

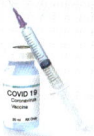

작년에 새로운 항바이러스제가 개발되었다.

타동사 뒤에 목적어가 없으면 대부분 수동태로 표현합니다. 동사 뒤에 〈by + 행위자〉가 오기도 하나 보통 생략되는 경우가 많고, 주로 시간, 장소, 방법 등을 나타내는 부사구가 뒤따라 나옵니다.

The job fair **was hosted** by the mayor's office. 취업 박람회가 시청에 의해 주최되었다.
　　　　　　　　　　　by + 행위자
Our refund policy **is listed** on our Web site. 저희의 환불 정책은 웹사이트에 나와 있습니다.
　　　　　　　　　　　장소
The annual sales report **should be submitted** by next week. 연간 매출 보고서는 다음 주까지 제출되어야 합니다.
　　　　　　　　　　　　　　　　　　　　시간
The copy of your contract **will be sent** by express mail. 계약서 사본은 빠른 우편으로 보내 드릴 겁니다.
　　　　　　　　　　　　　　　　　방법

🏁 고난도 JUMP UP

직접 목적어와 간접 목적어를 함께 수반하는 동사의 경우 수동태 뒤에 직접 목적어인 사물 목적어가 올 수 있습니다.

| buy 사다 | give 주다 | offer 제공하다 | send 보내다 | show 보여 주다 |

Attendees **are given** nametags at the entrance. 참석자들은 입구에서 이름표를 배부받습니다.
　　　　　　　　　목적어
The entire staff **will be offered** a bonus this year. 전 직원은 올해 보너스를 받게 됩니다.
　　　　　　　　　　　　　　목적어

연습문제

1. The keynote speaker of Renewable Energy Convention will ------- by the chairman.
   (A) introduce
   (B) have introduced
   (C) be introducing
   (D) be introduced

2. Prescription medication is always ------- behind the counter rather than on the display shelves.
   (A) stores
   (B) storing
   (C) storage
   (D) stored

3. Ms. Hanz anticipates that her painting will be ------- as an entry to the art contest.
   (A) considered
   (B) considering
   (C) consider
   (D) consideration

4. Customers ------- a cost estimate after a specialist checks the kitchen to be remodeled.
   (A) will be sent
   (B) has sent
   (C) are sending
   (D) be sent

수동태 구문 1: be + p.p. + 전치사

Customers **are satisfied with** its fast delivery service.
　　　　　 be p.p.　　전치사

고객들은 빠른 배송 서비스에 만족해합니다.

수동태가 감정이나 상태를 나타낼 때 다양한 전치사와 짝처럼 어울려 쓰입니다. 이 경우 대개의 과거분사는 타동사의 수동형으로 이해하기보다는 -ed로 끝나는 하나의 형용사로 보면 됩니다.

be satisfied[pleased] with ~에 만족해하다	be dedicated to ~에 헌신하다
be concerned with ~와 관련되다	be related to ~에 관련되다
be equipped with ~을 갖추고 있다	be accustomed[used] to ~에 익숙하다
be involved in ~에 연관되다	be concerned about ~에 대해 걱정하다
be interested in ~에 흥미가 있다	be excited about ~에 대해 들뜨다

My wife and I **were pleased with** the car rental company.
제 아내와 저는 그 자동차 대여점에 만족했습니다.

We **are** very **excited about** the renovations to our office space.
우리는 우리 사무실 공간 개조에 무척 들떠 있습니다.

문맥에 따라 수동태 뒤에 다양한 전치사가 붙을 수도 있어요.

Meals **are** not **included in** the package. 식사는 패키지에 포함되지 않습니다.
Details **are included on** the Web site. 세부 사항은 웹사이트에 올라가 있습니다.
A receipt **is included with** the e-mail. 영수증이 이메일에 첨부되어 있습니다.

연습문제　　　　　　　　　　　　　　　　　　　　　　　　　　　정답 및 해설 p.055

1 The choice of the Best Employee Award winner ------- on performance and attitude.

　(A) based　　　　(B) bases
　(C) basing　　　 (D) is based

2 The computer is ------- with a camera ideal for online meetings.

　(A) equipped　　(B) related
　(C) designed　　(D) concerned

3 Several of the experienced designers ------- in the creation of the new company logo.

　(A) were involving　(B) were involved
　(C) have involved　 (D) involve

4 Yending Cosmetics is dedicated ------- keeping the price of its products reasonable.

　(A) with　　(B) to
　(C) on　　　(D) for

4 수동태 구문 2: be + p.p. + to do

The renovation **is projected to end** next month.
                be p.p.   to do

그 보수 공사는 다음 주에 끝날 예정입니다.

수동태가 to부정사와 짝꿍처럼 쓰이는 형태도 자주 출제되는데 이 표현들은 문법뿐 아니라 듣기와 독해 지문에도 자주 나옵니다.

예정, 기대	be scheduled to *do* ~하기로 예정되다 be supposed to *do* ~하기로 되어 있다	be expected to *do* ~할 것으로 기대되다 be projected to *do* ~하기로 예정되다
요청, 요구	be required to *do* ~하도록 요구받다 be advised to *do* ~하도록 조언받다	be asked to *do* ~하도록 요청받다 be directed to *do* ~하도록 안내받다
허가	be permitted/allowed to *do* ~하는 것이 허락되다, ~할 수 있다	
의무	be forced/obliged to *do* ~하도록 강요받다	

Customers **are asked to** participate in a survey after shopping.
고객들은 쇼핑 후에 설문에 참여하도록 요청받습니다.

Business visitors **are permitted to** enter without a visa.
사업차 방문하시는 분들은 비자 없이 입국이 허가됩니다.

수동태 뒤에 절이 올 수도 있어요.

It **is expected** that the model will be renewed next year.
그 모델은 내년에 새롭게 바뀔 것으로 기대됩니다.

Please **be advised** that your flight was canceled.
귀하의 항공편이 취소되었음을 알려 드립니다.

연습문제

정답 및 해설 p.056

1 Visitors of the factory floor ------- to wear a safety helmet at all times.
   (A) are asked   (B) to ask
   (C) asking   (D) asks

2 Only members of the IT department ------- to install software on the laptops.
   (A) are permitted   (B) permitting
   (C) permissible   (D) permits

3 Tickets must be purchased in advance and are ------- to sell out quickly.
   (A) allowed   (B) obliged
   (C) expected   (D) advised

4 The airlines were forced ------- all flights due to the severe snowstorm.
   (A) to cancel   (B) canceled
   (C) canceling (D) be canceled

빈출 유형 풀이 전략

1. 태를 묻는 문제

STEP에 따라 실제 토익 문제를 푸는 순서와 요령을 익혀 보세요.

All current job openings at Sensen Inc. ------- a minimum of ten years' experience.

(A) are required
(B) requiring
(C) require
(D) will be required

STEP 1 선택지 구성 파악하기

선택지에 능동태와 수동태가 섞여 있음.
→ 적절한 동사 형태를 묻는 문제.

All current job openings at Sensen Inc. ------- a minimum of ten years' experience.

(A) are required
(B) requiring
(C) require
(D) will be required

STEP 2 빈칸 주변에서 단서 찾기

All current job openings가 주어,
a minimum of ten years' experience가 목적어
→ 적절한 능동태를 찾아야 함.

All current job openings at Sensen Inc. ------- a minimum of ten years' experience.

(A) are required
(B) requiring
(C) ✓ require
(D) will be required

STEP 3 정답 찾기

능동태는 (C) require뿐이다.

해석 센센 사의 현 모든 일자리는 최소 10년간의 경력을 요구하고 있다.

어휘 current 현재의   job opening 일자리, 공석 (=job vacancy)   require 요구하다, 필요로 하다

2. 태와 시제의 복합 문제

STEP에 따라 실제 토익 문제를 푸는 순서와 요령을 익혀 보세요.

The annual business plan for next year
------- at the board of directors meeting on Thursday.

(A) is presenting
(B) will be presented
(C) is presented
(D) presenting

STEP 1 선택지 구성 파악하기

선택지에 능동 및 수동, 현재 시제 및 미래 시제가 섞여 있음.
→ 적절한 동사 형태를 묻는 문제.

The annual business plan for next year
------- at the board of directors meeting on Thursday.

(A) is presenting
(B) will be presented
(C) is presented
(D) presenting

STEP 2 빈칸 주변에서 단서 찾기

The annual business plan이 주어,
동사 present가 타동사인데 빈칸 뒤에 목적어가 없음.
→ 수동태가 와야 함.

The annual business plan for next year
------- at the board of directors meeting on Thursday.

(A) is presenting
(B̸) will be presented
(C) is presented
(D) presenting

STEP 3 정답 찾기

연간 사업 계획은 목요일마다 반복적으로 발표되는 것이 아니므로 현재 시제는 어색.
→ is presented는 오답으로 제거.
→ 남은 미래 시제 (B)가 정답.

해석 내년 연간 사업 계획이 목요일에 이사회 회의에서 발표될 것이다.

어휘 annual 연간의 present 제시하다, 제출하다; 현재의 board of directors 이사회

VOCABULARY

빈출 동사 어휘 (4)

promote	홍보하다; 승진시키다	**promote** a new line of beverages 새로운 음료 제품을 홍보하다 be **promoted** to division manager 부장으로 승진되다
resume	재개하다	**resume** the meeting after lunch 점심 후에 회의를 재개하다 **resume** production of the vehicle 차량 생산을 재개하다
recruit	채용하다, 모집하다	**recruit** 100 new staff each year 매년 신규 직원 100명을 채용하다 **recruit** volunteers to help 도움을 줄 자원봉사자들을 모집하다
assure	장담하다, 확언하다	**assure** them of our support 그들에게 우리의 지원을 장담하다 be virtually **assured** 사실상 확실시되다
pursue	추구하다, 밀고 나가다	**pursue** new business opportunities 새로운 사업 기회를 추구하다 **pursue** a career in marketing 마케팅에서 경력을 밀고 나가다[쌓다]
yield	도출하다, 산출하다	**yield** promising results 희망적인 결과를 도출하다 **yield** substantial feedback 상당한 피드백을 이끌어 내다
withhold	(정보, 허가 등을) 주지 않다	**withhold** information for security reasons 보안상의 이유로 정보를 주지 않다 be **withheld** for income tax 소득세로 공제되다
grant	허락하다, 승인하다	**grant** employees more paid leave 직원들에게 더 많은 연차를 허락하다 **grant** permission to build on the site 그 부지에 건축하는 걸 허가하다 **grant** your request 당신의 요구를 승인하다

연습문제

1. Mr. Luca introduced a plan to ------- workers permission to work remotely.

   (A) conceive (B) pursue
   (C) grant   (D) presume

2. Due to its increasing popularity, Tanya's Burgers has been ------- staff to keep up with demand.

   (A) resuming   (B) tasting
   (C) recruiting (D) renovating

3. To attract more tourists, Lakefront Hotel plans to ------- the local region through advertising.

   (A) promote (B) direct
   (C) withhold (D) classify

4. The company's spokesperson has ------- the press that it will reopen its Denver factory.

   (A) compiled (B) yielded
   (C) assured (D) reinstated

establish	설립하다, 수립하다; (제도 등을) 확립하다	**establish** a good relationship with the local community 그 지역 사회와 좋은 관계를 수립하다 **establish** procedures for complaints 불만 대응 절차를 수립하다
coordinate	조직화하다, 조정하다	**coordinate** the work of the team 그 팀의 업무를 조직화하다 **coordinate** all the relevant information 모든 관련 정보를 체계화하다
commence	시작하다, 시작되다	**commence** building next month 다음 달에 건설 공사를 시작하다 **commence** after the holiday 연휴 후에 시작하다
predict ❀ forecast	예상하다, 예측하다	**predict** job growth in the region 그 지역의 일자리 증가를 예상하다 **predict** heavy snow for tomorrow 내일 폭설을 예상하다
finalize	마무리하다, 완성하다	**finalize** the arrangements 준비를 마무리 짓다 **finalize** his contract 계약을 마무리 짓다
accommodate	수용하다, 받아들이다	**accommodate** 500 people 500명을 수용하다 **accommodate** customer demand 고객의 요구를 수용하다
encounter	맞닥뜨리다, 부딪히다	**encounter** serious problems 심각한 문제들에 맞닥뜨리다 **encounter** strong opposition 강한 반대에 부딪히다
analyze	분석하다	**analyze** marketing data 마케팅 데이터를 분석하다 **analyze** the problem and arrive at a solution 그 문제를 분석하고 해결책에 이르다

정답 및 해설 p.057

5 After considering each proposal, the management ------- its decision to relocate the office.

(A) finalized (B) coordinated
(C) investigated (D) reassured

6 Dr. Foster is working to ------- sanitary protocol that everyone in the food service industry follows.

(A) succeed (B) establish
(C) discover (D) encounter

7 Mosquito pesticide spraying operations are scheduled to ------- before tourists come on vacation.

(A) commence (B) predict
(C) announce (D) intervene

8 The Sky Room can ------- up to 50 guests, while the Wind Room seats between 80 and 100 people comfortably.

(A) arrange (B) accommodate
(C) represent (D) allot

ACTUAL TEST

1. The branch managers ------- through their company e-mail accounts.
   (A) have to contact
   (B) may contact
   (C) can be contacted
   (D) have contacted

2. Scientific advancements ------- BV Laboratories to complete its experiments earlier than planned.
   (A) to allow
   (B) allowing
   (C) allowed
   (D) are allowed

3. The orchestra music for Jeremy Berman's new play is being ------- by Rosanna Russo.
   (A) composed
   (B) composing
   (C) composition
   (D) composes

4. The Mountain Spa hand soap that ------- last month had the wrong packaging.
   (A) produced
   (B) to produce
   (C) was produced
   (D) producing

5. The department head is ------- whether to ask team members to work overtime or hire some temporary employees.
   (A) decide
   (B) decided
   (C) decides
   (D) deciding

6. The entrance fees to all museums are ------- in the price of the city tour.
   (A) involved
   (B) included
   (C) related
   (D) based

7. At the law firm, all confidential documents ------- to remain in locked cabinets unless someone uses them.
   (A) require
   (B) requires
   (C) are required
   (D) is required

8. Reader's comments may be posted on the magazine's Web site, but their personal details will not be -------.
   (A) publication
   (B) publicized
   (C) publicizing
   (D) publicity

어휘 branch manager 지점장 e-mail account 이메일 계정 advancement 진보; 승진 compose 작곡하다
temporary employee 임시직, 비정규직 confidential 기밀의 publicize 알리다, 홍보하다

Questions 9-12 refer to the following e-mail.

To: All Employees <stafflist@guerrafilbert.com>
From: Michelle Wynn <m.wynn@guerrafilbert.com>
Date: March 15
Subject: Business expenses

Dear Employees,

Our company is looking for ways to better monitor expenses. In light of this, a new policy for receiving reimbursement payments ------- on April 1. From that date, you must get approval for business expenses from the human resources department. -------. We ask that you do so at least one week in advance, if possible. In cases where last-minute spending is necessary, receipts ------- in order to receive reimbursement from the company.

For business trips, please think about whether an in-person visit is necessary. Employees ------- to use video conferencing whenever possible. This will help to save both time and money.

Thank you for your cooperation in this matter.

Sincerely,

Michelle Wynn

9
(A) was implemented
(B) implementing
(C) implemented
(D) will be implemented

10
(A) Please send requests to Katie Lopez before the expected purchase.
(B) The management team reviewed the average spending for the year.
(C) The department is responsible for hiring new employees.
(D) These changes will ensure that equipment is working properly.

11
(A) submit
(B) to submit
(C) are submitting
(D) must be submitted

12
(A) advise
(B) advising
(C) are advised
(D) advised

어휘 monitor 감독하다, 관찰하다　in light of ~을 감안하여　reimbursement 상환, 환급, 배상　implement 시행하다

UNIT 07

형용사와 부사

1. 형용사 자리
2. 수량을 나타내는 형용사
3. 혼동하기 쉬운 형용사
4. 부사 자리
5. 다양한 형태의 부사
6. 혼동하기 쉬운 부사

빈출 유형 풀이 전략
Vocabulary
Actual Test

TOEIC Grammar

약 20%

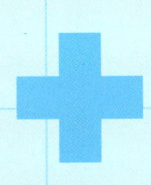

UNIT 07 형용사와 부사

형용사 문제는 매회 적게는 1문제에서 많게는 3문제 정도 출제됩니다. 부사 문제 역시 매회 3~4문제 정도 출제되는 영역으로 출제 빈도가 꽤 높은 편입니다. 높은 출제 빈도에 비해 문제 난이도는 그리 높지 않아서 기본기를 잘 다져 두면 어렵지 않게 풀 수 있습니다.

 스피드 진단 테스트

(A), (B) 중 알맞은 것을 고르세요.

1. She is a very ------- writer.

    (A) create　　　(B) creative

2. Mr. Baker ------- explained the procedure.

    (A) brief　　　(B) briefly

정답 및 해석

1. (B), 그녀는 매우 창의적인 작가이다.
2. (B), 베이커 씨는 그 절차를 간략하게 설명했다.

형용사와 부사란?

형용사는 사람이나 사물의 상태나 성질을 설명하는 말이며, 명사를 수식하거나 서술하는 역할을 합니다.

The **compact** car is **popular** with young people.
　　형용사　　명사　be동사+형용사
그 소형차는 젊은이들에게 인기 있다.

부사는 동사나 형용사, 부사 혹은 문장 전체를 수식하면서 시간, 장소, 방법, 목적, 이유, 정도 등에 대한 정보를 더해 줍니다.

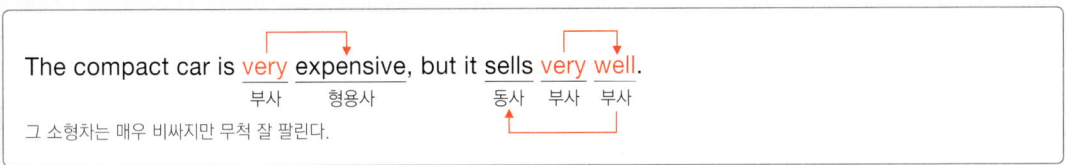

The compact car is **very** expensive, but it sells **very well**.
　　　　　　　　　부사　형용사　　　　　동사　부사　부사
그 소형차는 매우 비싸지만 무척 잘 팔린다.

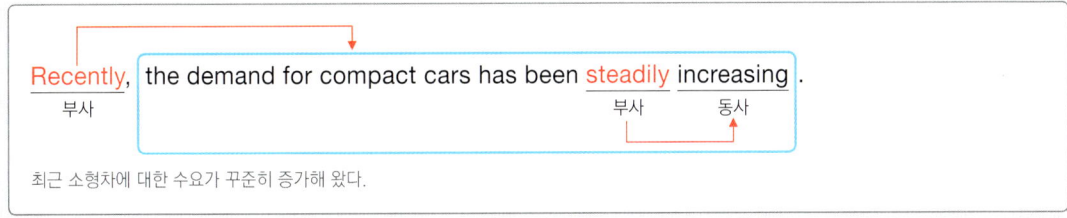

Recently, the demand for compact cars has been **steadily** increasing.
　부사　　　　　　　　　　　　　　　　　　　　　　　부사　　　동사
최근 소형차에 대한 수요가 꾸준히 증가해 왔다.

● 형용사와 부사의 형태

형용사는 주로 명사나 동사에 다양한 형용사형 접미어가 붙어서 만들어지며, 부사는 형용사에 부사형 접미어 -ly가 붙어 만들어집니다.

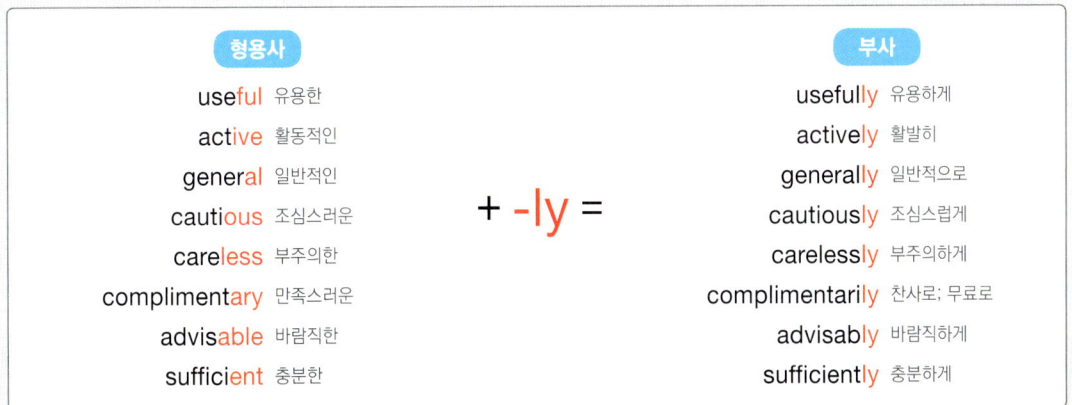

형용사		부사	
use**ful**	유용한	useful**ly**	유용하게
act**ive**	활동적인	active**ly**	활발히
gener**al**	일반적인	general**ly**	일반적으로
cauti**ous**	조심스러운	cautious**ly**	조심스럽게
care**less**	부주의한	careless**ly**	부주의하게
complimen**tary**	만족스러운	complimentari**ly**	찬사로; 무료로
advis**able**	바람직한	advisab**ly**	바람직하게
suffici**ent**	충분한	sufficient**ly**	충분하게

+ -ly =

1 형용사 자리

The Internet is **useful** for searching for information.
　　　　주어　동사　형용사

인터넷은 정보를 검색하는 데 **유용하다**.

The Internet is a **useful** tool for investors.
　　　　　　　　형용사　명사

인터넷은 투자자에게 **유용한** 도구다.

형용사는 명사 앞에 위치하여 명사를 수식합니다. 또한 보어 자리에 위치하여 주어나 목적어를 보충 설명하기도 합니다.

❶ 명사 앞

They provided **technical** support. 그들은 **기술적인** 지원을 제공했다.
　　　　　　　　　　　　명사

❷ 보어 자리

The data was **incorrect**. 그 데이터는 **부정확했다**.
주어　　　주격 보어

They found the data **incorrect**. 그들은 그 데이터가 **부정확하다는** 걸 알게 되었다.
　　　　목적어　목적격 보어

⬆ 고난도 JUMP UP

형용사는 명사를 뒤에서 수식할 수도 있습니다.

We have five jobs **available** at Houston City Library. 휴스턴 시립 도서관에는 다섯 개의 일자리가 있습니다.
　　　　명사　형용사

연습문제　　　　　　　　　　　　　　　　　정답 및 해설 p.062

1 Please note that as per company regulations, excessive spending on trips is not -------.

(A) accepting　　(B) acceptable
(C) acceptance　(D) accepts

2 The ------- intern finished the work in only two hours.

(A) energy　　　(B) energies
(C) energetically　(D) energetic

3 Ms. Bills had to pay an ------- charge for the repair of the wall.

(A) addition　　(B) additionally
(C) additional　(D) adding

4 The publisher of some of the best-selling books has called Adrian's novel too -------.

(A) predictable　(B) predicted
(C) prediction　(D) predictably

118

2 수량을 나타내는 형용사

There is **a lot of** / **much** traffic because of **many** visitors.
　　　　　　　　　　셀 수 없는 명사　　　　　　　　　　　복수 명사

방문객이 많아서 차가 막힌다.

수량을 나타내는 형용사는 뜻이 유사하지만 쓰임이 달라서 이를 활용한 문제가 종종 출제됩니다.

수량 형용사 + 복수 명사	수량 형용사 + 셀 수 없는 명사
a few people 몇몇 사람들	a little water 약간의 물
many companies 많은 회사들	much money 많은 돈
a lot of employees 많은 직원들	a lot of advice 많은 조언
plenty of chances 많은 기회들	plenty of time 많은 시간
other questions 다른 질문들	other information 다른 정보

🔼 고난도 JUMP UP

every와 all은 둘 다 '모든'을 뜻하지만 every는 단수 명사 앞에만, all은 복수 명사와 셀 수 없는 명사 앞에만 씁니다.

The CEO tried to answer <u>all</u> questions. 최고 경영자는 모든 질문에 답하기 위해 노력했다.
　　　　　　　　　　　　every (×)

<u>Every</u> hotel is completely booked. 모든 호텔이 예약이 꽉 찼다.
All (×)

연습문제

정답 및 해설 p.063

1 The marketing employees are expected to suggest ------- proposals regarding the new ad campaign.

(A) many　　(B) every
(C) each　　(D) much

2 Although ------- salespeople searched for new buyers last month, Mr. Thompson focused on contacting his former buyers.

(A) each　　(B) other
(C) every　　(D) another

3 The training session is for ------- employees in the HR Department.

(A) all　　(B) few
(C) each　　(D) enough

4 The curator has confirmed that ------- statue in the museum is real.

(A) all　　(B) every
(C) some　　(D) few

ㅋ 혼동하기 쉬운 형용사

confidential documents 기밀문서 | **confident** attitude 자신 있는 태도

❶ 형태는 비슷하지만 뜻이 다른 형용사

생김새는 비슷하지만 뜻은 전혀 다른 형용사를 알아봅시다.

considerable 상당한 considerate 사려 깊은	favorable 호의적인; 유리한 favorite 가장 좋아하는	dependable 믿을 만한 dependent 의존하는
successful 성공한 successive 연속의	complimentary 무료의; 칭찬하는 complementary 보완하는	last 마지막의; 지난 lasting 지속적인
respectable 존경할 만한 respective 각자의, 각각의	sensible 분별 있는 sensitive 세심한; 예민한	economic 경제의 economical 경제적인
advisable 바람직한 advisory 자문의	manageable 처리하기 쉬운 managerial 경영상의	reliable 믿을 수 있는 reliant 의존적인

considerable amount of money 상당한 양의 돈
considerate behavior 사려 깊은 행동
favorite flavor 좋아하는 맛
favorable impression 호감 가는 인상

❷ -ly 형용사

접미어 -ly 때문에 부사처럼 보이지만 사실은 형용사인 단어들을 알아봅시다.

friendly 친절한, 상냥한 costly 비싼, 비용이 많이 드는 orderly 정돈된, 질서 있는	timely 시기적절한, 때맞춘 likely ~할 것 같은 elderly 나이가 지긋한	oily 기름 같은, 기름진 neighborly (이웃 간에) 우호적인 lively 활발한

an **elderly** guest 나이 든 손님
a **lively** discussion 활발한 토론
oily food 기름진 음식
costly equipment 비싼 장비

연습문제

정답 및 해설 p.064

1. Kitchen appliances made by Weston, Inc. are considered ------- by many foreign consumers.

   (A) dependent (B) depending
   (C) dependable (D) depend

2. All customer service representatives should be ------- of client requests and questions.

   (A) considerate (B) considerable
   (C) consideration (D) considerately

3. Ms. Jenkins instructed her workers to respond to every e-mail in a ------- manner.

   (A) timer (B) timing
   (C) timely (D) time

4. A ------- applicant at J.B. Hooper will be offered a job immediately.

   (A) success (B) successful
   (C) successfully (D) successive

4 부사 자리

The book (**quickly**) became a best seller (**quickly**).
　　　　　　부사　　　　　　　　　　　　　　　부사

그 책은 (**금방**) 베스트셀러가 되었다.

부사는 명사를 제외한 모든 품사를 수식할 수 있고, 문장 앞에 위치하여 문장 전체도 수식할 수 있어요.

① 동사 앞뒤

A planning meeting **normally** takes 30 minutes. 기획 회의는 **보통** 30분 정도 걸린다.
　　　　　　　　　　부사 + 동사

단, 〈be동사 + 현재분사/과거분사〉 구조에서는 부사가 be동사와 현재분사/과거분사 사이에 위치합니다.

Mr. Lee is **currently** working with various IT companies. 이 씨는 **현재** 많은 IT 회사와 일하고 있다.
　　　　be동사 + 부사 + 현재분사

The machine was **temporarily** shut down for repairs. 그 기계는 수리를 위해 **잠시** 정지되었다.
　　　　　　be동사 + 부사 + 과거분사

② 형용사와 부사 앞

The solution was **surprisingly** simple. 그 해결책은 **놀랍도록** 간단했다.
　　　　　　　　부사 + 형용사

The game industry grew **extremely** fast. 게임 산업은 **매우 빠르게** 성장했다.
　　　　　　　　　　　부사 + 부사

③ 문장 앞

Unfortunately, the tickets are sold out. [부사 + 문장]
아쉽게도 티켓은 매진되었어요.

연습문제

정답 및 해설 p.065

1 Construction on the apartment complex by the beach is ------- happening.

(A) swiftness (B) swiftest
(C) swift (D) swiftly

2 The outdoor event was only ------- successful due to a weather problem.

(A) parting (B) partly
(C) parted (D) part

3 Mr. Jackson is ------- considering opening a second restaurant downtown next year.

(A) careful (B) carefully
(C) carefulness (D) cared

4 The forklift drivers ------- moved the large boxes from the high shelf to the floor.

(A) safe (B) safety
(C) safely (D) safeness

5 다양한 형태의 부사

The venue is large **enough** for the event.
형용사 large를 수식하는 부사
그 장소는 행사에 쓰기에 **충분히** 넓다.

보통은 형용사에 접미어 -ly가 붙어 부사가 되지만 고유한 형태를 가진 부사들도 있습니다.

방법	well 잘, 제대로	instead 대신에	straight 똑바로, 곧장
정도	enough (만족스럽게) 충분히	quite 꽤; 완전히	almost 거의
빈도	always 항상 often 자주	sometimes 가끔 seldom 거의 ~ 않는	never 절대 ~ 않는
시간	soon 곧 yet 아직, 이미, 벌써	so far 지금까지 still 여전히, 아직도	now 지금
장소	nearby 근처에	everywhere 도처에	there 그곳에
가능성	perhaps 아마도	maybe 아마도	

고난도 JUMP UP

접속부사는 앞 문장과 뒤 문장의 문맥을 연결하면서 뒤 문장을 수식하는 부사입니다.

therefore 그러므로
nevertheless 그럼에도 불구하고

however 하지만
likewise 마찬가지로

then 그러면, 그런 다음
in fact 사실은, 실제로는

I like the marketing idea. However, the problem is the cost.
그 마케팅 아이디어는 마음에 들어요. 하지만 문제는 비용이죠.

연습문제

정답 및 해설 p.066

1 Sylvester found several mistakes in the report, but ------- it was insightful.

(A) meanwhile (B) nevertheless
(C) how (D) occasionally

2 Ms. Carter is on vacation tomorrow but will ------- be informed about the meeting.

(A) still (B) quite
(C) already (D) very

3 Mr. Watkins ------- commutes by train except when it rains or snows.

(A) almost (B) seldom
(C) yet (D) quite

4 Mr. Jabili's proposal was not what the CEO expected but it was quite innovative -------.

(A) for example (B) consequently
(C) otherwise (D) instead

6 혼동하기 쉬운 부사

a **hard** worker
열심인 (형용사)
열심히 일하는 사람

work **hard**
열심히 (부사)
열심히 일하다

hardly know
거의 ~ 않는 (부사)
거의 모른다

형용사와 생김새가 똑같거나 비슷한 부사들을 알아봅시다.

❶ 형용사와 형태가 같은 부사

enough 충분한; 충분히	long 오랜; 오래	early 이른; 일찍
far 먼; 멀리; 훨씬	fast 빠른; 빨리	pretty 예쁜; 꽤

The products were released in early March. 그 제품들은 3월 초에 출시되었다.
　　　　　　　　　　　　　명사 March를 수식하는 형용사

The restaurant opens early on Saturdays. 그 식당은 토요일엔 일찍 문을 연다.
　　　　　　　　　　동사 open을 수식하는 부사

❷ -ly가 붙어 뜻이 달라지는 부사

late 늦은; 늦게	most 대부분의; 가장	near 가까운; 가까이	deep 깊은; 깊이
lately 최근에	mostly 대개, 주로	nearly 거의	deeply 매우, 깊이
high 높은; 높이	hard 열심인; 열심히	close 가까운; 가까이	short 짧은; 짧게
highly 매우	hardly 거의 ~ 않는	closely 면밀히	shortly 곧, 이내

The meeting started late. 그 회의는 늦게 시작했다.
I've been a little busy lately. 전 요즘 조금 바빴어요.

연습문제　　　　　　　　　　　　　　　　　　　　정답 및 해설 p.067

1 The auditorium was ------- full when Dr. Burgess began her speech.

(A) near　　　　(B) nearly
(C) nearest　　(D) nearing

2 The workers in the lab tried exceptionally ------- to discover the source of the disease.

(A) hard　　　　(B) hardness
(C) hardly　　　(D) hardest

3 Ms. Sanderson has been ------- impressed with the quality of Mr. Bream's analysis.

(A) deepen　　(B) deeply
(C) deep　　　(D) deepest

4 Mr. Martin will offer the position to a ------- qualified applicant.

(A) highest　　(B) higher
(C) high　　　 (D) highly

빈출 유형 풀이 전략

1. 형용사 자리

STEP에 따라 실제 토익 문제를 푸는 순서와 요령을 익혀 보세요.

Kelly came up with a ------- solution to the firm's budget crisis.

(A) reason
(B) reasons
(C) reasonable
(D) reasonably

STEP 1 선택지 구성 파악하기

reason의 다양한 형태가 제시되어 있으므로 빈칸에 들어갈 적절한 품사를 묻는 문제.

Kelly came up with a ------- solution to the firm's budget crisis.

(A) reason
(B) reasons
(C) reasonable
(D) reasonably

STEP 2 빈칸 주변에서 단서 찾기

빈칸 앞에 부정관사 a가 있고 뒤에는 명사 solution이 있으므로 빈칸은 형용사 자리.

Kelly came up with a ------- solution to the firm's budget crisis.

(A) reason
(B) reasons
(C) ✓ reasonable
(D) reasonably

STEP 3 정답 찾기

선택지 중 형용사인 (C) reasonable이 정답.

해석 켈리는 회사의 예산 위기에 대한 합리적인 해결책을 생각해 냈다.

어휘 come up with ~을 생각해 내다   reasonable 합리적인   solution to ~에 대한 해결책

2. 부사 자리

STEP에 따라 실제 토익 문제를 푸는 순서와 요령을 익혀 보세요.

Ms. Watson ------- signed the legal documents after a long evaluation period.

(A) finally
(B) finalize
(C) finalizing
(D) final

STEP 1 선택지 구성 파악하기

final의 활용형으로 다양하게 구성된 것으로 보아 빈칸에 알맞은 final의 형태를 묻는 문제.

Ms. Watson ------- signed the legal documents after a long evaluation period.

(A) finally
(B) finalize
(C) finalizing
(D) final

STEP 2 빈칸 주변에서 단서 찾기

빈칸 앞에 주어 Ms. Watson이 있고 뒤에는 동사 signed가 있음. 따라서 빈칸은 동사를 수식하는 부사 자리.

Ms. Watson ------- signed the legal documents after a long evaluation period.

(A) ✓ finally
(B) finalize
(C) finalizing
(D) final

STEP 3 정답 찾기

선택지 중 부사인 (A) finally가 정답.
이 문제처럼 주어와 동사 사이에 빈칸이 있고 선택지에 부사가 보인다면 부사가 정답일 확률이 높습니다.

해석 왓슨 씨는 오랜 검토 기간을 거친 후에 그 법률 문서에 마침내 서명했다.
어휘 finally 마침내 sign 서명하다 legal 법률의 evaluation 검토, 평가, 분석

VOCABULARY 빈출 형용사 어휘 (1)

reliable 동 dependable	믿을 만한, 신뢰할 만한	**reliable** information 믿을 만한 정보 **reliable** and hard-working 믿을 만하고 성실한
attentive	주의를 기울이는; 신경 쓰는	friendly and **attentive** staff 친절하고 세심한 직원들 **attentive** to the needs of customers 고객이 필요로 하는 것에 신경을 쓰는
mandatory 동 compulsory	의무적인	**mandatory** for all departments 모든 부서에 의무적인 **mandatory** retirement age 정년
upcoming 동 forthcoming	다가오는, 곧 있을	prepare for the **upcoming** event 다가오는 행사를 준비하다 an **upcoming** exhibit[exhibition] 곧 있을 전시회
potential 동 possible	가능성 있는, 잠재적인; 가능성	be aware of **potential** problems 잠재적 문제들을 알아차리다 attract **potential** customers 잠재 고객들을 끌어들이다
gradual 반 sudden 갑작스런	점진적인, 단계적인	a **gradual** improvement in sales figures 매출의 점진적인 향상 forecast a **gradual** recovery 점진적인 회복을 예상하다
possible 동 potential	있을 수 있는, 가능한	if (at all) **possible** 가능하다면 do everything **possible** 가능한 모든 것을 하다
primary 동 main	주요한	the course's **primary** purpose[aim] 그 수업의 주된 목표 be of **primary** importance 가장 중요하다

연습문제

1 Several noted experts will be speaking at the ------- marketing seminar.
 (A) upcoming (B) possible
 (C) various   (D) canceled

2 Following the safety regulations at the construction site is ------- for all visitors.
 (A) potential (B) specific
 (C) mandatory (D) invited

3 Safeway Garage has been providing ------- service to motor vehicle owners for two decades.
 (A) gradual   (B) prior
 (C) implied   (D) reliable

4 Menhaden, Inc. makes numerous appliances, but its ------- focus is on televisions.
 (A) primary   (B) informative
 (C) attentive (D) estimated

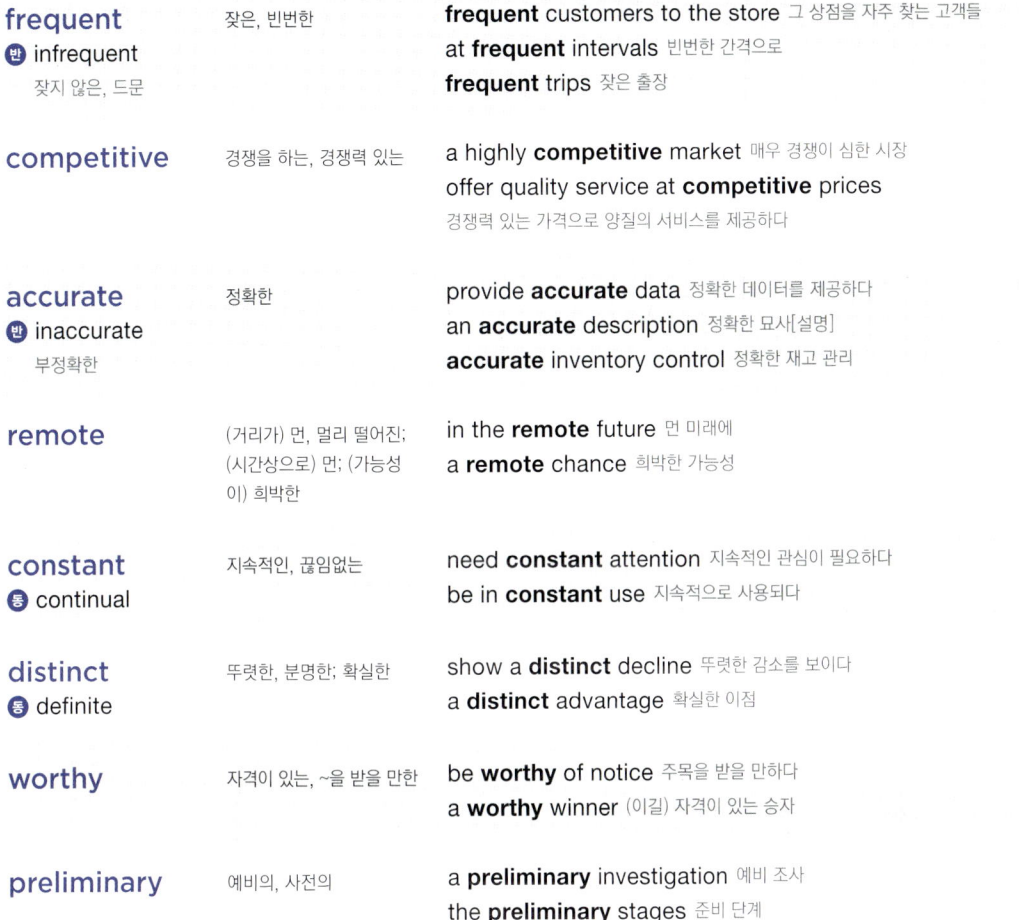

5 The ------- logo on the clothes clearly indicates they were made by Waltham Textiles.

(A) distinct (B) worthy
(C) reported (D) constant

6 The results of the ------- product test suggest the motor is not strong enough.

(A) expected (B) inexpert
(C) permanent (D) preliminary

7 The accountants working on the audit must make sure their numbers are as ------- as possible.

(A) hesitant (B) accurate
(C) competitive (D) revised

8 Mary is considering changing suppliers due to their ------- production delays.

(A) remote (B) dependent
(C) frequent (D) efficient

ACTUAL TEST

1. The researchers at Dynamo Metals are ------- when handling chemicals.
   (A) caution
   (B) cautious
   (C) cautions
   (D) cautiously

2. The factory inspector examined each of the manufactured items -------.
   (A) careful
   (B) caring
   (C) carefully
   (D) cared

3. Before every product launching, the CEO of TJ Electronics ------- tries to conduct a live product demonstration.
   (A) instead
   (B) always
   (C) therefore
   (D) well

4. ------- customer at Paulson Groceries receives a free gift on holidays.
   (A) None
   (B) A few
   (C) Most
   (D) Every

5. To reduce ------- spending, we're asking everyone to request approval before any large purchases.
   (A) excessive
   (B) excessively
   (C) excess
   (D) excesses

6. Guests at the Jackson Hotel are welcome to enjoy a ------- breakfast following the night of your stay.
   (A) complimentary
   (B) compliment
   (C) complementary
   (D) complemented

7. Individuals who wish to see the opera must book tickets ------- in advance.
   (A) very
   (B) much
   (C) far
   (D) hardly

8. Scott stated he would be ------- for the Web site redesign project.
   (A) responsible
   (B) to respond
   (C) responsibly
   (D) responding

어휘 cautious 조심스러운   handle 다루다, 처리하다   chemical 화학 물질; 화학의   inspector 검사관, 조사관   conduct 실시하다   approval 승인   book 예약하다

Questions 9-12 refer to the following article.

OLYMPIA (August 2)—The second annual Olympia Summer Festival will begin tomorrow morning at 9:00 at Landside Park. The festival is expected to be attended by an ------- 9. crowd of local residents.

Last year's festival featured games, rides, arts and crafts, and numerous local delicacies. ------- 10. . The festival's organizer, Marilyn Stewart, has high hopes for the event. "We expect large numbers of people to come every day. ------- 11. , the festival won't be too crowded as Landside Park covers a large area." Ms. Stewart assured that festival-goers will have fun in a safe and entertaining environment.

Attendance at the festival is $2 per day. ------- 12. profits from the festival will be donated to the local community center.

9 (A) enthusiasm
   (B) enthusiastic
   (C) enthusing
   (D) enthusiastically

11 (A) Apparently
   (B) However
   (C) In addition
   (D) Therefore

10 (A) This year's event includes musical performances.
   (B) Most attendees enjoyed going to the festival.
   (C) Games are popular with local children.
   (D) Most residents will attend the festival once.

12 (A) All
   (B) Each
   (C) Little
   (D) Much

어휘 annual 연례의   a crowd of 많은, 한 무리의   feature ~을 특색으로 하다   craft 공예   delicacy (지역의) 별미, 진미   organizer 주최자, 조직자   have high hopes 포부[기대]가 크다   crowded 혼잡한, 붐비는   cover (언급된 지역에) 걸치다   assure 장담하다   festival-goer 축제에 가는 사람   entertaining 재미있는, 즐거움을 주는

UNIT 08

전치사

1. 전치사 자리
2. 시간 · 장소 전치사
3. 기간 전치사
4. 기타 전치사
5. 혼동하기 쉬운 전치사: until vs. by
6. -ing형 전치사

빈출 유형 풀이 전략
Vocabulary
Actual Test

TOEIC Grammar

약 20%

UNIT 08 전치사

전치사 문제는 매회 3~4문제가 출제될 정도로 출제 비율이 높은 영역입니다. 토익에 자주 출제되는 전치사의 뜻과 쓰임을 정확히 알고 있어야 하며 전치사 관용 표현도 함께 알아 두는 것이 좋습니다.

스피드 진단 테스트

(A), (B) 중 알맞은 것을 고르세요.

1. Mr. Robert will arrive at the station ------- lunch.

    (A) after   (B) already

2. Applicants should submit their résumés ------- May 5.

    (A) by   (B) until

정답 및 해석

1. (A), 로버트 씨는 점심 이후에 역에 도착할 것이다.
2. (A), 지원자들은 이력서를 5월 5일까지 제출해야 한다.

🎯 전치사란?

전치사는 '앞前에 위치位하는 말詞'이라는 뜻으로, 명사 역할을 하는 말(명사, 대명사, 동명사) 앞에 위치하여 시간, 장소, 방향 등의 의미를 나타내는 말입니다.

on the table

under the table

● 전치사의 형태

전치사는 in, on처럼 한 단어로 된 것도 있고, such as, in front of와 같이 둘 이상의 단어가 결합하여 한 덩어리로 쓰이는 전치사도 있습니다.

한 단어 전치사	두 단어 전치사	세 단어 이상 전치사
among ~ 사이에 toward(s) ~ 쪽으로 throughout ~ 전역에, ~ 도처에	such as ~와 같은 according to ~에 따르면 regardless of ~에 관계없이	in front of ~ 앞에 on behalf of ~을 대표[대신]하여 in regard to ~와 관련하여

● 전치사구의 쓰임

전치사구란 '전치사 + 명사/대명사/동명사'를 이르는 말이며, 문장에서 형용사나 부사 역할을 합니다.
전치사 뒤에 있는 명사 상당어구들을 흔히 전치사의 목적어라고 부릅니다.

> The flight <u>from London</u> has arrived. 영국에서 오는 비행기가 도착했다. [형용사 역할]
>
> The meeting starts <u>at noon</u>. 회의는 12시에 시작한다. [부사 역할]

전치사가 동사와 짝을 지어 하나의 구동사를 이루는 경우가 있는데, 이 경우에는 전치사 뒤에 명사가 오더라도 전치사구로 묶을 수 없습니다.

> Did you have a chance to <u>look at</u> <u>the report</u>? 그 보고서 볼 기회가 있었나요?
>   구동사 목적어

UNIT 08 전치사 133

1 전치사 자리

The equipment is **from** Germany.
전치사   명사

그 장비는 **독일산**이다.

전치사는 명사나 목적격 대명사, 동명사 앞에 위치합니다.

❶ 명사 앞

The company made a considerable investment in security. 그 회사는 보안에 막대한 투자를 했다.
명사

Tickets for the concert are $30. 그 콘서트 표는 30달러입니다.
명사

❷ 목적격 대명사 앞

A package was delivered to him. 택배가 그에게 배달되었다.
목적격 대명사

❸ 동명사 앞

You can save 3 dollars by using a coupon. 쿠폰을 사용하면 3달러를 아낄 수 있습니다.
동명사

Please excuse my delay in replying. 답장이 늦어서 죄송합니다.
동명사

연습문제 정답 및 해설 p.073

1 Timesheets submitted ------- 5:00 P.M. today will be applied to the next pay period.

(A) later (B) sometimes
(C) after (D) than

2 ------- providing online services, Bikers Fabric could break into new markets.

(A) From (B) By
(C) Indeed (D) Likewise

3 Non-members are required to register online ------- arrival at the convention center.

(A) about (B) still
(C) upon (D) even

4 Visitors must put on a hardhat ------- entering the construction site.

(A) quite (B) out of
(C) before (D) then

2 시간·장소 전치사

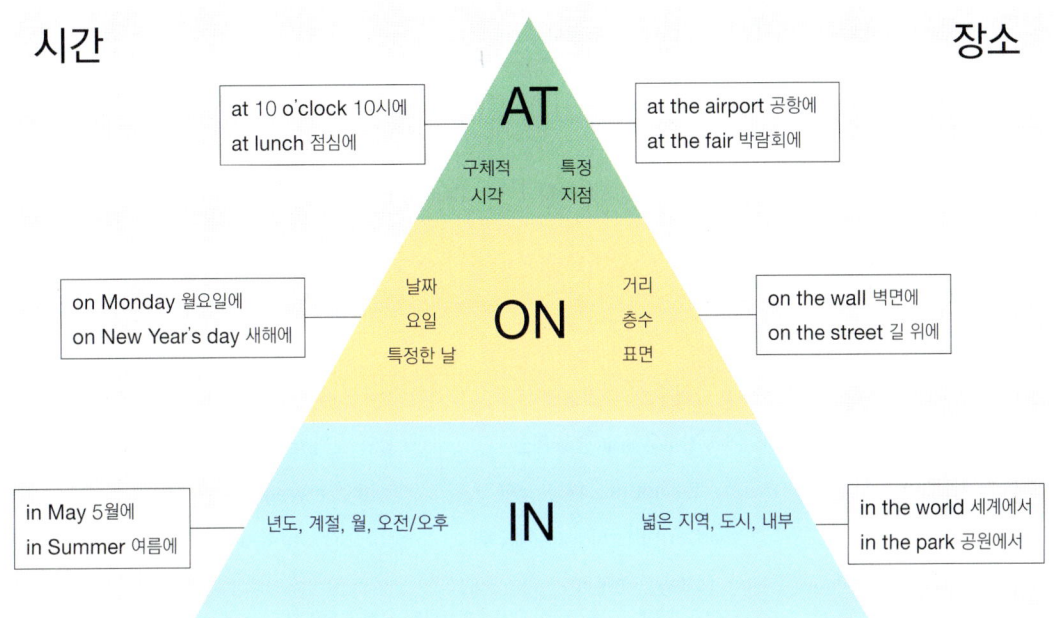

The store closes at 5:30 P.M. [시간]
그 가게는 오후 5시 30분에 닫는다.

The photography class is on Friday. [시간]
사진 수업은 금요일에 있다.

The merger took place in April. [시간]
합병은 4월에 이루어졌다.

They're staying at the Pristy Hotel. [장소]
그들은 프리스티 호텔에 묵고 있다.

The key to the cabinet is on John's desk. [장소]
캐비닛 열쇠는 존의 책상 위에 있다.

Smoking is prohibited in the building. [장소]
건물 안에서는 금연입니다.

연습문제

정답 및 해설 p.074

1. Mr. Masters hopes to open a café ------- the theater district downtown next month.

    (A) on (B) to
    (C) among (D) in

2. Ms. Wellborn had a taxi drop her off ------- the Clyburn Community Center.

    (A) for (B) on
    (C) at (D) up

3. The wood flooring ------- the second floor of the building will be replaced.

    (A) between (B) in
    (C) against (D) on

4. The keynote speech at the biotechnology conference is scheduled to start ------- 9:30 A.M.

    (A) at (B) in
    (C) for (D) of

기간 전치사

The warranty lasts for two years.
숫자로 표현된 기간

품질 보증은 2년 **동안** 지속됩니다.

Many shops were closed during the holidays.
행사 등이 일어난 때

많은 가게가 **연휴 동안** 문을 닫았다.

for + 숫자로 표현된 기간	for an hour 한 시간 동안	for two days 이틀 동안
during + 행사 등이 일어난 때	during the event 행사 동안	during the meeting 회의 동안
within + 기간	within 24 hours 24시간 내에	within a week 일주일 내에
throughout + 기간	throughout the night 밤새도록	throughout the performance 공연 내내
from + 시작 시점	from today 오늘부터 from 10 A.M. to 5 P.M. 오전 10시부터 오후 5시까지	

Packaged fruit juice should be consumed **within** a week.
시판 과일 주스는 일주일 **내에** 소비해야 한다.

The gallery is open daily **throughout** the year.
그 미술관은 1년 **내내** 매일 문을 연다.

packaged fruit juice

연습문제

정답 및 해설 p.075

1 ------- his business trip to Europe, Dr. Gills attended the Svalbard Science Conference.

(A) Without (B) Upon
(C) For (D) During

2 The sales figures ------- last week to this week increased sharply, marking a new record.

(A) within (B) from
(C) to (D) before

3 Decisions regarding employee transfers will be made ------- the next forty-eight hours.

(A) behind (B) toward
(C) from (D) within

4 Dr. Stephen from Barshire University was very cooperative ------- the entire interview session.

(A) from (B) throughout
(C) within (D) by

4 기타 전치사

Refund requests will not be accepted **through** e-mail.
~을 통해

이메일을 **통해서는** 환불 요청이 받아들여지지 않을 것입니다.

토익에 자주 출제되는 다양한 전치사를 살펴봅시다.

수단, 목적	through the Web site 웹사이트를 통해	for the museum tour 박물관 투어를 위해
동반, 보유	with new ideas 새 아이디어를 가지고	without permission 허가 없이
주제, 분야	about the topic 그 주제에 대해서	on legal matters 법적인 문제들에 관해
추가, 제외	besides cost 가격 외에도	except Sunday 일요일을 제외하고
기타	as a volunteer 자원봉사자로서	under construction/repair 공사/수리 중인

The two companies came to an agreement **on** the price. 두 회사는 가격에 관해 의견 일치를 봤다.

A new airport is **under** construction. 새 공항이 건설중이다.

고난도 JUMP UP

besides ~ 이외에도	vs.	**beside** ~ 옆에
Besides Italian, he also speaks English.		An extinguisher is beside the stage.
그는 이탈리아어 **외에** 영어도 구사한다.		소화기는 무대 **옆에** 있다.

연습문제

정답 및 해설 p.076

1 The intern will replace Ms. Reed ------- a junior accountant after he graduates.

(A) like (B) on
(C) as (D) about

2 All the problems with the product ------- its design were discussed at the board meeting.

(A) beside (B) besides
(C) through (D) for

3 When the investors heard ------- the upcoming product plan, they were eager to sign the investment contract.

(A) about (B) without
(C) through (D) except

4 Mr. Teakwood had to submit his reimbursement form ------- any receipts after losing them.

(A) with (B) without
(C) through (D) except

5 혼동하기 쉬운 전치사: until vs. by

stay **until** next week [지속]	submit the form **by** Friday [완료]
~까지 (지속)	~까지 (완료)
다음 주까지 (계속) 머무르다	그 양식을 금요일까지 (완료해서) 제출하다

뜻은 유사하지만 쓰임이 확연히 다른 until과 by의 차이를 알아봅시다.

❶ until + 지속 시점

until은 '지속'의 뜻을 내포하고 있어서 특정 시점까지 행위나 동작이 계속되는 것을 나타낼 때 씁니다.

| stay (머무르다) | continue (계속되다) | be valid (유효하다) | + until + 때 |

The clearance sale <u>continues</u> until tomorrow. 재고 정리 세일은 내일까지 계속됩니다.

This coupon <u>is valid</u> until December 31. 이 쿠폰은 12월 31일까지 (계속) 유효합니다.

❷ by + 완료 시점

by는 '(늦어도) 특정 시점'까지는 행위나 동작이 완료되는 기한을 표현할 때 씁니다.

| finish (마치다) | complete (완료하다) | submit (제출하다) | + by + 때 |

New recruits must <u>complete</u> the training program by the end of next month.
신입 사원들은 훈련 프로그램을 **(늦어도)** 다음 달 말까지 완료해야 합니다.

연습문제

정답 및 해설 p.077

1 The Cumberland Gallery will remain open ------- 8:00 P.M. this weekend.
(A) by   (B) for
(C) until   (D) on

2 The second round of interviews will continue ------- the end of the day.
(A) until   (B) for
(C) by   (D) over

3 Clients must submit their completed customer service surveys ------- 9:00 A.M. Monday morning.
(A) at   (B) by
(C) with   (D) until

4 All construction workers should enter their hours into the computer ------- 4:00 P.M. on Friday.
(A) by   (B) until
(C) with   (D) in

6 -ing형 전치사

The purse is 50 dollars including tax.
　　　　　　　　　　　　　　　　　　명사

그 지갑은 세금을 **포함해서** 50달러입니다.

Following the speech, he attended a luncheon.
　　　　　　　　　　명사

연설 **이후에** 그는 오찬에 참석했다.

-ing형 전치사는 형태 때문에 진행 시제나 동명사로 착각하기 쉽습니다. 이러한 전치사들은 시험에도 자주 출제되는 편이니 꼭 알아 둬야 합니다.

concerning the proposal	그 제안에 관하여	following the speech	그 연설 이후에
regarding the work	그 작업에 관하여	including tax	세금을 포함하여
considering the price	그 가격을 고려[감안]하면	excluding bonuses	보너스를 제외하고

If you have any questions **concerning** the schedule, please let me know.
　　　　　　　　　　　　　　　　= about, regarding
일정에 대해 문의 사항이 있으면 제게 말씀해 주세요.

I was impressed with how well he's done **considering** his lack of experience.
그의 경험 부족을 **고려하면** 그가 정말 잘해서 인상적이었습니다.

The books are on sale at $50, **excluding** postage.
그 책들은 우송료를 **제외하고** 50달러에 판매 중이다.

연습문제
정답 및 해설 p.078

1 The regulations ------- usage of company vehicles were altered at Monday's staff meeting.
　(A) through　　(B) concerning
　(C) though　　(D) excluding

2 All coupons for Zack's, ------- those issued online, will expire on December 31.
　(A) included　　(B) includes
　(C) including　　(D) inclusion

3 Ms. Toole's response ------- the missing laptop stressed the need for security.
　(A) as　　(B) regarding
　(C) following　　(D) onto

4 ------- the release of the movie, Anne Stanton became famous all around the world.
　(A) About　　(B) Following
　(C) Including　　(D) Regarding

빈출 유형 풀이 전략

1. 전치사 자리

STEP에 따라 실제 토익 문제를 푸는 순서와 요령을 익혀 보세요.

Lucas Legal Solutions is located directly ------- the gas station on Washington Avenue.

(A) opposite
(B) cautiously
(C) yet
(D) when

STEP 1 선택지 구성 파악하기

선택지가 각기 다른 품사로 구성되어 있는 것으로 보아 빈칸에 들어갈 적절한 품사를 묻는 문제.

Lucas Legal Solutions is located directly ------- the gas station on Washington Avenue.

(A) opposite
(B) cautiously
(C) yet
(D) when

STEP 2 빈칸 주변에서 단서 찾기

빈칸 뒤에 명사구(the gas station on Washington Avenue)가 이어지므로 빈칸은 명사구 앞에 위치할 수 있는 전치사 자리.

Lucas Legal Solutions is located directly ------- the gas station on Washington Avenue.

(A) opposite ✓
(B) cautiously
(C) yet
(D) when

STEP 3 정답 찾기

선택지 중 전치사 (A) opposite가 정답.

해석 루카스 리걸 솔루션스는 워싱턴 가의 주유소 바로 맞은편에 위치해 있다.

어휘 be located 위치되다 gas station 주유소 opposite 맞은편에 cautiously 조심스럽게, 신중하게 yet 아직; 그렇지만 when ~할 때

2. -ing형 전치사

STEP에 따라 실제 토익 문제를 푸는 순서와 요령을 익혀 보세요.

Calls ------- exchanges and refunds should be forwarded to Ms. Sellers's office.

(A) regards
(B) regarding
(C) regarded
(D) to regard

STEP 1 선택지 구성 파악하기

regard의 활용형으로 다양하게 구성된 것으로 보아 빈칸에 알맞은 regard의 형태를 묻는 문제.

Calls ------- exchanges and refunds should be forwarded to Ms. Sellers's office.

(A) regards
(B) regarding
(C) regarded
(D) to regard

STEP 2 빈칸 주변에서 단서 찾기

빈칸 뒤에 나오는 〈조동사+동사〉인 should be forwarded가 문장의 본동사 역할을 하고 있으므로 '------- exchanges and refunds'는 주어 Calls를 꾸며 주는 수식어구임.
따라서 빈칸에는 명사구(exchanges and refunds)를 목적어로 취할 수 있는 말이 들어가야 함.

Calls ------- exchanges and refunds should be forwarded to Ms. Sellers's office.

(A) regards
(B) ✓ regarding
(C) regarded
(D) to regard

STEP 3 정답 찾기

선택지 중 명사구를 목적어로 취하면서 문맥상 '교환과 환불에 관한 연락'이라는 의미를 완성할 수 있는 것은 전치사인 (B) regarding.

해석 교환 및 환불 관련 전화는 셀러 씨의 사무실로 돌려져야 한다.

어휘 exchange 교환 refund 환불 forward 전달하다, 보내다

VOCABULARY

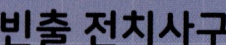 빈출 전치사구

as of[from]	~ 일자로, ~부터 (시작하여)	**as of** mid-July 7월 중순부터 **as from** next Monday 다음 주 월요일부로
next to	~ 옆에	be located **next to** the building 그 건물 옆에 위치해 있다 be **next to** each other 서로 바로 옆에[나란히] 있다
along with	~와 함께	serve sandwiches **along with** soft drinks 탄산음료와 함께 샌드위치를 제공하다 submit your résumé **along with** your application 지원서와 함께 이력서를 제출하다
in favor of	~에 찬성하여	vote **in favor of** the project 그 프로젝트에 찬성표를 던지다 be **in favor of** the plan 그 계획에 찬성하다
in (the) light of 동 considering	~을 고려하여, ~을 감안하여	**in (the) light of** the bad weather 악천후를 고려하여 **in the light of** the current situation 현 상황을 고려하여
instead of	~ 대신에	hang curtains **instead of** blinds 블라인드 대신 커튼을 달다 **instead of** waiting until next week 다음 주까지 기다리는 대신
in spite of 동 despite	~에도 불구하고	succeed **in spite of** all difficulties 모든 어려움에도 불구하고 성공하다 fail **in spite of** their efforts 그들의 노력에도 불구하고 실패하다
in response to	~에 대응하여	**in response to** customer demand 고객 요구에 응하여 **in response to** these issues 이 사안들에 대한 대처로

연습문제

1 As ------- Monday, January 19, the company's name will change to Data Xpress.

(A) for (B) on
(C) of (D) by

2 ------- paying employees cash bonuses, vacation packages were awarded by the firm.

(A) In favor of (B) Due to
(C) Instead of (D) Aware of

3 Applicants must submit a résumé ------- three letters of recommendation to Mr. Pruitt.

(A) along with (B) as well
(C) in light of (D) in case of

4 In ------- to increasing demand, the assembly line will now operate 24 hours a day.

(A) variety (B) fact
(C) access (D) response

by means of	(특정 방법이나 시스템 등을) 이용하여	**by means of** hard work 각고의 노력으로 afford a house **by means of** a loan 대출을 받아서 집을 마련하다
except for	~을 제외하고는, ~ 외에는	refund everything **except for** the shipping cost 배송비를 제외하고 환불해 주다 be open daily **except for** Mondays 월요일을 제외하고 매일 문을 열다
prior to 🔵 before	~ 전에	**prior to** the meeting 회의 전에 **prior to** use 사용 전에
in terms of	~의 관점에서, ~에 있어서	**in terms of** beauty 미의 관점에서 **in terms of** time and money 시간과 돈이라는 측면에서
depending on 🔵 according to	~에 따라	cancel the event **depending on** the weather 날씨에 따라 행사를 취소하다 change plans **depending on** the situation 상황에 따라 계획을 변경하다
because of 🔵 owing to	~ 때문에	**because of** heavy traffic 교통 체증 때문에 **because of** ongoing construction 진행 중인 공사 때문에
ahead of	~에 앞서	several days **ahead of** the deadline 마감일 며칠 전에 be completed **ahead of** schedule 예정보다 일찍 완료되다
aside from 🔵 apart from	~ 이외에도, ~ 뿐만 아니라; ~을 제외하고는, ~ 외에는	**aside from** her earnings as a musician 음악가로 얻는 수입 이외에도; 음악가로 얻는 수입을 제외하고는 **aside from** the low salary 낮은 급여 이외에도; 낮은 급여 외에는

정답 및 해설 p.079

5 ------- the significant increase in cost, many members have expressed dissatisfaction with some of the services at the fitness center.

(A) Owing to (B) Aside from
(C) According to (D) By means of

6 Charles's team has a reputation for completing projects ------- schedule.

(A) in particular (B) with regard
(C) ahead of (D) onto

7 Customers will retain all membership points accumulated ------- the merger.

(A) as to (B) in terms of
(C) without (D) prior to

8 The legal document has all the required signatures ------- Mr. Roswell's.

(A) depending on (B) instead
(C) throughout (D) except for

ACTUAL TEST

1. Ms. Carter has a layover in Dublin ------- arriving in Copenhagen tomorrow.

    (A) before
    (B) about
    (C) while
    (D) because

2. The supervisors always submit employee evaluations ------- the end of the month.

    (A) by
    (B) under
    (C) until
    (D) throughout

3. Mitch Stallings will be working in the PR Department ------- next Monday onward.

    (A) from
    (B) since
    (C) for
    (D) within

4. ------- the size of the parcel, it might leave the warehouse tomorrow morning.

    (A) Dependent to
    (B) Depending on
    (C) Depended
    (D) To depend on

5. Duncan Groceries sells all kinds of imported foods, ------- African and Asian delicacies.

    (A) starting
    (B) providing
    (C) including
    (D) avoiding

6. Hillside apartment residents have a view of mountains ------- the windows on the eastern side.

    (A) on
    (B) through
    (C) with
    (D) except

7. The downtown roads were closed for a while due to a thick blanket of -------.

    (A) snow
    (B) snowy
    (C) snowier
    (D) snowed

8. Jacob Interior will be providing free bathtub installations ------- next Sunday, March 11.

    (A) by
    (B) during
    (C) until
    (D) at

어휘 layover (일시적인) 체류, 경유 evaluation 평가(서) onward(s) 앞으로, (특정 시점부터) 계속 leave 떠나다 warehouse 물류 창고 delicacy (특정 지역의) 별미, 진미 for a while 한동안 installation 설치

Questions 9-12 refer to the following memo.

To: All Employees
From: Doug Lasker, IT Supervisor
Date: October 12
Subject: Web Site Maintenance

Please be aware that the company Web site is scheduled for some routine maintenance tomorrow starting at 8:00 A.M. The Web site ------- offline for at least seven hours. ------- that time, nobody will be able to access the Web site for any reason. It will take longer time than usual because our team is not only working on maintenance this time. ------- . When service resumes, please be sure to browse our Web site to check out its ------- features. We would appreciate your feedback regarding them.

Please be sure not to schedule anything requiring access to the company Web page tomorrow. If you have any questions, feel free to contact me at extension 845.

9. (A) was
   (B) will be
   (C) has been
   (D) is

10. (A) In
    (B) Instead
    (C) During
    (D) Despite

11. (A) No work was done on the upgrade yet.
    (B) I appreciate all of your suggestions.
    (C) We're sorry you couldn't access the site.
    (D) The site will also be given an upgrade.

12. (A) improved
    (B) proposed
    (C) attempted
    (D) reported

UNIT 09

to부정사

1. to부정사의 명사 역할
2. to부정사의 형용사 역할
3. to부정사의 부사 역할
4. 가주어와 의미상의 주어
5. to부정사와 어울려 쓰이는 동사
6. to부정사와 어울려 쓰이는 형용사

빈출 유형 풀이 전략
Vocabulary
Actual Test

TOEIC Grammar

약 10%

UNIT 09 to부정사

to부정사 문제는 매회 1문제 정도 출제됩니다. to부정사의 여러 역할 중에서 '~할'을 뜻하는 형용사 역할과 '~하기 위해서'를 뜻하는 부사 역할이 자주 출제되는 편입니다. 그 외에 to부정사의 의미상의 주어, to부정사와 어울려 쓰이는 동사와 형용사도 익혀 두어야 합니다.

 스피드 진단 테스트

(A), (B) 중 알맞은 것을 고르세요.

1. There's an easy way ------- online.

   (A) to pay   (B) pays

2. They want ------- the contract.

   (A) extension   (B) to extend

> 정답 및 해석
> 1. (A), 온라인으로 지불하는 쉬운 방법이 있다.
> 2. (B), 그들은 계약을 연장하기를 원한다.

💡 to부정사란?

to부정사는 동사원형 앞에 to를 붙여 문장에서 다양한 역할(명사, 형용사, 부사)을 수행할 수 있습니다. 아래의 예시에서는 동사 make가 to부정사로 쓰여 어떻게 명사, 형용사, 부사 역할을 하는지를 보여줍니다.

명사 역할

We asked them to make a quick decision.
　　　　　　　　　　빨리 결정을 내릴 것을
우리는 그들에게 빨리 결정을 내릴 것을 요청했다.

형용사 역할

We have some major decisions to make this week.
　　　　　　　　　　　　　　　　　내려야 할
우리는 금주에 내려야 할 몇 가지 중요한 결정들이 있다.

부사 역할

To make a decision, I asked my accountant for some financial advice.
　결정을 내리기 위해
결정을 내리기 위해 나는 회계사에게 재정적인 조언을 구했다.

● 헷갈리기 쉬운 to부정사

used to는 토익에서 매우 자주 쓰이는 표현입니다. 하지만 다음과 같이 형태는 비슷하지만 그 용법과 의미가 다르게 쓰이는 경우들이 있으므로 반드시 구분해 두도록 해야 합니다.

He used to work with Ms. Watson at Upcity. 그는 업시티에서 왓슨 씨와 함께 일했었다.
　　~하곤 했다

The data can be used to predict demand. 그 데이터는 수요를 예측하는 데 사용될 수 있다.
　　　　　　　　~하기 위하여 사용되다

　　　　　　　전치사
I'm not used to such spicy food. 저는 그런 매운 음식에 익숙하지 않아요.
~에 익숙하다(be/get used to 명사)

1 to부정사의 명사 역할

They wanted to develop a creative design.
명사 역할을 하는 to부정사구
그들은 **창의적인 디자인을 개발하길** 원했다.

to부정사가 문장에서 명사 역할을 할 땐 주어, 목적어, 보어 자리에 위치할 수 있습니다.

❶ 주어 자리

To reduce expenses is our goal.
↳ to부정사 주어는 단수 취급하므로 단수 동사를 씁니다.
지출을 줄이는 것이 우리의 목표이다.

❷ 목적어 자리

They want to build a new factory.
그들은 새 공장을 짓기를 원한다.

❸ 보어 자리

Your job is to analyze financial data.
　　　　　　주격 보어
당신이 할 일은 **금융 데이터를 분석하는** 것입니다.

He asked me to change the meeting date.
　　　　　　　목적격 보어
그는 내게 **회의 날짜를 변경할 것을** 요청했다.

연습문제　　　　　　　　　　　　　　　　　　　정답 및 해설 p.084

1 The task of the Hoody's Green Management is ------- recyclables from our office and dispose of them properly.

(A) collected　　(B) to collect
(C) collection　　(D) to collecting

2 By next year, Joyce Watters aims ------- at least 20 more part-time employees.

(A) to recruit　　(B) recruited
(C) recruiting　　(D) have recruited

3 Mr. Wang guarantees ------- the profit margins of any company that hires him as a consultant.

(A) increased　　(B) to increase
(C) increasing　　(D) having increased

4 Due to growing environmental concerns, the government is asking citizens ------- the use of disposable plastics.

(A) minimizing　　(B) minimized
(C) to minimize　　(D) for minimizing

2 to부정사의 형용사 역할

I couldn't find a place to park.
명사 ← 형용사 역할을 하는 to부정사

나는 **주차할 곳**을 찾을 수 없었다.

to부정사는 명사를 뒤에서 수식하여 형용사 역할을 할 수 있습니다. 이때 to부정사는 '~할', '~하는'으로 해석합니다.

❶ 명사 수식

I have an online meeting to attend.
← 명사구 an online meeting 수식

저는 **참석할** 화상 회의가 있어요.

I have a report to look at.
← 명사 a report 수식

저는 **살펴봐야 할** 보고서가 있어요.

online meeting

❷ 토익에 자주 출제되는 <명사+to부정사> 묶음 표현

plan to *do*	~할 계획	time to *do*	~할 시간
ability to *do*	~할 능력	chance to *do*	~할 기회
attempt to *do*	~하려는 시도	opportunity to *do*	~할 기회
way to *do*	~할 방법	effort to *do*	~하려는 노력

You'll have the opportunity to ask questions after the talk.

연설이 끝난 후에 **질문할 기회**가 있을 겁니다.

연습문제 정답 및 해설 p.085

1 Brookville Industries has been implementing a plan ------- its new staff members more quickly.

(A) to train   (B) trains
(C) trained   (D) will train

2 Executives at Franklin Auto agreed that it was time ------- electronic vehicles.

(A) manufactures   (B) will manufacture
(C) to manufacture   (D) manufacturing

3 Atlantis Resort added a new diving pool in an ------- to attract more visitors.

(A) attempting   (B) attempted
(C) attempts   (D) attempt

4 Pinceps Academy researches new ways ------- the learning efficiency of young students.

(A) improve   (B) improving
(C) to improve   (D) improves

to부정사의 부사 역할

Please fill out this form to sign up. 신청하시려면 이 양식을 작성해 주세요.
부사 역할을 하는 to부정사구

❶ 동사와 문장 수식

to부정사가 동사나 문장을 수식할 때는 주로 행위의 목적을 나타내며 '~하기 위해' 또는 '~하려면'으로 해석합니다.

Please press 2 **to place** an order. 주문하시려면 2번을 눌러 주세요.
　　　　　　　　동사 press 수식

To simplify the process, the company will introduce a new system.
　　　　문장 수식
절차를 간소화하기 위해 그 회사는 새로운 시스템을 도입할 것이다.

❷ 형용사 수식

to부정사가 형용사를 수식할 때는 주로 '~하게 되어' 또는 '~하다니'라고 해석합니다. 이때 to부정사 앞에 감정 형용사가 위치하기도 합니다.

We are sorry **to inform** you so late. 너무 늦게 알려 드려서 죄송합니다.
　　　　　　형용사 sorry 수식

⬆ 고난도 JUMP UP

too + 형용사/부사 + to *do* 너무 ~해서 …할 수 없는	형용사/부사 + enough to *do* ~하기에 충분히 …한
This place is **too** small **to hold** 200 people. 이 장소는 너무 작아서 200명을 수용할 수 없다.	This place is large **enough to hold** 200 people. 이 장소는 200명을 수용하기에 충분히 넓다.

연습문제
정답 및 해설 p.086

1 Great Eastern Inc. is happy ------- the news of our expansion to 25 cities in Asia.

(A) share　　　　(B) shared
(C) to share　　　(D) will share

2 Our restaurant's seating area has been renovated ------- outdoor dining when the weather is favorable.

(A) is offered　　(B) will offer
(C) to offer　　　(D) offers

3 Gamma Tech's rates are too ------- to outsource our company's Internet security management.

(A) expensively　(B) expenditure
(C) expenses　　 (D) expensive

4 An administrator will provide test takers with the tools necessary ------- each given task.

(A) complete　　(B) completed
(C) to complete　(D) will complete

4 가주어와 의미상의 주어

It is important **to calculate** the exact cost.
가주어 / 진주어
정확한 비용을 계산하는 것은 중요합니다.

❶ 가주어 it

주어 자리에 위치한 to부정사가 너무 길면 문장 맨 뒤로 보내고 주어 자리에 가주어 it을 쓸 수 있어요.

To improve the customer experience is important.
= It is important to improve the customer experience.
  가주어   진주어
고객 경험을 향상시키는 것은 중요하다.

❷ 의미상의 주어: for + 명사/목적격 대명사

to부정사가 나타내는 행위의 주체를 따로 밝힐 경우에는 to부정사 앞에 〈for + 명사/목적격 대명사〉로 표시합니다.

It is impossible for us to finish this project in two days.
가주어   의미상의 주어   진주어
우리가 이 프로젝트를 이틀 만에 끝내는 것은 불가능합니다.

The meeting was an opportunity for the two leaders to exchange views.
                              의미상의 주어   to부정사구
그 회의는 두 리더가 의견을 교환할 수 있는 기회였다.

연습문제 정답 및 해설 p.087

1 It is generally preferable ------- a letter of recommendation when applying for a position.

(A) inclusion   (B) included
(C) including   (D) to include

2 It is ------- to use the metric system when reporting data to an international audience.

(A) advice   (B) advisors
(C) to advise (D) advisable

3 The critics analyzed that it is necessary ------- Pullman Deli to make changes to some of its menus.

(A) except   (B) along
(C) to   (D) for

4 It is mandatory for staff ------- the refresher training because of the recent curriculum changes.

(A) attend   (B) attendance
(C) to attend (D) attended

5 to부정사와 어울려 쓰이는 동사

They decided **to hire** the engineer.
　　　　동사　　　　목적어 (to부정사)
그들은 그 엔지니어를 **고용하기로** 결정했다.

to부정사를 목적어와 목적격 보어로 취하는 특정 동사들을 알아봅시다.

❶ to부정사를 목적어로 쓰는 동사들

plan to *do*	~하기를 계획하다	promise to *do*	~하기로 약속하다
ask to *do*	~할 것을 요청하다	pledge to *do*	~하기로 맹세하다
choose to *do*	~하는 것을 선택하다	would like to *do*	~하고 싶다
expect to *do*	~하기를 기대하다	wish to *do*	~하기를 바라다

They promised <u>to deliver</u> the package within two days.
그들은 그 택배를 이틀 내에 **배송할 것을** 약속했다.

❷ to부정사를 목적격 보어로 쓰는 동사들

allow A to *do*	A가 ~하는 것을 허락하다	would like A to *do*	A가 ~하기를 원하다
expect A to *do*	A가 ~할 거라고 예상하다	encourage A to *do*	A에게 ~하라고 권장하다
remind A to *do*	A에게 ~하라고 상기시키다	advise A to *do*	A에게 ~하라고 충고하다

The company <u>encouraged</u> employees <u>to work</u> remotely.
그 회사는 직원들에게 **재택근무를** 권장했다.

연습문제　　　　　　　　　　　　　　　　　　　　　　정답 및 해설 p.088

1. Hank was deeply impressed by the interviewee because he ------- to improve the workplace atmosphere.

    (A) invited　　　(B) regarded
    (C) assumed　　(D) pledged

2. Mr. Byrd would like all volunteers ------- early on the day of the event.

    (A) arrives　　　(B) arriving
    (C) to arrive　　(D) will arrive

3. Shareholders ------- to earn high returns on their initial investments by January.

    (A) tested　　　(B) warranted
    (C) encouraged　(D) expected

4. The game console's seamless interface allows users ------- between its functions instantly.

    (A) switch　　　(B) switched
    (C) switching　　(D) to switch

6 to부정사와 어울려 쓰이는 형용사

The startup is ready to launch their new wireless earphones.
be ready to *do*
그 스타트업은 새로운 무선 이어폰을 **출시할 준비를** 하고 있다.

일부 형용사는 〈be 형용사 to *do*〉의 형태로 하나의 패턴처럼 쓰이기도 합니다. 아래의 패턴들은 토익에서 빈번하게 등장하니 꼭 하나의 덩어리로 외워 두세요.

be available to *do*	~하는 데 이용 가능하다	be advisable to *do*	~하는 것을 권하다
be eligible to *do*	~할 자격이 있다	be proud to *do*	~해서 자랑스럽다
be willing to *do*	기꺼이 ~하다	be scheduled to *do*	~할 예정이다
be able to *do*	~할 수 있다	be supposed to *do*	~하기로 되어 있다

Mr. John **is not available to attend** the seminar.
존 씨는 세미나에 **참석하지 못합니다**.

New employees **are eligible to receive** paid vacation time after three months of full-time employment.
신입 사원들은 정규직으로 3개월을 근무한 후 휴가 혜택을 **받을 자격이 된다**.

The elevator is out of order and **is scheduled to be repaired** this week.
그 엘리베이터는 고장나서 이번 주에 **수리될 예정이다**.

out of order

연습문제

정답 및 해설 p.089

1 Venice Tech is ------- to unveil its new mobile device, the Venice Z9.
  (A) praised   (B) proud
  (C) compatible (D) applicable

2 Ms. Marino is ------- to discuss design proposals with clients on Tuesdays and Thursdays.
  (A) diligent   (B) available
  (C) initial   (D) cautious

3 Mr. Clark is always ------- to provide technical assistance and advice to junior staff members.
  (A) willing   (B) acclaimed
  (C) cheery   (D) popular

4 Melton Outfitters' club members are ------- to receive free shipping on online orders.
  (A) eligible   (B) reviewed
  (C) comfortable (D) capable

빈출 유형 풀이 전략

1. to부정사의 형용사 역할

STEP에 따라 실제 토익 문제를 푸는 순서와 요령을 익혀 보세요.

The management has an obligation ------- carefully to its staff's safety concerns.

(A) listen
(B) listens
(C) listening
(D) to listen

STEP 1 선택지 구성 파악하기

선택지가 listen의 활용형으로 구성된 것으로 보아 빈칸에 알맞은 listen의 형태를 묻는 문제.

The management has an obligation ------- carefully to its staff's safety concerns.

(A) listen
(B) listens
(C) listening
(D) to listen

STEP 2 빈칸 주변에서 단서 찾기

빈칸 앞에 〈주어(The management)+동사(has)+목적어(an obligation)〉 구조로 완전한 절이 있음. 동사인 (A) listen과 단수 동사인 (B) listens는 오답으로 소거.

The management has an obligation ------- carefully to its staff's safety concerns.

(A) listen
(B) listens
(C) listening
(D) ✓ to listen

STEP 3 정답 찾기

동명사 또는 현재분사인 (C) listening과 to부정사인 (D) to listen 중에서 빈칸 앞에 있는 명사 an obligation을 수식할 수 있는 것은 (D) to listen.

해석 경영진은 직원들의 안전 문제들을 주의 깊게 들을 의무가 있다.

어휘 management 경영(진)　obligation 의무　carefully 주의 깊게　safety 안전　concern 우려, 관심사

2. to부정사와 어울려 쓰이는 동사

STEP에 따라 실제 토익 문제를 푸는 순서와 요령을 익혀 보세요.

All golf club members must agree ------- to the guidelines and pay a monthly fee.

(A) adhere
(B) to adhere
(C) be adhered
(D) adhering

STEP 1 선택지 구성 파악하기

선택지가 adhere의 활용형으로 구성된 것으로 보아 빈칸에 알맞은 adhere의 형태를 묻는 문제.

All golf club members must agree ------- to the guidelines and pay a monthly fee.

(A) adhere
(B) to adhere
(C) be adhered
(D) adhering

STEP 2 빈칸 주변에서 단서 찾기

〈주어(All golf club members)+동사(must agree)+-------+전치사구(to the guidelines)〉 구조이므로 빈칸은 동사 agree의 목적어 자리.

All golf club members must agree ------- to the guidelines and pay a monthly fee.

(A) adhere
(B) to adhere ✓
(C) be adhered
(D) adhering

STEP 3 정답 찾기

agree는 to부정사를 목적어로 쓰는 대표적인 동사임. 따라서 선택지 중 to부정사인 (B) to adhere가 정답.

해석 모든 골프 클럽 회원들은 지침을 준수하는 데 동의하고 매월 이용료를 지불해야 한다.

어휘 agree to *do* ~하는 데 동의하다 adhere to ~을 준수하다 guideline 지침 fee 요금

VOCABULARY 빈출 형용사 어휘 (2)

entire 동 whole	전체의	give one's **entire** attention to the task 그 일에 온 신경을 쏟다 cover the **entire** fee 모든 비용을 대다
absolute	완전한, 완벽한; 확실한	a workshop for **absolute** beginners 완전 초보들을 위한 워크숍 have **absolute** trust in her ability 그녀의 능력을 전적으로 신뢰하다
additional	추가의	receive **additional** discounts 추가 할인을 받다 at no **additional** cost 추가 비용 없이
hesitant	망설이는, 주저하는	be **hesitant** to accept the job 그 일을 수락하는 걸 망설이다 be **hesitant** about trying new things 새로운 일을 시도하길 망설이다
likely	~할 것 같은; 적당한, 알맞은	be **likely** to remain unchanged 계속 변하지 않을 것 같다 a **likely** candidate for the position 그 자리에 적당한 후보자
expert 반 inexpert 미숙한	전문적인; 숙련된	provide **expert** advice 전문적인 조언을 하다 be **expert** at finding information 정보를 찾는 데 숙련되다
sure 동 certain	분명히[반드시] ~할; 확실한	be **sure** to bring an ID card 반드시 신분증을 챙기다 a **sure** sign of rain 비가 내릴 확실한 징조
partial	부분적인	a **partial** solution 부분적인 해결책 get a **partial** refund 일부 환불을 받다

연습문제

1 The percentage of job applicants with certifications is ------- to increase over the next decade.
(A) acceptable (B) absolute
(C) studious   (D) likely

2 With the backing of ------- investors, the company was able to increase production.
(A) doubtful   (B) entitled
(C) additional (D) inexpert

3 Be ------- to inspect your rental vehicle for any damage before signing for it.
(A) entire   (B) sure
(C) reasonable (D) utmost

4 Due to several recalls in recent years, customers are ------- to purchase Dupont's kitchen appliances.
(A) hesitant   (B) beneficial
(C) partial   (D) granted

eager	열렬한, 열심인	be **eager** to get approval 승인받기를 간절히 바라다 **eager** crowds 열렬한 관중들
pleased	기쁜, 흡족한, 만족한	be **pleased** to help 돕게 되어 기쁘다 be **pleased** with the results 그 결과에 흡족하다
profitable	수익성이 있는; 유익한	a highly **profitable** market 매우 수익성 있는 시장 achieve **profitable** results 유익한 결과를 얻다
able 🔄 unable ~을 할 수 없는	~을 할 수 있는, 능력 있는	be **able** to attend 참석할 수 있다 an **able** secretary 능력 있는 비서
previous	이전의	**previous** experience 이전의 경험, 예전 경력 arrive the **previous** day 그 전날 도착하다
vacant	비어 있는	fill **vacant** seats 빈자리를 채우다 fall[become] **vacant** 결원이 되다, 일자리에 공석이 생기다
direct	직접적인; 직행의	have a **direct** effect on the plan 그 계획에 직접적인 영향을 미치다 a **direct** flight to Florida 플로리다행 직항
hospitable	환대하는, 친절한, 호의적인; 쾌적한	**hospitable** to new ideas 새로운 아이디어에 호의적인 a **hospitable** environment 쾌적한 환경

정답 및 해설 p.090

5 The musicians were ------- to perform the piece from memory thanks to their rehearsals.

(A) able (B) talented
(C) applauded (D) hospitable

6 It is no longer ------- for Ricardo's Ristorante to use cheese imported directly from Italy.

(A) delicious (B) profitable
(C) eager (D) gradual

7 The theater staff was disappointed by the number of ------- seats at the last performance.

(A) direct (B) vacant
(C) helpful (D) sequential

8 Our community center was ------- to host another local graduation ceremony this year.

(A) congratulated (B) previous
(C) committed (D) pleased

ACTUAL TEST

1. All kitchen staff are reminded ------- their hands regularly while working.

   (A) can wash
   (B) having washed
   (C) to wash
   (D) washing

2. Marches Meals planned ------- into the American market but decided to wait another year.

   (A) expand
   (B) to expand
   (C) expanding
   (D) expandable

3. Airport security is expected to ------- any items that could be hazardous on a plane.

   (A) will identify
   (B) identifying
   (C) identified
   (D) identify

4. Mr. Barkley, the ------- training manager, prepared resources for his replacement to use.

   (A) worthy
   (B) sociable
   (C) previous
   (D) partial

5. Margot Legal is a reputable law firm ------- to represent business and individuals alike.

   (A) accused
   (B) profitable
   (C) rare
   (D) eager

6. It is mandatory ------- loan applicants to disclose all of their personal financial history.

   (A) for
   (B) from
   (C) unless
   (D) until

7. Ms. O'Connell would like ------- your proposal for the Brooklyn project this afternoon.

   (A) to discuss
   (B) discussing
   (C) having discussed
   (D) discussion

8. In an effort ------- accidents, we have issued a recall on our toasters.

   (A) to avoid
   (B) avoided
   (C) has avoided
   (D) avoiding

어휘 regularly 정기적으로 hazardous 위험한 resource 자료; 재료 replacement 후임자; 대체물 reputable 평판이 좋은 represent 대변하다, 변호하다; 대표하다 mandatory 의무적인 disclose 밝히다, 공개하다 issue 발표하다; 발행하다

Questions 9-12 refer to the following e-mail.

To: All Staff Members <allstaff@qit.com>
From: Melissa Peck <m.peck@qit.com>
Subject: Helping Hands
Date: May 8

Attention Staff Members,

I was recently contacted by the charity organization Helping Hands, and I have some good news to pass on to all of you. It is my pleasure to inform you of an opportunity ------- and help out the local community here in Plattsburgh by working with them. Helping Hands provides services for those who have trouble getting around. ------- .
9.   10.

Specific ------- are assigned only to those who sign up. You will not be paid for your service.
11.
-------, the company will grant a half day off work each week for participants. Please
12.
contact me for more details.

Regards,

Melissa Peck
Director, QIT Human Resources

9   (A) to volunteer
    (B) volunteering
    (C) volunteers
    (D) having volunteered

10 (A) Please renew your driver's license.
    (B) More people are needed to help them run errands.
    (C) The group has drawn national attention.
    (D) Your assistance is greatly appreciated.

11 (A) associations
    (B) tasks
    (C) groceries
    (D) routes

12 (A) Likewise
    (B) Meanwhile
    (C) Moreover
    (D) However

어휘   recently 최근에   contact 연락하다   charity 자선 (단체)   pass on to ~에게 전달하다   inform A of B A에게 B를 알리다
by *doing* ~함으로써   have trouble *doing* ~하는 데 어려움을 겪다   get around 돌아다니다   grant 허락하다, 승인하다
details ((보통 복수형)) 세부 정보

UNIT 10

동명사

1. 동명사 자리
2. 동명사를 목적어로 쓰는 동사
3. 동명사와 to부정사 둘 다 목적어로 쓰는 동사 ①
4. 동명사와 to부정사 둘 다 목적어로 쓰는 동사 ②
5. 동명사 vs. 명사
6. 동명사 관용 표현

빈출 유형 풀이 전략
Vocabulary
Actual Test

TOEIC Grammar

약 5%

UNIT 10 동명사

동명사 문제는 두세 달에 1문제 정도 출제됩니다. 전치사의 목적어 자리에 들어갈 말로 동명사를 고르는 문제가 자주 출제되는 편이며, 동명사와 일반 명사를 구별하는 문제도 간혹 출제됩니다.

 스피드 진단 테스트

(A), (B) 중 알맞은 것을 고르세요.

1. He played an important role in ------- the center.

    (A) to open   (B) opening

2. Experts say that credit card ------- is declining.

    (A) usage   (B) using

정답 및 해석
1. (B), 그는 그 센터를 개관하는 데 중요한 역할을 했다.
2. (A), 전문가들은 신용 카드 사용량이 감소하고 있다고 말한다.

동명사란?

동명사는 동사를 명사처럼 활용하기 위해 동사원형에 -ing를 붙인 것으로, '~하는 것' 또는 '~하기'라고 해석하며 문장에서 명사 역할을 합니다.

● **동명사의 형태**

동명사와 현재분사 모두 철자 끝에 -ing를 붙여 만듭니다. 하지만 동사의 철자에 따라 살짝 변형이 일어납니다.

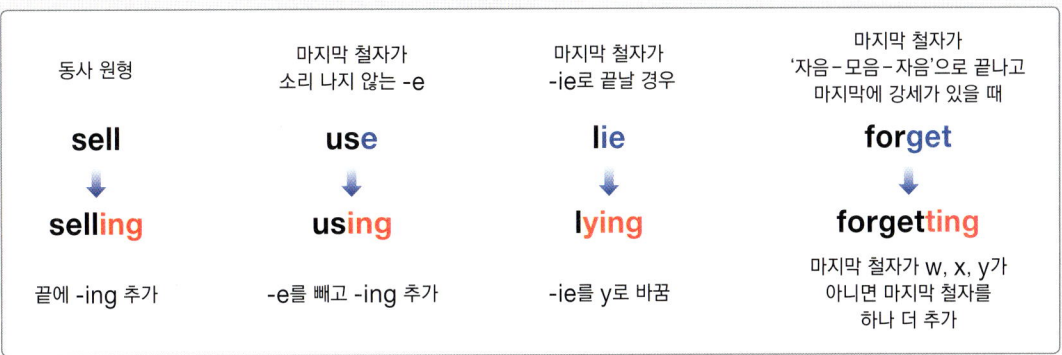

He is very good at using computers. 그는 컴퓨터 사용에 매우 능숙하다.
(use / 동명사)

The reports are lying on my desk. 그 보고서들은 내 책상 위에 놓여 있습니다.
(lie / 현재분사)

Ms. Taylor is interested in running her own business. 테일러 씨는 자신의 사업체를 운영하는 데 관심이 있다.
(run / 동명사)

● **동명사 vs. 현재분사**

동명사와 현재분사는 모두 동사 뒤에 -ing가 붙어서 헷갈릴 수 있지만 그 기능이 각각 다릅니다.

> He is considering selling his car. 그는 자신의 차를 파는 걸 고려하는 중이다.
> (considering → 동사의 현재진행형)
> (selling → 동명사 (consider의 목적어))

위에서 considering은 앞의 be동사(is)와 결합하여 현재진행형을 나타내는 현재분사입니다. 뒤에 명사구인 selling his car를 목적어로 취하고 있으므로 동사 역할을 하며, 명사로서의 기능은 없습니다.

하지만 selling은 뒤에 his car라는 목적어를 취함으로써 동사 sell(팔다)의 본래 기능을 하기도 하지만 동시에 consider의 목적어로 쓰여 명사 역할을 하기도 합니다.

1　동명사 자리

The consultant recommended **exercising regularly**.
　　　　　　　　　　　　　　　　　recommend의 목적어
그 상담사는 **규칙적으로 운동할 것**을 추천했다.

동명사는 문장에서 명사 역할을 하므로 주어, 목적어, 보어 자리에 위치할 수 있습니다.

❶ 주어 자리

Designing the best product requires considerable investment.
　　주어　　　　　　　　　　→ 동명사 주어는 단수 취급하므로 단수 동사를 씁니다.
최고의 제품들을 디자인하는 것은 상당한 투자를 필요로 한다.

❷ 목적어 자리

I really enjoyed staying at this hotel.
　　　　　　　　동사 enjoy의 목적어
이 호텔에 묵은 것은 정말 즐거운 일이었습니다.

This Web site is full of useful tips about storing food.
　　　　　　　　　　　　　　　　　　　전치사 about의 목적어
이 웹사이트는 **음식물을 보관하는 것**에 대한 유용한 정보로 가득하다.

❸ 보어 자리

Our speciality is building eco-friendly furniture.
　　주어　　　　　　　주격 보어
우리의 전문 분야는 **친환경 가구를 만드는 것**입니다.

연습문제　　　　　　　　　　　　　　　　　　　　　　　　　정답 및 해설 p.095

1　Mr. Arnold is in the process of ------- new customer data into the computer system.

　　(A) enter　　　　(B) enters
　　(C) entered　　　(D) entering

2　------- a thorough evaluation is crucial before a product launching.

　　(A) Performed　　(B) Performing
　　(C) Performs　　　(D) Performance

3　Peter Mayfield plays a vital role ------- assisting clients with their personal finances.

　　(A) in　　　　　(B) and
　　(C) though　　　(D) at

4　After ------- your magazine subscription, we will refund next month's pre-payment.

　　(A) canceled　　(B) canceling
　　(C) cancels　　　(D) cancelation

동명사를 목적어로 쓰는 동사

Please consider **accepting** our offer.
　　　　동사　　　　목적어 (동명사)

우리의 제안을 **받아들이는 걸** 고려해 주세요.

동명사를 목적어로 쓰는 대표 동사들을 알아봅시다.

consider *doing*	~하는 것을 고려하다	suggest *doing*	~하는 것을 제안하다
include *doing*	~하는 것을 포함하다	recommend *doing*	~하는 것을 추천하다
admit *doing*	~한 것을 인정하다	deny *doing*	~한 것을 부정하다
avoid *doing*	~하는 것을 피하다	give up *doing*	~하는 것을 포기하다
stop *doing*	~하는 것을 멈추다	postpone *doing*	~하는 것을 보류하다
discontinue *doing*	~하는 것을 중단하다	delay *doing*	~하는 것을 늦추다

You can avoid waiting in line by making an appointment online.
온라인으로 예약함으로써 줄 서서 **기다리는 것을 피할 수** 있습니다.

They postponed building a new factory because of high interest rates.
그들은 높은 금리 때문에 새 공장을 **짓는 걸 연기했다**.

My car's air conditioner stopped working.
내 차의 에어컨이 **작동을 멈췄다**.

연습문제

1. Mr. Deacon is ------- approving Ms. Elton's request to visit Dallas on business.
   (A) planning　　(B) asking
   (C) considering　(D) making

2. Amazon Airways wants passengers to postpone ------- online until it upgrades its Web site.
   (A) check in　　(B) checked in
   (C) checking in　(D) to check in

3. Improvements to the employee lounge include ------- more comfortable chairs to the room.
   (A) to add　　(B) addition
   (C) being added　(D) adding

4. Construction crews have closed parts of Mountainview Avenue, so officials ------- taking an alternative route downtown.
   (A) suggest　　(B) pledge
   (C) think　　　(D) admit

3 동명사와 to부정사 둘 다 목적어로 쓰는 동사 ①

It began { to rain / raining } heavily.

비가 세차게 내리기 시작했다.

몇몇 동사는 동명사와 to부정사를 모두 목적어로 쓸 수 있으며 의미에 변화가 없습니다.

| like 좋아하다 | begin 시작하다 | attempt 시도하다 | continue 계속하다 |
| prefer 선호하다 | start 시작하다 | propose 제안하다 | intend 의도하다 |

We will continue making / to make improvements to the security system.
우리는 그 보안 시스템을 계속해서 개선해 나갈 것이다.

He preferred resolving / to resolve the problem.
그는 그 문제를 해결하길 원했다.

They proposed changing / to change the event date.
그들은 행사 날짜를 바꿀 것을 제안했다.

연습문제

정답 및 해설 p.097

1. Ms. Sullivan continues to ------- her team by giving them difficult tasks.

    (A) challenging (B) challenge
    (C) challenged   (D) challenges

2. Farnsworth, Inc. expects to begin ------- its new sneakers line on June 11.

    (A) production (B) produce
    (C) producing   (D) produces

3. Marbury Books recommends ------- an advance copy of Dave Hiller's newest fantasy novel.

    (A) order   (B) orders
    (C) to order (D) ordering

4. Top saleswoman Clara Thomas prefers ------- the vacuum cleaner in person on January 15.

    (A) to demonstrate
    (B) demonstrated
    (C) demonstration
    (D) being demonstrated

4 동명사와 to부정사 둘 다 목적어로 쓰는 동사 ②

I tried using the car-sharing service. 나는 자동차 공유 서비스를 **이용해 봤다.**
try *doing* (시험 삼아) ~해 보다

We tried to meet the deadline. 우리는 마감일을 **맞추기 위해 노력했다.**
try *to do* ~하기 위해 노력하다

어떤 동사는 동명사가 목적어일 때와 to부정사가 목적어일 때 문장의 의미가 달라집니다. 동명사가 목적어일 때는 주로 과거의 일을, to부정사가 목적어일 때는 미래의 일을 나타냅니다.

remember *doing*	~했던 것을 기억하다	forget *doing*	~했던 것을 잊다
remember *to do*	~할 것을 기억하다	forget *to do*	~할 것을 잊다
regret *doing*	~했던 것을 후회하다	try *doing*	(시험 삼아) ~해 보다, 시도하다
regret *to do*	~하게 되어 유감이다	try *to do*	~하기 위해 노력하다

Remember to switch off the lights when leaving the office.
사무실을 나서기 전에 **잊지 말고** 불을 **끄세요.**

We regret to inform you that the parking lot is closed.
그 주차장이 폐쇄되었다는 것을 **알리게 되어 유감입니다.**

switch off

연습문제   정답 및 해설 p.098

1 Workers must not forget ------- their belongings before the moving of the office.

(A) packing   (B) package
(C) to pack   (D) packed

2 Several individuals tried ------- rooms at the Moonlight Hotel, but there were no vacancies.

(A) book   (B) booking
(C) booked   (D) have booked

3 Please don't forget ------- all open windows before leaving your hotel room.

(A) to close   (B) close
(C) closing   (D) closed

4 We regret ------- that Mr. Sanders will no longer work at Ziti Pharmaceutical as of May 1.

(A) announced   (B) to announce
(C) announcement   (D) announces

5 동명사 vs. 명사

Improving service quality is the key to success.
Improvement (×)   improving의 목적어
서비스 질을 **향상시키는 것이** 성공의 핵심이다.

동명사는 문장에서 명사 역할을 하지만 동사의 성질이 남아 있기 때문에 특정 쓰임에서는 명사와 차이가 있습니다.

❶ 동명사는 목적어를 취할 수 있지만 명사는 목적어를 취할 수 없다.

            → managing의 목적어
Managing employees is more difficult than you may think.
Management (×)
직원들을 **관리하는 것은** 생각보다 어렵다.

❷ 명사 앞에는 부정관사가 위치할 수 있지만 동명사는 쓸 수 없다.

We had a **discussion** about the enrollment issues.
          discussing (×)
우리는 등록 문제들에 관해 **논의를** 했다.

❸ 동명사는 부사의 수식을 받고 명사는 형용사의 수식을 받는다.

They suggested **investing** heavily in new product development.

그들은 신제품 개발에 **막대하게 투자하는 걸** 제안했다.

They made a heavy **investment** in new product development.

그들은 신제품 개발에 **막대한 투자를** 했다.

연습문제 정답 및 해설 p.099

1 ------- the city job fair is one of Ms. Hasting's major accomplishments this year.

(A) Organization (B) Organizing
(C) Organized   (D) Being organized

2 In a ------- written in February, Davidson Holdings stated they will stop investing in real estate.

(A) reporter (B) report
(C) reporting (D) reported

3 ------- of homes in Oakdale are required to register any significant home renovation projects.

(A) Owning (B) Owned
(C) Owners (D) Ownership

4 Mr. Green's method of ------- workers has resulted in higher productivity.

(A) train (B) training
(C) trainer (D) trains

동명사 관용 표현

The idea is worth considering.
to consider (×)

그 아이디어는 고려할 가치가 있다.

동명사 관용 표현은 한 덩어리로 외워 두세요.

❶ 동명사 관용 표현

be busy *doing*	~하느라 바쁘다	cannot help *doing*	~하지 않을 수 없다
be worth *doing*	~할 가치가 있다	feel like *doing*	~하고 싶다
be capable of *doing*	~할 능력이 있다	spend 돈/시간 *doing*	~하는 데 돈/시간을 쓰다
have difficulty (in) *doing*	~하는 데 어려움이 있다	(up)on *doing*	~하자마자

We **had difficulty in finding** a replacement for the secretary.
우리는 그 비서의 후임을 찾는 데 어려움이 있었다.

❷ '전치사 to + (동)명사' 표현

전치사 to 다음에 동명사가 오는 표현입니다. 이때 to를 보고 to부정사로 혼동하지 않도록 해야 합니다.

be used to *doing*	~하는 데 익숙하다	contribute to *doing*	~하는 데 기여하다
be committed to *doing*	~하는 데 전념하다	object to *doing*	~하는 데 반대하다
look forward to *doing*	~하는 것을 고대하다	in addition to *doing*	~에 더하여, ~ 외에도

I **look forward to hearing** from you.
연락 기다리겠습니다.

연습문제

정답 및 해설 p.100

1 In addition to ------- the retirement party, Janet May purchased a gift for Todd Arnold.

(A) arranged (B) arranging
(C) arrange (D) arranges

2 Jeff Cartwright stated that he is committed to ------- half of his fortune to charity.

(A) donating (B) donation
(C) donations (D) donates

3 Everyone at Rutherford Tech is looking forward to ------- Dr. Powell's talk on computer chips.

(A) having attended (B) attendance
(C) attended (D) attending

4 ------- receiving the package, Ms. Lowell restocked the items that were sold out previously.

(A) Upon (B) With
(C) Into (D) As for

빈출 유형 풀이 전략

1. 동명사 자리

STEP에 따라 실제 토익 문제를 푸는 순서와 요령을 익혀 보세요.

The vice president is responsible for
------- solutions to marketing problems.

(A) provide
(B) to provide
(C) providing
(D) provides

STEP 1 선택지 구성 파악하기

선택지가 provide의 활용형으로 구성되어 있으므로 빈칸에 알맞은 provide의 형태를 묻는 문제.

The vice president is responsible for
------- solutions to marketing problems.

(A) provide
(B) to provide
(C) providing
(D) provides

STEP 2 빈칸 주변에서 단서 찾기

빈칸 앞에 전치사 for가 있고 뒤에는 명사 solutions가 있음.
따라서 빈칸에는 전치사의 목적어 역할을 하는 동시에 명사를 목적어로 취할 수 있는 형태가 들어가야 함.

The vice president is responsible for
------- solutions to marketing problems.

(A) provide
(B) to provide
(C) ✓ providing
(D) provides

STEP 3 정답 찾기

동명사인 (C) providing이 정답.
to부정사인 (B) to provide는 전치사를 앞에 둘 수 없기 때문에 오답.

해석 부사장은 마케팅 문제들에 대한 해결책을 제공할 책임이 있다.

어휘 vice president 부사장   be responsible for ~에 책임이 있다   provide 제공하다, 공급하다   solution 해결책, 해법

2. 동명사 vs. 명사

STEP에 따라 실제 토익 문제를 푸는 순서와 요령을 익혀 보세요.

Mr. Harper reviews everything in the museum, including ------- of the items on display.

(A) describes
(B) descriptions
(C) described
(D) describing

STEP 1 선택지 구성 파악하기

선택지가 describe의 활용형으로 구성되어 있으므로 빈칸에 알맞은 describe의 형태를 묻는 문제.

Mr. Harper reviews everything in the museum, including ------- of the items on display.

(A) describes
(B) descriptions
(C) described
(D) describing

STEP 2 빈칸 주변에서 단서 찾기

빈칸 앞에 전치사 including이 있으므로 빈칸은 전치사의 목적어 역할을 할 수 있는 명사 자리.

Mr. Harper reviews everything in the museum, including ------- of the items on display.

(A) describes
(B) descriptions ✓
(C) described
(D) describing

STEP 3 정답 찾기

빈칸 뒤 전치사구(of the items on display)의 수식을 받을 수 있는 것은 명사인 (B) descriptions. 동명사인 (D) describing은 뒤에 목적어, 즉 명사가 이어져야 하므로 오답.

해석 하퍼 씨는 전시된 물품들의 설명서를 포함해 박물관의 모든 것을 검토한다.

어휘 review 검토하다   including ~을 포함하여   description 설명(서), 해설   item 물품, 품목   on display 전시된, 전시 중인   describe 묘사하다, 설명하다

VOCABULARY 빈출 명사/동사 어휘

function	기능; 기능하다, 작동하다	perform a **function** 기능을 수행하다 continue to **function** normally 계속 정상적으로 작동하다
finance	재정, 금융; 자금을 공급하다	**finance** office 회계팀, 재무팀 **finance** the building project 건설 사업에 자금을 공급하다
position	위치, 자리; (특정한 위치에) 두다, 놓다	resign from her **position** 그녀의 자리에서 물러나다 be perfectly **positioned** 완벽한 위치에 놓이다
file	파일, 서류철; (문서 등을 철하여) 보관하다	transfer **files** 파일을 전송하다 **file** the contracts alphabetically 그 계약서들을 알파벳순으로 보관하다
extract	발췌(문); 추출; 추출하다; 뽑다	publish a short **extract** 짧은 발췌문을 게재하다 **extract** financial data 금융 데이터를 추출하다
question	질문, 문제; 질문하다, 이의를 제기하다	ask tough **questions** 어려운 질문을 하다 **question** customers about the new product 고객들에게 새 제품에 대해 물어보다
address	주소; 연설; 연설하다; (문제 등을) 다루다	deliver the keynote **address** 기조연설을 하다 **address** security concerns 보안 문제를 해결하다
reserve	비축(물); 예약하다; (권한 등을) 보유하다	**reserve** funds 예비 자금 **reserve** a table for two 두 자리를 예약하다

연습문제

1 All reports must be ------- by the engineer who wrote them.
(A) filed   (B) repeated
(C) positioned   (D) appeared

2 Mr. Grimes gave the keynote ------- at the IT and security conference last Thursday.
(A) receiver   (B) reserve
(C) arrangement   (D) address

3 The company's ------- are suffering due to a lack of funding.
(A) souvenirs   (B) appeals
(C) finances   (D) questions

4 Ms. Lewis could ------- the necessary information from the data on customer preferences.
(A) extract   (B) deserve
(C) function   (D) reverse

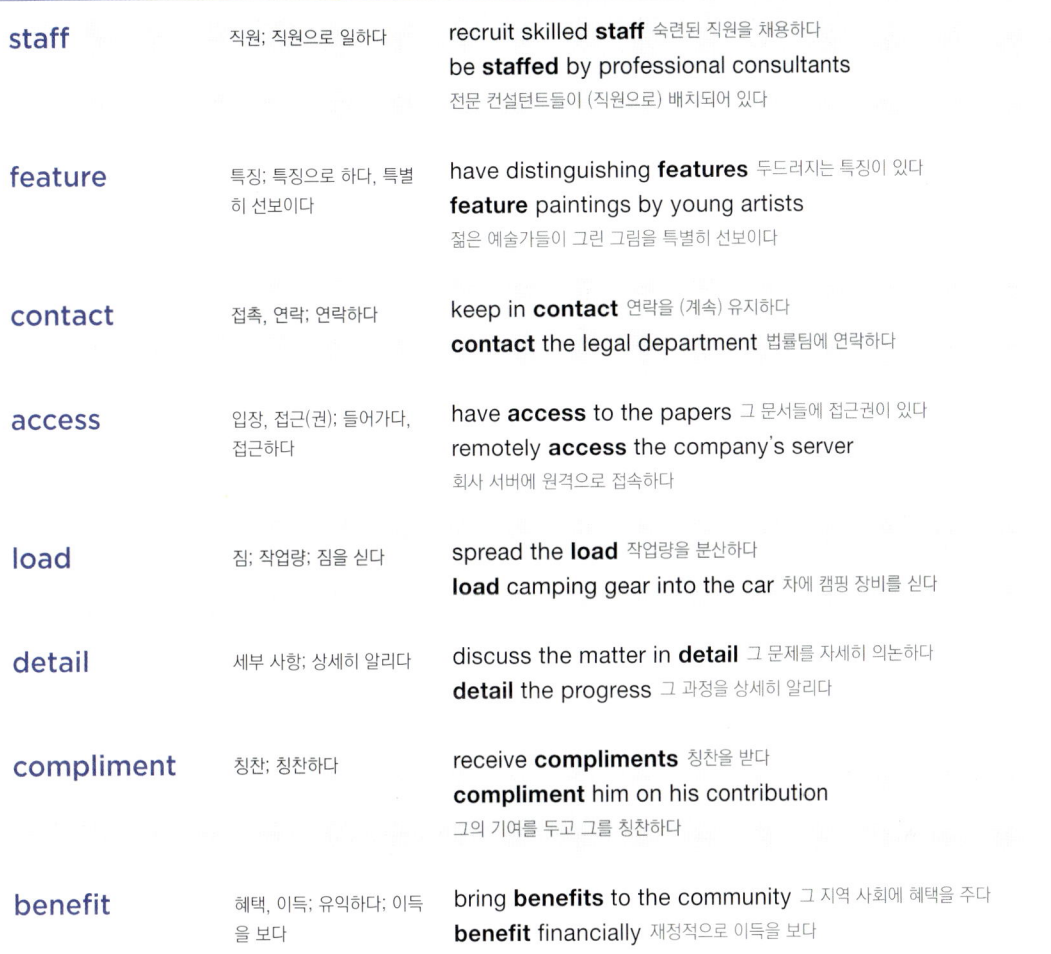

5 Solid Mech needs some workers to ------- its booth at the job fair.

(A) produce (B) staff
(C) load (D) combine

6 Mr. Ito required thirty minutes to ------- the planned renovations to the building manager.

(A) result (B) contact
(C) appear (D) detail

7 The employee ------- at Boone Furniture will be improved for full-time workers.

(A) respect (B) benefits
(C) features (D) styles

8 Ms. Worthy will receive temporary ------- to the company warehouse in Medford.

(A) permit (B) compliment
(C) access (D) favor

ACTUAL TEST

1 Several stores reported a large ------- in the number of customers on Mondays.

(A) increases
(B) increase
(C) increasingly
(D) increasing

2 Golden Light stops ------- survey calls to customers at 4:00 P.M. every day.

(A) making
(B) made
(C) makes
(D) to make

3 Cindy Holmes paid for her schooling by ------- part-time every evening.

(A) works
(B) working
(C) worked
(D) work

4 Customers are urged to ------- the customer service team with their complaints or suggestions.

(A) avoid
(B) announce
(C) contact
(D) reserve

5 Ms. Vela will consider ------- the plans to open a branch office in Tokyo.

(A) approve
(B) approving
(C) to approve
(D) has approved

6 All homes in Delmont Park ------- two floors and a spacious backyard.

(A) feature
(B) compliment
(C) involve
(D) construct

7 The mayor ------- to initiate a volunteer program for youths in the city.

(A) objects
(B) describes
(C) plans
(D) stops

8 ------- working at Marlin Fisheries, Eric Lewis was employed by Stoddard, Inc.

(A) If
(B) Prior to
(C) Even though
(D) For

어휘 report 보고하다   number 수, 인원수   make a call 전화하다   pay for ~을 지급하다, ~을 내다   schooling 학비, 수업료
urge 촉구하다, 거듭 권유하다   complaint 불만, 불평   suggestion 제안   branch office 지점, 지사   floor (건물의) 층
spacious 넓은   backyard 뒤뜰, 뒷마당   initiate 착수시키다, 시작하다   volunteer 자원봉사   youth 젊은이, 청소년

Questions 9-12 refer to the following memo.

To: All Employees, Hastings, Inc.

From: Chelsea Fitzgerald

Subject: Parking Lot

Date: April 28

You should all be happy to know that work on the employee parking lot is nearly finished. The lot will be ------- no later than this Friday.
            9.

The parking lot will have a capacity of 200 standard-sized vehicles. ------- . So there should
                                                                       10.
be more than enough space for every employee.

New parking passes will be required to park there. To acquire one, download an application from our Web site. ------- , submit the completed form to Jeb Walker in room 201. Mr. Walker
                         11.
is in charge of ------- parking passes and is also available to answer questions about the lot.
                12.

9 (A) approachable
   (B) viable
   (C) accessible
   (D) portable

11 (A) Therefore
   (B) Nevertheless
   (C) If so
   (D) Then

10 (A) This is 50 more spots than the old lot featured.
   (B) The work has taken two months to complete.
   (C) There are signs showing the lot's location.
   (D) Richard Barrow is responsible for the project.

12 (A) distributes
   (B) distributed
   (C) distribution
   (D) distributing

어휘 parking lot 주차장   no later than 늦어도 ~까지는   capacity 수용 능력, 용량   standard-sized 보통 크기의   vehicle 차량   require 요구하다, 필요로 하다   acquire 얻다, 취득하다   download 내려받다   application 신청서, 지원서   in charge of ~을 담당하고 있는

UNIT
11

분사

1. 분사 자리
2. 현재분사와 과거분사
3. 감정을 나타내는 분사
4. 분사구문

빈출 유형 풀이 전략
Vocabulary
Actual Test

TOEIC Grammar

약 10%

UNIT 11 분사

분사 문제는 매회 1문제 이상 출제됩니다. 분사가 들어갈 자리임을 파악하고 현재분사나 과거분사 선택지를 고르거나, 빈칸에 들어갈 말이 현재분사인지 과거분사인지 구별하는 문제가 자주 출제됩니다.

스피드 진단 테스트

(A), (B) 중 알맞은 것을 고르세요.

1. The CEO kept the reporters ------- for more than an hour.

   (A) wait   (B) waiting

2. They were looking for the ------- file last night.

   (A) losing   (B) lost

정답 및 해석

1. (B), 그 대표 이사는 기자들을 한 시간 이상이나 기다리게 했다.
2. (B), 그들은 어젯밤에 분실된 파일을 찾고 있었다.

분사란?

분사는 일종의 동작 형용사라고 할 수 있는데, 동사를 특정 형태로 바꾸어 문장에서 형용사 역할을 할 수 있도록 만든 것을 말합니다. 분사에는 현재분사와 과거분사가 있습니다.

● 분사의 형태

현재분사는 '동사원형 + -ing' 형태로 능동과 진행의 의미를 나타냅니다. 과거분사는 '동사원형 + -ed' 형태로 수동 또는 완료의 의미를 나타냅니다. 단, 과거분사의 경우 형태 변화가 불규칙한 동사에 유의하세요.

● 분사가 명사를 뒤에서 수식

분사는 위에서처럼 명사 앞에 오기도 하지만 명사의 뒤에서 명사를 꾸며 주는 역할을 하기도 합니다.

A trailer <u>carrying</u> cars overturned. 차량을 싣고 가던 트레일러가 전복되었다.

Several people <u>injured</u> in the accident were taken to the hospital. 그 사고로 다친 몇몇 사람들이 병원으로 옮겨졌다.

● 분사의 동사적 성질

to부정사, 동명사와 마찬가지로 분사 역시 문장에서 동사의 기능을 하지 않지만 동사적 성질을 그대로 가지고 있습니다. 그렇기 때문에 분사 뒤에 목적어나 보어를 쓸 수 있고, 수식어구의 꾸밈을 받을 수도 있습니다.

They built a highway <u>connecting</u> the two cities. 그들은 그 두 도시를 **연결하는** 고속 도로를 건설했다.
　　　　　　　　　　　현재분사　　목적어

They deleted the photos <u>stored</u> on the server. 그들은 서버에 **저장된** 사진들을 삭제했다.
　　　　　　　　　　　　과거분사　수식어구

1 분사 자리

the **attached** form	the form **attached** below
첨부된 양식	아래 첨부된 양식

분사는 문장에서 형용사 역할을 하기 때문에 명사 앞이나 뒤에서 명사를 꾸며 주거나 보어 자리에 위치할 수 있습니다.

❶ 명사 앞뒤

The city has several **fascinating** world cultural heritage sites.
　　　　　　　　　　　현재분사　　　　　명사구
그 도시에는 멋진 세계 문화유산들이 몇 가지 있다.

분사에 목적어나 보어, 전치사(구), 부사(구) 등이 붙어 길이가 길어지면 명사 뒤에 위치합니다.

The manager sent an e-mail **explaining the sign-up process**.
　　　　　　　　명사　　　　　현재분사구
매니저는 그 등록 과정을 설명하는 이메일을 보냈다.

We have a meeting **scheduled for Monday, May 3, at 9:30 A.M.**
　　　　　명사　　　　　과거분사구
우리는 5월 3일, 월요일, 오전 9시 30분에 회의가 잡혀 있다.

❷ 보어

The contract will be **finalized** on 25 May.
　주어　　　　　　주격 보어
그 계약은 5월 25일에 마무리될 것이다.

Mr. Jones wants the job **done** by tomorrow.
　　　　　　목적어　목적격 보어
존스 씨는 내일까지 그 일을 끝내기를 원합니다.

연습문제

정답 및 해설 p.106

1 Renovations are scheduled for the customs checkpoint ------- San Diego and Tijuana.

　(A) divide　　(B) divides
　(C) dividing　(D) division

2 The shipping company we use hasn't kept us ------- of their new shipping schedule.

　(A) to inform　(B) informed
　(C) informs　　(D) informative

3 To become a member of Fit Gym, please complete the ------- form.

　(A) attached　　(B) attach
　(C) attachment　(D) attachable

4 The labor union accepted the new benefits package ------- by the company.

　(A) had offered　(B) is offering
　(C) to offer　　 (D) offered

현재분사와 과거분사

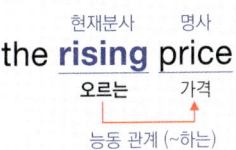   

현재분사 + 명사
the **rising** price
오르는 / 가격
능동 관계 (~하는)

과거분사 + 명사
damaged goods
파손된 / 상품들
수동 관계 (~된)

① 현재분사

현재분사는 '동사원형 + -ing' 형태이며, 분사와 수식받는 명사가 능동 관계일 때 씁니다.

The number of <u>participating</u> <u>businesses</u> has increased significantly since last year.
　　　　　　　　현재분사　　　명사
지난해 이래로 **참가하는** 업체들의 수가 상당히 늘었다.

② 과거분사

과거분사는 '동사원형 + -ed' 형태이며, 대개는 수동의 의미를 지니지만 그렇지 않은 경우도 있습니다.

a <u>revised</u> schedule 수정된 일정　　　　an <u>accomplished</u> musician 성공한 음악가
　　수동　　　　　　　　　　　　　　　　　　　수동 아님

🔺 고난도 JUMP UP

> 분사가 명사를 뒤에서 수식할 때, 현재분사는 뒤에 목적어를 둘 수 있으나 과거분사는 목적어를 둘 수 없습니다.
>
> Please send me <u>the report</u> <u>including</u> <u>the sales figures</u> by noon.
> 　　　　　　　　　명사　　　현재분사　　현재분사의 목적어
> 12시까지는 매출액을 포함한 보고서를 제게 보내 주세요.
>
> Please wear <u>the ID badge</u> <u>included</u> <u>in the information packet</u>.
> 　　　　　　　　명사　　　과거분사　　　　전치사구
> 자료집에 포함된 신분증을 착용해 주세요.

연습문제

정답 및 해설 p.107

1 Guard Corp., an agency ------- private security services to celebrities, is hiring qualified candidates.

　(A) providing　　(B) provision
　(C) provides　　(D) provided

2 The ------- changes are specified in the checklist that Ms. O'Hare filled out.

　(A) recommending　(B) recommendation
　(C) recommended　(D) recommends

3 Thanks to ------- repairs, the shuttle was able to return to operation quickly.

　(A) rush　　　　(B) rushed
　(C) rushing　　(D) had rushed

4 ------- staff members are asked to use street parking until further notice.

　(A) To commute　(B) Commuting
　(C) Commuted　　(D) Commute

감정을 나타내는 분사

The company's Web site is **confusing**.
현재분사

그 회사의 웹사이트는 **어수선하다**.

People are **confused** by the company's Web site.
과거분사

사람들은 그 회사의 웹사이트를 **혼란스러워**한다.

감정을 나타내는 분사는 수식하는 명사가 감정을 느끼게 하는 주체면 현재분사로 쓰고, 감정을 느끼는 대상이면 과거분사로 씁니다. 이러한 분사 형태의 단어들은 문장에서 하나의 형용사로 쓰입니다.

exciting 신나는	excited 신난	surprising 놀라운	surprised 놀란
delighting 기쁨을 주는	delighted 기뻐하는	pleasing 즐거운, 만족을 주는	pleased 기뻐하는
thrilling 아주 신나는	thrilled 아주 신난	disappointing 실망스러운	disappointed 실망한
satisfying 만족스러운	satisfied 만족스러워하는	interesting 흥미로운	interested 흥미 있는

The restaurant provides a <u>satisfying</u> meal.
　　　　　　　　　　　　감정을 느끼게 하는 주체

그 식당은 **만족스러운** 식사를 제공한다.

We were <u>satisfied</u> with the meal at the restaurant.
　　　　감정을 느끼는 대상

우리는 그 식당의 식사에 **만족했습니다**.

연습문제

정답 및 해설 p.108

1 Stephanie McQueen is the author of dozens of ------- books on the best-sellers list.

(A) thrill　　　　　(B) thrilled
(C) thrills　　　　(D) thrilling

2 Beacon Athletics ------- to open its first international retail location in Toronto.

(A) is pleasing　　(B) is pleased
(C) will please　　(D) pleases

3 Despite positive reviews from critics, actor Billy Brandt's latest film's box office numbers were -------.

(A) disappoints　　(B) disappointed
(C) disappointing　(D) disappointment

4 Our software firm would be ------- to have you work in our training division.

(A) delighting　　(B) delighted
(C) to delight　　(D) delights

4 분사구문

Not wanting to be late, they decided to take a taxi.
= **Because they didn't want** to be late, they decided to take a taxi.

늦고 싶지 않았기에 그들은 택시를 타기로 했다.

이유, 동시 상황, 연속된 일을 나타내는 종속절은 분사구문으로 바꿀 수 있습니다.

❶ 이유를 나타낼 때

Written in an easy-to-read style, the book is widely read by beginners.
= Because the book is written in an easy-to-read style
읽기 쉬운 스타일로 쓰여서 그 책은 입문자들에게 널리 읽힌다.

❷ 동시/연속 상황을 나타낼 때

Arriving in Chicago, I called Mr. Smith. 시카고에 도착한 다음 나는 스미스 씨에게 연락했다.
= After I arrived in Chicago

A truck overturned near Boston, **causing** long delays. 보스턴 근처에서 트럭 한 대가 전복되어 긴 정체를 **야기했다**.
= and caused

❸ 접속사가 있는 분사구문

부사절을 분사구문으로 만들 때, 접속사가 없어도 문맥을 통해 의미를 알 수 있기 때문에 부사절 접속사는 대개 생략합니다. 하지만 접속사가 없어서 문맥이 헷갈릴 수 있을 때에는 접속사를 남겨 둡니다.

Before giving a speech, Mr. Calvert distributed a handout.
연설을 시작하기 전에 캘버트 씨는 유인물을 나눠 줬다.

연습문제 정답 및 해설 p.109

1 Our startup business' stock value was up again, ------- another company record.

(A) marking (B) marked
(C) is marking (D) had marked

2 When recently -------, Atilla Auto's latest engine proved to be highly energy-efficient.

(A) test (B) tester
(C) tested (D) testing

3 The fundraising event raised $11,000, ------- its initial goal by 10 percent.

(A) exceeding (B) exceedingly
(C) is exceeding (D) exceeded

4 ------- his company's reputation, Brian Mars promised compensation to customers for the product recall.

(A) Defense (B) Defender
(C) Defended (D) Defending

빈출 유형 풀이 전략

1. 분사 자리

STEP에 따라 실제 토익 문제를 푸는 순서와 요령을 익혀 보세요.

A mixture ------- of various herbs is celebrity chef Tanya Li's top-selling item online.

(A) consistent
(B) consisting
(C) consistently
(D) consist

STEP 1 선택지 구성 파악하기
선택지가 consist의 활용형으로 구성되어 있으므로 빈칸에 알맞은 consist의 형태를 묻는 문제.

A mixture ------- of various herbs is celebrity chef Tanya Li's top-selling item online.

(A) consistent
(B) consisting
(C) consistently
(D) consist

STEP 2 빈칸 주변에서 단서 찾기
빈칸 뒤의 전치사구(of various herbs)와 함께 주어 (A mixture)를 수식해야 하므로 빈칸은 형용사 자리.

A mixture ------- of various herbs is celebrity chef Tanya Li's top-selling item online.

(A) consistent
(B) consisting ✓
(C) consistently
(D) consist

STEP 3 정답 찾기
선택지 중 형용사 역할을 할 수 있는 현재분사인 (B) consisting이 정답.

해석 다양한 약초로 구성된 혼합물은 유명 요리사 타냐 리의 온라인 몰에서 가장 잘 팔리는 제품이다.

어휘 mixture 혼합물, 혼합 재료 consist of ~로 구성되다 various 다양한 herb 약초 top-selling 가장 잘 팔리는 consistent 한결같은, 일관된 consistently 한결같이, 일관되게

2. 현재분사 vs. 과거분사

STEP에 따라 실제 토익 문제를 푸는 순서와 요령을 익혀 보세요.

This ------- plan would help the participants in each department do their part successfully.

(A) outline
(B) outlined
(C) outliner
(D) outlining

STEP 1 선택지 구성 파악하기

선택지가 outline의 활용형으로 구성되어 있으므로 빈칸에 알맞은 outline의 형태를 묻는 문제.

This ------- plan would help the participants in each department do their part successfully.

(A) outline
(B) outlined
(C) outliner
(D) outlining

STEP 2 빈칸 주변에서 단서 찾기

〈지시형용사(This) + ------- + 명사(plan) + 동사(would help)〉 구조이므로 빈칸은 명사 plan을 꾸며 주는 형용사 자리.
선택지 중 형용사 역할을 할 수 있는 것은 과거분사 (B) outlined와 현재분사 (D) outlining.

This ------- plan would help the participants in each department do their part successfully.

(A) outline
(B) outlined
(C) outliner
(D) outlining

STEP 3 정답 찾기

계획(plan)은 '개요가 잡히는' 대상이므로 빈칸과 수동 관계임. 따라서 과거분사인 (B) outlined가 정답.

해석 개요가 잡힌 이 계획은 각 부서의 참가자들이 그들의 역할을 성공적으로 해내도록 도울 것이다.

어휘 outline 개요를 잡다, 윤곽을 그리다   participant 참가자   department 부서   part 역할   successfully 성공적으로

UNIT 11 분사 187

VOCABULARY 빈출 형용사 어휘 (3)

surrounding	인근의, 주위의	the **surrounding** areas 주변 지역 the controversy **surrounding** the decision 그 결정을 둘러싼 논란
rising	증가하는, 상승하는	concerns about **rising** oil prices 증가하는 유가에 대한 염려 **rising** energy consumption 증가하는 에너지 소비
challenging	(어렵지만) 도전적인, 도전의식을 불러일으키는	**challenging** problems 도전적인 문제들 the most **challenging** aspect of the job 그 일에서 가장 어려운 측면
existing	기존의	**existing** equipment 기존 장비 improve **existing** products 기존 제품들을 향상시키다
lasting ⓢ long-lasting	지속적인, 오래 가는	leave a **lasting** impression 지속적인[깊은] 인상을 남기다 be of no **lasting** value 지속적인 가치가 없다
missing	없어진, 분실한; 빠진, 누락된	look for the **missing** file 분실한 파일을 찾다 **missing** from the list 목록에서 빠진
leading	선두의, 주요한, 가장 중요한	the area's **leading** manufacturer 그 분야의 주요 제조사 play a **leading** part in the project 그 프로젝트에서 가장 중요한 역할을 하다
rewarding	가치 있는, 보람 있는; 많은 수익이 나는	a **rewarding** experience 가치 있는 경험 find the job **rewarding** 그 일이 가치 있다는 걸 알게 되다

연습문제

1 Increased temperatures in the Golden Coast will have ------- harmful effects on the environment.

(A) descending (B) existing
(C) lasting (D) parting

2 The ------- demand for organic fruits and vegetables is changing the agricultural industry.

(A) profiting (B) rising
(C) converting (D) surrounding

3 The marketing firm's application procedure is -------, so applicants are encouraged to submit impressive résumés.

(A) missing (B) including
(C) challenging (D) reacting

4 Tech Brite is a ------- firm in renewable energy technology.

(A) rewarding (B) graduating
(C) saving (D) leading

repeated	반복된	**repeated** changes in plans 반복된 계획 변경 make **repeated** efforts 거듭 노력하다
accomplished ❸ skilled, skillful	(기량이) 뛰어난	an **accomplished** actor 기량이 뛰어난 배우 a highly **accomplished** and consistent performer 매우 기량이 뛰어나고 기복이 없는 연주자
complicated ❸ complex	복잡한	**complicated** problems 복잡한 문제들 go through **complicated** procedures 복잡한 절차를 밟다
customized	주문 제작된	a **customized** design 주문 제작된 디자인 provide **customized** fitness programs 맞춤형 운동 프로그램을 제공하다
advanced	진보된; 고급[상급]의	**advanced** technology 진보된 기술 require **advanced** degrees 고학력을 요구하다
dedicated	헌신적인, 전념하는; 특정 목적으로 만들어진[사용되 는], ~ 전용의	be **dedicated** to the research 그 연구에 전념하다 **dedicated** bus lanes 버스 전용 차선
extended	연장된	work **extended** hours 초과 근무를 하다 purchase an **extended** warranty 품질 보증 연장 서비스를 구입하다
experienced	숙련된, 경험이 풍부한	**experienced** staff 숙련된 직원들 **experienced** in dealing with demanding customers 까다로운 고객들을 다루는 데 노련한

정답 및 해설 p.110

5 Due to ------- noise complaints, pets will no longer be allowed in the apartment building.

(A) repeated (B) conducted
(C) dedicated (D) respected

6 Only highly ------- leaders get promoted to upper management at most companies.

(A) customized (B) compensated
(C) introduced (D) experienced

7 The ------- product designer was awarded with the industry's top honors.

(A) assisted (B) extended
(C) accomplished (D) refunded

8 McCain Pharmaceuticals' main lab only employs scientists with ------- degrees in their fields.

(A) accrued (B) advanced
(C) complicated (D) educated

UNIT 11 분사 189

ACTUAL TEST

1. To learn more about insurance plans from Prime State, speak with one of our ------- representatives.

   (A) certify
   (B) certified
   (C) certifying
   (D) certification

2. Anyone ------- in joining the charity run should register online by this Friday.

   (A) to interest
   (B) interesting
   (C) interests
   (D) interested

3. The receptionist apologized for the delay, ------- that there had been a problem with their online system.

   (A) explained
   (B) will explain
   (C) explaining
   (D) explains

4. All guests planning an ------- vacation at our hotel will be gifted free room upgrades and dining coupons.

   (A) accomplished
   (B) objective
   (C) equal
   (D) extended

5. Whitehall Library is asking for ------- speakers to volunteer as guest lecturers.

   (A) regarded
   (B) imposed
   (C) experienced
   (D) customized

6. Dentists recommend extra ------- process which includes using floss or mouthwash after brushing teeth.

   (A) cleanses
   (B) cleansing
   (C) cleansed
   (D) to cleanse

7. Refer to the ------- packet for information on your first day's orientation session.

   (A) enclosing
   (B) enclosed
   (C) enclosure
   (D) enclose

8. At the product launch, Mr. Hilton gave an ------- presentation that everyone enjoyed.

   (A) excitingly
   (B) excitement
   (C) excited
   (D) exciting

어휘 insurance 보험 join 합류하다; 가입하다 charity 자선 (단체) register 등록하다 delay 지연 gift (선물 따위를) 주다 ask for ~을 찾다, ~을 요청하다 volunteer 자원봉사를 하다 lecturer 강연자 floss 치실 mouthwash 구강 청결제 refer to ~을 참조하다 launch 출시

Questions 9-12 refer to the following e-mail.

To: r.ford@smithtowndental.com
From: i.kelsey@digione.com
Date: 12 June
Subject: Re: Database Services

Dear Mr. Ford,

I am glad you contacted me about setting up a secure database for your dental clinic. Digi One offers a wide array of services, ---9.--- your business' digital operations. After reviewing the attached service plan options, please ---10.--- the one that would best fit your needs. A service representative can help you with that if you need assistance. ---11.--- , your specific plan can be customized if necessary.

With our most popular plan, one of our computer technicians will visit your office weekly to perform maintenance and updates. ---12.--- .

I look forward to hearing back from you soon.

Sincerely,

Ian Kelsey
Service Representative, Digi One

9 (A) optimize
   (B) optimizes
   (C) optimizer
   (D) optimizing

10 (A) select
   (B) remove
   (C) depend
   (D) refer

11 (A) As in
   (B) Although
   (C) In addition
   (D) Likewise

12 (A) Our databases are simple to browse and update.
   (B) This can also be done remotely if you prefer.
   (C) Digi One is updated bi-weekly for system improvements.
   (D) You can read client testimonials on our homepage.

어휘 set up ~을 설치하다 secure 안전한 a wide array of 다양한, 많은 operation 운영 attached 첨부된 fit 맞다 specific 구체적인 necessary 필요한, 필수적인 maintenance 유지 보수

UNIT 12

등위 접속사와 부사절 접속사

1. 등위 접속사
2. 상관 접속사
3. 부사절 접속사: 시간, 조건
4. 부사절 접속사: 이유, 양보/대조
5. 부사절 접속사: 목적, 결과
6. 접속사 vs. 전치사

빈출 유형 풀이 전략
Vocabulary
Actual Test

TOEIC Grammar

약 10%

UNIT 12 등위 접속사와 부사절 접속사

등위 접속사와 부사절 접속사 문제는 각각 매회 1문제 이상 출제됩니다. 각 접속사의 뜻과 쓰임을 제대로 이해하여 문맥에 맞는 접속사를 고르는 게 중요합니다.

 스피드 진단 테스트

(A), (B) 중 알맞은 것을 고르세요.

1. ------- the CEO and the CTO attended the exhibition.

   (A) Both   (B) Either

2. Ms. Weston was absent ------- she didn't feel well.

   (A) when   (B) because

정답 및 해석

1. (A), 최고 경영자와 최고 기술 책임자 둘 다 그 전시회에 참석했다.
2. (B), 웨스턴 씨는 몸이 좋지 않아서 결근했다.

접속사란?

접속사는 문장에서 단어와 단어, 구와 구, 또는 절과 절을 잇는 역할을 합니다.

● 등위 접속사

등위 접속사는 단어와 단어, 구와 구, 또는 절과 절을 문법상 대등한 관계로 이어 주는 접속사입니다.

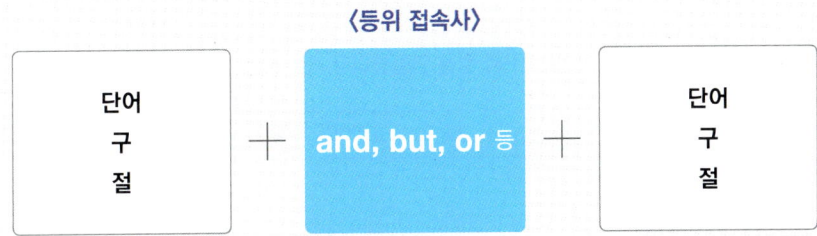

I bought her **a pearl necklace** and **a luxury bag** for her birthday, but she wanted to **return** or **exchange** both of them.
나는 그녀에게 생일 선물로 진주 목걸이와 명품 가방을 사 줬지만, 그녀는 그 둘 다 반품하거나 교환하기를 원했다.

● 부사절 접속사

부사절은 '부사절 접속사 + 주어 + 동사 ~' 구조로 문장에서 부사 역할을 합니다. 시간, 이유, 조건 등의 다양한 의미로 부사절을 이끄는 종속 접속사를 부사절 접속사라고 합니다.

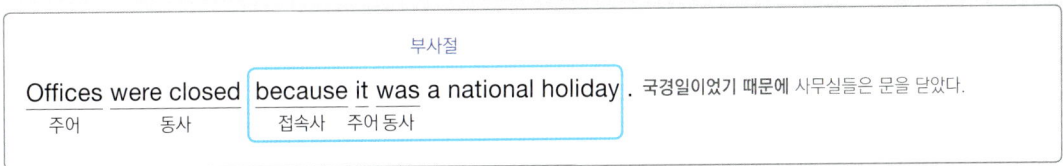

● 부사절의 위치

부사절은 부사처럼 주절의 앞이나 뒤에 올 수 있고, 주절의 앞에 올 때는 항상 쉼표(,)를 붙인다는 것을 기억하세요.

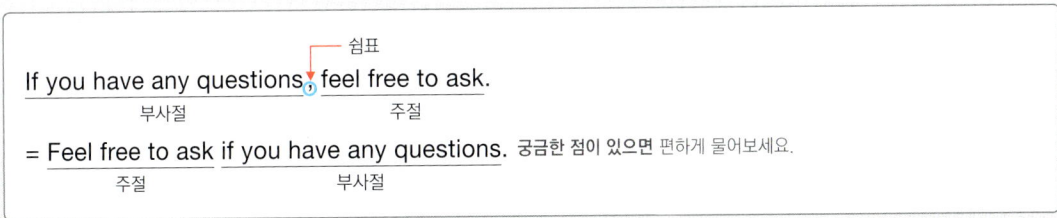

1 등위 접속사

The event includes free foods **and** drinks.

그 행사에는 무료 음식과 음료가 포함되어 있다.

등위 접속사는 품사가 같은 단어나 구조가 같은 구와 절을 연결합니다. 단, so는 절만 연결합니다.

| and 그리고 | but 그러나 | yet 그렇지만, 그런데도 | or 또는 | so 그래서 |

❶ 단어 + 등위 접속사 + 단어

Guests can enjoy coffee and tea in the lobby.
　　　　　　　　명사　　　명사

손님들은 로비에서 **커피와 차**를 즐길 수 있다.

❷ 구 + 등위 접속사 + 구

Tickets can be purchased at the park ticket booth or through our Web site.
　　　　　　　　　　　전치사구　　　　　　　　　전치사구

티켓은 **공원 매표소에서 또는 우리의 웹사이트를 통해서** 구입할 수 있습니다.

❸ 절 + 등위 접속사 + 절

My flight was delayed so I was late for the meeting.
　　　절　　　　　　　　　절

비행기가 연착되어서 회의에 늦었다.

연습문제　　　　　　　　　　　　　　　　정답 및 해설 p.115

1. The Duncan Roughrider is the safest ------- most powerful pickup truck on the market.

    (A) and　　　(B) but
    (C) either　　(D) both

2. The new recliner design is focused on ------- and overall size.

    (A) comfort　　　(B) comfortable
    (C) comfortably　(D) comforted

3. Several items in the package were broken, ------- the customer requested a refund.

    (A) or　　(B) while
    (C) yet　 (D) so

4. Mr. Boothe applied for the open position ------- hasn't heard back from them yet.

    (A) both　(B) but
    (C) so　　(D) for

2 상관 접속사

The book offers **both** information **and** entertainment.

그 책은 정보**와** 재미 **둘 다** 제공한다.

and, or, but 등의 등위 접속사가 다른 단어와 짝을 이루어 한 덩어리로 쓰일 때 이것을 상관 접속사라고 합니다.

both A and B	A와 B 둘 다	either A or B	A나 B 둘 중 하나
not A but B	A가 아니라 B	neither A nor B	A와 B 둘 다 아닌
not only A but (also) B	A뿐만 아니라 B도	B as well as A	A뿐만 아니라 B도

Please submit both an application form and a reference letter by July 8.
지원서와 추천서 둘 다 7월 8일까지 제출해 주세요.

The position requires not only technical ability but also creativity.
= The position requires creativity as well as technical ability.
그 자리는 기술적 능력뿐만 아니라 창의성도 요한다.

🏁 고난도 JUMP UP

주어가 상관 접속사로 연결되어 있을 때 동사는 B에 수 일치를 합니다. (단, both A and B는 항상 복수 동사를 씁니다.)

Neither the manager nor the employees were aware of the problem.
　　　　　A　　　　　　　B (복수 명사)　　복수 동사
부장과 직원들 누구도 그 문제를 알아차리지 못했다.

연습문제

정답 및 해설 p.116

1 Waitstaff should work ------- the morning shift or the evening shift each week.

(A) both　　　　(B) neither
(C) either　　　(D) not only

2 Not only the diners but also the famous critic, John Hemmings, ------- food at Joy's Bistro is exceptional.

(A) comment　　　(B) comments
(C) commentary　 (D) commenting

3 After lunch, neither the conference room ------- the auditorium will be available to use.

(A) but　　(B) nor
(C) and　　(D) so

4 The menu at the Western Steakhouse includes regular dishes ------- seasonal specialties.

(A) nor　　　　　(B) either
(C) as well as　(D) but also

부사절 접속사: 시간, 조건

When you arrive at the airport, I'll be waiting for you.
　　　　　　　　시간 부사절

If you can't find me, please call me or my assistant.
　　　　조건 부사절

공항에 도착하면 제가 기다리고 있을 거예요. **저를 못 찾으시면** 저나 제 비서에게 전화 주세요.

❶ 시간을 나타내는 부사절 접속사

| when ~할 때 | before/after ~ 전에/~ 후에 | until ~할 때까지 |
| while ~하는 동안 | as soon as ~하자마자 | |

The interview continued <u>until</u> it got dark. 날이 어두워질 때까지 인터뷰가 계속되었다.

❷ 조건을 나타내는 부사절 접속사

| once 일단 ~하면 | if 만약 ~라면 | unless 만약 ~가 아니라면 |
| as long as ~하는 한 | provided/providing (that) 만약 ~라면 | |

<u>If you have any questions</u>, don't hesitate to ask me. 궁금한 점이 있으면 주저 말고 물어보세요.

⬆ 고난도 JUMP UP

> 시간이나 조건을 나타내는 부사절에서는 현재 시제가 미래 시제를 대신합니다.
>
> They will make an announcement **once** the date of the event is / ~~will be~~ scheduled.
> 일단 행사 날짜가 정해지면 그들이 공지할 겁니다.

연습문제　　　　　　　　　　　　　　　　　　　　　정답 및 해설 p.117

1 Restaurant owners should apply for a permit ------- they start serving customers.

(A) since　　　(B) before
(C) as well as　(D) while

2 ------- Ms. Montpelier got off the plane, she went to the baggage claim area.

(A) As soon as　(B) While
(C) Until　　　(D) Although

3 The opening ceremony will proceed as scheduled ------- it rains tomorrow morning.

(A) whereas　(B) unless
(C) while　　(D) as long as

4 When you ------- any issue on your computer, contact Jay at extension 56.

(A) encountered　(B) encounter
(C) will encounter　(D) encountering

4 부사절 접속사: 이유, 양보/대조

Because the traffic was terrible, he was late for the meeting.
　　　　　　이유 부사절

길이 엄청 막혔기 때문에 그는 회의에 늦었다.

Although the traffic was terrible, he wasn't late for the meeting.
　　　　　　양보 부사절

길이 엄청 막혔지만 그는 회의에 늦지 않았다.

❶ 이유를 나타내는 부사절 접속사

| because | ~하기 때문에 | as | ~하기 때문에 |
| since | ~하기 때문에 | now (that) | (이제) ~이므로 |

Now that I live close to work, I walk to work.
이제 직장 근처에 살아서 나는 직장까지 걸어간다.

❷ 양보/대조를 나타내는 부사절 접속사

although	비록 ~일지라도	while	~한 반면
though	비록 ~일지라도	whereas	~한 반면
even though	비록 ~일지라도		

Although the building is old, it is well maintained.
그 건물은 오래되었지만 관리가 잘 되어 있다.

연습문제　　　　　　　　　　　　　　　　　　정답 및 해설 p.118

1 ------- the Milton Hotel had no vacancies, rooms were available at the Greenbrier Resort.

　(A) Because　　(B) Instead
　(C) Since　　　(D) Whereas

2 ------- the attorney reviewed the contract thoroughly, Mr. Wakefield was hesitant to sign it.

　(A) As soon as　(B) Now that
　(C) Even though　(D) Once

3 ------- a gym membership was free, few employees are taking advantage of it.

　(A) Although　　(B) If
　(C) Since　　　(D) In order that

4 Dayton Moore surpassed his monthly quota ------- Kevin Harold was unable to sell any vehicles.

　(A) while　　　(B) nor
　(C) provided that　(D) as

5 부사절 접속사: 목적, 결과

We left early **so that** we could arrive on time.
　　　　행동　　　　　　　　　　목적
우리는 제때 도착하기 위해 일찍 떠났다.

We left **so** early **that** we had to wait an hour.
　　　　원인　　　　　　　　　　결과
우리는 너무 일찍 떠나서 한 시간을 기다려야 했다.

❶ 목적을 나타내는 부사절 접속사

| so that ~하기 위해서 | in order that ~하기 위해서 |

Please let me know your arrival time **so that** I can pick you up at the airport.
제가 공항에 당신을 데리러 갈 수 있도록 도착 시간을 알려 주세요.

A reminder e-mail will be sent **in order that** you don't miss your appointment.
귀하가 예약을 놓치지 않으시도록 예약 알림 이메일이 발송될 겁니다.

❷ 결과를 나타내는 부사절 접속사

so 형용사/부사 that+주어+동사 너무 ~해서 …하다

The traffic was **so** bad **that** she had to change the meeting time.
　　　　　　형용사　　주어　　　동사
길이 너무 막혀서 그녀는 회의 시간을 바꿔야 했다.

연습문제　　　　　　　　　　　　　정답 및 해설 p.119

1 Ms. Denton postponed her trip to France ------- she could attend Dr. Pollard's speech.

(A) that　　　　(B) as
(C) so that　　(D) when

2 Mr. Marino, the head trainer, was sent to the Toledo factory ------- the workers could work efficiently.

(A) because　　(B) that
(C) as well as　(D) in order that

3 The revolutionary laptop was so ------- that more than 300 people invested in it.

(A) succession　(B) successful
(C) successfully　(D) success

4 The interior design by Fredrick Lee was ------- innovative that it won several awards.

(A) so　　　　(B) in order
(C) very　　　(D) such

6 접속사 vs. 전치사

while he gives a presentation
접속사 주어 동사
그가 발표를 하는 동안에

during the presentation
전치사 명사
발표 동안에

접속사 뒤에는 '주어 + 동사'를 갖춘 절이 이어지고, 전치사 뒤에는 명사(구)가 이어집니다.

혼동하기 쉬운 접속사와 전치사

종류	뜻	접속사 + 주어 + 동사	전치사 + 명사(구)
시간	~ 동안 ~ 전에/~ 후에 ~까지	while before/after until, by the time	during, for before, prior to/after, following until, by
조건	~가 아니라면	unless	without
이유	~ 때문에	because, since, as	because of, due to, owing to
양보/대조	비록 ~일지라도	although, though, even though	despite, in spite of

All arrangements will be completed **before** they arrive. 그들이 도착하기 전에 모든 준비가 완료될 것이다.
　　　　　　　　　　　　　　　　　　접속사　주어　동사

All arrangements will be completed **prior to** their arrival. 그들이 도착하기 전에 모든 준비가 완료될 것이다.
　　　　　　　　　　　　　　　　　　전치사　　명사구

All arrangements will be completed **before** noon. 정오 전에 모든 준비가 완료될 것이다.
　　　　　　　　　　　　　　　　　　전치사　명사

연습문제

정답 및 해설 p.120

1 The Mobile Towers construction project is behind schedule ------- government regulations.

(A) because　　(B) while
(C) although　　(D) because of

2 Jared feels that ------- companies have membership programs, shoppers make regular purchases.

(A) before　　(B) in spite of
(C) when　　(D) owing to

3 The new video game is popular with players ------- its minor design flaws.

(A) by the time　　(B) due to
(C) until　　(D) despite

4 Mr. Rodgers will lead the Personnel Department ------- Ms. Rodriguez attends the seminar abroad.

(A) while　　(B) during
(C) so that　　(D) prior to

UNIT 12 등위 접속사와 부사절 접속사 201

빈출 유형 풀이 전략

1. 상관 접속사

STEP에 따라 실제 토익 문제를 푸는 순서와 요령을 익혀 보세요.

All exchanges and refunds are handled by ------- Mr. Jackson or Ms. Hand.

(A) either
(B) both
(C) neither
(D) when

STEP 1 선택지 구성 파악하기

선택지가 다양한 접속사로 구성되어 있으므로 빈칸에 알맞은 접속사를 고르는 문제.

All exchanges and refunds are handled by ------- Mr. Jackson or Ms. Hand.

(A) either
(B) both
(C) neither
(D) when

STEP 2 빈칸 주변에서 단서 찾기

빈칸 뒤에 〈명사 or 명사〉 구조가 이어지므로 문장을 연결하는 접속사인 (D) when은 오답으로 소거.

All exchanges and refunds are handled by ------- Mr. Jackson or Ms. Hand.

(A) either ✓
(B) both
(C) neither
(D) when

STEP 3 정답 찾기

〈명사 or 명사〉 구조를 연결하면서 'A나 B 둘 중 하나'를 뜻할 수 있는 (A) either가 정답.

해석 모든 교환과 환불은 잭슨 씨나 핸드 씨 중 한 사람에 의해 처리된다.

어휘 exchange 교환; 교환하다 refund 환불; 환불하다 handle 처리하다, 다루다

2. 부사절 접속사

STEP에 따라 실제 토익 문제를 푸는 순서와 요령을 익혀 보세요.

Tom Diego speaks Spanish fluently ------- Angela Panini deals with all Italian clients.

(A) while
(B) before
(C) due to
(D) as long as

STEP 1 선택지 구성 파악하기

선택지가 다양한 접속사로 구성되어 있으므로 빈칸에 알맞은 접속사를 고르는 문제.

Tom Diego speaks Spanish fluently ------- Angela Panini deals with all Italian clients.

(A) while
(B) before
(C) due to
(D) as long as

STEP 2 빈칸 주변에서 단서 찾기

빈칸 뒤에 주어(Angela Panini)와 구동사(deals with)가 있으므로 빈칸은 접속사 자리.
또한 빈칸 앞뒤가 서로 상반된 내용을 언급하고 있으므로 '대조'를 의미하는 접속사가 두 문장을 이어 줘야 함.

Tom Diego speaks Spanish fluently ------- Angela Panini deals with all Italian clients.

(A) ✓ while
(B) before
(C) due to
(D) as long as

STEP 3 정답 찾기

따라서 '반면에'를 뜻하는 (A) while이 정답.

해석 앤젤라 파니니가 모든 이탈리아 고객들을 응대하는 반면, 톰 디에고는 스페인어를 유창하게 한다.

어휘 fluently 유창하게 deal with ~을 처리하다, ~을 다루다 client 고객, 의뢰인

VOCABULARY 빈출 부사 어휘 (1)

diligently	부지런히, 애써	work **diligently** 부지런히 일하다 **diligently** complete the task 그 업무를 부지런히 완료하다
approximately 동 roughly	대략, 약	last **approximately** three hours 세 시간 가까이 지속되다 take **approximately** three weeks 대략 3주 정도 걸리다
occasionally 동 from time to time	가끔, 때때로	**occasionally** provide rare chances 가끔 드문 기회를 제공하다 see each other **occasionally** 가끔 서로를 만나다
unanimously	만장일치로	**unanimously** agree 만장일치로 동의하다 be **unanimously** approved 만장일치로 승인되다
properly 반 improperly 부적절하게	적절하게, 제대로	function **properly** 제대로 기능하다 **properly** trained staff 제대로 훈련을 받은 직원들
entirely 동 completely	전적으로, 완전히	**entirely** agree with the idea 그 의견에 전적으로 동의하다 an **entirely** new approach 완전히 새로운 접근법
especially 동 particularly	특히	**especially** helpful in developing writing skills 특히 작문 능력 개발에 도움이 되는 be **especially** fond of poetry 특히 시를 좋아하다
recently	최근에	until **recently** 최근까지 a **recently** launched novel 최근에 출간된 소설

연습문제

1. Ms. Badger ------- offered Terry Haas a promotion to senior vice president.
   (A) partially (B) visually
   (C) recently   (D) entirely

2. Deliveries from Delmont Logistics ------- arrive two or three days ahead of schedule.
   (A) occasionally (B) fairly
   (C) temporarily   (D) approximately

3. When the software is installed -------, the computer will work better than ever.
   (A) properly   (B) apparently
   (C) especially (D) randomly

4. Pierre Argent studied ------- for weeks to be accredited as an accountant.
   (A) unanimously (B) readily
   (C) diligently   (D) approvingly

eventually	결국, 마침내	find a job **eventually** 결국 취직을 하다 **eventually** succeed in computer business 마침내 컴퓨터 업계에서 성공을 거두다
thoroughly 🔄 completely	완전히, 철저히	clean up spills **thoroughly** 쏟은 것을 제대로 닦다 **thoroughly** confused 몹시 혼란스러운
helpfully	도움이 되도록, 유용하게	**helpfully** provide a manual 도움이 되도록 설명서를 제공하다 **helpfully** suggest 도움이 되는 제안을 하다
busily	바쁘게, 분주하게	**busily** write down orders 바쁘게 주문을 받아 적다 **busily** keep up with the demand 분주하게 수요를 맞추다
brightly	밝게; (표정 등이) 환하게	wear a **brightly** colored scarf 밝은 색 스카프를 매다 smile **brightly** 환하게 미소 짓다
adequately 🔄 sufficiently	충분히	**adequately** test the product 그 제품을 충분히 테스트하다 be **adequately** funded 충분히 자금을 조달받다
originally	원래, 애초에	**originally** scheduled for Friday 원래는 금요일로 예정된 earlier than **originally** intended 원래 의도했던 것보다 더 이른
exactly 🔄 precisely	정확하게	look **exactly** the same 정확히 똑같이 보이다 **exactly** the opposite 정반대

정답 및 해설 p.121

5 Lionel Parker is unable to ------- describe the problem with the machinery.

(A) highly (B) adequately
(C) previously (D) brightly

6 Roland Motors executives expect the Norfolk factory to employ ------- 1,200 workers next year.

(A) approximately (B) sincerely
(C) helpfully (D) repeatedly

7 Workplaces should be cleaned ------- at the end of each workday.

(A) vitally (B) thoroughly
(C) evenly (D) busily

8 The new Garmacore laptop fits ------- into its newly designed packing box.

(A) decisively (B) exactly
(C) originally (D) promptly

ACTUAL TEST

1 All commemorative T-shirts are sold out, ------- postcards may still be purchased.

(A) so
(B) but
(C) because
(D) nor

2 It is ------- safe to repair the machine if the batteries are removed.

(A) unanimously
(B) exactly
(C) repeatedly
(D) entirely

3 ------- Mr. Howard resigns, he will remain the head of the Mumbai office.

(A) Until
(B) As long as
(C) Yet
(D) Prior to

4 ------- the anticipated improvements were made, customer satisfaction at Demarche greatly improved.

(A) While
(B) After
(C) In spite of
(D) So that

5 Mr. Nealon possesses not only a law degree ------- a degree in business.

(A) unless
(B) in order that
(C) as well as
(D) but also

6 Ms. Sanderson will calculate the money left in the budget before she ------- the expense request.

(A) will approve
(B) approves
(C) had approved
(D) approving

7 ------- the night manager or the custodian should have the keys to the office.

(A) Both
(B) Even though
(C) Either
(D) As

8 The company picnic will be scheduled ------- the weather forecast is reviewed.

(A) not only
(B) once
(C) whereas
(D) owing to

어휘 commemorative 기념하는 sold out 매진된, 다 팔린 resign 사직하다, 물러나다 remain 계속 ~이다, 남아 있다 head 책임자 anticipated 기대하던, 대망의 improvement 개선, 향상 customer satisfaction 고객 만족(도) possess 소유하다, 보유하다 expense request 지출 요청(서) custodian 관리인

Questions 9-12 refer to the following article.

SAN FREDO (July 14)—Tycho, Inc. recently released its newest software, called Alpha Tech. Alpha Tech -------- users to organize their budgets for both personal and professional purposes. -------- users download the software, it starts with a comprehensive tutorial, which makes it very user-friendly. This permits users to understand every -------- that the software provides. The software is currently available at a discounted price of $99. -------- .
9.   10.   11.   12.

9. (A) enabling
   (B) to enable
   (C) will have enabled
   (D) enables

10. (A) Instead of
    (B) Although
    (C) Despite
    (D) When

11. (A) price
    (B) award
    (C) service
    (D) utilization

12. (A) Those interested should order it at once.
    (B) The new budgeting seminar is expected to be a success.
    (C) Thank you very much for your recent purchase.
    (D) The software should be available in two months.

어휘   release 출시하다, 공개하다   organize 조직하다, 체계화하다   personal 개인적인   professional 직업의, 전문적인   comprehensive 포괄적인, 종합적인   tutorial 사용 지침 프로그램; 개별 지도   user-friendly 사용자 친화적인   permit A to *do* A가 ~하는 것을 가능하게 하다[허락하다]   currently 현재, 지금

에듀윌이
너를
지지할게

ENERGY

내를 건너서 숲으로
고개를 넘어서 마을로

어제도 가고 오늘도 갈
나의 길 새로운 길

– 윤동주, '새로운 길'

UNIT
13

명사절 접속사

1. 명사절 자리
2. 명사절을 이끄는 의문사
3. 명사절 접속사: that
4. 명사절 접속사: if, whether

빈출 유형 풀이 전략
Vocabulary
Actual Test

TOEIC Grammar

약 10%

UNIT 13 명사절 접속사

명사절 접속사 문제는 매회 1문제 이상 출제됩니다. 단순히 접속사의 뜻으로 정답을 고를 수 있는 문제보다는 전체 문장 구조를 보고 쓰임에 맞는 접속사를 고르는 문제가 자주 출제됩니다.

 스피드 진단 테스트

(A), (B) 중 알맞은 것을 고르세요.

1. Regulations require ------- all staff wear safety helmets.
   (A) about
   (B) that

2. They will decide ------- or not to continue the work.
   (A) that
   (B) whether

정답 및 해석

1. (B), 규정들은 모든 직원이 안전모를 착용할 것을 요구한다.
2. (B), 그들은 그 일을 계속할지 말지 결정할 것이다.

명사절이란?

명사절은 '명사절 접속사 + 주어 + 동사 ~' 구조로 쓰이며 문장에서 명사 역할을 합니다. 명사 역할을 한다는 것은 문장의 주어, 목적어, 보어 자리에 위치할 수 있다는 걸 뜻합니다.

● **명사절의 형태: 명사절 접속사 + 주어 + 동사**

The good news is <u>that the machine has been fixed</u>. 좋은 소식은 기계가 수리되었다는 것이다.
- The good news: 주어 / is: 동사
- that: 명사절 접속사
- the machine: 주어 / has been fixed: 동사
- that the machine has been fixed: 명사절 (보어 역할)

● **명사절 접속사의 종류**

명사절을 이끄는 접속사에는 크게 세 가지가 있습니다.

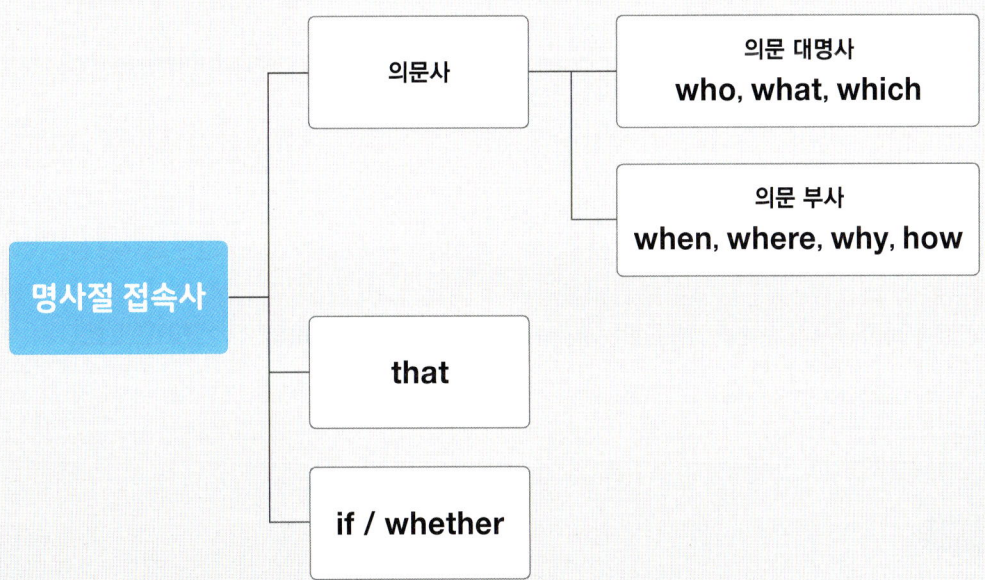

I don't know how long it will take. 시간이 얼마나 오래 걸릴지 모르겠다.
I don't know if it will take an hour or two. 한 시간이 걸릴지 두 시간이 걸릴지 모르겠다.
I didn't know that it would take that much time. 그렇게 많은 시간이 걸릴지 몰랐다.

1 명사절 자리

The only problem is **that** price is a little high.
명사절 (보어 역할)

유일한 문제는 **가격이 약간 높다는 것**이다.

명사절은 주어와 보어, 그리고 목적어 자리에 위치할 수 있습니다.

❶ 주어

<u>What</u> we need <u>is</u> to secure funding. 우리에게 필요한 것은 자금을 확보하는 겁니다.
　단수 주어　　　단수 동사

❷ 보어

A key benefit of the product is <u>that it is recyclable</u>. 그 제품의 핵심 장점은 **재활용할 수 있다는 점**이다.

❸ 목적어

The red light indicates <u>that the microphone is turned on</u>. 빨간 불은 마이크가 켜져 있다는 것을 나타낸다.
　　　　　　　　　　indicate의 목적어 역할을 하는 명사절

🔼 고난도 JUMP UP

that절을 주어로 쓸 때는 가주어 it을 문장 앞에 두고 that절을 문장 뒤로 보냅니다.

That we provide our customers with expert assistance is important.
→ <u>It</u> is important <u>that</u> we provide our customers with expert assistance.
　가주어　　　　　진주어
우리의 고객들에게 전문적인 도움을 제공하는 것은 중요합니다.

연습문제　　　　　　　　　　　　　　　　　　　　　　　　정답 및 해설 p.126

1　Ms. Corbett argued ------- increasing the perks of the company could attract better qualified employees.

　(A) for　　　　(B) about
　(C) that　　　(D) towards

2　Please let the agent at check-in know ------- you would like an aisle or window seat.

　(A) which　　(B) but
　(C) about　　(D) whether

3　Ahmed Abadi conducted a survey to determine ------- JNG Motors can reach younger generations.

　(A) how　　　(B) unless
　(C) among　　(D) with

4　The problem with the project plan is ------- the deadlines are not realistic.

　(A) that　　　(B) whether
　(C) due to　　(D) of

2 명사절을 이끄는 의문사

의문 대명사

who 누가   what 무엇을

which 어느 것을

의문 부사

when 언제   where 어디에

why 왜   how 어떻게

의문사가 이끄는 명사절은 문장의 주어와 보어, 그리고 목적어 자리에 위치하여 명사 역할을 할 수 있습니다. 의문 대명사는 명사절 내에서 대명사 역할을 하며, 의문 부사는 부사 역할을 합니다.

❶ 의문 대명사

I don't know who is in charge of advertising the product.
　　　　　　　who가 의문사인 동시에 명사절의 주어 역할을 대신함

누가 그 제품 광고를 담당하는지 모르겠어요.

The business course may be what you're seeking.
　　　　　　　　　　　　　what이 의문사인 동시에 동사 seek의 목적어 역할을 대신함

그 비즈니스 수업은 아마도 **당신이 찾던 것**일 겁니다.

❷ 의문 부사

Mr. West asked when the new boss was coming.
　　　　　　　 의문 부사　　 주어　　　　동사

웨스트 씨는 **새 상사가 언제 오는지** 물었다.

　　　　　　　　　　┌─ 주어
The point is how we meet customers' needs.
　　　　　　 의문 부사　동사　　　목적어

요점은 **우리가 고객의 요구를 어떻게 충족하느냐**는 것이다.

연습문제　　　　　　　　　　　　　　　　　　　　　　　　정답 및 해설 p.127

1 Check the software company's Web site to find out ------- the next update will be out.

(A) when　　(B) which
(C) who　　(D) whether

2 The mentors will explain ------- the trainees will be doing each day.

(A) how　　(B) that
(C) where　(D) what

3 The advertisement successfully portrayed ------- life can change with Goodwill's new dishwasher.

(A) where　(B) how
(C) what　　(D) who

4 The security guards at the entrance know ------- is on the guest list.

(A) where　(B) when
(C) whether　(D) who

3 명사절 접속사: that

The survey results indicate that consumers prefer to shop online.
명사절 (indicate의 목적어 역할)
설문 조사 결과는 소비자들이 온라인 쇼핑을 선호한다는 것을 나타낸다.

명사절 접속사 that은 확실하고 단정적인 사실을 표현할 때 쓰며 '~하는 것'이라고 해석합니다. 특히 명사절 접속사 that절을 목적어로 취하는 타동사를 함께 알아 두면 좋습니다.

that절을 목적어로 취하는 타동사

announce that ~을 발표하다	claim that ~을 주장하다	mention that ~을 언급하다
complain that ~을 불평하다	admit that ~을 인정하다	agree that ~을 동의하다
answer that ~라고 대답하다	state that (공식적으로) ~을 말하다; (문서 등에) ~을 명시하다	

They mentioned that the event will take place in March.
그들은 그 행사가 3월에 있을 거라고 언급했다.

⬆ 고난도 JUMP UP

제안/충고/요구/요청의 의미가 있는 동사는 '타동사 + that + 주어 + (should) 동사원형' 구조로 씁니다.

- 제안 suggest, propose
- 권고/조언 recommend, advise
- 요구/요청 demand, require, ask, request

} + that + 주어 + (should) 동사원형

He requested that all electronic devices be turned off during the meeting.
동사 — that절의 주어 — that절의 동사구 (should 생략)
그는 회의 동안 모든 전자 기기의 전원을 끌 것을 요청했다.

연습문제 정답 및 해설 p.128

1. Park regulations ------- that visitors are not allowed to eat on the grass.
   (A) restrict (B) state
   (C) authorize (D) forbid

2. Hanik Electronics has announced ------- Howard Cross will take over the position of CFO.
   (A) that (B) who
   (C) while (D) though

3. Ms. Denzel requests that a limousine ------- for Denton Inc.'s CEO at the airport.
   (A) wait (B) is waiting
   (C) waits (D) will wait

4. The technician ------- that an anti-virus software be installed on the computer.
   (A) downloaded (B) registered
   (C) recommended (D) transferred

명사절 접속사: if, whether

The question is whether we can meet the deadline.
명사절 (be동사의 주격 보어 역할)
문제는 우리가 마감일을 맞출 수 있을 것인가이다.

if나 whether가 이끄는 명사절은 불확실한 사실을 전달할 때 쓰며 '~인지 아닌지'라고 해석합니다. 명사절 접속사 if와 whether는 뜻은 유사하지만 쓰임이 다르기 때문에 각각의 쓰임을 제대로 익혀야 합니다.

명사절 접속사 if와 whether의 쓰임 정리

	if	whether
주어 자리	×	○
보어 자리	×	○
동사의 목적어	○	○
전치사의 목적어	×	○
or not	if or not (×)	whether or not (○)
to부정사구	if to do (×)	whether to do (○)

I asked **if/whether** the ticket was still valid. 나는 그 티켓이 아직 유효한지 물어봤다.
동사 ask의 목적어 역할을 하는 if/whether절

if (×)
It depends on **whether** you travel by train or plane. 그것은 당신이 기차를 탈지 비행기를 탈지에 달려 있어요.
전치사 on의 목적어 역할을 하는 whether절

연습문제

정답 및 해설 p.129

1 ------- the meeting is in the morning or afternoon, the project manager will be there.

(A) If (B) However
(C) Only (D) Whether

2 Mr. Gartner asked the designers if ------- could work on a new logo design.

(A) them (B) themselves
(C) theirs (D) they

3 The hotel receptionist checked to see ------- there were any free rooms left.

(A) though (B) if
(C) however (D) for

4 The HR manager wanted to know ------- or not the workshop materials were ready.

(A) if (B) that
(C) how (D) whether

UNIT 13 명사절 접속사 217

빈출 유형 풀이 전략

1. 명사절 접속사 자리

STEP에 따라 실제 토익 문제를 푸는 순서와 요령을 익혀 보세요.

The airline requires ------- passengers be at the airport two hours before their flight.

(A) of
(B) from
(C) which
(D) that

STEP 1 선택지 구성 파악하기

선택지가 각기 다른 품사로 구성되어 있는 것으로 보아 빈칸에 알맞은 품사를 묻는 문제.

The airline requires ------- passengers be at the airport two hours before their flight.

(A) of
(B) from
(C) which
(D) that

STEP 2 빈칸 주변에서 단서 찾기

〈주어(The airline) + 동사(requires) + ------- + 주어(passengers) + 동사원형(be)〉 구조.
따라서 빈칸은 require의 목적어 역할을 하면서 빈칸 뒤의 절을 연결할 수 있는 접속사 자리.

The airline requires ------- passengers be at the airport two hours before their flight.

(A) of
(B) from
(C) which
(D) that ✓

STEP 3 정답 찾기

require는 that절을 목적어로 취하므로 (D) that이 정답.

해석 그 항공사는 승객들이 비행 2시간 전에 공항에 와 있을 것을 요구한다.

어휘 airline 항공사   require 요구하다, 필요로 하다   passenger 승객, 여객   airport 공항   flight 비행, 항공편

2. 명사절 접속사 whether

STEP에 따라 실제 토익 문제를 푸는 순서와 요령을 익혀 보세요.

Ms. Turner asked the real estate agent
------- the apartment was furnished.

(A) whether
(B) for
(C) that
(D) wherever

STEP 1 선택지 구성 파악하기

선택지가 각기 다른 품사로 구성되어 있는 것으로 보아 빈칸에 알맞은 품사를 묻는 문제.

Ms. Turner asked the real estate agent
------- the apartment was furnished.

(A) whether
(B) for
(C) that
(D) wherever

STEP 2 빈칸 주변에서 단서 찾기

빈칸 앞에 완전한 절이 있고 뒤에도 절이 이어지므로 빈칸은 절과 절을 연결하는 접속사 자리.
빈칸 앞에 있는 동사 asked는 간접목적어와 직접목적어를 취하는 4형식 동사이며, '------- ~ furnished'는 asked의 직접목적어 역할을 함.

Ms. Turner asked the real estate agent
------- the apartment was furnished.

(A) whether
(B) for
(C) that
(D) wherever

STEP 3 정답 찾기

문맥상 아파트에 가구가 갖추어져 있는지 아닌지 물어보았다는 내용이 되는 게 자연스러움.
따라서 〈주어 + 동사〉 구조의 절과 함께 목적어 자리에 위치할 수 있고 '~인지 아닌지'를 뜻하는 (A) whether가 정답.

해석 터너 씨는 부동산 중개인에게 그 아파트에 가구가 갖추어져 있는지를 물었다.
어휘 real estate agent 부동산 중개인 apartment 아파트(의 한 세대) be furnished 가구가 비치되다

VOCABULARY

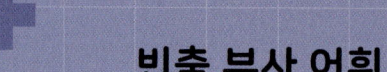
빈출 부사 어휘 (2)

rapidly	빠르게, 급속히	grow/increase **rapidly** 빠르게 성장하다/증가하다 the **rapidly** changing world of online shopping 빠르게 변화하는 온라인 쇼핑업계
randomly	무작위로	be **randomly** selected 무작위로 선택되다 arrange books **randomly** 책들을 아무렇게나 꽂다
expertly	능숙하게, 전문적으로	be **expertly** performed 능숙하게 연주되다[행해지다] an **expertly** crafted work 전문가의 솜씨로 만들어진 작품
efficiently	능률적으로, 효율적으로	an **efficiently** run company 능률적으로 운영되는 회사 function **efficiently** 효율적으로 기능하다
readily ⑤ easily 쉽게 willingly 기꺼이	손쉽게, 순조롭게; 선뜻, 기꺼이	**readily** resolve the issue 손쉽게 그 문제를 해결하다 **readily** agree to the interview 선뜻 인터뷰에 응하다
anonymously	익명으로	make a donation **anonymously** 익명으로 기부하다 be posted **anonymously** 익명으로 게재되다
conveniently	편리하게, 편의상	be **conveniently** located 편리한 위치에 있다 **conveniently** provide a service 편의상 서비스를 제공하다
neatly	깔끔하게	arrange one's work area **neatly** 근무 공간을 깔끔하게 정리하다 summarize the information **neatly** 그 정보를 깔끔하게 요약하다

연습문제

1 Timi Cosmetics processed the order ------ and shipped it the same day.

(A) conveniently (B) rapidly
(C) strongly (D) temporarily

2 The orchestra ------ executed the symphony at last night's concert.

(A) efficiently (B) slightly
(C) likewise (D) expertly

3 Most survey respondents selected the option to submit their answers ------.

(A) anonymously (B) constantly
(C) readily (D) analytically

4 The winner of the PBX Radio concert tickets will be chosen ------ among the callers.

(A) randomly (B) neatly
(C) thoroughly (D) briefly

exclusively ⓢ only	독점적으로, 오로지	available **exclusively** to frequent customers 단골들만 이용 가능한 **exclusively** produce milk products 오로지 유제품만 생산하다
finally ⓢ eventually	마침내; 마지막으로	**finally** close the deal 마침내 거래를 성사시키다 **finally** approve the plan 마침내 그 계획을 승인하다
frequently	자주, 빈번히	run **frequently** (버스, 기차 등이) 자주 다니다 **frequently** asked questions 자주 받는 질문들
generally	일반적으로, 대개; 개괄적으로	be **generally** regarded as essential 대개 필수적이라고 여겨지다 a **generally** accepted approach 일반적으로 받아들여지는 접근(법)
shortly ⓢ soon	곧, 얼마 안 되어	contact the customer **shortly** 그 고객에게 바로 연락하다 begin the task **shortly** 업무를 바로 시작하다
completely ⓢ totally	완전히, 전적으로	fill out the form **completely** 그 양식을 빠짐없이 작성하다 agree with her **completely** 그녀의 의견에 전적으로 동의하다
punctually	정각에, 시간에 맞춰서	start **punctually** at ten 10시 정각에 시작하다 arrive **punctually** 시간에 맞춰 도착하다
precisely ⓢ exactly	정확히, 확실히	be measured **precisely** 정확히 측정되다 know **precisely** what they want 그들이 원하는 걸 정확히 알다

정답 및 해설 p.130

5 After a four-hour delay, the plane ------- took off from O'Hara Airport.

(A) frequently (B) preferably
(C) especially (D) finally

6 The committee will review your proposal and give you their feedback -------.

(A) completely (B) shortly
(C) essentially (D) wrongly

7 Vocanix Academy is ------- considered the most prestigious music school in the region.

(A) precisely (B) promptly
(C) sharply (D) generally

8 Nina Abbas runs a restaurant that ------- serves vegetarian dishes.

(A) punctually (B) exclusively
(C) lately (D) significantly

ACTUAL TEST

1. The event organizer will decide ------- will speak first at the ceremony.

   (A) who
   (B) when
   (C) what
   (D) which

2. The Pim Pro software helps companies manage their human resources data more -------.

   (A) efficiently
   (B) randomly
   (C) commonly
   (D) repeatedly

3. The director asked that Mr. Thibault ------- present at the weekly board meeting.

   (A) was
   (B) had been
   (C) be
   (D) will be

4. Ms. Kino is analyzing the data to find out how consumers ------- their cosmetics.

   (A) chosen
   (B) choose
   (C) to choose
   (D) are chosen

5. Please keep your seat belt fastened until the plane has ------- stopped.

   (A) frequently
   (B) completely
   (C) quickly
   (D) neatly

6. The quarterly report indicates ------- sales increased by 14 percent compared to last year.

   (A) what
   (B) that
   (C) much
   (D) since

7. At the convention, Limbda Corp.'s spokesperson described ------- their new tablet will look like.

   (A) which
   (B) what
   (C) that
   (D) when

8. Ms. Mitsuni called the museum to ask ------- it gives guided tours.

   (A) in order to
   (B) that
   (C) whether
   (D) what

어휘 organizer 조직자, 주최자 human resources 인적 자원, 인력 director 이사 present 출석한, 참석한 cosmetics ((항상 복수형)) 화장품 fasten 매다, 채우다 quarterly 연 4회의, 분기별의 compared to ~에 비해 spokesperson 대변인 guided tour 가이드 동반 관람

Questions 9-12 refer to the following advertisement.

Is your company planning on expanding overseas? ---9.---. However, with the right preparation, it can bring about exceptional ---10.--- for your business. Broad Horizons can help you with that. Just tell us where you want to go. We will provide you with an exhaustive country profile, and guide you through the necessary paperwork. Our experts will then show you ---11.--- your marketing techniques should be adapted to reach the local culture. ---12.---, we'll be assisting you in every step of accomplishing your sales goal. Thanks to our services, your company will become an international success in no time.

9 (A) There are many wonderful touristic sites to visit.
   (B) This product is finally available in your country.
   (C) You may have to pay an additional delivery fee.
   (D) Breaking into the international market can be difficult.

10 (A) similarities
   (B) consequences
   (C) negotiations
   (D) opportunities

11 (A) how
   (B) why
   (C) for
   (D) because

12 (A) However
   (B) Apparently
   (C) Above all
   (D) Instead

어휘 expand 확장하다, 성장하다 preparation 준비, 대비 bring about ~을 가져오다, ~을 초래하다 provide A with B A에게 B를 제공하다 exhaustive 철저한, 총망라한 guide A through B A에게 B(복잡한 것)를 단계별로 안내하다 adapt 각색하다, 조정하다 reach 도달하다, 닿다 in no time 즉시

UNIT 14

가정법

1. 가정법 현재
2. 가정법 과거와 과거완료
3. 가정법 미래
4. if 생략

빈출 유형 풀이 전략
Vocabulary
Actual Test

TOEIC Grammar

약 5%

UNIT 14 가정법

가정법 문제는 출제 빈도가 그리 높지는 않지만 가정법 과거완료와 if를 생략한 가정법 도치 구문이 간혹 출제됩니다. 가정법은 언뜻 보면 마냥 복잡해 보이지만 기본 구조를 숙지하고 문제 출제 유형에 익숙해지면 그다지 어렵지 않게 문제를 풀 수 있습니다.

 스피드 진단 테스트

(A), (B) 중 알맞은 것을 고르세요.

1. If I had taken the job, I ------- about $500 a week.

    (A) would make   (B) would have made

2. ------- you need further information, please visit our Web site.

    (A) Should   (B) After

정답 및 해석

1. (B), 내가 그 일을 맡았다면 일주일에 약 500달러를 벌었을 것이다.
2. (A), 혹시라도 더 많은 정보가 필요하시면 우리의 웹사이트를 방문해 주세요.

💡 가정법이란?

가정법은 실제로 일어나지 않았거나 앞으로 일어날지 아닐지 분명하지 않은 것을 가정할 때 씁니다.

● 가정법의 구조

가정법은 가정을 하는 if절과 그로 인해 발생할 결과인 주절로 구성되어 있습니다.

| If you leave now, | you will get there on time. | 지금 출발하면 그곳에 제시간에 도착할 거예요. |
| if절 (가정) | 주절 (결과) | |

● 가정법의 종류

가정법은 if절의 시제에 따라 가정법 현재, 과거, 과거완료, 미래로 나눕니다.

가정법 현재 (현재나 미래 가정)	If the weather is fine 만약 날씨가 좋다면
가정법 과거 (현재의 반대 가정)	If I were not busy 만약 내가 바쁘지 않다면
가정법 과거완료 (과거의 반대 가정)	If we had started earlier 만약 우리가 더 빨리 시작했다면
가정법 미래 (혹시라도 일어날 수 있는 상황 가정)	If you should need more information 혹시라도 더 많은 정보가 필요하면

● 가정법과 조동사

가정법은 실제로 일어나지 않은 상황을 추측하기 위한 방법이며, 조동사로 추측의 강도를 나타냅니다.

강한 추측	약한 추측		약한 추측의 과거형
will ~할 것이다	would 아마도 ~할 것이다	→	would have p.p. 아마도 ~했을 것이다
can ~할 수 있다	could 아마도 ~할 수 있다	→	could have p.p. 아마도 ~할 수 있었다
may ~할지도 모른다	might 아마도 ~할지도 모른다	→	might have p.p. 아마도 ~했을지도 모른다

I will go to the festival. 나는 그 축제에 갈 거야.
I would go to the festival. 나는 (아마도) 그 축제에 갈 거야.
I would have gone to the festival. 나는 (아마도) 그 축제에 갔을 거야.

1 가정법 현재

If you **order** the books now, they **will arrive** by tomorrow.
　　　　동사 현재형　　　　　　　　　　　　will + 동사원형

지금 그 책들을 **주문하면** 내일까지 **도착할 겁니다**.

가정법 현재는 미래에 일어날 가능성이 높은 일, 즉 조건이 맞으면 일어날 수 있는 일을 표현할 때 씁니다.

If + 주어 + 동사 현재형 ~, 주어 + will/can/may + 동사원형 ~
If + 주어 + 동사 현재형 ~, 동사원형 ~

If the property **is** left in a good condition, the deposit **will be** returned.
(임차한) 그 집[건물]이 양호한 **상태라면** 보증금은 **반환될 것입니다**.

If you **are** interested, please **call** our customer service department at 202-555-0173.
관심 **있으시다면** 저희 고객 서비스 센터(202-555-0173)로 **전화 주세요**.

고난도 JUMP UP

주절에 〈조동사 현재형 + 동사원형〉 대신 〈동사 현재형〉을 쓰면 보편적이며 일반적인 현재 사실을 나타내게 됩니다.

A free 30-day trial **is** available if you want to try before purchase.
　　　　　　　　　동사 현재형
구입 전에 시험 삼아 써 보고 싶다면 30일 무료 체험판이 이용 가능합니다.

연습문제

정답 및 해설 p.135

1 If the printer ------ well, it will make clearer copies of documents.

(A) maintains
(B) is maintained
(C) will maintain
(D) will be maintaining

2 If you ------ receive the reservation e-mail by today, call Mr. Sandro.

(A) do not
(B) had not been
(C) were not
(D) did not

3 If Mr. Arnold arrives on time, he ------ the presentation to the clients.

(A) gives
(B) to give
(C) gave
(D) will give

4 If the alarm ------, look at the monitor to check for problems.

(A) goes off
(B) going off
(C) will go off
(D) had gone off

2 가정법 과거와 과거완료

If we **took** a taxi, we **wouldn't miss** the flight.
　　　동사 과거형　　　　　　　would + 동사원형

택시를 **탄다면** 우리는 비행기를 **놓치지 않을** 텐데. (택시를 탈 수 없는 상황임.)

If we **had taken** a taxi, we **wouldn't have missed** the flight.
　　　had p.p.　　　　　　　　　would + have p.p.

택시를 **탔다면** 우리는 비행기를 **놓치지 않았을** 텐데.

가정법 과거는 현재 사실과 반대되는 가정을 할 때, 가정법 과거완료는 과거 사실과 반대되는 가정을 할 때 씁니다.

❶ **가정법 과거 (현재 사실을 다르게 가정)**: ~라면 …할 텐데

> If + 주어 + 동사 과거형 / were ~, 주어 + would/could/might + 동사원형 ~

If the bag **had** a big front pocket, I **would buy** it. 그 가방에 큰 앞주머니가 있다면 그것을 살 텐데.
If he **were** here, he **might help** us. 그가 여기에 있다면 그는 우리를 도울 텐데.

❷ **가정법 과거완료 (과거 사실을 다르게 가정)**: ~했다면 …했을 텐데

> If + 주어 + had p.p. ~, 주어 + would/could/might + have p.p. ~

If you **had called** me, I **would have picked** you up at the airport.
제게 **전화했다면** 제가 공항에 당신을 데리러 갔을 거예요.

연습문제

1. If the order had been placed on Monday, it ------- by Thursday.
   (A) would have arrived
   (B) has arrived
   (C) is being arrived
   (D) would have been arrived

2. They ------- a 20% discount if they had ordered a day earlier.
   (A) received
   (B) have received
   (C) would have received
   (D) will have received

3. If Mark ------- the error, we would have had a huge complaint from the customer.
   (A) didn't catch
   (B) hadn't been caught
   (C) hadn't caught
   (D) caught

4. If the weather had been nicer, the groundbreaking ceremony ------- outdoors.
   (A) has taken place
   (B) had taken place
   (C) would have taken place
   (D) will have taken place

가정법 미래

If it should rain tomorrow, the game will be canceled.
    should + 동사원형   will + 동사원형
혹시라도 내일 비가 오면 그 경기는 취소될 것이다.

가정법 미래는 가능성이 낮은 미래의 일을 표현할 때 쓰며, '혹시라도 ~하면 …할 것이다'라고 해석합니다.
이 구문은 주로 if를 생략하고 〈Should + 주어 + 동사 ~〉의 형태로 자주 사용됩니다.
(ex. Should it rain tomorrow, the game will be canceled.)

If + 주어 + should + 동사원형 ~, 주어 + will/can/may + 동사원형 ~

If you **should need** to cancel your reservation, we **will refund** half of your deposit.
= Should you need to cancel your reservation
혹시라도 예약을 취소해야 한다면 보증금 절반을 환불해 드릴 겁니다.

고난도 JUMP UP

가정법 미래의 주절은 〈조동사 현재형 + 동사원형〉 대신 동사원형으로 시작하는 명령문이나 **please**로 시작하는 청유문으로도 쓸 수 있습니다.

If you **should need** any assistance, **please** let me know.
                                      청유문
혹시라도 도움이 필요하다면 제게 알려 주세요.

연습문제

정답 및 해설 p.137

1. If Mr. Simmons ------- have any questions, you can tell him to call me.
   (A) would
   (B) should
   (C) will
   (D) could

2. If the train should arrive late, Ms. Kerry ------- the person meeting her.
   (A) will inform
   (B) informs
   (C) have informed
   (D) would have informed

3. If company revenues should increase, all employees ------- a cash bonus.
   (A) receive
   (B) will be received
   (C) received
   (D) will receive

4. If the demonstration were successful, the marketing team ------- new advertisements.
   (A) would create
   (B) creates
   (C) has created
   (D) will create

4 if 생략

Should you have any questions, please let me know.
  = If you (should) have any questions
혹시라도 궁금한 점이 있으면 제게 말씀해 주세요.

가정법에서 if를 생략하면 조동사 또는 be동사가 문장 앞으로 도치됩니다.

❶ 가정법 미래

Should you cancel after that date, a fee will be charged.
  = If you (should) cancel after that date
그 날짜 이후로 취소하시게 되면 수수료가 청구될 것입니다.

❷ 가정법 과거

Were Ms. Nakamura in New York, she would attend the trade fair.
  = If Ms. Nakamura were in New York
나카무라 씨가 뉴욕에 있다면 무역 박람회에 참석할 텐데.

❸ 가정법 과거완료

Had she left early, she wouldn't have been late for the meeting.
  = If she had left early
그녀가 일찍 떠났다면 회의에 늦지 않았을 텐데.

연습문제

1. Had Fletcher explained the problem clearly, the repairman ------- the freezer quickly.
   (A) might fix
   (B) will fix
   (C) would have fixed
   (D) has fixed

2. ------- the results of the customer survey been sent earlier, we could have shown the CEO.
   (A) Except
   (B) Should
   (C) Had
   (D) Instead of

3. ------- your ID card fail to work properly, someone from maintenance will reset it.
   (A) Should
   (B) Had
   (C) What
   (D) Were

4. Were the applicants hired, the Sales Department ------- more than thirty employees.
   (A) would have
   (B) will have
   (C) having
   (D) have

빈출 유형 풀이 전략

1. 가정법 과거완료

STEP에 따라 실제 토익 문제를 푸는 순서와 요령을 익혀 보세요.

If the price of land -------, Mr. Williams would have considered selling his property.

(A) increases
(B) had increased
(C) increased
(D) be increased

STEP 1 선택지 구성 파악하기
선택지가 increase의 활용형으로 다양하게 구성된 것으로 보아 빈칸에 알맞은 increase의 형태를 묻는 문제.

If the price of land -------, Mr. Williams would have considered selling his property.

(A) increases
(B) had increased
(C) increased
(D) be increased

STEP 2 빈칸 주변에서 단서 찾기
주절이 〈주어 + would + have p.p.〉 구조이므로 가정법 과거완료 문장임을 알 수 있음.

If the price of land -------, Mr. Williams would have considered selling his property.

(A) increases
(B) had increased ✓
(C) increased
(D) be increased

STEP 3 정답 찾기
가정법 과거완료 문장의 if절 구조는 〈If + 주어 + had p.p.〉이므로 (B) had increased가 정답.

해석 땅값이 인상되었다면 윌리엄스 씨가 부동산을 파는 것을 고려했을 것이다.
어휘 price 값, 가격 land 땅, 토지 increase 증가하다, 인상되다 consider 고려하다 property 부동산, 소유지

2. if 생략

STEP에 따라 실제 토익 문제를 푸는 순서와 요령을 익혀 보세요.

Were Ms. Sanders available, she ------- the conference call with Parker Associates.

(A) participates in
(B) would participate in
(C) to participate in
(D) will have participated in

STEP 1 선택지 구성 파악하기

선택지가 participate의 활용형으로 다양하게 구성된 것으로 보아 빈칸에 알맞은 participate의 형태를 묻는 문제.

Were Ms. Sanders available, she ------- the conference call with Parker Associates.

(A) participates in
(B) would participate in
(C) to participate in
(D) will have participated in

STEP 2 빈칸 주변에서 단서 찾기

if절에서 Were가 앞에 위치한 것으로 보아 'If Ms. Sanders were available'에서 if가 생략되어 주어와 동사가 도치된 것임을 알 수 있음.

Were Ms. Sanders available, she ------- the conference call with Parker Associates.

(A) participates in
(B) ✓ would participate in
(C) to participate in
(D) will have participated in

STEP 3 정답 찾기

If절의 구조가 〈If + 주어 + 동사 과거형〉이면 가정법 과거 문장이므로 주절은 〈주어 + would/could/might + 동사원형〉으로 써야 함.
따라서 (B) would participate in이 정답.

 샌더스 씨가 시간이 있다면 파커 어소시에이츠와의 전화 회의에 참여할 것이다.

 available (만날) 시간이 있는, 바쁘지 않은   participate in ~에 참여하다   conference call 전화 회의

UNIT 14 가정법 233

VOCABULARY 빈출 부사 어휘 (3)

commonly 동 widely	흔히, 보통	occur **commonly** 흔히 발생하다 a **commonly** used device 흔히 사용되는 장치
proficiently	숙련되게, 능숙하게	speak English **proficiently** 영어를 능숙하게 하다 deal with the problem **proficiently** 그 문제를 능숙하게 처리하다
officially 동 publicly 공식적으로 formally 정식으로	공식적으로, 정식으로	announce **officially** 공식적으로 발표하다 launch the new model **officially** 새 모델을 정식으로 출시하다
curiously	호기심에; 이상하게	ask **curiously** 호기심에 물어보다 **curiously** quiet 이상하게 조용한
patiently	끈기 있게, 참을성 있게	**patiently** answer all the questions 모든 질문에 끈기 있게 답하다 wait **patiently** 참을성 있게 기다리다
electronically	전자식으로	withdraw funds **electronically** 자금을 전자식으로 인출하다 pay the bill **electronically** 청구서를 전자식으로 결제하다
sharply	(비판 등을) 날카롭게, 신랄하게; 급격히	be **sharply** criticized 날카롭게 비판을 받다 increase **sharply** 급격히 증가하다
equally	똑같이, 동일[동등]하게	be **equally** divided 똑같이 나뉘다 **equally** important 똑같이 중요한

연습문제

1 Heather Fashion waited ------- to unveil their limited edition series for this winter.

(A) patiently (B) severely
(C) equally (D) apparently

2 Once the new cosmetics went on sale, revenues at JT Bradford increased -------.

(A) proficiently (B) sharply
(C) reportedly (D) very

3 Milton Furniture will ------- open for business this coming Friday.

(A) commonly (B) practically
(C) officially (D) accidentally

4 Most messages between colleagues at Dillon, Inc. are sent -------.

(A) curiously (B) busily
(C) electronically (D) fairly

particularly ≒ especially	특히	a **particularly** dry winter 특히 건조한 겨울 not **particularly** interesting 특별히 흥미롭지는 않은	
successfully	성공적으로	**successfully** negotiate a deal 성공적으로 거래를 성사시키다 **successfully** complete the course 그 과정을 성공적으로 마치다	
tightly	단단히, 꽉; 엄격히	close the windows **tightly** 창문들을 꽉 닫다 be **tightly** controlled 엄격히 통제되다	
safely	안전하게, 무사히	drive **safely** 안전하게 운전하다 be **safely** stored 안전하게 보관되다	
normally ≒ usually	보통; 정상적으로	**normally** take an hour 보통은 한 시간이 걸리다 operate **normally** 정상적으로 작동되다	
locally	(특정 지역) 근방에서; 국지적으로	manufacture **locally** 지역[국내]에서 제조하다 **locally** produced goods 지역[국내]에서 생산된 상품	
wisely	현명하게	act **wisely** and quickly 현명하고 빠르게 행동하다 invest **wisely** 현명하게 투자하다	
purposely ≒ on purpose	고의로, 일부러	**purposely** avoid 일부러 피하다 **purposely** develop good relations 의도적으로 좋은 관계를 쌓다	

정답 및 해설 p.139

5 This program teaches clients how to invest ------- so as to avoid losing any money.

(A) wisely   (B) steadily
(C) tightly   (D) randomly

6 Eric Watson ------- organized his company's summer picnic for the third straight year.

(A) viciously   (B) purposely
(C) slightly   (D) successfully

7 While Ms. Klein ------- interviews job candidates, Mr. Popper handled them this week.

(A) normally   (B) peacefully
(C) safely   (D) unanimously

8 The keynote speech by Dr. Reaver was considered ------- influential by attendees.

(A) coherently (B) particularly
(C) prettily   (D) locally

ACTUAL TEST

1. If Mr. Gill had not attended the AI conference, he ------- not have gotten a chance to get funding.

   (A) can
   (B) would
   (C) must
   (D) will

2. Some manufacturing companies ------- locate their warehouses near their factories.

   (A) purposely
   (B) proficiently
   (C) variously
   (D) partially

3. ------- Ms. Baker not reviewed the hotel invoice closely, she might have been overcharged.

   (A) Have
   (B) Had
   (C) Has
   (D) Having

4. If Ms. Kenneth ------- for the job earlier, she could have been the new secretary.

   (A) had applied
   (B) applied
   (C) apply
   (D) should apply

5. If Eric ------- the material, he could have caught the mistakes.

   (A) reviewed
   (B) will review
   (C) had reviewed
   (D) have reviewed

6. Power Books will provide a 10% discount ------- you use the following coupon code.

   (A) neither
   (B) therefore
   (C) if
   (D) whereas

7. Mr. Parker ------- his project report if his supervisor requested he do so.

   (A) completes
   (B) will complete
   (C) would complete
   (D) has completed

8. Denton Industries prefers to acquire supplies ------- to support companies in Rockport.

   (A) locally
   (B) seriously
   (C) sharply
   (D) variably

Questions 9-12 refer to the following posting on a Web site.

Spring Flower Festival 》 Home 》 Forum Page

What a great festival!
by David Harper

This year's Cumberland Spring Flower Festival was the best ever. As the ------- (9.) of the event, I know exactly how well everything went. Things couldn't have been better. I'd especially like to thank all of our volunteers. If we hadn't gotten so many of them, the festival ------- (10.) so successful. Thanks to all of you for the help you provided. ------- (11.) . I was also impressed by the musical performers. I saw the performances ------- (12.) on Friday and the following day. The fans loved those shows almost as much as I did. I'd say it was an amazing festival overall.

9 (A) organizer
　　(B) performer
　　(C) speaker
　　(D) designer

10 (A) is not
　　(B) will not be
　　(C) has not been
　　(D) would not have been

11 (A) You'll be paid for your time soon.
　　(B) Schedules will be posted online.
　　(C) I hope you enjoyed yourselves, too.
　　(D) We've got a great show coming up.

12 (A) little
　　(B) each
　　(C) none
　　(D) both

어휘　forum 포럼, 공개 토론방　the best ever 역대 최고의 것　exactly 정확히　couldn't have been better 더할 나위 없이 좋았다　especially 특히　volunteer 자원봉사자　be impressed 깊은 인상을 받다　the following day 그 다음 날　amazing (놀랄 만큼) 훌륭한　overall 전체적으로

UNIT 15

관계사

1. 주격 관계대명사
2. 목적격 관계대명사
3. 소유격 관계대명사
4. 관계대명사 what
5. 관계부사: where, when
6. 관계부사: why, how

빈출 유형 풀이 전략
Vocabulary
Actual Test

TOEIC Grammar

약 15%

UNIT 15 관계사

관계사 문제는 매회 1문제 이상 꾸준히 출제됩니다. 빈칸 뒤에 이어지는 절을 보고 빈칸에 들어갈 말이 주격/목적격/소유격 관계대명사인지 아니면 관계부사인지 구별하는 문제가 자주 출제됩니다.

 스피드 진단 테스트

(A), (B) 중 알맞은 것을 고르세요.

1. Sue is replacing Chris ------- is retiring this month.

    (A) who   (B) whose

2. I know a store ------- you can buy in bulk.

    (A) which   (B) where

정답 및 해석

1. (A), 수는 이번 달에 은퇴하게 될 크리스 씨를 대신할 것이다.
2. (B), 저는 대량 구매가 가능한 상점을 알아요.

관계사란?

관계사는 반복을 피하기 위해 두 문장의 공통된 부분을 하나로 연결시키는 말로, 이때 관계사가 이끄는 절은 앞에 있는 명사(선행사)를 수식하는 형용사적 역할을 합니다.

> John is a journalist. + He won the Journalist of the Year Award. 존은 기자이다. 그는 올해의 기자상을 받았다.
>
> John is a journalist who won the Journalist of the Year Award. 존은 올해의 기자상을 받은 기자이다.
> 선행사

● 관계대명사의 종류

관계대명사는 두 문장을 하나로 연결하는 접속사인 동시에 대명사 역할을 합니다. 관계대명사가 이끄는 절 안에서 어떤 역할을 하는지에 따라 주격, 목적격, 소유격으로 나눌 수 있습니다.

선행사 \ 격	주격	목적격	소유격
사람	who	who(m)	whose
사물, 동물	which	which	whose / of which
사람, 사물, 동물	that	that	-

● 관계부사

관계부사는 두 문장을 하나로 연결하는 접속사인 동시에 부사 역할을 합니다. 선행사에 따라 where, when, why, how를 씁니다.

선행사	관계부사
장소 (the place)	where
시간 (the time, the day)	when
이유 (the reason)	why
방법 (the way)	how

1 주격 관계대명사

She is a designer. + The designer worked for WeGraphics.

She is the designer **who** worked for WeGraphics.
　　　　　선행사　　　　　　　관계대명사절

그녀는 위그래픽스에서 일했던 디자이너이다.

주격 관계대명사가 쓰인 관계대명사절에는 주어가 없으며, 관계대명사가 꾸미는 선행사가 사람이면 who, 사물이면 which를 씁니다. who나 which 대신 that을 쓰기도 합니다.

All customers who make reservations today will receive a 10% discount.
　선행사　　　　　　관계대명사절

오늘 예약하는 모든 고객은 10% 할인을 받습니다.

The houses which overlook Victoria Street cost a lot.
　선행사　　　　　관계대명사절

빅토리아 거리가 내려다보이는 집들은 비싸다.

고난도 JUMP UP

주격 관계대명사만 단독으로 생략할 수는 없지만 〈주격 관계대명사 + be동사〉는 생략할 수 있습니다.

The computer (which is) used for graphic design is so slow.
　선행사　　　　　　관계대명사절

그래픽 디자인용으로 사용되는 그 컴퓨터는 무척 느리다.

연습문제

정답 및 해설 p.144

1 R&D staff members ------- can work next weekend should contact Ms. Gordon immediately.

(A) what　　　(B) which
(C) who　　　(D) they

2 Mr. Collins takes the train ------- departs from Central Station at 7:00 A.M.

(A) which　　　(B) who
(C) it　　　(D) but

3 Owning an apartment ------- is located downtown is important to Mr. Wendell.

(A) what　　　(B) this
(C) who　　　(D) that

4 A free T-shirt is available to anybody who ------- at Carter Park next weekend.

(A) volunteer　　　(B) volunteering
(C) volunteers　　　(D) volunteered

2 목적격 관계대명사

She is a designer. + Mr. Kim recommended the designer.

She is the designer **who(m)** Mr. Kim recommended.
선행사   관계대명사절

그녀는 **김 씨가 추천한 디자이너**이다.

목적격 관계대명사가 쓰이는 관계대명사절에는 목적어가 없으며, 관계대명사가 꾸며 주는 선행사가 사람이면 who(m), 사물이면 which를 씁니다. who(m)나 which 대신 that을 쓰기도 합니다.

The woman **whom** I met at the fair works in the sales department.
선행사   관계대명사절

내가 박람회에서 만난 그 여자는 영업부에서 일한다.

The supermarket offers a delivery service **which** customers can use for free.
                      선행사   관계대명사절

그 슈퍼마켓은 **고객들이 무료로 이용할 수 있는 배달 서비스**를 제공한다.

🔼 고난도 JUMP UP

목적격 관계대명사는 생략할 수 있습니다.

The bookstore didn't have the book (which) I was looking for. 그 서점에는 내가 찾는 책이 없었다.
                선행사   관계대명사절

연습문제   정답 및 해설 p.145

1 Mr. Erikson recovered one of the suitcases ------- he had lost at the airport.

   (A) it   (B) that
   (C) who   (D) whom

2 The doubtful customers were pleased to know that the appliances ------- purchased work properly.

   (A) that   (B) which
   (C) they   (D) themselves

3 Mr. Montpelier contacted the woman ------- he wanted to offer a marketing position to.

   (A) herself   (B) which
   (C) what   (D) whom

4 Please review the employee evaluation ------- I have attached to this message.

   (A) whom   (B) how
   (C) that   (D) who

UNIT 15 관계사 243

3 소유격 관계대명사

She is a designer. + The designer's specialty is typography.

She is the designer **whose** specialty is typography.
선행사   관계대명사절

그녀는 **특기가 타이포그래피인** 디자이너이다.

소유격 관계대명사 whose는 바로 뒤에 소유격이나 관사 없이 명사가 이어지고, 선행사가 사람이거나 사물일 때 씁니다. 소유격 관계대명사는 that으로 바꿔 쓰거나 생략할 수 없습니다.

┌─── The novel's author ───┐
The novel, whose author won a Pulitzer Prize, has become a bestseller.
선행사 (사물)   관계대명사절

저자가 퓰리처상을 수상한 그 소설은 베스트셀러가 되었다.

┌─── Mr. Hofsteader's presentation ───┐
Ms. Denver mentioned Mr. Hofsteader whose presentation was remarkable.
              선행사 (사람)   관계대명사절

덴버 씨는 **발표가 인상적이었던** 호프스테더 씨를 언급했다.

┌─── Jump&High Sportswear's popularity ───┐
Jump&High Sportswear, whose popularity is widespread among athletes, will launch a line of
     선행사 (기업)   관계대명사절
children's clothes soon.

선수들 사이에서 인기 있는 점프앤하이 스포츠웨어는 곧 아동복을 출시할 것이다.

연습문제   정답 및 해설 p.146

1 The curator will meet the donors ------- financial support keeps the museum operating.

  (A) whose   (B) what
  (C) which   (D) why

2 After lunch, Beth Armstrong will demonstrate the new product ------- computing capabilities are impressive.

  (A) which   (B) who
  (C) whom   (D) whose

3 The award was given to the contestant whose ------- was loved by the audience.

  (A) perform   (B) the performance
  (C) performance   (D) performers

4 All owners ------- property must be inspected should contact the relevant government agency.

  (A) which   (B) whose
  (C) who   (D) that

244

4 관계대명사 what

> 관계대명사절
> **What** we need to do is to improve the internship program.
> = The thing which
> 우리가 해야 할 것은 그 인턴십 프로그램을 개선하는 것입니다.

관계대명사 what은 '~ 것'이라고 해석하며 the thing(s) which로 바꿔 쓸 수 있습니다. 여기서 알 수 있듯 관계대명사 what은 the thing(s)라는 선행사를 이미 포함하고 있기 때문에 what 앞에는 선행사가 위치할 수 없습니다.

❶ 주어 자리

What makes this product special is its unique color. 이 제품을 특별하게 만드는 것은 독특한 색깔이다.
주어 역할을 하는 관계대명사절 → 관계대명사 what 주어는 단수 취급하므로 단수 동사를 씁니다.

❷ 보어 자리

This is not what I ordered. 이것은 제가 주문한 것이 아닙니다.
주어 주격 보어 역할을 하는 관계대명사절

❸ 목적어 자리

By using this research tool, you'll learn what customers want.
learn의 목적어 역할을 하는 관계대명사절
이 조사 도구를 사용하면 **고객들이 원하는** 것을 알게 될 것입니다.

From what she said, I thought she was new.
전치사 from의 목적어 역할을 하는 관계대명사절
그녀가 말하는 것을 듣고 나는 그녀가 신입이라고 생각했어요.

연습문제 정답 및 해설 p.147

1 Ms. Stallings read the product reviews ------- included complaints and attempted to solve the problems.

(A) who   (B) whose
(C) what   (D) which

2 ------- impressed the overseas clients the most was Mr. Reardon's attention to detail.

(A) Who   (B) What
(C) This   (D) These

3 The supervisor decided to ask about ------- Mr. Leonard wanted for his next assignment.

(A) whom   (B) that
(C) what   (D) when

4 The user manual for the order processing system is ------- Mr. Hand requested last week.

(A) it   (B) that
(C) whose   (D) what

5 관계부사: where, when

The apartment is old. + Jake lives in the apartment.

The apartment [**where** Jake lives] is old.
　　　　　　　= in which

제이크가 살고 있는 아파트는 오래되었다.

관계부사는 선행사가 장소면 where, 시간이면 when으로 나타내고, 관계부사 뒤에는 완전한 절이 이어집니다. 관계부사 when과 where는 〈전치사 + which〉와 바꿔 쓸 수 있는데, 선행사에 따라 전치사가 달라질 수 있습니다.

❶ 관계부사 where

My office is close to the area **where** the apartment is located.
　　　　　　　　　　　　선행사　　관계부사 (= in which)
제 사무실은 그 아파트가 위치해 있는 지역에 가깝습니다.

The hotel [**where** we will be staying] is not far from the museum.
　선행사　관계부사 (= at which)
우리가 묵을 호텔은 그 박물관에서 멀지 않아요.

❷ 관계부사 when

Monday is the day **when** a weekly meeting takes place. 월요일은 주간 회의가 열리는 날이다.
　　　　　선행사　관계부사 (= on which)

They weathered a difficult time **when** they suffered major financial loss.
　　　　　　　선행사　　　관계부사 (= at which)
그들은 상당한 재정적 손실을 겪는 힘든 시기를 잘 헤쳐 나갔다.

연습문제　　　　　　　　　　　　　　　　　　　　　정답 및 해설 p.148

1 The weekend is the time ------- the amusement park has the most visitors.

(A) where　　(B) what
(C) why　　　(D) when

2 The basement laboratory is the place ------- most cutting-edge research is done.

(A) how　　(B) which
(C) where　(D) when

3 Dr. Sandoval will announce the names of the nurses ------- are working the night shift.

(A) who　　(B) which
(C) where　(D) when

4 Mr. Filmore will receive a box in ------- product samples have been packed.

(A) when　　(B) where
(C) which　　(D) what

6 관계부사: why, how

This is the reason. + We decided to move for that reason.

This is the reason [**why** we decided to move].
　　　　선행사　　　관계부사 (= for which)

이것이 **우리가 이사를 결심한 이유**이다.

관계부사는 선행사가 이유면 why, 방법이면 how로 나타냅니다. 관계부사 why의 선행사인 the reason은 생략할 수 있습니다. 하지만 관계부사 how는 선행사 the way와 함께 쓸 수 없습니다.

❶ 관계부사 why

Mr. Grant explained to his manager the reason **why** he was late.
　　　　　　　　　　　　　　　　　　　선행사　　관계부사 (= for which)

그랜트 씨는 부장에게 **자신이 늦은 이유**를 설명했다.

I'd like to know the reason **why** we need such a big budget for this project.
　　　　　　　　선행사　　관계부사 (= for which)

이 프로젝트에 **그렇게 많은 예산이 필요한 이유**를 알고 싶습니다.

❷ 관계부사 how

We will change **how** we support our staff. 우리는 **우리의 직원을 지원하는 방식**을 바꿀 것입니다.
　　　　　　　　관계부사

We will change the way we support our staff.
　　　　　　　선행사　↳ 관계부사 how 생략

연습문제　　　　　　　　　　　　　　　　　　　　　정답 및 해설 p.149

1 Mr. Bonaventure is planning ------- he can expand his textile business.

(A) how　　　　(B) that
(C) which　　　(D) why

2 Dylan West explained the reason for ------- he wanted to transfer to the Madrid office.

(A) which　　　(B) where
(C) how　　　　(D) why

3 ------- can cause a delay for a flight is a mechanical problem.

(A) Which　　　(B) How
(C) Why　　　　(D) What

4 The mayor wants to understand ------- the money in the budget will be spent.

(A) whose　　　(B) what
(C) how　　　　(D) whom

빈출 유형 풀이 전략

1. 관계대명사

STEP에 따라 실제 토익 문제를 푸는 순서와 요령을 익혀 보세요.

Ms. Ashburn found an agent ------- contacts in the publishing industry were exceptional.

(A) whose
(B) which
(C) whom
(D) what

STEP 1 선택지 구성 파악하기
선택지가 모두 관계대명사로 구성되어 있음.

Ms. Ashburn found an agent ------- contacts in the publishing industry were exceptional.

(A) whose
(B) which
(C) whom
(D) what

STEP 2 빈칸 주변에서 단서 찾기
빈칸 뒤에 〈주어(contacts ~ industry) + 동사(were) + 주격 보어(exceptional)〉 구조로 완전한 문장이 있음.
빈칸 뒤 주어 contacts에 관사가 없음.

Ms. Ashburn found an agent ------- contacts in the publishing industry were exceptional.

(A) ✓ whose
(B) which
(C) whom
(D) what

STEP 3 정답 찾기
빈칸 앞 명사 an agent와 빈칸 뒤 명사 contacts가 an agent's contacts로 소유 관계 성립.
따라서 빈칸은 소유격 관계대명사 자리이므로 (A) whose가 정답.

 해석 애쉬번 씨는 출판업계에 특별한 연줄이 있는 중개인을 찾았다.

어휘 agent 대리인, 중개인 contact 연고, 연줄 publishing 출판(업) industry 산업, 업계 exceptional 예외적인, 특별한

2. 관계부사

STEP에 따라 실제 토익 문제를 푸는 순서와 요령을 익혀 보세요.

Mr. Ortego will meet Ms. Simon at the airport exit ------- pickups are allowed.

(A) which
(B) where
(C) how
(D) what

STEP 1 선택지 구성 파악하기

선택지에 관계대명사와 관계부사가 섞여 있음.

Mr. Ortego will meet Ms. Simon at the airport exit ------- pickups are allowed.

(A) which
(B) where
(C) how
(D) what

STEP 2 빈칸 주변에서 단서 찾기

빈칸 앞에 선행사 the airport exit가 있고 뒤에는 〈주어(pickups) + 동사구(are allowed)〉 구조로 완전한 문장이 있음.
따라서 관계부사인 (B) where와 (C) how가 정답 후보.

Mr. Ortego will meet Ms. Simon at the airport exit ------- pickups are allowed.

(A) which
(B) where ✓
(C) how
(D) what

STEP 3 정답 찾기

선행사(the airport exit)가 장소를 나타내므로 (B) where가 정답.

해석 오르테고 씨는 픽업이 허용되는 공항 출구에서 사이먼 씨를 만날 것이다.
어휘 airport 공항 exit 출구 pickup 픽업 (사람을 차에 태움) allow 허용하다, 허락하다

VOCABULARY 빈출 부사 어휘 (4)

significantly 상당히		rise **significantly** 상당히 증가하다 **significantly** lower price 상당히 낮은 가격
mutually 서로, 상호 간에		**mutually** beneficial relationship 서로 득이 되는 관계 a **mutually** convenient time 서로에게 편한 시간
currently 현재, 지금 동 now		**currently** available products 현재 이용 가능한 제품들 be **currently** working as a designer 현재 디자이너로 일하고 있다
promptly 지체 없이; 정확히 제시간에 동 immediately 즉시		get it started **promptly** 그것을 즉시 시작하다 arrive **promptly** 제시간에 도착하다
consistently 지속적으로, 꾸준히		maintain **consistently** high grades 꾸준히 높은 성적을 유지하다 **consistently** provide high-quality work 꾸준히 양질의 작업물을 제공하다
accurately 정확하게, 정밀하게		**accurately** reflect popular opinion 여론을 정확하게 반영하다 **accurately** identify customer needs 고객 니즈를 정확하게 파악하다
strictly 엄격하게		be **strictly** regulated 엄격하게 규제받다 **strictly** speaking 엄밀히 말하면
increasingly 점점, 더욱 더 동 more and more		**increasingly** popular 점점 인기를 끄는 **increasingly** competitive job markets 점점 경쟁이 심해지는 고용 시장

연습문제

1 Many electronic exports related to computing are ------- regulated by the government.
 (A) strictly (B) arguably
 (C) mutually (D) brightly

2 All staff members ------- on business trips are exempt from the budget committee meeting.
 (A) consistently (B) instantly
 (C) fairly (D) currently

3 The keynote speech is scheduled to begin ------- at 9:15 A.M.
 (A) cautiously (B) promptly
 (C) seriously (D) accurately

4 The CEO expects this quarter's profits to improve ------- thanks to the booming economy.
 (A) significantly (B) increasingly
 (C) reportedly (D) approvingly

urgently	급히, 긴급히	**urgently** schedule a meeting 급하게 회의 일정을 잡다 **urgently** take measures 급하게 대책을 마련하다
widely	널리, 폭넓게; 대단히, 크게	**widely** advertise the event 그 행사를 널리 알리다 be **widely** reported in the newspaper 신문에 크게 보도되다
closely ⑧ very carefully	면밀히; 밀접하게	examine the proposals **closely** 그 제안들을 면밀히 검토하다 work **closely** with the technicians 기술자들과 긴밀하게 작업하다
highly ⑧ very	매우, 많이	**highly** proficient with the software 그 소프트웨어에 매우 능숙한 the most **highly**-paid professions 가장 소득이 높은 직종들
evenly	공평하게; 고르게, 골고루	**evenly** distributed 공평하게 분배된 apply the paint **evenly** 페인트를 골고루 바르다
moderately ⑧ reasonably	적당히, 알맞게	**moderately** priced 적당한 가격의 a **moderately** successful businessman 나름대로 성공한 사업가
definitely ⑧ certainly	분명히, 확실히	be **definitely** decided 확실히 결정되다 **definitely** worth a visit 확실히 방문할 가치가 있는
temporarily	일시적으로, 임시로	**temporarily** unavailable 일시적으로 이용할 수 없는 close **temporarily** for maintenance work 정비 작업을 위해 임시로 닫다

정답 및 해설 p.150

5 The lawyer read the contract ------- to ensure there were no problems.

(A) naturally (B) closely
(C) jointly (D) moderately

6 The ------- anticipated release of the software was a success for Data Pro.

(A) purposely (B) definitely
(C) apparently (D) highly

7 The parking lot on Waverly Street was ------- closed during the holiday.

(A) sincerely (B) temporarily
(C) importantly (D) evenly

8 Ms. Dillon is ------- respected as an expert in the field of civil engineering.

(A) widely (B) effectively
(C) urgently (D) daily

ACTUAL TEST

1. Mr. Montrose shops at a grocery store that ------- delicacies from Europe.
   (A) import
   (B) to import
   (C) importing
   (D) imports

2. Ms. Ball booked a room at the hotel ------- she had previously stayed.
   (A) where
   (B) who
   (C) when
   (D) what

3. Mr. Truss takes graduate classes in the city in which ------- lives.
   (A) himself
   (B) his
   (C) he
   (D) him

4. Jasmine Polymers has ------- beneficial contracts with several suppliers.
   (A) mutually
   (B) temporarily
   (C) hopefully
   (D) virtually

5. Individuals ------- plan to travel abroad must make sure their passports are valid for the duration of their trip.
   (A) how
   (B) whose
   (C) whom
   (D) who

6. All timesheets, ------- are available in Mr. Green's office, should be submitted to Carol Roth.
   (A) whose
   (B) they
   (C) these
   (D) which

7. The Galley is a restaurant ------- diners enjoy top-flight service and food.
   (A) for whom
   (B) which
   (C) what
   (D) at which

8. We are preparing for the conference ------- many local businesspeople are planning to attend.
   (A) which
   (B) who
   (C) whose
   (D) what

어휘 delicacy 진미, 별미   previously 이전에, 그에 앞서   graduate class 대학원 수업   beneficial 유익한, 유리한   contract 계약, 협약   supplier 공급자, 공급업체   individual 개인   make sure 확인하다, 확실히 하다   valid (법적으로) 유효한   top-flight 최고의, 일류의   prepare for ~을 준비하다, ~에 대비하다

Questions 9-12 refer to the following company newsletter.

Cynthia Watts, our vice president, has just published the book *Be Yourself at Work*. Ms. Watts mentioned that she decided to write it because she saw too many workers hiding their real selves from their colleagues. "I sometimes pretended to be someone I wasn't. But I realized that I needed to show my actual ---9.--- all the time," said Ms. Watts. The book provides information that ---10.--- by people to improve their relationships at work. They can also find tips on how to become better workers. ---11.--- .

Next week, all Bertrom employees will be given signed copies of the book, courtesy of Ms. Watts. She hopes everyone ---12.--- the confidence to be themselves after reading this book.

9 (A) performance
   (B) standard
   (C) personality
   (D) opportunity

10 (A) it was using
   (B) will use
   (C) were used
   (D) can be used

11 (A) There is something for everyone inside this book.
   (B) Ms. Watts has worked here for ten years.
   (C) A book signing was held last weekend.
   (D) The book's cover was designed by a Bertrom employee.

12 (A) finds
   (B) writes
   (C) receives
   (D) appears

어휘 vice president 부사장 publish 출판하다 be oneself 자연스럽게 행동하다 at work 직장에서, 근무 중 mention 언급하다, (간단히) 말하다 real self 실제 자기, 본모습 actual 실제의 all the time 언제나, 항상 signed copy 사인본, 서명본 courtesy of (무료로) ~가 제공한

UNIT
16

비교 구문

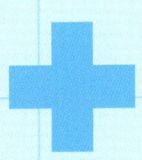

1. 원급 비교
2. 비교급 비교
3. 최상급 비교
4. 비교급과 최상급 강조

빈출 유형 풀이 전략
Vocabulary
Actual Test

TOEIC Grammar

약 5%

UNIT 16 비교 구문

비교 구문 문제는 2회에 1문제 정도 출제됩니다. 원급과 비교급, 그리고 최상급의 형태와 구조를 정확히 이해해야 하고, 비교급과 최상급 강조 표현도 종종 출제되니 꼭 알아 두어야 합니다.

 스피드 진단 테스트

(A), (B) 중 알맞은 것을 고르세요.

1. This new laptop is ------- than the old one.

    (A) lighter   (B) lightest

2. It is one of the ------- buildings in New York.

    (A) taller   (B) tallest

정답 및 해석

1. (A), 이 새 노트북은 예전 것보다 더 가볍다.
2. (B), 그것은 뉴욕에서 가장 높은 건물 중 하나이다.

💡 비교 구문이란?

비교란 형용사나 부사에 -er, -est를 붙이거나 more, most를 덧붙여 성질이나 상태, 수량의 정도를 서로 비교하는 것을 말합니다.

One World Trade Center is the tallest building in New York.
원월드 무역 센터는 뉴욕에서 가장 높은 빌딩이다.

The Empire State Building is smaller than Central Park Tower.
엠파이어 스테이트 빌딩은 센트럴 파크 타워보다 작다.

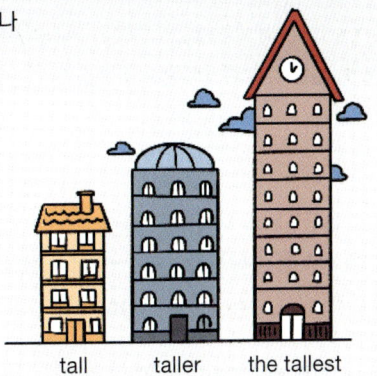

tall   taller   the tallest

● 비교급과 최상급의 형태

형용사나 부사를 비교급이나 최상급 형태로 쓸 때는 아래와 같이 몇 가지 규칙에 따라 써야 합니다.

	원급	비교급	최상급
1음절 단어	fast large	faster larger	the fastest the largest
2음절 이상 단어	difficult	more difficult less difficult	the most difficult the least difficult
불규칙 변화	good / well bad / ill many / much little	better worse more less	best worst most least

● 비교 구문의 종류

원급 비교는 비교하는 두 대상이 동등할 때, 비교급 비교는 두 비교 대상의 우열을 가릴 때 씁니다. 최상급 비교는 셋 이상의 비교 대상 중 하나가 가장 두드러질 때 씁니다.

원급 비교 (as 원급 as)	비교급 비교 (비교급 + than)	최상급 비교 (the + 최상급)
as fast as ~만큼 빠른 as difficult as ~만큼 어려운 as importantly as ~만큼 중요하게	faster than ~보다 빠른 more difficult than ~보다 어려운 less importantly than ~보다 덜 중요하게	the fastest 가장 빠른 the most difficult 가장 어려운 the least importantly 가장 중요하지 않게

1 원급 비교

Service is **as** important **as** product.
서비스는 제품**만큼** 중요하다.

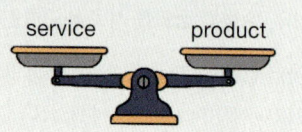

❶ as 형용사/부사 as: ~만큼 …한/하게

as ~ as 사이에 오는 말이 주격 보어 역할을 하면 형용사를 쓰고, 동사를 수식하면 부사를 씁니다.

The company's latest audio speaker is **as** thin **as** a book. 그 회사의 최신 스피커는 책**만큼** 얇다.
(주어) (주격 보어)

Media industry grew **as** quickly **as** sports industry. 미디어 산업은 스포츠 산업**만큼** 빠르게 성장했다.

❷ as + many/much (복수 명사/셀 수 없는 명사) + as: ~만큼 많이, 많게는; ~만큼 많은

Pick **as** many **as** you want out of the options listed below.
아래 나열된 옵션들 중에서 원하는 **만큼 많이** 고르세요.

Some audience members paid **as** much **as** $500 a ticket.
몇몇 관객은 티켓 한 장에 **많게는** 500달러를 지불했다.

⬆ 고난도 JUMP UP

배수 + as much as: ~보다 … 배 많은

This year's revenues are **twice as much as** last year's.
올해 수익은 작년**보다 두 배 많다**.

연습문제

정답 및 해설 p.155

1. People traveling on unpaved roads should drive as ------- as possible.

    (A) cautious (B) cautiously
    (C) caution (D) cautioning

2. Some items at retail stores cost twice as ------- as those sold online.

    (A) much (B) often
    (C) still (D) quite

3. The hiring committee believes Mr. Roberts's qualifications are ------- those of Tina Johnson.

    (A) impressively
    (B) as impressive as
    (C) more impressive
    (D) the most impressive

4. Trains can travel to Baltimore from New York as ------- as cars or buses.

    (A) swift (B) swifter
    (C) swiftly (D) swiftness

2 비교급 비교

Service is **more** important **than** product.
서비스는 제품**보다** **중요하다**.

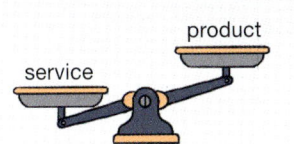

❶ 형용사/부사의 비교급 + than

This year's unemployment rate was lower than last year's. 올해 실업률은 작년보다 더 낮았다.
　　　　　　　　　　　　　　　　　　형용사 low의 비교급

The new copy machine works better than the old one. 새 복사기는 예전 것보다 더 잘 작동한다.
　　　　　　　　　　　　　부사 well의 비교급

❷ more/less + 형용사/부사 + than

Home cooking is more economical than dining out. 집밥이 외식보다 더 경제적이다.
　주어　　　　　　주격 보어 (형용사)

During the festival, the bus operates less frequently than the subway.
축제 동안에는 버스가 지하철**보다** **덜** **자주** 운행된다.

⬆ 고난도 JUMP UP

The + 비교급, the + 비교급: ~하면 할수록 더 …하다

The higher the price is, the less people want the product.
가격이 **높으면 높을수록** 사람들은 그 제품을 **덜** 원한다.

연습문제
정답 및 해설 p.156

1 Heath Catering claims that their revised menus are ------- than the previous menus.

(A) healthy　　(B) healthily
(C) healthier　(D) healthiest

2 Repeated surveys prove that regular customers make purchasing decisions ------- than new ones.

(A) fastest　(B) fast
(C) faster　(D) the fastest

3 The chief reporter at the magazine is more ------- than any of the reporters.

(A) response　　(B) responses
(C) responsible　(D) responsively

4 At Robinson's, cashiers say that the upgraded system makes assisting customers ------- than ever before.

(A) so convenient　(B) as convenient
(C) more convenient　(D) convenient

3 최상급 비교

Service quality is **the most** important factor affecting customer satisfaction.
　　　　　　　　　　the most + 형용사

서비스의 질이 고객 만족에 영향을 미치는 **가장 중요한** 요소다.

❶ the + 형용사/부사의 최상급

We are striving to offer the highest quality coffee.
　　　　　　　　　　　high의 최상급

우리는 **가장 높은** 품질의 커피를 제공하기 위해 전력을 다하고 있습니다.

❷ the most/least + 형용사/부사

Among the automotive rivals, Automoco Inc. is the most fully stocked.
　　　　　　　　　　　　　　　　　　　　　　　　the most + 부사

자동차 라이벌 회사들 중에서 오토모코 사가 **가장 충분하게** 재고가 비축되어 있다.

Mr. Hansen is the least experienced candidate of the interviewees.
　　　　　　　　the least + 형용사

핸슨 씨는 면접자들 중에서 **가장 경력이 적은** 지원자이다.

⬆ 고난도 JUMP UP

one of the 최상급 + 복수 명사: 가장 ~한 것들 중 하나

It is one of the most attractive cities in the world.
그곳은 세계에서 **가장 매력적인 도시 중 한 곳**이다.

연습문제　　　　　　　　　　　　　　　　　정답 및 해설 p.157

1　Dietrich Pro has many fun games, and the ------- one is called Dynamo.

　　(A) most popular　　(B) more popular
　　(C) popularly　　　 (D) popularity

2　The most ------- salesman in PJ Electronics is Jacob Mercer.

　　(A) successful　　(B) successfully
　　(C) success　　　(D) successes

3　Of the offices in Garner Towers, the basement units are the ------- to rent.

　　(A) more cheaply　(B) cheapest
　　(C) most cheaply　(D) cheaper

4　Griswold, Inc., one of the region's ------- manufacturers, will be constructing three new factories.

　　(A) stead　　　(B) more steadily
　　(C) steadily　 (D) steadiest

4 비교급과 최상급 강조

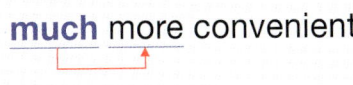

훨씬 더 편리한

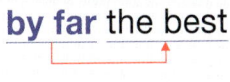

단연코 가장 좋은

❶ **비교급 강조 부사:** much, even, still, far, a lot (훨씬 더 ~한)

The honeycomb packaging design is much more cost-effective than pulp packaging.

벌집 모양 포장지 디자인은 펄프 포장지보다 **훨씬 더** 비용 효율이 좋다.

The demand for drive-through is far higher than eat-in customers in the country.

그 나라에서 드라이브스루 수요는 매장 손님보다 **훨씬 더 높다**.

❷ **최상급 강조 부사:** by far, much, very, quite, even (단연 가장 ~한)

최상급 강조 부사는 보통 〈최상급 강조 부사 + the + 최상급〉 구조로 씁니다.

The CEO of Technics Co. is by far the most influential figure.

테크닉스 사의 최고 경영자는 **단연코 가장 영향력 있는** 인물이다.

단, very는 〈the + very + 최상급〉 구조로 씁니다.

Please visit our Web site for the very latest news and updates.

가장 최신 뉴스와 정보를 보시려면 우리의 웹사이트를 방문해 주세요.

연습문제

정답 및 해설 p.158

1 The factory manager noticed Kevin Thomas was ------- more productive than other employees.

   (A) very   (B) quite
   (C) much   (D) by far

2 The entry submitted by Sabrina Duncan was ------- the most outstanding one.

   (A) less   (B) very
   (C) by far   (D) a lot

3 Mr. Kay's speech was a lot ------- than the keynote speech at the conference.

   (A) impressive
   (B) impressively
   (C) more impressive
   (D) most impressively

4 Imported foreign items are much ------- expensive than domestic goods these days.

   (A) more   (B) far
   (C) many   (D) most

빈출 유형 풀이 전략

1. 비교급 vs. 최상급

STEP에 따라 실제 토익 문제를 푸는 순서와 요령을 익혀 보세요.

Dr. Roth provides the ------- essays for readers on his personal Web site.

(A) as insight as
(B) more insightfully
(C) most insightful
(D) insightfully

STEP 1 선택지 구성 파악하기
선택지가 insight의 활용형으로 다양하게 구성된 것으로 보아 빈칸에 알맞은 insight의 형태를 묻는 문제.

Dr. Roth provides the ------- essays for readers on his personal Web site.

(A) as insight as
(B) more insightfully
(C) most insightful
(D) insightfully

STEP 2 빈칸 주변에서 단서 찾기
빈칸 앞에 정관사 the가 있고 뒤에는 명사 essays가 있으므로 빈칸은 명사를 수식하는 형용사 자리.

Dr. Roth provides the ------- essays for readers on his personal Web site.

(A) as insight as
(B) more insightfully
(C) ✓ most insightful
(D) insightfully

STEP 3 정답 찾기
정관사 the와 어울려 최상급을 나타내는 (C) most insightful이 정답.

해석 로스 박사는 개인 웹사이트에 독자들을 위해 가장 통찰력 있는 글들을 제공한다.
어휘 provide 제공하다   insightful 통찰력 있는   personal 개인의, 개인적인

2. 비교급과 최상급 강조

STEP에 따라 실제 토익 문제를 푸는 순서와 요령을 익혀 보세요.

When customers add several options, the car's price becomes ------- higher than the original price.

(A) more
(B) such
(C) this
(D) much

STEP 1 선택지 구성 파악하기

선택지가 다양한 품사로 구성되어 있으므로 빈칸에 알맞은 품사를 고르는 문제.

When customers add several options, the car's price becomes ------- higher than the original price.

(A) more
(B) such
(C) this
(D) much

STEP 2 빈칸 주변에서 단서 찾기

빈칸 앞에 동사 becomes가 있고 뒤에는 비교급 higher than이 있으므로 빈칸은 비교급을 수식하는 부사 자리.

When customers add several options, the car's price becomes ------- higher than the original price.

(A) more
(B) such
(C) this
(D) much ✓

STEP 3 정답 찾기

비교급을 수식할 수 있는 부사인 (D) much가 정답.

해석 고객이 몇 가지 옵션을 추가하면 자동차 가격은 원래 가격보다 훨씬 더 높아진다.

어휘 add 추가하다; 합하다   option 선택(권)   original 원래의

VOCABULARY 빈출 형용사 어휘 (4)

superior 반 inferior 하위의, 낮은	우수한, 우월한	vastly **superior** 훨씬 우수한 **superior** to previous models 예전 모델들보다 더 우수한
accessible	접근[이용] 가능한; 이해하기 쉬운	not **accessible** to the public 일반인은 접근할 수 없는 a very **accessible** account 매우 이해하기 쉬운 설명
joint	공동의, 합동의	a **joint** effort 공동의 노력 finish in **joint** first place 공동 1위를 하다
constructive	건설적인	**constructive** advice 건설적인 충고 play a **constructive** role 건설적인 역할을 하다
affordable	(가격 등이) 알맞은	at **affordable** prices 알맞은 가격에 **affordable** overseas destinations 저렴한 해외 여행지들
meaningful	의미 있는, 중요한	a **meaningful** experience 의미 있는 경험 in a **meaningful** way 의미 있는 방식으로
typical	전형적인, 대표적인; 보통의	a **typical** example 전형적인 예 a **typical** week 평범한 한 주
adequate 동 sufficient	충분한, 적절한	give an **adequate** answer 충분한 답변을 하다 make **adequate** provisions 적절한 준비[대비]를 하다

연습문제

1 Thomas Carter's ------- people skills make him an ideal salesperson.

(A) surrounding (B) superior
(C) eventual (D) accessible

2 The new lotion provides ------- protection from the sun's rays.

(A) cheerful (B) constructive
(C) instinctive (D) adequate

3 The ------- employee at J.T Bosworth has a graduate degree in engineering.

(A) joint (B) typical
(C) sufficient (D) confidential

4 Property in the suburban region of Milton is ------- to many young couples.

(A) meaningful (B) approved
(C) affordable (D) decisive

considerate ᭢ thoughtful	사려 깊은, (남을) 배려하는	polite and **considerate** 공손하고 사려 깊은 a kind and **considerate** host 친절하고 배려하는 진행자
dependent on	~에 좌우되는; ~에 의존[의지]하는	**dependent on** the weather 날씨에 좌우되는 **dependent on** online shopping 온라인 쇼핑에 의존하는
prompt ᭢ immediate	즉각적인	**prompt** payment 즉각적인 지불, 즉시 결제 call for **prompt** action 즉각적인 조치를 요하다
ambitious	야심 있는, 야심 찬	an **ambitious** plan 야심 찬 계획 an **ambitious** attempt 야심 찬 시도
durable ᭢ hard-wearing 내구성 있는, 튼튼한	내구성이 있는; 오래가는	a **durable** material 내구성 있는 물질 find a **durable** solution 장기적인 해결책을 찾다
prosperous ᭢ affluent	번창한, 부유한	increasingly **prosperous** 점점 번창하는 a more **prosperous** future 보다 풍요로운 미래
tentative ᭢ provisional	잠정적인	**tentative** conclusions 잠정적인 결론 take **tentative** steps 잠정적인 조치를 취하다
utmost	최고의, 최대한	**utmost** assistance 전폭적인 지원 make **utmost** efforts 최대한 노력하다

정답 및 해설 p.159

5 Martin Textiles remains ------- on the sales of cotton fibers for its profits.

(A) dependent (B) certain
(C) clear   (D) tentative

6 Completing the budget report on time is of ------- importance to Ms. Washington.

(A) considerate (B) efficient
(C) utmost   (D) partial

7 Mitch Stallings set the ------- goal of increasing revenues by 40% this year.

(A) ambitious (B) cooperative
(C) repealed   (D) prosperous

8 Customer service agents were taught to provide ------- responses to customer inquiries.

(A) severe   (B) prompt
(C) durable (D) impractical

ACTUAL TEST

1. If the sale takes place, DataQuest will acquire one of the ------- firms in the industry.
   (A) newer than
   (B) as new as
   (C) newly
   (D) newest

2. Being transferred abroad is less appealing to Mr. Argus ------- accepting a pay cut.
   (A) than
   (B) for
   (C) so
   (D) still

3. The survey shows that the new copier causes paper jams ------- than the previous one did.
   (A) frequent
   (B) frequently
   (C) more frequently
   (D) the most frequently

4. The two scientists made a ------- presentation about their cancer research.
   (A) commercial
   (B) durable
   (C) reported
   (D) joint

5. While ------- than expected, the Forest Ranger SUV from Damon Motors handles well.
   (A) heavy
   (B) heavier
   (C) heaviest
   (D) heavily

6. Employees at Chandler, Inc. are encouraged to provide ------- suggestions regarding workplace improvements.
   (A) level
   (B) prosperous
   (C) customary
   (D) meaningful

7. Since Mr. Halls is expecting a lot from this survey, we should analyze the data as ------- as possible.
   (A) accuracy
   (B) accurate
   (C) accurately
   (D) more accurate

8. While work experience is important, Ms. Cole says that personality is the ------- feature.
   (A) vitality
   (B) more vitally
   (C) vitally
   (D) most vital

어휘 take place 일어나다, 발생하다   transfer 옮기다, 이동하다   appeal to ~의 관심을 끌다   copier 복사기
make a presentation 발표하다   handle well (차량 등이) 잘 조향되다, 방향 컨트롤이 잘 되다   regarding ~에 관해
improvement 향상, 개선   work experience 경력   personality 인성, 성격   feature 특징, 특성

Questions 9-12 refer to the following article.

Big Change by Local Restaurant

RICHMOND—The Hilltop, a local restaurant, just announced it is making a big change. After receiving numerous ----9.---- from customers, the restaurant is finally introducing outdoor dining. The restaurant is currently in the process of adding a dining area behind the restaurant. There will be enough room for approximately ten tables. The purpose is to encourage diners to spend ----10.---- time indoors and to let them enjoy the warm spring and summer evenings in Richmond. The Hilltop will also be open later at night as long as the weather stays nice. ----11.---- . Other restaurants in the same region ----12.---- of adding their own outdoor dining areas in response.

9 (A) requests
   (B) orders
   (C) deliveries
   (D) reservations

10 (A) some
   (B) more
   (C) few
   (D) less

11 (A) Owner Tina Blair hopes customers will respond positively.
   (B) The Hilltop is one of the premier dining locations in the city.
   (C) Customers are already enjoying meals while sitting outdoors.
   (D) The menu at the Hilltop will be expanding soon.

12 (A) thinks
   (B) to think
   (C) are thinking
   (D) being thought

어휘 make a change 변화하다 numerous 많은 outdoor 야외의 currently 현재 in the process of ~의 과정에 있는, ~을 진행 중인 approximately 거의, 대략 as long as ~하는 한 in response 대응하여

PART 7

UNIT 17

문제 유형별 (1)

1. 주제/목적 문제
2. 세부 사항 문제
3. True/NOT 문제
4. 추론/암시 문제

Actual Test

Unit 17에서 다루는 문제들은 Part 7에서 가장 빈도가 높은 유형들입니다. **주제/목적을 묻는 문제**와 각 글의 자세한 내용을 바탕으로 정답을 찾는 **세부 사항을 묻는 문제**들은 지문의 종류에 상관없이 자주 출제됩니다. 그 외에 **글에 언급된 내용 및 언급되지 않은 것을 찾는 문제**와 특정 내용을 바탕으로 내포된 의미를 파악하는 **추론 문제**는 난이도가 높아 정답을 찾는 데 시간이 다소 소요되는 유형입니다.

1 주제/목적 문제

글을 읽을 때 글의 주제나 글을 쓴 목적은 반드시 파악해야 합니다. 주제나 목적에 관련된 단서는 글의 초반에 나타나는 경우가 많으나, 글의 전반에 걸쳐 나오거나 부탁의 경우 글의 후반부에 언급되기도 합니다.

● 문제 유형

What is the letter **mainly about**? 편지는 주로 무엇에 대한 것인가?
What is the **purpose** of the advertisement? 광고의 목적은 무엇인가?
Why was this e-mail **written**? 이 이메일이 작성된 이유는?

● 문제 풀이 전략

Q. What is the purpose of the e-mail?

STEP 1 문제 확인
문제에 목적(purpose)이 포함된 경우 글의 주제를 묻는 대표적인 문제입니다.

To: Management Team 〈managers@v-tech.com〉
From: Frank Klein 〈f_klein@v-tech.com〉
Date: December 2
Subject: Employee Evaluations

Dear Managers,

I would like to remind you that you must finish your employee evaluation forms by December 6. You should complete a separate form for each employee. Detailed notes about employees help us to improve our staff training events. The evaluation form can be downloaded from the company Web site. Please submit the completed evaluation forms to the HR department.

Sincerely,

Frank Klein
Human Resources Manager, V-Tech

STEP 2 지문에서 주제 관련 단서 찾기
글의 주제는 주로 글의 초반에 언급되는 경우가 많습니다. 첫 번째 문장의 I would like to remind you 이하에서 12월 6일까지 직원 평가서를 완료해야 한다고 알리고 있습니다.

(A) To introduce a new employee
(B) To adjust a schedule
(C) To emphasize a deadline
(D) To announce a training session

STEP 3 단서를 바탕으로 정답 찾기
단서 부분에서 12월 6일까지 끝내 달라고 했으므로 이를 deadline으로 표현한 선택지가 정답입니다.

해석 p.164

어휘 evaluation 평가   separate 분리된   detailed 자세한   submit 제출하다   adjust 조정하다   emphasize 강조하다

패러프레이징 다음을 읽고 지문을 가장 잘 패러프레이징한 것을 고르세요.

1 What is the e-mail mainly about?

> Dear Employees,
> The staff cafeteria will be closed for renovations from June 3. The upgrade to the facilities will take approximately three weeks.

(A) To notify employees of workplace improvements
(B) To promote meal options in a cafeteria

2 What is the purpose of the article?

> Cookex, Canada's leading kitchenware retailer, has opened its first store abroad in Milan, Italy. Cookex has built a reputation for style and quality.

(A) To seek job applicants in Milan
(B) To highlight an overseas expansion

미니 테스트

Question 1 refers to the following notice.

> Dear visitors,
>
> Here at the Aurora National Park, we do not allow dogs in certain areas, even if they are on a leash. We aim to provide an enjoyable experience for all of our visitors. Unfortunately, the noise and mess created by dogs can be an inconvenience to our staff as well as other visitors. This is particularly necessary in our picnic areas. Dog-free zones are clearly marked with signs, so please watch for those if you have a dog with you.
>
> Thank you for your understanding.
>
> Sincerely,
>
> Aurora National Park Management

1 Why was the notice written?

(A) To promote a new picnic area
(B) To apologize for a park closure
(C) To announce a park improvement project
(D) To explain a policy decision

2 세부 사항 문제

세부 내용을 묻는 문제는 누가(Who), 언제(When), 어디서(Where), 무엇을(What), 어떻게(How), 왜(Why)의 육하원칙을 바탕으로 만들어집니다. 글을 처음부터 읽는 것보다 문제의 키워드를 지문에서 찾아 그 주변 내용을 살피는 것이 중요합니다.

● 문제 유형

Who is Mr. Jones? 존스 씨는 누구인가?
What do customers receive for free? 고객들이 무료로 받는 것은 무엇인가?
When will the shipment arrive? 배송물이 도착하는 것은 언제인가?
How can applicants learn about the position? 지원자들이 그 직책에 대해 어떻게 알 수 있는가?

● 문제 풀이 전략

Q. How can customers receive a refund?

If an event at Marigold Outdoor Theater is canceled because of bad weather, you are entitled to a full refund of the ticket price. To claim your refund, bring your ticket to the box office and present it to one of our staff members. We require an in-person visit for our refund process.

We do not accept tickets by mail. Additionally, we cannot assist with a refund request over the phone. We apologize for any inconvenience.

(A) By completing an online form
(B) By visiting the theater ✓
(C) By mailing a ticket
(D) By calling the box office

STEP 1 문제에서 키워드 파악하기
문제를 먼저 읽고 세부 사항을 묻는 문제임을 파악합니다. 문제에 언급된 키워드(refund)에 표시를 합니다. 환불을 받을 수 있는 '방법'을 묻는 문제입니다.

STEP 2 지문에서 문제의 키워드 찾기
문제의 키워드가 언급된 부분을 지문에서 찾아 표시하고 키워드가 포함된 문장의 앞뒤 부분을 읽어 봅니다. 환불 절차를 위해서는 직접 방문해야 한다고 했으므로 정답에서 이와 비슷한 표현을 찾습니다.

STEP 3 정답 찾기
단서 부분의 an in-person visit란 표현이 (B)에서 visiting the theater로 표현되었습니다.

해석 p.166

어휘 be entitled to ~할 자격이 있다   full refund 전액 환불   claim (환불, 보상금 등을) 신청하다, 청구하다; 주장하다, 요구하다   present 제시하다, 보여 주다   in-person 직접   assist with ~을 돕다   apologize for ~을 사과하다   inconvenience 불편함

패러프레이징 다음을 읽고 지문을 가장 잘 패러프레이징한 것을 고르세요.

1 What will happen on September 4?

> Before the new features of the security system are used companywide, the security department has selected ten staff members to perform system tests on September 4.

(A) The security team will install equipment.
(B) Appointed employees will take part in some testing.

2 Why is a bridge being closed?

> Due to routine repairs on a support beam, Ellis Bridge will be closed from today for approximately two weeks. Alternative routes for commuters can be found online.

(A) Commuters have complained about traffic.
(B) Maintenance work will be carried out.

미니 테스트

Question 1 refers to the following notice.

> **Notice to Duncan Airlines Passengers:**
> We do our best to ensure the safe and timely transport of your luggage. Do not pack fragile items in checked luggage, as bags may be handled roughly or stacked while in our care. Scratches and dirt marks are not compensated, as these are normal wear and tear. In addition, ripped pockets or exterior fabric also cannot be included in damage claims. If your bag has damage to major components such as the handles, wheels, or zippers, please let us know. If a Duncan Airlines employee has caused damage to one of these areas, you will be compensated. For more information, visit www.duncanairlines.com.

1 What type of damage can passengers receive compensation for?

(A) Torn pockets
(B) Dirt marks
(C) A broken wheel
(D) Scratches

3 True/NOT 문제

Part 7의 True/NOT 문제는 지문의 내용과 일치하는 부분이나 일치하지 않는 부분을 선택지에서 고르는 문제입니다. 일치하거나 불일치하는 부분을 지문에 표시해 가며 선택지와 대조해 정답을 골라야 합니다.

● 문제 유형

What is **true about** the Web site? 웹사이트 대해 사실인 것은 무엇인가?
What is **mentioned about** the work? 업무에 대해 언급된 것은 무엇인가?
= What is **indicated about** the work?
= What is **stated about** the work?
What is **NOT** indicated about the service? 서비스에 대해 언급되지 않은 것은 무엇인가?

● 문제 풀이 전략

Q. What is NOT indicated as a job duty of the position?

STEP 1 문제에서 키워드 파악하기
문제를 먼저 읽고 업무(job duty)로 언급되지 '않은' 것을 찾는 문제임을 파악합니다.

Bank Teller Position at Avila Bank

Avila Bank has job openings for a full-time bank teller at its Warren Avenue branch. We are currently seeking a friendly and professional individual for this role.

Duties include receiving cash deposits and processing withdrawals, answering customers' questions both in person and over the phone. In addition, bank tellers will suggest other bank services, such as loans and business banking, as needed.

We offer a competitive hourly wage along with paid vacation time. Visit our Web site for further details.

STEP 2 지문의 내용과 선택지 대조하기
지문에서 Duties 이하에 업무가 나열된 부분을 찾아 선택지와 하나씩 대조합니다. 단서에 표시하며 언급된 부분은 선택지에서 소거합니다. 눈으로만 보지 말고 지문에 표시를 해 가며 대조해야 정확하게 정답을 찾을 수 있습니다.

(A) Responding to inquiries
(B) Recommending other services
(C) Handling cash transactions
(D) Approving loan applications ✓

STEP 3 정답 찾기
대출(loan)과 관련해서는 대출과 같은 서비스를 제안해 준다고 했을 뿐, 승인해 주는 것은 아니므로 Approving loan applications는 오답임을 알 수 있습니다.

해석 p.168

어휘 duty 업무 bank teller 은행 창구 직원 job opening 일자리 공석 currently 지금, 현재 seek 찾다 individual 개인
deposit 예금 withdrawal 출금 such as ~와 같은 competitive 경쟁력이 있는 wage 급여 along with ~와 함께
paid vacation time 유급 휴가 inquiry 문의 사항 transaction 거래 approve 승인하다

패러프레이징 패러프레이징을 통해 문제의 정답을 찾아 보세요. 정답 및 해설 p.168

1 What do the meeting rooms NOT offer?

> Each meeting room features:
> - Comfortable chairs
> - Wireless Internet
> - A large whiteboard
> - Complimentary tea and coffee

(A) Free beverages (B) Printing equipment

2 What is true about *Round-Up*?

> Raymond Jordan will replace Caroline Ladner as the lead anchor for Channel 7's Saturday morning news broadcast, *Round-Up*. Mr. Jordan brings twenty years of experience to the role.

(A) It is a weekly broadcast. (B) It has been on TV for twenty years.

미니 테스트 정답 및 해설 p.169

Question 1 refers to the following e-mail.

```
========================= E-Mail Message =========================

To:       Ted Emerson <ted.emerson@tedsgardening.com>
From:     Rosa Ocasio <rocasio@elmsford1.com>
Subject:  Web site
Date:     July 10
```

Dear Mr. Emerson,

I was delighted to discover your gardening Web site when I was trying to identify a weed in my garden. Your online tool made it easy to figure out what it was.

I now visit your site frequently. I have even used ideas from your Design of the Week in my own garden. I also love how you provide a directory of companies that sell gardening supplies.

I do have one suggestion, however. It would be great if you could include information about garden pests. I'm sure a lot of your readers are dealing with snails, bugs, and so on.

Many thanks,
Rosa Ocasio

1 What is NOT mentioned about the Web site in the e-mail?

(A) It includes a list of businesses.

(B) It has a chat section for gardeners.

(C) It offers a plant identification tool.

(D) It provides a weekly design suggestion.

4 추론/암시 문제

추론 문제는 지문에 언급된 내용을 바탕으로 그 안에 숨겨진 의미를 파악하여 이를 가장 잘 표현한 선택지를 고르는 문제입니다. 숨겨진 의미를 파악해야 하므로 난이도가 높은 문제 유형에 속합니다.

● 문제 유형

Where is the notice **most likely** posted? 공지문이 게시된 곳은 어디인 것 같은가?
What is **suggested about** the company? 그 회사에 대해 암시된 것은?
= What is **inferred about** the company?
= What is **implied about** the company?

● 문제 풀이 전략

Q. What is suggested about *The Whispering Winds*?

STEP 1 문제에서 키워드 파악하기
suggested about이란 표현을 보고 추론 문제임을 확인합니다. 이탤릭체로 써 있는 고유 명사 The Whispering Winds에 대한 문제이므로 글의 전반적인 내용을 확인해야 합니다.

Join us for an evening to remember!

Harron Publishing is pleased to announce the launch of

The Whispering Winds

January 19, 3 P.M. ~ 6 P.M.

Braxton Bookstore, 2020 Washburn Street

Author Arnold Edmunds will be reading excerpts from his debut novel. He will also discuss his friend, whose life story provided the main plot for the novel. Mr. Edmunds will sign copies of the book at the end.

Light refreshments will be served. Please confirm your attendance by e-mailing lauch@harronpublishing.com.

STEP 2 지문에서 문제의 단서 찾기
지문에서는 신간 소설 출시 행사를 알리고 있으며 단서 부분에서 작가는 그의 친구의 인생 이야기를 소재로 했다고 언급하고 있습니다.

(A) It is the author's second novel.
(B) It was published on January 19.
(C) It is based on a true story. ✓
(D) It is a best-selling book.

STEP 3 단서를 바탕으로 추론하여 정답 찾기
친구의 인생 이야기는 허구적인 내용이 아니라 '실제 이야기'이므로 사실적인 이야기를 바탕으로 했음을 알 수 있습니다. 이처럼 추론 문제는 단서를 바탕으로 한 번 더 생각해야 정확한 답을 찾을 수 있습니다.

해석 p.170

어휘 launch 출시 author 작가, 저자 excerpt 발췌문 plot 줄거리 refreshments 다과 confirm 확인하다 attendance 참석 publish 출판하다 be based on ~을 바탕으로 하다

패러프레이징

다음을 읽고 지문을 가장 잘 패러프레이징한 것을 고르세요.

1 What is suggested about Mr. Fleming?

> Fortunately, Ms. Brandt's uncle, Norm Fleming, has received many business loans over the years, so he was able to advise her.

(A) He invested in Ms. Brandt's business.
(B) He is familiar with the loan process.

2 What is implied about Mr. Sherman?

> Dear Mr. Sherman,
>
> I have checked our database for the books you said you needed for a medical assistant certification program. Unfortunately, we are completely sold out, so I recommend contacting other businesses.

(A) He made changes to a database.
(B) He is training to work in medicine.

미니 테스트

Question 1 refers to the following advertisement.

Canterbury Dairy Farm

Milk ◆ Cheese ◆ Ice Cream

The freshest milk in the region!

Get a free sample of ice cream at our visitor center.

Just 2 miles ahead!

Exit 42, 806 Durham Road

---

1 Where would people most likely see this advertisement?

(A) On a roadside billboard
(B) In a travel magazine
(C) At a supermarket
(D) On a Web site

ACTUAL TEST

Questions 1-2 refer to the following coupon.

Camptime Winter Sale

Get a 50% discount on
all camping clothing

Coupon valid at any Camptime branch. No minimum purchase required. Expires January 10.

1. What item is offered at a lower price?

    (A) A flashlight
    (B) A tent
    (C) A sweatshirt
    (D) A sleeping bag

2. What will happen after January 10?

    (A) An offer will not be valid.
    (B) A new branch will open.
    (C) A price will decrease.
    (D) A shipment will arrive.

Questions 3-4 refer to the following information.

Dayton Hotel Shuttle Bus

(7 A.M. to 9 P.M.)

Dayton Hotel offers a free shuttle bus service between our site and the city center. From June 1, the bus will run more frequently than before. Every Saturday and Sunday, the bus will depart from the hotel every 15 minutes instead of every 30 minutes. Weekday departures will remain the same. The shuttle will leave the hotel every 90 minutes Monday through Thursday and every 60 minutes on Fridays. We have made these adjustments for our guests' convenience. For a complete schedule, visit www.daytonhotel.com/services.

3 Why was the information written?

(A) To recommend a shorter bus route
(B) To notify bus passengers of safety rules
(C) To apologize for shuttle bus delays
(D) To explain changes to a schedule

4 How often does the shuttle bus run on Fridays?

(A) Every 15 minutes
(B) Every 30 minutes
(C) Every 60 minutes
(D) Every 90 minutes

Questions 5-6 refer to the following memo.

MEMO

To: All Mayorga Inc. Employees
From: Corey Jensen, Office Manager
Date: February 11
Subject: Encouraging teamwork

From March 1, Mayorga Inc. will launch the Mayorga Teamwork Prize (MTP). The MTP aims to formally recognize employees for their cooperation with their coworkers. One winner will be announced on the first of each month. The person will be allowed to leave work one hour early on each Friday in that month. We hope that this benefit will be enjoyable to the winner.

All employees are eligible for the MTP, and anyone can submit a nomination. However, the same person cannot win the MTP twice within six months. If you would like to make a nomination, please pick up a form from the HR office.

5 What is the purpose of the memo?

(A) To announce new job duties
(B) To congratulate employees
(C) To introduce a new award system
(D) To explain a vacation policy

6 What is NOT mentioned about the MTP?

(A) It can be received by any employee.
(B) It will be announced once a month.
(C) It includes a shorter work schedule.
(D) Its nominations are valid for six months.

Questions 7-9 refer to following e-mail.

E-Mail Message

To: Samuel Valdez <svaldez@freesemail.com>
From: Westline Railway <contact@westlinerailway.com>
Date: June 19
Subject: A special offer!

Dear Mr. Valdez,

I would like to inform you about a survey we are currently conducting. Sharing your opinions about Westline Railway's new online booking process can help us to make further improvements. You will be rewarded with a discount on your next ticket purchase. To participate, please follow the steps below.

1. Visit www.westlinerailway.com/survey and complete the survey.

2. Enter your e-mail address at the end of the survey.

3. You will receive a voucher code in your inbox. You can use it to get 25% off your next Westline Railway journey.

If you have any questions, please feel free to e-mail me at this address.
Thank you!

Diane Harper
Customer Care Center, Westline Railway

---

7 Why did Ms. Harper write to Mr. Valdez?

(A) To thank him for a purchase
(B) To request some feedback
(C) To introduce a new product
(D) To apologize for an error

8 What should Mr. Valdez provide to get a discount on his next journey?

(A) An account number
(B) A photo ID
(C) An original receipt
(D) A coupon code

9 What is suggested about Ms. Harper?

(A) She has designed a Web site.
(B) She will answer questions directly.
(C) She will send a sample to Mr. Valdez.
(D) She is a new Westline Railway employee.

UNIT 18

문제 유형별 (2)

1. 문장 삽입 문제
2. 의도 파악 문제
3. 동의어 찾기 문제

Actual Test

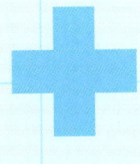

Unit18에서 다루는 문제들은 출제되는 개수는 적지만 난이도가 높아 고득점을 받기 위해서는 반드시 정리해 두어야 하는 유형입니다. 주어진 문장이 글의 흐름상 들어가기 적절한 곳을 고르는 **문장 삽입 문제**와 문자 메시지 대화문에만 출제되는 **화자의 의도 파악 문제**는 평균 2문제씩 출제되며, **동의어 찾기**는 2~3문제가 출제됩니다.

1 문장 삽입 문제

문장 삽입 문제는 글을 읽으며 주어진 문장이 들어가기에 가장 적절한 자리를 찾는 문제입니다.

● 문제 유형

In which of the positions marked [1], [2], [3], and [4] does the following sentence best belong?
[1], [2], [3], [4]로 표시된 곳 중에서 다음 문장이 들어가기에 가장 적절한 곳은?

● 문제 풀이 전략

Q. In which of the positions marked [1], [2], [3], and [4] does the following sentence best belong?
"Redmond Financial is considered the most trustworthy company in the industry."

STEP 1 제시된 문장 먼저 읽기
문제에 주어진 문장을 먼저 읽고 단서가 될 만한 단어나 표현들을 찾습니다. 앞의 내용을 가리키는 지시어나 앞뒤 흐름을 자연스럽게 이어 주는 연결어 등이 있다면 표시해 둡니다.

To: All Redmond Financial Employees
From: Adeline Bates
Date: March 9
Subject: Approved changes

Dear Staff,

I am pleased to announce that Redmond Financial will expand its compensation package for employees from next quarter. —[1]—. Our number of paid vacation days for employees is already well above average compared to other businesses across the country. However, we will still add three more. Performance bonuses will also be increased by 10%. —[2]—.

—[3]—. This trust is made possible through the dedication of our staff. —[4]—. We hope these changes will make you feel valued.

Warmest regards,

Adeline Bates, HR Director

STEP 2 문장의 앞뒤 연결 확인
글을 읽으며 번호 앞뒤의 문장들이 자연스럽게 연결되는지 파악합니다. 앞뒤의 흐름이 끊기거나 번호 뒤의 문장에서 가리키는 대상이 앞에 없다면 그 자리에 주어진 문장을 넣어 앞뒤로 다시 읽어 봅니다.

STEP 3 문장 넣고 해석해 보기
[3]번 뒤의 문장에서 This가 가리키는 대상이 앞에 언급되어 있지 않습니다. 따라서 주어진 문장을 이곳에 넣어 보면 This trust가 trustworthy company를 가리키는 말이며, 그 흐름이 자연스러우므로 [3]번이 정답임을 알 수 있습니다.

(A) [1]   (B) [2]   (C) [3] ✓   (D) [4]

해석 p.176

어휘 trustworthy 가치 있는   above average 평균 이상   compared to ~와 비교하여   valued 가치 있는

미니 테스트 1 다음을 읽고 주어진 문장이 들어가기에 가장 적절한 곳을 고르세요. 정답 및 해설 p.176

—[1]—. Conference participants can attend talks given by a variety of speakers. Also, they can register for a workshop on leadership. —[2]—.

1 "This session is limited to the first thirty people who sign up."

(A) [1] (B) [2]

Your membership will expire on July 31. —[1]—. Please reply to this e-mail before the date to renew your membership. —[2]—.

2 "Alternatively, you can use the address to cancel your membership."

(A) [1] (B) [2]

미니 테스트 2 정답 및 해설 p.177

Question 1 refers to the following article.

VANCOUVER, 24 Feb.—Kerr Sports has announced that it has taken over MV Footwear for $18.5 million. —[1]—. Kerr Sports is known for its basketball and baseball equipment. —[2]—. The company's CEO wants to start selling shoes as well. The acquisition will help Kerr Sports expand its product line. —[3]—. That's because MV Footwear is popular with young consumers. Ann Engel, a spokesperson for Kerr Sports, said that negotiations took several weeks. —[4]—. The company will work to keep all MV Footwear employees on staff.

1 In which of the positions marked [1], [2], [3] and [4] does the following sentence best belong?

"In addition, the move is expected to bring in new customers."

(A) [1]
(B) [2]
(C) [3]
(D) [4]

2 의도 파악 문제

의도 파악 문제는 대화 지문에 출제되는 문제입니다. 특정 시간에 언급된 표현이 문맥상 어떠한 의미로 쓰였는지를 파악하는 문제입니다.

● 문제 유형

At 9:51 A.M., what does Ms. Sheehan mean when she writes, "I'll be on it shortly"?
오전 9시 51분에, 시핸 씨가 "제가 곧 시작할 거예요"라고 한 의도는 무엇인가?

● 문제 풀이 전략

Q. At 9:51 A.M., what does Ms. Sheehan mean when she writes, "I'll be on it shortly"?

STEP 1 인용구 확인하고 본문에 표시하기
오전 9시 51분에 질문에 나타난 표현을 찾아 표시를 해 둡니다. '그것을 곧 할게요'라고 했으므로 '그것'이 무엇인지를 유념하며 대화를 읽습니다.

Gabriel Ruiz (9:48 A.M.)
Hello, Vanessa. Have you started painting the stairway railings yet?

Vanessa Sheehan (9:51 A.M.)
Hi, Gabriel. I'll be on it shortly. I just need to hang up some signs first to warn people about the wet paint.

STEP 2 인용구 앞뒤 내용 읽기
대화하는 사람들 사이의 관계와 대화 주제를 파악해가며 대화를 읽어 갑니다. 표시해 둔 표현의 바로 앞과 뒤 문장을 주의 깊게 읽습니다.

Gabriel Ruiz (9:52 A.M.)
All right. Do you think the smell will bother people in the building?

Vanessa Sheehan (9:54 A.M.)
Most of the building's windows are open, so it shouldn't be a problem.

Gabriel Ruiz (9:55 A.M.)
I'm glad to hear that!

STEP 3 문맥상 적절한 의도 찾기
표현의 바로 앞부분에서 '페인트 작업을 시작했냐'고 물었고 '곧 할 것이다'라고 했으므로 페인트 작업을 곧 시작할 것임을 알 수 있습니다. 따라서 페인트 작업을 some work로, shortly를 soon으로 바꿔 표현한 문장인 (B)가 정답입니다.

(A) She will explain a new project.
(B) She will start some work soon. ✓
(C) She will print some signs.
(D) She will meet Mr. Ruiz quickly.

해석 p.178

어휘 shortly 곧 stairway 계단 railing 난간 hang up ~을 걸다 warn 경고하다 wet 젖은, 축축한 bother 귀찮게 하다

미니 테스트 1 다음을 읽고 밑줄 친 부분의 의도를 가장 잘 표현한 것을 고르세요.

1

Daniel Hampton (11:19 A.M.)
We still cannot get the copy machine to work, so a technician will need to fix it.

Grand Office Inc. (11:21 A.M.)
No problem. One of our technicians can go there now.

(A) He can replace Mr. Hampton's copy machine.
(B) He will send someone to make a repair.

2

Bruno Marchesi (1:25 P.M.)
Would you mind hooking up the projector and laptop? We'll need them for the meeting.

Emily Rourke (1:30 P.M.)
Done. Is that all?

(A) She has set up some equipment.   (B) She has contacted some employees.

미니 테스트 2

Question 1 refers to the following text-message chain.

Linda Harrison (2:43 P.M.)
Matthew, I've emailed you the first draft of the catalog. Have you had time to look at it?

Matthew Kemp (2:46 P.M.)
I've just opened the file. It looks like the photos are very small. They will be difficult for customers to see.

Linda Harrison (2:47 P.M.)
I thought I needed to fit a lot onto each page. I guess I will do it all again.

Matthew Kemp (2:48 P.M.)
Not necessarily. The colors and text look great. You can just change the picture size and have more pages.

Linda Harrison (2:50 P.M.)
What a relief. That won't take me long.

1 At 2:48 P.M., what does Mr. Kemp mean when he writes, "Not necessarily"?

(A) Ms. Harrison should not get help with a task.
(B) Ms. Harrison will not have to start a project over.
(C) Ms. Harrison should not delete some photos.
(D) Ms. Harrison will not have to send an e-mail.

③ 동의어 찾기 문제

동의어를 묻는 문제는 특정 단어가 문장에서 어떠한 의미로 쓰였는지를 묻는 문제입니다. 단어의 일반적인 의미를 묻기도 하지만, 다양한 의미를 가진 단어를 주고 문맥상 그 단어의 의미와 일치하는 단어를 고르게 하는 문제가 주를 이룹니다.

● 문제 유형

In the e-mail, the word "immediate" in paragraph 1, line 5 is closest in meaning to
이메일에서 첫 번째 단락 다섯 번째 줄의 "immediate"와 의미상 가장 가까운 것은?

● 문제 풀이 전략

Q. In the e-mail, the word "immediate" in paragraph 1, line 5 is closest in meaning to

STEP 1 지문에서 질문의 단어 찾기
글을 읽기 전에 질문에 나타난 단어를 해당 위치에서 찾아 표시를 해 둡니다.

From: Patricia Lee ⟨leepatricia@kentrock.com⟩
To: Jerry Callahan ⟨j.callahan@greenwood.gov⟩
Date: April 14
Subject: Meeting

Dear Ms. Callahan,

I am writing to express my appreciation to the city council. I attended the feedback session for residents on April 10. The participants shared ideas about improvements for the City Hall building and its immediate surroundings. The council members carefully listened to everyone's suggestions. I look forward to seeing the new changes to the area.

Sincerely,

Patricia Lee

STEP 2 문장 내에서의 의미 파악
단어가 포함된 문장의 앞뒤 문장을 읽으며 단어의 의미를 유추합니다. 단어의 본래 의미가 아닌 주어진 문장 내에서의 의미를 파악해야 하는 것이 핵심입니다.

(A) next
(B) current
(C) nearby ✓
(D) prompt

STEP 3 문맥에 적절한 동의어 고르기
주어진 단어 immediate는 주로 '즉각적인'이란 뜻으로 쓰이지만 위치나 장소를 나타내는 말을 수식할 때는 '근처의, 가까운'이란 의미로 쓰입니다.

해석 p.180

어휘 express 표현하다 appreciation 감사 council 의회 resident 거주자, 주민 participant 참여자 share 공유하다
improvement 개선 사항 surroundings 주변 환경 suggestion 제안 사항 look forward to *doing* ~하는 것을 기대하다
area 지역 current 현재의 nearby 가까운, 근처의 prompt 즉각적인

미니 테스트 1 다음을 읽고 밑줄 친 부분과 의미상 가장 가까운 것을 고르세요. 정답 및 해설 p.180

1

We understand that you are very busy. Even so, could you please spare a few minutes to give us your feedback?

(A) give (B) ask

2

If you have any further issues with your computer, please contact the IT team. They can be reached at IT@brisbandsales.net.

(A) problems (B) versions

미니 테스트 2 정답 및 해설 p.181

Question 1 refers to the following e-mail.

```
================= E-Mail Message =================
To:       Josephine Frazier
From:     Eric Stanfield
Date:     July 19
Subject:  Digital Marketing
```

Dear Ms. Frazier,

I am the vice president of the Salisbury Small Business Association (SSBA). I recently saw your talk on digital marketing at the Essex Center. I found it to be very informative. I am wondering if you could teach one of our monthly workshops on the same topic. Our members would love to learn new skills in your area of expertise.

The SSBA was founded fifteen years ago to support small businesses. Members can get help obtaining a business loan, access up-to-date information about the current market, and get discounts from suppliers.

If you are available, please let me know the most convenient dates.

Sincerely,
Eric Stanfield

1 In the e-mail, the word "area" in paragraph 1, line 4, is closest in meaning to

(A) distance (B) subject (C) level (D) portion

ACTUAL TEST

Questions 1-3 refer to the following e-mail.

From:	Travis Baxley
To:	Movie Pass Customer Service
Date:	August 6
Subject:	Account #59250

I am writing about my Movie Pass subscription. —[1]—. I signed up for the video-streaming service in June and selected an annual subscription. I was surprised to see a charge on my credit card for $12.95 from your company. A payment of $139.95 for the entire one-year subscription was made up front, so there should be no additional fees until next year. —[2]—.

I logged into my account on your Web site this morning to see what previous payments were listed. Only the original $139.95 transaction was there. —[3]—. Would you mind letting me know how often the site is updated? I would also like a refund of $12.95 issued as soon as possible. —[4]—.

Sincerely,

Travis Baxley

1. What is the purpose of the e-mail?

    (A) To take advantage of an offer
    (B) To cancel an online service
    (C) To upgrade an account
    (D) To report a payment issue

2. Why did Mr. Baxley visit the Web site this morning?

    (A) To change his contact information
    (B) To sign up for a subscription
    (C) To check an account history
    (D) To watch some movies

3. In which of the positions marked [1], [2], [3], and [4] does the following sentence best belong?

    "However, I don't know whether any information was missing."

    (A) [1]
    (B) [2]
    (C) [3]
    (D) [4]

Questions 4-5 refer to the following text-message chain.

Pamela Boyer, 11:31 A.M.
Hi, Andre. Are you busy right now?

Andre Hyland, 11:35 A.M.
I'm working on an expense report. What's going on?

Pamela Boyer, 11:36 A.M.
My inspection at the Veltri Building ran later than I expected. It would be really helpful if you could set up the chairs and tables in the training room for me.

Andre Hyland, 11:37 A.M.
Sure. Do you have a layout in mind?

Pamela Boyer, 11:38 A.M.
Yes, I'll take a picture of the layout and send it to you by phone. Fortunately, I picked up the handouts from the printer yesterday.

4 What is Mr. Hyland asked to do?

(A) Proofread a handout
(B) Arrange some furniture
(C) Print some materials
(D) Reserve a meeting room

5 At 11:37 A.M., what does Mr. Hyland mean when he writes, "Sure"?

(A) He is available to assist Ms. Boyer.
(B) He will explain a process to Ms. Boyer.
(C) He agrees with Ms. Boyer's complaint.
(D) He has found Ms. Boyer's belongings.

Questions 6-8 refer to the following article.

Northwest Rail Going Strong

PHILADELPHIA (April 6)—Northwest Rail has announced that it will begin offering several express train routes from next month. —[1]—. The company expects that the new service will boost the number of passengers by approximately fifteen percent. Commuters between Philadelphia and New York are expected to make up the majority of the new business. —[2]—.

"We have listened to feedback from passengers and worked to make more convenient options available," said Jessie Cohn, Northwest Rail's vice president.

The change is part of a larger plan to improve services overall. For example, in January, a complimentary Wi-Fi network was added to all Northwest Rail trains. In addition, passengers will no longer have to visit the ticket window to buy tickets. —[3]—. The company also plans to invest in new trains with more space for luggage. —[4]—.

6 What is mentioned about Northwest Rail?

(A) It will start charging passengers for excess luggage.
(B) It recently began offering an express service.
(C) It will relocate its head office to New York.
(D) It is likely to serve more travelers from May.

7 What happened in January?

(A) Northwest Rail hired more staff members.
(B) Ms. Cohn was promoted to vice president.
(C) Passengers were given free Internet access.
(D) A ticket exchange policy changed.

8 In which of the positions marked [1], [2], [3], and [4] does the following sentence best belong?

"They can instead use the automated machines near the platform."

(A) [1]
(B) [2]
(C) [3]
(D) [4]

Questions 9-11 refer to the following Web page.

---

http://www.summitenterprises.com

Modern transportation companies face unique challenges in an ever-changing industry. Fluctuations in demand, unpredictable fuel prices, evolving customer expectations, and increased competition are just a few aspects of the industry that businesses must respond to.

Summit Enterprises is here to help! Thanks to our large team of consultants, you can be sure to find an expert with experience that meets your particular needs. For example:

- Training staff members
- Following environmental regulations
- Maximizing automation
- Growing your customer base

Call us at 555-8181 today to discuss how we can help you take your transportation business to the next level. There is no charge for the initial consultation.

---

9 For whom is the Web page written?

(A) Professors teaching finance
(B) Owners of transportation businesses
(C) Students studying business
(D) Employees in HR team

10 What is suggested about Summit Enterprises?

(A) It has branches in many locations.
(B) It mainly works with large corporations.
(C) It has specialists in a variety of areas.
(D) It will merge with a competitor.

11 In the Web page, the word "just" in paragraph 1, line 3, is closest in meaning to

(A) correct
(B) lately
(C) only
(D) fair

에듀윌이
너를
지지할게

ENERGY

작은 성공부터 시작하라.

성공에 익숙해지면 무슨 목표든지 이룰 수 있다는
자신감이 생긴다.

– 데일 카네기(Dale Carnegie)

UNIT 19

지문 유형별 (1)

1. 이메일/편지
2. 광고
3. 공고/회람
4. 기사

Actual Test

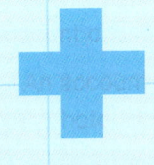

Unit 19에서 다루는 지문들은 Part 7에서 가장 많이 출제되는 유형들입니다. 각 지문마다 글의 서식이나 흐름이 대략적으로 정해져 있기 때문에 이러한 패턴들을 잘 익혀 두면 독해 시간을 줄이는 데 큰 도움이 될 수 있습니다. 또한, 각 지문별로 자주 쓰이는 표현을 학습하여 정답의 단서를 빠르게 파악할 수 있는 훈련을 해야 합니다.

1 이메일/편지

이메일과 편지는 Part 7에서 출제 빈도가 높은 지문 유형입니다. 주로 고객과 회사 간의 제품 구입 및 환불에 대한 내용이나 회사 내부에서의 업무에 관한 내용을 다룹니다.

● **지문의 기본 구조**

To: Malcolm Haynes 〈haynesm@auto-world.net〉
From: Serena Dolan 〈serena@stahrtires.com〉
Subject: Your order
Date: June 20

Dear Mr. Haynes,

I am writing to inform you that your order of 35-inch tires will be late.

Unfortunately, some of our factory's equipment has broken down. We are making repairs as quickly as possible. The order can be sent by June 26.

Please let us know whether you would like to cancel your order. There would be no fee in this case, as outlined in our cancellation policy, which is attached. We apologize for any inconvenience.

Sincerely,

Serena Dolan
Shipping Manager, Auto World

수신인, 발신인, 제목 확인
이메일을 받는 사람과 보내는 사람의 이름, 그리고 제목을 확인합니다.

글을 쓴 목적
주로 글의 앞부분에 글을 쓴 목적이 언급되지만 글의 후반부에 언급되는 경우도 있습니다.

[빈출 문제]
Q. What is the purpose of the e-mail?
이메일의 목적은 무엇인가?

세부 내용
지문에 나타난 키워드를 중심으로 세부적인 사항이 언급됩니다.

[빈출 문제]
Q. According to Ms. Dolan, what has caused a problem?
돌란 씨에 따르면, 문제를 일으킨 것은 무엇인가?

요청 사항 및 첨부 파일
글의 마지막에는 문제의 해결책이나 요청 사항 및 첨부 파일 등이 언급되며 이와 관련된 문제들이 출제됩니다.

[빈출 문제]
Q. What does Ms. Dolan ask Mr. Haynes to do?
돌란 씨가 헤인즈 씨에게 요청한 것은 무엇인가?
Q. What is included in the e-mail?
이메일에 포함된 것은 무엇인가?

해석 p.186

어휘 unfortunately 안타깝게도   equipment 장비   break down 고장 나다   repair 수리   whether ~인지 아닌지   cancel 취소하다
fee 요금   outline 개요를 서술하다   cancellation 취소   policy 정책   attach 첨부하다   apologize for ~에 대해 사과하다

빈출 표현

주제/목적 관련 표현

I'm writing to ~	제가 글을 쓰는 이유는
I would like to inform you ~	당신께 ~을 알려 드리고 싶습니다
This is to let you know that ~	이는 당신께 ~을 알려 드리는 것입니다
This is a reminder to ~	이는 ~을 상기시켜 드리기 위함입니다
I regret to inform you that ~	당신께 ~을 알려 드리게 되어 유감입니다

사과, 감사, 첨부 파일 안내, 문의 사항

I apologize for ~	~에 사과드립니다
We would appreciate ~	~에 감사드리고 싶습니다
Please find enclosed[attached/included]	첨부된 것을 확인해 주세요
Stop by ~	~에 들러 주세요
Feel free to contact ~	언제든 연락 주세요
Please let me know	저희에게 ~을 알려 주세요

미니 테스트

Question 1 refers to the following letter.

Gretchen Anderson
1190 Tyson Road
Tucson, AZ 85709

Dear Ms. Anderson,

This letter is provided to alert you to a potential issue. Our records show that your electricity usage has recently increased significantly. Specifically, the usage for May was nearly double the usage for April. It is also much higher than other households of your size.

If you cannot identify the reason for this increase, there may be an issue with your electricity meter. Should you like a technician to visit your home for an inspection, please fill out the enclosed form and return it to us.

Sincerely,

The Southwest Electricity Team

Enclosure

---

1 What is attached in the letter?

(A) An overdue bill
(B) A request form
(C) A confirmation letter
(D) A discount voucher

2 광고

광고 지문은 크게 제품 및 서비스 광고와 구인 광고로 나누어집니다. 제품이나 서비스의 장점 및 혜택을 광고하는 내용과 일자리의 업무 및 자격 요건을 알리는 내용을 다룹니다.

● 지문의 기본 구조

LUXURY APARTMENT FOR RENT

Located in the Cambridge Building at 703 Kovar Road. Three bedrooms, two bathrooms, spacious kitchen with modern appliances, and balcony with coastal views.

Tenants can use the on-site pool and fitness center. The monthly rent is $3,500. Available from July 1.

To book a tour of the apartment unit and building, call Rhapsody Realty at 555-7930.

광고하는 제품 및 서비스

광고 지문은 제목이 눈에 띄게 언급되는 경우가 많으며 이를 통해 광고하는 것이 무엇인지를 파악할 수 있습니다.

> 빈출 문제
>
> Q. What is being advertised?
> 광고되고 있는 것은 무엇인가?

제품 / 서비스의 특징 및 혜택

광고 지문의 주요 내용은 광고하는 제품이나 서비스 등에 대한 특징 및 혜택에 관한 것이며, 이는 글의 가장 중요한 부분입니다.

> 빈출 문제
>
> Q. What feature of the Cambridge Building is mentioned?
> 케임브리지 빌딩의 특징으로 언급된 것은 무엇인가?

구입 및 이용 방법

광고의 마지막 부분에는 주로 제품이나 서비스의 이용 방법 및 연락처가 언급됩니다.

> 빈출 문제
>
> Q. How can people schedule a tour?
> 사람들이 방문 일정을 잡을 수 있는 방법은 무엇인가?

해석 p.188

어휘 rent 임대(료) located in ~에 위치하는 spacious (공간이) 넓은 modern 현대적인, 최신의 appliance 가전제품 coastal 해안의 view 경치, 경관 tenant 세입자 available 이용 가능한 book 예약하다

빈출 표현

일반 광고 주요 표현

benefit	혜택	for more details	보다 자세한 사항은
feature	특징	purchase	구입하다
take advantage of	~을 이용[활용]하다	order by phone	전화로 주문하다
offer	할인	gift certificate	상품권
discount	할인	valid	유효한
complimentary	무료의	sign up for	~을 신청하다
free parking available	무료 주차 가능	register for	~에 등록하다
flyer	전단지	stop by	~에 들르다

구인 광고 주요 표현

full-time	정규직의	degree	학위
part-time	시간제의	preferred	선호되는, 우대되는
temporary job	임시직	application	신청서, 지원서
vacancy	공석	competitive salary	경쟁력 있는 급여
position	자리	paid vacation	유급 휴가
requirement	필수 조건	certificate	자격증
qualification	자격 요건	résumé	이력서
be eligible to *do*	~할 자격이 되다	cover letter	자기 소개서

미니 테스트

정답 및 해설 p.188

Question 1 refers to the following job posting.

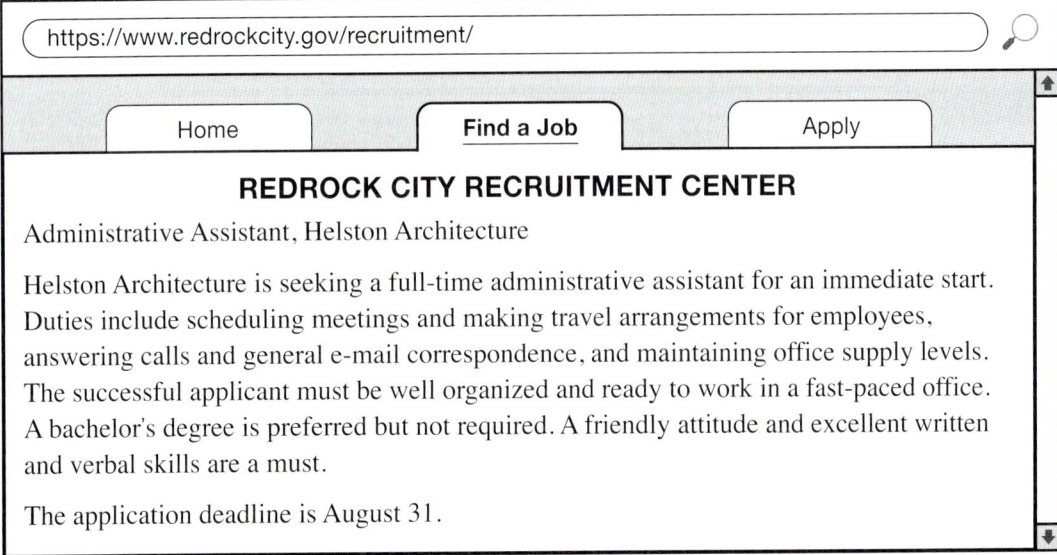

1 What qualification is required for the position?

(A) A driver's license
(B) Experience managing a team
(C) Strong writing skills
(D) A bachelor's degree

3 공고/회람

공고와 회람은 특정 대상에게 어떠한 사실을 알리는 글입니다. 주로 공사나 일정 변경 등을 알리는 내용이며, 공고하는 글은 글의 초반에 공지하는 바를 명확하게 언급하는 것이 특징입니다.

● 지문의 기본 구조

Notice to Arlington City Residents: Planned Road Closure

The express lanes of Highway 129 from Exit 16 to Exit 21 will be closed from July 2. The other two lanes in both directions will remain open. The closure will take place so that work crews can repair sections of the road.

Drivers are encouraged to allow for extra travel time through the area. Alternatively, they may take other routes to avoid using Highway 129. The work will take approximately three weeks. For the latest details on the reopening date, visit the city's Web site.

공고 목적 및 대상

공지문의 경우 짧은 제목이나 문장으로 공지 내용 및 대상을 초반에 강조합니다.

빈출 문제
Q. For whom is this notice intended?
이 공지문은 누구를 위해 의도된 것인가?

공지 내용에 대한 세부 사항 (날짜, 장소 등)

본문에는 공지하고자 하는 시간, 장소 등이 나타나 있습니다. 질문의 키워드와 대조하여 해당 내용을 자세히 읽고 정답을 고릅니다.

빈출 문제
Q. What will take place in July?
7월에 발생할 일은 무엇인가?

요청 사항 및 추가 정보

공지 내용과 관련해 부탁하는 내용이나 기타 추가적인 정보가 마지막에 언급됩니다.

빈출 문제
Q. How can people get up-to-date information on the project?
사람들이 프로젝트에 대한 최신 정보를 얻을 수 있는 방법은 무엇인가?

해석 p.189

어휘 resident 주민 express lane 추월 차선 closure 폐쇄 take place 발생하다 crew 작업자 repair 수리하다 section 부분 be encouraged to do ~하도록 권장받다 allow for 감안하다 alternatively 대신에 approximately 대략

빈출 표현

공고/회람 관련 어휘

passenger	승객	alert, warn	경고하다
resident	거주자, 주민	unavailable	이용할 수 없는
recipient	받는 사람, 수취인	accessible	접근할 수 있는
attention	집중, 주의	suspend	중단하다
repair	수리	install	설치하다
renovation	보수	temporary	임시의
construction	공사, 건설	policy	정책
expansion	확장, 확대	inspect	검사하다, 점검하다

공고/회람 관련 표현

Please speak with ~	~와 이야기하십시오
Please note that ~	~을 유념하십시오
Please be aware that ~	~을 알고 계십시오
For more information, please visit ~	더 많은 정보는 ~을 방문하십시오
We apologize for any inconvenience.	불편을 끼쳐 죄송합니다.
take effect	시행되다
take place	발생하다, 일어나다

미니 테스트

Question 1 refers to the following memo.

MEMO

From: Heather Colbert
To: All staff
Date: Tuesday, December 8
Subject: For your information

The office Internet connection will be unavailable this Thursday, December 10, from 11:30 A.M. to approximately 1:30 P.M. The system will undergo an upgrade during this time, which will result in faster speeds for all users. Your supervisors will notify you when the system is working again.

Please plan ahead in order to minimize the disruption to your workflow. If you need to use the Internet urgently during this time, the IT team can set up a temporary mobile hotspot. Please call extension 31 in that case.

Thank you for your cooperation.

1. What does Ms. Colbert indicate in the memo?

   (A) Some security cameras will undergo testing.
   (B) Employees should not visit certain Web sites.
   (C) The office will be temporarily closed on Thursday.
   (D) An Internet connection will be upgraded.

4 기사

기사 지문은 경제 및 경영에 관한 내용들을 주로 다루며 난이도가 높은 편입니다. 회사들 간의 인수 합병이나 회사의 핵심 인물의 인사 발령, 사업 및 행사 소개 등의 내용이 자주 출제됩니다.

● 지문의 기본 구조

Pierce Sports Sees Changes Ahead

BOSTON (February 7)—Pierce Sports has announced the acquisition of Larson Apparel for $3.4 million. Taking over the clothing company is the next step in Pierce's plans to expand its product lines.

"Larson Apparel is famous for its modern style in sportswear," explained Paul Goodwin, a spokesperson for Pierce Sports. "We are excited about offering our customers high-quality clothes for their workouts."

Pierce Sports is based in Boston and mainly serves domestic customers. However, next year it will open its first branch abroad in London. This is expected to create at least 80 new jobs.

기사 제목 및 첫 번째 문장 확인

기사 지문의 경우 첫 문장에서 육하원칙을 바탕으로 한 글의 주제가 대략적으로 나타납니다. 기사가 작성된 날짜도 단서가 될 수 있으므로 미리 확인해 둡니다.

빈출 문제
Q. Why was the article written?
기사가 쓰인 이유는 무엇인가?

기사 세부 내용 확인

기사의 세부 사항 질문은 회사명, 사람 이름 등 고유명사가 많이 출제되니 이에 주목하며 글을 읽습니다.

빈출 문제
Q. What is Larson Apparel known for?
라슨 어패럴은 무엇으로 유명한가?

앞으로의 계획 및 추가 정보

기사의 마지막에는 앞으로의 계획이나 추가 정보를 얻을 수 있는 방법 등이 언급됩니다.

빈출 문제
Q. What will Pierce Sports do next year?
피어스 스포츠 사는 내년에 무엇을 할 것인가?

해석 p.190

어휘 acquisition 인수 expand 확장하다 be famous for ~으로 유명하다 spokesperson 대변인 workout 운동 mainly 주로 domestic 국내의 branch 지점, 지사 at least 최소한, 적어도

빈출 표현

기사 관련 표현

acquisition	(회사) 인수	resign	사임하다
merger	(회사) 합병	fund raising	자금 모금
take over	~을 인수하다	headquarters	본사
revenue	이익	based in	~에 본사를 둔
profit	이익, 수익	branch	지점, 지사
get a promotion	승진하다	subsidiary	부수적인, 자(子)회사의
transfer	이동하다; 전근 가다; 이전; 전근	commemorative	기념하는
retire	은퇴하다	fluctuate	변동을 거듭하다

직책 관련 표현

president	사장	CEO (= Chief Executive Officer)	대표 이사
vice president	부사장	COO (= Chief Operating Officer)	최고 운영 담당자
chairperson	의장	CFO (= Chief Financial Officer)	최고 재무 담당자
secretary	비서		
spokesperson	대변인		

미니 테스트

정답 및 해설 p.190

Question 1 refers to the following article.

NAIP Conference to Be Postponed

The National Association of Insurance Providers (NAIP) has postponed its annual conference for industry professionals. The event, which was originally scheduled for November 9, will now take place on November 16.

NAIP President Marjorie McGuire cited emergency repairs at the conference venue, Evergreen Hall, as the reason behind the date change. Ticketholders are able to get a full refund if they cannot attend the event on the new date.

The conference will include a talk from Natalie Parsons entitled "Making Public-Private Partnerships Work". There will also be opportunities to network with other professionals in the insurance industry. More information can be found at www.naipevents.com.

1 Why was NAIP's conference rescheduled?

(A) A presenter could not attend the event.
(B) Building repairs were needed unexpectedly.
(C) Not enough tickets had been sold.
(D) There was a booking error at the venue.

ACTUAL TEST

Questions 1-2 refer to the following advertisement.

Help your business look great!

You've researched the market, found the right employees, and provided a high-quality service. But are you making a good first impression? Make sure your workplace is sparkling clean from the moment your customers walk through the door!

For a limited time, business owners in Worthington can get a discount on cleaning services from Enhance Cleaning. Schedule your first visit before October 1 and get 50% off the regular fees.

We can handle any cleaning job, big or small, and our experienced employees will ensure that a thorough cleaning job is done. Call us today to find out more!

Enhance Cleaning
(879) 555-6477

1 For whom is the advertisement intended?

(A) Property developers
(B) People who own a business
(C) Cleaning supplies merchants
(D) Job seekers in Worthington

2 How can customers be eligible for an offer?

(A) By posting a review on a Web site
(B) By recommending the business to a friend
(C) By booking a service by September 30
(D) By spending at least $50

308

Questions 3-4 refer to the following article.

Friday, February 4, from 10 A.M. to 4 P.M., a food festival will be held at Diamond Hotel to showcase local restaurants.

Visitors can sample a variety of cuisines for free or purchase full meals at a discounted rate. There will be something for everyone, from elaborate seafood dishes to simple deli sandwiches.

Lori Boehm, general manager of the Diamond Hotel, said she was delighted to have the hotel host the festival. Thanks to her previous work as a cook at the Beam Café, she is confident that the festival will help to boost interest in local businesses.

"Restaurants in the area need to show diners what they have to offer," Ms. Boehm said. "This festival is a great way for people to try something new."

3 Why was the article written?

(A) To announce a training session
(B) To highlight a manager's achievements
(C) To advertise an investment opportunity
(D) To promote an upcoming event

4 What is indicated about Ms. Boehm?

(A) She is looking for a temporary job.
(B) She has experience in the restaurant business.
(C) She will prepare some food on February 4.
(D) She made a business environmentally friendly.

Questions 5-7 refer to the following letter.

18 September

Dayoung Lee
873 Waterview Lane
TORONTO, ON M5B 2L3

Dear Ms. Lee,

Thank you for choosing a Pulaski wall-mounted air conditioner.

Your purchase includes a six-month warranty, which is set to expire on October 31. It's not too late to enroll in our extended warranty program. Enjoy the peace of mind that comes from protecting your appliance. You'll be able to take advantage of the following benefits:

- As many in-person repairs as needed
- Online chat support 24 hours a day, 7 days a week
- New air filters sent every three months (the recommended changing period)
- Free download of our energy-saving tips smartphone application

We offer a two-, five-, and ten-year warranty. Register for the warranty length that best meets your needs using the enclosed form. Please feel free to check out our Frequently Asked Questions page at www.pulaski.com/warranty/FAQ.

Sincerely,

Luis Costa

Luis Costa
Enclosure

5. Why is Mr. Costa writing to Ms. Lee?
   (A) Because she discovered some missing parts
   (B) Because she bought a Pulaski product
   (C) Because she contacted a customer service team
   (D) Because she made a request online

6. What is NOT mentioned as a benefit of the extended warranty?
   (A) Unlimited repairs
   (B) Free shipping on returned items
   (C) Air filter replacements
   (D) Access to assistance anytime

7 What is included with the letter?

(A) An instruction manual
(B) A product catalog
(C) A registration document
(D) A discount voucher

Questions 8-9 refer to the following job advertisement.

Salvidar Inc.

Job Title: IT Support Technician

Description: Salvidar Inc. is a well-respected IT firm with a fast-growing client base using our helpdesk service. We are seeking an experienced IT professional with excellent communication skills and extensive knowledge of business-related software programs.

Key Duties: Answer customer inquiries at our call center to find a solution to technical problems. Record details of customer issues. Schedule follow-up assistance if needed.

An online skills test is required as part of the application. To request a practice version of the test, e-mail HR Director Aaron Bryson at abryson@salvidarinc.com. To apply for the position, upload your résumé at salvidarinc.com/HR.

8 What is a responsibility of the role?

(A) Resolving technical issues over the phone
(B) Writing new versions of software programs
(C) Training coworkers in IT skills
(D) Visiting customers' homes in person

9 How can applicants receive a sample test?

(A) By visiting a Web site
(B) By calling Mr. Bryson
(C) By sending an e-mail
(D) By attending an event

ACTUAL TEST

Questions 10-11 refer to the following notice.

NOTICE TO ELLISON BANK CUSTOMERS

Please be aware that we will be remodeling the first floor of our bank, including the waiting area. The hours of operation will not change during the work. They will still be Monday to Friday from 8 A.M. to 6 P.M. and Saturday from 10 A.M. to 3 P.M. The project will begin this Monday, October 5, and it is supposed to be completed by the end of the month. All banking services will still be available during this time. The work crew will try to minimize disruption. However, there may be supplies or wires in some areas, so please take care when walking around the first floor.

Thank you for your understanding.

Timothy Sotelo, Branch Manager

10 What is the purpose of the notice?

(A) To explain the reason for a building closure
(B) To warn customers about a reduction in services
(C) To ask customers to be careful during renovations
(D) To introduce a bank's new hours of operation

11 When will the notice most likely be removed?

(A) October 1
(B) October 5
(C) October 31
(D) November 5

Questions 12-13 refer to the following e-mail.

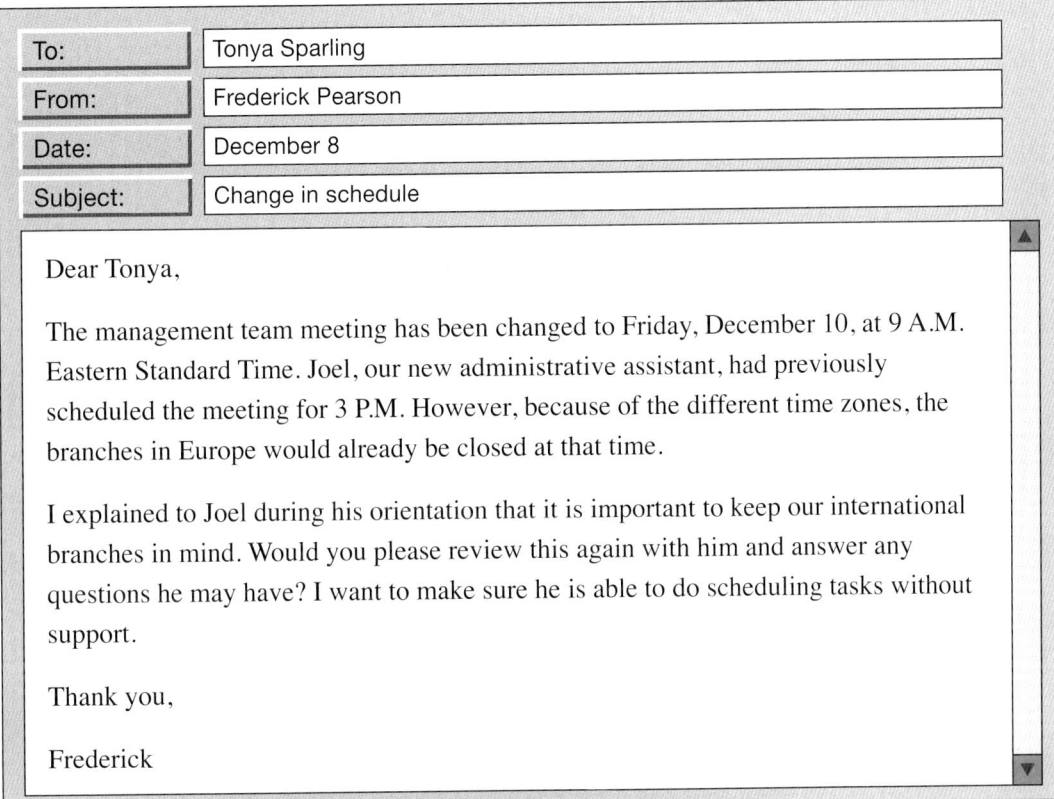

To: Tonya Sparling
From: Frederick Pearson
Date: December 8
Subject: Change in schedule

Dear Tonya,

The management team meeting has been changed to Friday, December 10, at 9 A.M. Eastern Standard Time. Joel, our new administrative assistant, had previously scheduled the meeting for 3 P.M. However, because of the different time zones, the branches in Europe would already be closed at that time.

I explained to Joel during his orientation that it is important to keep our international branches in mind. Would you please review this again with him and answer any questions he may have? I want to make sure he is able to do scheduling tasks without support.

Thank you,

Frederick

12 Why did Mr. Pearson send the e-mail?

(A) To introduce an employee to a manager
(B) To provide an agenda for a meeting
(C) To request additional training for an employee
(D) To schedule an interview with a job candidate

13 What problem with the original meeting does Mr. Pearson mention?

(A) Some equipment was not ready for use.
(B) Mr. Pearson had another schedule at that time.
(C) It was arranged for a national holiday.
(D) It was after working hours for some branches.

UNIT 20

지문 유형별 (2)

1. 양식(form)
2. 메시지 대화문
3. 연계 지문_이중 지문
4. 연계 지문_삼중 지문

Actual Test

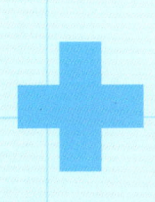

다양한 형식으로 출제되는 **양식 지문**은 정보를 나열하는 글이므로, 질문에 해당하는 정보를 찾는 능력이 필요합니다. **메시지 대화문**은 2지문씩 출제되며 일상에서 자주 사용하는 문자 메시지 형태로, 간단한 일상 대화 표현들을 학습해 두어야 합니다. 총 25문제가 출제되는 **연계 지문**의 경우 두 개, 세 개 지문을 빠르게 훑으며 서로의 관련성을 파악하는 것이 문제 풀이의 관건입니다.

1 양식(form)

양식 지문은 정보가 나열되는 형식의 글이므로, 자세히 읽기보다는 질문을 보며 필요한 정보를 찾아내는 것이 중요합니다. 양식은 웹페이지, 일정표, 정보, 설문지, 우편엽서 등의 다양한 종류가 출제됩니다.

● **지문의 기본 구조**

10th Annual Design Innovation Conference
Woodby Center, Toronto ◆ April 28–30

Day 1 Schedule

9:00 A.M. Registration and refreshments

10:00 A.M. Presentation: "Boosting Your Design Creativity" by Isabella Hovis

11:00 A.M. Presentation: "Managing Client Expectations" by Tiffany Bartlett

12:30 P.M. Lunch break

1:30 P.M. Workshop: "Software Programs That Improve Efficiency" by Simon Belmore

3:00 P.M. Presentation: "Trends in Graphic Design" by Diane Atkins

5:00 P.M. Question-and-Answer Session with small business owners in the field

NOTE: A buffet lunch is included in the registration fee.

읽는 대상 및 글의 목적 파악

행사의 종류와 글을 읽는 대상 등 전반적인 사항을 먼저 파악합니다. 이 글은 디자인 업계 사람들을 위해 쓰인 글입니다.

빈출 문제
Q. Who is the intended audience of this schedule?
이 일정표의 의도된 독자는 누구인가?

양식 세부 사항 확인

일정표처럼 정보가 나열되어 있는 경우는 전체를 읽는 것보다는 부분을 보면서 질문에 해당하는 정보를 찾습니다. 아래 질문의 경우 벨모어 씨가 나온 부분을 찾아 그가 발표하는 내용을 찾습니다.

빈출 문제
Q. What will Mr. Belmore do?
벨모어 씨가 할 것은 무엇인가?

주의 사항 및 추가 정보 확인

양식 지문에서 주의 사항이나 추가 정보를 알리는 문장이 있다면 반드시 읽고 관련 문제가 있는지 확인합니다. 학회 등록비에는 식사비가 포함되어 있음을 추가로 알리고 있습니다.

빈출 문제
Q. What is indicated about the conference?
학회에 대해 언급된 것은 무엇인가?

해석 p.197

어휘 innovation 혁신 registration 등록 refreshments 다과 boost 북돋우다 creativity 창의력 expectation 기대 improve 향상시키다 efficiency 효율성 owner 소유주 buffet 뷔페 fee 요금

빈출 표현

review	평가, 논평	warranty	품질 보증서
testimonial	추천서	keynote address	기조연설
questionnaire	설문지	instructions	설명서
complete	작성하다; 완료하다	annual	연례의, 1년마다의
submit	제출하다	refreshments	다과
register for	~에 등록하다	beverage	음료
sign up for	~을 신청하다	RSVP	(초대장에서) 회답 주시기 바랍니다

미니 테스트

Question 1 refers to the following online form.

1. What type of business is Howard and Mitchell Inc.?

    (A) An inspection service
    (B) A moving company
    (C) A landscaping firm
    (D) A real estate agency

2 메시지 대화문

메시지 대화문은 2인 대화와 3인 대화로 나뉩니다. 주로 회사 업무에 관한 내용이 다루어지며, 대화 상대들이 서로 어떤 관계에 있는지 파악해 가며 글을 읽어야 합니다.

● 지문의 기본 구조

Erwin, Katherine [10:45 A.M.]
Levi, I need you to come to the Danby Bank construction site.

Rossi, Levi [10:47 A.M.]
What's going on?

Erwin, Katherine [10:48 A.M.]
The cement mixer has broken down. It needs to be fixed right away so we don't fall behind schedule.

Rossi, Levi [10:49 A.M.]
You've got to be kidding. I inspected it yesterday.

Erwin, Katherine [10:51 A.M.]
I know.

Rossi, Levi [10:52 A.M.]
All right. I'll be there as soon as I can.

대화 상대 및 글의 주제 파악
메시지를 주고받는 사람들의 관계를 파악해 가며 글을 읽습니다. 두 사람은 공사장과 관련된 이야기를 나누고 있습니다.

빈출 문제
Q. What are the writers mainly discussing?
화자들이 주로 논의하고 있는 것은 무엇인가?

세부 사항 확인
대화 중에는 문제점이나 요청 사항들이 주로 언급됩니다.

빈출 문제
Q. What problem does Ms. Erwin mention?
어윈 씨가 언급한 문제점은 무엇인가?

의도를 묻는 문제
해당 문장이 나온 부분에 표시를 해 두고 앞뒤 문맥을 파악해야 합니다. 지문에서 '말도 안 된다'고 한 것은 어제 이미 점검을 하고 왔다는 것을 강조하기 위한 표현입니다.

빈출 문제
Q. At 10:49 A.M., what does Mr. Rossi mean when he writes, "You've got to be kidding"?
오전 10시 49분에, 로시 씨가 "말도 안 돼요"라고 말한 의도는 무엇인가?

해석 p.198

어휘 construction 공사, 건설 site 장소, 현장 mixer 혼합기 break down 고장 나다 fix 고치다 behind schedule 일정보다 늦은 inspect 검사하다, 점검하다

● 빈출 표현

Absolutely.	그럼요., 당연하죠.	I'll take care of it.	제가 처리할게요.
That's no problem.	문제없어요.	Are you available?	시간 있으신가요?
Done.	다 됐어요.	What's going on?	무슨 일이죠?
Good to know.	알려 줘서 고마워요.	I can make it.	해낼 수 있어요.; (약속 시간 등에) 맞출 수 있어요.
Sounds good.	좋아요.		

미니 테스트

정답 및 해설 p.198

Question 1 refers to the following text-message chain.

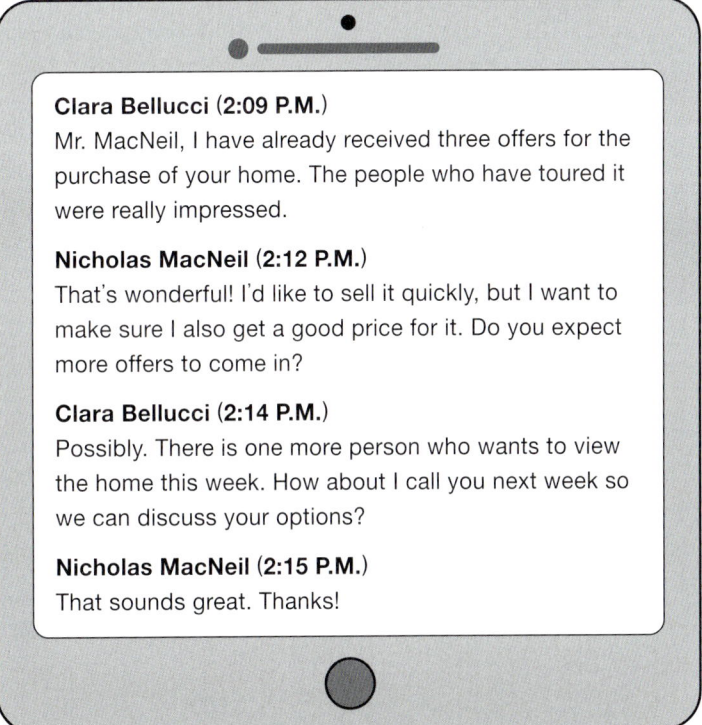

1 What are the writers mainly discussing?

   (A) A business loan
   (B) A renovation project
   (C) A travel schedule
   (D) A property sale

3 연계 지문_이중 지문

이중 지문은 지문 간의 연관성을 파악한 후 두 지문에 연계되어 있는 단서를 통해 정답을 찾아야 합니다.

● 문제 풀이 전략

Ace Flooring Specialists Cost Estimate

Client: Brentwood Community Center

DESCRIPTION OF WORK	ESTIMATED COST
Removal of 5,000 sq. ft. of old carpet	$3,750
Disposal of carpet	$800
5,000 sq. ft. of hardwood flooring (materials and labor)	$54,250
Estimated Total	$58,800

Prepared by Vince Ramos on November 8, (697) 555-8140

두 지문의 연관 관계 파악
첫 번째 지문의 견적서를 바탕으로 아래 이메일이 작성되었으므로 둘의 관계를 파악합니다. 표가 나오는 경우는 그 안에 있는 정보를 묻는 문제가 출제될 확률이 높습니다.

연계 질문 확인
질문에서 언급하고 있는 대상이 하나의 지문에 나와 있지만 그 지문 안에서 답을 찾을 수 없다면 정답의 단서는 나머지 지문에 있게 마련입니다.

[연계 질문]
Q. How many square feet is the community center's lobby?
커뮤니티 센터의 로비는 몇 평방피트인가?

To: Ruth Clark, Brentwood Community Center Director
From: Joseph Landrum, Maintenance Manager
Subject: Budget
Date: November 10

Dear Ruth,

I'd like to reserve $58,800 in next year's budget to replace the lobby's carpet with hardwood flooring. The carpet is badly worn because of our 2,000 visitors monthly, so it's time for a change anyway.

Thanks,

Joseph

연계 질문의 단서 확인
두 번째 지문인 이메일에서 로비 카펫을 교체해야 함을 언급하고 있으며 첫 번째 지문의 견적서 표에서 카펫이 5,000평방피트임을 알 수 있으므로 이 둘을 연계하여 정답을 찾습니다.

[질문 정답]
A. 5,000

어휘 estimate 견적서 removal 제거 material 재료 labor 노동 reserve (나중을 위해) 따로 남겨 두다 replace 교체하다, 대체하다

Question 1 refers to the following brochure and sales report.

Colonial Lumber Company

630 Berkeley Street
Philadelphia, PA 19103

Colonial Lumber Company supplies high-quality wood products to individuals for woodworking projects. We offer a wide range of sizes in the following options:

Pine: A soft wood that is popular with woodworkers at the basic level.	**Cedar**: A beautiful wood known for its red tones and pleasant scent.
Oak: A sturdy wood with distinct patterns in the wood grain.	**Engineered Wood**: A manufactured wood made from recycled wood pieces.

We offer free delivery on orders exceeding $100. To place an order, or for inquiries, please call 267-555-9663.

Colonial Lumber Company: Sales Summary for March and April

Units Sold:

Wood Type	March	April
Pine	8,965	9,177
Oak	6,287	6,501
Cedar	4,884	4,960
Engineered Wood	3,133	3,279
Total	23,269	23,917

1 What is indicated about Colonial Lumber Company's top-selling product?

(A) It is used by beginners.
(B) It has a nice smell.
(C) It has noticeable patterns.
(D) It is made from recycled materials.

4 연계 지문_삼중 지문

대개 다섯 문제 중 두 문제가 연계 문제로 출제됩니다. 삼중 지문의 연계 문제를 풀 때는 문제의 키워드가 등장하는 지문 내용을 파악한 후 나머지 지문에서 연계 단서를 찾아야 합니다. 연계 단서는 주로 포괄적인 표현이나 유사 표현 등으로 패러프레이징된다는 점에 유의하세요.

● 문제 풀이 전략

Garden in the Sky
The Verona Community Center has just opened its new rooftop garden. It features flower gardens designed by Joshua Duarte as well as metal sculptures created by artist Loretta Cole.

To: Violet Piper ⟨vpiper@waukeshainc.com⟩
From: Jackson Higgins ⟨jhiggins@waukeshainc.com⟩
Date: August 1
Subject: Verona trip

Dear Violet,

The travel arrangements have been made for your trip to Verona. You will be staying at the Rubin Hotel. I hope you enjoy touring the community center's new garden. I found out that Loretta Cole will be there to answer your questions on August 5.

Sincerely,

Jackson

http://rubinhotel.com/home

At Rubin Hotel, we aim to provide guests with a relaxing and comfortable atmosphere. We have just completed construction on our building and we are excited to share it with you. Visit our Booking page to make a reservation.

세 지문의 연관 관계 파악

삼중 지문은 세 지문 간의 관계를 먼저 빠르게 파악하는 것이 중요합니다. 첫 번째 지문은 커뮤니티 센터를 광고하는 글이며, 두 번째 지문은 이메일로 출장 장소(커뮤니티 센터)와 숙소(루빈 호텔)를 안내하는 내용입니다. 마지막으로 세 번째 지문은 루빈 호텔의 웹사이트입니다.

연계 문제 풀이 1

파이퍼 씨는 8월 5일에 콜(Cole) 씨를 만난다고 했는데, 콜 씨는 첫 번째 지문에서 조각상을 만든 예술가라고 언급되어 있습니다.

빈출 문제

Q. Who will Ms. Piper meet on August 5?
파이퍼 씨가 8월 5일에 만나는 사람은 누구인가?

A. A sculptor
조각가

연계 문제 풀이 2

두 번째 지문에서 파이퍼 씨는 루빈 호텔에 머물 예정이라고 했는데, 세 번째 지문에서 루빈 호텔 공사가 이제 막 완료되었다고 했으므로 새로 지어진 호텔임을 알 수 있습니다.

빈출 문제

Q. What is indicated about Ms. Piper?
파이퍼 씨에 대해 언급된 것은 무엇인가?

A. She will stay at a newly built hotel.
그녀는 새로 지어진 호텔에 체류할 것이다.

해석 p.201

어휘 rooftop 옥상 feature 특색을 이루다 as well as ~뿐만 아니라 metal 금속 sculpture 조각상 arrangement 준비
aim to do ~하는 것을 목표로 하다 comfortable 편안한 atmosphere 분위기

Question 1-2 refer to the following article, job posting, and e-mail.

VITORIA (February 17)—Salvim Laboratories has confirmed that the company has nearly completed the development of a new variety of soybean called Formosa. The plant needs much less water compared to other soybeans. Upon the completion of this project, the next generation of Formosa will begin to be developed. It will have a much shorter growing time than previous varieties.

Salvim Laboratories is Hiring!

We have openings in Information Technology, Research and Development, Human Resources, and Sales as we begin the development of Damasio, the next generation of the popular Formosa soybean plant. Previous experience is required for all positions. In addition, Research and Development applicants must have a degree in a scientific field. Apply online at salvimlabs.com.

E-Mail

To: Yasmin Santos
From: Matheus Costa
Date: July 31
Subject: Document

Dear Ms. Santos,

I would like to thank you once again for the job offer. I am excited about joining the Salvim Laboratories staff. Please find attached proof of my degree, which is required for the position. If you need anything else, please let me know.

Warmest regards,

Matheus Costa

1 What is a feature of Damasio?

(A) It will produce more beans.
(B) It will use less water.
(C) It will have a better flavor.
(D) It will grow more quickly.

2 In which department will Mr. Costa work?

(A) Information Technology
(B) Research and Development
(C) Sales
(D) Human Resources

ACTUAL TEST

Questions 1-2 refer to the following postcard.

POSTCARD

Dobson Resort
1317 Columbia Road
Denver, CO 80231
Telephone: 720-555-3216

Dear Brett Lewis,

We would like to remind you that your membership will expire on August 31. Be sure to renew it so that you can continue playing golf at our site. In addition to giving you unlimited time on the course, membership also allows you to get 10 percent off all equipment at the Dobson Resort clubhouse and 15 percent off meals at our restaurant.

To make a renewal, visit www.dobsonresort.com.

1 Who most likely is Mr. Lewis?

(A) A business investor
(B) A resort owner
(C) A golf instructor
(D) A golf club member

2 What is indicated about Dobson Resort?

(A) It provides customers with free equipment.
(B) Its prices will increase after August 31.
(C) It has an on-site dining facility.
(D) It will open a new location soon.

Questions 3-4 refer to the following text-message chain.

Eva Peralta [11:03 A.M.]
What was the magazine you needed for the training workshop? I'm at a newsstand. I could look for it now.

Spencer Gresham [11:07 A.M.]
It's called World Finance, and I need the June edition. There's an interesting article in it that I wanted to share.

Eva Peralta [11:08 A.M.]
All right. I'll check for you.

Eva Peralta [11:12 A.M.]
They have it! I'll pay cash for it and get a receipt. Please submit that so I can get reimbursed. It's a small amount, but it's still a business expense.

Spencer Gresham [11:13 A.M.]
I'll do that. Thanks!

3. What is probably true about the magazine?

(A) It is not sold at most newsstands.
(B) It will be used in a training session.
(C) It has an article about Ms. Peralta.
(D) It is published once a week.

4. At 11:13 A.M., what does Mr. Gresham mean when he writes, "I'll do that"?

(A) He will meet Ms. Peralta.
(B) He will submit a receipt.
(C) He will withdraw some cash.
(D) He will check a policy.

ACTUAL TEST

Questions 5-9 refer to the following e-mail and form.

To:	Timothy Hensley
From:	Zaida Dawson
Subject:	Reimbursement request
Date:	June 18
Attachment:	business expenses form, Dawson receipts

Hi Mr. Hensley,

I started working at Medina Enterprises a couple of weeks ago, and I've already completed my first business trip. My manager told me that I should send the receipts for my business expenses to the finance team, along with a completed form. As I understand it, the cost of the airline tickets, hotel, and taxi fares are covered. In addition, I can receive reimbursement for up to $45 per day for my meals.

Please find the necessary details on the attached form. Scans of the relevant receipts are also attached. I used taxis to travel between the airport and the hotel as well as between the hotel and the convention center. If you need further details, please let me know.

Sincerely,

Zaida Dawson

Medina Enterprises Business Expenses Form

To receive reimbursement, please complete this form and submit it to the finance team. Receipts should be provided. The reimbursement will be processed within five business days.

Employee Name: Zaida Dawson
Reason for Expenses: Business trip to attend annual sales convention in Dallas, Texas

Category	Dates			
	June 12	June 13	June 14	June 15
Airline Tickets	$235.00	—	—	$235.00
Taxi Fares	$56.00	$14.80	$15.90	$53.00
Hotel	$129.00	$129.00	$129.00	$129.00
Meals	$28.50	$52.00	$43.50	$18.00

5. What is the purpose of the e-mail?

   (A) To comply with a process
   (B) To sign up for an event
   (C) To schedule a meeting
   (D) To recommend a job opportunity

6. What does Ms. Dawson mention about herself?

   (A) She gave a talk at a conference.
   (B) She has lost a receipt.
   (C) She used to live in Texas.
   (D) She is a new employee.

7. What is suggested about Mr. Hensley?

   (A) He works at a different branch from Ms. Dawson.
   (B) He is Ms. Dawson's manager.
   (C) He is in charge of scheduling business trips.
   (D) He is a member of the finance team.

8. In the e-mail, the word "covered" in paragraph 1, line 4, is closest in meaning to

   (A) wrapped up
   (B) kept safe
   (C) paid for
   (D) stored away

9. For which day's expenses will Ms. Dawson not receive full reimbursement?

   (A) June 12
   (B) June 13
   (C) June 14
   (D) June 15

ACTUAL TEST

Questions 10-14 refer to the following memo, telephone message, and e-mail.

From: Christina Irving, General Manager
To: All Charleston branch employees
Date: April 3
Subject: Building closure

The Hodge Building will be closed from 4 P.M. on Friday, April 7, to both employees and visitors so that a new air conditioning system can be installed. The new system will be more energy efficient than the current one. It will consume much less electricity each month.

Employees can leave work at 4 P.M. without using any vacation time. Please note that the building will also be closed for part of Saturday, as the work is expected to be completed by Saturday morning around 11 A.M. To prevent dust from getting into your work computers, please cover them with plastic sheets before you leave on Friday. Materials are provided in the Human Resources office.

TELEPHONE MESSAGE

For: Christina Irving
Caller (Company): Samuel Cordova (Nelson Inc.)
Date: Thursday, April 6
Time: 10:52 A.M.

☑ New call   ☐ Returning your call
☐ Please call back   ☑ Caller left a message (see below)

Message:
Some of the components needed for the installation will not be delivered until Friday evening. Because of this, we cannot begin the work as planned. That also means the work will be completed about three hours later than we had originally promised.

Message taken by: Aaron Trin

E-Mail Message

From: Dean Boyd
To: Finance Team
Date: April 6
Subject: Closure

Dear Team,

I have just been informed that tomorrow's installation work will begin later than planned. If you have any work projects to finish up, you do not need to leave the building at four o'clock. Whether you leave early or on time, please remember to carry out the necessary preparations requested by Ms. Irving in her memo.

Thanks!

Dean

---

10. According to the memo, why will the Hodge Building be temporarily closed?

    (A) A potential buyer will take a tour.
    (B) Safety inspections will be conducted.
    (C) A cooling system will be installed.
    (D) Some walls will be painted.

11. What benefit of the change does Ms. Irving mention?

    (A) Increasing security
    (B) Using less energy
    (C) Saving time
    (D) Attracting new clients

12. Why did Mr. Cordova call Ms. Irving?

    (A) To ask how to access a building
    (B) To explain a problem with some parts
    (C) To report an issue with a regulation
    (D) To get approval on a budget increase

13. What is the new expected time for the project to be completed?

    (A) Friday evening
    (B) Saturday morning
    (C) Saturday afternoon
    (D) Sunday morning

14. What does Mr. Boyd remind his team to do?

    (A) Use a different entrance
    (B) Move some office furniture
    (C) Take personal items home
    (D) Cover some equipment

RC

실전
모의고사

READING TEST

In the Reading test, you will read a variety of texts and answer several different types of reading comprehension questions. The entire Reading test will last 75 minutes. There are three parts, and directions are given for each part. You are encouraged to answer as many questions as possible within the time allowed.

You must mark your answers on the separate answer sheet. Do not write your answers in your test book.

PART 5

Directions: A word or phrase is missing in each of the sentences below. Four answer choices are given below each sentence. Select the best answer to complete the sentence. Then mark the letter (A), (B), (C), or (D) on your answer sheet.

101. All valuables are stored ------- in the hotel's safe.
    (A) secures
    (B) securely
    (C) security
    (D) secure

102. Following an intense -------, the Alvarado Inc. managers were able to finalize the contract's terms.
    (A) negotiate
    (B) negotiated
    (C) negotiating
    (D) negotiation

103. A reception was held to welcome Ms. Dennis and ------- team.
    (A) her
    (B) hers
    (C) she
    (D) herself

104. The human resources department ------- the compliance records required by the federal government.
    (A) maintains
    (B) cultivates
    (C) persuades
    (D) associates

105. Fairway Shipping cannot issue refunds for delays caused by circumstances ------- its control.
    (A) below
    (B) before
    (C) behind
    (D) beyond

106. ------- can be spent on repairs without the written consent of the building manager.
    (A) Nothing
    (B) Never
    (C) Somebody
    (D) Another

107. Under the new policy, salespeople are responsible for ------- their own clients.
    (A) to find
    (B) find
    (C) found
    (D) finding

108. The shuttle bus was running behind schedule due to getting ------- in rush-hour traffic.
    (A) forced
    (B) stuck
    (C) rejected
    (D) stood

109. The theater's parking lot fills up quickly, so we ------- arriving early to find a spot.
(A) recommend
(B) recommendation
(C) to recommend
(D) recommending

110. Banquet guests received a bag of party ------- when they arrived.
(A) favored
(B) to favor
(C) favors
(D) favorably

111. New safety measures will be implemented at the factory ------- this month.
(A) soon
(B) later
(C) often
(D) almost

112. The hotel's lobby will be repainted because the current color is too -------.
(A) bright
(B) brightly
(C) brighter
(D) brightest

113. The Harrison Gym invited all its members ------- a class on proper weightlifting techniques.
(A) to
(B) out
(C) of
(D) about

114. While other talks at the journalism conference were ------- brief, the keynote speech lasted two hours.
(A) comparison
(B) comparing
(C) comparatively
(D) compare

115. This file cabinet contains health insurance certificates along with other confidential -------.
(A) documents
(B) treatments
(C) structures
(D) events

116. The ------- partner should provide help such as administrative support when needed.
(A) cooperates
(B) cooperate
(C) cooperating
(D) cooperatively

117. ------- Mr. Jenkins received a better offer from the competitor, she decided to stay at her current company.
(A) Rather
(B) Whether
(C) Although
(D) As well as

118. There are several projects that need attention, but the sales pitch for Purnell Enterprises is the -------.
(A) most urgent
(B) urgent
(C) more urgently
(D) urgently

119. Participants are expected to write down their questions instead of asking them ------- the workshop.
(A) directly
(B) in case
(C) during
(D) while

120. Stimson Automotive is ------- changing the sales commission plan for its full-time employees.
(A) completely
(B) completeness
(C) complete
(D) completed

GO ON TO THE NEXT PAGE

121. Low-income patients are ------- to receive free medication through the patient support program.
    (A) typical
    (B) eligible
    (C) accurate
    (D) unfair

122. The total number of bike ------- in the city has nearly doubled in the past decade.
    (A) message
    (B) messaging
    (C) messengers
    (D) messaged

123. Because the department has a small budget, purchases of ------- $50 must be approved by a manager.
    (A) except
    (B) than
    (C) over
    (D) toward

124. At the moment, Morgan Industries ------- to renew its contract with the supplier.
    (A) hesitant
    (B) is hesitant
    (C) was hesitant
    (D) to be hesitant

125. You will not be reimbursed for company expenses ------- you provide a receipt.
    (A) since
    (B) whereas
    (C) unless
    (D) while

126. Using his ------- experience, the real estate agent was able to provide an accurate estimate of the home's value.
    (A) apart
    (B) once
    (C) either
    (D) past

127. By this time tomorrow, the hiring committee ------- its decision on who will replace Ms. Gibbs.
    (A) finalizes
    (B) had finalized
    (C) is finalizing
    (D) will have finalized

128. Answers to the most ------- asked questions will be posted on the company Web site.
    (A) actively
    (B) finally
    (C) frequently
    (D) absolutely

129. Boar County will oversee the installation of the jogging trails, the purpose of ------- is to fulfill the demand for outdoor exercise.
    (A) any
    (B) whom
    (C) one
    (D) which

130. The ------- reason for the newly imposed regulations is to improve the factory's safety rating.
    (A) intensive
    (B) creative
    (C) primary
    (D) dependable

PART 6

Directions: Read the texts that follow. A word, phrase, or sentence is missing in parts of each text. Four answer choices for each question are given below the text. Select the best answer to complete the text. Then mark the letter (A), (B), (C), or (D) on your answer sheet.

Questions 131-134 refer to the following article.

BEAUMONT, TX (April 20)—As part of the celebration of our city's history, Centennial Hall ------- an orchestra concert featuring the work of local composer Emilia Oyola. Tickets go on
131.
sale at the box office and online tomorrow. The show is set for June 3 at 7:30 P.M.

While Ms. Oyola will be the conductor, some of the pieces will not be ------- . Two songs
132.
written by other local composers are also part of the lineup. ------- .
133.

The concert will mark the first performance of the Beaumont City Orchestra since the concert hall was renovated. ------- attendees to Centennial Hall will certainly notice a vast
134.
improvement in sound quality thanks to sound reflectors added to the ceiling.

131. (A) host
 (B) hosted
 (C) will host
 (D) has hosted

132. (A) hers
 (B) ours
 (C) theirs
 (D) its

133. (A) Ms. Oyola grew up just outside of Beaumont.
 (B) The orchestra is looking for new members.
 (C) Ms. Oyola plays the piano and violin.
 (D) It is these composers' official debut.

134. (A) Authorized
 (B) Sensible
 (C) Preceding
 (D) Regular

GO ON TO THE NEXT PAGE

Questions 135-138 refer to the following e-mail.

To: Ivan Bryson <ivanb@brysonart.com>
From: Heather Wallace <heather@zamora-gallery.com>
Date: June 10
Subject: Zamora Gallery plans

Dear Mr. Bryson,

On behalf of the Zamora Gallery, I would like to say how pleased we are to be featuring some of your work at our upcoming exhibit. Our marketing team uses a variety of ------- to **135.** highlight new artists such as yourself. For instance, we ------- you on our homepage so that **136.** visitors can learn more about your work. ------- . Therefore, we would like you to write a brief **137.** biography of yourself, around two hundred words. You can see examples of other artists' biographies on our Web site if you are not sure what should be included. Upon completion, please send ------- to me as soon as possible. **138.**

Should you have any questions, I would be more than happy to answer them. I can be reached at this e-mail address.

Warmest regards,

Heather Wallace

135. (A) strategies
(B) investigations
(C) assets
(D) competitions

136. (A) will promote
(B) promoting
(C) had promoted
(D) promotes

137. (A) Over time, it is very common for the artwork to increase in value.
(B) A senior marketer oversees all parts of the campaign from start to finish.
(C) This is most effective when we have more information about your background.
(D) Each painting is carefully wrapped and labeled before being transported.

138. (A) it
(B) them
(C) your
(D) some

Questions 139-142 refer to the following advertisement.

Reiko Refrigerated Transportation Services

Do you need to ship goods that must be refrigerated while in transit? ------- **139.** . Reiko has been in the shipping industry for decades, and we can help you whether you are transporting medications, perishable food, or more.

We have a variety of vehicle sizes to suit your shipment. ------- **140.** include small vans, mid-sized trucks, and large trailers. We only work with refrigerated items, and we have done so throughout our company's history. This ------- **141.** means our employees are highly experienced in keeping a controlled environment for your goods.

We want potential customers ------- **142.** confident in our services. That's why we insure all items and offer a money-back guarantee.

139. (A) We can ensure your items stay at the right temperature.
(B) The thermometer can detect even the smallest changes.
(C) Reiko may be under new ownership soon.
(D) An insulating layer in the packaging would be better.

140. (A) Anything
(B) These
(C) Everyone
(D) Both

141. (A) manuscript
(B) incentive
(C) specialization
(D) routine

142. (A) have felt
(B) to feel
(C) and felt
(D) who feels

Questions 143-146 refer to the following letter.

Duane Shepherd
215 Fairfield Road
Cambridge, MA 02142

September 3

Dear Valued Patient,

The Patterson Dental Clinic ------- to 1575 Kerry Way on November 1. From that date, ------- appointments will take place at the new location. We are excited to offer our patients more modern facilities, a larger waiting area, and better parking options at our new site. We are also considering expanding our business hours to make it easier for people working full-time to find an appointment after work or on weekends. ------- , the final schedule has not been determined yet.

We are excited to serve you at our new office. ------- . One of our staff members would be happy to give you directions.

Sincerely,

The Patterson Dental Clinic Team

143. (A) relocated
(B) relocate
(C) will relocate
(D) relocating

144. (A) other
(B) those
(C) all
(D) they

145. (A) However
(B) Similarly
(C) Above all
(D) For example

146. (A) A new dentist will be joining our practice soon.
(B) If you have difficulty finding the building, please feel free to call us.
(C) Your personal dental records will be kept confidential at all times.
(D) The variety of services offered by our clinic remain the same as before.

PART 7

Directions: In this part you will read a selection of texts, such as magazine and newspaper articles, e-mails, and instant messages. Each text or set of texts is followed by several questions. Select the best answer for each question and mark the letter (A), (B), (C), or (D) on your answer sheet.

Questions 147-148 refer to the following memo.

MEMO

To: Prolance Customer Service Team
From: Olivia Cronin
Re: Customer complaints
Date: September 2

The August electricity bills were calculated incorrectly, so customers received bills that were too high. We're issuing new bills this week, so please explain this to customers if needed.

Additionally, we are receiving a lot of positive feedback from customers. Therefore, starting next month, we will make printouts of what customers are saying and hang them up in the break room to help motivate the staff.

147. Why did Ms. Cronin send the message?

(A) To describe a policy
(B) To explain a problem
(C) To introduce new equipment
(D) To announce a staff change

148. When can employees start to see comments from customers?

(A) In September
(B) In October
(C) In November
(D) In December

GO ON TO THE NEXT PAGE

Questions 149-150 refer to the following notice.

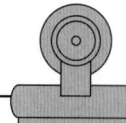

NOTICE

On Wednesday, August 4, Ocala Electricity Services will repair the main breaker here at Avalon Suites. This requires shutting off the electricity to all units. Those living in the building will not have electricity during the maintenance work, which will start at 10 A.M. Prior to this time, we recommend that you power down computers and other electrical devices to avoid damage. Refrigerators can remain without electricity for up to four hours without affecting the food, as long as the door is kept closed. The work will be completed by 11 A.M. We apologize for any inconvenience this may cause.

149. Who is the intended audience of this notice?

(A) Electricians
(B) Tenants
(C) Building owners
(D) Maintenance workers

150. What most likely will happen at Avalon Suites at 11 A.M. on August 4?

(A) New computers will be set up.
(B) An entrance will be off limits.
(C) Some units will be inspected.
(D) People can use the electricity again.

Questions 151-152 refer to the following text-message chain.

Charles Griffith (9:58 A.M.)
Hi, Penelope. I'm here at the factory, and I just found out that the delivery from Treetop Textiles is late. We were supposed to get the leather for the front-pocket handbags yesterday.

Penelope Lapierre (10:01 A.M.)
Not again! I think we need to start looking for another supplier for our leather. This is the third late delivery from Treetop Textiles this month.

Charles Griffith (10:04 A.M.)
I agree, but wouldn't there be a penalty for canceling the contract?

Penelope Lapierre (10:06 A.M.)
The current one is coming to an end in just a few weeks.

Charles Griffith (10:07 A.M.)
Oh, really? Then let's get on with it.

Penelope Lapierre (10:10 A.M.)
Sounds good to me. But as for today, does that mean there is nothing for the production floor workers to do?

Charles Griffith (10:12 A.M.)
I'll assign the handbag workers to something else now. That way, we won't lose any working hours while we wait for the delivery from Treetop.

151. At 10:07 A.M., what does Mr. Griffith mean when he writes, "Then let's get on with it"?

(A) They should pay a fee for rush delivery.
(B) They should start working on the handbags.
(C) They should update some contract terms.
(D) They should try to find a new supplier.

152. What will Mr. Griffith probably do next?

(A) Inspect some finished handbags
(B) Check a delivery address
(C) Reassign employees to other tasks
(D) Order leather from another business

GO ON TO THE NEXT PAGE

Questions 153-154 refer to the following advertisement.

Preston Swim Center

The days are getting colder, but that doesn't mean you have to give up swimming. You can swim indoors with Preston Swim Center. We offer two Olympic-size swimming pools and one shallow junior pool. And from October 10, we will stay open one hour later on weekdays and two hours later on weekends.

Special Offer: Purchase a 30-day pass and get a free towel. The pass can be used by the purchaser or their family. It is valid for all Preston Swim Center activities, including group classes, and it will save you 60% compared to the daily rate.

153. What is true about Preston Swim Center?

(A) It has four indoor swimming pools.
(B) It will extend its hours of operation.
(C) It sells swimming accessories on site.
(D) It was not open on weekends previously.

154. What is NOT mentioned about the 30-day pass?

(A) It is cheaper than paying the daily rate.
(B) It is replaced for free if lost.
(C) It can be transferred to another person.
(D) It includes group activities.

Questions 155-157 refer to the following advertisement.

TRUE TO THE FRUIT
May 1–14

Available at participating supermarkets nationwide!

At TC Beverage Co., we don't add any artificial flavors to our line of Refresh juice. That means each bottle of Refresh is both healthy and delicious, and it tastes the same as if you squeezed fresh fruit yourself at home.

No other juice on the market can compete with Refresh's natural taste. But don't take our word for it—in our nationwide "True to the Fruit" event, you can do a blind taste-test of Refresh and another brand to see how they compare. Look for the "True to the Fruit" kiosk at your local supermarket. Anyone who participates in the store taste-test will be given a code to use on our Web site to get 50% off any Refresh product.

For further details about the event, visit www.tcbevco.com, call our help line at 1-800-555-6600, or talk to a customer service agent at your local supermarket.

155. Why is TC Beverage Co. holding the event?
(A) To compare its products to those of its competitors
(B) To promote recipes made with its products
(C) To thank customers for their business
(D) To introduce a new product line

156. What will participants in the event be given?
(A) A TC Beverage Co. T-shirt
(B) A prize drawing entry
(C) A discount code
(D) Samples to take home

157. What is NOT mentioned as a way to get more information about the event?
(A) Signing up for a newsletter
(B) Visiting a Web site
(C) Making a phone call
(D) Speaking to a supermarket employee

GO ON TO THE NEXT PAGE

Questions 158-160 refer to the following article.

Centennial Stadium Strikes Out

November 22, SARASOTA — Centennial Stadium, owned by Arcadia Corp., submitted plans for a second stadium, but permission to start construction was denied by the city's planning commission.

The proposed plan would have used 6 acres of non-developed land in the Hampton neighborhood, directly across the street from the current stadium. Arcadia Corp. purchased the land three years ago with the intention of creating a second stadium. However, as the land is classified as a wetland and is the natural habitat of many birds and reptiles, environmental groups are pushing to protect the area, and they have worked to block the proposal.

The head of Arcadia Corp., Craig Amos, argues that Sarasota needs a second stadium. "We need a site for the stadium, and this is the best neighborhood for attracting visitors and keeping heavy traffic out of the city center," Amos said in a recent statement.

Amos says the new sports facility would create hundreds of jobs for the city and give a boost to the tourism sector. He has scheduled a meeting with Sarasota city council members for next Tuesday in hopes of reviving the proposal.

---

158. What is the topic of the article?

(A) The closure of a stadium
(B) The announcement of a sports tournament
(C) The rejection of a building project
(D) The opening of an environmental park

159. What is suggested about the Hampton neighborhood?

(A) It enforces strict traffic regulations.
(B) It is the home of some wildlife.
(C) It includes several tourist attractions.
(D) It has changed a lot in three years.

160. What does Mr. Amos plan to do next week?

(A) Propose a city tour
(B) Start a new job
(C) Take part in a competition
(D) Meet with local officials

Questions 161-163 refer to the following announcement.

Attention: Wadena LTD Employees

—[1]—. The Wadena LTD management team is thrilled to inform everyone that we have been nominated for the Innovative Workplace Award. The winner will be announced on July 10.

—[2]—. As you know, this is a highly prestigious award. Great job, everyone! Over the past years, we have restructured our management system and provided intensive training to employees. —[3]—.

We plan to continue to strive for improvement at all levels of the company, and the HR department would love to hear your ideas on how to do so. Please e-mail Helen Callaway at h.callaway@wadenaltd.com if you have anything to share. —[4]—.

---

161. What is the purpose of the announcement?
(A) To introduce a new management structure
(B) To congratulate employees on an achievement
(C) To encourage staff to attend a training session
(D) To confirm an award winner

162. What is true about the HR department?
(A) Its manager will be promoted soon.
(B) It will assess employees' performance.
(C) Its newest employee is Helen Callaway.
(D) It is seeking feedback from employees.

163. In which of the positions marked [1], [2], [3], and [4] does the following sentence best belong?

"These measures have clearly been effective."

(A) [1]
(B) [2]
(C) [3]
(D) [4]

Questions 164-167 refer to the following brochure.

Turn your garden into a new income stream!

Fairmont Skills Center Course #5892: Growing Herbs for Profit

Fresh herbs are a popular product all year round, including in winter. With just a few skills, you can operate your own business growing and selling herbs.

The ongoing work for an herb garden is minimal, meaning you won't have to spend endless hours tending to your plants.

Fairmont Skills Center offers:

- Experienced instructors who can personalize class materials to the students' needs
- A range of class structures to suit the schedules of busy people
  Course A: Mondays 6 P.M. – 8 P.M.
  Course B: Wednesdays 1 P.M. – 3 P.M.
  Course C: Saturdays 9 A.M. – 11 A.M.
- Lower course fee with proof of residence in Fairmont
- A complete explanation on the process from start to finish, including teaching you the best ways to market your herbs to local restaurants and individuals
- Upon completing the course, you will be given a password that gives you access to our exclusive online forum, where you can ask questions and get help from other herb growers.

How much can you make by selling herbs? Here are the prices currently paid by local restaurants.

Basil	$14.00/lb.	Chives	$13.50/lb.
Oregano	$13.75/lb.	Coriander	$17.00/lb.

Enroll by March 1 at www.fairmontsc.com!

164. What benefit of growing herbs as a business is mentioned in the brochure?

(A) Small space needed
(B) Guaranteed large profits
(C) Ease of using equipment
(D) Short time commitment

165. Who can get a discount on the course?

(A) Advanced gardeners
(B) Restaurant owners
(C) Students with high grades
(D) People who live in Fairmont

166. What is true about the course?

(A) It will have ten total hours of training.
(B) It offers information about marketing.
(C) It will be taught outdoors.
(D) It is offered only in winter.

167. What will course participants receive?

(A) Ongoing online support
(B) Some gardening supplies
(C) A certificate of completion
(D) A contract with a local restaurant

Questions 168-171 refer to the following online chat discussion.

Kayla Lambert (9:05 A.M.):	Hi, Tara and Sven. Is the due date for the spring catalog still March 6?
Tara Hull (9:07 A.M.):	It needs to be sent to the printer on March 3.
Kayla Lambert (9:08 A.M.):	I hadn't heard about that change.
Tara Hull (9:09 A.M.):	Sorry, Kayla! We discussed it at Monday's meeting, but I forgot that you took that day off.
Kayla Lambert (9:10 A.M.):	I should still be able to make that work.
Tara Hull (9:11 A.M.):	I'm glad to hear that.
Kayla Lambert (9:12 A.M.):	How are you two doing with your catalog assignments?
Tara Hull (9:14 A.M.):	Actually, I've finished preparing the cover and the layout. If either of you need some help, I'm available.
Kayla Lambert (9:16 A.M.):	I'm fine.
Sven Ebersbach (9:17 A.M.):	Would you mind helping me write some of the product descriptions? They're taking a lot longer than I expected.
Tara Hull (9:19 A.M.):	Sure! I'll head over to your office. But first, let me stop by the warehouse to get some samples. It will be easier to do if we can see and touch the clothes in person.
Sven Ebersbach (9:21 A.M.):	That sounds perfect. Thanks!
Tara Hull (9:22 A.M.):	My pleasure.

168. What does Ms. Lambert want to know about?

(A) A project deadline
(B) A workshop date
(C) A printer function
(D) A meeting schedule

169. What is indicated about Ms. Lambert?

(A) She recently joined Ms. Hull and Mr. Ebersbach's team.
(B) She is unable to work additional hours.
(C) She supervised the catalog last time.
(D) She was not in the office on Monday.

170. At 9:16 A.M., what does Ms. Lambert mean when she writes, "I'm fine"?

(A) She is enjoying her part of the assignment.
(B) She is not upset about a miscommunication.
(C) She does not need any help from Ms. Hull.
(D) She would like to work with Mr. Ebersbach.

171. What will Ms. Hull most likely do next?

(A) Pick up some clothing items
(B) Meet some clients at her office
(C) Carry out a warehouse inspection
(D) Print descriptions of some products

Questions 172-175 refer to the following review.

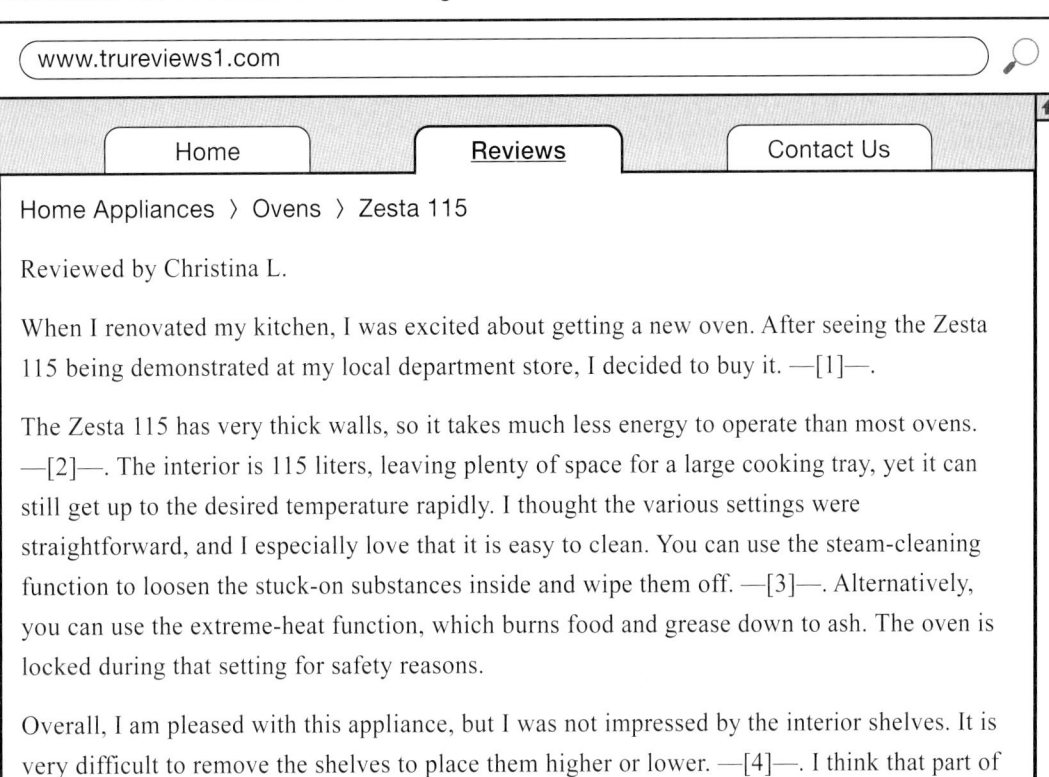

www.trureviews1.com

Home | **Reviews** | Contact Us

Home Appliances 〉 Ovens 〉 Zesta 115

Reviewed by Christina L.

When I renovated my kitchen, I was excited about getting a new oven. After seeing the Zesta 115 being demonstrated at my local department store, I decided to buy it. —[1]—.

The Zesta 115 has very thick walls, so it takes much less energy to operate than most ovens. —[2]—. The interior is 115 liters, leaving plenty of space for a large cooking tray, yet it can still get up to the desired temperature rapidly. I thought the various settings were straightforward, and I especially love that it is easy to clean. You can use the steam-cleaning function to loosen the stuck-on substances inside and wipe them off. —[3]—. Alternatively, you can use the extreme-heat function, which burns food and grease down to ash. The oven is locked during that setting for safety reasons.

Overall, I am pleased with this appliance, but I was not impressed by the interior shelves. It is very difficult to remove the shelves to place them higher or lower. —[4]—. I think that part of the design could have been improved.

172. Why most likely did the reviewer purchase the Zesta 115?
 (A) It is well known for its low price.
 (B) It had the most positive reviews.
 (C) It was recommended by her friend.
 (D) It was presented in a demonstration.

173. What is NOT a benefit of the Zesta 115 mentioned by the reviewer?
 (A) It has multiple shelves.
 (B) It is energy efficient.
 (C) It is an ample size.
 (D) It can heat up quickly.

174. What is true about the Zesta 115?
 (A) It is the company's newest model.
 (B) It offers two options for cleaning.
 (C) It is endorsed by professional chefs.
 (D) It comes with a free cooking tray.

175. In which of the positions marked [1], [2], [3], and [4] does the following sentence best belong?

 "This is a major issue if you have a wide variety in the sizes of foods you cook."

 (A) [1]
 (B) [2]
 (C) [3]
 (D) [4]

GO ON TO THE NEXT PAGE

Questions 176-180 refer to the following e-mail and notice.

E-Mail Message

From: Chun Liu ⟨liuc@raverdevelopment.com⟩
To: Matheus Jones ⟨jonesm@raverdevelopment.com⟩
Subject: Staff meeting
Date: January 18

Hi Matheus,

Thanks again for agreeing to conduct Thursday's staff meeting since I've changed my travel plans and won't be back in the office until next week. I know you're currently working on the notice for the new parking policy. If you need someone to look it over, please send it to Troy Saldana. I'd do it myself, but I didn't bring my laptop with me on vacation, and my phone does not have the encryption software needed to open confidential company files.

The monthly fee for on-site parking will be $160. The lot will open on February 1, and we are expecting a lot of people to be interested in getting a parking space.

Thanks!

Chun

Notice to Raver Development Staff

The new policy for our on-site lot will go into effect on February 1. Employees who wish to have a designated parking space should visit the administration department and complete the paperwork as below.

Terms and Conditions Agreement	Employees must sign this document to demonstrate that they will follow all parking rules and maintain the parking space. (no littering, no repair work on-site, responsible driving, etc.)
Banking Instructions	A fee of $125 will be charged automatically every month. This will be collected on the 25th of the month for use of the parking space the following month.
Vehicle Information	Employees should provide information about the make and model of their vehicle along with the license plate number. A parking pass with the plate number will be issued if you are selected for a space.
Employee Profile	As the demand is expected to exceed the availability, the spaces will be allocated in the following order: disabled employees, senior full-time employees, junior full-time employees, part-time employees. We may also leave five spaces for visitor use, but this has not been decided yet.

176. What does Ms. Liu indicate in the e-mail?
    (A) Mr. Jones can borrow her work laptop.
    (B) Mr. Jones should arrive to the meeting early.
    (C) She will send an updated notice to Mr. Jones.
    (D) She will not return to the office in time for a meeting.

177. Why will Ms. Liu be unable to review a policy document?
    (A) She is not familiar with the plans for the policy.
    (B) She does not have time to do it during her vacation.
    (C) She cannot open sensitive files on her phone.
    (D) She did not get permission in advance from Mr. Saldana.

178. What changed about Raver Development's parking policy after Ms. Liu's e-mail?
    (A) The person in charge of assigning spaces
    (B) The date the policy will take effect
    (C) The cost of using a parking space
    (D) The day of the month to pay a fee

179. What will employees do in the administration department?
    (A) Confirm they agree to set terms
    (B) Provide proof of their car insurance
    (C) Request reimbursement for vehicle repairs
    (D) Indicate the preferred location of a parking space

180. According to the notice, what is being considered?
    (A) Allocating spaces based on a lottery system
    (B) Purchasing another parking area
    (C) Adding parking for non-employees
    (D) Running a workshop on responsible driving

GO ON TO THE NEXT PAGE

Questions 181-185 refer to the following e-mail and article.

From:	Katrina Hume ⟨hume_k@barringtonconsultants.com⟩
To:	Barry Roderick ⟨barryroderick@green-world.org⟩
Date:	July 9
Subject:	Green World Annual Meeting

Dear Mr. Roderick,

I am honored that you have asked me to take part in the upcoming Green World Annual Meeting on August 20, and I am glad to say that I am able to do so. I always enjoy sharing my knowledge about improving recycling rates. It's always wonderful to have a reason to return to my hometown for a visit.

I understand that you have not finalized the start time yet. Due to another speaking engagement that I have on the same day, I would not be able to give the opening speech if you start before 10:00 A.M. If that is the case, I would be happy to be the closing speaker.

I truly appreciate the efforts your organization has made to help the environment, and I look forward to promoting recycling and sustainable living with you.

Sincerely,

Katrina Hume

Green World Hosts Annual Meeting

by Lisa Grise

The nonprofit environmental organization Green World hosted its annual meeting on August 20. The event took place in Huntsville on the Brookside University campus. The aim of the event was to raise awareness about environmental issues and provide practical advice. The event included speeches, workshops, and a session in which policymakers and business owners debated strategies for reducing single-use plastics.

With highly respected consultant Katrina Hume as the opening speaker and Reuse Manufacturing founder Eugene Akins as the closing speaker, there was a high level of expertise on display. Those interested in joining Green World or participating in future events are encouraged to visit www.green-world.org.

181. What is the purpose of the e-mail?

(A) To recommend an event
(B) To suggest a presentation topic
(C) To accept an invitation
(D) To change a date

182. In the e-mail, the word "appreciate" in paragraph 3, line 1, is closest in meaning to

(A) value
(B) realize
(C) enhance
(D) assess

183. What is true about Ms. Hume?

(A) She grew up in Huntsville.
(B) She started her own business.
(C) She graduated from Brookside University.
(D) She used to work with Mr. Roderick.

184. According to Ms. Grise, what happened on August 20?

(A) Environmental awards were presented.
(B) New Green World members were confirmed.
(C) A debate on disposable plastics was held.
(D) A new recycling policy was proposed.

185. What is implied about the Green World Annual Meeting?

(A) It started after 10:00 A.M.
(B) It had a speaker cancel at the last minute.
(C) It included a meal for attendees.
(D) It will be in the same location next year.

GO ON TO THE NEXT PAGE

Questions 186-190 refer to the following job posting, interview schedule, and e-mail.

Marketing Coordinator Position at Diaz&Associates

Diaz&Associates, a Seattle-based firm dedicated to providing financial planning services, is looking for a new marketing coordinator. We have been in operation for two decades, and, for the first time in our company's history, we are expanding our business into the insurance industry. Therefore, effective marketing will be crucial.

Position description: The marketing coordinator is primarily responsible for managing our social media accounts, writing articles for our online newsletter, and organizing in-person and virtual events.

Requirements: A bachelor's or master's degree in marketing, business administration, or advertising is required along with three years of project management experience. Proficiency in GoCreate design software is a plus.

Interested applicants should send a résumé to hr@diazandassoc.com.

Marketing Coordinator Interviews		
Applicant	Date & Time	Employment Details
Corina Geiger	October 8, 2:00 P.M.	Bachelor's degree in marketing; 2 years project management; proficient in GoCreate
Byoungmin Kim	October 8, 4:00 P.M.	Master's degree in business administration; 3 years project management; proficient in GoCreate
Darrell Crawford	October 9, 1:00 P.M.	Bachelor's degree in advertising; operates personal blog; 3 years project management
Sebastian Trevino	October 10, 3:30 P.M.	Master's degree in advertising; winner of Campaign Creativity Award; proficient in GoCreate
Margaret Echols	October 11, 10:00 A.M.	Master's degree in literature; 4 years project management; proficient in GoCreate

---

E-Mail Message

From: Rhonda Fitch ⟨rfitch@diazandassoc.com⟩
To: William Austell ⟨waustell@diazandassoc.com⟩
Subject: Interview
Date: October 3

Hi William,

I would like you to cover one of the interviews for the marketing coordinator position, as I don't want to reschedule it. Please interview Mr. Trevino on my behalf, as I've been invited to give a speech at a small business luncheon in Westerville on that day, and I think this would be great exposure for our company. We can meet when I get back to discuss what you thought of the candidate.

Thank you so much!

Rhonda

---

186. What is indicated about Diaz&Associates in the job posting?

(A) It is entering a new field.
(B) It was founded two years ago.
(C) It will open a new branch in Seattle.
(D) It specializes in security.

187. What is one responsibility mentioned in the job posting?

(A) Finding new customers
(B) Creating online content
(C) Traveling for events
(D) Conducting staff training

188. Who best matches the company's stated requirements and preferences?

(A) Ms. Geiger
(B) Mr. Kim
(C) Mr. Trevino
(D) Ms. Echols

189. In the e-mail, the word "cover" in paragraph 1, line 1, is closest in meaning to

(A) protect
(B) include
(C) conceal
(D) handle

190. When will Ms. Fitch give a talk?

(A) On October 8
(B) On October 9
(C) On October 10
(D) On October 11

Questions 191-195 refer to the following article, online form, and e-mail.

Home Matters
Does new insulation really make a difference?

An efficient insulation system offers both immediate and long-term benefits. The amount of energy needed to heat your home is greatly reduced when your walls and roof are properly insulated, making it both eco-friendly and economical. Without insulation, sounds can be easily carried between rooms. This can be corrected with thick insulation.

Some old types of insulation are hazardous to your health, and these are eligible for free removal and disposal through the government's recently launched Home Protections Program (HPP).

---

http://watsoninsulation.com/request

Watson Insulation Services: In-Home Visit Request

Name: Melinda Varner   **Date of request:** May 1

Address: 956 Straford Park Drive, Grand Rapids, MI 49503

Phone/E-mail: 948-555-8701/m.varner@santiagopro.com

Preferred form of contact: [ ] phone   [✓] e-mail

Best Date(s)/Time(s) to visit:

   Date(s): May 9 or 10

   Time(s): [✓] morning (9–noon)   [ ] early afternoon (noon–2)   [ ] late afternoon (2–4)

Type of request: [✓] provide pricing estimate   [ ] inspect previous work   [ ] other: _____

All Watson Insulation employees are required to successfully complete a comprehensive hands-on education program to ensure their level of expertise is fit for the job. This program is twice as long as those provided by our competitors, so you know you're getting the best of the best.

We will contact you within 2 business days of completing this form.

E-Mail

TO: Melinda Varner <m.varner@santiagopro.com>
FROM: Watson Insulation Services <reply@watsoninsulation.com>
DATE: May 9, 4:53 P.M.
SUBJECT: Insulation installation
ATTACHMENT: Price quote

Dear Ms. Varner,

I am following up on the home visit made by our technician, Jeremy Regan. I'm pleased that we could accommodate your request for the best time to visit. Please find attached the official price quote that Mr. Regan has prepared. You will see that you will not be charged for removing the insulation, as it is eligible for free removal through HPP. This quote is valid for thirty days, so please reply to this e-mail or call 555-9961 if you wish to go forward.

Warmest regards,

Curtis Donahue

---

191. What is NOT indicated in the article as a benefit of insulation?
(A) Saving money
(B) Keeping out moisture
(C) Helping the environment
(D) Reducing noise disturbances

192. What is mentioned about Watson Insulation Services?
(A) It only serves customers within Grand Rapids.
(B) It has lower prices than its competitors.
(C) Its staff members undergo extensive training.
(D) It does not offer visits on weekends.

193. What is suggested about Ms. Varner's property?
(A) It contains a harmful substance.
(B) It has insurance to cover repair work.
(C) It is owned by the government.
(D) It has some damage to its roof.

194. What is true about Mr. Regan?
(A) He visited Ms. Varner's home in the morning.
(B) He needed two days to prepare a report.
(C) He suggested making an adjustment to an estimate.
(D) He is a founding member of the company.

195. What does Mr. Donahue ask Ms. Varner to do?
(A) Call the company to resolve a problem
(B) Provide details about the size of her home
(C) Send a deposit before starting the work
(D) Indicate whether she wants the work completed

Questions 196-200 refer to the following e-mails and price list.

TO:	inquiries@valley-rentals.net
FROM:	Joseph Dansby <jdansby@avenueinsurance.net>
DATE:	August 6
SUBJECT:	Chair rental inquiry

To Whom It May Concern:

I am planning an awards banquet for my company, Avenue Enterprises, on Saturday, September 18. We will need three hundred chairs to accommodate our guests. I've never rented chairs before, but someone at my office used your business for her friend's retirement party and highly recommended you. Could you please let me know what options are available for us? We have a budget of three dollars per chair and can arrange to pick them up if necessary.

Sincerely,

Joseph Dansby

TO:	Joseph Dansby <jdansby@avenueinsrance.net>
FROM:	inquiries@valley-rentals.net
DATE:	August 7
SUBJECT:	RE: Chair rental inquiry
ATTACHMENT:	Price list

Dear Mr. Dansby,

Thank you for your interest in using Valley Rentals for your upcoming event. Please find attached our latest price list. You may place your rental order by replying to this e-mail. We are pleased to announce that we have just added a folding chair option. It is perfect for events in which you may need to clear the seating area quickly to make room for other activities. If you have any questions about the rental process, please let me know.

Warmest regards,

Marla Gonzalez

Valley Rentals: Chair Rentals Price List

Item #	Description	Color Options	Daily Rate
203	Plastic Patio Chair	white, green	$2.70
204	Plastic Patio Chair with Armrests	white, green	$3.20
317	Metal Folding Chair	silver	$3.80
487	Hardwood Chair with Slotted Back	light brown, dark brown	$5.40
495	Aluminum and Wood Café-Style Chair	silver/black, silver/brown	$6.00

- Open daily, excluding public holidays.
- Items are cleaned thoroughly before dispatch and can be used in all weather conditions.
- Customers may pick up items in person or pay a flat fee of $25.00 for delivery and pickup.
- Please call 697-555-0014 to inquire about getting up to sixty percent off rentals over extended periods.

196. What does Mr. Dansby indicate in the first e-mail?

(A) He has recently started working for Avenue Enterprises.
(B) He plans to use Valley Rentals' services regularly.
(C) He found out about the business through a coworker.
(D) He has been nominated for a company award.

197. Which item will Mr. Dansby most likely rent?

(A) Item 203
(B) Item 204
(C) Item 487
(D) Item 495

198. What is the daily charge for Valley Rentals' newest chair type?

(A) $2.70
(B) $3.80
(C) $5.40
(D) $6.00

199. According to the price list, what is true about Valley Rentals?

(A) It requires a $25 deposit for rental requests.
(B) It provides discounts for long-term rentals.
(C) It is open every day of the year.
(D) It operates at more than one location.

200. What is suggested in the price list about all Valley Rentals chairs?

(A) They will be delivered at no cost.
(B) They are inspected for damage before the rental.
(C) They are suitable to use outdoors.
(D) They should be cleaned before being returned.

ANSWER SHEET

TOEIC 실전 모의고사

응시일자	20 . .
이름	
맞은 개수	/100

LISTENING (Part I ~ IV)

READING (Part V ~ VII)

ANSWER SHEET

TOEIC 실전 모의고사

응시일자	20 . .
이름	
맞은 개수	/100

LISTENING (Part I ~ IV)

#		#		#		#	
1	ⓐⓑⓒ	21	ⓐⓑⓒ	41	ⓐⓑⓒⓓ	81	ⓐⓑⓒⓓ
2	ⓐⓑⓒ	22	ⓐⓑⓒ	42	ⓐⓑⓒⓓ	82	ⓐⓑⓒⓓ
3	ⓐⓑⓒ	23	ⓐⓑⓒ	43	ⓐⓑⓒⓓ	83	ⓐⓑⓒⓓ
4	ⓐⓑⓒ	24	ⓐⓑⓒ	44	ⓐⓑⓒⓓ	84	ⓐⓑⓒⓓ
5	ⓐⓑⓒ	25	ⓐⓑⓒ	45	ⓐⓑⓒⓓ	85	ⓐⓑⓒⓓ
6	ⓐⓑⓒ	26	ⓐⓑⓒ	46	ⓐⓑⓒⓓ	86	ⓐⓑⓒⓓ
7	ⓐⓑⓒ	27	ⓐⓑⓒ	47	ⓐⓑⓒⓓ	87	ⓐⓑⓒⓓ
8	ⓐⓑⓒ	28	ⓐⓑⓒ	48	ⓐⓑⓒⓓ	88	ⓐⓑⓒⓓ
9	ⓐⓑⓒ	29	ⓐⓑⓒ	49	ⓐⓑⓒⓓ	89	ⓐⓑⓒⓓ
10	ⓐⓑⓒ	30	ⓐⓑⓒ	50	ⓐⓑⓒⓓ	90	ⓐⓑⓒⓓ
11	ⓐⓑⓒ	31	ⓐⓑⓒ	51	ⓐⓑⓒⓓ	91	ⓐⓑⓒⓓ
12	ⓐⓑⓒ	32	ⓐⓑⓒ	52	ⓐⓑⓒⓓ	92	ⓐⓑⓒⓓ
13	ⓐⓑⓒ	33	ⓐⓑⓒ	53	ⓐⓑⓒⓓ	93	ⓐⓑⓒⓓ
14	ⓐⓑⓒ	34	ⓐⓑⓒ	54	ⓐⓑⓒⓓ	94	ⓐⓑⓒⓓ
15	ⓐⓑⓒ	35	ⓐⓑⓒ	55	ⓐⓑⓒⓓ	95	ⓐⓑⓒⓓ
16	ⓐⓑⓒ	36	ⓐⓑⓒ	56	ⓐⓑⓒⓓ	96	ⓐⓑⓒⓓ
17	ⓐⓑⓒ	37	ⓐⓑⓒ	57	ⓐⓑⓒⓓ	97	ⓐⓑⓒⓓ
18	ⓐⓑⓒ	38	ⓐⓑⓒ	58	ⓐⓑⓒⓓ	98	ⓐⓑⓒⓓ
19	ⓐⓑⓒ	39	ⓐⓑⓒ	59	ⓐⓑⓒⓓ	99	ⓐⓑⓒⓓ
20	ⓐⓑⓒ	40	ⓐⓑⓒ	60	ⓐⓑⓒⓓ	100	ⓐⓑⓒⓓ

READING (Part V ~ VII)

#		#		#		#		#	
101	ⓐⓑⓒⓓ	121	ⓐⓑⓒⓓ	141	ⓐⓑⓒⓓ	161	ⓐⓑⓒⓓ	181	ⓐⓑⓒⓓ
102	ⓐⓑⓒⓓ	122	ⓐⓑⓒⓓ	142	ⓐⓑⓒⓓ	162	ⓐⓑⓒⓓ	182	ⓐⓑⓒⓓ
103	ⓐⓑⓒⓓ	123	ⓐⓑⓒⓓ	143	ⓐⓑⓒⓓ	163	ⓐⓑⓒⓓ	183	ⓐⓑⓒⓓ
104	ⓐⓑⓒⓓ	124	ⓐⓑⓒⓓ	144	ⓐⓑⓒⓓ	164	ⓐⓑⓒⓓ	184	ⓐⓑⓒⓓ
105	ⓐⓑⓒⓓ	125	ⓐⓑⓒⓓ	145	ⓐⓑⓒⓓ	165	ⓐⓑⓒⓓ	185	ⓐⓑⓒⓓ
106	ⓐⓑⓒⓓ	126	ⓐⓑⓒⓓ	146	ⓐⓑⓒⓓ	166	ⓐⓑⓒⓓ	186	ⓐⓑⓒⓓ
107	ⓐⓑⓒⓓ	127	ⓐⓑⓒⓓ	147	ⓐⓑⓒⓓ	167	ⓐⓑⓒⓓ	187	ⓐⓑⓒⓓ
108	ⓐⓑⓒⓓ	128	ⓐⓑⓒⓓ	148	ⓐⓑⓒⓓ	168	ⓐⓑⓒⓓ	188	ⓐⓑⓒⓓ
109	ⓐⓑⓒⓓ	129	ⓐⓑⓒⓓ	149	ⓐⓑⓒⓓ	169	ⓐⓑⓒⓓ	189	ⓐⓑⓒⓓ
110	ⓐⓑⓒⓓ	130	ⓐⓑⓒⓓ	150	ⓐⓑⓒⓓ	170	ⓐⓑⓒⓓ	190	ⓐⓑⓒⓓ
111	ⓐⓑⓒⓓ	131	ⓐⓑⓒⓓ	151	ⓐⓑⓒⓓ	171	ⓐⓑⓒⓓ	191	ⓐⓑⓒⓓ
112	ⓐⓑⓒⓓ	132	ⓐⓑⓒⓓ	152	ⓐⓑⓒⓓ	172	ⓐⓑⓒⓓ	192	ⓐⓑⓒⓓ
113	ⓐⓑⓒⓓ	133	ⓐⓑⓒⓓ	153	ⓐⓑⓒⓓ	173	ⓐⓑⓒⓓ	193	ⓐⓑⓒⓓ
114	ⓐⓑⓒⓓ	134	ⓐⓑⓒⓓ	154	ⓐⓑⓒⓓ	174	ⓐⓑⓒⓓ	194	ⓐⓑⓒⓓ
115	ⓐⓑⓒⓓ	135	ⓐⓑⓒⓓ	155	ⓐⓑⓒⓓ	175	ⓐⓑⓒⓓ	195	ⓐⓑⓒⓓ
116	ⓐⓑⓒⓓ	136	ⓐⓑⓒⓓ	156	ⓐⓑⓒⓓ	176	ⓐⓑⓒⓓ	196	ⓐⓑⓒⓓ
117	ⓐⓑⓒⓓ	137	ⓐⓑⓒⓓ	157	ⓐⓑⓒⓓ	177	ⓐⓑⓒⓓ	197	ⓐⓑⓒⓓ
118	ⓐⓑⓒⓓ	138	ⓐⓑⓒⓓ	158	ⓐⓑⓒⓓ	178	ⓐⓑⓒⓓ	198	ⓐⓑⓒⓓ
119	ⓐⓑⓒⓓ	139	ⓐⓑⓒⓓ	159	ⓐⓑⓒⓓ	179	ⓐⓑⓒⓓ	199	ⓐⓑⓒⓓ
120	ⓐⓑⓒⓓ	140	ⓐⓑⓒⓓ	160	ⓐⓑⓒⓓ	180	ⓐⓑⓒⓓ	200	ⓐⓑⓒⓓ

ANSWER SHEET

TOEIC 실전 모의고사

응시일자	20 . .
이름	
맞은 개수	/100

LISTENING (Part I ~ IV)

#		#		#		#		#	
1	ⓐⓑⓒ	21	ⓐⓑⓒ	41	ⓐⓑⓒⓓ	61	ⓐⓑⓒⓓ	81	ⓐⓑⓒⓓ
2	ⓐⓑⓒ	22	ⓐⓑⓒ	42	ⓐⓑⓒⓓ	62	ⓐⓑⓒⓓ	82	ⓐⓑⓒⓓ
3	ⓐⓑⓒ	23	ⓐⓑⓒ	43	ⓐⓑⓒⓓ	63	ⓐⓑⓒⓓ	83	ⓐⓑⓒⓓ
4	ⓐⓑⓒ	24	ⓐⓑⓒ	44	ⓐⓑⓒⓓ	64	ⓐⓑⓒⓓ	84	ⓐⓑⓒⓓ
5	ⓐⓑⓒ	25	ⓐⓑⓒ	45	ⓐⓑⓒⓓ	65	ⓐⓑⓒⓓ	85	ⓐⓑⓒⓓ
6	ⓐⓑⓒ	26	ⓐⓑⓒ	46	ⓐⓑⓒⓓ	66	ⓐⓑⓒⓓ	86	ⓐⓑⓒⓓ
7	ⓐⓑⓒ	27	ⓐⓑⓒ	47	ⓐⓑⓒⓓ	67	ⓐⓑⓒⓓ	87	ⓐⓑⓒⓓ
8	ⓐⓑⓒⓓ	28	ⓐⓑⓒ	48	ⓐⓑⓒⓓ	68	ⓐⓑⓒⓓ	88	ⓐⓑⓒⓓ
9	ⓐⓑⓒⓓ	29	ⓐⓑⓒ	49	ⓐⓑⓒⓓ	69	ⓐⓑⓒⓓ	89	ⓐⓑⓒⓓ
10	ⓐⓑⓒⓓ	30	ⓐⓑⓒ	50	ⓐⓑⓒⓓ	70	ⓐⓑⓒⓓ	90	ⓐⓑⓒⓓ
11	ⓐⓑⓒⓓ	31	ⓐⓑⓒ	51	ⓐⓑⓒⓓ	71	ⓐⓑⓒⓓ	91	ⓐⓑⓒⓓ
12	ⓐⓑⓒⓓ	32	ⓐⓑⓒ	52	ⓐⓑⓒⓓ	72	ⓐⓑⓒⓓ	92	ⓐⓑⓒⓓ
13	ⓐⓑⓒⓓ	33	ⓐⓑⓒ	53	ⓐⓑⓒⓓ	73	ⓐⓑⓒⓓ	93	ⓐⓑⓒⓓ
14	ⓐⓑⓒⓓ	34	ⓐⓑⓒ	54	ⓐⓑⓒⓓ	74	ⓐⓑⓒⓓ	94	ⓐⓑⓒⓓ
15	ⓐⓑⓒⓓ	35	ⓐⓑⓒ	55	ⓐⓑⓒⓓ	75	ⓐⓑⓒⓓ	95	ⓐⓑⓒⓓ
16	ⓐⓑⓒⓓ	36	ⓐⓑⓒ	56	ⓐⓑⓒⓓ	76	ⓐⓑⓒⓓ	96	ⓐⓑⓒⓓ
17	ⓐⓑⓒⓓ	37	ⓐⓑⓒ	57	ⓐⓑⓒⓓ	77	ⓐⓑⓒⓓ	97	ⓐⓑⓒⓓ
18	ⓐⓑⓒⓓ	38	ⓐⓑⓒ	58	ⓐⓑⓒⓓ	78	ⓐⓑⓒⓓ	98	ⓐⓑⓒⓓ
19	ⓐⓑⓒⓓ	39	ⓐⓑⓒ	59	ⓐⓑⓒⓓ	79	ⓐⓑⓒⓓ	99	ⓐⓑⓒⓓ
20	ⓐⓑⓒⓓ	40	ⓐⓑⓒ	60	ⓐⓑⓒⓓ	80	ⓐⓑⓒⓓ	100	ⓐⓑⓒⓓ

READING (Part V ~ VII)

#		#		#		#		#	
101	ⓐⓑⓒⓓ	121	ⓐⓑⓒⓓ	141	ⓐⓑⓒⓓ	161	ⓐⓑⓒⓓ	181	ⓐⓑⓒⓓ
102	ⓐⓑⓒⓓ	122	ⓐⓑⓒⓓ	142	ⓐⓑⓒⓓ	162	ⓐⓑⓒⓓ	182	ⓐⓑⓒⓓ
103	ⓐⓑⓒⓓ	123	ⓐⓑⓒⓓ	143	ⓐⓑⓒⓓ	163	ⓐⓑⓒⓓ	183	ⓐⓑⓒⓓ
104	ⓐⓑⓒⓓ	124	ⓐⓑⓒⓓ	144	ⓐⓑⓒⓓ	164	ⓐⓑⓒⓓ	184	ⓐⓑⓒⓓ
105	ⓐⓑⓒⓓ	125	ⓐⓑⓒⓓ	145	ⓐⓑⓒⓓ	165	ⓐⓑⓒⓓ	185	ⓐⓑⓒⓓ
106	ⓐⓑⓒⓓ	126	ⓐⓑⓒⓓ	146	ⓐⓑⓒⓓ	166	ⓐⓑⓒⓓ	186	ⓐⓑⓒⓓ
107	ⓐⓑⓒⓓ	127	ⓐⓑⓒⓓ	147	ⓐⓑⓒⓓ	167	ⓐⓑⓒⓓ	187	ⓐⓑⓒⓓ
108	ⓐⓑⓒⓓ	128	ⓐⓑⓒⓓ	148	ⓐⓑⓒⓓ	168	ⓐⓑⓒⓓ	188	ⓐⓑⓒⓓ
109	ⓐⓑⓒⓓ	129	ⓐⓑⓒⓓ	149	ⓐⓑⓒⓓ	169	ⓐⓑⓒⓓ	189	ⓐⓑⓒⓓ
110	ⓐⓑⓒⓓ	130	ⓐⓑⓒⓓ	150	ⓐⓑⓒⓓ	170	ⓐⓑⓒⓓ	190	ⓐⓑⓒⓓ
111	ⓐⓑⓒⓓ	131	ⓐⓑⓒⓓ	151	ⓐⓑⓒⓓ	171	ⓐⓑⓒⓓ	191	ⓐⓑⓒⓓ
112	ⓐⓑⓒⓓ	132	ⓐⓑⓒⓓ	152	ⓐⓑⓒⓓ	172	ⓐⓑⓒⓓ	192	ⓐⓑⓒⓓ
113	ⓐⓑⓒⓓ	133	ⓐⓑⓒⓓ	153	ⓐⓑⓒⓓ	173	ⓐⓑⓒⓓ	193	ⓐⓑⓒⓓ
114	ⓐⓑⓒⓓ	134	ⓐⓑⓒⓓ	154	ⓐⓑⓒⓓ	174	ⓐⓑⓒⓓ	194	ⓐⓑⓒⓓ
115	ⓐⓑⓒⓓ	135	ⓐⓑⓒⓓ	155	ⓐⓑⓒⓓ	175	ⓐⓑⓒⓓ	195	ⓐⓑⓒⓓ
116	ⓐⓑⓒⓓ	136	ⓐⓑⓒⓓ	156	ⓐⓑⓒⓓ	176	ⓐⓑⓒⓓ	196	ⓐⓑⓒⓓ
117	ⓐⓑⓒⓓ	137	ⓐⓑⓒⓓ	157	ⓐⓑⓒⓓ	177	ⓐⓑⓒⓓ	197	ⓐⓑⓒⓓ
118	ⓐⓑⓒⓓ	138	ⓐⓑⓒⓓ	158	ⓐⓑⓒⓓ	178	ⓐⓑⓒⓓ	198	ⓐⓑⓒⓓ
119	ⓐⓑⓒⓓ	139	ⓐⓑⓒⓓ	159	ⓐⓑⓒⓓ	179	ⓐⓑⓒⓓ	199	ⓐⓑⓒⓓ
120	ⓐⓑⓒⓓ	140	ⓐⓑⓒⓓ	160	ⓐⓑⓒⓓ	180	ⓐⓑⓒⓓ	200	ⓐⓑⓒⓓ

에듀윌이
너를
지지할게

ENERGY

삶의 순간순간이
아름다운 마무리이며
새로운 시작이어야 한다.

– 법정 스님

에듀윌 토익 베이직 READING RC

발 행 일	2022년 3월 14일 초판
편 저 자	에듀윌 어학연구소
펴 낸 이	이중현
펴 낸 곳	(주)에듀윌
등록번호	제25100–2002–000052호
주 소	08378 서울특별시 구로구 디지털로34길 55 코오롱싸이언스밸리 2차 3층

* 이 책의 무단 인용 · 전재 · 복제를 금합니다.   ISBN 979-11-360-1567-9 (13740)

www.eduwill.net
대표전화 1600-6700

여러분의 작은 소리
에듀윌은 크게 듣겠습니다.

본 교재에 대한 여러분의 목소리를 들려주세요.
공부하시면서 어려웠던 점, 궁금한 점,
칭찬하고 싶은 점, 개선할 점, 어떤 것이라도 좋습니다.

에듀윌은 여러분께서 나누어 주신 의견을
통해 끊임없이 발전하고 있습니다.

에듀윌 도서몰 book.eduwill.net
- 부가학습자료 및 정오표: 에듀윌 도서몰 → 도서자료실
- 교재 문의: 에듀윌 도서몰 → 문의하기 → 교재(내용,출간) / 주문 및 배송

꿈을 현실로 만드는
에듀윌

DREAM

공무원 교육
- 선호도 1위, 신뢰도 1위! 브랜드만족도 1위!
- 합격자 수 2,100% 폭등시킨 독한 커리큘럼

종합출판
- 온라인서점 베스트셀러 1위!
- 출제위원급 전문 교수진이 직접 집필한 합격 교재

학점은행제
- 99%의 과목이수율
- 17년 연속 교육부 평가 인정 기관 선정

어학 교육
- 토익 베스트셀러 1위
- 토익 동영상 강의 무료 제공

자격증 교육
- 9년간 아무도 깨지 못한 기록 합격자 수 1위
- 가장 많은 합격자를 배출한 최고의 합격 시스템

콘텐츠 제휴·B2B 교육
- 고객 맞춤형 위탁 교육 서비스 제공
- 기업, 기관, 대학 등 각 단체에 최적화된 고객 맞춤형 교육 및 제휴 서비스

대학 편입
- 편입 교육 1위!
- 최대 200% 환급 상품 서비스

직영학원
- 검증된 합격 프로그램과 강의
- 1:1 밀착 관리 및 컨설팅
- 호텔 수준의 학습 환경

부동산 아카데미
- 부동산 실무 교육 1위!
- 상위 1% 고소득 창업/취업 비법
- 부동산 실전 재테크 성공 비법

국비무료 교육
- '5년우수훈련기관' 선정
- K-디지털, 산대특 등 특화 훈련과정
- 원격국비교육원 오픈

에듀윌 교육서비스 **공무원 교육** 9급공무원/소방공무원/계리직공무원 **자격증 교육** 공인중개사/주택관리사/손해평가사/감정평가사/노무사/전기기사/경비지도사/검정고시/소방설비기사/소방시설관리사/사회복지사1급/대기환경기사/수질환경기사/건축기사/토목기사/직업상담사/전기기능사/산업안전기사/건설안전기사/위험물산업기사/위험물기능사/유통관리사/물류관리사/행정사/한국사능력검정/한경TESAT/매경TEST/KBS한국어능력시험·실용글쓰기/IT자격증/국제무역사/무역영어 **어학 교육** 토익 교재/토익 동영상 강의 **세무/회계** 전산세무회계/ERP정보관리사/재경관리사 **대학 편입** 편입 영어·수학/연고대/의약대/경찰대/논술/면접 **직영학원** 공무원학원/소방학원/공인중개사 학원/주택관리사 학원/전기기사 학원/편입학원 **종합출판** 공무원·자격증 수험교재 및 단행본 **학점은행제** 교육부 평가인정기관 원격평생교육원(사회복지사2급/경영학/CPA) **콘텐츠 제휴·B2B 교육** 교육 콘텐츠 제휴/기업 맞춤 자격증 교육/대학취업역량 강화 교육 **부동산 아카데미** 부동산 창업CEO/부동산 경매 마스터/부동산 컨설팅 **주택취업센터** 실무 특강/실무 아카데미 **국비무료 교육(국비교육원)** 전기기능사/전기(산업)기사/소방설비(산업)기사/IT(빅데이터/자바프로그램/파이썬)/게임그래픽/3D프린터/실내건축디자인/웹퍼블리셔/그래픽디자인/영상편집(유튜브) 디자인/온라인 쇼핑몰광고 및 제작(쿠팡, 스마트스토어)/전산세무회계/컴퓨터활용능력/ITQ/GTQ/직업상담사

교육문의 **1600-6700** www.eduwill.net

쉬운 토익 공식
에듀윌 토익
동영상 강의 109강 무료 제공

입문부터 실전까지
스타강사 노하우 완벽 반영!

에듀윌 회원이면 토익 인강 & 학습 자료 무료 제공

최신 토익 인강
109강 무료

인공지능
토익 앱

최신 학습
맞춤 서비스

※ 에듀윌 회원 전원 베이직 & 실전 인강 109강이 무료 제공됩니다.
※ 강의 무료 수강 혜택 상세내용은 오른쪽 QR코드를 모바일로 스캔 후 확인 가능합니다.
※ 해당 강의는 에듀윌 토익 사이트에서도 회원가입 후 무료로 이용 가능합니다.
※ 무료 제공 이벤트는 예고없이 변경되거나 종료될 수 있습니다.

무료 혜택 받기

* 2022 대한민국 브랜드만족도 토익 교육 1위 (한경비즈니스)
* 알라딘 외국어 토익 실전 분야 베스트셀러 1위 (에듀윌 토익 실전 LC+RC, 2022년 3월 4~5주, 4월 1~2주 주간 베스트 기준)
* YES24 국어 외국어 사전 영어 토익/TOEIC 기출문제/모의고사 베스트셀러 1위(베이직 리딩, 2022년 4월 4주 주별 베스트)
* YES24 국어 외국어 사전 영어 토익/TOEIC 기출문제/모의고사 베스트셀러 1위(베이직 리스닝, 2022년 5월 4주 주별 베스트)

에듀윌 토익 베이직 READING RC
4주 끝장

정답 및 해설

에듀윌 토익 베이직 READING RC
정답 및 해설

기초부터 실전까지 한번에!

에듀윌 토익 베이직
READING RC
정답 및 해설

PART 5·6

UNIT 01 명사

1 명사 자리: 관사/한정사/소유격/형용사 뒤

본문 p.026

1. (B)   2. (B)   3. (B)   4. (D)

1.

The restaurant on Mesa Street is having a large **celebration** to mark its tenth anniversary.

(A) celebrate
(B) celebration
(C) celebrated
(D) celebrates

메사 가에 있는 그 식당은 10주년 기념일을 축하하기 위해 대규모 축하 행사를 열 것이다.

해설 **명사 자리 [형용사 뒤]** 빈칸은 관사 a와 형용사 large의 수식을 받는 자리이므로 명사인 (B) celebration이 정답이다. (A) celebrate와 (D) celebrates는 동사, (C) celebrated는 동사 또는 과거분사이므로 명사 자리에 올 수 없다.

어휘 have a celebration 축하 행사를 열다   mark 축하[기념]하다; 표시하다; 자국; 표시   anniversary 기념일

2.

Ricardo Sosa, the executive chef at Restaurant Dove, avoids making any **appointments** with food journalists during peak hours.

(A) appoint
(B) appointments
(C) appointed
(D) appoints

도브 식당의 총괄 주방장인 리카르도 소사는 가장 바쁜 시간에는 음식 저널리스트들과의 어떤 약속도 잡지 않는다.

해설 **명사 자리 [한정사 뒤]** any는 명사 앞에 쓰여 한정의 뜻을 나타내는 한정사이다. 빈칸 뒤에는 전치사구 with food journalists가 이어지므로 빈칸에는 한정사의 수식을 받을 수 있는 명사가 들어가야 한다. 따라서 선택지 중 명사인 (B) appointments가 정답이다.

어휘 make an appointment 예약하다, 약속하다   journalist 저널리스트, 기자   peak hours 가장 바쁜[혼잡한] 시간대

3.

For Dr. Saeb's retirement party, Ms. Decker hired a **caterer** to serve food.

(A) caters
(B) caterer
(C) cater
(D) catered

사에브 박사의 은퇴 기념 파티를 위해 데커 씨가 음식을 제공할 출장 연회 업체를 고용했다.

해설 **명사 자리 [관사 뒤]** 빈칸 앞에 관사 a가 있고 뒤에는 to부정사가 있으므로 빈칸은 명사 자리이다. 따라서 단수 명사인 (B) caterer가 정답이다. (A) caters와 (C) cater는 동사, (D) catered는 동사 또는 과거분사이므로 관사 a의 수식을 받는 명사 자리에 올 수 없다.

어휘 retirement 은퇴, 퇴직   hire 고용하다   caterer 출장 연회 업자, (행사의) 음식 공급자   serve food 음식을 내놓다

4.

Anne Withers, the billionaire entrepreneur, is known for her **dedication** to improving public healthcare access.

(A) dedicate
(B) dedicated
(C) dedicates
(D) dedication

억만장자 사업가인 앤 위더스는 공공 의료 접근성을 향상시키는 데 헌신한 것으로 알려져 있다.

해설 **명사 자리 [소유격 뒤]** 빈칸은 소유격 her의 수식을 받는 자리이므로 명사인 (D) dedication이 정답이다. (A) dedicate와 (C) dedicates는 동사, (B) dedicated는 동사 또는 형용사이다.

어휘 entrepreneur 사업가   be known for ~로 알려지다   dedication 헌신, 전념   improve 향상시키다

2 명사 자리: 주어와 보어

본문 p.027

1. (D)   2. (A)   3. (A)   4. (B)

1.

The letter of **acceptance** for the IT position was sent on August 8 by Martha Syngman.

(A) accepted
(B) acceptable
(C) accepts
(D) acceptance

그 IT직에 대한 합격 통지서가 8월 8일에 마사 싱먼에 의해 보내졌다.

해설 명사 자리 [주어] 빈칸에는 The letter of와 결합하여 문장의 주어 역할을 할 수 있는 말이 들어가야 한다. 따라서 명사인 (D) acceptance가 정답이다. (A) accepted는 동사 또는 과거분사, (B) acceptable은 형용사, (C) accepts는 동사이므로 빈칸에 적절하지 않다.

어휘 the letter of acceptance 합격 통지서   position 일자리, 직위   accept (기관 등에서) 받아 주다, 받아들이다   acceptable 받아들일 수 있는, 용인되는

2.

The store's holiday season sales event was an unprecedented **success**.

(A) success
(B) successful
(C) succeed
(D) successes

그 상점의 연휴 세일 행사가 전례 없는 성공을 거두었다.

해설 명사 자리 [주격 보어] 빈칸 앞에 be동사 was가 있으므로 빈칸은 주격 보어 자리이자 관사 an과 형용사 unprecedented의 수식을 받는 자리이다. 따라서 단수 명사인 (A) success가 정답이다. (B) successful은 형용사, (C) succeed는 동사이므로 명사 자리에 올 수 없고, (D) successes는 복수 명사이므로 부정관사의 수식을 받을 수 없기 때문에 오답이다.

어휘 unprecedented 전례 없는   success 성공   successful 성공적인   succeed 성공하다

3.

The department head called Mr. Reuben a great **leader** for finishing the project ahead of schedule.

(A) leader
(B) lead
(C) leadership
(D) leading

부서장은 프로젝트를 예정보다 빨리 끝냈다는 이유로 루벤 씨를 훌륭한 리더라고 칭했다.

해설 명사 자리 [목적격 보어] 빈칸은 동사 call의 목적격 보어 자리이자 관사 a와 형용사 great의 수식을 받는 자리이다. 따라서 명사인 (A) leader가 정답이다. (B) lead와 (C) leadership은 명사이지만 목적어인 Mr. Reuben과 동격의 관계가 성립하지 않기 때문에 오답이다. 동명사 또는 현재분사인 (D) leading 역시 동명사로 보더라도 목적어와 동격이 아니므로 빈칸에 부적절하다.

어휘 department head 부서장, 부서 책임자   ahead of schedule 예정보다 빨리   lead 선두, 우세; 안내하다, 이끌다

4.

Since the **satisfaction** of our clients is our biggest priority, we highly value your feedback.

(A) satisfied
(B) satisfaction
(C) satisfy
(D) satisfactory

우리 고객들의 만족이 우리의 최대 우선 사항이므로 우리는 당신의 의견을 매우 소중하게 생각합니다.

해설 명사 자리 [주어] 빈칸은 동사 is의 주어 자리이자 정관사 the의 수식을 받는 명사 자리이므로 (B) satisfaction이 정답이다. (A) satisfied는 동사 또는 형용사, (C) satisfy는 동사, (D) satisfactory는 형용사이므로 모두 명사 자리에 올 수 없다.

어휘 satisfaction 만족(감)   priority 우선 사항   highly 크게, 대단히, 매우   value 소중하게 생각하다; 가치   satisfy 만족시키다   satisfactory 만족스러운

3 명사 자리: 목적어

1. (C) 2. (A) 3. (B) 4. (C)

1.

The economic crisis has caused **decreases** in sales for businesses all over the country.

경제 위기가 전국적으로 기업들에게 매출 감소를 야기했다.

(A) to decrease (B) decreased
(C) **decreases** (D) will decrease

해설 명사 자리 [동사의 목적어] 빈칸은 타동사 has caused의 목적어 자리이므로 명사인 (C) decreases가 정답이다. (A) to decrease는 to부정사인데, 동사 cause는 to부정사를 목적어가 아닌 목적격 보어 자리에 쓰기 때문에 답이 될 수 없다. (B) decreased는 동사 또는 과거분사, (D) will decrease는 동사이므로 목적어 자리에 올 수 없다.

어휘 economic 경제의 crisis 위기 cause 야기하다; 원인 decrease 감소, 하락; 줄다, 감소하다

2.

The new intern needs **help** with the copier on the third floor.

새로운 인턴 사원은 3층에 있는 복사기에 대해 도움을 필요로 한다.

(A) **help** (B) helpful
(C) helpfully (D) helped

해설 명사 자리 [동사의 목적어] 빈칸은 타동사 needs의 목적어 자리이므로 명사인 (A) help가 정답이다. (B) helpful은 형용사, (C) helpfully는 부사, (D) helped는 동사 또는 과거분사이므로 오답이다.

어휘 intern 인턴 사원 copier 복사기 helpful 도움이 되는 helpfully 도움이 되도록, 유용하게

3.

The mayor announced a plan for the **development** of the empty lot near the park.

시장은 공원 근처의 공터 개발 계획을 발표했다.

(A) developing (B) **development**
(C) develops (D) develop

해설 명사 자리 [전치사의 목적어] 빈칸은 전치사 for의 목적어 자리이므로 명사인 (B) development가 정답이다. 동명사인 (A) developing 은 관사의 수식을 받을 수 없기 때문에 오답이다. (C) develops와 (D) develop은 동사이므로 목적어 자리에 올 수 없다.

어휘 announce 발표하다, 알리다 development 개발; 발달, 발전 empty lot 공터

4.

With just one year in **operation**, Cuff Motors is already turning record profits.

운영 1년 만에 커프 모터스는 이미 기록적인 수익을 내고 있다.

(A) operate (B) operated
(C) **operation** (D) operational

해설 명사 자리 [전치사의 목적어] 빈칸 앞에 전치사 in이 있으므로 빈칸에는 전치사의 목적어 역할을 할 수 있는 명사가 들어가야 한다. 따라서 (C) operation이 정답이다. (A) operate는 동사, (B) operated는 동사 또는 과거분사, (D) operational은 형용사이기 때문에 빈칸에 적절하지 않다.

어휘 in operation 운영하는, 가동하는 turn profits 수익을 내다 record 기록적인; 기록, 기록하다, 녹음하다

4 셀 수 있는 명사 vs. 셀 수 없는 명사

본문 p.029

1. (A)　　2. (D)　　3. (B)　　4. (D)

1.

The event organizer called the management office to ask for **permission** to use the event hall.

그 행사 기획자는 행사장을 사용하기 위한 허가를 요청하기 위해 관리실에 연락했다.

(A) **permission**　　(B) permit
(C) permitting　　(D) permitted

해설 셀 수 없는 명사 빈칸 앞에 부정관사 없이 전치사 for가 있으므로 빈칸에는 셀 수 없는 명사인 (A) permission이 들어가야 한다. (B) permit는 셀 수 있는 명사이므로 부정관사 없이 쓰려면 반드시 복수형인 permits로 써야 한다. (C) permitting은 동명사 또는 현재분사, (D) permitted는 동사 또는 과거분사이므로 빈칸에 적절하지 않다.

어휘 organizer 주최자, (행사 등의) 기획자　management office 관리실　ask for ~을 요청하다　permission 허락, 허가　permit 허가증; 허락하다

2.

Every year, City Hall receives **compliments** on the various events of the spring festival it organizes.

매년, 시청은 그들이 준비하는 다양한 봄 축제 행사에 대해 찬사를 받는다.

(A) complimented　　(B) complimentary
(C) compliment　　(D) **compliments**

해설 셀 수 있는 명사 빈칸은 동사 receives의 목적어 자리이므로 명사인 (C) compliment와 (D) compliments 중에서 답을 골라야 하는데, 빈칸 앞에 부정관사가 없기 때문에 복수 명사인 (D) compliments가 정답이다. (A) complimented는 동사 또는 과거분사, (B) complimentary는 형용사이므로 목적어 자리에 올 수 없다.

어휘 compliment 칭찬, 찬사; 칭찬하다　various 다양한　organize 준비하다, 조직하다　complimentary 칭찬하는; 무료의

3.

According to the job description, experience in **accounting** is required to work in the finance department.

직무 설명에 따르면 재무팀에서 일하기 위해서는 회계에서의 경력이 요구된다.

(A) accountant　　(B) **accounting**
(C) account　　(D) accountable

해설 셀 수 없는 명사 빈칸은 전치사 in의 목적어 자리이므로 명사가 들어가야 한다. 또한 빈칸 앞에 부정관사가 없기 때문에 빈칸에는 셀 수 없는 명사나 복수 명사가 들어가야 하므로 셀 수 없는 명사인 (B) accounting이 정답이다. (A) accountant와 (C) account는 셀 수 있는 명사이기 때문에 부정관사 없이 쓰려면 반드시 복수형으로 써야 한다. (D) accountable은 형용사이므로 명사 자리에 올 수 없다.

어휘 according to ~에 따르면　description 설명, 기술, 서술　require 요구하다; 필요로 하다　finance department 재무팀　accountant 회계사　accountable 책임이 있는

4.

The company is recruiting heavy machine operators with **certification** in forklifts and cranes.

그 회사는 지게차와 크레인에서 증명을 받은 중장비 기사들을 모집하고 있다.

(A) certify　　(B) certifying
(C) certificate　　(D) **certification**

해설 셀 수 없는 명사 빈칸은 전치사 with의 목적어 자리이므로 명사가 들어가야 한다. 또한 빈칸 앞에 부정관사가 없기 때문에 빈칸에는 셀 수 없는 명사나 복수 명사가 들어가야 하므로 셀 수 없는 명사인 (D) certification이 정답이다. (C) certificate는 셀 수 있는 명사이기 때문에 부정관사 없이 쓰려면 반드시 복수형으로 써야 한다.

어휘 recruit (신입 등을) 모집하다, 뽑다　heavy machine 중장비　operator (장비, 기계 등을) 조작하는 사람, 기사　forklift 지게차　crane 기중기, 크레인　certify 증명하다

5 사람 명사 vs. 추상 명사

1. (B)　　　2. (B)　　　3. (A)　　　4. (C)

1.

Many **visitors** of the museum sign the guest book after their tour.
(A) visits　　　(B) visitors
(C) visit　　　(D) visited

박물관의 많은 방문객들은 관람 후에 방명록을 작성한다.

해설　**사람 명사** 빈칸은 문장의 주어 자리이며, 방명록에 서명을 하는 주체는 사람이어야 하므로 (B) visitors(방문객들)가 정답이다.

어휘　sign 서명하다; 조짐, 징후　guest book 방명록

2.

The hotel collects **payment** when the guests check in rather than at booking.
(A) payers　　　(B) payment
(C) paid　　　(D) pays

그 호텔은 예약할 때보다는 투숙객이 체크인할 때 대금을 받는다.

해설　**추상 명사** 빈칸은 동사 collects의 목적어 자리이며, 문맥상 체크인할 때 대금을 받는다는 내용이 되는 게 자연스러우므로 (B) payment(납부, 지불(금))가 정답이다. (A) payers(지급인)와 (D) pays(급료, 보수)를 동사 collect와 함께 쓰면 각각 '지급인들을 모으다', '급료를 모으다'라는 의미가 되어 문맥상 어색하고, (C) paid는 동사 또는 과거분사이므로 목적어 자리에 들어갈 수 없다.

어휘　collect 수금하다, 징수하다; 모으다　check in (호텔 등에) 체크인하다, 탑승 수속을 밟다　rather than ~보다는　booking 예약

3.

Mesta Studios is a renowned **producer** of documentaries for young adults.
(A) producer　　　(B) production
(C) produces　　　(D) productive

메스타 스튜디오는 청소년들을 위한 유명 다큐멘터리 제작사이다.

해설　**사람 명사** 빈칸 앞에 be동사인 is가 있으므로 빈칸은 주격 보어 자리이며, 관사 a와 형용사 renowned의 수식을 받는 명사가 들어가야 한다. 주격 보어가 명사일 때는 주어와 동격이어야 하므로 주어 Mesta Studios와 동격 관계를 이룰 수 있는 (A) producer(제작자)가 정답이다. (B) production(생산)이 빈칸에 들어가면 '메스타 스튜디오는 생산이다'라는 의미가 되어 문맥상 어색하다.

어휘　renowned 유명한, 명성 있는　young adult 청소년　productive 생산적인, 생산하는

4.

Ms. Nguyen will interview **applicants** for the manager position starting on May 14.
(A) applied　　　(B) applicable
(C) applicants　　　(D) application

응우옌 씨는 5월 14일부터 관리직 지원자들을 면접할 것이다.

해설　**사람 명사** 빈칸은 동사 interview의 목적어 자리이며, 면접 대상은 사람이어야 하므로 '지원자들'을 뜻하는 (C) applicants가 정답이다. (D) application은 '지원(서); 응용'이라는 의미이므로 문맥상 적절하지 않다. (A) applied는 동사 또는 과거분사, (B) applicable은 형용사이므로 목적어 자리에 올 수 없다.

어휘　position 일자리; 직위　apply 지원하다; 적용하다　applicable 해당되는, 적용되는; 적절한

6 복합 명사

1. (B)   2. (D)   3. (C)   4. (A)

1.

Although it has a high admission **fee**, the golf club has a reasonable monthly rate.

(A) salary   (B) fee
(C) fair   (D) entry

그 골프 클럽은 입장 **요금**은 비싸도 월 이용료는 적당하다.

(A) 급여   (B) 요금
(C) 박람회 (D) 입장

해설 복합 명사 빈칸 앞의 명사 admission과 복합 명사를 이루어 '입장료'를 의미해야 하므로 (B) fee가 정답이다. 나머지 선택지들은 문맥상 admission과 어울리지 않는다.

어휘 reasonable (가격이) 적당한, 합리적인   monthly 매월의   rate 요금; 속도; 비율

2.

Please read the data **security** policy and sign the bottom of the page.

(A) advantage   (B) initials
(C) schedule   (D) security

데이터 **보안** 정책을 읽고 페이지 맨 아래에 서명하시기 바랍니다.

(A) 이점, 장점   (B) (이름의) 첫 글자
(C) 일정   (D) 보안

해설 복합 명사 빈칸 뒤의 명사 policy와 복합 명사를 이루어 '보안 정책'을 의미해야 하므로 (D) security가 정답이다.

어휘 sign 서명하다; 조짐, 징후

3.

Barsty Electronics has reported a budget **surplus** for the past three years.

(A) assembly   (B) account
(C) surplus   (D) proportion

바스티 일렉트로닉스는 지난 3년간 예산 **흑자**를 보고했다.

(A) 조립; 집회, 회합   (B) 계좌
(C) 흑자; 과잉   (D) 비율

해설 복합 명사 빈칸 앞의 명사 budget과 복합 명사를 이루어 '예산 흑자'를 의미해야 하므로 (C) surplus가 정답이다.

어휘 electronics ((항상 복수형)) 전자 제품, 전자 기기   past 지난

4.

A small service **charge** is added for orders that are less than 10 dollars.

(A) charge   (B) provider
(C) speed   (D) amount

10달러 미만의 주문에는 약간의 서비스 **요금**이 추가됩니다.

(A) 요금   (B) 공급자
(C) 속도   (D) 양; 총액

해설 복합 명사 빈칸 앞의 명사 service와 복합 명사를 이루어 '서비스 요금'을 의미해야 하므로 (A) charge가 정답이다.

어휘 add 추가하다   order 주문; 주문하다   less than ~보다 적은

VOCABULARY

본문 p.034

1. (A) 2. (D) 3. (A) 4. (C) 5. (C) 6. (A) 7. (C) 8. (D)

1.

Ms. Selbst asked the contractor to provide an **estimate** for the cost of renovating her kitchen.

(A) estimate (B) attempt
(C) industry (D) objective

젤프스트 씨는 계약업체에게 그녀의 주방 수리에 대한 **견적서**를 줄 것을 요청했다.

(A) 견적(서); 추정(치) (B) 시도
(C) 산업 (D) 목적, 목표

해설 명사 어휘 to provide의 목적어로 가장 자연스럽게 의미가 통하는 명사를 골라야 한다. 따라서 '견적(서)'이라는 의미의 (A) estimate가 정답이다.

어휘 contractor 계약자, 도급업자 provide 제공하다 renovate 수리하다; 혁신하다

2.

There has been a significant **drop** in market shares since the CEO's resignation.

(A) supplier (B) reason
(C) collaboration (D) drop

대표 이사의 사임 이후로 시장 점유율에 상당한 **하락**이 있었다.

(A) 공급자, 공급업체 (B) 이유
(C) 협업 (D) 하락, 감소

해설 명사 어휘 빈칸 뒤에 나오는 market shares(시장 점유율)에 어떠한 변화가 있었는지 나타낼 수 있는 명사를 골라야 한다. 문맥상 '시장 점유율이 현저하게 하락했다'는 내용이 되는 게 자연스러우므로 '하락, 감소'라는 의미의 (D) drop이 정답이다.

어휘 significant 상당한, 현저한; 중요한 resignation 사직, 사임

3.

It is necessary to raise **awareness** of the lack of access to proper healthcare in some areas.

(A) awareness (B) goals
(C) precision (D) issue

일부 지역에서 적절한 보건 의료 서비스에의 접근이 용이하지 않다는 **인식**을 높이는 것이 필수적이다.

(A) 인식, 의식, 관심 (B) 목표
(C) 정확(성), 정밀(성) (D) 쟁점

해설 명사 어휘 동사 raise의 목적어로 가장 자연스럽게 의미가 통하는 명사를 골라야 한다. 따라서 '인식, 의식'이라는 의미의 (A) awareness가 정답이다. raise awareness (of)는 '(~에 대한) 의식/인식을 높이다'를 뜻한다.

어휘 necessary 필수적인 lack of ~의 부족[결핍] access to ~에 대한 이용[접근] proper 적절한 healthcare 보건 의료

4.

The new employee took the **initiative** in redesigning the team's workspace.

(A) documentation (B) figures
(C) initiative (D) status

그 신입 직원은 팀의 작업 공간을 재설계하는 데 **솔선**했다.

(A) 문서 (B) 수치
(C) 주도권; 계획 (D) 자격, 지위

해설 명사 어휘 동사 took의 목적어로 가장 자연스럽게 의미가 통하는 명사를 골라야 한다. 따라서 '주도권'이라는 의미의 (C) initiative가 정답이다. 특히 initiative는 take the initiative (in)의 형태로 자주 쓰인다.

어휘 take the initiative 솔선하다; 주도권을 잡다 redesign 재설계[재계획]하다 workspace 작업 공간

5. The city councilor's speech helped increase **confidence** in the town's economic future.

(A) market   (B) delivery
(C) confidence   (D) assembly

시 의회 의원의 연설은 도시 경제의 앞날에 대한 **자신감**을 높이는 데 도움이 되었다.

(A) 시장   (B) 배달
(C) 자신감   (D) 조립; 집회, 회합

> **해설** 명사 어휘 동사 increase의 목적어로 가장 자연스럽게 의미가 통하는 명사를 골라야 한다. 따라서 '자신감'이라는 의미의 (C) confidence가 정답이다.
>
> **어휘** city councilor 시 의회 의원   increase 높이다, 증가시키다; 증가   economic 경제의

6. Please speak to one of our sales **associates** for information about our electronics.

(A) associates   (B) inventory
(C) promotion   (D) features

저희의 전자 제품들에 관한 정보는 저희 영업 **사원들** 중 한 명에게 말씀하시기 바랍니다.

(A) (직장) 동료   (B) 물품 목록; 재고(품)
(C) 판촉, 홍보   (D) 특징

> **해설** 명사 어휘 빈칸 앞의 명사 sales와 복합 명사를 이루어 '영업 사원, 판매 직원'을 의미해야 하므로 '(직장) 동료, 직원'이라는 의미의 (A) associates가 정답이다.
>
> **어휘** electronics ((항상 복수형)) 전자 제품, 전자 기기

7. On weekday nights, the restaurant rarely reaches its full **capacity**.

(A) referral   (B) cancelation
(C) capacity   (D) facility

평일 밤에 그 식당은 만석이 되는 일이 드물다.

(A) 위탁; 소개(서)   (B) 취소
(C) 용량, 수용력; 능력   (D) 시설

> **해설** 명사 어휘 형용사 full의 수식을 받아 한정된 공간에 사람이 가득 찬 정도를 나타낼 수 있는 명사를 골라야 한다. 따라서 '용량, 수용력'이라는 의미의 (C) capacity가 정답이다.
>
> **어휘** weekday 평일   rarely 거의 ~않는   reach 도달하다, 이르다, 닿다

8. In her presentation, Dr. Matvey acknowledged her partner's **contribution** to the research study.

(A) guidance   (B) venue
(C) separation   **(D) contribution**

그녀의 발표에서 마트베이 박사는 연구 조사에 대한 파트너의 **기여**에 감사를 표했다.

(A) 안내   (B) 장소
(C) 분리   **(D) 기여, 기부**

> **해설** 명사 어휘 동사 acknowledge(감사를 표하다)의 목적어로 가장 자연스럽게 의미가 통하는 명사를 골라야 한다. 따라서 '기여, 기부'라는 의미의 (D) contribution이 정답이다.
>
> **어휘** presentation 발표, 프레젠테이션   acknowledge ((공식적으로)) 감사를 표하다; 인정하다

ACTUAL TEST

본문 p.036

| 1. (A) | 2. (A) | 3. (C) | 4. (D) | 5. (C) | 6. (B) |
| 7. (C) | 8. (A) | 9. (B) | 10. (A) | 11. (B) | 12. (A) |

1.

Interns should obtain **approval** from their assigned mentors before leaving the office.

인턴들은 퇴근하기 전에 자신들에게 배정된 멘토에게 승인을 얻어야 한다.

(A) approval
(B) approvingly
(C) approved
(D) approve

해설 명사 자리 [목적어] 빈칸 앞에 주어(Interns)와 동사(should obtain)가 있는 것으로 보아 빈칸은 목적어 자리이므로 명사인 (A) approval이 정답이다. (B) approvingly는 부사, (C) approved는 동사 또는 과거분사, (D) approve는 동사이므로 오답이다.

어휘 obtain 얻다, 획득하다, 입수하다 approval 승인; 인정, 찬성 assign (일, 책임 등을) 맡기다, 배정하다
leave the office 퇴근하다

2.

Inventory must be checked for any items that are past their expiration date.

유효 기간을 넘긴 품목들이 있는지 **재고**가 확인되어야 한다.

(A) Inventory
(B) Security
(C) Referral
(D) Situation

(A) 재고
(B) 보안
(C) 위탁; 소개(서)
(D) 상황

해설 명사 어휘 유효 기간을 넘긴 품목이 있는지 보려면 재고를 확인해야 하므로 빈칸에 가장 적절한 말은 '재고'라는 의미의 (A) Inventory이다.

어휘 past 지난간 expiration date 유효 기간

3.

The majority of **subscribers** said they preferred receiving the newsletter by e-mail.

다수의 구독자가 이메일로 소식지를 받는 걸 선호한다고 말했다.

(A) subscribed
(B) subscribes
(C) subscribers
(D) subscriptions

해설 사람 명사 vs. 추상 명사 빈칸에는 The majority of와 결합하여 문장의 주어 역할을 할 수 있는 말이 들어가야 한다. 선택지 중 명사는 (C) subscribers와 (D) subscriptions인데, 문맥상 주어가 소식지를 받는 주체이므로 '구독자'를 뜻하는 (C) subscribers가 정답이다. (A) subscribed는 동사 또는 과거분사이고, (B) subscribes는 동사이므로 빈칸에 적절하지 않다.

어휘 majority of 다수의 subscriber 구독자 prefer ~을 (더) 선호하다 newsletter 소식지 subscribe 구독하다
subscription 구독(료)

4.

Our success in the third quarter is the **result** of an aggressive marketing campaign.

3/4분기의 성공은 공격적인 마케팅 캠페인의 결과이다.

(A) resulting
(B) resulted
(C) resultant
(D) result

해설 명사 자리 [주격 보어] 빈칸 앞에 be동사 is가 있으므로 빈칸은 주격 보어 자리이자 관사 the와 전치사구(of ~ campaign)의 수식을 받는 자리이므로 명사인 (D) result가 정답이다. (A) resulting은 동명사 또는 현재분사, (B) resulted는 동사 또는 과거분사, (C) resultant (그 결과로 생긴)는 형용사이므로 명사 자리에 들어갈 수 없다.

어휘 quarter 사분기; 4분의 1 result 결과; (~의) 결과로 발생하다 aggressive 공격적인 resultant 그 결과로 생긴, 그에 따른

010

5.

Ms. Lee expressed her **gratitude** for the opportunity to host the awards ceremony.	이 씨는 시상식을 주최할 기회를 가진 것에 대해 감사를 표했다.
(A) gratefully (B) grateful (C) **gratitude** (D) gratify	

> **해설** 명사 자리 [소유격 뒤] 빈칸은 소유격 her의 수식을 받는 자리이므로 명사인 (C) gratitude가 정답이다. (A) gratefully는 부사, (B) grateful은 형용사, (D) gratify는 동사이므로 소유격의 수식을 받을 수 없다.

> **어휘** express 표현하다 gratitude 감사 opportunity to do ~할 기회 host 주최하다 awards ceremony 시상식 grateful 고마워하는 gratify 기쁘게 하다

6.

Akasuki Tech is well known as the first software company that implemented lifetime **employment**.	아카스키 테크는 평생 고용을 시행한 첫 번째 소프트웨어 회사로 잘 알려져 있다.
(A) employs (B) **employment** (C) employer (D) employed	

> **해설** 사람 명사 vs. 추상 명사 빈칸은 lifetime과 복합 명사를 이루어 동사 implemented의 목적어 역할을 하는 명사 자리이다. 문맥상 평생 고용을 시행했다는 내용이 되는 게 자연스러우므로 (B) employment가 정답이다. (C) employer는 명사이긴 하지만 '평생 고용자를 시행했다'는 어색한 해석이 되므로 빈칸에 적절하지 않다.

> **어휘** be known as ~로 알려지다 implement 시행하다 lifetime employment (정년이 보장되는) 평생 고용, 종신 고용

7.

It is a rare **exception** for visitors to donate less than twenty dollars in the City Hall charity events.	시청 자선 행사에서 방문객들이 20달러 미만을 기부하는 것은 드물게 있는 이례적인 일이다.
(A) except (B) exceptions (C) **exception** (D) exceptional	

> **해설** 명사 자리 [관사/형용사 뒤] 빈칸은 관사 a와 형용사 rare의 수식을 받는 자리이므로 단수 명사인 (C) exception이 정답이다. (A) except는 전치사, (B) exceptions는 복수 명사, (D) exceptional은 형용사이므로 오답이다.

> **어휘** rare 드문 exception 이례, 예외 donate 기부[기증]하다 charity event 자선 행사 except ~을 제외하고 exceptional 예외의, 특별한

8.

The grocery store prides itself on using only local **suppliers** for its produce.	그 식료품점은 농산물에 대해서는 오직 지역의 **공급업체**들만 이용하는 데 자부심을 느낀다.
(A) **suppliers** (B) clients (C) administrations (D) figures	(A) 공급업체 (B) 고객 (C) 경영진 (D) 수치

> **해설** 명사 어휘 형용사 local의 수식을 받아 동명사 using의 목적어로 가장 자연스럽게 의미가 통하는 명사를 골라야 한다. 따라서 '공급업체'라는 의미의 (A) suppliers가 정답이다.

> **어휘** grocery store 식료품점 pride oneself 자부심을 느끼다 local 지역의 produce 농산물; 생산하다

Notice to all FFR Employees

We are happy to announce that ⁹**renovations** on the staff lunchroom are finally complete.

Starting Monday, the new area will be open ¹⁰**daily** from 8 A.M. until 8 P.M. We encourage everyone to use this space to eat together.

You may choose from various ¹¹**dining** options. Menus include styles of cuisines from around the world. The cafeteria also caters to vegan diets and those with special dietary needs.

¹²**Employees may also bring food from home.** Microwaves and refrigerators are available for those who wish to do so.

We hope you enjoy these new facilities.

FFR 직원들에게 알림

우리는 구내식당 ⁹**수리**가 마침내 끝났다는 것을 알리게 되어 기쁩니다.

월요일부터 새로운 구역이 ¹⁰**매일** 오전 8시부터 오후 8시까지 개방될 것입니다. 우리는 모두가 이 공간을 이용해 함께 식사하기를 권합니다.

여러분은 다양한 ¹¹**식사** 선택권에서 고를 수도 있습니다. 메뉴에는 전 세계 요리 스타일이 포함됩니다. 구내식당은 또한 채식주의 식단과 특별한 식단이 필요한 분들을 충족시킵니다.

¹²**직원들은 또한 집에서 음식을 가져와도 됩니다.** 전자레인지와 냉장고는 그렇게 하고 싶은 분들이 이용할 수 있습니다.

여러분이 이 새로운 시설을 마음껏 이용하시길 바랍니다.

어휘 notice 통지, 예고; 알아차리다 announce 알리다, 발표하다 renovation 수리, 수선; 혁신 lunchroom 구내식당 starting ~부터 daily 매일; 매일의 encourage A to do A가 ~하도록 권장[장려]하다 dining 식사, 정찬 option 선택(권) include 포함하다 cuisine 요리(법) cafeteria 구내식당 cater to ~을 충족시키다, ~의 구미에 맞추다 vegan 완전한 채식주의자; 완전한 채식주의자의 diet 식단, 식사 dietary 식단의, 음식의 need ((보통 복수형)) 요구, 필요; 필요로 하다 available 이용할 수 있는

9. (A) renovate (B) **renovations**
   (C) renovated (D) renovates

   해설 명사 자리 [that절의 주어] 빈칸 앞에 명사절 접속사 that이 있고 뒤에는 that절의 동사 are가 있으므로 빈칸에는 that절의 주어 역할을 할 수 있는 명사가 들어가야 한다. 따라서 선택지 중 명사인 (B) renovations가 정답이다. (A) renovate와 (D) renovates는 동사이고, (C) renovated는 동사 또는 과거분사이므로 빈칸에 적절하지 않다.

10. (A) **daily** (B) evenly (A) **매일** (B) 고르게
    (C) busily (D) locally (C) 바쁘게, 분주하게 (D) 장소상으로

    해설 부사 어휘 형용사 open을 수식해 가장 자연스럽게 의미가 통하는 부사를 골라야 한다. 따라서 '매일'이라는 의미의 (A) daily가 정답이다.

11. (A) display (B) **dining** (A) 전시, 진열 (B) **식사, 정찬**
    (C) stationery (D) career (C) 문구류 (D) 경력

    해설 명사 어휘 명사 options와 어울려 '식사로 선택할 수 있는 것들이 다양하다'는 내용이 되는 게 가장 자연스러우므로 '식사'라는 의미의 (B) dining이 정답이다.

12. (A) **Employees may also bring food from home.** (A) **직원들은 또한 집에서 음식을 가져와도 됩니다.**
    (B) Please let us know your preference. (B) 여러분이 선호하는 것을 우리에게 알려 주세요.
    (C) We expect many customers to come. (C) 우리는 많은 고객이 올 것으로 기대합니다.
    (D) However, there are no dishwashers. (D) 그러나 식기세척기는 없습니다.

    해설 알맞은 문장 고르기 빈칸 뒤 문장에서 '그렇게 하고 싶은 사람들은 전자레인지와 냉장고를 이용할 수 있다'고 했으므로 '그렇게 한다는 것'이 무엇인지 파악해야 한다. 집에서 음식을 갖고 오면 구내식당에 있는 전자레인지에 데우거나 냉장고에 보관할 수 있으므로 문맥상 (A)가 가장 적절하다.

    어휘 preference 선호(도), 선호하는 것 expect 기대하다, 예상하다 dishwasher 식기세척기

UNIT 02 대명사

1 인칭대명사

본문 p.042

1. (A)   2. (B)   3. (D)   4. (B)

1.

When Mr. Perkins goes to London, **he** will fly first class.

(A) he
(B) him
(C) his
(D) himself

퍼킨스 씨가 런던에 갈 때, 그는 일등석을 탈 것이다.

해설 인칭대명사 [주격] 빈칸은 동사 will fly 앞의 주어 자리이므로 주격 대명사인 (A) he가 정답이다. (B) him은 목적격 대명사, (C) his는 소유격 또는 소유대명사, (D) himself는 재귀대명사로 주어 자리에 들어갈 수 없다.

어휘 first class 일등석

2.

While the branch manager is on vacation, the assistant manager is filling in for **her**.

(A) herself
(B) her
(C) she
(D) hers

지점장이 휴가 중인 동안, 부매니저가 그녀를 대신할 것이다.

해설 인칭대명사 [목적격] 빈칸은 전치사 for의 목적어 자리이며, 문맥상 부매니저가 지점장을 대신할 거라는 내용이 되는 게 자연스러우므로 목적격 대명사인 (B) her가 정답이다. 여기서 her는 앞에 나온 the branch manager를 가리킨다. 소유대명사인 (D) hers는 '그녀의 것'이란 의미이므로 문맥에 적합하지 않다.

어휘 branch manager 지점장, 지사장 on vacation 휴가 중인 fill in for ~을 대신하다 assistant 부(副)-, 조(助)-; 조수

3.

Ms. Mensch gave the clients a presentation to convince **them** to work with their new providers.

(A) theirs
(B) they
(C) their
(D) them

멘슈 씨는 새로운 공급업자들과 작업하도록 고객들을 설득하기 위해 그들에게 발표를 했다.

해설 인칭대명사 [목적격] 빈칸은 to convince의 목적어 자리이며, 문맥상 '그들의 것'이 아니라 '그들(고객들)'이 새로운 공급업체와 일하도록 설득하는 것이므로 (D) them이 정답이다. 주격 대명사인 (B) they는 주어 자리에 들어가야 하며, 소유격인 (C) their는 수식할 명사가 있어야 하므로 모두 빈칸에 적절하지 않다.

어휘 give A a presentation A에게 발표하다 convince A to do A를 ~하도록 설득하다 provider 제공자, 공급자

4.

Ms. Flitzer could not use the copier because **it** broke down weeks ago.

(A) them
(B) it
(C) itself
(D) they

복사기가 몇 주 전에 고장났기 때문에 플리처 씨는 복사기를 사용할 수 없었다.

해설 인칭대명사 [주격] 빈칸은 구동사 broke down 앞의 주어 자리이며, 문맥상 빈칸의 주어는 앞에 나온 the copier를 가리키므로 단수 대명사인 (B) it이 정답이다. (A) them은 복수 명사를 대신하는 목적격 대명사이고, (C) itself는 재귀대명사이므로 주어 자리에 쓸 수 없다.

어휘 copier 복사기 break down 고장 나다, 망가지다

2 소유격과 소유대명사

본문 p.043

1. (C) 2. (B) 3. (D) 4. (B)

1.

Trainees using the equipment for the first time should ask for help from **their** mentors.

(A) themselves (B) them
(C) their (D) they

처음으로 그 장비를 사용하는 교육생들은 그들의 멘토에게 도움을 요청해야 한다.

해설 인칭대명사 [소유격] 빈칸 앞에 전치사 from이 있고 뒤에는 명사 mentors가 있으므로 빈칸에는 명사를 수식하는 말이 들어가야 한다. 따라서 소유격인 (C) their가 정답이다. (A) themselves는 재귀대명사, (B) them은 목적격 대명사, (D) they는 주격 대명사이므로 명사를 수식하는 자리에 들어갈 수 없다.

어휘 trainee 교육을 받는 사람 equipment ((집합적)) 장비, 용품 ask for ~을 요청하다 mentor 멘토, 좋은 조언자

2.

Ms. Casey left a bag with **her** personal belongings in her hotel room.

(A) she **(B) her**
(C) herself (D) hers

케이시 씨는 호텔 객실에 그녀의 개인 소지품이 담긴 가방을 두고 왔다.

해설 인칭대명사 [소유격] 빈칸 앞에 전치사 with가 있고 뒤에는 명사구 personal belongings가 있으므로 빈칸에는 명사를 수식하는 말이 들어가야 한다. 따라서 소유격인 (B) her가 정답이다. (A) she는 주격 대명사, (C) herself는 재귀대명사, (D) hers는 소유대명사이므로 명사를 수식하는 자리에 들어갈 수 없다.

어휘 leave 남겨 두다 personal belongings 개인 소지품

3.

All files were mixed up, so we had to check whether those were **ours**.

(A) our (B) we
(C) ourselves **(D) ours**

모든 파일들이 뒤섞여서 우리는 그것들이 우리의 것인지 확인해야 했다.

해설 인칭대명사 [소유대명사] 빈칸은 be동사 were의 주격 보어 자리이므로 명사나 형용사가 들어가야 한다. 따라서 소유대명사인 (D) ours가 정답이다. 여기서 ours는 our files를 의미한다. (A) our는 소유격, (B) we는 주격 대명사, (C) ourselves는 재귀대명사이므로 오답이다.

어휘 mix up ~을 뒤죽박죽으로 만들다, ~을 뒤섞다 check 확인하다 whether ~인지 아닌지

4.

Mr. Sheffield helped me during my presentation, so I will help him during **his**.

(A) him **(B) his**
(C) he (D) himself

셰필드 씨가 내 발표 시간에 나를 도와줘서 나도 그의 발표 시간에 그에게 도움을 줄 것이다.

해설 인칭대명사 [소유대명사] 빈칸 앞에 전치사 during이 있으므로 빈칸은 전치사의 목적어 자리이다. 또한 문맥상 셰필드 씨가 나의 발표 동안 도움을 줬기 때문에 그의 발표 동안에는 내가 도울 거라는 내용이 되는 게 자연스러우므로 선택지 중 소유대명사인 (B) his가 정답이다. 여기서 his는 his presentation을 의미한다. (A) him은 목적격 대명사, (C) he는 주격 대명사, (D) himself는 재귀대명사이므로 오답이다.

어휘 during ~ 동안 presentation 발표

3 재귀대명사

본문 p.044

1. (C) 2. (D) 3. (C) 4. (B)

1.

At Raya's Fashion, we make all of the clothes and accessories **ourselves**.

(A) us (B) we
(C) ourselves (D) our

라야 패션에서는 의류와 액세서리를 모두 우리가 직접 만듭니다.

해설 재귀대명사 [강조 용법] 빈칸 앞에 〈주어(we)+동사(make)+목적어(all ~ accessories)〉 구조로 완전한 문장이 있으므로 빈칸에는 생략해도 문장이 성립할 수 있는 말이 들어가야 한다. 따라서 재귀대명사 (C) ourselves가 정답이다. 재귀대명사가 강조 용법으로 쓰일 때는 주어나 목적어를 강조할 수 있으며, 재귀대명사를 생략해도 문장은 문법적으로 완전하다는 특징이 있다. 이 문장에서는 재귀대명사가 주어 we를 강조하는 역할을 한다.

어휘 clothes ((집합적)) 의류, 옷 accessory 액세서리

2.

If Ms. Kiko resigns this month, Mr. Baker should be able to supervise the construction on **his own**.

(A) he (B) his
(C) himself (D) his own

키코 씨가 이번 달에 사임하면 베이커 씨가 혼자서 공사를 감독할 수 있어야 한다.

해설 관용 표현 on one's own 빈칸 앞의 전치사 on과 함께 쓸 수 있는 말을 골라야 한다. on one's own은 '혼자서, 단독으로'라는 뜻이므로 (D) his own이 정답이다. '혼자서 공사를 감독해야 한다'는 의미가 되어 문맥상으로도 자연스럽다. (A) he는 주격 대명사, (B) his는 소유격 또는 소유대명사, (C) himself는 재귀대명사이다.

어휘 resign 사직하다, 물러나다 supervise 감독하다 construction 건설, 공사

3.

The CEO planned out a crisis management system **herself** to prevent for possible business threats.

(A) she (B) her
(C) herself (D) hers

대표 이사는 발생할 수 있는 사업상 위험을 방지하기 위해 직접 위기 관리 시스템을 계획했다.

해설 재귀대명사 [강조 용법] 빈칸 앞에 〈주어(The CEO)+구동사(planned out)+목적어(a crisis management system)〉 구조로 완전한 문장이 있으므로 빈칸에는 생략해도 문장이 성립할 수 있는 말이 들어가야 한다. 따라서 재귀대명사 (C) herself가 정답이다. 재귀대명사가 강조 용법으로 쓰일 때는 주어나 목적어를 강조할 수 있으며, 재귀대명사를 생략해도 문장은 문법적으로 완전하다는 특징이 있다. 이 문장에서는 재귀대명사가 주어 The CEO를 강조하는 역할을 한다.

어휘 plan out ~을 (세심히) 계획하다 crisis management 위기 관리 prevent 막다, 방지하다 possible 가능한, 있을 수 있는 threat 위협

4.

Marge and Gerald had to set up their stall for the expo by **themselves**.

(A) they (B) themselves
(C) them (D) theirs

마지와 제럴드는 박람회의 진열대를 알아서 설치해야 했다.

해설 재귀대명사 관용 표현 빈칸 앞의 전치사 by와 함께 쓸 수 있는 말을 골라야 한다. by oneself는 '혼자서, 다른 사람의 도움 없이'라는 뜻이므로 (B) themselves가 정답이다. 목적격 대명사인 (C) them과 소유대명사 (D) theirs도 전치사의 목적어로 쓸 수 있지만 각각 '그들에 의해', '그들의 것에 의해'라는 의미가 되어 문맥상 적절하지 않다. (A) they는 주격 대명사이므로 전치사 뒤에 올 수 없다.

어휘 set up ~을 설치하다 stall 진열대 expo 박람회, 전람회

4 지시대명사

본문 p.045

1. (A) 2. (C) 3. (B) 4. (D)

1.

Consumers find the Fex Electronics tablet's interfaces more stylish than **those** of their competitors.

(A) those (B) them
(C) they (D) that

소비자들은 펙스 일렉트로닉스 태블릿의 인터페이스가 경쟁사들의 인터페이스보다 더 멋지다고 생각한다.

해설 지시대명사 those 빈칸은 of their competitors의 수식을 받으면서 앞에 나온 복수 명사 interfaces를 대신하는 자리이므로 복수 지시대명사인 (A) those가 정답이다. (D) that은 단수 지시대명사이므로 빈칸에 적절하지 않다. (B) them은 목적격 대명사이고, (C) they는 주격 대명사이므로 오답이다.

어휘 tablet 태블릿 PC; 평판, 명판   competitor 경쟁자, 경쟁 상대

2.

Ms. Tesh asked **those** who volunteered for the fundraising event to meet at noon.

(A) these (B) them
(C) those (D) themselves

테시 씨는 모금 행사에 자원한 사람들에게 12시에 모일 것을 요청했다.

해설 지시대명사 those 빈칸은 동사 asked의 목적어 자리이자 뒤에 오는 관계사절(who ~ event)의 수식을 받는 자리이다. 선택지 중 관계사절의 수식을 받을 수 있는 것은 (C) those이다. 〈those who+동사〉는 '~하는 사람들'이라고 해석한다.

어휘 ask A to do A에게 ~할 것을 요청하다   volunteer 자원하다, 자원봉사하다; 자원봉사자   fundraising 모금, 자금 조달

3.

These people in the conference hall are not attending the forum.

(A) This **(B) These**
(C) That (D) They

회의장에 있는 이 사람들은 토론회에 참석하지 않을 것이다.

해설 지시형용사 these 빈칸은 명사 people을 수식하는 자리이므로 복수 명사를 수식할 수 있는 지시형용사인 (B) These가 정답이다. (A) This와 (C) That은 단수 명사를 수식하고, (D) They는 주격 대명사이므로 명사를 수식할 수 없다.

어휘 conference hall 회의장   attend 참석하다   forum 토론회, 공개 토론, 포럼

4.

Our newsletter is sent out more often than **that** of other IT startups.

(A) this (B) these
(C) their **(D) that**

우리 소식지는 다른 IT 스타트업들의 소식지보다 더 자주 발송됩니다.

해설 지시대명사 that 빈칸은 of other IT startups의 수식을 받으면서 앞에 나온 단수 명사 Our newsletter를 대신하는 자리이므로 단수 지시대명사인 (D) that이 정답이다. 단수 지시대명사 (A) this와 복수 지시대명사 (B) these는 다른 말의 수식을 받을 수 없다. (C) their는 소유격이므로 오답이다.

어휘 newsletter 소식지   send out ~을 발송하다   startup 스타트업, 신생 벤처 기업

5 부정대명사: one, another, the other(s)

본문 p.046

1. (B)   2. (B)   3. (C)   4. (A)

1.

Despite the low success of its first branch, Beanie Coffee has opened **another** in Paris.

(A) other (B) another
(C) any (D) all

첫 번째 지점의 저조한 성과에도 불구하고, 비니 커피는 파리에 또 다른 지점을 열었다.

해설 부정대명사 another 빈칸은 동사 has opened의 목적어 자리이며, 문맥상 첫 번째 지점 외에 또 다른 지점을 열었다는 내용이 되는 게 자연스러우므로 '또 하나, 또 다른 것[사람]'을 의미하는 부정대명사 (B) another가 정답이다. (A) other는 '다른'을 뜻하는 형용사이기 때문에 뒤에 수식할 명사가 있어야 한다. 다만 the other(나머지 하나)는 명사 역할을 할 수 있다. (C) any(일부; 아무 것)와 (D) all(모든 것) 모두 문맥상 적절하지 않으므로 오답이다.

어휘 despite ~에도 불구하고   success 성공, 성과   branch 지점, 지사

2.

One candidate had no prior work experience while **the other** was a senior accountant.

(A) other (B) the other
(C) ones (D) either

한 후보자는 이전 업무 경력이 없었다. 반면에 나머지 한 명은 상급 회계사였다.

해설 부정대명사 the other 빈칸은 접속사 while이 이끄는 절의 주어 자리이다. 빈칸 뒤에 be동사의 단수형인 was가 있으므로 주어 역시 단수형으로 수 일치를 해야 한다. 따라서 단수 대명사 (B) the other가 정답이다. 주절의 주어 One candidate도 중요한 단서인데, 둘 중 하나를 가리킬 때는 one, 나머지 하나를 가리킬 때는 the other라고 표현한다.

어휘 candidate 후보자   prior 이전의   while 반면에, ~인 반면   senior 선임의   accountant 회계사

3.

All volunteers are encouraged to help **each other** create a lively atmosphere in the event venue.

(A) other (B) another
(C) each other (D) the other

모든 자원봉사자들은 행사장에서 서로 활기찬 분위기를 조성하는 걸 돕도록 권장된다.

해설 부정대명사 each other 빈칸은 to help의 목적어 자리이며, 문맥상 서로 활기찬 분위기를 조성하도록 도와야 한다는 내용이 되는 게 자연스러우므로 '서로'라는 의미의 부정대명사 (C) each other가 정답이다. (A) other는 '다른'을 뜻하는 형용사이기 때문에 뒤에 수식할 명사가 있어야 한다. (B) another(또 하나, 또 다른 것[사람])와 (D) the other(나머지 하나)는 모두 문맥상 적절하지 않으므로 오답이다.

어휘 volunteer 자원봉사자; 자원봉사하다   be encouraged to do ~하도록 권장받다   create 만들어 내다; 창조하다   lively 활기 넘치는   atmosphere 분위기, 기운   venue (행사의) 장소

4.

Among the offers, the job in Springfield is the most interesting even though **the others** pay more.

(A) the others (B) another
(C) each (D) other

그 제안들 중에서, 비록 다른 곳들이 더 많은 급여를 주지만 스프링필드의 업무가 가장 흥미롭다.

해설 부정대명사 the others 빈칸은 접속사 even though가 이끄는 절의 주어 자리이다. 빈칸 뒤에 복수 동사 pay가 있으므로 주어 역시 복수형으로 수 일치를 해야 한다. 따라서 복수 대명사 (A) the others가 정답이다. (B) another(또 하나, 또 다른 것[사람])와 (C) each(각각)는 단수 대명사이고, (D) other는 '다른'을 뜻하는 형용사이기 때문에 뒤에 수식할 명사가 있어야 한다.

어휘 among (셋 이상일 때) ~ 사이에, ~ 중에   offer 제안   interesting 흥미로운   even though 비록 ~일지라도

6 수량을 나타내는 부정대명사

본문 p.047

1. (A)   2. (C)   3. (B)   4. (B)

1.

Before leaving the factory floor, please check that **all** of the machines are turned off.

공장의 작업 현장을 떠나기 전에 기계들 모두 전원이 꺼졌는지 확인하십시오.

(A) all   (B) another
(C) the other   (D) each

해설 all+of the 복수 명사+복수 동사 빈칸은 of the machines의 수식을 받는 자리이며, 뒤에 be동사의 복수형인 are가 있으므로 빈칸 역시 복수형으로 수 일치를 해야 한다. 따라서 〈all+of the 복수 명사+복수 동사〉 구조로 쓰이는 (A) all이 정답이다. (D) each는 〈each+of the 복수 명사+단수 동사〉 구조로 쓰이므로 오답이다.

어휘 floor 작업장 machine 기계 turn off (전원을) 끄다

2.

After the training, we expect **each** of the employees is well aware of the system.

교육이 끝나면 우리는 각 직원이 시스템을 잘 알게 될 것으로 예상한다.

(A) many   (B) every
(C) each   (D) all

해설 each+of the 복수 명사+단수 동사 빈칸은 of the employees의 수식을 받는 자리이며, 뒤에 be동사의 단수형인 is가 있으므로 빈칸 역시 단수형으로 수 일치를 해야 한다. 따라서 〈each+of the 복수 명사+단수 동사〉 구조로 쓰이는 (C) each가 정답이다. (A) many는 복수 동사로 수 일치하며, (D) all은 〈of the 복수 명사〉의 수식을 받으면 복수 동사로, 〈of the 셀 수 없는 명사〉의 수식을 받으면 단수 동사로 수 일치하므로 오답이다.

어휘 training 교육, 훈련 expect 예상하다, 기대하다 employee 직원 be aware of ~을 알다, ~을 인지하다

3.

Ms. McCarthy and Mr. Choi began working at ARFG Inc. when **both** of them were interns.

매카시 씨와 최 씨는 둘 다 인턴이었을 때 ARFG 사에서 일하기 시작했다.

(A) one   (B) both
(C) another   (D) every

해설 both+of the 복수 명사+복수 동사 빈칸은 of them의 수식을 받는 자리이며, 뒤에 be동사의 복수형인 were가 있으므로 빈칸 역시 복수형으로 수 일치를 해야 한다. 따라서 〈both+of the 복수 명사+복수 동사〉 구조로 쓰이는 (B) both가 정답이다. (A) one과 (C) another는 모두 단수 동사를 쓰므로 오답이다.

어휘 work at ~에서 일하다

4.

Instead of taking the bus up the mountain, **some** of our tourists like to hike it.

우리의 관광객 일부는 버스를 타고 산에 올라가는 대신 걸어서 올라가는 것을 좋아한다.

(A) someone   (B) some
(C) other   (D) each other

해설 some+of the 복수 명사+복수 동사 빈칸은 of our tourists의 수식을 받는 자리이며, 뒤에 복수 동사 like가 있으므로 빈칸 역시 복수형으로 수 일치를 해야 한다. 따라서 〈some+of the 복수 명사+복수 동사〉 구조로 쓰이는 (B) some이 정답이다.

어휘 instead of ~ 대신에 tourist 여행객 hike 도보 여행을 하다; 도보 여행

VOCABULARY

본문 p.050

1. (C) 2. (A) 3. (A) 4. (B) 5. (D) 6. (A) 7. (B) 8. (A)

1.

Marth Corp. always uses the TD Convention Center as its **venue** for company events.

(A) requirement (B) ceremony
(C) venue (D) enterprise

마스 사는 회사 행사를 위한 **장소**로 항상 TD 컨벤션 센터를 이용한다.

(A) 요구하는 것 (B) 의식, 식
(C) 장소 (D) 기업

해설 명사 어휘 빈칸 뒤의 전치사 for로 보아 회사의 행사를 위한 '장소'로 컨벤션 센터를 이용한다는 의미가 되어야 가장 자연스러우므로 (C) venue(장소)가 정답이다.

어휘 as ~로(써) event 행사

2.

To apply for the job, you must submit a recent **recommendation** letter from a former employer.

(A) recommendation (B) concern
(C) format (D) issue

그 직무에 지원하기 위해서는 이전 고용주로부터 받은 최근 **추천**서를 제출해야 한다.

(A) 추천 (B) 걱정; 관심사
(C) 포맷, 구성 방식 (D) 쟁점, 문제

해설 명사 어휘 [복합 명사] 빈칸 뒤에 나오는 명사 letter(편지)와 어울려 복합 명사로 쓰기에 알맞은 명사를 골라야 한다. 취업을 위해 이전 상사로부터 받을 만한 것은 '추천서'이므로 (A) recommendation이 빈칸에 가장 적절하다.

어휘 apply for ~에 지원하다 submit 제출하다 recent 최근의 former 이전의 employer 고용주

3.

All documents undergo an approval process for **compliance** with data protection laws.

(A) compliance (B) program
(C) expense (D) participation

모든 서류들은 자료 보호법의 **준수**를 위해 승인 절차를 밟는다.

(A) 준수 (B) 프로그램
(C) 비용 (D) 참여

해설 명사 어휘 전치사구 with data protection laws와 어울려 가장 자연스럽게 의미가 통하는 명사를 골라야 한다. 따라서 '준수, (명령, 요구 등에) 따름'이라는 의미의 (A) compliance가 정답이다.

어휘 document 서류 undergo (변화, 안 좋은 일 등을) 겪다, 받다 approval 승인 process 절차 protection 보호

4.

We require at least two weeks' **notice** to modify an event reservation.

(A) absence **(B) notice**
(C) delay (D) shipment

행사 예약을 변경하려면 최소 2주 전에 **통지**할 것을 요청합니다.

(A) 결석, 부재 **(B) 알림, 통지**
(C) 지연, 지체 (D) 수송(품)

해설 명사 어휘 빈칸 앞에 기간을 나타내는 말이 있고 뒤에는 to부정사구(to modify an event reservation)로 구체적인 상황 설명이 있다. 따라서 행사 예약을 바꾸려면 최소 2주 전에 통보하라는 내용이 되는 게 가장 자연스러우므로 (B) notice(통지)가 정답이다.

어휘 require 요청하다, 요구하다 modify 수정하다, 변경하다 reservation 예약

019

5.

Someone at TeK's Inc. signed a **proof** of delivery of the package on February 12.

(A) wealth (B) fare
(C) closure (D) **proof**

테크 사의 누군가가 2월 12일에 택배 배송 **증명서**에 서명했다.

(A) 부; 풍부 (B) 요금
(C) 폐쇄 (D) 증명(서)

> 해설 **명사 어휘** 전치사구 of delivery와 어울리면서 동사 signed의 목적어로 가장 자연스럽게 의미가 통하는 명사를 골라야 한다. 따라서 '증명(서)'이라는 의미의 (D) proof가 정답이다.

> 어휘 sign 서명하다 delivery 배송 package 소포

6.

Ms. Fuji made several **adjustments** to the company's Web site to make it look more modern.

(A) **adjustments** (B) standards
(C) maintenance (D) skills

푸지 씨는 회사 웹사이트가 더 현대적으로 보이게 하기 위해 몇 가지 **수정**을 했다.

(A) 수정, 조정 (B) 기준, 표준
(C) 유지 (D) 기술

> 해설 **명사 어휘** 동사 made의 목적어로 가장 자연스럽게 의미가 통하는 명사를 골라야 한다. 따라서 '수정, 조정'이라는 의미의 (A) adjustments가 정답이다. make an adjustment는 '수정하다'를 뜻한다.

> 어휘 several 몇몇의 modern 현대의, 최신의

7.

We have left a schedule of the cruise's events in your cabin for your **convenience**.

(A) enrollment (B) **convenience**
(C) collaboration (D) accuracy

귀하의 **편의**를 위해 선실 안에 유람선 행사 일정표를 남겨 두었습니다.

(A) 등록 (B) 편의, 편리
(C) 협업 (D) 정확성

> 해설 **명사 어휘** '귀하의 ----을 위해 유람선 행사 일정표를 남겨 두었다'라는 문장에서 빈칸에 가장 적합한 어휘는 (B) convenience (편리)이다. for one's convenience는 '~의 편의를 위해서'를 뜻한다.

> 어휘 leave 남겨 두다 schedule 일정표; 일정을 잡다 cruise 유람선 cabin (배의) 객실, 선실

8.

The housing market has benefited from recent economic **growth** in Share County district.

(A) **growth** (B) release
(C) accounts (D) layout

주택 시장은 셰어 카운티 구역의 최근 경제 **성장**으로부터 혜택을 받았다.

(A) 성장 (B) 발표, 공개
(C) 계정, 계좌 (D) 배치

> 해설 **명사 어휘** 형용사 economic의 수식을 받아 가장 자연스럽게 의미가 통하는 명사를 골라야 한다. 따라서 '성장'이라는 의미의 (A) growth가 정답이다.

> 어휘 benefit from ~로부터 이익[혜택]을 얻다 recent 최근의 economic 경제의 district 구역

ACTUAL TEST

본문 p.052

| 1. (A) | 2. (B) | 3. (A) | 4. (B) | 5. (B) | 6. (D) |
| 7. (B) | 8. (C) | 9. (A) | 10. (D) | 11. (C) | 12. (A) |

1.

Many stationery stores reported that **their** best-selling product is colored pencil set from Dendle Stationery Inc.

(A) their (B) they
(C) them (D) theirs

많은 문구점들은 자신들의 베스트셀러 상품이 덴들 문구사의 색연필 세트라고 전했다.

해설 인칭대명사 [소유격] 빈칸 앞에 명사절 접속사 that이 있고 뒤에는 명사구 best-selling product가 있으므로 빈칸에는 명사를 수식하는 말이 들어가야 한다. 따라서 소유격인 (A) their가 정답이다. (B) they는 주격 대명사, (C) them은 목적격 대명사, (D) theirs는 소유대명사이므로 명사를 수식하는 자리에 들어갈 수 없다.

어휘 stationery store 문구점 report 보고하다; 보고

2.

Contest entries will not be accepted if **they** are submitted after the deadline.

(A) it (B) they
(C) each (D) others

대회 출품작들은 마감일 이후에 제출되면 접수되지 않을 것이다.

해설 인칭대명사 [주격] 빈칸은 동사 are submitted 앞의 주어 자리이므로 주격 대명사인 (B) they가 정답이다. (A) it과 (C) each는 단수 대명사이므로 빈칸에 들어갈 수 없다. (D) others는 복수 대명사이지만 '다른 것들'을 의미하기 때문에 문맥상 적절하지 않으므로 오답이다.

어휘 contest 경연 대회 entry 출품작; 응모권 accept 받아들이다 submit 제출하다 deadline 마감일

3.

The first candidate demonstrated a **wealth** of expertise in various Paka Software programs.

(A) wealth (B) term
(C) growth (D) termination

첫 번째 후보자는 다양한 파카 소프트웨어 프로그램에 대한 전문 지식이 **풍부함**을 보여 주었다.

(A) 풍부, 다량; 부 (B) 용어, 말; 기간
(C) 성장, 증가 (D) 종료

해설 명사 어휘 전치사구 of expertise와 어울리면서 동사 demonstrated의 목적어로 가장 자연스럽게 의미가 통하는 명사를 골라야 한다. 따라서 '풍부, 다량'이라는 의미의 (A) wealth가 정답이다.

어휘 candidate 후보자 demonstrate 보여 주다, 입증하다 expertise 전문 지식 various 다양한

4.

Some of the speakers at the conference will be staying at Diamond Hotel.

(A) They (B) Some
(C) We (D) Much

학회 발표자들 중 몇몇은 다이아몬드 호텔에 묵을 것이다.

해설 some+of the 복수 명사 빈칸은 of the speakers, 즉 〈of the 복수 명사〉의 수식을 받는 자리이므로 (B) Some이 정답이다. 주격 인칭대명사인 (A) They와 (C) We는 전치사구의 수식을 받을 수 없고, (D) Much는 〈much+of the 셀 수 없는 명사+단수 동사〉의 구조로 쓰이므로 오답이다.

어휘 speaker 발표자 conference 학회, (대규모) 회의 stay 묵다, 머무르다

5.
Additional chairs are available in the next room if you need **them**.

(A) us (B) **them**
(C) you (D) their

의자들이 필요하면 옆방에 있는 여분의 의자들을 이용하실 수 있습니다.

해설 인칭대명사 [목적격] 빈칸은 동사 need의 목적어 자리이며, 문맥상 의자가 더 필요하면 옆방에서 가져다 쓰라는 내용이 되는 게 자연스러우므로 '그것들(의자들)'을 의미하는 목적격 대명사 (B) them이 정답이다. (A) us와 (C) you는 사람을 가리키는 목적격 대명사이고, (D) their는 소유격이므로 오답이다.

어휘 additional 추가의 available 이용 가능한

6.
Only **those** with valid licenses are authorized to operate heavy machinery.

(A) them (B) that
(C) this (D) **those**

유효한 면허증을 가진 사람들만 중장비를 가동시킬 권한을 부여받는다.

해설 지시대명사 those 빈칸은 with valid licenses의 수식을 받는 주어 자리이며, 뒤에 be동사의 복수형인 are가 있으므로 (D) those가 정답이다. those with는 '~을 가진 사람들'이라고 해석한다. (A) them은 목적격 대명사, (B) that과 (C) this는 단수 지시대명사이므로 오답이다.

어휘 valid 유효한 license 면허증 authorize 권한을 부여하다 operate 가동시키다, 운영하다 machinery ((집합적)) 기계류

7.
Do not hesitate to share all your questions and **concerns** with our customer service department.

(A) expenses (B) **concerns**
(C) promotions (D) values

주저하지 마시고 귀하의 모든 의문과 **우려**를 저희 고객 서비스 팀에 공유해 주십시오.

(A) 비용 (B) 걱정; 관심사
(C) 홍보, 승진 (D) 가치

해설 명사 어휘 '모든 의문과 ----을 고객 서비스 팀에 공유해 주십시오'라는 문장에서 빈칸에 가장 적합한 어휘는 (B) concerns(걱정; 관심사)이다.

어휘 hesitate to do ~하는 것을 망설이다 share 공유하다 department 부서

8.
Of the four houses, three were in poor condition while **the other** was recently renovated.

(A) other (B) another
(C) **the other** (D) each other

네 채의 주택 중에서 세 채는 상태가 좋지 않았다. 반면에 나머지 하나는 최근에 보수되었다.

해설 부정대명사 the other 빈칸은 접속사 while이 이끄는 절의 주어 자리이다. 빈칸 뒤에 be동사의 단수형인 was가 있으므로 주어 역시 단수형으로 수 일치를 해야 한다. 따라서 단수 대명사 (C) the other가 정답이다. (A) other는 '다른'을 뜻하는 형용사이기 때문에 뒤에 수식할 명사가 있어야 한다. (B) another는 '또 하나, 또 다른 것[사람]'을 뜻하므로 문맥상 적절하지 않고, (D) each other(서로)는 문맥상 알맞지 않을 뿐만 아니라 주어 자리에 쓸 수 없기 때문에 오답이다.

어휘 poor 좋지 못한 condition 상태 while 반면에 recently 최근에 renovate 개조하다, 보수하다

Dear Professor Saetang,

Thank you for contacting us on the subject of organizing a field trip to the Brandywine Art Museum. We would be glad to welcome you and your students.

In addition to the standard tour, we have several special **⁹ events** that you may be interested in. Most of these are **¹⁰ educational** activities relating to art history. There are hands-on workshops as well as seminars throughout the month of April. **¹¹ You can find the full schedule on our Web site.**

Please notify **¹² me** in advance of the date of your visit so that we may prepare.

We look forward to having you.

Regards,

Ethel Yeder

새탕 교수님께,

브랜디와인 아트 뮤지엄 견학 준비에 관해 저희에게 연락 주셔서 감사합니다. 저희는 귀하와 귀하의 학생들을 기쁜 마음으로 맞이할 것입니다.

일반 견학뿐만 아니라, 귀하께서 관심이 있으실지도 모르는 몇몇 특별 **⁹ 행사들**이 있습니다. 이것들 중 대부분은 미술사와 관련된 **¹⁰ 교육적인** 활동들입니다. 4월 한 달 동안 세미나뿐만 아니라 직접 해 보는 워크숍도 있습니다. **¹¹ 전체 일정은 저희 웹사이트에서 보실 수 있습니다.**

저희가 준비할 수 있도록 방문 날짜를 **¹² 저에게** 미리 알려 주시기 바랍니다.

귀하를 만나 뵙기를 기대합니다.

에델 예더

어휘 on the subject of ~에 관하여 organize 준비하다, 조직하다 field trip 견학, 현장 학습 welcome 맞이하다, 환영하다
in addition to ~ 뿐만 아니라, ~ 외에도 standard 일반적인 be interested in ~에 관심이 있다 activity 활동 relate to ~와 관련되다 hands-on 직접 해 보는 as well as ~ 뿐만 아니라 throughout ~ 동안, ~ 내내 notify A of B A에게 B를 알려 주다
in advance 미리, 사전에 so that ~하기 위해서 prepare 준비하다

9. (A) events   (B) treatments   (A) 행사   (B) 치료
    (C) venues   (D) prices   (C) 장소   (D) 가격

   해설 명사 어휘 일반 견학 외에 교수가 관심을 가질 만한 특별한 것이 있다는 내용이 되는 게 자연스러우며, 빈칸 뒤에 이어지는 문장에서 미술사와 관련된 활동이 있다고 했으므로 (A) events(행사들)가 빈칸에 가장 적절하다.

10. (A) executive   (B) dependent   (A) 경영의; 고급의   (B) 의존적인
    (C) likely   (D) educational   (C) ~일 것 같은   (D) 교육적인

   해설 형용사 어휘 명사 activities를 수식해 가장 자연스럽게 의미가 통하는 형용사를 골라야 한다. 빈칸 뒤에 이어지는 문장에서 워크숍과 세미나를 언급한 것으로 보아 교육에 관한 활동이라는 것을 알 수 있으므로 빈칸에 가장 적절한 어휘는 (D) educational(교육적인)이다.

11. (A) We'd like to thank you for your help.
    (B) However, I will not be available in May.
    (C) You can find the full schedule on our Web site.
    (D) Payment will be processed once you arrive.

    (A) 귀하의 도움에 감사드리고 싶습니다.
    (B) 하지만 저는 5월에 시간이 없을 것입니다.
    (C) 전체 일정은 저희 웹사이트에서 보실 수 있습니다.
    (D) 지불은 일단 도착하시면 처리될 것입니다.

   해설 알맞은 문장 고르기 빈칸 앞 문장에 '4월 한 달 동안'이라는 시간 표현이 언급되었고, 뒤 문장에서는 방문 날짜를 알려 달라고 했으므로 빈칸에는 일정에 관한 내용이 들어가는 게 가장 적절하다. 따라서 '전체 일정은 웹사이트에서 찾아볼 수 있다'고 한 (C)가 정답이다.

   어휘 would like to do ~하고 싶다 available 시간이 있는 payment 지불 process 처리하다 once 일단 ~하면

12. (A) me   (B) one
    (C) theirs   (D) my

   해설 인칭대명사 [목적격] 빈칸은 동사 notify의 목적어 자리이므로 목적격 대명사 (A) me가 정답이다. (B) one과 (C) theirs는 문맥상 알맞지 않고, (D) my는 소유격이므로 오답이다.

UNIT 03 동사

1 동사의 자리와 형태

본문 p.058

1. (D)   2. (B)   3. (C)   4. (C)

1.

Parjak Corp. **negotiated** a price reduction for buying out Gasny Inc.

(A) negotiating (B) negotiation
(C) negotiator   (D) **negotiated**

파작 사는 개스니 사 인수를 위한 가격 할인을 협상했다.

해설 주어+동사 동사 자리에 들어갈 동사 품사를 묻는 가장 간단한 형태의 문제이다. 주어가 Parjak Corp.이고 빈칸은 동사 자리인데 동사 품사는 (D) negotiated뿐이다.

어휘 negotiate 협상하다   reduction 할인, 삭감   buy out ~을 인수하다

2.

The managing director strongly **opposed** the budget cuts that the company had proposed.

(A) opposition (B) **opposed**
(C) opposing   (D) opposite

그 관리부장은 회사가 제안한 예산 삭감에 강하게 반대했다.

해설 주어+부사+동사 빈칸 앞의 The managing director가 주어, 빈칸 뒤의 the budget cuts는 목적어이므로 빈칸은 동사 자리이다. 따라서 동사 품사인 (B) opposed가 정답이다.

어휘 strongly 강하게, 거세게   oppose ~에 반대하다   budget cut 예산 삭감   propose 제안하다

3.

The cost of living **varies** from town to town even within the same region.

(A) variation   (B) various
(C) **varies** (D) to vary

주거비는 같은 지역 안에서조차 동네마다 다양하다.

해설 긴 주어+동사 The cost of living은 주어, 빈칸은 동사 자리이므로 동사 역할을 할 수 있는 (C) varies가 정답이다. 주어가 The cost로 단수이므로 단수 동사인 varies가 온 것도 참고로 알아 두자.

어휘 vary 다양하다

4.

Ms. McGee explained that changing the job requirements **would complicate** the hiring process.

(A) to complicate   (B) be complicating
(C) **would complicate** (D) be complicated

맥기 씨는 구직 요건을 변경하는 것이 채용 과정을 복잡하게 만들 것이라고 설명했다.

해설 조동사+동사원형 빈칸 앞의 changing the job requirements가 주어, 빈칸 뒤의 the hiring process가 목적어이므로 빈칸은 동사 자리이다. 선택지 중에서 동사 역할을 할 수 있는 것은 〈조동사+동사원형〉 형태의 (C) would complicate뿐이다. complicate의 형태 때문에 형용사로 착각하기 쉬운데 이는 동사 형태이고 형용사 형태는 complicated(복잡한)이다.

어휘 job requirement 구직 요건   complicate 복잡하게 만들다

2 동사원형 자리

본문 p.059

1. (A)　　2. (A)　　3. (B)　　4. (C)

1.

| On the collection day, residents must **separate** their household trash from their recyclable items. | 수거일에 주민 여러분은 가정용 쓰레기와 재활용 가능한 품목을 분리해 두셔야 합니다. |

(A) separate　　(B) to separate
(C) separation　(D) seperates

해설 **조동사＋동사원형** 조동사 뒤의 동사원형 자리를 묻는 문제로, 빈칸이 조동사 must 뒤에 있으므로 정답은 동사원형인 (A) separate이다. 참고로, separate는 동사뿐 아니라 형용사(분리된, 따로 떨어진)로 쓰인다는 정보도 챙겨 두자.

어휘 resident 주민　separate A from B A와 B를 구별하다　household 가정의; 가정　recyclable 재활용 가능한

2.

| Please **confirm** that all of the items you have ordered are in the package. | 주문하신 모든 제품이 포장 박스 안에 있는지 확인하시기 바랍니다. |

(A) confirm　　(B) confirming
(C) to confirm　(D) confirms

해설 **Please＋동사원형** 동사 자리를 묻는 문제에서 조동사 뒤의 동사원형 자리를 묻는 문제와 함께 기초 난이도에 해당하는 명령문 유형이다. 명령문은 주어 없이 동사원형 혹은 〈Please＋동사원형〉으로 문장이 시작되므로 정답은 (A) confirm이다.

어휘 confirm 확인하다　package 포장 상자, 포장품; 소포

3.

| When on the factory floor, **wear** your protective gear at all times. | 공장 현장에 있을 때에는 항상 안전 장비를 착용하세요. |

(A) wearing　　(B) wear
(C) wears　　　(D) to wear

해설 **명령문의 동사원형** 빈칸은 명령문의 동사원형 자리이므로 정답은 (B) wear이다. 이렇게 명령문으로 시작하는 주절이 문장의 뒤에 위치하는 경우도 있으니 유념해 두자. 참고로, When on the factory floor는 When과 on 사이에 you are가 생략된 문장으로, 부사절에서 주어와 be동사가 생략 가능하다는 것도 챙겨 둘 것.

어휘 protective gear 안전 장비

4.

| Experts recommend that passwords **be** at least 12 characters long. | 전문가들은 비밀번호가 최소 12자 이상은 되어야 한다고 권고한다. |

(A) are　　(B) were
(C) be　　(D) being

해설 **recommend＋that＋주어＋동사원형** 동사 recommend가 보이고 의미상 '비밀번호가 12자 이상이 되어야 한다'는 당위의 내용을 담고 있으므로 that절의 동사 형태는 〈should＋동사원형〉 혹은 〈동사원형〉의 형태가 되어야 한다. 따라서 동사원형인 (C) be가 정답이다.

어휘 expert 전문가　recommend 권고하다　character 글자, 부호; 성격, 특징

3 자동사

본문 p.060

1. (C) 2. (A) 3. (A) 4. (B)

1.

The harvest festival **occurs** every year in the last week of October.

(A) occurring   (B) occurrence
(C) occurs   (D) to occur

추수 감사절은 매년 10월 마지막 주에 열린다.

> **해설** 주어+동사 주어가 The harvest festival이고 빈칸 뒤에 오는 성분들은 부사구들이므로 빈칸에는 자동사가 와야 한다. 선택지 중 동사 역할을 할 수 있는 것은 (C) occurs뿐이다.
>
> **어휘** harvest festival 추수 감사절   occurrence 발생, 나타남

2.

A slight difference **exists** between the items which sell well online and in store.

(A) exists   (B) to exist
(C) existing   (D) existence

온라인에서 잘 팔리는 품목과 상점에서 잘 팔리는 품목 사이에는 약간의 차이가 존재한다.

> **해설** 주어+자동사+부사구 빈칸은 주어와 부사구 사이에 위치한 동사 자리이므로 쉽게 정답이 (A) exists임을 가려낼 수 있다. 참고로, which 관계사절의 동사 sell은 '~을 팔다'라는 타동사뿐만 아니라 '~이 팔리다'라는 자동사로 쓰이기도 한다는 것을 알아 두자.
>
> **어휘** slight 약간의   sell 팔리다, ~을 팔다

3.

The new headquarters building **relies** on solar energy for its power.

(A) relies   (B) deals
(C) agrees   (D) turns

새로운 본사 건물은 전력을 태양 에너지에 의존하고 있다.

> **해설** 자동사 어휘 선택지를 보니 적절한 동사 어휘를 고르는 문제로, 빈칸 뒤의 전치사 on과 어울리면서 문맥상 적절한 동사를 골라야 한다. 전치사 on과 어울려 뒤에 목적어를 취할 수 있는 동사로 (A) relies와 (C) agrees가 가능한데 문맥상 '동의하다'보다는 '의존하다'라는 의미가 적절하므로 정답은 (A) relies이다.
>
> **어휘** headquarters 본사   rely on ~에 의존하다

4.

Ms. Vowsky contributed **to** the project by taking and organizing all of the meeting notes.

(A) at   (B) to
(C) on   (D) for

보스키 씨는 모든 회의 메모를 기록하고 정리함으로써 프로젝트에 기여했다.

> **해설** 자동사+전치사 선택지를 보니 contributed와 짝꿍을 이루는 전치사를 묻는 문제로 contribute to(~에 기여하다)를 바로 떠올릴 수 있어야 한다. 문맥상 '프로젝트에 기여했다'라는 의미가 적절하므로 (B) to가 정답이다.
>
> **어휘** take notes 메모하다

4 타동사

1. (D)   2. (A)   3. (C)   4. (D)

1.

You can **reach** our customer service representative by phone or chat.

(A) be reached (B) were reached
(C) has reached (D) reach

여러분은 전화나 채팅으로 저희 고객 서비스 담당 직원과 연락할 수 있습니다.

해설 타동사의 능동태 조동사 뒤의 빈칸은 동사원형만 올 수 있으므로 (A) be reached와 (D) reach가 정답 후보이다. reach는 '~에 도착하다, ~에게 연락하다'라는 우리말 해석 때문에 자동사로 혼동하기 쉬우나 목적어를 취할 수 있는 타동사이다. 빈칸 뒤에 목적어 our customer service representative가 있으므로 정답은 능동태인 (D) reach이다.

어휘 reach (타동사로) ~에게 연락하다; ~에 도착하다

2.

The start-up's CEO **addressed** the people at the press conference with a lot of confidence.

(A) addressed (B) spoke
(C) handled (D) dealt

그 스타트업 회사의 대표는 자신감으로 충만해서 기자 회견에서 대중들에게 연설했다.

해설 타동사 어휘 빈칸에 들어갈 적절한 동사 어휘를 고르는 문제인데, 빈칸 뒤에 바로 목적어가 온 것으로 보아 타동사 어휘가 와야 함을 알 수 있다. (A) addressed의 기본형 address는 '(미팅, 콘퍼런스 등)에서 연설하다' 또는 '(청중)에게 연설하다'라는 뜻의 타동사로 쓰일 수 있으므로 정답이다. (B) spoke는 동사 speak의 과거형으로 '~에게 말하다'라고 할 때 speak to의 형태가 되어야 하므로 오답이다. (C) handle은 타동사이나 '~을 처리하다'의 의미로 문맥상 적절하지 않고, deal의 과거형인 (D) dealt는 의미상으로도 부적절할 뿐만 아니라 dealt with의 형태로 쓰여야 한다.

어휘 address 연설하다 press conference 기자 회견 confidence 자신감

3.

You must **reply** to this e-mail to verify your attendance at the convention.

(A) answer (B) oppose
(C) reply (D) object

여러분은 여러분의 총회 참석을 확정하기 위해 이 이메일에 응답해야 합니다.

해설 타동사 vs. 자동사 빈칸은 조동사 must 뒤에 위치하는 동사 자리로, 빈칸 뒤의 전치사 to와 어울리면서 문맥상 적절한 어휘를 골라야 한다. (A) answer와 (B) oppose는 타동사이므로 오답으로 제외시킨다. (C) reply와 (D) object가 전치사 to와 어울리는데, 의미상 '~에 반대하다'보다는 '~에 응답하다'의 의미가 적절하므로 정답은 (C) reply이다.

어휘 verify 확인해 주다 (=confirm) oppose ~에 반대하다

4.

Nearly 200 employees participated **in** the team building exercise event organized by J&A Inc.

(A) with (B) to
(C) of **(D) in**

거의 200명의 직원들이 제이앤에이 사가 마련한 팀 빌딩 훈련 행사에 참여했다.

해설 자동사+전치사 빈칸 앞의 동사 participate를 보자마자 '~에 참석하다'라는 의미의 participate in (=take part in, attend)을 떠올릴 수 있어야 한다. 정답은 (D) in이다.

어휘 exercise 훈련, 연습 organize 준비하다, 마련하다

VOCABULARY

본문 p.064

1. (B) 2. (A) 3. (B) 4. (C) 5. (C) 6. (D) 7. (B) 8. (C)

1.

To lead a team project, staff must first **submit** their plan to Ms. Jansen.

(A) maintain (B) submit
(C) discuss (D) afford

팀 프로젝트를 이끌려면 직원들은 우선 젠슨 씨에게 그들의 계획을 **제출해야** 합니다.

(A) 유지하다 (B) 제출하다
(C) 논의하다 (D) 여유가 되다

해설 **동사 어휘** 목적어인 their plan(그들의 계획)과 의미상 어울리는 동사는 (B) submit(제출하다)와 (C) discuss(논의하다)이다. (C) discuss는 〈discuss A with B(A를 B와 함께 논의하다)〉의 형태로 쓰이므로 적절하지 않다. 따라서 정답은 (B) submit.

어휘 lead 이끌다, 지휘하다 staff 직원들

2.

The HR manager **invited** all team members to participate in the optional workshops.

(A) **invited** (B) grouped
(C) anticipated (D) responded

인사팀장은 모든 팀원들에게 자율 워크숍에 참석하라고 **초대했다**.

(A) 초대하다 (B) (그룹으로) 나누다
(C) 기대하다 (D) 응답하다

해설 **동사 어휘** 빈칸 뒤에 바로 목적어가 있으므로 자동사인 (D) responded는 우선 오답으로 제외시켜야 한다. 뒤에 목적어와 to부정사 목적어를 취하면서 의미상 적절한 동사는 (A) invited뿐이다. 동사 invite는 invite A to do 혹은 be invited to do의 형태로 자주 쓰이니 기억해 둘 것.

어휘 optional 선택적인, 자율의 (↔ mandatory 의무적인)

3.

Each model is expected to **comply** with the brand's strict safety standards.

(A) fulfill (B) **comply**
(C) confirm (D) extend

각각의 모델은 브랜드의 엄격한 안전 기준을 **따를** 것이 요구된다.

(A) 충족시키다 (B) 따르다
(C) 확인하다 (D) 늘리다

해설 **동사 어휘** 빈칸 바로 뒤의 전치사 with와 함께 쓸 수 있는 동사는 (B) comply뿐이다. comply는 자동사로, 목적어를 수반하려면 comply with(~을 따르다)의 형태가 되어야 하는데 문맥상으로도 '안전 기준을 따르다'라는 의미로 적절하다.

어휘 be expected to do ~할 것으로 기대되다 strict 엄격한 safety standards 안전 기준 fulfill (요구 조건을) 충족시키다, (목표나 의무를) 달성하다 extend (기간, 길이, 공간 등을) 늘리다

4.

All items will be heavily **discounted** during tomorrow's grand opening sale.

(A) lasted (B) applied
(C) **discounted** (D) simplified

내일 있을 개업 기념 특별 세일 동안 모든 제품은 엄청나게 **할인될** 것이다.

(A) 지속되다 (B) 적용되다
(C) 할인되다 (D) 간소화되다

해설 **동사 어휘** All items를 수동태의 주어로 취해 의미가 가장 자연스러운 과거분사를 골라야 한다. 따라서 '할인하다'를 뜻하는 discount의 과거분사인 (C) discounted가 정답이다.

어휘 heavily (양, 정도 등을) 아주 많이 grand opening sale 개업 기념 특별 세일

028

5.

The charity Run for Life **donates** thousands of dollars for cancer research annually.	런포라이프 자선 단체는 암 연구를 위해 매년 수천 달러를 **기부하고** 있습니다.
(A) suspends (B) proves **(C) donates** (D) cures	(A) 보류하다 (D) 증명하다 **(C) 기부하다** (D) 치료하다

> 해설 동사 어휘 thousands of dollars와 의미상 어울리는 동사는 '기부하다'라는 뜻의 (C) donates이므로 정답은 (C)이다. 문장 뒷부분의 cancer research를 보고 (B) proves나 (D) cures를 정답으로 혼동할 수 있으나 목적어인 thousands of dollars와의 연결이 부자연스럽다.

> 어휘 charity 자선 단체   annually 매년, 연간   suspend (공식적으로) 보류하다, 일시 중지하다   cure 치료하다; 치료법, 치료제

6.

For a leave of absence, staff members are required to **obtain** prior approval from their supervisor.	휴가를 위해 직원들은 상사로부터 사전 승인을 **받아야** 합니다.
(A) designate (B) compete (C) assign **(D) obtain**	(A) 지명하다 (B) 경쟁하다 (C) 할당하다 **(D) 얻다**

> 해설 동사 어휘 빈칸 뒤의 목적어 prior approval(사전 승인)과 가장 자연스럽게 어울리는 동사는 '얻다, 받다'라는 뜻의 (D) obtain뿐이다. 따라서 정답은 (D).

> 어휘 leave of absence 휴가   be required to do ~할 필요가 있다, ~해야 하다   prior 사전의   approval 승인   supervisor 상사, 감독관   designate (자리나 직책에) 지명하다; (장소를) 지정하다   compete 경쟁하다, 겨루다   assign 할당하다, 배치하다

7.

For a small fee, Pet Power **assists** dog owners who have trouble training their pets.	적은 비용으로 펫파워는 반려동물을 훈련시키는 데 어려움을 겪고 있는 견주들을 **돕고** 있습니다.
(A) charges **(B) assists** (C) introduces (D) consumes	(A) 부과하다 **(B) 돕다** (C) 소개하다 (D) 소비하다

> 해설 동사 어휘 목적어 dog owners와 함께 쓰여 문맥상 어울리는 동사 어휘를 골라야 한다. 문장 앞의 fee(요금)라는 단어만 보고 fee와 어울려 쓰이는 charge(부과하다, 청구하다)를 성급히 정답으로 고르지 않도록 해야 한다.

> 어휘 have trouble doing ~하는 데 어려움을 겪다   charge (비용을) 부과하다, 청구하다; 요금   introduce 소개하다, 도입하다   consume (시간, 에너지, 상품 등을) 소비하다

8.

The completion of the restoration project is expected to **coincide** with the building's bicentennial.	복원 프로젝트의 완성은 그 건물의 200주년 기념일과 **일치하게** 될 것으로 예상된다.
(A) collaborate (B) uphold **(C) coincide** (D) announce	(A) 협력하다 (B) 옹호하다 **(C) 일치하다** (D) 알리다

> 해설 동사 어휘 with와 함께 쓰이는 동사로 (A) collaborate와 (C) coincide가 가능한데, collaborate with 뒤에는 주로 협력하는 사람이 와야 하므로 오답이다. 따라서 정답은 (C) coincide로, 프로젝트 완성일과 건물의 기념일이 일치한다는 내용이 잘 들어맞는다.

> 어휘 restoration 복원   be expected to do ~할 것으로 예상되다   bicentennial 200주년   uphold (법, 원칙 등을) 옹호하다, 유지하다

ACTUAL TEST

본문 p.066

1. (D)   2. (B)   3. (A)   4. (B)   5. (C)   6. (D)
7. (D)   8. (A)   9. (D)   10. (B)   11. (A)   12. (C)

1.

Light refreshments will **be provided** to all guests who wish to attend a guided tour.

(A) provides
(B) provided
(C) to provide
(D) be provided

가이드 투어 참여를 원하시는 모든 방문객들께는 가벼운 다과가 제공될 것입니다.

해설 조동사＋동사원형 선택지의 능동, 수동의 동사 형태를 보고 복잡하게 생각할 수 있으나 빈칸이 조동사 will 뒤에 위치하므로 동사원형만 고르면 된다. 능동, 수동의 여부를 판별할 필요도 없이 정답은 동사원형으로 시작하는 (D) be provided임을 알 수 있다.

어휘 refreshments ((항상 복수형)) 다과   guided tour 가이드가 안내하는 관광

2.

The Trimble Gallery **celebrated** its twenty-fifth anniversary with a large reception last week.

(A) celebrate
(B) celebrated
(C) celebrating
(D) being celebrated

트림블 미술관은 지난주에 성대한 연회로 25주년을 축하했다.

해설 동사 자리 빈칸은 동사 자리이므로 동사 자리에 올 수 없는 (C)와 (D)는 오답으로 제외시키자. (A) celebrate가 오려면 주어가 복수 명사여야 하는데 단수 명사이므로 정답이 될 수 없다. 더구나 last week라는 과거를 나타내는 시간 부사구가 있으므로 현재 시제도 어색하다. 따라서 정답은 과거 시제인 (B) celebrated이다.

어휘 reception 축하 연회

3.

The airplane's equipment has to **comply** with the latest safety regulations before it is used.

(A) comply
(B) depend
(C) submit
(D) adopt

비행기의 장비는 사용되기 전에 최신 안전 규정을 따라야 합니다.

해설 자동사＋전치사 빈칸 뒤의 전치사 with와 어울리면서 문맥상 자연스러운 동사 어휘를 고르는 문제이다. (C) submit(제출하다)와 (D) adopt(채택하다)는 타동사이므로 바로 오답으로 제외시킨다. (B) depend는 전치사 on, upon과 짝을 이루므로 오답이다. 따라서 with와 짝을 이루는 (A) comply가 정답이다. '최신 안전 규정을 따르다'라는 의미도 자연스럽다.

어휘 comply with ~을 준수하다   latest 최신의   safety regulations ((주로 복수형)) 안전 규정

4.

Sales of Mako Co.'s new hybrid car already **surpassed** the projections made by analysts.

(A) surpassing
(B) surpassed
(C) being surpassed
(D) have surpassed

마코 사의 하이브리드 신차 매출은 이미 분석가들의 예측을 초과했다.

해설 부사＋동사 빈칸 앞에 부사 already가 있고 빈칸 뒤에는 목적어 명사구가 왔으므로 빈칸은 동사 자리이다. 따라서 정답이 (B) surpassed임을 쉽게 알 수 있다. 현재완료 시제인 (D)를 정답으로 착각할 수 있는데, 현재완료가 올 수는 있으나 have already surpassed의 순서가 되어야 하므로 오답이다.

어휘 surpass 뛰어넘다, 능가하다   projection 예상, 추정

5.

Please **be** aware that some of the part-time jobs are as demanding as full-time ones.

(A) to be (B) being
(C) be (D) been

어떤 파트타임직은 정규직만큼이나 힘들다는 것을 알아 두시기 바랍니다.

해설 명령문 Please 뒤의 동사원형 자리를 묻는 가장 기초적인 문제이다. 정답은 (C) be이다. 참고로, 'Please be aware that …' 뿐만 아니라 'Please be aware of (명사)'의 형태로도 쓰인다는 것을 챙겨 두자.

어휘 demanding 힘든, 부담이 큰

6.

Association members are allowed to register **for** the conference one week before non-members.

(A) as (B) from
(C) onto **(D) for**

협회 회원들은 비회원들보다 일주일 먼저 회의에 등록하실 수 있습니다.

해설 자동사+전치사 빈칸 앞의 동사 register를 보자마자 register for(~에 등록하다)를 떠올릴 수 있으면 해석할 필요 없이 정답이 (D)임을 쉽게 알아챌 수 있다. 토익에 자주 등장하는 표현을 암기해 두면 시간을 절약할 수 있으므로 부지런히 암기해 두자.

어휘 association 협회, 연계 be allowed to do ~하는 것이 허락되다, ~할 수 있다 one week before ~보다 일주일 앞서

7.

The electronics company **has sold** more than one million copies of its new game console.

(A) to sell (B) was sold
(C) selling **(D) has sold**

그 전자 회사는 새로운 게임기를 백만 대 넘게 팔았다.

해설 주어+타동사+목적어 The electronics company는 주어이고 빈칸은 동사 자리이다. 빈칸 뒤에 목적어가 있으므로 빈칸에는 능동태인 (D) has sold가 와야 한다. 동사 sell은 자동사와 타동사로 모두 쓰이는 동사이므로 주의해서 기억해 두자.

어휘 electronics company 전자 회사 game console 게임기

8.

Mr. Timmins has asked that a taxi **be** ready for him when he arrives.

(A) be (B) were
(C) has been (D) being

티민즈 씨는 그가 도착할 때 그가 탈 택시가 준비될 것을 요청했다.

해설 ask that+주어+(should)+동사원형 that절 앞의 동사 has asked를 보자마자 '~해야 한다'고 요구 및 제안을 나타내는 경우가 아닌지 의심해 봐야 한다. 택시를 준비해 달라고 요구하는 것이므로 that절의 동사는 〈should+동사원형〉이나 〈동사원형〉이 와야 하므로 정답은 (A) be이다. 요구, 제안 등을 나타내는 동사 ask, request, demand, suggest, recommend 등의 동사를 기억하고 있으면 어렵지 않게 정답을 찾을 수 있다.

어휘 be ready for ~할 준비가 되다 (=be ready to do)

To: Lakeland Residents
From: Lakeland City Council
Subject: Project Update
Date: March 4

The Lakeland City Council would like to provide an update on the 2nd Avenue project, as below.

A permit has been granted for the construction of a new mini shopping center on 2nd Avenue. A recent survey of citizens **9 indicated** that there is a need for more retail businesses in Lakeland. Krefton Contractors has been selected to construct the building. TC Property Management will **10 handle** renting out the units.

The building will house more than 30 shops and restaurants. **11 It is** supposed to be completed by next December. Other businesses in the area will remain open during the construction. **12 Shoppers and workers in the area may notice an increase in noise.** However, the work crews will do their best to minimize disruptions.

수신: 레이크랜드 주민 여러분
발신: 레이크랜드 시청
제목: 프로젝트 관련 최신 정보
날짜: 3월 4일

레이크랜드 시청에서 아래와 같이 2번가 프로젝트에 대한 최신 정보를 전해 드리고자 합니다.

2번가에 신규로 작은 쇼핑몰을 건설하는 것에 대한 허가를 받았습니다. 최근에 시민들을 설문한 결과 레이크랜드에 소매상점이 더 많았으면 하는 요구가 있는 것으로 **9 나타났습니다**. 크래프트 건설사가 시공사로 선정되었습니다. TC 자산 관리에서 그 공간의 임대를 **10 처리할** 것입니다.

그 건물은 30개 이상의 상점과 식당을 수용할 것입니다. **11 건물은** 내년 12월까지 완공되기로 되어 있습니다. 그 지역의 다른 상점들은 공사 기간 동안 문을 계속 열 것입니다. **12 그 지역의 쇼핑객 분들과 점원 분들은 소음의 증가에 신경이 쓰일 수 있습니다.** 하지만 공사 인부들은 소음을 최소화하기 위해 최선을 다할 것입니다.

어휘 permit 허가; 허가하다 grant 승인하다, 허락하다; 보조금 indicate 나타내다, 보여 주다 retail 소매 property 재산, 자산, 부동산 rent out ~을 세놓다, ~을 임대하다 unit (건물 내의) 한 단위 house 수용하다; 집

---

9. (A) indicative (B) indication (C) indicating **(D) indicated**

해설 동사 자리 주어는 A recent survey of citizens이고, that 이하는 목적어이므로 빈칸은 동사 자리이다.

---

10. (A) point **(B) handle** (C) observe (D) deal

(A) 가리키다 **(B) 처리하다** (C) 관찰하다 (D) 처리하다

해설 동사 어휘 빈칸 뒤에 전치사 없이 목적어가 나오므로 타동사인 (B) handle이 정답이다. (D) deal이 '처리하다'를 뜻하려면 전치사 with와 함께 써야 하므로 이 문장에서는 오답이다.

---

11. **(A) It is** (B) Yours are (C) Theirs are (D) There is

해설 대명사 주어+동사 앞 문장의 The building이나 more than 30 shops and restaurants를 대명사 주어로 대신하려면 It이나 They가 와야 한다.

---

12. (A) Revenue from tourists may increase because of the change.
(B) Safety regulations have become stricter recently.
(C) Shoppers and workers in the area may notice an increase in noise.
(D) Other projects are being considered to promote the area.

(A) 관광 수익은 그 변화로 증가할 것입니다.
(B) 안전 규정은 최근에 더 엄격해졌습니다.
(C) 그 지역의 쇼핑객 분들과 점원 분들은 소음의 증가에 신경이 쓰일 수 있습니다.
(D) 그 지역을 홍보할 다른 프로젝트들도 고려되고 있습니다.

해설 알맞은 문장 고르기 역접의 접속부사인 However를 통해 빈칸 뒤의 내용과 반대되는 내용이 빈칸에 와야 함을 유추할 수 있다. 소음을 최소화하기 위해 노력하겠다는 내용과 반대되는 선택지는 소음에 신경이 쓰일 수 있다는 내용의 (C)이다.

UNIT 04 수 일치

1 긴 주어의 수 일치

본문 p.072

1. (A)   2. (C)   3. (D)   4. (A)

1.

Logan Tech's new recruitment drive **has** already attracted five hundred applicants.

(A) has
(B) to have
(C) having
(D) have

로건 테크 사의 새로운 채용 캠페인은 이미 5백 명의 지원자를 끌어모았다.

해설 긴 주어+수 일치 선택지를 보니 have 동사의 적절한 형태를 묻는 문제로, 뒤에 already attracted가 나오므로 (B)와 (C)는 오답으로 제거해야 한다. 주어가 Logan Tech's new recruitment drive로 명사와 명사가 결합한 복합 명사의 경우 뒤쪽 명사의 수만 보면 된다. 단수 명사 drive에 어울리는 단수 동사는 (A) has이다.

어휘 recruitment 채용   drive (조직적인) 운동, 캠페인; 운전하다   attract 끌어모으다

2.

Kembery, a sustainable fashion brand, **manufactures** casual clothing for women.

(A) manufacturing
(B) are manufactured
(C) manufactures
(D) to manufacture

지속 가능한 패션 브랜드인 캠버리는 여성용 캐주얼 의류를 생산한다.

해설 주어+동격어구+동사 주어인 Kembery가 단수이고 casual clothing이 목적어이므로 단수 동사이며 능동태인 (C)가 정답이다. 빈칸 앞에 sustainable이라는 다소 생소한 어휘가 등장해 당황할 수 있으나, 토익 문법 문제의 경우 해석 문제라기보다는 구조를 파악하는 문제가 많으므로 겁먹지 말 것.

어휘 sustainable (환경 파괴 없이) 지속 가능한   manufacture 제조하다, 생산하다

3.

An appliance with these labels **conforms** to all energy-efficiency regulations.

(A) to conform
(B) conforming
(C) conform
(D) conforms

이 표식이 붙어 있는 기기는 모든 에너지 효율 규정을 따르고 있습니다.

해설 주어+전치사구+동사 빈칸 바로 앞에 오는 labels를 주어로 오해하면 함정에 빠질 수 있는 문제이다. 주어는 An appliance로 단수 명사이므로 정답은 단수 동사인 (D) conforms이다. 참고로, conform은 자동사로 뒤에 목적어를 취하려면 conform to, conform with로 쓰인다는 것을 기억해 둘 것.

어휘 appliance (가정용) 전자 제품   conform to[with] (규정이나 관습 등을) 따르다 (=obey)

4.

The article that will be published tomorrow **highlights** Escobar Inc.'s efforts to expand overseas.

(A) highlights
(B) highlight
(C) were highlighted
(D) to highlight

내일 출간될 기사는 해외로 사업을 확장하려는 에스코바 사의 노력을 중점적으로 다루고 있다.

해설 주어+수식절+동사 주어가 절의 수식을 받아 길어진 형태이다. 주어는 The article이고, that부터 tomorrow까지는 주어를 수식하는 주격 관계대명사절이다. 주어인 The article이 단수 주어이므로 정답은 단수 동사인 (A) highlights이다.

어휘 publish 발행하다, 출간하다   highlight 중점적으로 다루다, 강조하다   expand 확대하다, 확장하다   overseas 해외로

033

2 주의해야 할 주어의 수

본문 p.073

1. (D)   2. (A)   3. (B)   4. (D)

1.

> By the end of this month, Samco Fashions **is** going to release a new line of swimwear.
>
> (A) were   (B) are
> (C) be   **(D) is**

이번 달 말까지 샘코 패션즈는 수영복 신제품을 출시할 예정입니다.

해설 **회사명 + 단수 동사** 회사명인 Samco Fashions를 복수 명사로 착각하면 오답 함정에 빠지기 쉬운 문제이다. 회사명은 복수 형태를 취한다 하더라도 단수 취급하므로 정답은 단수 동사인 (D) is이다.

어휘 release 출시하다, 내놓다   swimwear 수영복

2.

> The customs officer **checks** the passport and other documents of people entering the country.
>
> **(A) checks**   (B) checking
> (C) check   (D) to check

세관 직원은 입국하는 사람들의 여권과 기타 서류들을 확인한다.

해설 **복합 명사의 수 일치** 주어는 The customs officer로 단수 명사이므로 단수 동사인 (A) checks가 정답임을 쉽게 알 수 있다. 복합 명사의 경우 뒤의 명사의 수에 동사의 형태를 일치시킨다는 것을 다시 한번 기억하자.

어휘 enter ~에 들어가다

3.

> The human resources department of most corporations **is training** new staff members through online-based courses.
>
> (A) train   **(B) is training**
> (C) to train   (D) training

대부분 회사의 인사팀은 온라인 강좌를 통해 신입 직원들을 훈련시키고 있습니다.

해설 **복합 명사의 수 일치** 문장의 주어는 The human resources department로, 복합 명사의 경우 맨 마지막 명사의 수에 동사의 형태를 일치시킨다는 것을 알고 있으면 쉽게 해결되는 문제이다. 주어가 단수 명사이므로 단수 동사인 (B) is training이 정답이다. 빈칸 바로 앞의 corporations를 주어로 착각하지 않도록 주의할 것.

어휘 human resources department 인사부[팀]   corporation 회사   online-based 온라인으로 진행되는

4.

> Pressing the red button on the wall **activates** the alarm system for the laboratory.
>
> (A) activating   (B) activate
> (C) active   **(D) activates**

벽에 있는 빨간 버튼을 누르면 실험실의 경보 시스템이 작동됩니다.

해설 **동명사 주어 + 단수 동사** 주어가 동명사구(Pressing the red button on the wall)이므로 단수 취급한다. 따라서 단수 동사인 (D) activates가 정답이다. 동명사뿐 아니라 긴 주어인 명사절도 단수 취급한다는 것을 참고로 기억해 두자.

어휘 activate 작동시키다, 활성화하다

3 주의해야 할 수량 표현

본문 p.074

1. (B)   2. (A)   3. (B)   4. (A)

1.

Each of the Camdex-360 laptops **is** equipped with a battery that lasts for six hours.

(A) are   (B) is
(C) be   (D) were

각각의 캠덱스-360 노트북은 6시간 동안 지속되는 배터리를 내장하고 있다.

> **해설** each of the+복수 명사+단수 동사 부정대명사 each의 수 일치 법칙을 기억하고 있으면 정답이 단수 동사인 (B) is임을 쉽게 찾을 수 있다. 빈칸 바로 앞에 오는 복수 명사 laptops에 낚여서는 안 된다.
>
> **어휘** be equipped with ~을 갖추다

2.

A large number of businesses **use** a recruitment firm to find new employees.

(A) use   (B) uses
(C) using   (D) to use

많은 사업체들이 신규 인력을 찾기 위해 채용 전문 회사를 이용한다.

> **해설** a large number of a large number of(많은)를 보자마자 뒤에 복수 명사와 복수 동사가 온다는 것을 예측하고 있으면 정답이 (A) use임을 쉽게 알아챌 수 있다. 단, the number of(~의 수)가 주어로 올 경우에는 단수 취급한다는 것을 알아 두자.
>
> **어휘** recruitment firm 채용 전문 회사

3.

The event planning team will go home early because most of the preparation **has** been completed.

(A) have   (B) has
(C) to have   (D) having

행사 기획팀은 대부분의 준비가 완료되었기 때문에 일찍 퇴근할 것이다.

> **해설** most of the+셀 수 없는 명사+단수 동사 부정대명사 all, most, some, any는 바로 뒤따라오는 명사의 수에 동사를 일치시킨다. preparation이 단수 형태이므로 정답은 단수 동사인 (B) has가 된다.
>
> **어휘** preparation 준비

4.

All of the clients of Parkway Accounting **are invited** to attend the year-end banquet.

(A) are invited   (B) is invited
(C) are inviting   (D) invites

파크웨이 회계 법인의 모든 고객들은 송년회에 참석하도록 초대를 받습니다.

> **해설** all of the+복수 명사+복수 동사 주어가 All of the clients of Parkway Accounting인데, 부정대명사 all의 경우 바로 뒤에 수반되는 명사의 수에 동사를 일치시킨다. clients가 복수 명사이므로 복수 동사인 (A)와 (C)가 정답 후보인데, 고객들은 초대를 받는 대상이고 동사 invite는 〈invite+목적어+to do〉나 〈be invited to do〉의 형태로 쓰이므로 수동태인 (A) are invited가 정답이다.
>
> **어휘** be invited to do ~하도록 초대를 받다   year-end banquet 송년회

035

4 태와 시제가 결합된 수 일치

1. (B)   2. (D)   3. (A)   4. (C)

1.

> All of the new Max cars **provide** a warranty that covers three years.
>
> (A) providing   (B) **provide**
> (C) provides   (D) are provided

모든 맥스 신차는 3년간 보장되는 보증서를 제공합니다.

해설 수 일치 주어가 All of the new Max cars인데, 부정대명사 all의 경우 바로 뒤에 수반되는 명사의 수에 동사를 일치시킨다. cars가 복수이므로 복수 동사가 와야 하며, 빈칸 뒤에 목적어가 있으므로 능동태인 (B) provide가 정답이다.

어휘 warranty 보증서   cover (보험이) 보장하다; 덮다, 가리다

2.

> A number of keynote speakers **are chosen** because of their expertise in product marketing.
>
> (A) choose   (B) is chosen
> (C) chooses   (D) **are chosen**

많은 기조 연설자들은 상품 마케팅 분야에서의 그들의 전문 지식 때문에 선정됩니다.

해설 수 일치+태 주어는 A number of keynote speakers이며, speakers가 복수이므로 복수 동사가 와야 한다. 주의해야 할 것은 the number of는 뒤에 나오는 명사가 복수라 하더라도 단수 동사를 사용하며, a number of는 뒤에 복수 명사가 나오며 복수 동사를 쓴다는 점이다. 복수 동사는 (A)와 (D)이다. choose는 타동사인데 뒤에 목적어가 없으므로 수동태가 와야 한다. 따라서 정답은 (D) are chosen이다.

어휘 keynote speaker 기조 연설자   expertise 전문 지식

3.

> The report about Calvin Turner's sudden retirement **has generated** a great deal of interest among analysts.
>
> (A) **has generated**   (B) generate
> (C) generating   (D) was generated

칼빈 터너의 갑작스러운 은퇴 발표는 분석가들 사이에 많은 관심을 일으켰다.

해설 수 일치+태 주어 The report가 단수 명사이므로 (A) has generated와 (D) was generated가 정답 후보인데, 빈칸 뒤에 목적어 a great deal of interest가 있으므로 정답은 능동태인 (A) has generated이다. 참고로 a great deal of는 '(양이) 많은'이라는 뜻으로 뒤에 셀 수 없는 명사와 단수 동사를 취한다는 것도 챙겨 두자.

어휘 report 발표, 보도   retirement 은퇴   generate 발생시키다

4.

> The logistics department **has experienced** some issues with the distribution network but can resolve them soon.
>
> (A) experience   (B) are experiencing
> (C) **has experienced** (D) to experience

그 물류팀은 유통망에 문제를 겪었으나 곧 그것들을 해결할 수 있다.

해설 수 일치+시제 주어 The logistics department의 logistics가 복수 형태이므로 복수 명사로 착각할 수 있으나 복합 명사는 뒤의 명사에 수 일치를 시키면 된다. 따라서 단수 동사인 (C) has experienced가 정답이다.

어휘 logistics department 물류팀   experience 겪다, 경험하다   distribution 유통, 분배

VOCABULARY

본문 p.078

1. (C) 2. (A) 3. (D) 4. (B) 5. (A) 6. (C) 7. (C) 8. (A)

1.

| This training program focuses on **implementing** innovative teaching strategies developed by leading educators.

(A) committing　　(B) allowing
(C) **implementing**　(D) transporting | 이 훈련 프로그램은 최고의 교육자들이 개발한 혁신적인 교수 전략을 **실행하는** 것에 초점을 두고 있다.

(A) 저지르다　(B) 허락하다
(C) **실행하다**　(D) 운송하다 |

[해설] 동사 어휘 빈칸 뒤의 innovative teaching strategies를 수반하면서 문맥상 자연스러운 동사 어휘는 '실행하다'라는 뜻의 implementing뿐이다. 동사 implement는 목적어로 strategy(전략), policy(정책), measure(조치), plan(계획) 등을 주로 수반한다.

[어휘] focus on ~에 초점을 두다, ~을 강조하다 (=emphasize)　innovative 혁신적인　leading 최고의, 선두의

2.

| Ms. Burr's impressive educational background makes up for the fact that she **lacks** experience.

(A) **lacks**　　　(B) borrows
(C) imposes　　(D) accomplishes | 버 씨의 인상적인 학력은 그녀가 경험이 **부족하다는** 사실을 만회한다.

(A) **부족하다**　(B) 빌리다
(C) 도입하다　(D) 달성하다 |

[해설] 동사 어휘 make up for가 '(부족한 것이나 손실 등을) 만회하다'라는 뜻이므로 impressive educational background에 반대되는 내용이 뒤에 들어가야 함을 예측할 수 있다. 따라서 정답은 (A) lacks이다. lack은 토익에서 '부족, 결핍'이란 뜻의 명사로도 자주 쓰인다. (예: the lack of parking facilities 주차 시설의 부족)

[어휘] impressive 인상적인　educational background 학력　make up for ~을 벌충하다, ~을 만회하다, ~을 보상하다　impose (새로운 법 등을) 도입하다; (제약 등을) 부과하다

3.

| All prices will be **reduced** during the first hour of the store's special event.

(A) combined　　(B) declined
(C) attributed　　(D) **reduced** | 상점의 특별 행사가 시작되는 1시간 동안에는 모든 가격이 **할인될** 것입니다.

(A) 결합하다　(B) 감소하다
(C) ~의 탓으로 돌리다　(D) **할인하다** |

[해설] 동사 어휘 수동태가 포함된 빈칸이므로 주어인 All prices와 자연스럽게 어울리는 동사 어휘를 골라야 한다. 가격과 어울리는 동사로는 '할인하다'라는 뜻의 reduce가 가장 적절하므로 정답은 과거분사형인 (D) reduced이다.

[어휘] decline 감소하다, 줄어들다; 거절하다

4.

| Staff at Brenner's Deli don't **accept** personal checks without the holder's signature.

(A) afford　　　(B) **accept**
(C) refund　　(D) allocate | 브레너 델리의 직원들은 소유주의 서명이 없는 개인 수표는 **수락하지** 않습니다.

(A) 여유가 되다　(B) **수락하다**
(C) 환불하다　(D) 할당하다 |

[해설] 동사 어휘 빈칸 뒤의 personal checks(개인 수표)와 자연스럽게 어울리는 동사 어휘는 '수락하다'라는 의미의 (B) accept뿐이다. 다음과 같이 accept와 어울려 쓰이는 표현들을 꼭 익혀 두도록 하자. (accept the terms 조건을 수락하다　accept a job offer 입사 제안을 수락하다　accept an assignment 임무/부서 배치를 수락하다)

[어휘] afford (금전적, 시간적으로) 여유가 되다　allocate (특정 목적을 위해) 할당하다, 배정하다

5.

Nashville Library will offer résumé writing classes once the city council **approves** its educational budget.

(A) **approves** (B) cuts
(C) invites (D) convenes

내슈빌 도서관은 시 의회가 교육 예산을 **승인하면** 이력서 작성 수업을 제공할 것이다.

(A) 승인하다 (B) 삭감하다
(C) 초대하다 (D) 소집하다

> **해설** 동사 어휘 빈칸 뒤의 its educational budget과 어울릴 수 있는 동사 어휘로 우선 (A) approves(승인하다)와 (B) cuts(삭감하다)가 가능하다. 문맥상 '예산을 승인해야 수업을 제공할 수 있는' 것이므로 정답은 (A) approves이다.

> **어휘** city council 시 의회   convene (회의 등을) 소집하다

6.

Most people these days use their smartphone's GPS when **exploring** places they haven't been to before.

(A) cultivating (B) investing
(C) **exploring** (D) ensuring

요즘 대부분의 사람들은 전에 가 보지 못한 장소를 **돌아다닐** 때 스마트폰의 GPS 기능을 사용한다.

(A) 재배하다 (B) 투자하다
(C) 탐험하다 (D) 확실히 하다

> **해설** 동사 어휘 문맥상 '못 가 본 장소를 가 볼 때 GPS를 사용한다'는 의미가 적절하므로 '탐험하다, 살피다'라는 뜻의 동사 exploring이 가장 적절하다. 따라서 정답은 (C)이다.

> **어휘** cultivate (식물, 작물을) 재배하다; (스킬, 자질 등을) 기르다   ensure 확실히 하다 (=make sure)

7.

As per the employment contract, workers **retain** their right to form a labor union.

(A) classify (B) accumulate
(C) **retain** (D) agree

고용 계약서에 따르면 직원들은 노동조합을 설립할 권리를 **보유합니다**.

(A) 분류하다 (B) 축적하다
(C) 보유하다 (D) 동의하다

> **해설** 동사 어휘 내용상 '권리를 가지고 있다'라는 의미의 동사 어휘가 들어가야 적절하므로 '보유하다'라는 뜻의 (C) retain이 정답이다.

> **어휘** as per ~에 따르면 (=according to)   employment contract 고용 계약서   form 설립하다, 형성하다   labor union 노동조합   accumulate 축적하다, 모으다

8.

Orion Tech's planning committee will **distribute** pamphlets with details of the company's anniversary celebration to its employees.

(A) **distribute** (B) arrange
(C) observe (D) register

오리온 테크의 기획 위원회는 회사의 기념 축하연의 세부 사항이 담긴 팸플릿을 직원들에게 **나눠 줄** 것이다.

(A) 나눠 주다 (B) 준비하다
(C) 관찰하다 (D) 등록하다

> **해설** 동사 어휘 '팸플릿을 직원들에게 ----할 것이다'에 들어갈 적절한 동사 어휘를 고르는 문제로, '직원들에게 팸플릿을 나눠 준다'는 의미가 가장 자연스럽다. 따라서 정답은 (A) distribute이다.

> **어휘** planning committee 기획 위원회   distribute 나눠 주다 (=hand out)   celebration 축하, 기념, 기념 행사

ACTUAL TEST

本文 p.080

| 1. (B) | 2. (C) | 3. (D) | 4. (B) | 5. (A) | 6. (D) |
| 7. (D) | 8. (C) | 9. (A) | 10. (D) | 11. (B) | 12. (C) |

1.

The self-driving cars made by the Amarillo Corporation **represent** a major advancement in the automotive industry.

(A) representing
(B) **represent**
(C) represents
(D) representation

아마릴로 사에서 생산한 자율 주행차는 자동차 산업의 큰 발전을 대변한다.

해설 긴 주어의 수 일치 주어가 길어 복잡해 보이지만 주어는 The self-driving cars로 복수 명사이다. 따라서 정답은 복수 동사인 (B) represent임을 쉽게 알 수 있다.

어휘 self-driving car 자율 주행차 represent 대표하다, 대변하다 major 주요한, 중대한 advancement 진보, 발전 automotive 자동차의

2.

Employees are encouraged to help each other with projects if the opportunity **arises**.

(A) to arise
(B) arise
(C) arises
(D) had arisen

직원들은 기회가 생기면 서로의 프로젝트를 도와주도록 권고받는다.

해설 단수 명사+단수 동사 빈칸은 if 부사절의 동사 자리로 주어(the opportunity)가 단수 명사이므로 단수 동사 (C) arises가 정답임을 쉽게 알 수 있다.

어휘 be encouraged to do ~하도록 권고받다 help A with B A가 ~하는 것을 돕다 arise 발생하다

3.

Waldeck's newly released tablet **features** a higher-resolution screen.

(A) to feature
(B) feature
(C) is featured
(D) features

왈덱에서 새로 출시된 태블릿은 고해상도 화면이 주요 특징이다.

해설 긴 주어의 수 일치 주어가 소유격과 수식어구의 결합으로 길어 보이지만 단수 형태(tablet)를 취하고 있다. 따라서 (C) is featured와 (D) features가 정답 후보인데 빈칸 뒤에 목적어가 있으므로 정답은 능동태인 (D) features이다.

어휘 newly released 새로 출시된 feature ~을 특징으로 하다 high-resolution 고해상도

4.

Burnam and Cohen Landscaping **provides** an initial consultation to new customers at no charge.

(A) provide
(B) provides
(C) providing
(D) is provided

버남 앤 코헨 조경 회사는 신규 고객들에게 무료로 최초 상담을 제공한다.

해설 수 일치+태 주어가 A and B의 형태여서 복수 명사로 착각할 수 있으나 회사명이므로 단수 취급해야 한다. 따라서 단수 동사인 (B)와 (D)가 정답 후보인데 빈칸 뒤에 목적어가 있으므로 정답은 능동태인 (B) provides이다. 참고로 동사 provide는 provide A with B 혹은 provide B to[for] A의 형태로 자주 쓰인다는 것도 챙겨 둘 것.

어휘 landscaping 조경 initial 최초의, 처음의 consultation 상담 at no charge 무료로

039

5.

Some of the candidates for the position **hold** a master's degree in a relevant field.

(A) **hold** (B) holds
(C) holding (D) to hold

그 자리에 지원한 몇몇 지원자들은 관련 분야에 석사 학위를 보유하고 있다.

> 해설 some of the+복수 명사+복수 동사 부정대명사 some, any, all, most의 경우 뒤의 명사 형태에 동사의 수를 일치시킨다. Some of the 뒤의 명사가 candidates로 복수 명사이므로 복수 동사인 (A) hold가 정답이다.

> 어휘 candidate 지원자, 후보자   position 자리, 직책   relevant 관련 있는, 적절한

6.

Market surveys analyzing the financial sector **have been conducted** by a team of leading experts.

(A) has been conducted
(B) have conducted
(C) will be conducting
(D) **have been conducted**

금융 분야를 분석하는 시장 조사는 최고 전문가 팀에 의해 수행되어 왔다.

> 해설 수 일치+태 analyzing the financial sector는 Market surveys를 수식해 주는 분사구이므로 주어는 복수 명사이다. 따라서 빈칸은 복수 동사 자리이며, 빈칸 뒤의 by 이하를 통해 수동태가 되어야 함을 알 수 있다.

> 어휘 market survey 시장 조사   financial 금융의, 재무의   sector 분야   conduct 수행하다   leading 선두의, 최고의, 주요한

7.

Attendees at the banquet **were entertained** by musicians who play classical music.

(A) entertain (B) is entertaining
(C) was entertained (D) **were entertained**

연회 참석자들은 클래식 음악을 연주하는 음악가들 덕분에 귀가 즐거웠다.

> 해설 수 일치+태 빈칸은 동사 자리로 주어는 banquet이 아닌 Attendees라는 점에 주목해야 한다. 복수 형태의 주어이므로 복수 동사가 와야 하는데 뒤에 〈by+행위자〉 형태인 by musicians가 왔으므로 수동태가 와야 적절하다. 따라서 정답은 (D) were entertained이다.

> 어휘 attendee 참석자   entertain 접대하다, 즐겁게 해 주다

8.

The number of video streaming platforms **has increased** substantially over the past few years.

(A) are increased (B) have increased
(C) **has increased** (D) increasing

동영상 스트리밍 플랫폼의 수가 과거 몇 년간 상당히 증가해 왔다.

> 해설 the number of+복수 명사+단수 동사 The number of를 보자마자 뒤에 복수 명사와 단수 동사를 취한다는 법칙을 떠올릴 수 있어야 한다. 복수 명사와 복수 동사를 취하는 a number of, a large number of와 헷갈려서는 안 된다. (B)는 복수 동사이므로 소거되며, 과거부터 현재까지의 기간을 나타내는 over the past few years의 시간 부사구와 함께 쓰였으므로 현재완료형인 (C)가 정답이 된다.

> 어휘 substantially 상당히, 많이 (=greatly, considerably)

Operating Expenses for Small Businesses

If you are starting a new business, it is a good idea to calculate your expected operating expenses in advance. Operating expenses **9 include** payments for rent, utilities, and taxes. **10 Those** costs are usually easy to predict, as they do not fluctuate much from month to month. Employees' wages are somewhat stable but don't forget to add additional items such as health insurance.

For companies that produce a product, the cost of the necessary raw materials **11 depends** on the volume of goods produced. When production levels are high, more raw materials are needed. Fortunately, for most businesses, this means sales are higher as well.

12 There are many financial matters to consider. Therefore, it is important to get advice from a certified accountant.

소규모 사업 운영 경비

당신이 신규 사업을 시작하는 중이라면 사전에 예상 운영 경비를 계산해 보는 것이 좋습니다. 운영 경비는 임대료, 공과금, 세금을 **9 포함합니다**. **10 그** 비용들은 달마다 변동이 크지 않기 때문에 보통 예측하기 쉽습니다. 직원들의 임금은 다소 안정적이나 의료 보험과 같은 부가적인 품목들을 더하는 것을 잊지 마세요.

제품을 생산하는 회사의 경우 필요한 원자재 비용은 생산되는 상품의 양에 **11 달려 있습니다**. 생산 수준이 높을 때는 더 많은 원자재가 필요합니다. 다행히도 대부분의 사업에 있어 이는 매출도 또한 더 높다는 것을 의미합니다.

12 고려할 재무적 문제들이 많이 있습니다. 그러므로 공인 회계사로부터 조언을 받는 것이 중요합니다.

어휘 start a business 사업을 시작하다 calculate 계산하다 in advance 미리 include 포함하다 utilities 공과금 predict 예측하다 fluctuate 오르락내리락하다, 요동치다 wage 임금 stable 안정적인 raw material 원자재 depend (up)on ~에 달려 있다 financial 재정의, 금융의 certified 공인된

9. (A) include (B) includes
   (C) included (D) had included

   해설 수 일치+시제 빈칸 앞에 온 Operating expenses가 주어, 빈칸 뒤의 payments는 목적어이다. 따라서 빈칸은 동사 자리인데 주어가 복수 명사이므로 우선 단수 동사인 (B) includes는 오답으로 제외시킨다. 운영 경비에 대한 일반적인 사실을 이야기하는 것이므로 현재 시제인 (A) include가 오는 것이 가장 자연스럽다.

10. (A) Each (B) All (A) 각각의 (B) 모든
    (C) Another (D) Those (C) 또 다른 (D) 그

    해설 지시형용사 빈칸 뒤의 복수 명사 costs를 수식하면서 문맥상 적절한 지시형용사나 부정형용사를 고르는 문제이다. 우선 (A) Each와 (C) Another는 단수 명사에만 올 수 있으므로 오답으로 제외시킨다. 문맥상 빈칸 앞 문장에 등장한 payments for rent, utilities, and taxes를 지칭하는 내용이 되어야 하므로 '그 비용들은'이란 의미를 나타내려면 (D) Those가 와야 한다.

11. (A) depend (B) **depends**
    (C) depending (D) to depend

    해설 긴 주어의 수 일치 주어 the cost와 빈칸 사이에 of the necessary raw materials라는 전치사구가 삽입된 형태로 주어를 빈칸 바로 앞의 materials로 착각해서는 안 된다. 주어인 the cost가 단수이므로 단수 동사인 (B) depends가 정답이다.

12. (A) Small businesses have a higher chance of success.
    (B) After all, many people enjoy running their own business.
    (C) There are many financial matters to consider.
    (D) The business can boost sales through online marketing.

    (A) 소규모 사업들은 성공할 가능성이 더 높습니다.
    (B) 결국 많은 사람들은 사업을 운영하는 것을 즐깁니다.
    (C) 고려할 재무적 문제들이 많이 있습니다.
    (D) 사업은 온라인 마케팅을 통해 매출을 증가시킬 수 있습니다.

    해설 알맞은 문장 고르기 빈칸 뒤 인과 관계를 나타내는 접속부사인 Therefore를 통해 빈칸에는 뒤 문장의 이유에 해당하는 내용이 올 것임을 유추할 수 있다. 빈칸 문장 뒤에는 공인 회계사로부터 조언을 받으라는 내용이 나오고, 빈칸 앞부분에는 사업의 운영 경비 예측이 중요함을 이야기했으므로 이와 일맥상통하는 내용은 비용과 관련된 (C)이다.

    어휘 boost 신장시키다, 증가시키다

UNIT 05 시제

1 기본 시제
본문 p.086

1. (D)   2. (C)   3. (B)   4. (D)

1.

The department head sometimes **asks** team members to work in pairs.

(A) ask (B) is asked
(C) asking (D) asks

그 부서장은 때때로 팀원들에게 짝을 지어 일할 것을 요청한다.

해설 현재 시제 빈칸 앞의 빈도 부사인 sometimes(때때로)를 통해 빈칸이 현재 시제 자리임을 알아챌 수 있다. 빈도 부사는 반복적으로 행하는 행동이 얼마나 자주 일어나는지의 빈도를 나타내는 부사이므로 현재 시제와 주로 어울리고 동사 앞에 위치한다는 것도 참고로 알아 두자.

어휘 head 책임자   in pairs 짝을 지어

2.

It **seemed** interesting to lead the workshop last month, but Mr. Norwood is not willing to do so in the future.

(A) will seem (B) seems
(C) seemed (D) be seeming

지난달에 워크숍을 이끌었던 것은 흥미로웠던 것 같지만, 노어우드 씨는 향후 그렇게 할 의향이 없습니다.

해설 과거 시제 선택지를 보니 빈칸에 들어갈 적절한 시제를 묻는 문제이므로 단서가 될 시간 부사구가 있는지부터 확인해야 한다. 빈칸 문장에 last month라는 시간 부사구가 왔으므로 정답은 과거 시제인 (C) seemed이다.

어휘 seem ~인 것 같다, ~처럼 보이다   be willing to do ~할 의향이 있다

3.

Bryson Auto **relocated** its central office to Berlin several months ago.

(A) will relocate (B) relocated
(C) relocates (D) has relocated

브라이슨 자동차는 몇 달 전에 본사를 베를린으로 이전했다.

해설 과거 시제 문장 맨 뒷부분의 several months ago의 ago를 보자마자 과거 시제를 떠올릴 수 있어야 한다. 정답은 과거 시제인 (D) relocated이다.

어휘 relocate 이전시키다   central office 본사, 본점

4.

Darren Wilson, the head of the security team, **will review** our emergency procedures next Wednesday.

(A) reviewed (B) reviewing
(C) has reviewed (D) will review

보안팀장인 대런 윌슨 씨는 다음 주 수요일에 우리의 비상 처리 절차를 검토할 것이다.

해설 미래 시제 Darren Wilson이 주어, the head of the security team이 주어의 동격어구, 빈칸은 동사 자리이므로 (B)는 오답으로 제외시키자. 문장 맨 끝에 next Wednesday라는 미래 시제를 나타내는 시간 부사구가 있으므로 정답은 미래 시제인 (D) will review이다.

어휘 security 보안, 경비   procedure 절차, 순서

2 진행형

본문 p.087

1. (A) 2. (B) 3. (B) 4. (C)

1.

At present, VC Laboratories **is developing** a new treatment for seasonal allergies.

(A) is developing (B) was developing
(C) developing (D) has been developed

현재 VC 연구소는 계절성 알레르기를 위한 새로운 치료법을 개발 중이다.

해설 **현재진행형** 문장 맨 앞의 시간 부사구인 At present(현재)를 통해 적절한 시제를 판단할 수 있어야 한다. 선택지 중 at present와 함께 어울릴 수 있는 시제는 현재진행형인 (A) is developing뿐이다. VC 연구소가 현재 하는 일을 사실대로 설명한다는 면에서 현재 시제가 가능한 것도 참고로 알아 두자.

어휘 laboratory 실험실, 연구소   treatment 치료, 처치

2.

All employees need to behave responsibly when they **are traveling** on company business.

(A) traveled (B) are traveling
(C) to travel (D) has traveled

모든 직원은 출장을 가 있는 동안 책임감 있게 행동해야 합니다.

해설 **현재진행형** 부사절 안의 they는 주어, on company business는 부사구이므로 빈칸에는 to부정사가 들어갈 수 없다. 문맥상 '출장을 다니는 동안'이므로 현재진행형이 가장 적절하다.

어휘 responsibly 책임감 있게   on company business 업무상

3.

Triumph Gallery **will be accepting** paintings for its annual art competition until next Friday.

(A) accepting (B) will be accepting
(C) has been accepting (D) acceptable

트라이엄프 미술관은 다음 주 금요일까지 연례 미술 대회를 위한 그림을 접수받을 것이다.

해설 **미래진행형** 빈칸은 동사 자리이므로 동사 역할을 할 수 없는 (A)와 (D)는 오답이다. next라는 형용사가 미래 시점을 의미하므로 과거부터 현재까지의 일을 표현하는 현재완료형인 (C)는 정답이 될 수 없다. 따라서 정답은 '다음 주 금요일까지'라는 미래의 특정 시점과 어울릴 수 있는 시제인 미래진행형 (B) will be accepting이다.

어휘 annual 연례의, 연간의   competition 대회, 경쟁

4.

Starting next month, employees at Richmond Co. **will be volunteering** at local charities.

(A) volunteering (B) have been volunteering
(C) will be volunteering (D) were volunteering

다음 달부터는 리치몬드 사의 직원들이 지역 자선 단체에서 봉사 활동을 할 것이다.

해설 **미래진행형** Starting next month의 시간 부사구를 통해 미래의 일임을 알 수 있다. 미래 시제를 정답으로 떠올릴 수 있는데, 미래 시제가 선택지에 없으므로 미래의 일을 나타낼 수 있는 미래진행형인 (C) will be volunteering이 정답이다. 하나의 시제가 하나의 특정 시점과 일대일로 호응하는 것은 아니므로 소거법을 통해 가장 자연스러운 시제를 고르는 것이 문제 해결의 핵심이다.

어휘 charity 자선 단체

3 현재 시제가 미래를 대신하는 경우

본문 p.088

1. (B) 2. (A) 3. (B) 4. (D)

1.

Ms. Mitchell will negotiate her salary when she **renews** her contract on Friday.

(A) renewing (B) renews
(C) had renewed (D) to renew

미첼 씨는 금요일에 계약을 갱신할 때 연봉을 협상할 것이다.

해설 시간 부사절에서의 시제 주절이 미래 시제이므로 부사절도 미래 시제가 적절하나 시간 및 조건의 부사절에서는 미래 대신 현재 시제를 사용하므로 현재 시제인 (B) renews가 정답이다.

어휘 negotiate one's salary 연봉 협상을 하다 renew one's contract 계약을 갱신하다

2.

If the landlord **neglects** to repair items quickly, make a formal complaint.

(A) neglects (B) had neglected
(C) will be neglecting (D) neglect

집주인이 빨리 물건을 고쳐 주는 것을 소홀히 한다면 정식으로 불만을 제기하세요.

해설 조건 부사절에서의 시제+수 일치 의미상 미래의 일을 이야기하고 있으나 조건의 부사절에서는 현재 시제가 미래 시제를 대신하므로 현재 시제를 써야 한다. 주어인 the landlord가 단수 명사이므로 단수 동사인 (A) neglects가 정답이다.

어휘 landlord 집주인 neglect 소홀히 하다, 방치하다 make a complaint 불만을 제기하다 formal 공식의, 정식의

3.

The train **leaves** in about ten minutes, so passengers should get on board.

(A) leave (B) leaves
(C) left (D) leaving

기차는 약 10분 후에 출발하오니 승객 분들은 탑승하세요.

해설 현재 시제가 미래를 나타내는 경우+수 일치 in about ten minutes(약 10분 후에)와 가장 어울리는 시제는 미래 시제이다. 하지만 미래 시제가 없으므로 미래의 의미를 나타낼 수 있는 현재 시제나 현재진행형이 있는지 확인해야 한다. 현재 시제인 (A)와 (B)가 정답으로 가능한데, 주어인 The train이 단수 명사이므로 단수 동사인 (B) leaves가 정답이다. 이렇게 시간표, 계획표에 있는 확정된 일의 경우 현재 시제로 미래의 일을 나타낼 수 있다.

어휘 get on board 승선하다, 탑승하다

4.

A maintenance worker **is installing** new lights in the hallway later this week.

(A) to install (B) will be installed
(C) installed (D) is installing

정비 직원이 이번 주 말에 복도에 새로운 전등을 설치할 것입니다.

해설 현재진행형이 미래를 나타내는 경우 문장 맨 끝의 later this week를 통해 미래 시제가 와야 함을 알 수 있다. 가까운 미래의 일을 표현할 때는 현재진행형을 쓸 수 있으므로 정답은 (D) is installing이다. (B)도 미래 시제이기는 하나 빈칸 뒤에 목적어가 있으므로 수동태는 올 수 없다.

어휘 maintenance worker 정비 직원 install 설치하다

4 현재완료

1. (D)　　　2. (B)　　　3. (A)　　　4. (D)

1.

Bailey Sportswear **has improved** its employee training program since February of last year.

(A) will improve
(B) improving
(C) to improve
(D) has improved

베일리 스포츠웨어는 작년 2월 이래로 직원 훈련 프로그램을 개선해 왔다.

해설 **현재완료형** 빈칸은 동사 자리이므로 동사 역할을 할 수 있는 (A) will improve(미래 시제)와 (D) has improved(현재완료형) 중 적절한 시제를 골라야 한다. 문장 맨 끝의 시간 부사구 since February of last year의 since(~ 이래로 쭉)를 보자마자 현재완료형을 떠올려야 한다. 정답은 (D).

2.

The holiday party is several weeks away, but the receptionist **decorated** the office yesterday.

(A) decorate
(B) decorated
(C) to decorate
(D) have decorated

연말 파티가 몇 주 남았지만 접수 담당자는 어제 사무실을 장식했다.

해설 **과거 시제** 빈칸 문장의 yesterday를 통해 빈칸에 과거 시제가 와야 함을 알 수 있다. 정답은 (B) decorated이다.

어휘 holiday party (주로 회사에서 한 해를 마무리하기 위해 여는) 연말 파티   receptionist 접수 담당자

3.

Last month, Ms. Nelson **authorized** company funds to be used for an office renovation project.

(A) authorized
(B) authorizing
(C) has authorized
(D) will authorize

지난달에 넬슨 씨는 사무실 보수 프로젝트에 사용될 회사 자금을 재가했다.

해설 **과거 시제** Last month라는 명확한 과거 시점이 있으므로 빈칸에는 과거 시제가 와야 옳다. 따라서 정답은 (A) authorized이다.

어휘 authorize 재가하다, 권한을 부여하다   fund 자금, 기금

4.

The number of newspaper subscribers **has decreased** by fifteen percent over the past year.

(A) decreased
(B) decreasing
(C) will decrease
(D) has decreased

신문 구독자의 수가 작년 동안 15% 감소해 왔다.

해설 **현재완료형** over the past year는 '작년 한 해에 걸쳐'라는 기간을 뜻하므로 현재완료형인 (D) has decreased가 정답이다. 참고로 the number of는 단수 동사, a number of는 복수 동사로 수 일치한다는 점을 기억하자.

어휘 subscriber 구독자   decrease 감소하다

5 기타 완료 시제

본문 p.090

1. (D)   2. (D)   3. (D)   4. (D)

1.

Mr. Frost designed one of the most creative marketing campaigns the company **had seen**.

(A) was seen (B) sees
(C) will have seen (D) **had seen**

프로스트 씨는 회사가 본 것 중 가장 창의적인 마케팅 캠페인 중 하나를 기획했다.

해설 과거완료형 프로스트 씨가 마케팅 캠페인을 기획하기 전에 이미 그 회사는 다른 캠페인들을 목격해 왔다. 프로스트 씨가 기획한 때가 과거이므로(designed) 빈칸에는 그보다 앞선 과거완료 시제가 와야 한다.

어휘 design 기획하다, 고안하다, 설계하다

2.

By the end of next year, Ferretti Electronics **will have opened** three new retail branches.

(A) opened (B) had opened
(C) will be opened (D) **will have opened**

내년 말까지 페레티 전자는 세 군데의 신규 소매점을 오픈할 것이다.

해설 미래완료형 By the end of next year라는 미래의 기한을 나타내는 시간 부사구가 왔으므로 미래완료형을 떠올릴 수 있어야 한다. 미래의 특정 시점까지 완료될 것이라는 의미의 미래완료형인 (D) will have opened가 정답이다.

어휘 electronics 전자 기술, 전자 제품 retail branch 소매점

3.

McKinney Enterprises **will have signed** the licensing agreement with GT Media by this time next week.

(A) signs (B) has been signing
(C) had signed (D) **will have signed**

맥키니 사는 다음 주 이맘때까지 GT 미디어와 저작권 사용 계약에 서명할 것이다.

해설 미래완료형 by this time next week라는 미래의 완료 기한이 등장했으므로 미래완료형이 가장 적절하다. 따라서 정답은 (D) will have signed이다.

어휘 enterprise 기업, 회사 licensing agreement 라이선스 계약

4.

Chavez Engineering **has been serving** the Philadelphia area for over two decades.

(A) is serving (B) was served
(C) to be served (D) **has been serving**

차베즈 엔지니어링은 20년 넘게 필라델피아 지역에서 서비스를 제공해 오고 있다.

해설 현재완료진행형 for over two decades라는 기간을 나타내는 시간 부사구가 왔으므로 '계속'의 의미를 가지는 현재완료형을 정답으로 떠올릴 수 있어야 한다. 현재완료형과 마찬가지로 현재완료진행형도 과거부터 현재까지 계속되는 일을 나타내므로 (D) has been serving이 가장 적절하다.

어휘 serve 일하다, 근무하다; (음식을) 제공하다

6 문맥으로 판단해야 하는 시제 문제

1. (A)   2. (C)   3. (B)   4. (C)

1.

The work crew repainted the hallway walls and then **cleaned** the carpet thoroughly.

(A) cleaned   (B) clean
(C) cleans   (D) cleaning

인부들은 복도 벽에 페인트를 다시 칠한 다음에 카펫을 꼼꼼하게 청소했다.

해설 **과거 시제** 시제의 단서가 될 만한 시간 부사구가 없는 경우 문맥을 통해 적절한 시제를 판단해야 한다. 빈칸 앞의 절이 과거 시제이고 부사 then(그런 다음에)을 통해 이어진 행동임을 알 수 있으므로 과거 시제가 가장 자연스럽다. 따라서 정답은 (A) cleaned이다.

어휘 hallway 복도   thoroughly 완전히, 철저히

2.

After Ms. Caruso **rearranged** the furniture in the waiting area, the space looked much larger.

(A) to rearrange   (B) is rearranging
(C) rearranged   (D) having rearranged

카루소 씨가 대기실의 가구를 재배치한 이후에 그 공간은 훨씬 더 넓어 보였다.

해설 **과거 시제** 시제의 단서가 되는 시간 부사구가 따로 없으므로 다른 절의 내용을 통해 시제를 판단해야 한다. 주절의 시제가 looked로 과거 시제인데, 접속사 After를 통해 주절의 내용은 After절의 이후 내용임을 알 수 있다. 따라서 선택지 중 가장 적절한 것은 주절과 같은 과거 시제인 (C) rearranged이다.

어휘 rearrange 재배치하다   waiting area 대기실

3.

Dr. Panidos **is performing** surgery and cannot be contacted under any circumstances.

(A) was performing   (B) is performing
(C) has performed   (D) had performed

파니도스 선생님은 수술 집도 중이어서 어떤 상황이라도 연락을 받으실 수 없습니다.

해설 **현재진행형** 문맥상 '현재 수술을 하는 중이어서 연락을 받을 수 없다'는 내용이 가장 자연스럽다. 따라서 정답은 현재진행형인 (B) is performing이다.

어휘 perform surgery 수술을 집도하다   under any circumstances 어떤 상황이라도, 어떤 경우라도

4.

Although she **had not examined** the device carefully, Ms. Jackson was confident that it was working well.

(A) was not examined   (B) is not examined
(C) had not examined   (D) is not examining

잭슨 씨는 그 장비를 주의 깊게 검사하지 않았음에도 장비가 잘 작동할 거라는 확신에 차 있었다.

해설 **과거완료형** 빈칸 뒤에 목적어가 있으므로 선택지 중 수동태인 (A)와 (B)는 오답으로 제거해야 한다. 주절이 과거의 일을 나타내고 있는데 장비를 검사한 것은 그보다 더 과거의 일이므로 과거완료인 (C) had not examined가 알맞다.

어휘 examine 검사하다, 조사하다   device 장비   confident 확신에 찬, 자신만만한   work 작동하다

VOCABULARY

본문 p.094

1. (C) 2. (C) 3. (B) 4. (D) 5. (A) 6. (D) 7. (A) 8. (C)

1.

If we **secure** funding from government grants, we won't need to lay off any assembly line workers.

(A) attempt (B) advise
(C) secure (D) withdraw

우리가 정부 보조금으로 자금을 **확보한다면** 조립 라인 근로자를 해고할 필요가 없을 것이다.

(A) 시도하다 (B) 충고하다
(C) 확보하다 (D) 인출하다

해설 동사 어휘 목적어인 funding(자금)과 어울리는 동사 어휘는 (C) secure(확보하다)와 (D) withdraw(인출하다)이다. 문맥상 자금을 인출하는 것이 아니라 가지고 있어야 근로자를 해고할 필요가 없는 것이므로 정답은 (C) secure이다.

어휘 funding 자금; 자금 조달 grant 보조금; 주다, 승인하다 lay off ~을 해고하다 assembly line 조립 라인

2.

This coupon is for full-price products only and cannot be **redeemed** on clearance items.

(A) deferred (B) assumed
(C) redeemed (D) complied

이 쿠폰은 정가 제품에만 해당되고 재고 정리 중인 제품에는 **교환될** 수 없습니다.

(A) 연기하다 (B) 가정하다
(C) 교환하다 (D) 따르다

해설 동사 어휘 redeem a coupon(쿠폰을 교환하다), redeem a voucher(상품권을 교환하다)의 어구를 알고 있으면 쉽게 해결할 수 있는 문제다. 문맥상 '쿠폰이 정가 제품을 위한 것으로 재고 정리 중인 제품에는 해당이 안 된다'는 의미가 되어야 자연스러우므로 '(쿠폰 등을) 상품으로 바꾸다'라는 의미의 (C) redeemed가 정답이다.

어휘 full-price 정가의 clearance 재고 정리 판매 defer 미루다, 연기하다 assume 가정[추측]하다; (직책을) 맡다 comply 지키다, 따르다

3.

The Blake Historical House will be **undergoing** repairs after the peak visiting season.

(A) educating **(B) undergoing**
(C) hosting (D) importing

블레이크 고택은 성수기 방문 시즌 이후에 보수 공사에 **들어갈** 것입니다.

(A) 교육시키다 **(B) 겪다**
(C) 주최하다 (D) 수입하다

해설 동사 어휘 빈칸 뒤의 목적어 repairs와 의미상 어울리는 동사는 '(변화 등을) 겪다'라는 뜻의 (B) undergoing뿐이다. 수리 관련 내용은 토익에 자주 등장하는 주제로, '수리하다'라는 뜻의 동사구인 make repairs, do repairs, undergo repairs, carry out repairs를 한꺼번에 기억해 두자.

어휘 undergo repairs[renovations] 보수 공사를 하다 peak 성수기의, 절정의; 절정, 최고조

4.

To improve employee morale, MT Corporation has **initiated** a flexible working hour system.

(A) demanded (B) surveyed
(C) vacated **(D) initiated**

직원 사기를 증진시키기 위해 MT 사는 유연 근무제를 **시작했다**.

(A) 요구하다 (B) 설문 조사를 하다
(C) 비우다 **(D) 시작하다**

해설 동사 어휘 목적어인 a flexible working hour system(유연 근무제)을 수반하기에 적절한 동사 어휘는 (A) demanded와 (D) initiated뿐인데, 주어인 MT Corporation은 새로운 제도를 요구한 주체라기보다는 실행한 주체이므로 정답은 (D) initiated이다.

어휘 morale 사기, 의욕 flexible working hour system 유연 근무제 vacate (자리, 직책 등을) 비우다

5.

The merchandising team designed a new clothing line to **launch** in time for baseball's playoff season.	상품 기획팀은 야구 플레이오프 시즌에 맞춰 제때에 **출시할** 신상 의류 제품을 디자인했다.
(A) launch (B) attract (C) resolve (D) represent	**(A)** 출시하다 (B) 유인하다 (C) 해결하다 (D) 대표하다

> **해설** 동사 어휘 '제때에 ----할 신상 의류 제품을 디자인했다'라는 의미로 a new clothing line을 수식하기에 자연스러우면서 in time의 수식을 받기에도 적절한 동사 어휘를 골라야 한다. 따라서 '제때에 출시할 신상 의류 제품을 디자인했다'라는 의미를 이루는 (A) launch가 빈칸에 가장 적절하다.

> **어휘** line 제품군 in time 제때, 시간에 맞춰

6.

Hartman's Groceries **pledged** to reduce its use of plastic by 50% by next year.	하트만 식료품은 자사의 플라스틱 사용을 내년까지 50% 줄이겠다고 **약속했다**.
(A) warranted (B) inhibited (C) reassured **(D) pledged**	(A) 보증하다 (B) 억제하다 (C) 안심시키다 **(D) 약속하다**

> **해설** 동사 어휘 문맥상 '플라스틱 사용을 줄일 것을 ----했다'에 들어갈 적절한 동사 어휘를 고르는 문제로, '약속했다'라는 뜻의 (D) pledged가 들어가는 것이 가장 자연스럽다.

> **어휘** pledge to do ~하기로 약속하다 warrant 보증하다; 보증서 inhibit 억제하다, 못 하게 하다

7.

If clients do not **specify** the brand of materials they want, then generic ones will be used.	고객들이 별도로 자재 브랜드를 **명시하지** 않으면 브랜드가 없는 일반 자재가 사용될 것입니다.
(A) specify (B) charge (C) inspect (D) delegate	**(A)** 명시하다 (B) 부과하다 (C) 검사하다 (D) 위임하다

> **해설** 동사 어휘 '브랜드를 알려 주지 않으면 브랜드가 없는 자재가 사용될 것이다'라는 뜻이 되어야 적절하므로 정답은 (A) specify이다.

> **어휘** generic 브랜드가 별도로 없는; 포괄적인, 통칭의

8.

Mario's Pizzeria announced that it will **waive** the charge for delivery this December.	마리오 피자는 이번 12월에 배송비를 **감면해** 주겠다고 안내했다.
(A) proceed (B) arrange **(C) waive** (D) summarize	(A) 진행되다 (B) 준비하다 **(C)** 감면하다 (D) 요약하다

> **해설** 동사 어휘 평소에 waive the charge(비용을 감면해 주다), waive the fee(수수료를 감면해 주다), waive the fine(벌금을 감면해 주다)의 어구를 기억해 두었으면 쉽게 정답을 고를 수 있는 문제이다. 비용(the charge)과 자연스럽게 어울리는 동사 어휘는 (C) waive뿐이다. 참고로 엄밀히 말하면 waive는 '감면하다'가 아니라 '(권리, 요구 등을) 포기하다'를 뜻한다. 다만 비용과 관련된 말과 함께 쓰이면 권리자가 자신의 권리를 포기하고 비용을 받지 않는다는 의미가 되기 때문에 우리말로 의역했을 때 '감면하다'가 되는 것이다.

> **어휘** pizzeria 피자 가게 delivery 배송

ACTUAL TEST

1. (D)	2. (A)	3. (D)	4. (B)	5. (C)	6. (C)
7. (D)	8. (D)	9. (B)	10. (A)	11. (A)	12. (C)

1.

The water to the building will be shut off while the plumber **is investigating** the issue.

(A) investigated
(B) will investigate
(C) has investigated
(D) is investigating

배관공이 문제를 조사하는 동안 그 건물의 수도가 끊길 것이다.

해설 시간 부사절의 시제 주절의 내용이 미래 시제이지만 while, when, before 등의 시간을 나타내는 부사절에서는 현재가 미래를 대신하므로 현재진행 시제인 (D)가 적절하다. 또한 while은 '~하는 동안'이란 의미이므로 현재진행형이 문맥상으로도 가장 어울린다.

어휘 plumber 배관공 investigate 조사하다, 살피다

2.

Before he **starts** the workshop, the manager is going to summarize the aim of each session.

(A) starts
(B) start
(C) will start
(D) is starting

그 관리자는 워크숍을 시작하기 전에 각 세션의 목표를 요약해 줄 것이다.

해설 시간 부사절의 시제 주절의 시제가 is going to로 미래이므로 종속절에도 미래 시제가 오는 것이 자연스럽다. 하지만 종속절의 접속사가 시간의 접속사인 Before이므로 시간 및 조건의 부사절에서는 현재 시제가 미래를 대신한다는 법칙을 떠올려야 한다. 주어가 he로 3인칭 단수이므로 단수 동사인 (A) starts가 정답이다.

어휘 summarize 요약하다

3.

Dave Aldrich **was named** the city's most recognizable architect last year.

(A) names
(B) is named
(C) has named
(D) was named

데이브 알드리치 씨는 작년에 시에서 가장 저명한 건축가로 선정되었다.

해설 과거 시제 문장 맨 끝의 last year를 통해 과거 시제가 와야 함을 알 수 있으므로 정답은 쉽게 (D) was named임을 알 수 있다. 선택지에 수동태가 와서 태까지 판별해야 하는 문제로 생각할 수 있으나 이렇게 시제만 판별해도 문제가 해결될 수 있다. 참고로 동사 name은 수동태가 될 경우 목적격 보어인 명사가 수동태 동사 뒤에 남는다는 것도 챙겨 두자.

어휘 name 임명하다, 지명하다 recognizable 알아볼 수 있는

4.

The building's exterior walls **have deteriorated** in recent years and should be repaired soon.

(A) deteriorating
(B) have deteriorated
(C) to deteriorate
(D) deteriorated

최근 몇 년 사이에 그 건물의 외벽 상태가 나빠져서 곧 수리되어야 합니다.

해설 현재완료형 in recent years는 '최근 몇 년간, 최근 몇 년 동안'이라는 뜻으로 기간을 의미하는 시간 부사구이므로 현재완료형과 자주 어울려 쓰인다. 따라서 정답은 (B) have deteriorated이다.

어휘 exterior 외관의 deteriorate 악화되다, 더 나빠지다

5.

The interns **will have assisted** each department in the firm by the time they complete the training program.

(A) had assisted   (B) are assisting
(C) will have assisted (D) will assist

인턴들이 교육 프로그램을 마칠 때쯤이면 회사의 각 부서를 돕게 될 것입니다.

해설 **미래완료형** by the time 뒤에 현재 시제가 오면 일부 예외적인 경우를 제외하고는 주절에는 미래완료형이, 과거 시제가 오면 주절에는 과거완료형이 온다. by the time 뒤에 현재 시제가 왔으므로 미래완료형이 와야 적절하다.

어휘 assist 돕다

6.

After the mechanic **had inspected** the vehicle, he recommended replacing some worn components.

(A) inspects   (B) have inspected
(C) had inspected (D) is inspecting

정비공은 자동차를 점검한 후에 마모된 몇몇 부품을 교체할 것을 권고했다.

해설 **과거완료형** 문맥상 점검을 한 후에 교체할 것을 추천한 것이므로 After절의 내용이 더 과거의 일이다. 따라서 정답은 과거완료형인 (C) had inspected이다. 과거완료의 경우 사건의 전후 관계를 명확히 밝히기 위해 주로 사용되는데, 접속사 after(~ 후에)는 뜻에 이미 전후 관계가 포함되어 있으므로 과거완료 대신 과거 시제를 사용할 수 있다는 점도 참고로 알아 두자.

어휘 mechanic 정비공   inspect 점검하다   recommend 권고하다, 제안하다   replace 교체하다   worn 해진, 닳은   component 부품

7.

The director explained her reasons for promoting the least experienced employee but **was criticized**.

(A) being criticized   (B) is criticized
(C) criticized   **(D) was criticized**

그 관리자는 경력이 가장 적은 직원을 승진시킨 것에 대한 이유를 설명했으나 비난을 받았다.

해설 **과거 시제** 시제의 단서가 될 만한 시간 부사구가 따로 없는 문장이므로 앞뒤 절의 내용을 통해 적절한 시제를 판별해야 한다. but 앞의 절이 과거 시제이므로 빈칸에도 과거 시제가 오는 것이 가장 자연스러운데 주어진 The director가 비난을 받았다는 것이 적절하므로 정답은 수동태 과거 시제인 (D) was criticized이다.

어휘 promote 승진시키다   the least 가장 적은, 최소의

8.

Streaming Central gives customers three warnings about late payments, after which the account **is suspended**.

(A) suspended   (B) be suspended
(C) had been suspended **(D) is suspended**

스트리밍 센트럴은 지불 체납에 대해 고객에게 세 번 경고를 주는데, 그 후에는 계정이 정지됩니다.

해설 **현재 시제** 시간 부사구가 따로 없으므로 다른 절의 시제를 통해 빈칸에 들어갈 적절한 시제를 판단해야 한다. after 앞의 주절에 현재 시제가 왔고 문맥상 일반적인 정책을 설명하는 내용이다. after which에는 지불 체납에 대한 경고 조치 이후의 내용이 나와 있으므로 일반적인 정책을 설명하는 현재 시제나 미래의 일을 나타내는 미래 시제가 가장 적절하다. 선택지에 현재 시제가 있으므로 정답은 (D) is suspended이다. 참고로 after which에서 which는 앞 문장을 받는 관계대명사로 '그 이후에'라는 뜻으로 해석하면 된다.

어휘 warning 경고   account 계정   suspend 유예시키다, 보류하다, 정지하다

TO ALL DEXTER PET STORE CUSTOMERS

Dexter Pet Store boasts the largest collection of animal-related merchandise in the region. Since 2002, our business **9 has provided** high-quality products and expert advice to keep your pets happy and healthy. After much consideration, we decided that we want to spend more time with our family. As a result, we are planning to **10 close** at the end of the month. We **11 are holding** our final day of business on Saturday, September 30. In the meantime, please don't hesitate to visit the store to take advantage of substantial discounts in all departments. We need to get rid of our entire inventory of stock. **12 Therefore, it's a great time to stock up on supplies.** We appreciate your patronage through the years, and we wish you and your pets all the best.

덱스터 펫 스토어의 모든 고객 분께

덱스터 펫 스토어는 지역에서 동물 관련 용품을 가장 많이 보유하고 있는 것을 자랑합니다. 2002년 이래로 저희 가게는 고객님들의 반려동물이 행복하고 건강할 수 있는 고품질의 상품과 전문적인 조언을 9 제공해 왔습니다. 많은 고심 끝에 저희는 가족과 더 많은 시간을 보내고 싶다고 결심을 내렸습니다. 따라서 저희는 이번 달 말에 10 가게를 정리할 계획입니다. 저희는 9월 30일 토요일에 마지막 영업을 11 할 예정입니다. 그 사이에 주저하지 말고 상점을 방문하셔서 모든 품목에서 상당한 할인 기회를 이용하시기 바랍니다. 우리는 재고 전체를 처리해야 합니다. 12 그러므로 물품을 쟁여 둘 아주 좋은 기회입니다. 수년 동안 이용해 주셔서 감사드리며 고객 여러분과 여러분의 반려동물에게 행운이 함께 하기를 바랍니다.

어휘 boast 자랑하다, 뽐내다　merchandise (집합 명사) 상품　expert 전문적인; 전문가　consideration 고려, 숙고　in the meantime 그 동안에　don't hesitate to do 주저하지 말고 ~하다　take advantage of ~을 이용하다　substantial 상당한 (=considerable)　get rid of ~을 없애다　entire 전체의, 전부의　inventory 재고 목록, 재고　patronage 애용

9. (A) provided　　　　　(B) has provided
   (C) is providing　　　 (D) was being provided

   해설 현재완료형 적절한 시제를 묻는 문제이므로 단서가 되는 시간 부사구가 있는지부터 빠르게 찾아야 한다. 빈칸 문장 맨 앞에 Since 2002라는 기간을 나타내는 시간 부사구가 있으므로 단번에 현재완료형인 (B) has provided가 정답임을 알 수 있다.

10. (A) close　　　　　(B) invest　　　　(A) 폐점하다　(B) 투자하다
    (C) acknowledge　(D) eliminate　　(C) 인정하다　(D) 제거하다

    해설 동사 어휘 빈칸 앞의 want to spend more time with our family와 뒤 문장의 final day of business를 통해 문을 닫는다는 내용임을 알 수 있다. 따라서 폐점한다는 의미의 (A) close가 문맥상 가장 자연스럽다.

11. (A) are holding　　(B) had to hold
    (C) will be held　　(D) have held

    해설 미래를 나타내는 현재진행형 문맥상 9월 30일 토요일에 마지막 영업을 가질 것이라는 미래의 의미가 적절하다. 미래 시제인 (C) will be held를 정답으로 고를 수 있으나 빈칸 뒤에 목적어가 있으므로 수동태는 올 수 없다. 현재진행형이 미래의 일을 나타낼 수 있으므로 정답은 (A) are holding이다.

12. (A) Nevertheless, the industry is growing steadily.
    (B) Some pets are easier to care for than others.
    (C) Therefore, it's a great time to stock up on supplies.
    (D) The new location will be announced soon.

    (A) 그럼에도 불구하고 그 산업은 끊임없이 성장 중입니다.
    (B) 몇몇 반려동물은 다른 동물들보다 돌보기 쉽습니다.
    (C) 그러므로 물품을 쟁여 둘 아주 좋은 기회입니다.
    (D) 새로운 위치는 곧 안내될 것입니다.

    해설 알맞은 문장 고르기 빈칸 앞에서 재고를 처리하기 위해 할인 행사를 한다고 했고, 빈칸 뒤에서는 영업 종료를 앞두고 마지막 인사를 하고 있다. 따라서 빈칸에는 재고 구입 독려를 유도하는 내용인 (C)가 가장 자연스럽다.

    어휘 steadily 끊임없이　stock up on (필요할 때 쓰려고) ~을 쟁여 두다　supplies 소모품, 용품, 물품

UNIT 06 태

1 능동태

본문 p.104

1. (A)   2. (B)   3. (C)   4. (C)

1.

Royas, a jewelry manufacturer, **operates** several store branches in the region.

(A) operates (B) is operated
(C) operating (D) to operate

주얼리 제조업체인 로야스는 그 지역에 여러 개의 지점을 운영한다.

해설　**주어+동격어구+동사** Royas는 주어, 쉼표 사이는 Royas가 무엇인지를 설명해 주는 동격어구로, 빈칸은 동사 자리이다. 동사 자리 뒤에 목적어가 있으므로 능동태인 (A) operates가 와야 옳다.

어휘　manufacturer 제조사 operate (사업체, 기관 등을) 운영하다; (기계를) 작동시키다 branch 지점, 지사

2.

The recruiter **considers** Mr. Hark to be the best candidate because of his certifications.

(A) is considered (B) considers
(C) was considered (D) considering

채용 담당자는 하크 씨의 자격증 때문에 그가 가장 적임자라고 생각한다.

해설　**타동사의 능동태** 빈칸 뒤의 Mr. Hark가 목적어이므로 빈칸에는 동사의 능동태가 올 확률이 높다. 의미상으로도 '채용 담당자는 하크 씨가 가장 적임의 후보자라고 생각한다'라는 능동의 의미가 적절하므로 정답은 (B) considers이다.

어휘　recruiter 채용 담당자 consider A to do A를 ~라고 여기다 certification 자격증, 증명서; 증명

3.

The summer sales event **will last** throughout the whole month of July.

(A) is lasted (B) will be lasted
(C) will last (D) to last

여름철 할인 행사는 7월 내내 계속될 것이다.

해설　**자동사** 선택지의 동사 last를 보자마자 last가 자동사이므로 수동태를 오답으로 제거할 줄 알아야 한다. 빈칸 앞의 주어, 빈칸 뒤는 시간의 부사구, 빈칸은 동사 자리이므로 정답은 능동태인 (C) will last뿐이다.

어휘　last 지속되다 throughout ~동안 쭉, ~ 내내 whole 전체의, 전부의

4.

Ms. Bellido **returned** to her hotel room because she had forgotten her bag.

(A) is returned (B) were returned
(C) returned (D) returning

벨리도 씨는 가방을 깜빡했기 때문에 호텔 방으로 되돌아갔다.

해설　**자동사** 동사 return이 '~로 돌아가다'라는 뜻일 때는 자동사로 쓰이므로 정답은 능동태 과거형인 (C) returned이다. 한편, return이 '(물건 등을) 되돌려 주다, 반환하다'의 뜻일 때는 타동사로 쓰일 수 있다.

어휘　forget 잊다, 깜박하다

2 수동태

본문 p.105

1. (D)   2. (D)   3. (A)   4. (A)

1.

> The keynote speaker of Renewable Energy Convention will **be introduced** by the chairman.
>
> (A) introduce   (B) have introduced
> (C) be introducing   **(D) be introduced**

재생 에너지 총회의 기조 연설자는 의장에 의해 소개될 것이다.

[해설] **수동태** 빈칸 뒤의 by the chairman이 수동태의 근거가 되므로 정답이 (D)임을 바로 알아챌 수 있다.

[어휘] keynote speaker 기조 연설자   renewable energy 재생 에너지   convention 총회, 대회; 관습, 관례   chairman 의장

2.

> Prescription medication is always **stored** behind the counter rather than on the display shelves.
>
> (A) stores   (B) storing
> (C) storage   **(D) stored**

처방전이 있어야 구입 가능한 의약품은 진열대가 아닌 계산대 뒤쪽에 항시 보관됩니다.

[해설] **수동태** 빈칸 앞에 be동사인 is가 있으므로 (B) storing과 (D) stored가 정답일 가능성이 높다. 빈칸 뒤에 목적어가 없으므로 정답은 수동태인 (D) stored가 된다. 의미상 '의약품이 항시 보관된다'라는 수동의 의미도 적절하다.

[어휘] prescription medication 처방전이 있어야 구입 가능한 약 (↔ over-the-counter drug 처방전 없이 구입 가능한 일반 의약품)   store 저장하다, 보관하다   counter 판매대, 계산대   display shelf 진열대, 매대

3.

> Ms. Hanz anticipates that her painting will be **considered** as an entry to the art contest.
>
> **(A) considered**   (B) considering
> (C) consider   (D) consideration

한즈 씨는 그녀의 그림이 미술 대회 출품작으로 고려될 수 있기를 기대하고 있다.

[해설] **수동태** 빈칸 뒤에 목적어가 없으므로 가장 먼저 수동태를 의심해 봐야 한다. 의미상으로도 '그림이 출품작으로 고려되다'라는 의미가 자연스러우므로 정답은 (A) considered이다. consider A as B는 'A를 B로 여기다'는 뜻이며 수동태로 전환되면 A is considered as B의 형태가 된다.

[어휘] anticipate 기대하다, 고대하다   entry 출품작

4.

> Customers **will be sent** a cost estimate after a specialist checks the kitchen to be remodeled.
>
> **(A) will be sent**   (B) has sent
> (C) are sending   (D) be sent

고객들은 전문가가 리모델링이 될 주방을 확인한 후에 비용 견적서를 받게 될 겁니다.

[해설] **수여동사의 수동태** 빈칸 뒤에 목적어가 있으므로 능동태를 고려할 수 있으나 send가 목적어를 2개 취하는 수여동사라는 점에 주목해야 한다. 문맥상 '고객은 비용 견적서를 받는 것'이 자연스러우므로 수동태가 되어야 하며, after절이 현재이므로 그보다 뒤인 미래 수동이 적절하다. send는 수동태가 되어도 직접 목적어가 뒤에 남는다.

[어휘] cost estimate 비용 견적서   specialist 전문가   remodel 개조하다, 리모델링하다

3 수동태 구문 1: be + p.p. + 전치사

본문 p.106

1. (D) 2. (A) 3. (B) 4. (B)

1.

The choice of the Best Employee Award winner **is based** on performance and attitude.	최우수 직원상 수상자의 선정은 성과와 태도를 근거로 한다.
(A) based (B) bases (C) basing **(D) is based**	

해설 be based on 주어 The choice가 뒤에 오는 전치사구의 수식을 받고 있다. 빈칸은 동사 자리로 뒤에 목적어가 없으므로 수동태를 의심해 봐야 한다. be based on은 '~에 근거를 두다'라는 의미의 토익 빈출 동사구로, 문맥상 '성과와 태도를 근거로 한다'라는 의미도 자연스러우므로 정답은 (D) is based이다.

어휘 be based on ~을 근거로 하다, ~을 기반으로 하다   performance (업무의) 성과; (음악 등의) 공연   attitude 태도

2.

The computer is **equipped** with a camera ideal for online meetings.	그 컴퓨터는 온라인 회의에 이상적인 카메라를 갖추고 있다.
(A) equipped (B) related (C) designed (D) concerned	

해설 be equipped with 전치사 with와 어울리면서 문맥상 자연스러운 분사 형태의 어휘를 골라야 한다. 의미상 '컴퓨터에 카메라가 내장되어 있다'라는 내용이 적절하므로 '(장비 등을) 갖춘'이라는 뜻의 (A) equipped가 가장 적절하다.

어휘 be equipped with (장비 등을) 갖추다   ideal 이상적인

3.

Several of the experienced designers **were involved** in the creation of the new company logo.	경험 많은 여러 명의 디자이너들이 회사의 새로운 로고를 만드는 데 참여했다.
(A) were involving **(B) were involved** (C) have involved (D) involve	

해설 be involved in 선택지의 동사가 involve이고 빈칸 뒤에 전치사 in이 온 것으로 보아 토익에 빈출되는 be involved in이 정답이 아닌지 의심해 봐야 한다. 의미상으로도 '여러 명의 디자이너들이 만드는 데 참여했다'라는 의미가 자연스러우므로 정답은 (B) were involved이다.

어휘 experienced 숙련된, 경험 많은, 노련한   be involved in ~에 관련되다, ~에 참여하다

4.

Yending Cosmetics is dedicated **to** keeping the price of its products reasonable.	옌딩 코스메틱스는 자사 제품의 가격을 적절하게 유지하는 데 전념하고 있다.
(A) with **(B) to** (C) on (D) for	

해설 be dedicated to 빈칸 앞의 is dedicated를 보자마자 be dedicated to(~에 헌신하다, ~에 전념하다)가 떠올라야 한다. 정답은 (B) to이다.

어휘 keep 유지하다   reasonable (가격이) 적당한, 합리적인

4 수동태 구문 2: be + p.p. + to do

본문 p.107

1. (A)   2. (A)   3. (C)   4. (A)

1.

Visitors of the factory floor **are asked** to wear a safety helmet at all times.

(A) are asked (B) to ask
(C) asking   (D) asks

공장의 작업 현장 방문객들은 항상 안전모를 쓰도록 요청받습니다.

해설 be asked to *do* Visitors of the factory floor가 주어이고 빈칸 뒤에 to부정사가 보이므로 빈칸은 동사 자리이다. 문맥상 방문객들이 요청을 받는 것이 자연스러우므로 수동이 되어야 적절하다. 따라서 정답은 (A) are asked이다.

어휘 be asked to *do* ~하도록 요청받다   safety helmet 안전모   at all times 항상, 언제나 (=always)

2.

Only members of the IT department **are permitted** to install software on the laptops.

(A) are permitted (B) permitting
(C) permissible   (D) permits

IT 부서원만이 노트북에 소프트웨어를 설치하도록 허가된다.

해설 be permitted to *do* be permitted to *do*(~하도록 허가되다)라는 표현을 알고 있으면 단번에 정답을 찾아낼 수 있다. 문맥상으로도 'IT 부서원만이 설치가 허가된다'라는 의미가 자연스러우므로 정답은 (A)이다.

어휘 install 설치하다

3.

Tickets must be purchased in advance and are **expected** to sell out quickly.

(A) allowed   (B) obliged
(C) expected (D) advised

표는 미리 예매해야 하며, 빠르게 매진될 것으로 예상된다.

해설 be expected to *do* 빈칸에 적절한 분사 어휘를 묻는 문제로 모두 to부정사를 동반하는 어휘들이다. 문맥상 '빠르게 매진될 것이다'라는 의미가 적절하므로 예정을 의미하는 (C) expected가 오는 것이 가장 자연스럽다.

어휘 in advance 미리   be expected to *do* ~하도록 기대되다   sell out 매진되다

4.

The airlines were forced **to cancel** all flights due to the severe snowstorm.

(A) to cancel   (B) canceled
(C) canceling   (D) be canceled

그 항공사들은 심한 눈보라로 인해 모든 비행을 취소할 수밖에 없었다.

해설 be forced to *do* be forced to *do*(~하도록 강요받다, ~할 수밖에 없다)를 기억하고 있으면 해석할 필요도 없이 바로 정답을 가려낼 수 있는 문제이다. be forced 뒤에는 to부정사가 뒤따라야 하므로 정답은 (A) to cancel이다.

어휘 severe 심한

VOCABULARY

본문 p.110

1. (C)   2. (C)   3. (A)   4. (C)   5. (A)   6. (B)   7. (A)   8. (B)

1.

Mr. Luca introduced a plan to **grant** workers permission to work remotely.	루카 씨는 직원들이 원격 근무를 할 수 있도록 허가를 **해 주는** 계획안을 도입했다.
(A) conceive (B) pursue **(C) grant** (D) presume	(A) 상상하다 (B) 추구하다 **(C) 주다** (D) 추정하다

> 해설 동사 어휘 문맥상 2개의 목적어인 workers, permission과 자연스럽게 어울릴 수 있는 동사 어휘를 골라야 한다. '직원들에게 허가를 주다'라는 의미가 가장 적절하므로 정답은 '주다'라는 뜻의 (C) grant이다.

> 어휘 introduce 도입하다; 소개하다 grant 주다, 허가하다; 보조금 permission 허가 remotely 멀리 떨어져, 원격으로

2.

Due to its increasing popularity, Tanya's Burgers has been **recruiting** staff to keep up with demand.	상승하는 인기 때문에 타냐스 버거는 수요를 따라잡기 위해 직원들을 **채용해** 오고 있다.
(A) resuming (B) tasting **(C) recruiting** (D) renovating	(A) 재개하다 (B) 맛보다 **(C) 채용하다** (D) 수리하다

> 해설 동사 어휘 목적어인 staff를 보자마자 (C) recruiting이 정답임을 쉽게 알 수 있는 문제이다. 이렇게 동사 어휘의 경우 전체 문장을 해석하기보다 목적어와의 의미 관계만 봐도 답이 보이는 경우가 많으므로 기억해 두자.

> 어휘 keep up with ~을 따라잡다, ~에 뒤처지지 않다 demand 수요 resume (일 등을) 다시 시작하다, 재개하다

3.

To attract more tourists, Lakefront Hotel plans to **promote** the local region through advertising.	더 많은 관광객들을 유인하기 위해 레이크프론트 호텔은 광고를 통해 현지 지역을 **홍보할** 계획이다.
(A) promote (B) direct (C) withhold (D) classify	**(A) 홍보하다** (B) 안내하다 (C) 보류하다 (D) 분류하다

> 해설 동사 어휘 문맥상 적절한 동사 어휘를 고르는 문제이므로 가장 먼저 목적어와의 의미 관계부터 판단해야 한다. 목적어인 the local region(현지 지역) 외에도 동사를 수식하는 전치사구 through advertising(광고를 통해)의 단서를 통해 '홍보하다'라는 뜻의 (A) promote가 가장 자연스러움을 알 수 있다.

> 어휘 attract 끌어당기다, 유인하다 plan to do ~할 계획이다 withhold (비용 지급, 정보 제공 등을) 보류하다

4.

The company's spokesperson has **assured** the press that it will reopen its Denver factory.	회사의 대변인은 덴버 공장을 다시 열 것이라고 언론에게 **확인시켜** 주었다.
(A) compiled (B) yielded **(C) assured** (D) reinstated	(A) 편집하다 (B) 생산하다 **(C) 확언하다** (D) 복귀시키다

> 해설 동사 어휘 동사 assure는 '~에게 …을 확신[확인]시켜 주다'는 의미로 〈assure A that + 주어 + 동사〉 혹은 〈assure A of B〉의 형태로 자주 쓰인다.

> 어휘 compile 편집하다, 엮다 yield (농산물을) 생산하다; (결과를) 낳다 reinstate (직책 등으로) 복귀시키다, (법률 등을 원래 상태로) 회복시키다

5.

After considering each proposal, the management **finalized** its decision to relocate the office.

(A) finalized   (B) coordinated
(C) investigated   (D) reassured

각각의 제안서를 고려한 이후에 경영진은 사무실을 이전하려는 그들의 결정을 **최종 확정했다**.

(A) 최종 확정하다   (B) 조직화하다
(C) 조사하다   (D) 안심시키다

> [해설] 동사 어휘 문맥상 '사무실을 이전시키려는 결정을 ----'에 가장 적절한 동사 어휘를 골라야 한다. 따라서 정답은 '최종 확정했다'라는 의미의 (A) finalized이다.

> [어휘] management 경영진 relocate 이전시키다

6.

Dr. Foster is working to **establish** sanitary protocol that everyone in the food service industry follows.

(A) succeed   (B) **establish**
(C) discover   (D) encounter

포스터 박사는 음식 서비스업의 모든 종사자들이 따라야 하는 위생 규약을 **수립하기** 위해 작업 중이다.

(A) 성공하다   (B) **수립하다**
(C) 발견하다   (D) 맞닥뜨리다

> [해설] 동사 어휘 문맥상 '제도 등을 수립하다'라는 의미의 동사 어휘가 들어가야 자연스러우므로 정답은 '(제도나 기관 등을) 수립하다'라는 뜻의 (B) establish이다.

> [어휘] sanitary 위생의 (=hygiene) protocol 규약, 협약 encounter (문제, 어려움, 저항 등에) 맞닥뜨리다, 부딪히다

7.

Mosquito pesticide spraying operations are scheduled to **commence** before tourists come on vacation.

(A) **commence**   (B) predict
(C) announce   (D) intervene

모기 살충제 살포 작업은 휴가차 관광객들이 오기 전에 **시작할** 예정입니다.

(A) **시작하다**   (B) 예상하다
(C) 안내하다   (D) 개입하다

> [해설] 동사 어휘 '모기 살충제 살포 작업이 ----될 예정이다'라는 문맥에 적절한 동사 어휘를 골라야 한다. 시작하거나 착수한다는 의미가 적절하므로 정답은 '시작하다'라는 뜻의 (A) commence가 정답이다.

> [어휘] pesticide 살충제 spray 뿌리다 be scheduled to do ~할 예정이다 on vacation 휴가차
> intervene (논쟁 등의 어려운 상황을 개선하기 위해) 개입하다, 끼어들다

8.

The Sky Room can **accommodate** up to 50 guests, while the Wind Room seats between 80 and 100 people comfortably.

(A) arrange   (B) **accommodate**
(C) represent   (D) allot

스카이 룸은 50명의 손님을 수용할 수 있는 한편, 윈드 룸은 80명에서 100명을 무리 없이 **수용할** 수 있습니다.

(A) 준비하다   (B) **수용하다**
(C) 대표하다   (D) 할당하다

> [해설] 동사 어휘 접속사 while(~한 반면)을 통해 앞뒤의 문장이 서로 대칭 구조임을 알 수 있다. 종속절에 쓰인 seat가 동사로 사용될 때는 '특정 수의 인원을 수용할 수 있는 좌석을 가지고 있다'라는 뜻이 되므로, 주절의 빈칸에는 seat에 상응하는 동사가 들어가야 한다. 따라서 '수용하다'라는 뜻의 (B) accommodate가 정답이다.

> [어휘] up to (최대) ~까지 comfortably 수월하게, 무리 없이; 편안하게

ACTUAL TEST

본문 p.112

| 1. (C) | 2. (C) | 3. (A) | 4. (C) | 5. (D) | 6. (B) |
| 7. (C) | 8. (B) | 9. (D) | 10. (A) | 11. (D) | 12. (C) |

1.

The branch managers **can be contacted** through their company e-mail accounts.

(A) have to contact (B) may contact
(C) can be contacted (D) have contacted

그 지점장들은 회사 이메일 계정을 통해 연락을 취할 수 있습니다.

해설 **조동사+수동태** 동사 contact는 '~에게 연락하다'라는 뜻의 타동사이다. 따라서 빈칸 뒤에 목적어가 없으므로 수동태가 와야 하는데 수동태는 (C) can be contacted뿐이다.

어휘 branch manager 지점장 e-mail account 이메일 계정

2.

Scientific advancements **allowed** BV Laboratories to complete its experiments earlier than planned.

(A) to allow (B) allowing
(C) allowed (D) are allowed

과학의 진보는 BV 연구소가 계획했던 것보다 일찍 실험을 완료할 수 있도록 해 주었다.

해설 **능동태** 사람 명사는 능동태의 주어, 사물 명사는 수동태의 주어라고 알고 있으면 오답 함정에 빠지기 쉬운 문제이다. 〈allow 목적어 to do〉의 구조로 '과학의 진보가 ~할 수 있게 해 주었다'라는 능동의 의미가 적절하므로 정답은 (C) allowed이다.

어휘 advancement 진보; 승진 earlier than ~보다 일찍

3.

The orchestra music for Jeremy Berman's new play is being **composed** by Rosanna Russo.

(A) composed (B) composing
(C) composition (D) composes

제레미 버만의 새로운 연극에 들어갈 오케스트라 음악은 로자나 루소에 의해 작곡되는 중이다.

해설 **수동태** 빈칸 뒤에 by Rosanna Russo라는 행위자가 있고 의미상 '음악이 작곡되고 있다'라는 수동의 의미가 자연스러우므로 정답은 (A) composed이다. 한편, compose는 '작곡하다'의 의미 외에 '구성하다'라는 의미를 가져 be composed of의 형태로 자주 쓰인다는 것도 알아 두자.

어휘 play 연극; 경기 compose 작곡하다; 작성하다, 쓰다; 구성하다

4.

The Mountain Spa hand soap that **was produced** last month had the wrong packaging.

(A) produced (B) to produce
(C) was produced (D) producing

지난달에 생산된 마운틴 스파 손 세정제는 포장이 잘못되어 있었다.

해설 **수동태** 선행사인 The Mountain Spa hand soap은 생산하는 주체가 아닌 생산되는 대상이므로 수동태인 (C) was produced가 정답이다. 이때, that was는 생략 가능하다는 것도 참고로 알아 둘 것.

어휘 hand soap 손 세정제 packaging 포장

5.

The department head is **deciding** whether to ask team members to work overtime or hire some temporary employees.

(A) decide (B) decided
(C) decides **(D) deciding**

그 부서장은 팀원들에게 야근을 요청할지 아니면 임시직을 고용할지 결정을 내리는 중이다.

해설 능동태 빈칸이 be동사 뒤에 있으므로 (A) decide와 (C) decides는 바로 오답으로 제거한다. 빈칸 뒤에 whether가 이끄는 목적어가 왔으므로 정답은 능동태인 (D) deciding이다. 참고로 whether to do A or do B는 'A할지 혹은 B할지'라는 뜻으로 기억해 두자.

어휘 department head 부서장 work overtime 야근하다, 특근하다 temporary employee 임시직, 비정규직

6.

The entrance fees to all museums are **included** in the price of the city tour.

(A) involved **(B) included**
(C) related (D) based

모든 박물관의 입장료는 시티 투어 비용에 포함되어 있습니다.

해설 be included in 선택지를 보니 빈칸 뒤의 전치사 in과 어울리면서 문맥상 적절한 분사 어휘를 고르는 문제이다. (C) related는 be related to(~와 관련되다), (D) based는 be based on(~에 근거를 두다)의 형태로 쓰이므로 오답으로 제거한다. 문맥상 '포함되어 있다'라는 의미가 자연스러우므로 정답은 (B) included이다.

어휘 entrance fee 입장료

7.

At the law firm, all confidential documents **are required** to remain in locked cabinets unless someone uses them.

(A) require (B) requires
(C) are required (D) is required

법률 회사에서 모든 기밀문서는 누군가가 사용하지 않는 경우에는 잠금 장치가 된 캐비닛에 두어야 합니다.

해설 be required to do 선택지의 동사 require를 보자마자 토익 빈출 표현인 〈be required to do〉 혹은 〈require A to do〉를 바로 떠올릴 수 있어야 한다. 빈칸 뒤에 목적어 없이 바로 to부정사가 이어지므로 정답은 〈be required to do〉의 형태가 되어야 하는데, 주어가 documents로 복수이므로 정답은 (C) are required이다. 이렇게 태를 묻는 문제는 시제 혹은 수 일치와 자주 결합되어 등장하므로 꼼꼼히 정답을 확인하는 과정을 거치는 것이 좋다.

어휘 confidential 기밀의 remain ~에 남다

8.

Reader's comments may be posted on the magazine's Web site, but their personal details will not be **publicized**.

(A) publication **(B) publicized**
(C) publicizing (D) publicity

독자 비평은 잡지의 웹사이트에 게시될 수 있으나 독자들의 개인 상세 정보는 공개되지 않을 것입니다.

해설 문맥상 '개인 상세 정보는 공개되지 않을 것이다'라는 수동의 의미가 자연스러우므로 수동태를 이루는 과거분사인 (B) publicized가 와야 적절하다.

어휘 post 게시하다, 공고하다; (우편물을) 발송하다; 우편 publication 발표, 공개 publicize 알리다, 홍보하다 publicity (언론의) 주목, 관심, 홍보

To: All Employees 〈stafflist@guerrafilbert.com〉
From: Michelle Wynn 〈m.wynn@guerrafilbert.com〉
Date: March 15
Subject: Business expenses

Dear Employees,

Our company is looking for ways to better monitor expenses. In light of this, a new policy for receiving reimbursement payments ⁹**will be implemented** on April 1. From that date, you must get approval for business expenses from the human resources department. ¹⁰**Please send requests to Katie Lopez before the expected purchase.** We ask that you do so at least one week in advance, if possible. In cases where last-minute spending is necessary, receipts ¹¹**must be submitted** in order to receive reimbursement from the company.

For business trips, please think about whether an in-person visit is necessary. Employees ¹²**are advised** to use video conferencing whenever possible. This will help to save both time and money.

Thank you for your cooperation in this matter.

Sincerely,

Michelle Wynn

수신: 전 직원
발신: 미셸 윈
날짜: 3월 15일
제목: 업무 경비

임직원 분들께,

우리 회사는 비용을 더 잘 관리 감독할 방법을 찾는 중입니다. 이런 상황을 감안하여, 환급금을 받는 새로운 정책이 4월 1일부터 ⁹**시행될 것입니다**. 그날부터는 업무 경비에 대해 인사팀으로부터 승인을 받아야 합니다. ¹⁰**구매 예정일 전에 케이티 로페즈에게 요청서를 보내 주세요.** 가능하다면 최소한 일주일 전에 미리 해 주시기를 바랍니다. 임박해서 비용 지출이 필요한 경우에는 회사로부터 환급을 받기 위해서는 영수증이 ¹¹**제출되어야만 합니다**.

출장의 경우에는 면대면 방문이 꼭 필요한지를 생각해 보시기 바랍니다. 직원들은 가능한 한 화상 회의 시스템을 사용하시길 ¹²**권해 드립니다**. 이는 시간과 비용 모두 줄이는 데 도움이 될 겁니다.

이 사안에 대해 협조해 주셔서 감사합니다.

미셸 윈

어휘 monitor 감독하다, 관찰하다   in light of ~을 감안하여, ~을 고려하여   reimbursement 상환, 환급, 배상   implement 시행하다
approval 승인   in case ~한 경우에   last-minute 마지막 순간의, 막바지의

---

9. (A) was implemented   (B) implementing   (C) implemented   **(D) will be implemented**

해설 동사 자리+수동태+시제 빈칸 뒤에 목적어가 없으므로 수동태가 와야 하는데 향후 있을 새로운 정책에 대해 소개하고 있으므로 미래 시제인 (D) will be implemented가 정답이다.

---

10. **(A) Please send requests to Katie Lopez before the expected purchase.**
(B) The management team reviewed the average spending for the year.
(C) The department is responsible for hiring new employees.
(D) These changes will ensure that equipment is working properly.

(A) 구매 예정일 전에 케이티 로페즈에게 요청서를 보내 주세요.
(B) 관리팀은 일 년간의 평균 지출을 검토했습니다.
(C) 그 부서는 신규 직원을 채용하는 업무를 책임지고 있습니다.
(D) 이 변화는 장비가 제대로 작동하도록 보장해 줄 것입니다.

해설 알맞은 문장 고르기 빈칸 바로 뒤 문장으로 미루어 보아 빈칸에는 환급 절차와 관련하여 요청하는 내용이 나와야 한다. (A)의 send requests to Katie Lopez before the expected purchase가 빈칸 다음 문장에서 do so로 간략하게 표현되었다.

---

11. (A) submit   (B) to submit   (C) are submitting   **(D) must be submitted**

해설 수동태 주어가 receipts, 빈칸 뒤에 목적어가 없는 문장이다. 선택지의 동사 submit가 타동사이므로 목적어를 수반하지 않으려면 수동태가 와야 한다. 선택지 중 수동태는 (D) must be submitted뿐이다.

---

12. (A) advise   (B) advising   **(C) are advised**   (D) advised

해설 수동태 advise가 능동태로 쓰이면 'advise+사람+to do'의 형태로 쓰이며, 수동태로 쓰일 경우 '사람 be advised to do'의 형태가 된다. 빈칸 뒤에 to use가 나왔으므로 수동태인 are advised가 적절하다.

UNIT 07 형용사와 부사

1 형용사 자리

본문 p.118

1. (B)   2. (D)   3. (C)   4. (A)

1.

Please note that as per company regulations, excessive spending on trips is not **acceptable**.

(A) accepting (B) **acceptable**
(C) acceptance (D) accepts

회사 규정에 따라 출장에 과도한 지출을 하는 것은 허용되지 않음을 유념하십시오.

해설 형용사 자리 [주격 보어] 빈칸은 be동사 is 뒤의 주격 보어 자리로 주어인 excessive spending(과도한 지출)의 상태를 나타내는 형용사가 와야 한다. 따라서 부정어 not과 함께 쓰여 '허용되지 않는다'라는 뜻을 만드는 (B) acceptable이 정답이다. (A) accepting은 현재분사 또는 동명사로, 현재분사일 경우 be동사 is와 함께 현재진행형 구문을 만들 수 있지만, 이 경우 accept가 타동사이므로 뒤에 목적어가 와야 한다. (C) acceptance는 명사로, 주어와 동격 관계일 때만 보어 자리에 올 수 있고, (D) accepts는 동사이므로 오답이다.

어휘 note that ~을 유념하다   as per ~에 따라   regulation ((보통 복수형)) 규정   excessive 지나친, 과도한   spending 지출   acceptable 허용할 수 있는, 받아들여지는   acceptance 수용, 받아들임

2.

The **energetic** intern finished the work in only two hours.

(A) energy (B) energies
(C) energetically (D) **energetic**

그 활기 넘치는 인턴은 업무를 단 2시간 만에 완료했다.

해설 형용사 자리 [명사 앞] 빈칸 앞에 정관사 The가 있고 뒤에는 명사 intern이 있는 것으로 보아 빈칸은 명사를 수식하는 자리이므로 형용사인 (D) energetic이 정답이다. (A) energy와 (B) energies는 명사, (C) energetically는 부사이다.

어휘 energetic 활동적인, 활기에 찬   energetically 활동적으로

3.

Ms. Bills had to pay an **additional** charge for the repair of the wall.

(A) addition (B) additionally
(C) **additional** (D) adding

빌스 씨는 벽 수리에 대해 추가 요금을 지불해야 했다.

해설 형용사 자리 [명사 앞] 빈칸 앞에 관사 an이 있고 빈칸 뒤에 명사 charge가 있는 것으로 보아 빈칸은 명사를 수식하는 자리이므로 형용사인 (C) additional이 정답이다.

어휘 pay a charge 요금을 내다   additional 추가의   repair 수리, 보수; 수리하다   addition 추가, 추가된 것

4.

The publisher of some of the best-selling books has called Adrian's novel too **predictable**.

(A) **predictable** (B) predicted
(C) prediction (D) predictably

몇몇 베스트셀러 도서들의 출판사에서는 에이드리언의 소설이 너무 뻔하다고 했다.

해설 형용사 자리 [목적격 보어] 빈칸은 〈call+목적어+목적격 보어〉 구조의 목적격 보어 자리이므로 목적어 novel의 보어 역할을 하는 형용사인 (A) predictable이 정답이다. 목적격 보어 자리에 명사가 올 수도 있지만 (C) prediction은 novel과 동격 관계가 성립하지 않으므로 오답이다. (B) predicted는 과거분사로 형용사 역할을 하지만, 여기서는 '에이드리언의 소설이 너무 예측된다'는 어색한 의미가 되어 부적합하다. (D) predictably는 부사로 보어 자리에 올 수 없다.

어휘 call A(목적어) B(목적격 보어) A를 B라고 부르다   predictable 예측할 수 있는   predict 예측하다   prediction 예측, 예견

2 수량을 나타내는 형용사

본문 p.119

1. (A)   2. (B)   3. (A)   4. (B)

1.

The marketing employees are expected to suggest **many** proposals regarding the new ad campaign.

(A) many (B) every
(C) each (D) much

마케팅 직원들은 새로운 광고 캠페인에 관한 많은 제안서를 제안해야 한다.

해설 수량을 나타내는 형용사 빈칸은 명사 proposals를 수식하는 자리이므로 복수 명사를 수식하는 수량 형용사인 (A) many가 정답이다. (B) every와 (C) each는 셀 수 있는 명사의 단수형을 수식하고, (D) much는 셀 수 없는 명사를 수식하므로 오답이다.

어휘 be expected to do 마땅히 ~을 해야만 하다; ~할 것으로 예상되다   suggest 제안하다   proposal 제안서
regarding ~에 관하여

2.

Although **other** salespeople searched for new buyers last month, Mr. Thompson focused on contacting his former buyers.

(A) each (B) other
(C) every (D) another

지난달에 다른 영업 사원들은 신규 구매자들을 찾았지만 톰슨 씨는 자신의 예전 구매자들에게 연락하는 데 집중했다.

해설 수량을 나타내는 형용사 빈칸은 명사 salespeople을 수식하는 자리이므로 복수 명사를 수식하는 수량 형용사인 (B) other가 정답이다. salespeople은 -s 같은 복수형 접미어가 없지만 그 자체로 복수 형태임을 알아 두자. (A) each, (C) every, (D) another는 모두 셀 수 있는 명사의 단수형을 수식하며, 이 중 each와 another 뒤에 of가 오면 〈each/another+of+(the) 복수 명사〉 형태로 쓴다.

어휘 although ~에도 불구하고   search for ~을 찾다   focus on ~에 집중하다   contact 연락하다; 연락   former 이전의

3.

The training session is for **all** employees in the HR Department.

(A) all (B) few
(C) each (D) enough

그 교육 과정은 인사부의 모든 직원들을 위한 것이다.

해설 수량을 나타내는 형용사 빈칸은 명사 employees를 수식하는 자리이므로 복수 명사를 수식하는 수량 형용사가 와야 한다. (A) all(모든)과 (B) few(거의 없는) 둘 다 복수 명사를 수식할 수 있지만, 문맥상 '모든 직원들을 위한 것'이라는 의미가 되어야 자연스러우므로 (A) all이 정답이다. (C) each는 셀 수 있는 명사의 단수형을 수식하며, (D) enough는 '충분한'이라는 뜻의 형용사로 문맥에 어울리지 않는다.

어휘 training 교육   HR 인적 자원 (=Human Resources)   department 부서

4.

The curator has confirmed that **every** statue in the museum is real.

(A) all (B) every
(C) some (D) few

큐레이터는 박물관의 모든 조각상이 진품이라는 것을 확인해 주었다.

해설 수량을 나타내는 형용사 빈칸은 명사 statue를 수식하는 자리이므로 셀 수 있는 명사의 단수형을 수식하는 수량 형용사인 (B) every가 정답이다. (A) all과 (C) some은 복수 명사나 셀 수 없는 명사를 수식하고, (D) few는 복수 명사를 수식하기 때문에 빈칸에 적절하지 않다.

어휘 confirm 확인하다, 확정하다   statue 조각상   real 진짜의

3 혼동하기 쉬운 형용사

본문 p.120

1. (C) 2. (A) 3. (C) 4. (B)

1.

> Kitchen appliances made by Weston, Inc. are considered **dependable** by many foreign consumers.
>
> 웨스턴 사가 만든 주방 가전제품들은 많은 외국 소비자들에게 믿을 만한 것으로 여겨진다.
>
> (A) dependent (B) depending
> **(C) dependable** (D) depend

해설 혼동하기 쉬운 형용사 이 문장은 〈consider+목적어+목적격 보어〉 구조의 5형식 구문이 수동태로 변환된 것으로, 주어 Kitchen appliances는 원래 능동태 문장의 목적어였다. 따라서 빈칸에는 kitchen appliances의 보어 역할을 할 수 있는 형용사 (C) dependable(믿을 만한)이 와야 한다. (A) dependent(의존적인)도 형용사이지만 의미가 어울리지 않고, (B) depending은 현재분사일 경우 형용사 보어 역할을 할 수 있지만 역시 의미상 어색하며, (D) depend는 동사이다.

어휘 appliance 가전제품 consider A(목적어) B(목적격 보어) A를 B라고 여기다 dependable 믿을 수 있는 foreign 외국의 consumer 소비자

2.

> All customer service representatives should be **considerate** of client requests and questions.
>
> 모든 고객 서비스 담당자들은 고객의 요청 사항과 문의 사항을 배려해야 한다.
>
> **(A) considerate** (B) considerable
> (C) consideration (D) considerately

해설 혼동하기 쉬운 형용사 빈칸은 be동사 뒤의 주격 보어 자리로, 주어인 All customer service representatives의 상태를 나타내는 형용사나 주어와 동격을 이루는 명사가 와야 하는데, 특히 여기서는 빈칸 뒤의 전치사 of와 함께 쓰일 수 있는 것을 골라야 한다. 정답은 형용사 (A) considerate로 be considerate of는 '~을 배려하다'라는 뜻이다. 형용사인 (B) considerable(상당한)은 의미가 알맞지 않고, 명사인 (C) consideration은 주어와 동격 관계가 성립하지 않으므로 오답이며, (D) considerately는 부사이다.

어휘 representative 대표자, 담당자 considerate 배려하는, 사려 깊은 client 고객 request 요청 사항

3.

> Ms. Jenkins instructed her workers to respond to every e-mail in a **timely** manner.
>
> 젠킨스 씨는 그녀의 직원들에게 모든 이메일에 제때에 답하도록 지시했다.
>
> (A) timer (B) timing
> **(C) timely** (D) time

해설 혼동하기 쉬운 형용사 빈칸은 관사 a와 명사 manner 사이의 형용사 자리이므로 (C) timely가 정답이다. timely는 -ly 형태지만 부사가 아니라 형용사임에 주의하자. (A) timer, (B) timing, (D) time은 모두 명사이다.

어휘 instruct A to do A가 ~하게 지시하다 respond to ~에 답하다 in a timely manner 시기적절하게 timer 타임 스위치, 타이머 timing 타이밍, 적당한 시기(를 택하기)

4.

> A **successful** applicant at J.B. Hooper will be offered a job immediately.
>
> 제이비 후퍼 사의 합격자는 즉시 업무를 받게 될 것이다.
>
> (A) success **(B) successful**
> (C) successfully (D) successive

해설 혼동하기 쉬운 형용사 빈칸 앞에 관사 A가 있고 뒤에는 명사 applicant가 있으므로 빈칸은 명사를 수식하는 형용사 자리다. 형용사인 (B) successful(성공한)과 (D) successive(연속적인) 중에서 의미상 applicant를 수식하기에 적합한 (B)가 정답이다. successful applicant는 '합격자'라는 의미다. (A) success는 명사로 applicant와 복합 명사를 이루지 않으며, (C) successfully는 부사이므로 명사를 수식할 수 없다.

어휘 successful applicant 합격자 offer 제공하다 job 업무 immediately 즉시, 바로

4 부사 자리

본문 p.121

1. (D) 2. (B) 3. (B) 4. (C)

1.

Construction on the apartment complex by the beach is **swiftly** happening.

(A) swiftness (B) swiftest
(C) swift **(D) swiftly**

해변 옆의 아파트 단지 공사는 신속히 이루어지고 있다.

해설 부사 자리 [be동사+부사+현재분사] 빈칸은 be동사 is와 현재분사 happening 사이의 부사 자리이므로 (D) swiftly가 정답이다. (A) swiftness는 명사, (B) swiftest는 형용사의 최상급, (C) swift는 형용사이다.

어휘 construction 공사, 건설   complex (건물) 단지   happen 일어나다, 발생하다   swiftness 신속, 빠름   swift 신속한, 빠른

2.

The outdoor event was only **partly** successful due to a weather problem.

(A) parting **(B) partly**
(C) parted (D) part

야외 행사는 날씨 문제로 부분적으로만 성공적이었다.

해설 부사 자리 [형용사 앞] 빈칸은 형용사 successful을 수식하는 자리이므로 부사인 (B) partly가 정답이다. 이 문장의 only처럼 부사는 다른 부사를 수식하기도 한다는 것을 알아 두자. (A) parting은 동명사 또는 현재분사, (C) parted는 동사의 과거형 또는 과거분사, (D) part는 명사 또는 동사로 형용사를 수식할 수 없다.

어휘 outdoor 야외의   partly 부분적으로   successful 성공한, 성공적인   due to ~ 때문에   part 부분; 나누다, 가르다

3.

Mr. Jackson is **carefully** considering opening a second restaurant downtown next year.

(A) careful **(B) carefully**
(C) carefulness (D) cared

잭슨 씨는 내년에 시내에 두 번째 음식점을 열 것을 신중히 고려 중이다.

해설 부사 자리 [be동사+부사+현재분사] 빈칸은 be동사 is와 현재분사 considering 사이의 부사 자리이므로 (B) carefully가 정답이다. (A) careful은 형용사, (C) carefulness는 명사, (D) cared는 동사의 과거형 또는 과거분사이므로 부사 자리에 올 수 없다.

어휘 carefully 신중히, 주의 깊게   consider doing ~하는 것을 고려하다   downtown 시내에   care 보살피다, 마음을 쓰다; 돌봄, 주의

4.

The forklift drivers **safely** moved the large boxes from the high shelf to the floor.

(A) safe (B) safety
(C) safely (D) safeness

지게차 운전자들이 높은 선반에 있는 대형 상자들을 바닥으로 안전하게 운반했다.

해설 부사 자리 [동사 앞] 빈칸은 동사 moved를 수식하는 자리이므로 부사인 (C) safely가 정답이다. (A) safe는 형용사, (B) safety와 (D) safeness는 명사이다.

어휘 forklift 지게차   safely 안전하게   from A to B A부터 B까지   shelf 선반   safety 안전(성)

5 다양한 형태의 부사

1. (B)   2. (A)   3. (B)   4. (D)

1.

Sylvester found several mistakes in the report, but **nevertheless** it was insightful.

(A) meanwhile (B) **nevertheless**
(C) how (D) occasionally

실베스터 씨는 그 보고서에서 몇몇 실수를 발견했지만, **그럼에도 불구하고** 그 보고서는 통찰력이 있었다.

(A) 그 사이에 (B) **그럼에도 불구하고**
(C) 어떻게 (D) 때때로

해설 **다양한 형태의 부사** 빈칸이 없어도 필수 성분을 모두 갖춘 완전한 문장이므로 빈칸은 부사 자리이다. 선택지 대부분이 부사로 구성되어 있으므로 문맥에 알맞은 것을 골라야 한다. '보고서에 실수가 있기는 했지만 통찰력이 있었다'는 맥락이므로, '그럼에도 불구하고'라는 뜻으로 양보의 의미를 전달하는 부사인 (B) nevertheless가 정답이다.

어휘 several 몇몇의   mistake 실수   insightful 통찰력 있는

2.

Ms. Carter is on vacation tomorrow but will **still** be informed about the meeting.

(A) **still** (B) quite
(C) already (D) very

카터 씨는 내일 휴가이지만 **그런데도** 회의에 관해 통보를 받을 것이다.

(A) **그런데도** (B) 꽤, 상당히
(C) 이미 (D) 매우

해설 **다양한 형태의 부사** 빈칸은 조동사 will과 동사 be informed 사이의 부사 자리이다. '휴가이지만 회의에 관해 통보를 받을 것이다'라는 의미이므로 '그런데도, 그럼에도 불구하고'라는 의미가 있는 (B) still이 알맞다.

어휘 on vacation 휴가 중인   inform 알리다, 통지하다

3.

Mr. Watkins **seldom** commutes by train except when it rains or snows.

(A) almost (B) **seldom**
(C) yet (D) quite

왓킨스 씨는 비가 오거나 눈이 올 때를 제외하고는 기차로는 **좀처럼** 출근하지 않는다.

(A) 거의 (B) **좀처럼 ~ 않는**
(C) 아직 (D) 꽤, 상당히

해설 **다양한 형태의 부사** 빈칸은 동사 commutes를 수식하는 부사 자리로, '비나 눈이 올 때를 제외하고는 기차로 출근하지 않는다'는 의미가 되어야 자연스러우므로 부정의 의미를 갖는 부사가 와야 한다. 따라서 '좀처럼 ~ 않는'이란 뜻의 부사인 (B) seldom이 정답이다. 나머지 부사는 의미상 적합하지 않다.

어휘 commute 출퇴근하다, 통근하다   except ~을 제외하고

4.

Mr. Jabili's proposal was not what the CEO expected but it was quite innovative **instead**.

(A) for example (B) consequently
(C) otherwise (D) **instead**

자빌리 씨의 제안은 대표가 예상했던 것이 아니었으나, **대신에** 꽤 획기적이었다.

(A) 예를 들어 (B) 그 결과
(C) 그렇지 않으면 (D) **대신에**

해설 **다양한 형태의 부사** 빈칸이 없어도 필수 성분을 모두 갖춘 완전한 문장이므로 빈칸은 부사 자리이다. 의미상 적합하면서 문장의 맨 마지막에 와도 어색하지 않은 부사를 골라야 한다. 정답은 (D) instead(대신에)로, '제안이 기대와는 달랐지만 대신에 획기적이었다'라는 의미가 되어 자연스럽다. instead를 포함해 나머지 선택지는 모두 접속부사로, 단독으로 접속사 역할을 할 수는 없지만 앞 문장과 뒤 문장을 의미적으로 연결해 준다.

어휘 proposal 제안   expect 기대하다, 예상하다   innovative 혁신적인

6 혼동하기 쉬운 부사

본문 p.123

1. (B)　　2. (A)　　3. (B)　　4. (D)

1.

The auditorium was **nearly** full when Dr. Burgess began her speech.	버제스 박사가 연설을 시작했을 때 강당은 거의 만석이었다.
(A) near　　　　　　(B) **nearly** (C) nearest　　　　　(D) nearing	

해설 혼동하기 쉬운 부사 빈칸은 형용사 full을 수식하는 부사 자리이므로 (B) nearly(거의)가 정답이다. '강당이 거의 만석이었다'라는 뜻이 되어 문맥상으로도 자연스럽다. (A) near는 형용사, 부사, 전치사, 동사로 쓰이는데, 부사일 때는 '가까이'라는 의미이므로 빈칸에 알맞지 않다. (C) nearest는 형용사 near의 최상급이며, (D) nearing은 동사 또는 현재분사이다.

어휘 auditorium 강당　nearly 거의　full 가득 찬　speech 연설　near 가까운; 가까이; ~ 근처에; 가까워지다

2.

The workers in the lab tried exceptionally **hard** to discover the source of the disease.	연구실의 직원들은 그 질병의 원인을 찾기 위해 특별히 열심히 노력했다.
(A) **hard**　　　　　(B) hardness (C) hardly　　　　　(D) hardest	

해설 혼동하기 쉬운 부사 빈칸 앞의 exceptionally는 '특별히'라는 의미로 다른 부사나 형용사 앞에서 강조의 의미로 쓰이는 부사이고, 빈칸이 동사 뒤에 온 것으로 보아 빈칸은 부사 자리이다. 따라서 '열심히'라는 의미의 부사로 쓰이는 (A) hard가 정답이다. hard는 형용사와 부사의 형태가 같다. (C) hardly 역시 부사이지만 '거의 ~않는'이라는 부정의 의미로 쓰이므로 문맥에 어울리지 않는다. (B) hardness는 '단단함'이라는 의미의 명사이고, (D) hardest는 hard의 최상급이다.

어휘 lab 연구실 (=laboratory)　exceptionally 특별히　discover 찾다, 발견하다　source 원천, 근원

3.

Ms. Sanderson has been **deeply** impressed with the quality of Mr. Bream's analysis.	샌더슨 씨는 브림 씨의 분석의 우수함에 깊은 인상을 받아 왔다.
(A) deepen　　　　　(B) **deeply** (C) deep　　　　　　(D) deepest	

해설 혼동하기 쉬운 부사 빈칸은 be동사와 과거분사 impressed 사이의 부사 자리로, '깊은 인상을 받았다'라는 의미가 되어야 하므로 (B) deeply가 정답이다. 이때의 deeply는 '대단히, 몹시'라는 의미다. (C) deep은 형용사와 부사로 모두 쓰이지만 부사일 때는 주로 물리적 깊이를 나타내므로 빈칸에 어울리지 않는다. (A) deepen은 동사, (D) deepest는 deep의 최상급이다.

어휘 be impressed with ~에 깊은 인상[감동]을 받다　quality 품질, 우수함　analysis 분석　deepen 깊어지다, 깊게 하다

4.

Mr. Martin will offer the position to a **highly** qualified applicant.	마틴 씨는 고도의 자격을 갖춘 지원자에게 그 직책을 제안할 것이다.
(A) highest　　　　　(B) higher (C) high　　　　　　(D) **highly**	

해설 혼동하기 쉬운 부사 빈칸은 형용사 qualified를 수식하는 부사 자리로, '자격을 아주 잘 갖춘 지원자'라는 의미가 되어야 하므로 '대단히, 매우'를 뜻하는 정도를 나타내는 부사 (D) highly가 정답이다. (C) high는 형용사와 부사로 모두 쓰이지만 부사일 때는 주로 물리적 높이를 나타내므로 문맥에 맞지 않다. (A) highest와 (B) higher는 각각 high의 최상급과 비교급이다.

어휘 offer 제안하다　position 직책　highly 매우, 대단히　qualified 자격을 갖춘　applicant 지원자

VOCABULARY

본문 p.126

1. (A) 2. (C) 3. (D) 4. (A) 5. (A) 6. (D) 7. (B) 8. (C)

1.

Several noted experts will be speaking at the **upcoming** marketing seminar.

(A) upcoming (B) possible
(C) various   (D) canceled

몇몇 유명한 전문가들이 **곧 있을** 마케팅 세미나에서 연설할 것이다.

(A) 곧 있을   (B) 가능한
(C) 다양한   (D) 취소된

> **해설** 형용사 어휘 '---- 마케팅 세미나에서 연설할 것이다'라는 문장에서 빈칸에 가장 적합한 어휘는 (A) upcoming(곧 있을, 다가오는)이다. '곧 있을 마케팅 세미나'라는 의미가 되어 이 문장의 미래 시제와도 잘 어울린다. '다양한'이라는 의미의 (C) various는 뒤에 복수 명사가 와야 한다.
>
> **어휘** noted 유명한 expert 전문가

2.

Following the safety regulations at the construction site is **mandatory** for all visitors.

(A) potential (B) specific
(C) mandatory (D) invited

건설 현장에서 안전 규정을 따르는 것은 모든 방문객들에게 **의무적**이다.

(A) 가능성 있는 (B) 구체적인
(C) 의무적인   (D) 초대받은

> **해설** 형용사 어휘 빈칸은 주어인 동명사구 Following the safety regulations(안전 규정을 따르는 것)의 보어 자리이다. '규정 준수는 의무적'이라는 의미가 되어야 가장 자연스러우므로 (C) mandatory가 정답이다.
>
> **어휘** follow 따르다, 준수하다 safety 안전 regulation ((보통 복수형)) 규정 construction 건설, 공사 site 현장, 장소

3.

Safeway Garage has been providing **reliable** service to motor vehicle owners for two decades.

(A) gradual   (B) prior
(C) implied   (D) reliable

세이프웨이 개러지 사는 20년 동안 자동차 소유주들에게 **믿을 만한** 서비스를 제공해 오고 있는 중이다.

(A) 점차적인 (B) 이전의
(C) 암시적인 (D) 믿을 만한

> **해설** 형용사 어휘 '회사가 20년 동안 ---- 서비스를 제공해 왔다'라는 문장에서 빈칸에 가장 적합한 어휘는 (D) reliable(믿을 만한)이다. 참고로 reliable과 reliant(의존하는)를 혼동하지 않도록 주의한다.
>
> **어휘** provide A to B A를 B에게 제공하다 motor vehicle 자동차 owner 소유주 decade 10년

4.

Menhaden, Inc. makes numerous appliances, but its **primary** focus is on televisions.

(A) primary   (B) informative
(C) attentive (D) estimated

맨헤이든 사는 많은 가전제품을 만들지만 **주된** 초점은 텔레비전에 두고 있다.

(A) 주된, 주요한   (B) 유익한
(C) 주의를 기울이는 (D) 추정된

> **해설** 형용사 어휘 명사 focus에 어울리는 형용사를 골라야 한다. '많은 제품을 만들지만 ---- 초점은 텔레비전에 두고 있다'라는 문장에서 빈칸에 가장 적합한 어휘는 (A) primary(주된, 주요한)이다. primary focus 외에도 main/central focus가 자주 쓰인다.
>
> **어휘** numerous 많은 appliance (가정용) 기기 focus 집중; 집중하다

5.

The **distinct** logo on the clothes clearly indicates they were made by Waltham Textiles.

(A) distinct (B) worthy
(C) reported (D) constant

옷에 있는 **뚜렷한** 로고는 그것들이 월섬 텍스타일 사가 만든 것임을 분명히 보여 준다.

(A) 뚜렷한 (B) ~을 받을 만한
(C) 보도된, 알려진 (D) 끊임없는

해설 형용사 어휘 명사 logo에 어울리는 형용사를 골라야 한다. '옷에 있는 ---- 로고가 분명히 나타내 준다'라는 문장에서 빈칸에 가장 적합한 어휘는 (A) distinct(뚜렷한, 분명한)이다.

어휘 clearly 분명히   indicate 나타내다, 보여 주다

6.

The results of the **preliminary** product test suggest the motor is not strong enough.

(A) expected (B) inexpert
(C) permanent (D) preliminary

예비 제품 시험의 결과는 모터가 충분히 강력하지 않음을 나타낸다.

(A) 예상되는 (B) 미숙한
(C) 영구적인 (D) 예비의

해설 형용사 어휘 복합 명사 product test를 수식하기에 적합한 형용사를 골라야 한다. '---- 제품 시험의 결과는 모터가 충분히 강력하지 않음을 나타낸다'라는 문장에서 빈칸에 가장 적합한 어휘는 (D) preliminary(예비의)이다. preliminary test는 '예비 시험[실험]'이라는 뜻이다.

어휘 result 결과   suggest 시사하다, 암시하다; 제안하다   enough 충분히; 충분한

7.

The accountants working on the audit must make sure their numbers are as **accurate** as possible.

(A) hesitant (B) accurate
(C) competitive (D) revised

회계 감사 작업을 하는 회계사들은 반드시 수치들이 가능한 한 **정확하도록** 해야 한다.

(A) 망설이는 (B) 정확한
(C) 경쟁력 있는 (D) 수정된

해설 형용사 어휘 빈칸 앞의 as와 빈칸 뒤의 as possible로 보아 as ~ as possible(가능한 ~한/하게) 구문임을 알 수 있다. 따라서 their numbers의 상태를 나타내는 보어 역할을 하기에 적합한 형용사가 와야 한다. '수치가 정확하다'라는 의미가 되어야 가장 자연스러우므로 정답은 (B) accurate(정확한)이다.

어휘 accountant 회계사, 회계원   audit 회계 감사   make sure (that) ~을 확실히 하다, 반드시 ~하다

8.

Mary is considering changing suppliers due to their **frequent** production delays.

(A) remote (B) dependent
(C) frequent (D) efficient

메리 씨는 납품업체의 **잦은** 생산 지연 때문에 업체를 바꾸는 걸 고려하고 있다.

(A) 외진, 먼 (B) 의존적인
(C) 잦은, 빈번한 (D) 능률적인, 효율적인

해설 형용사 어휘 production delays를 수식하기에 적합한 형용사를 골라야 한다. '---- 생산 지연 때문에 업체 변경을 고려하고 있다'는 문장에서 빈칸에 가장 적합한 어휘는 (C) frequent(잦은, 빈번한)이다.

어휘 supplier 공급업체, 공급자   due to ~ 때문에   production 생산, 제작; 제품   delay 지연, 연기

ACTUAL TEST

본문 p.128

| 1. (B) | 2. (C) | 3. (B) | 4. (D) | 5. (A) | 6. (A) |
| 7. (C) | 8. (A) | 9. (B) | 10. (A) | 11. (B) | 12. (A) |

1.

The researchers at Dynamo Metals are **cautious** when handling chemicals.

(A) caution (B) **cautious**
(C) cautions (D) cautiously

다이나모 메탈 사의 연구원들은 화학 물질을 다룰 때 조심스럽다.

해설 형용사 자리 빈칸은 be동사 are 뒤의 보어 자리로 주어 The researchers(연구원들)의 상태를 나타내는 말이 와야 하므로 형용사인 (B) cautious가 정답이다. 주격 보어 자리에는 명사도 올 수 있는데, 이때 명사는 주어와 동격 관계를 이루어야 한다. 따라서 caution이 명사로 쓰였다고 해도 주어와 동격이 아니므로 오답이다.

어휘 researcher 연구원 cautious 조심스러운 handle 다루다, 처리하다 chemical 화학 물질; 화학의

2.

The factory inspector examined each of the manufactured items **carefully**.

(A) careful (B) caring
(C) **carefully** (D) cared

공장 검사관은 제조된 제품들 각각을 주의 깊게 살펴보았다.

해설 부사 자리 필수 성분을 모두 갖춘 완전한 문장의 맨 마지막에 빈칸이 왔으므로 부사인 (C) carefully가 정답이다. (A) careful은 형용사, (B) caring은 동명사, 현재분사 또는 형용사, (D) cared는 동사의 과거형 또는 과거분사이다.

어휘 inspector 검사관, 조사관 examine 조사하다, 살펴보다 manufactured 제조된 item 제품, 물건 carefully 주의 깊게 caring 배려하는, 보살피는 care 돌보다, 주의하다; 돌봄, 주의

3.

Before every product launching, the CEO of TJ Electronics **always** tries to conduct a live product demonstration.

(A) instead (B) **always**
(C) therefore (D) well

TJ 일렉트로닉스의 대표는 모든 제품의 출시에 앞서 **항상** 라이브 제품 시연을 하려고 한다.

(A) 대신에 (B) 항상
(C) 그러므로 (D) 잘

해설 다양한 형태의 부사 '제품 출시에 앞서 ---- 라이브 제품 시연을 하려고 한다'라는 문장에서 빈칸에 가장 적합한 어휘는 (B) always(항상)이다.

어휘 launch 출시하다, 착수하다 conduct 실시하다, 수행하다 product demonstration 제품 시연[설명]

4.

Every customer at Paulson Groceries receives a free gift on holidays.

(A) None (B) A few
(C) Most (D) **Every**

폴슨 그로서리 사의 모든 고객은 휴일에 무료 사은품을 받는다.

해설 수량을 나타내는 형용사 빈칸은 명사 customer를 수식하는 자리이므로 셀 수 있는 명사의 단수형을 수식하는 수량 형용사로 쓰이는 (D) Every(모든)가 정답이다. (A) None(아무것도)은 대명사이므로 연이어 명사가 올 수 없고, (B) A few(조금 있는)는 복수 명사를 수식하며, (C) Most(대부분)는 복수 명사 또는 셀 수 없는 명사를 수식한다.

어휘 customer 고객 free gift 무료 사은품

070

5.

To reduce **excessive** spending, we're asking everyone to request approval before any large purchases.

(A) excessive (B) excessively
(C) excess (D) excesses

과도한 지출을 줄이기 위해 대량 구매 전에는 모두가 승인을 요청할 것을 부탁드리는 바입니다.

> 해설 형용사 자리 빈칸은 동사 reduce와 명사 spending 사이의 형용사 자리이므로 (A) excessive가 정답이다. (B) excessively는 부사이고, (C) excess와 (D) excesses는 명사이므로 형용사를 수식할 수 없다.

> 어휘 reduce 줄이다 excessive 지나친, 과도한 spending 지출 ask A to do A에게 ~하라고 부탁[요청]하다 request 요청하다, 신청하다 approval 승인 large purchase 대량 구매 excessively 과도하게, 지나치게 excess 초과, 과잉

6.

Guests at the Jackson Hotel are welcome to enjoy a **complimentary** breakfast following the night of your stay.

(A) complimentary (B) compliment
(C) complementary (D) complemented

잭슨 호텔의 투숙객들은 숙박한 다음 날 무료 조식을 즐기는 것을 환영합니다.

> 해설 형용사 자리 빈칸은 관사 a와 명사 breakfast 사이의 형용사 자리이므로 (A) complimentary가 정답이다. complimentary breakfast는 '무료 아침 식사'라는 의미이므로 문맥상으로도 자연스럽다. (C) complementary(보완하는)도 형용사이지만 의미상 부적합하고, (B) compliment는 명사로 '칭찬', 동사로 '칭찬하다'를 뜻하므로 역시 빈칸에 올 수 없다.

> 어휘 welcome (사람들이) 환영받는 complimentary 무료의 following 다음의 complement 보완하다, 보충하다; 보완물

7.

Individuals who wish to see the opera must book tickets **far** in advance.

(A) very (B) much
(C) far (D) hardly

그 오페라를 관람하기를 바라는 사람들은 표를 훨씬 전에 미리 예약해야만 한다.

> 해설 부사의 쓰임 완전한 문장 중간에 빈칸이 있고, 빈칸 뒤에 '미리, 사전에'를 뜻하는 부사구 in advance가 온 것으로 보아 다른 부사를 강조하는 부사가 와야 한다. 따라서 '훨씬'의 뜻을 지닌 부사 (C) far가 와서 in advance를 강조하여 '훨씬 전에 미리 예약해야 한다'라는 의미가 되는 것이 가장 적절하다. (A) very는 주로 형용사/부사의 원급이나 최상급을 수식하고, (B) much는 동사를 수식하거나 형용사/부사의 비교급과 최상급을 수식하며, (D) hardly(거의 ~ 않는)는 부정의 의미를 나타내는 부사로 문맥에 적합하지 않다.

> 어휘 individual 개인, 사람 book 예약하다 in advance 미리

8.

Scott stated he would be **responsible** for the Web site redesign project.

(A) responsible (B) to respond
(C) responsibly (D) responding

스콧 씨는 자신이 웹사이트 리뉴얼 프로젝트를 맡게 될 것이라고 말했다.

> 해설 형용사 자리 빈칸은 be동사 뒤의 주격 보어 자리로, 빈칸 뒤의 전치사 for와 어울리면서 주어 he의 상태를 나타내는 형용사를 골라야 하므로 (A) responsible이 정답이다. be responsible for는 '~에 책임이 있다'라는 뜻이다. (B) to respond는 to부정사, (C) responsibly는 부사이고, (D) responding은 be동사와 함께 진행 시제로 쓰일 수 있으나 문맥상 적절하지 않다.

> 어휘 state 말하다, 진술하다 responsible 책임이 있는 redesign 다시 디자인하다, 외관[기능]을 고치다

OLYMPIA (August 2)—The second annual Olympia Summer Festival will begin tomorrow morning at 9:00 at Landside Park. The festival is expected to be attended by an ⁹**enthusiastic** crowd of local residents.

Last year's festival featured games, rides, arts and crafts, and numerous local delicacies. ¹⁰ **This year's event includes musical performances.** The festival's organizer, Marilyn Stewart, has high hopes for the event. "We expect large numbers of people to come every day. ¹¹ **However**, the festival won't be too crowded as Landside Park covers a large area." Ms. Stewart assured that festival-goers will have fun in a safe and entertaining environment.

Attendance at the festival is $2 per day. ¹² **All** profits from the festival will be donated to the local community center.

올림피아 (8월 2일) - 제2회 연례 올림피아 서머 페스티벌이 내일 아침 9시에 랜드사이드 파크에서 시작될 것이다. 축제에는 ⁹ **열정적인** 지역 주민들이 대거 참석할 것으로 예상된다.

작년 축제는 게임, 놀이 기구, 미술, 공예 및 많은 지역 별미들을 특색으로 했다. ¹⁰ **올해의 행사에는 음악 공연이 포함된다.** 축제 주최자인 매릴린 스튜어트는 행사에 거는 기대가 크다. "저희는 매일 수많은 사람들이 올 것으로 예상합니다. ¹¹ **하지만** 랜드사이드 파크가 넓은 지역에 걸쳐 있으므로 그리 혼잡하지는 않을 것입니다." 스튜어트 씨는 축제 참가자들이 안전하고 즐거운 환경에서 재미있는 시간을 보내게 될 것이라고 장담했다.

축제 참가는 하루에 2달러이다. 축제의 ¹² **모든** 수익은 지역 문화 센터에 기부될 것이다.

어휘 annual 연례의 be expected to *do* ~할 것으로 예상되다 enthusiastic 열정적인 local 지역의 resident 주민, 거주자 feature 특색으로 하다 craft 공예 delicacy (지역의) 별미, 진미 include 포함하다 performance 공연 organizer 주최자, 조직자 have high hopes 포부가 크다 crowded 혼잡한, 붐비는 cover (언급된 지역에) 걸치다 assure 장담하다 festival-goer 축제에 가는 사람 entertaining 재미있는, 즐거움을 주는 attendance 참석, 참여 profit 이익, 수익

---

9. (A) enthusiasm (B) **enthusiastic**
(C) enthusing (D) enthusiastically

해설 형용사 자리 빈칸은 관사 an 뒤에서 명사 crowd를 수식하는 자리이므로 형용사인 (B) enthusiastic(열정적인)이 정답이다. (C) enthusing은 동명사 또는 현재분사로, 형용사 자리 문제에서 의미가 비슷한 형용사와 현재분사가 함께 선택지로 제시될 경우 형용사가 우선한다는 것도 알아 두자. (A) enthusiasm은 명사, (D) enthusiastically는 부사이므로 빈칸에 올 수 없다.

어휘 enthusiasm 열정 enthuse 열변을 토하다

---

10. (A) **This year's event includes musical performances.**
(B) Most attendees enjoyed going to the festival.
(C) Games are popular with local children.
(D) Most residents will attend the festival once.

(A) 올해의 행사에는 음악 공연이 포함된다.
(B) 대부분의 참석자들은 축제에 가는 것을 즐겼다.
(C) 게임은 지역 아이들에게 인기가 있다.
(D) 대부분의 주민들은 축제에 한 번 참석할 것이다.

해설 알맞은 문장 고르기 빈칸 앞에서 작년 행사의 특징들을 나열했으므로 빈칸에서는 올해의 행사 내용을 언급하는 것이 자연스럽다. 따라서 '올해의 행사에는 음악 공연이 포함된다'고 한 (A)가 정답이다.

어휘 attendee 참석자 be popular with ~에게 인기가 있다

---

11. (A) Apparently (B) **However**
(C) In addition (D) Therefore

(A) 보아하니 (B) **하지만**
(C) 게다가, 또한 (D) 그러므로

해설 접속부사 빈칸 앞의 문장에서는 '수많은 사람들이 올 것으로 예상된다'고 했고, 빈칸 뒤의 문장에서는 '그다지 혼잡하지 않을 것'이라고 했으므로 서로 대조적인 내용을 자연스럽게 이어 주는 접속부사로 쓰이는 (B) However가 정답이다.

---

12. (A) **All** (B) Each
(C) Little (D) Much

(A) **모든** (B) 각각
(C) 거의 없는 (D) 많은

해설 수량을 나타내는 형용사 빈칸은 명사 profits를 수식하는 자리이므로 셀 수 있는 명사의 복수형을 수식하는 수량 형용사로 쓰이는 (A) All이 정답이다. all 뒤에는 셀 수 없는 명사도 올 수 있다. (B) Each는 뒤에 셀 수 있는 명사의 단수 형태가 오며, (C) Little과 (D) Much는 뒤에 셀 수 없는 명사가 오므로 오답이다.

UNIT 08 전치사

1 전치사 자리

본문 p.134

1. (C)   2. (B)   3. (C)   4. (C)

1.

Timesheets submitted **after** 5:00 P.M. today will be applied to the next pay period.

(A) later (B) sometimes
(C) after (D) than

오늘 오후 5시 이후에 제출되는 근무 시간 기록표는 다음 급여 지급 주기에 적용될 것입니다.

해설 전치사 자리 [명사 앞] 빈칸 뒤에 명사 5:00 P.M.이 있으므로 빈칸에는 명사를 목적어로 취할 수 있는 전치사가 들어가야 한다. 문맥상 오후 5시 이후에 제출되는 근무 기록표가 다음 급여 지급 주기에 적용될 것이라는 내용이 되어야 자연스러우므로 (C) after가 정답이다. (A) later(나중에)와 (B) sometimes(때때로)는 부사이므로 오답이다.

어휘 timesheet 근무 시간 기록표 apply 적용하다 pay period 급여 지급 주기

2.

By providing online services, Bikers Fabric could break into new markets.

(A) From   (B) By
(C) Indeed (D) Likewise

온라인 서비스를 제공함으로써 바이커스 패브릭은 새로운 시장으로 진입할 수 있었다.

해설 전치사 자리 [동명사 앞] 빈칸 뒤에 동명사 providing이 있으므로 빈칸에는 명사를 목적어로 취할 수 있는 전치사가 들어가야 한다. 문맥상 온라인 서비스를 제공함으로써 새로운 시장으로 진입할 수 있었다는 내용이 되어야 자연스러우므로 방법이나 수단을 나타내는 전치사 (B) By가 정답이다. (C) Indeed(정말로)와 (D) Likewise(마찬가지로)는 부사이므로 오답이다.

어휘 provide 제공하다, 공급하다 break into ~에 진입하다; ~에 침입하다

3.

Non-members are required to register online **upon** arrival at the convention center.

(A) about (B) still
(C) upon   (D) even

회원이 아닌 사람들은 컨벤션 센터에 도착하는 대로 온라인으로 등록해야 한다.

해설 전치사 자리 [명사 앞] 빈칸 뒤에 명사 arrival이 있으므로 빈칸에는 명사를 목적어로 취할 수 있는 전치사가 들어가야 한다. 문맥상 회원이 아니면 컨벤션 센터에 도착하는 대로 온라인으로 등록해야 한다는 내용이 되어야 자연스러우므로 '~하자마자'라는 뜻의 전치사인 (C) upon이 정답이다. 이때의 upon은 on으로 바꾸어 쓸 수 있다. (B) still(아직도)과 (D) even(~조차; 훨씬)은 부사이므로 오답이다.

어휘 be required to do ~하는 것이 요구되다 register 등록하다 arrival 도착

4.

Visitors must put on a hardhat **before** entering the construction site.

(A) quite   (B) out of
(C) before (D) then

방문객들은 공사 현장에 들어가기 전에 안전모를 착용해야 한다.

해설 전치사 자리 [동명사 앞] 빈칸 뒤에 동명사 entering이 있으므로 빈칸에는 명사를 목적어로 취할 수 있는 전치사가 들어가야 한다. 문맥상 공사 현장에 들어가기 전에는 반드시 안전모를 착용해야 한다는 내용이 되어야 자연스러우므로 (C) before가 정답이다. (B) out of(~에서; ~ 밖으로)는 전치사이지만 의미상 어울리지 않고, (A) quite(꽤)와 (D) then(그때; 그러면)은 부사이므로 오답이다.

어휘 put on ~을 착용하다, ~을 입다 hardhat 안전모 enter 들어가다, 입장하다 construction 공사, 건설 site 현장, 장소

2 시간·장소 전치사

본문 p.135

1. (D)   2. (C)   3. (D)   4. (A)

1.

Mr. Masters hopes to open a café **in** the theater district downtown next month.

(A) on
(B) to
(C) among
(D) in

마스터스 씨는 다음 달에 시내의 극장가에 카페를 열기를 바란다.

> [해설] 장소 전치사 in 빈칸 뒤에 장소를 나타내는 명사 the theater district가 있으므로 비교적 넓은 장소를 나타낼 때 쓰는 전치사인 (D) in이 정답이다. (A) on은 표면에 맞닿은 것이나 거리, 층수 또는 날짜, 요일을 말할 때 쓰고, (B) to는 방향을 나타내며, (C) among은 셋 이상에서 '~ 사이에'의 의미로 쓰이므로 모두 오답이다.

> [어휘] hope to do ~하기를 바라다   district 구역, 지역   downtown 시내에

2.

Ms. Wellborn had a taxi drop her off **at** the Clyburn Community Center.

(A) for
(B) on
(C) at
(D) up

웰본 씨는 택시 기사에게 클라이번 커뮤니티 센터에 내려 달라고 했다.

> [해설] 장소 전치사 at 빈칸 뒤의 장소 명사 the Clyburn Community Center는 웰본 씨가 가려고 하는 특정 목적지이다. 따라서 '특정 지점'을 나타내는 장소 전치사인 (C) at이 정답이다. (A) for는 목적, 방향, 기간을 나타내고, (B) on은 표면에 맞닿은 것이나 거리, 층수 또는 날짜, 요일을 말할 때 쓰고, (D) up(~ 위로)은 방향을 나타낸다.

> [어휘] have+사람+do ~가 ~하게 만들다(설득하다, 명령하다)   drop off ~을 내려 주다

3.

The wood flooring **on** the second floor of the building will be replaced.

(A) between
(B) in
(C) against
(D) on

건물 2층에 있는 원목 바닥재는 교체될 것이다.

> [해설] 장소 전치사 on 빈칸 뒤에 층수를 나타내는 명사 the second floor가 있으므로 (D) on이 정답이다. (B) in 역시 장소 전치사로 쓰이기는 하지만 비교적 넓은 장소나 무언가의 내부를 나타낼 때 쓰기 때문에 이 문장에는 적절하지 않다. (A) between(~ 사이에)과 (C) against(~에 맞서, ~에 반대하여)도 의미상 적절하지 않으므로 오답이다.

> [어휘] flooring 바닥재   replace 교체하다

4.

The keynote speech at the biotechnology conference is scheduled to start **at** 9:30 A.M.

(A) at
(B) in
(C) for
(D) of

생명 공학 학회에서의 기조연설은 오전 9시 30분에 시작될 예정이다.

> [해설] 시간 전치사 at 빈칸 뒤에 구체적인 시각을 나타내는 명사 9:30 A.M.이 있으므로 (A) at이 정답이다. (B) in은 연도, 월, 계절 등을 나타내는 명사와 함께 쓰이고, (C) for(~ 동안)는 기간을 나타내며, (D) of는 앞뒤 명사가 소유 관계일 때 쓴다.

> [어휘] keynote speech 기조연설   biotechnology 생명 공학   conference 학회   be scheduled to do ~할 예정이다

3 기간 전치사

본문 p.136

1. (D)   2. (B)   3. (D)   4. (B)

1.

> **During** his business trip to Europe, Dr. Gills attended the Svalbard Science Conference.
>
> (A) Without   (B) Upon
> (C) For   **(D) During**

유럽 출장 동안 길스 박사는 스발바르 과학 콘퍼런스에 참석했다.

해설 기간 전치사 during 문맥상 유럽 출장 동안 과학 콘퍼런스에 참석했다는 내용이 되어야 자연스러우므로 '~ 동안'을 뜻하는 (D) During이 정답이다. (C) For 역시 기간 전치사로 쓰이지만 뒤에 숫자로 표현된 기간이 와야 하므로 이 문장에는 적절하지 않다.

어휘 business trip 출장   attend 참석하다, 출석하다

2.

> The sales figures **from** last week to this week increased sharply, marking a new record.
>
> (A) within   **(B) from**
> (C) to   (D) before

지난주부터 이번 주까지 매출액이 급격하게 증가하여 최고치를 기록했다.

해설 기간 전치사 from 문맥상 지난주부터 이번 주까지 매출액이 급격하게 증가했다는 내용이 되어야 자연스러우므로 '~부터'를 뜻하는 (B) from이 정답이다. (A) within(~ 내에)은 기간을 나타내지만 의미상 적절하지 않으므로 오답이다. (C) to(~ 쪽으로, ~까지)는 방향이나 도달점을 나타내며, (D) before(~ 전에, ~ 앞에는) 시간 또는 위치상의 전후 관계를 나타낸다.

어휘 sales figures 매출액   sharply 급격히; 날카롭게   mark a record 기록을 남기다, 기록을 세우다

3.

> Decisions regarding employee transfers will be made **within** the next forty-eight hours.
>
> (A) behind   (B) toward
> (C) from   **(D) within**

인사 이동에 관한 결정은 다음 48시간 이내에 이뤄질 것이다.

해설 기간 전치사 within 문맥상 48시간 이내에 결정이 이뤄질 것이라는 내용이 되어야 자연스러우므로 '~ 이내에'를 뜻하는 (D) within이 정답이다. (C) from(~부터)이 기간 전치사로 쓰이면 시작 시점을 나타내고, (A) behind(~ 뒤에)와 (B) toward(~ 쪽으로, ~을 향하여)는 장소를 나타내는 전치사이므로 오답이다.

어휘 make a decision 결정하다   regarding ~에 관하여   employee transfer 인사 이동

4.

> Dr. Stephen from Barshire University was very cooperative **throughout** the entire interview session.
>
> (A) from   **(B) throughout**
> (C) within   (D) by

바샤이어 대학의 스티븐 박사는 인터뷰 시간 내내 매우 협조적이었다.

해설 기간 전치사 throughout 문맥상 스티븐 박사는 인터뷰 내내 협조적이었다는 내용이 되어야 자연스러우므로 '~ 내내'를 뜻하는 (B) throughout이 정답이다. (A) from은 시작 시점을 나타내며, (C) within(~ 내에)은 정해진 시간 안에 무언가를 한다는 맥락에서 쓰이고, (D) by는 특정 시점까지 행위나 동작이 완료되는 것을 강조하는 전치사이므로 모두 이 문장에는 적절하지 않다.

어휘 cooperative 협조하는; 협력[협동]하는   entire 전체의

4 기타 전치사

본문 p.137

1. (C)   2. (B)   3. (A)   4. (B)

1.

The intern will replace Ms. Reed **as** a junior accountant after he graduates.	그 인턴은 졸업 후에 신참 회계사로서 리드 씨를 대체할 것이다.
(A) like   (B) on
(C) as (D) about	

해설 기타 전치사 문맥상 그 인턴이 신참 회계사라는 역할로 리드 씨의 자리를 대신할 거라는 내용이 되어야 자연스러우므로 역할 또는 자격을 나타내는 전치사 (C) as(~로서)가 정답이다. (A) like(~처럼)와 (B) on(~에), 그리고 (D) about(~에 대해서)은 모두 의미상 어울리지 않는 전치사이므로 오답이다.

어휘 replace 교체하다, 대체하다   accountant 회계사, 회계원   graduate 졸업하다

2.

All the problems with the product **besides** its design were discussed at the board meeting.	디자인 외에도 제품에 대한 모든 문제점들이 이사회 회의에서 논의되었다.
(A) beside   (B) besides
(C) through (D) for	

해설 기타 전치사 문맥상 디자인 외에도 제품의 전반적인 문제점들이 모두 논의되었다는 내용이 되어야 자연스러우므로 '~ 이외에도'를 뜻하는 (B) besides가 정답이다. 형태가 유사한 (A) beside는 '~ 옆에'라는 의미이기 때문에 이 문장에는 적절하지 않다.

어휘 discuss 논의하다, 상의하다   board 이사회

3.

When the investors heard **about** the upcoming product plan, they were eager to sign the investment contract.	투자자들이 곧 나올 상품 계획에 대해 들었을 때, 그들은 투자 계약을 체결하고 싶어 했다.
(A) about   (B) without
(C) through (D) except	

해설 기타 전치사 문맥상 상품 계획에 대해 들었을 때 투자 계약을 체결하고 싶어 했다는 내용이 되어야 자연스러우므로 '~에 대해서'를 뜻하는 (A) about이 정답이다. (B) without(~ 없이)과 (C) through(~을 통해), 그리고 (D) except(~을 제외하고)는 모두 의미상 어울리지 않는 전치사이므로 오답이다.

어휘 upcoming 다가오는, 곧 있을   be eager to do ~하기를 간절히 바라다   sign the contract 계약을 체결하다

4.

Mr. Teakwood had to submit his reimbursement form **without** any receipts after losing them.	틱우드 씨는 영수증을 잃어버린 후에 그것들 없이 환급 서식을 제출해야 했다.
(A) with   (B) without
(C) through (D) except	

해설 기타 전치사 문맥상 losing them에서 them이 receipts를 가리키므로 영수증 없이 환급 서식을 제출했다는 내용이 되어야 자연스럽다. 따라서 '~ 없이'를 뜻하는 (B) without이 정답이다. (A) with(~와 함께, ~을 가지고)와 (C) through(~을 통해), 그리고 (D) except(~을 제외하고)는 모두 의미상 어울리지 않는 전치사이므로 오답이다.

어휘 submit 제출하다   reimbursement 환급, 배상   form 서식   receipt 영수증

5 혼동하기 쉬운 전치사: until vs. by

본문 p.138

1. (C)　　2. (A)　　3. (B)　　4. (A)

1.

The Cumberland Gallery will remain open **until** 8:00 P.M. this weekend.	컴벌랜드 갤러리는 이번 주말에 오후 8시까지 문을 열어 둘 것이다.
(A) by　　　　　　　(B) for **(C) until**　　　　　　(D) on	

해설 until vs. by 빈칸 앞에 remain open이 있는 것으로 보아 이번 주말에는 오후 8시까지 '계속' 문을 열어 둔다는 내용이 되어야 한다. 따라서 '지속'의 의미가 있는 (C) until이 정답이다. (A) by는 특정 시점까지 행위나 동작이 '완료'되는 것을 강조하는 전치사이므로 이 문장에는 적절하지 않다. (B) for는 뒤에 구체적인 기간을 나타내는 말이 이어져야 하며, (D) on은 날짜와 요일, 그리고 특정한 날을 가리키는 말과 어울리기 때문에 빈칸에 적절하지 않다.

어휘 remain ~한 상태로 남다

2.

The second round of interviews will continue **until** the end of the day.	2차 면접은 하루가 끝날 무렵까지 계속될 것이다.
(A) until　　　　　　(B) for (C) by　　　　　　　(D) over	

해설 until vs. by 빈칸 앞에 continue가 있는 것으로 보아 2차 면접은 하루가 끝날 때까지 '계속' 진행될 것이라는 내용이 되어야 한다. 따라서 '지속'의 의미가 있는 (A) until이 정답이다. (C) by는 특정 시점까지 행위나 동작이 '완료'되는 것을 강조하는 전치사이므로 이 문장에는 적절하지 않다. (B) for는 구체적인 기간을 나타내는 말이 이어져야 하며, (D) over가 기간을 나타내는 말과 함께 쓰일 땐 '~ 동안에, ~에 걸쳐서'를 뜻하는데 이 문장에는 어울리지 않는 의미이므로 오답이다.

어휘 interview 면접　continue 계속되다

3.

Clients must submit their completed customer service surveys **by** 9:00 A.M. Monday morning.	고객들은 월요일 오전 9시까지 작성이 완료된 고객 서비스 설문지를 제출해야 한다.
(A) at　　　　　　　**(B) by** (C) with　　　　　　(D) until	

해설 until vs. by 빈칸 앞에 동사 submit이 있는 것으로 보아 작성이 완료된 설문지는 월요일 오전까지 제출을 '완료'해야 한다는 내용이 되어야 한다. 따라서 '완료'의 의미가 있는 (B) by가 정답이다. (D) until은 특정 시점까지 행위나 동작이 '지속'되는 것을 강조하는 전치사이므로 이 문장에는 적절하지 않다. (A) at은 구체적이고 특정한 시점에 어떤 행위가 일어난다는 걸 나타내는 말이며, (C) with는 '~와 함께'를 뜻하기 때문에 오답이다.

어휘 client 고객　submit 제출하다　complete (서식 등을) 빠짐없이 작성하다 (= fill in)　survey 설문 조사

4.

All construction workers should enter their hours into the computer **by** 4:00 P.M. on Friday.	모든 건설 작업자들은 금요일 오후 4시까지 그들의 근무 시간을 컴퓨터에 입력해야 한다.
(A) by　　　　　　　(B) until (C) with　　　　　　(D) in	

해설 until vs. by 문맥상 작업자들은 금요일 오후 4시까지 근무 시간 입력을 '완료'해야 한다는 내용이 되어야 한다. 따라서 '완료'의 의미가 있는 (A) by가 정답이다. (B) until은 특정 시점까지 행위나 동작이 '지속'되는 것을 강조하는 전치사이므로 이 문장에는 적절하지 않다. (C) with는 '~와 함께'를 뜻하며, (D) in은 비교적 길고 광범위한 기간을 나타내는 말과 함께 쓰기 때문에 이 문장에는 어울리지 않는 전치사이다.

어휘 construction 건설, 공사　enter one's hours ~의 근무 시간을 입력하다

6 -ing형 전치사

본문 p.139

1. (B) 2. (C) 3. (B) 4. (B)

1.

The regulations **concerning** usage of company vehicles were altered at Monday's staff meeting.

회사 차량 사용에 관한 규정들이 월요일 직원 회의에서 변경되었다.

(A) through (B) **concerning**
(C) though (D) excluding

해설 -ing형 전치사 concerning 빈칸 뒤에 명사구(usage ~ vehicles)가 있으므로 빈칸은 명사구를 목적어로 취하는 전치사 자리이다. 문맥상 '회사 차량 사용에 관한 규정들'이 되어야 자연스러우므로 '~에 관하여'를 뜻하는 (B) concerning이 정답이다. (A) through(~을 통하여)와 (D) excluding(~을 제외하고)은 전치사이지만 모두 문맥에 어울리지 않기 때문에 오답이다. (C) though는 접속사 또는 부사이므로 빈칸에 적절하지 않다.

어휘 regulation ((보통 복수형)) 규정 usage 사용 alter 변경하다, 고치다 though 비록 ~일지라도; 그래도, 그렇지만

2.

All coupons for Zack's, **including** those issued online, will expire on December 31.

온라인에서 발급받은 것들을 포함해 잭스의 모든 쿠폰은 12월 31일에 만료될 것이다.

(A) included (B) includes
(C) including (D) inclusion

해설 -ing형 전치사 including 빈칸 뒤에 대명사 those가 있으므로 빈칸은 명사를 목적어로 취하는 전치사 또는 현재분사 자리이다. 따라서 -ing형 전치사로 쓰이는 한편 그 자체가 분사 형용사인 (C) including(~을 포함하여)이 정답이다. (A) included는 동사 또는 과거분사, (B) includes는 동사, (D) inclusion은 명사이므로 오답이다.

어휘 issue 발급하다 expire 만료되다 include 포함하다 inclusion 포함

3.

Ms. Toole's response **regarding** the missing laptop stressed the need for security.

분실한 노트북에 관한 툴 씨의 답변은 보안의 필요성을 강조했다.

(A) as (B) **regarding**
(C) following (D) onto

해설 -ing형 전치사 regarding 문맥상 '분실한 노트북에 관한 답변'이 되어야 자연스러우므로 '~에 관하여'를 뜻하는 (B) regarding이 정답이다. (A) as(~로서)와 (C) following(~ 이후에), 그리고 (D) onto(~ 위로; ~ 쪽으로)는 모두 문맥에 어울리지 않는다.

어휘 response 답변, 반응 missing 분실한 laptop 노트북 컴퓨터 stress 강조하다 need 필요(성) security 보안

4.

Following the release of the movie, Anne Stanton became famous all around the world.

그 영화의 개봉 후에 앤 스탠턴은 전 세계적으로 유명해졌다.

(A) About **(B) Following**
(C) Including (D) Regarding

해설 -ing형 전치사 following 문맥상 영화의 개봉 이후에 전 세계적으로 유명해졌다는 내용이 되어야 자연스러우므로 '~ 이후에'라는 의미로 시간의 전후 관계를 나타내는 (B) Following이 정답이다. (A) About(~에 대하여)과 (C) Including(~을 포함하여), 그리고 (D) Regarding(~에 관하여)은 모두 문맥에 어울리지 않는다.

어휘 release 출시, 개봉; 출시[개봉]하다 famous 유명한 all around the world 전 세계적으로

VOCABULARY

본문 p.142

1. (C) 2. (C) 3. (A) 4. (D) 5. (B) 6. (C) 7. (D) 8. (D)

1.

As **of** Monday, January 19, the company's name will change to Data Xpress.	1월 19일 월요일**부터** 회사명이 데이터 엑스프레스로 변경될 것이다.
(A) for (B) on **(C) of** (D) by	

해설 전치사구 문맥상 월요일부터 회사명이 변경될 것이라는 내용이 되어야 자연스러우므로 빈칸 앞의 As와 어울려 '~ 일자로, ~부터'를 뜻하는 (C) of가 정답이다. as for는 '~에 관해 말하자면'을 의미하기 때문에 (A) for는 빈칸에 적절하지 않다.

어휘 change 변경되다

2.

Instead of paying employees cash bonuses, vacation packages were awarded by the firm.	직원들에게 현금 보너스를 지급하는 **대신에** 회사에 의해 휴가 패키지 여행 상품이 주어졌다.
(A) In favor of (B) Due to **(C) Instead of** (D) Aware of	(A) ~에 찬성하여 (B) ~ 때문에 **(C) ~ 대신에** (D) ~을 인지하는

해설 전치사구 문맥상 현금 보너스 대신 휴가 패키지가 주어졌다는 내용이 되어야 자연스러우므로 '~ 대신에'라는 의미의 (C) Instead of가 정답이다.

어휘 pay+간목+직목 ~에게 ~를 지급하다, 지불하다 vacation 휴가 award (돈이나 상 등을) 주다, 수여하다

3.

Applicants must submit a résumé **along with** three letters of recommendation to Mr. Pruitt.	지원자들은 프루이트 씨에게 추천서 세 부**와 함께** 이력서를 제출해야 한다.
(A) along with (B) as well (C) in light of (D) in case of	**(A) ~와 함께** (B) 또한 (C) ~을 고려하여 (D) ~의 경우에

해설 전치사구 문맥상 추천서와 함께 이력서를 제출해야 한다는 내용이 되어야 자연스러우므로 '~와 함께'라는 의미의 (A) along with가 정답이다.

어휘 applicant 지원자 submit 제출하다 résumé 이력서 letter of recommendation 추천서

4.

In **response** to increasing demand, the assembly line will now operate 24 hours a day.	증가하는 수요에 **대응**하여 이제 조립 라인은 24시간 가동될 것이다.
(A) variety (B) fact (C) access **(D) response**	(A) 다양성 (B) 사실 (C) 접근 **(D) 대응**

해설 전치사구 문맥상 증가하는 수요에 대응하여 조립 라인을 하루 종일 가동할 거라는 내용이 되어야 자연스러우므로 빈칸 앞뒤의 In, to와 어울려 '~에 대응하여'를 의미할 수 있는 (D) response가 정답이다.

어휘 demand 수요 assembly line (공장 등의) 조립 라인 operate 운영되다

5.

Aside from the significant increase in cost, many members have expressed dissatisfaction with some of the services at the fitness center.

(A) Owing to (B) Aside from
(C) According to (D) By means of

큰 폭의 가격 인상 **외에도** 많은 회원들이 그 체육관의 여러 가지 서비스에 불만을 드러냈다.

(A) ~ 때문에 (B) ~ 이외에도
(C) ~에 따라 (D) ~을 이용하여

해설 전치사구 문장 뒷부분에서 고객들이 여러 서비스에 불만을 표출했다고 했고, 빈칸 바로 뒷부분에서도 불만의 요소가 될 수 있는 '가격 상승'에 대해 언급하고 있으므로 문두에는 '~을 포함하여' 또는 '~ 이외에도'라는 전치사구가 오는 것이 적절하다. 따라서 (B) Aside from(=Apart from)이 정답이다.

어휘 significant 상당한 express 표현하다, 나타내다 dissatisfaction 불만

6.

Charles's team has a reputation for completing projects **ahead of** schedule.

(A) in particular (B) with regard
(C) ahead of (D) onto

찰스의 팀은 프로젝트를 일정보다 **앞서** 완료한다는 평판을 듣는다.

(A) 특히 (B) ~와 관련하여
(C) ~에 앞서 (D) ~ 위로; ~ 쪽으로

해설 전치사구 빈칸 뒤에 명사 schedule이 있는 것으로 보아 시간의 전후 관계를 나타내는 전치사가 적절한 자리이다. 문맥상 프로젝트를 일정보다 앞서 완료한다는 내용이 되어야 자연스러우므로 (C) ahead of(~에 앞서)가 정답이다. (B) with regard는 with regard to의 형태로 '~와 관련하여'를 뜻하기 때문에 빈칸에 적절하지 않다.

어휘 have a reputation for ~라는 평판을 얻다, ~로 명성이 있다 complete 완료하다

7.

Customers will retain all membership points accumulated **prior to** the merger.

(A) as to (B) in terms of
(C) without (D) prior to

고객들은 합병 **전에** 누적된 모든 멤버십 포인트를 계속 유지할 것이다.

(A) ~에 관하여 (B) ~의 관점에서
(C) ~ 없이 (D) ~ 전에

해설 전치사구 문맥상 고객들은 합병 전에 누적된 포인트를 모두 그대로 유지할 것이라는 내용이 되어야 자연스러우므로 '~ 전에'라는 의미의 (D) prior to가 정답이다.

어휘 retain (계속) 보유하다, 유지하다 accumulate 누적하다, 축적하다 merger 합병

8.

The legal document has all the required signatures **except for** Mr. Roswell's.

(A) depending on (B) instead
(C) throughout (D) except for

그 법률 서류에는 로스웰 씨의 것**을 제외하고** 모든 필요한 서명이 있다.

(A) ~에 따라 (B) 대신에
(C) ~ 내내 (D) ~을 제외하고

해설 전치사구 문맥상 법률 서류에는 로스웰 씨의 서명을 제외한 모든 서명이 있다는 내용이 되어야 자연스러우므로 '~을 제외하고'라는 의미의 (D) except for가 정답이다.

어휘 legal 법률의 require 요구하다, 필요로 하다 signature 서명

ACTUAL TEST

본문 p.144

1. (A) 2. (A) 3. (A) 4. (B) 5. (C) 6. (B)
7. (A) 8. (C) 9. (B) 10. (C) 11. (D) 12. (A)

1.

Ms. Carter has a layover in Dublin **before** arriving in Copenhagen tomorrow.

(A) before (B) about
(C) while (D) because

카터 씨는 내일 코펜하겐에 도착하기 전에 더블린에서 경유를 한다.

해설 전치사 자리 [동명사 앞] 빈칸 뒤에 동명사 arriving이 있으므로 빈칸에는 명사를 목적어로 취할 수 있는 전치사가 들어가야 한다. 문맥상 코펜하겐에 도착하기 전에 더블린에서 경유를 한다는 내용이 되어야 하므로 '~ 전에'라는 의미의 (A) before가 정답이다. (B) about(~에 대해서)은 전치사이지만 의미상 적절하지 않다. (C) while(~ 동안)과 (D) because(~ 때문에)는 접속사이므로 뒤에 주어와 동사를 갖춘 절이 이어져야 하기 때문에 오답이다.

어휘 layover (일시적인) 체류, 경유

2.

The supervisors always submit employee evaluations **by** the end of the month.

(A) by (B) under
(C) until (D) throughout

상사들은 항상 매월 말까지 직원 평가서를 제출한다.

해설 until vs. by 빈칸 앞에 동사 submit가 있는 것으로 보아 항상 월말까지 직원 평가서 제출을 '완료'해야 한다는 내용이 되어야 한다. 따라서 '완료'의 의미가 있는 (A) by가 정답이다. (C) until은 특정 시점까지 행위나 동작이 '지속'되는 것을 강조하는 전치사이므로 여기서는 적절하지 않다. (B) under와 (D) throughout은 각각 '~ 아래에; ~하는 중이'과 '~ 내내'를 뜻하는데 이 문장에는 어울리지 않는 의미이므로 오답이다.

어휘 supervisor 상사, 감독관 submit 제출하다 evaluation 평가(서)

3.

Mitch Stallings will be working in the PR Department **from** next Monday onward.

(A) from (B) since
(C) for (D) within

밋치 스톨링스는 앞으로 다음 주 월요일부터 홍보 부서에서 일하게 될 것이다.

해설 기간 전치사 from 문맥상 월요일부터 홍보 부서에서 일할 거라는 내용이 되어야 하므로 시작 시점을 나타내는 전치사인 (A) from(~부터)이 정답이다. (B) since(~ 이래로)는 주로 현재완료 시제와 어울려 쓰이며, 의미상으로도 빈칸에 적절하지 않다.

어휘 department 부서 onward(s) 앞으로, (특정 시점부터) 계속

4.

Depending on the size of the parcel, it might leave the warehouse tomorrow morning.

(A) Dependent to (B) **Depending on**
(C) Depended (D) To depend on

소포의 크기에 따라 내일 오전에 물류 창고에서 출고될 수도 있다.

해설 전치사구 빈칸 뒤에 명사구(the size of the parcel)가 있으므로 빈칸은 명사구를 목적어로 취하는 전치사 자리이다. 문맥상 소포의 크기에 따라 내일 오전에 출고될 수 있는지 정해진다는 내용이 되어 자연스러우므로 '~에 따라'를 뜻하는 (B) Depending on이 정답이다. to부정사인 (D) To depend on도 수식어구 역할을 할 수 있지만 '소포의 크기에 의존하기 위해서'라는 의미가 되어 문맥상 적절하지 않다.

어휘 parcel 소포, 꾸러미 leave 떠나다 warehouse 물류 창고

5.

Duncan Groceries sells all kinds of imported foods, **including** African and Asian delicacies.

(A) starting (B) providing
(C) including (D) avoiding

던컨 식자재 마트는 아프리카와 아시아의 별미를 포함하여 모든 종류의 수입 식품을 판매한다.

해설 -ing형 전치사 including 빈칸 뒤에 명사구(African and Asian delicacies)가 있으므로 빈칸은 명사구를 목적어로 취하는 전치사 자리이다. 문맥상 아프리카와 아시아의 별미를 포함하여 모든 수입 식품을 판매한다는 내용이 되어야 자연스러우므로 '~을 포함하여'를 뜻하는 (C) including이 정답이다. (B) providing은 '만약 ~라면'이라는 의미의 조건 접속사로도 쓰이는데, 이때는 provided와 바꿔 쓸 수 있다.

어휘 import 수입하다 delicacy (특정 지역의) 별미, 진미

6.

Hillside apartment residents have a view of mountains **through** the windows on the eastern side.

(A) on **(B) through**
(C) with (D) except

힐사이드 아파트 주민들은 동쪽 창문을 통하여 산이 바라다보인다.

해설 기타 전치사 문맥상 창문을 통하여 산이 보인다는 내용이 되어야 자연스러우므로 '~을 통해'를 뜻하는 (B) through가 정답이다. (A) on(~에)과 (C) with(~와 함께, ~을 가지고), 그리고 (D) except(~을 제외하고)는 모두 의미상 어울리지 않는 전치사이므로 오답이다.

어휘 resident 거주자, 주민 view 조망, 경치 eastern 동쪽의 side 측면

7.

The downtown roads were closed for a while due to a thick blanket of **snow**.

(A) snow (B) snowy
(C) snowier (D) snowed

시내 도로는 두텁게 내려앉은 눈 때문에 한동안 통제되었다.

해설 명사 자리 [전치사 뒤] 빈칸은 전치사 of 뒤의 명사 자리이므로 (A) snow가 정답이다. (B) snowy는 형용사, (C) snowier는 snowy의 비교급, (D) snowed는 동사 또는 과거분사이므로 오답이다.

어휘 for a while 한동안 due to ~ 때문에 a blanket of 두텁게 내려앉은 snowy 눈에 덮인; 눈이 많이 내리는

8.

Jacob Interior will be providing free bathtub installations **until** next Sunday, March 11.

(A) by (B) during
(C) until (D) at

제이콥 인테리어는 3월 11일인 다음 주 일요일까지 욕조 무료 설치를 제공할 것이다.

해설 until vs. by 문맥상 인테리어 업체가 다음 주 일요일까지 무료로 욕조 설치를 '계속' 진행하게 될 것이라는 내용이 되어야 한다. 따라서 '지속'의 의미가 있는 (C) until이 정답이다. (A) by는 특정 시점까지 행위나 동작이 '완료'되는 것을 강조하는 전치사이므로 이 문장에서는 적절하지 않다. (B) during은 뒤에 구체적인 행사나 사건을 나타내는 말이 이어져야 하며, (D) at은 구체적이고 특정한 시점을 나타내는 명사 앞에 오므로 빈칸에 적절하지 않다.

어휘 bathtub 욕조 installation 설치

To: All Employees
From: Doug Lasker, IT Supervisor
Date: October 12
Subject: Web Site Maintenance

Please be aware that the company Web site is scheduled for some routine maintenance tomorrow starting at 8:00 A.M. The Web site ⁹**will be** offline for at least seven hours. ¹⁰**During** that time, nobody will be able to access the Web site for any reason. It will take longer time than usual because our team is not only working on maintenance this time. ¹¹**The site will also be given an upgrade.** When service resumes, please be sure to browse our Web site to check out its ¹²**improved** features. We would appreciate your feedback regarding them.

Please be sure not to schedule anything requiring access to the company Web page tomorrow. If you have any questions, feel free to contact me at extension 845.

수신: 전 직원
발신: IT 관리자 더그 래스커
날짜: 10월 12일
제목: 웹사이트 유지 보수

내일 오전 8시부터 회사 웹사이트에 정기 유지 보수 작업이 진행될 예정이라는 걸 알아 두시길 바랍니다. 웹사이트는 최소 7시간 동안 오프라인 상태가 ⁹**될 것입니다**. 그 시간 ¹⁰**동안**, 어떠한 이유로든 아무도 웹사이트에 접속할 수 없을 것입니다. 이번에는 우리 팀이 유지 보수 작업만 할 게 아니기 때문에 평소보다 시간이 더 걸릴 것입니다. ¹¹**사이트는 업그레이드도 될 것입니다.** 서비스가 재개될 때, ¹²**개선된** 특징들을 확인하기 위해 반드시 웹사이트를 둘러보시기 바랍니다. 그것들과 관련해 여러분의 의견을 주시면 감사하겠습니다.

내일은 회사 웹페이지에 접속이 필요한 어떤 것도 일정을 잡지 마십시오. 궁금한 점이 있으면 내선 번호 845로 제게 언제든지 연락 주십시오.

어휘 be aware that ~라는 걸 알다[인지하다]   be scheduled for ~가 예정되다   routine 정례적인, 일상적인   maintenance 유지 보수   at least 최소한, 적어도   access 접속하다   resume 다시 시작하다, 재개하다   browse 돌아다니다, 둘러보다   feature 특징, 특색   appreciate 고마워하다, 감사하다   regarding ~에 관하여   require 필요로 하다, 요구하다   extension 내선 번호

9. (A) was (B) will be (C) has been (D) is

해설 동사 시제 빈칸 앞 문장에서 내일 오전 8시부터 웹사이트 유지 보수 작업이 진행될 예정이라고 했으며, 빈칸이 있는 문장에서는 유지 보수 작업으로 인해 발생할 일을 서술하고 있으므로 미래 시제로 표현하는 게 적절하다. 따라서 (B) will be가 정답이다.

10. (A) In (B) Instead (C) During (D) Despite

해설 기간 전치사 during 빈칸 뒤에 명사구 that time이 있으며 문맥상 유지 보수 작업이 진행되는 동안에는 웹사이트에 접속할 수 없을 거라는 내용이 되어야 자연스러우므로 '~ 동안'을 뜻하는 전치사인 (C) During이 정답이다.

11. (A) No work was done on the upgrade yet.
(B) I appreciate all of your suggestions.
(C) We're sorry you couldn't access the site.
(D) The site will also be given an upgrade.

(A) 업그레이드 작업은 아직 완료되지 않았습니다.
(B) 여러분의 모든 제안에 감사드립니다.
(C) 여러분이 사이트에 접속할 수 없었던 점을 사과드립니다.
(D) 사이트는 업그레이드도 될 것입니다.

해설 알맞은 문장 고르기 빈칸 앞에서 이번에는 단순 유지 보수만 하는 게 아니기 때문에 시간이 오래 걸릴 거라고 했으므로 빈칸에는 어떤 작업이 추가적으로 진행되는지 언급하는 게 흐름상 적절하다. 따라서 사이트가 업그레이드될 것이라는 내용의 (D)가 정답이다. (C)는 과거의 일에 대해 사과하고 있으므로 적절하지 않다.

12. (A) improved (B) proposed (C) attempted (D) reported

(A) 개선된 (B) 제안된 (C) 시도된 (D) 보고된

해설 형용사 어휘 명사 features를 수식해 가장 자연스럽게 의미가 통하는 형용사를 골라야 한다. 따라서 '개선된'이라는 의미의 (A) improved가 정답이다.

UNIT 09　to부정사

1　to부정사의 명사 역할
본문 p.150

1. (B)　　2. (A)　　3. (B)　　4. (C)

1.

The task of the Hoody's Green Management is **to collect** recyclables from our office and dispose of them properly.

(A) collected　　　　(B) to collect
(C) collection　　　　(D) to collecting

후디스 그린 매니지먼트의 업무는 우리 사무실로부터 재활용품을 수거하여 그것들을 적절하게 처리하는 것이다.

해설 to부정사의 명사 역할 [보어 자리] 빈칸은 be동사 is의 주격 보어 자리이다. to부정사가 명사 역할을 할 때는 보어 자리에 올 수 있으므로 (B) to collect가 정답이다. '후디스 그린 매니지먼트의 업무는 재활용품을 수거하는 것'이라는 의미가 되어 문맥에도 알맞다. (C) collection은 명사이지만 주격 보어 자리에 명사가 들어가려면 <주어=주격 보어>가 성립해야 하는데, 이 문장의 주격 보어 자리에 명사 collection이 들어가면 <후디스 그린 매니지먼트의 업무=수집품>이 되어 문맥상 어색하므로 답이 될 수 없다.

어휘 task 직무, 과업　collect 모으다, 수집하다　recyclables ((항상 복수형)) 재활용품　dispose of ~을 처리하다, ~을 없애다

2.

By next year, Joyce Watters aims **to recruit** at least 20 more part-time employees.

(A) to recruit　　　　(B) recruited
(C) recruiting　　　　(D) have recruited

내년까지 조이스 워터스는 시간제 근무 직원들을 최소한 20명 더 채용하는 것을 목표로 하고 있다.

해설 to부정사의 명사 역할 [목적어 자리] 빈칸은 동사 aims의 목적어 자리이며, aim은 to부정사를 목적어로 취해 aim to do(~하는 것을 목표로 하다) 형태로 쓰이므로 (A) to recruit가 정답이다. 동명사인 (C) recruiting이 aim의 목적어로 쓰이려면 aim at이 되어야 하기 때문에 답이 될 수 없다. (B) recruited는 동사 또는 과거분사이고, (D) have recruited는 현재완료이므로 오답이다.

어휘 recruit 채용하다　at least 최소한, 적어도

3.

Mr. Wang guarantees **to increase** the profit margins of any company that hires him as a consultant.

(A) increased　　　　(B) to increase
(C) increasing　　　　(D) having increased

왕 씨는 그를 컨설턴트로 고용하는 어떤 회사에게든 수익률을 증가시켜 줄 것을 보장한다.

해설 to부정사의 명사 역할 [목적어 자리] 빈칸은 동사 guarantees의 목적어 자리이며, guarantee는 to부정사를 목적어로 취해 guarantee to do(~하는 것을 약속하다) 형태로 쓰이므로 (B) to increase가 정답이다.

어휘 guarantee 보장[약속]하다　profit margin 이윤[이익] 폭, 수익률　hire 고용하다, 채용하다　consultant 상담가, 자문 위원

4.

Due to growing environmental concerns, the government is asking citizens **to minimize** the use of disposable plastics.

(A) minimizing　　　　(B) minimized
(C) to minimize　　　　(D) for minimizing

증가하는 환경적인 우려 때문에 정부는 시민들에게 일회용 플라스틱 사용을 최소화할 것을 요청하고 있다.

해설 to부정사의 명사 역할 [목적격 보어 자리] 빈칸은 is asking의 목적격 보어 자리이며, ask는 to부정사를 목적격 보어로 취해 ask A to do(A가 ~할 것을 요청하다) 형태로 쓰이므로 to부정사인 (C) to minimize가 정답이다.

어휘 due to ~ 때문에　concern 우려, 관심사　citizen 시민　minimize 최소화하다　disposable 일회용의

2 to부정사의 형용사 역할

본문 p.151

1. (A)   2. (C)   3. (D)   4. (C)

1.

Brookville Industries has been implementing a plan **to train** its new staff members more quickly.

(A) to train   (B) trains
(C) trained   (D) will train

브루크빌 인더스트리는 신입 직원들을 보다 빠르게 교육시키기 위한 계획을 실행해 왔다.

해설 to부정사의 형용사 역할 빈칸 앞이 완전한 절이므로 빈칸 이하가 명사 plan을 뒤에서 수식하는 구조가 되어야 한다. 그러므로 빈칸 뒤의 명사구(its new staff members)를 목적어로 취하면서 명사 plan을 뒤에서 수식할 수 있는 (A) to train이 정답이다. 동사 또는 명사인 (B) trains와 동사인 (D) will train은 명사를 수식할 수 없으며, 과거분사인 (C) trained가 명사를 뒤에서 수식하는 경우에는 뒤에 목적어를 동반하지 않으므로 오답이다.

어휘 implement 실행하다, 수행하다   train 교육시키다, 훈련시키다

2.

Executives at Franklin Auto agreed that it was time **to manufacture** electronic vehicles.

(A) manufactures   (B) will manufacture
(C) to manufacture   (D) manufacturing

프랭클린 오토의 임원들은 전기 차를 제조해야 할 시기라는 데 동의했다.

해설 to부정사의 형용사 역할 빈칸 이하가 명사 time을 뒤에서 수식하는 구조가 되어야 하므로 형용사 역할을 할 수 있는 to부정사인 (C) to manufacture가 정답이다.

어휘 executive 임원, 중역   it's time to do ~할 시간이다   manufacture 제조하다   electronic vehicle 전기 차

3.

Atlantis Resort added a new diving pool in an **attempt** to attract more visitors.

(A) attempting   (B) attempted
(C) attempts   (D) attempt

아틀란티스 리조트는 더 많은 방문객을 유치하려는 시도로 새로운 다이빙 수영장을 추가했다.

해설 명사 자리 빈칸 앞에 부정관사 an이 있고 뒤에는 to부정사인 to attract가 있으므로 빈칸은 단수 명사 자리이다. 따라서 (D) attempt가 정답이다. in an attempt to do는 '~하려는 시도로'를 의미한다. (A) attempting은 동명사 또는 현재분사, (B) attempted는 동사 또는 과거분사, (C) attempts는 동사 또는 복수 명사이므로 모두 빈칸에 적절하지 않다.

어휘 add 더하다, 추가하다   attempt 시도   attract 유치하다, 끌어들이다

4.

Pinceps Academy researches new ways **to improve** the learning efficiency of young students.

(A) improve   (B) improving
(C) to improve   (D) improves

핀셉스 아카데미는 어린 학생들의 학습 효율을 증진시키는 새로운 방법들을 연구한다.

해설 to부정사의 형용사 역할 빈칸 앞이 완전한 절이므로 빈칸 이하가 명사구 new ways를 수식하는 구조가 되어야 한다. 그러므로 빈칸 뒤의 명사구(the learning ~ students)를 목적어로 취하면서 new ways를 뒤에서 수식할 수 있는 (C) to improve가 정답이다. (A) improve와 (D) improves는 동사, (B) improving은 동명사 또는 현재분사이므로 오답이다.

어휘 research 연구하다, 조사하다   improve 개선하다   efficiency 효율성

3 to부정사의 부사 역할

본문 p.152

1. (C)   2. (C)   3. (D)   4. (C)

1.

Great Eastern Inc. is happy **to share** the news of our expansion to 25 cities in Asia.

(A) share (B) shared
(C) to share (D) will share

그레이트 이스턴 사는 아시아의 25개 도시로 확장한다는 소식을 전하게 되어 기쁩니다.

해설 **to부정사의 부사 역할** 빈칸에는 형용사 happy를 수식할 수 있는 말이 들어가야 한다. to부정사는 형용사를 뒤에서 수식하는 부사 역할을 할 수 있으므로 (C) to share가 정답이다. (A) share는 동사 또는 명사, (B) shared는 동사 또는 과거분사, (D) will share는 동사이므로 모두 빈칸에 적절하지 않다.

어휘 share 공유하다; 나누다; 몫, 지분   expansion 확장, 확대

2.

Our restaurant's seating area has been renovated **to offer** outdoor dining when the weather is favorable.

(A) is offered (B) will offer
(C) to offer (D) offers

저희 음식점의 좌석 구역은 날씨가 좋을 때 야외 식사를 제공하기 위해 개조되었습니다.

해설 **to부정사의 부사 역할** 빈칸 앞이 완전한 절이므로 빈칸 이하는 부사 역할을 해야 한다. 선택지에서 부사 역할을 할 수 있는 것은 to부정사인 (C) to offer뿐이다. (A) is offered와 (B) will offer는 동사, (D) offers는 동사 또는 명사이므로 모두 빈칸에 적절하지 않다.

어휘 renovate 개조하다, 수리하다   outdoor 야외의   dining 식사   favorable (날씨 등이) 좋은; 호의적인

3.

Gamma Tech's rates are too **expensive** to outsource our company's Internet security management.

(A) expensively (B) expenditure
(C) expenses **(D) expensive**

감마 테크의 요금은 너무 비싸서 우리 회사의 인터넷 보안 관리를 위탁할 수 없다.

해설 **형용사 자리** 빈칸 앞뒤로 too와 to가 있으므로 ⟨too 형용사/부사 to do(너무 ~해서 …할 수 없는)⟩ 구조임을 알 수 있다. 따라서 부사인 (A) expensively와 형용사인 (D) expensive 중에서 답을 골라야 하는데, 문장의 동사가 be동사 are인 것으로 보아 빈칸은 주격 보어 자리이므로 (D) expensive가 정답이다.

어휘 rate 요금   expensive 비싼, 돈이 많이 드는   outsource (회사가 작업, 생산을) 외부에 위탁하다   security 보안, 안전   expenditure 지출   expense 비용

4.

An administrator will provide test takers with the tools necessary **to complete** each given task.

(A) complete (B) completed
(C) to complete (D) will complete

관리자는 각각의 주어진 임무를 완수하는 데 필요한 도구들을 수험자들에게 제공할 것이다.

해설 **to부정사의 부사 역할** 빈칸에는 형용사 necessary를 수식할 수 있는 말이 들어가야 한다. to부정사는 형용사를 뒤에서 수식하는 부사 역할을 할 수 있으므로 (C) to complete가 정답이다. (A) complete는 동사 또는 형용사, (B) completed는 동사 또는 과거분사, (D) will complete는 동사이므로 부사 역할을 할 수 없다.

어휘 administrator 관리자, 행정인   provide A with B A에게 B를 제공하다   test taker 수험자, 시험을 보는 사람   necessary 필수적인, 필요한   complete 완료하다

4 가주어와 의미상의 주어

본문 p.153

1. (D)   2. (D)   3. (D)   4. (C)

1.

> It is generally preferable **to include** a letter of recommendation when applying for a position.
>
> (A) inclusion   (B) included
> (C) including   **(D) to include**

일자리에 지원할 때는 추천서를 포함하는 것이 일반적으로 선호된다.

해설 **가주어와 진주어** 문장의 주어 자리에 It이 있는데, 지칭하는 대상이 없는 것으로 보아 대명사가 아닌 가주어로 쓰인 것임을 알 수 있다. 또한 빈칸 뒤에 명사구(a letter of recommendation)가 있으므로 빈칸에는 문장의 진짜 주어 역할을 하는 동시에 명사구 목적어를 취할 수 있는 말이 들어가야 한다. 따라서 to부정사인 (D) to include가 정답이다.

어휘 generally 일반적으로   preferable 선호되는; 더 좋은   a letter of recommendation 추천서   apply for ~에 지원하다

2.

> It is **advisable** to use the metric system when reporting data to an international audience.
>
> (A) advice   (B) advisors
> (C) to advise   **(D) advisable**

국제적인 청중들을 대상으로 자료를 보고할 때는 미터법을 사용하는 것이 바람직하다.

해설 **형용사 자리** 빈칸은 be동사 is의 주격 보어 자리이므로 명사나 형용사가 들어가야 한다. 문맥상 빈칸에는 진짜 주어(to use ~ system)의 상태를 나타내는 말이 들어가야 하므로 형용사인 (D) advisable이 정답이다. '미터법을 사용하는 것이 바람직하다'는 의미가 되어 문맥에도 알맞다. (A) advice와 (B) advisors는 명사이지만 주격 보어 자리에 명사가 들어가려면 〈주어=주격 보어〉가 성립해야 하는데, 이 문장의 주격 보어 자리에 명사 advice 또는 advisors가 들어가면 〈미터법을 사용하는 것=조언/조언자들〉이 되어 문맥상 어색하므로 답이 될 수 없다.

어휘 advisable 바람직한, 권할 만한   metric system 미터법   report 보고하다   audience 청중, 관중

3.

> The critics analyzed that it is necessary **for** Pullman Deli to make changes to some of its menus.
>
> (A) except   (B) along
> (C) to   **(D) for**

비평가들은 풀먼 델리가 일부 메뉴에 변화를 주는 것이 필요하다고 분석했다.

해설 **의미상의 주어** 명사절 접속사 that의 주어 자리에 it이 있고 뒤에는 to부정사구(to make ~ menus)가 이어지는 것으로 보아 가주어-진주어 구문임을 알 수 있다. 또한 빈칸 뒤에 있는 Pullman Deli는 문맥상 to부정사구가 언급하는 행위, 즉 메뉴에 변화를 주는 행위의 주체이다. 다시 말해 Pullman Deli가 to부정사의 의미상 주어이며, 이때는 〈for+명사/목적격 대명사〉로 써야 하므로 (D) for가 정답이다.

어휘 critic 비평가   analyze 분석하다   make a change 변경하다

4.

> It is mandatory for staff **to attend** the refresher training because of the recent curriculum changes.
>
> (A) attend   (B) attendance
> **(C) to attend**   (D) attended

최근 교육 과정 변경 때문에 직원들이 재직자 훈련에 참석하는 것은 의무이다.

해설 **가주어와 진주어** 문장의 주어 자리에 It이 있는데, 지칭하는 대상이 없는 것으로 보아 대명사가 아닌 가주어로 쓰인 것임을 알 수 있다. 또한 빈칸 앞에 〈for+명사〉로 의미상의 주어가 있고 뒤에는 명사구(the refresher training)가 있으므로 빈칸에는 문장의 진짜 주어 역할을 하는 동시에 명사구 목적어를 취할 수 있는 말이 들어가야 한다. 따라서 to부정사인 (C) to attend가 정답이다.

어휘 mandatory 의무적인   refresher training 재직자 훈련, 재교육   curriculum 교육 과정   attendance 참석, 출석

5 to부정사와 어울려 쓰이는 동사

본문 p.154

1. (D)   2. (C)   3. (D)   4. (D)

1.

Hank was deeply impressed by the interviewee because he **pledged** to improve the workplace atmosphere.

(A) invited   (B) regarded
(C) assumed   **(D) pledged**

행크 씨가 그 면접자에게 깊은 감명을 받은 이유는 그가 업무 환경을 개선하겠다고 다짐했기 때문이다.

해설 to부정사를 목적어로 쓰는 동사 [pledge to *do*] 빈칸 뒤에 to부정사인 to improve가 있으므로 선택지 중 to부정사를 목적어로 취하는 동사인 (D) pledged가 정답이다. pledge to *do*는 '~하기로 맹세[약속]하다'라는 뜻이며, '업무 환경을 개선하기로 약속했다'는 의미가 되어 문맥에도 알맞다. (A) invited는 invite A to *do*(A에게 ~하라고 요청하다) 형태로 쓰인다.

어휘 be impressed by ~에 감명을 받다   interviewee 면접 대상자   improve 개선하다, 향상시키다   workplace 직장, 업무 현장   atmosphere 분위기   regard ~로 여기다, 간주하다   assume 추정하다; (일을) 맡다

2.

Mr. Byrd would like all volunteers **to arrive** early on the day of the event.

(A) arrives   (B) arriving
(C) to arrive   (D) will arrive

버드 씨는 모든 자원봉사자들이 행사 당일에 일찍 도착하기를 바란다.

해설 to부정사를 목적격 보어로 쓰는 동사 [would like A to *do*] 빈칸 앞에 있는 would like는 to부정사를 목적격 보어로 취하는 동사이므로 (C) to arrive가 정답이다. would like A to *do*는 'A가 ~하기를 원하다[바라다]'라는 뜻이며, '모든 자원봉사자들이 행사 당일에 일찍 도착하기를 바란다'는 의미가 되어 문맥에도 알맞다.

어휘 would like A to *do* A가 ~하는 것을 바라다   volunteer 자원봉사자

3.

Shareholders **expected** to earn high returns on their initial investments by January.

(A) tested   (B) warranted
(C) encouraged   **(D) expected**

주주들은 1월까지 그들의 초기 투자금에 대한 고수익을 얻기를 기대했다.

해설 to부정사를 목적어로 쓰는 동사 [expect to *do*] 빈칸 뒤에 to부정사인 to earn이 있으므로 선택지 중 to부정사를 목적어로 취하는 동사인 (D) expected가 정답이다. expect to *do*는 '~하기를 기대하다'라는 뜻이며, '투자금에 대한 고수익을 얻기를 기대한다'는 의미가 되어 문맥에도 알맞다. (C) encouraged는 encourage A to *do*(A에게 ~하라고 권장하다) 형태로 쓰인다.

어휘 shareholder 주주   return 수익   initial 초기의, 처음의   investment 투자(금)   warrant 보증하다

4.

The game console's seamless interface allows users **to switch** between its functions instantly.

(A) switch   (B) switched
(C) switching   **(D) to switch**

그 게임기의 매끄러운 인터페이스는 사용자들이 기능 전환을 바로바로 할 수 있게 한다.

해설 to부정사를 목적격 보어로 쓰는 동사 [allow A to *do*] 빈칸 앞에 있는 allows는 to부정사를 목적격 보어로 취하는 동사이므로 (D) to switch가 정답이다. allow A to *do*는 'A가 ~하는 것을 허락하다[가능하게 하다]'라는 뜻이며, '사용자들이 기능 전환을 바로바로 하는 걸 가능하게 한다'는 의미가 되어 문맥에도 알맞다. (A) switch는 동사 또는 명사, (B) switched는 동사 또는 과거분사, (C) switching은 동명사 또는 현재분사이므로 모두 빈칸에 부적절하다.

어휘 game console 게임기   seamless 매끄러운; 이음매가 없는   switch 전환하다   function 기능   instantly 즉시

6 to부정사와 어울려 쓰이는 형용사

본문 p.155

1. (B) 2. (B) 3. (A) 4. (A)

1.

Venice Tech is **proud** to unveil its new mobile device, the Venice Z9.

(A) praised (B) **proud**
(C) compatible (D) applicable

베니스 테크는 새로운 모바일 장치인 베니스 Z9을 발표하게 되어 자랑스러워한다.

해설 to부정사와 어울려 쓰이는 형용사 [be proud to do] 빈칸 앞에 be동사 is가 있고 뒤에는 to부정사가 있으므로 빈칸에는 to부정사와 어울려 쓰이는 형용사가 들어가야 한다. be proud to do는 '~해서 자랑스럽다'라는 뜻이며, '신제품을 발표해서 자랑스럽다'는 의미가 되어 문맥에도 알맞으므로 (B) proud가 정답이다.

어휘 unveil 발표하다 device 장치 praise 칭찬하다 compatible 호환이 되는 applicable 적용할 수 있는

2.

Ms. Marino is **available** to discuss design proposals with clients on Tuesdays and Thursdays.

(A) diligent (B) **available**
(C) initial (D) cautious

마리노 씨는 화요일과 목요일마다 고객들과 디자인 제안에 관해 논의할 시간이 있다.

해설 to부정사와 어울려 쓰이는 형용사 [be available to do] 빈칸 앞에 be동사 is가 있고 뒤에는 to부정사가 있으므로 빈칸에는 to부정사와 어울려 쓰이는 형용사가 들어가야 한다. be available to do는 '~하는 데 이용 가능하다, ~할 시간[여유]이 있다'라는 뜻이며, '마리노 씨는 화요일과 목요일마다 논의할 시간이 된다'는 의미가 되어 문맥에도 알맞으므로 (B) available이 정답이다.

어휘 discuss 논의하다 proposal 제안 client 고객 diligent 부지런한 initial 초기의 cautious 조심스러운

3.

Mr. Clark is always **willing** to provide technical assistance and advice to junior staff members.

(A) **willing** (B) acclaimed
(C) cheery (D) popular

클라크 씨는 언제나 부하 직원들에게 기술적인 도움과 조언을 기꺼이 제공한다.

해설 to부정사와 어울려 쓰이는 형용사 [be willing to do] 빈칸 앞에 be동사 is가 있고 뒤에는 to부정사가 있으므로 빈칸에는 to부정사와 어울려 쓰이는 형용사가 들어가야 한다. be willing to do는 '기꺼이 ~하다'라는 뜻이며, '기술적인 도움과 조언을 기꺼이 제공한다'는 의미가 되어 문맥에도 알맞으므로 (A) willing이 정답이다.

어휘 assistance 도움, 지원 junior 하급의, 부하의 acclaimed 찬사를 받는 cheery 쾌활한 popular 인기 있는

4.

Melton Outfitters' club members are **eligible** to receive free shipping on online orders.

(A) **eligible** (B) reviewed
(C) comfortable (D) capable

멜턴 아웃피터스 클럽 회원들은 온라인 주문에 대해 무료 배송을 받을 자격이 있다.

해설 to부정사와 어울려 쓰이는 형용사 [be eligible to do] 빈칸 앞에 be동사 are가 있고 뒤에는 to부정사가 있으므로 빈칸에는 to부정사와 어울려 쓰이는 형용사가 들어가야 한다. be eligible to do는 '~할 자격이 있다'는 뜻이며, '클럽 회원들은 무료 배송을 받을 자격이 있다'는 의미가 되어 문맥에도 알맞으므로 (A) eligible이 정답이다. (D) capable은 be capable of(~할 수 있다)로 쓰인다는 점에 유의해야 한다.

어휘 shipping 배송, 운송 order 주문(품); 주문하다 review 검토하다 comfortable 편안한

VOCABULARY

본문 p.158

1. (D) 2. (C) 3. (B) 4. (A) 5. (A) 6. (B) 7. (B) 8. (D)

1.

The percentage of job applicants with certifications is **likely** to increase over the next decade.

(A) acceptable (B) absolute
(C) studious (D) likely

향후 10년에 걸쳐 자격증을 가진 구직자들의 비율이 증가**할 것 같다**.

(A) 받아들일 수 있는 (B) 완전한, 완벽한
(C) 학구적인 (D) ~할 것 같은

해설 형용사 어휘 to부정사와 어울려 가장 자연스럽게 의미가 통하는 형용사를 골라야 한다. 따라서 '~할 것 같은'이라는 의미의 (D) likely가 정답이다.

어휘 percentage 비율 job applicant 취업 지원자 certification 증명(서) decade 10년

2.

With the backing of **additional** investors, the company was able to increase production.

(A) doubtful (B) entitled
(C) additional (D) inexpert

추가 투자자들의 지원으로 그 회사는 생산을 늘릴 수 있었다.

(A) 의심스러운 (B) 자격이 되는
(C) 추가의 (D) 미숙한

해설 형용사 어휘 명사 investors를 수식해 가장 자연스럽게 의미가 통하는 형용사를 골라야 한다. 따라서 '추가의'라는 의미의 (C) additional이 정답이다.

어휘 with the backing of ~의 지원[후원]으로 investor 투자자 be able to do ~할 수 있다 production 생산

3.

Be **sure** to inspect your rental vehicle for any damage before signing for it.

(A) entire (B) sure
(C) reasonable (D) utmost

차량 수령 서명을 하기 전에 임대 차량에 손상이 있는지 **반드시** 점검하십시오.

(A) 전체의 (B) 분명히 ~할; 확실한
(C) 합리적인 (D) 최고의, 최대한

해설 형용사 어휘 to부정사와 어울려 가장 자연스럽게 의미가 통하는 형용사를 골라야 한다. 따라서 '분명히 ~할'이라는 의미의 (B) sure가 정답이다.

어휘 inspect 점검하다, 검사하다 rental 임대의, 대여의 vehicle 차량 damage 손상, 피해 sign for ~을 수령했다고 서명하다

4.

Due to several recalls in recent years, customers are **hesitant** to purchase Dupont's kitchen appliances.

(A) hesitant (B) beneficial
(C) partial (D) granted

최근 몇 해에 걸친 리콜 때문에 고객들은 듀폰의 주방 가전제품을 구입하는 걸 **망설인다**.

(A) 망설이는 (B) 이로운, 유익한
(C) 부분적인 (D) 승인받은

해설 형용사 어휘 to부정사와 어울려 가장 자연스럽게 의미가 통하는 형용사를 골라야 한다. 따라서 '망설이는'이라는 의미의 (A) hesitant가 정답이다.

어휘 due to ~ 때문에 recall 회수, 리콜 recent 최근의 purchase 구매하다; 구매 appliance 가전제품

5.

The musicians were **able** to perform the piece from memory thanks to their rehearsals.

(A) able (B) talented
(C) applauded (D) hospitable

음악가들은 리허설 덕분에 작품을 외워서 공연할 수 있었다.

(A) ~을 할 수 있는 (B) 재능이 있는
(C) 박수를 받는 (D) 환대하는

해설 형용사 어휘 to부정사와 어울려 가장 자연스럽게 의미가 통하는 형용사를 골라야 한다. 따라서 '~을 할 수 있는'이라는 의미의 (A) able이 정답이다.

어휘 piece (미술, 음악 등의) 작품 from memory 외워서 thanks to ~ 덕분에 rehearsal 리허설, 예행연습

6.

It is no longer **profitable** for Ricardo's Ristorante to use cheese imported directly from Italy.

(A) delicious (B) profitable
(C) eager (D) gradual

리카르도 레스토랑이 이탈리아에서 직수입된 치즈를 사용하는 것은 더 이상 **수익성**이 없다.

(A) 맛있는 (B) 수익성이 있는
(C) 열렬한, 열심인 (D) 점진적인

해설 형용사 어휘 빈칸은 주격 보어 자리이므로 진주어(to use ~ Italy)의 상태나 상황을 표현하는 말이 들어가야 한다. 문맥상 이탈리아에서 직수입한 치즈를 쓰는 건 수익성이 없다는 내용이 되는 게 자연스러우므로 '수익성이 있는'이라는 의미의 (B) profitable이 정답이다.

어휘 no longer 더 이상 ~않는 import 수입하다 directly 직접, 바로

7.

The theater staff was disappointed by the number of **vacant** seats at the last performance.

(A) direct (B) vacant
(C) helpful (D) sequential

극장 직원들은 지난 공연에서 **빈** 좌석 수에 실망했다.

(A) 직접적인 (B) 비어 있는
(C) 도움이 되는 (D) 순차적인

해설 형용사 어휘 명사 seats를 수식해 가장 자연스럽게 의미가 통하는 형용사를 골라야 한다. 따라서 '비어 있는'이라는 의미의 (B) vacant가 정답이다.

어휘 be disappointed by ~에 실망하다 the number of ~의 수

8.

Our community center was **pleased** to host another local graduation ceremony this year.

(A) congratulated (B) previous
(C) committed (D) pleased

저희 커뮤니티 센터는 올해 또 한 번의 지역 졸업식을 주최하게 되어 **기뻤습니다**.

(A) 축하받는 (B) 이전의
(C) 헌신적인 (D) 기쁜

해설 형용사 어휘 to부정사와 어울려 가장 자연스럽게 의미가 통하는 형용사를 골라야 한다. 따라서 '기쁜'이라는 의미의 (D) pleased가 정답이다. (C) committed는 be committed to doing(~하는 데 헌신하다) 형태로 쓰이므로 이 문장에는 적절하지 않다.

어휘 host 주최하다 another 또 하나의 local 지역의 graduation ceremony 졸업식

ACTUAL TEST

본문 p.160

| 1. (C) | 2. (B) | 3. (D) | 4. (C) | 5. (D) | 6. (A) |
| 7. (A) | 8. (A) | 9. (A) | 10. (B) | 11. (B) | 12. (D) |

1.

All kitchen staff are reminded **to wash** their hands regularly while working.

(A) can wash (B) having washed
(C) to wash (D) washing

모든 주방 직원들은 근무 중에 주기적으로 손을 씻으라는 주의를 받는다.

해설 to부정사를 목적격 보어로 쓰는 동사 [remind A to *do*] 동사 remind는 to부정사를 목적격 보어로 취한다. 또한 〈주어+동사+목적어+목적격 보어(to부정사)〉 문장이 수동태 문장으로 바뀌면 〈목적어+be p.p.+목적격 보어(to부정사)〉가 되므로 to부정사인 (C) to wash가 정답이다. remind A to *do*는 be reminded to *do*와 같이 수동태 표현으로도 자주 쓰이며 '~하라고 주의받다'를 뜻한다.

어휘 regularly 정기적으로   while ~ 동안

2.

Marches Meals planned **to expand** into the American market but decided to wait another year.

(A) expand (B) **to expand**
(C) expanding (D) expandable

마치스 밀스는 미국 시장으로 확장할 계획이었으나 한 해 더 기다리기로 결정했다.

해설 to부정사를 목적어로 쓰는 동사 [plan to *do*] 빈칸 앞에 있는 planned는 to부정사를 목적어로 취하는 동사이므로 (B) to expand가 정답이다. plan to *do*는 '~하기를 계획하다'라는 뜻이며, '미국 시장으로 확장할 계획이었다'는 의미가 되어 문맥에도 알맞다. (A) expand는 동사, (C) expanding은 동명사 또는 현재분사, (D) expandable은 형용사로 모두 빈칸에 알맞지 않다.

어휘 expand into ~로 확장하다   decide to *do* ~하기로 결정하다   expandable 확장할 수 있는

3.

Airport security is expected to **identify** any items that could be hazardous on a plane.

(A) will identify (B) identifying
(C) identified (D) **identify**

공항 보안 직원은 비행기에서 위험할 수 있는 물건들을 모두 확인해야 한다.

해설 to부정사를 목적격 보어로 쓰는 동사 [expect A to *do*] 동사 expect는 to부정사를 목적격 보어로 취한다. 또한 〈주어+동사+목적어+목적격 보어(to부정사)〉 문장이 수동태 문장으로 바뀌면 〈목적어+be p.p.+목적격 보어(to부정사)〉가 되므로 to부정사인 (D) identify가 정답이다. expect A to *do*는 be expected to *do*와 같이 수동태 표현으로도 자주 쓰이며 '마땅히 ~을 해야 하다; ~할 것으로 예상되다'를 뜻한다.

어휘 security 보안, 안전   identify 확인하다   hazardous 위험한

4.

Mr. Barkley, the **previous** training manager, prepared resources for his replacement to use.

(A) worthy (B) sociable
(C) **previous** (D) partial

이전 교육 매니저였던 바클리 씨는 그의 후임자가 사용할 자료들을 준비해 두었다.

(A) 가치가 있는 (B) 사교적인
(C) 이전의 (D) 부분적인

해설 형용사 어휘 명사구 training manager를 수식해 가장 자연스럽게 의미가 통하는 형용사를 골라야 한다. 따라서 '이전의'라는 의미의 (C) previous가 정답이다.

어휘 prepare 준비하다   resource 자료; 재료   replacement 후임자; 대체물

5.

Margot Legal is a reputable law firm **eager** to represent business and individuals alike.

(A) accused (B) profitable
(C) rare **(D) eager**

마고 법률 사무소는 기업과 개인 모두를 대변하길 **열망하는** 평판이 좋은 법률 회사이다.

(A) 고발된 (B) 수익성이 있는
(C) 드문, 희귀한 **(D) 열망하는**

해설 형용사 어휘 to부정사와 어울려 가장 자연스럽게 의미가 통하는 형용사를 골라야 한다. 따라서 '열망하는'이라는 의미의 (D) eager가 정답이다.

어휘 reputable 평판이 좋은 represent 대변하다, 변호하다; 대표하다 individual 개인 alike 둘 다, 똑같이

6.

It is mandatory **for** loan applicants to disclose all of their personal financial history.

(A) for (B) from
(C) unless (D) until

대출 신청자들이 그들의 개인 재무 기록을 모두 공개하는 것은 의무이다.

해설 의미상의 주어 문장의 주어 자리에 It이 있고 뒤에는 to부정사구(to disclose ~ history)가 이어지는 것으로 보아 가주어-진주어 구문임을 알 수 있다. 또한 빈칸 뒤에 있는 loan applicants는 문맥상 to부정사구가 언급하는 행위, 즉 개인 재무 기록을 공개하는 행위의 주체이다. 다시 말해 loan applicants가 to부정사의 의미상 주어이며, 이때는 〈for+명사/목적격 대명사〉로 써야 하므로 (A) for가 정답이다.

어휘 mandatory 의무적인 loan 대출 applicant 신청자, 지원자 disclose 밝히다, 공개하다 financial 재무의

7.

Ms. O'Connell would like **to discuss** your proposal for the Brooklyn project this afternoon.

(A) to discuss (B) discussing
(C) having discussed (D) discussion

오코넬 씨는 오늘 오후에 브루클린 프로젝트에 대한 당신의 제안서를 논의하고 싶어 합니다.

해설 to부정사를 목적어로 쓰는 동사 [would like to do] 빈칸 앞에 있는 would like는 to부정사를 목적어로 취하는 동사이므로 (A) to discuss가 정답이다. would like to do는 '~하고 싶다'라는 뜻이며, '오코넬 씨가 제안서를 논의하고 싶어 한다'는 의미가 되어 문맥에도 알맞다. (B) discussing과 (C) having discussed는 동명사 또는 현재분사, (D) discussion은 명사이므로 모두 빈칸에 알맞지 않다.

어휘 discuss 논의하다 proposal 제안서 discussion 논의, 상의

8.

In an effort **to avoid** accidents, we have issued a recall on our toasters.

(A) to avoid (B) avoided
(C) has avoided (D) avoiding

사고를 방지하려는 노력으로 우리는 토스터기에 대해 리콜을 발표했습니다.

해설 to부정사의 형용사 역할 빈칸 앞뒤에 각각 명사 effort와 accidents가 있으므로 빈칸에는 앞에 있는 명사를 수식하는 형용사 역할을 하는 동시에 뒤에 있는 명사를 목적어로 취할 수 있는 말이 들어가야 한다. 따라서 to부정사인 (A) to avoid가 정답이다. in an effort to do는 '~하려는 노력으로'를 의미한다. (B) avoided는 동사 또는 과거분사, (C) has avoided는 현재완료, (D) avoiding은 동명사 또는 현재분사이므로 모두 빈칸에 적절하지 않다.

어휘 avoid 피하다 accident 사고 issue 발표하다; 발행하다 recall 회수, 리콜

To: All Staff Members 〈allstaff@qit.com〉
From: Melissa Peck 〈m.peck@qit.com〉
Subject: Helping Hands
Date: May 8

Attention Staff Members,

I was recently contacted by the charity organization Helping Hands, and I have some good news to pass on to all of you. It is my pleasure to inform you of an opportunity **9 to volunteer** and help out the local community here in Plattsburgh by working with them. Helping Hands provides services for those who have trouble getting around. **10 More people are needed to help them run errands.**

Specific **11 tasks** are assigned only to those who sign up. You will not be paid for your service. **12 However**, the company will grant a half day off work each week for participants. Please contact me for more details.

Regards,

Melissa Peck
Director, QIT Human Resources

수신: 전 직원 〈allstaff@qit.com〉
발신: 멜리사 펙 〈m.peck@qit.com〉
제목: 도움의 손길
날짜: 5월 8일

전 직원들은 주목해 주세요.

저는 최근 자선 단체인 도움의 손길로부터 연락을 받았으며, 여러분에게 전해 드릴 좋은 소식이 있습니다. 그들과 함께 일함으로써 **9 자원봉사를 하고** 이곳 플래츠버그 지역 사회를 도울 기회를 여러분에게 알려 드리게 되어 기쁩니다. 도움의 손길은 거동이 불편한 분들에게 봉사를 제공합니다. **10 그들이 용무를 보는 데 도움을 줄 사람들이 더 필요합니다.**

구체적인 **11 업무**는 신청을 하는 사람들에게만 할당됩니다. 여러분의 봉사에 대해 대가가 지급되지 않을 것입니다. **12 하지만**, 회사는 참여자들에게 매주 반차를 승인할 것입니다. 보다 자세한 정보를 원하시면 제게 연락 주세요.

멜리사 펙
QIT 인사팀 부장

어휘) recently 최근에   contact 연락하다   charity 자선 (단체)   pass on to ~에게 전달하다   inform A of B A에게 B를 알리다
have trouble *doing* ~하는 데 어려움을 겪다   get around 돌아다니다   specific 구체적인   assign 할당하다   grant 승인하다

---

9. (A) **to volunteer** (B) volunteering
 (C) volunteers (D) having volunteered

해설) **to부정사의 형용사 역할** 빈칸 이하가 명사 opportunity를 뒤에서 수식하는 구조가 되어야 하므로 형용사 역할을 할 수 있는 to부정사인 (A) to volunteer가 정답이다.

---

10. (A) Please renew your driver's license.
 (B) **More people are needed to help them run errands.**
 (C) The group has drawn national attention.
 (D) Your assistance is greatly appreciated.

(A) 여러분의 운전면허증을 갱신하시기 바랍니다.
(B) **그들이 잡다한 일을 하는 데 도움을 줄 사람들이 더 필요합니다.**
(C) 그 단체는 국가적인 관심을 끌어냈습니다.
(D) 여러분의 도움에 매우 감사드립니다.

해설) **알맞은 문장 고르기** 빈칸 앞에서 도움의 손길이라는 단체는 거동이 불편한 분들에게 봉사를 한다고 했다. 따라서 빈칸에는 봉사 활동을 할 때 여러 잡다한 일을 도와줄 사람이 더 필요하다는 내용이 들어가는 게 적절하므로 (B)가 정답이다.

어휘) renew 갱신하다   run an errand 볼일을 보다, 심부름을 하다   draw attention 관심을 끌다   appreciate 감사하다

---

11. (A) associations (B) **tasks** (A) 협회, 제휴 (B) **업무**
 (C) groceries (D) routes (C) 식료품 (D) 길, 노선

해설) **명사 어휘** 빈칸 앞에 있는 형용사 Specific의 수식을 받고 동사 are assigned와 어울려 가장 자연스럽게 의미가 통하는 명사를 골라야 한다. 따라서 '업무'라는 의미의 (B) tasks가 정답이다.

---

12. (A) Likewise (B) Meanwhile (A) 마찬가지로 (B) 그동안
 (C) Moreover (D) **However** (C) 게다가 (D) **하지만**

해설) **접속부사** 빈칸 앞에서 봉사 대가가 지급되지 않는다고 했는데, 뒤에서는 회사에서 반차를 제공한다고 했으므로 앞뒤 내용이 서로 대조적이다. 따라서 대조적인 두 문장을 의미적으로 자연스럽게 연결해 주는 접속부사인 (D) However(하지만)가 정답이다.

UNIT 10 동명사

1 동명사 자리

본문 p.166

1. (D) 2. (B) 3. (A) 4. (B)

1.

Mr. Arnold is in the process of **entering** new customer data into the computer system.

(A) enter
(B) enters
(C) entered
(D) entering

아널드 씨는 컴퓨터 시스템에 새 고객 데이터를 입력하는 과정에 있다.

해설 동명사 자리 [전치사의 목적어] 빈칸 앞에 전치사 of가 있고 뒤에는 명사구 new customer data가 이어지므로 빈칸에는 명사구를 목적어로 취할 수 있는 동명사가 들어가야 한다. 따라서 (D) entering이 정답이다.

어휘 in the process of ~하는 중인, ~하는 과정에 있는   enter 입력하다   customer 고객   data 데이터, 자료

2.

Performing a thorough evaluation is crucial before a product launching.

(A) Performed
(B) **Performing**
(C) Performs
(D) Performance

제품 출시 전에 철저한 평가를 수행하는 것은 중요하다.

해설 동명사 자리 [주어] 빈칸 뒤에 be동사 is가 있으므로 빈칸에는 명사구인 a thorough evaluation과 함께 문장의 주어 역할을 할 수 있는 말이 들어가야 한다. 따라서 동명사 (B) Performing이 정답이다. 참고로 이 문장에서 a thorough evaluation은 동명사 Performing의 목적어 역할을 하고 있다. 일반 명사인 (D) Performance는 목적어를 취할 수 없기 때문에 빈칸에 들어갈 수 없다. (A) Performed는 동사 또는 과거분사, (C) Performs는 동사이므로 모두 오답이다.

어휘 perform 수행하다, 실시하다; 공연하다   thorough 철저한   evaluation 평가   performance 실행, 수행; 실적, 성과; 공연

3.

Peter Mayfield plays a vital role **in** assisting clients with their personal finances.

(A) **in**
(B) and
(C) though
(D) at

피터 메이필드는 고객들의 개인 자산 관리를 돕는 데 중요한 역할을 한다.

해설 전치사 자리 [동명사 앞] 빈칸 앞에 〈주어(Peter Mayfield)+동사(plays)+목적어(a vital role)〉 구조로 완전한 절이 있고 뒤에는 동명사 assisting이 있다. 따라서 빈칸에는 동명사를 목적어로 취할 수 있는 전치사가 들어가야 하며, plays a vital role과 어울려 가장 자연스럽게 의미가 통하는 것은 (A) in이다.

어휘 play a vital role in ~에서 중요한[필수적인] 역할을 하다   assist 돕다   client (업체의) 고객, 의뢰인

4.

After **canceling** your magazine subscription, we will refund next month's pre-payment.

(A) canceled
(B) **canceling**
(C) cancels
(D) cancelation

귀하의 잡지 구독을 취소한 후에 우리는 미리 납부된 다음 달 구독료를 환불해 드릴 것입니다.

해설 동명사 자리 [전치사의 목적어] 빈칸 앞에 전치사 After가 있고 뒤에는 명사구 your magazine subscription이 이어지므로 빈칸에는 명사구를 목적어로 취할 수 있는 동명사가 들어가야 한다. 따라서 (B) canceling이 정답이다.

어휘 cancel 취소하다   magazine 잡지   subscription 구독   refund 환불하다

2 동명사를 목적어로 쓰는 동사

본문 p.167

1. (C)   2. (C)   3. (D)   4. (A)

1.

Mr. Deacon is **considering** approving Ms. Elton's request to visit Dallas on business.

(A) planning
(B) asking
(C) considering
(D) making

디컨 씨는 댈러스에 출장을 가게 해 달라는 엘튼 씨의 요청을 승인하는 걸 고려하고 있다.

해설 동명사를 목적어로 쓰는 동사 [consider *doing*] 빈칸 앞에 주어 Mr. Deacon이 있고 뒤에는 동명사구 목적어(approving ~ business)가 이어지므로 빈칸에는 동명사를 목적어로 취하는 동사가 들어가야 한다. 따라서 정답은 (C) considering이다. (A) planning과 (B) asking은 to부정사를 목적어로 취하는 동사이므로 답이 될 수 없다.

어휘 consider 고려하다 approve 찬성하다, 승인하다 request 요청, 신청 visit 방문하다 on business 볼일이 있어, 업무로

2.

Amazon Airways wants passengers to postpone **checking in** online until it upgrades its Web site.

(A) check in
(B) checked in
(C) checking in
(D) to check in

아마존 항공은 자사 웹사이트를 업그레이드할 때까지는 승객들이 온라인으로 탑승 수속하는 것을 미루길 바란다.

해설 동명사 자리 빈칸은 to부정사인 to postpone의 목적어가 들어갈 자리이다. postpone은 동명사를 목적어로 취하므로 (C) checking in이 정답이다.

어휘 passenger 승객, 여객 postpone 연기하다, 미루다 check in 탑승 수속을 하다 online 온라인으로

3.

Improvements to the employee lounge include **adding** more comfortable chairs to the room.

(A) to add
(B) addition
(C) being added
(D) adding

직원 휴게실의 개선 공사에는 그 방에 편안한 의자들을 더 많이 추가하는 것이 포함된다.

해설 동명사 자리 빈칸은 동사 include의 목적어가 들어갈 자리이다. include는 동명사를 목적어로 취하므로 (D) adding이 정답이다. (C) being added는 동명사구이긴 하나 수동형이므로 목적어(more comfortable chairs to the room)를 취할 수 없기 때문에 오답이다.

어휘 improvement 개선 (공사), 향상 include 포함되다, 포함하다 add 더하다, 추가하다 comfortable 편안한, 안락한 addition 추가된 것, 부가물

4.

Construction crews have closed parts of Mountainview Avenue, so officials **suggest** taking an alternative route downtown.

(A) suggest
(B) pledge
(C) think
(D) admit

공사 팀이 마운틴뷰 거리의 일부를 막아서 당국자들은 시내로 향하는 대체 경로를 이용할 것을 권한다.

해설 동명사를 목적어로 쓰는 동사 [suggest *doing*] 빈칸 앞에 주어 officials가 있고 뒤에는 동명사구 목적어(taking ~ downtown)가 이어지므로 빈칸에는 동명사를 목적어로 취하는 동사가 들어가야 한다. 문맥상 거리 일부가 폐쇄되었기 때문에 다른 길로 돌아서 가는 걸 제안하는 게 가장 자연스러우므로 정답은 (A) suggest이다. (B) pledge는 to부정사를 목적어로 취하는 동사이므로 답이 될 수 없다.

어휘 construction 건설, 공사 crew (특별한 기술을 가지고 공동으로 작업하는) 팀, 조; 승무원 avenue 대로, 큰길 official 당국자, 관계자 suggest 제안하다, 권하다 alternative 대체 가능한 downtown 시내에, 시내로

3 동명사와 to부정사 둘 다 목적어로 쓰는 동사 ①

본문 p.168

1. (B)   2. (C)   3. (D)   4. (A)

1.

Ms. Sullivan continues to **challenge** her team by giving them difficult tasks.

(A) challenging (B) challenge
(C) challenged (D) challenges

설리번 씨는 자기 팀에게 어려운 업무를 줌으로써 팀원들을 계속 분발시킨다.

> [해설] **동사 자리** 빈칸은 동사 continues의 목적어가 들어갈 자리이다. continue는 동명사와 to부정사를 모두 목적어로 취하는데, 빈칸 앞에 to가 있으므로 동사원형인 (B) challenge가 정답이다.
>
> [어휘] continue to do 계속 ~하다   challenge 자극하다, 분발시키다

2.

Farnsworth, Inc. expects to begin **producing** its new sneakers line on June 11.

(A) production (B) produce
(C) producing (D) produces

판즈워스 사는 6월 11일에 새 운동화 제품군을 생산하기 시작할 것으로 예상한다.

> [해설] **동명사 자리** 빈칸은 to부정사인 to begin의 목적어가 들어갈 자리이다. begin은 동명사와 to부정사를 모두 목적어로 취하므로 선택지 중 동명사인 (C) producing이 정답이다.
>
> [어휘] Inc. 주식회사 (=Incorporated)   expect to do ~하기를 기대[예상]하다   produce 생산하다, 제조하다   sneakers (고무창) 운동화   line 제품군   production 생산, 제조

3.

Marbury Books recommends **ordering** an advance copy of Dave Hiller's newest fantasy novel.

(A) order (B) orders
(C) to order (D) ordering

마버리 북스는 데이브 힐러의 최신 판타지 소설의 신간 견본을 주문할 것을 권장한다.

> [해설] **동명사 자리** 빈칸은 동사 recommends의 목적어가 들어갈 자리이다. recommend는 동명사를 목적어로 취하므로 (D) ordering이 정답이다.
>
> [어휘] recommend 추천하다, 권장하다   order 주문하다   advance copy 신간 견본

4.

Top saleswoman Clara Thomas prefers **to demonstrate** the vacuum cleaner in person on January 15.

(A) to demonstrate (B) demonstrated
(C) demonstration (D) being demonstrated

최고의 판매원인 클라라 토마스는 1월 15일에 직접 진공청소기를 시연할 것을 원한다.

> [해설] **to부정사 자리** 빈칸은 동사 prefers의 목적어가 들어갈 자리이다. prefer는 동명사와 to부정사를 모두 목적어로 취하므로 선택지 중 to부정사인 (A) to demonstrate가 정답이다.
>
> [어휘] saleswoman 여자 영업직원   prefer 원하다, ~하고 싶어 하다   demonstrate 시연하다, 사용 시범을 보이다   vacuum cleaner 진공청소기   in person 직접, 몸소   demonstration 시연, 사용 시범

4 동명사와 to부정사 둘 다 목적어로 쓰는 동사 ②

본문 p.169

1. (C)   2. (B)   3. (A)   4. (B)

1.

Workers must not forget **to pack** their belongings before the moving of the office.

(A) packing   (B) package
(C) to pack   (D) packed

직원들은 사무실 이사 전에 자기 소지품을 싸는 것을 잊지 말아야 한다.

> **해설** to부정사 자리 빈칸은 동사 forget의 목적어가 들어갈 자리이다. forget은 목적어가 동명사일 때는 과거의 일을, to부정사일 때는 미래의 일을 나타낸다. 문맥상 이사 전에 소지품을 싸는 걸 잊지 말아야 한다는 미래의 의미가 되어야 하므로 (C) to pack이 정답이다.

> **어휘** forget to do ~할 것을 잊다   pack 포장하다, 싸다   belongings ((항상 복수형)) 소유물, 소지품   moving 이동, 이사   package 소포, 꾸러미

2.

Several individuals tried **booking** rooms at the Moonlight Hotel, but there were no vacancies.

(A) book   **(B) booking**
(C) booked   (D) have booked

몇몇 개인이 문라이트 호텔에 방을 예약하려고 해 보았지만 빈방이 하나도 없었다.

> **해설** 동명사 자리 빈칸은 동사 tried의 목적어가 들어갈 자리이다. try는 동명사와 to부정사를 모두 목적어로 취할 수 있으므로 동명사인 (B) booking이 정답이다. try는 목적어가 동명사면 어떤 일을 시도해 본다는 걸 의미하고, to부정사면 어떤 일을 하기 위해 노력한다는 걸 의미한다.

> **어휘** individual 개인   try doing ~을 시도하다, (시험 삼아) ~해 보다   book 예약하다   vacancy 빈방, 빈집

3.

Please don't forget **to close** all open windows before leaving your hotel room.

(A) to close   (B) close
(C) closing   (D) closed

호텔 객실을 나서기 전에 창문을 모두 닫는 걸 잊지 마세요.

> **해설** to부정사 자리 빈칸은 동사 forget의 목적어가 들어갈 자리이다. forget은 목적어가 동명사일 때는 과거의 일을, to부정사일 때는 미래의 일을 나타낸다. 문맥상 객실을 떠나기 전에 창문 닫는 걸 잊지 말아야 한다는 미래의 의미가 되어야 하므로 (A) to close가 정답이다.

> **어휘** leave (장소에서) 떠나다, 출발하다

4.

We regret **to announce** that Mr. Sanders will no longer work at Ziti Pharmaceutical as of May 1.

(A) announced   **(B) to announce**
(C) announcement   (D) announces

저희는 샌더스 씨가 5월 1일자로 더 이상 지티 제약에 근무하지 않을 것이라고 발표하게 되어 유감입니다.

> **해설** to부정사 자리 빈칸은 동사 regret의 목적어가 들어갈 자리이다. regret는 동명사와 to부정사를 모두 목적어로 취할 수 있으므로 to부정사인 (B) to announce가 정답이다. 참고로 regret는 목적어가 동명사일 때는 과거의 일을, to부정사일 때는 미래의 일을 나타낸다.

> **어휘** regret to do ~하게 되어 유감이다   announce 발표하다   no longer 더 이상 ~ 않는   pharmaceutical 약, 제약   as of ~일자로

5 동명사 vs. 명사

본문 p.170

1. (B) 2. (B) 3. (C) 4. (B)

1.

> **Organizing** the city job fair is one of Ms. Hasting's major accomplishments this year.
>
> (A) Organization (B) **Organizing**
> (C) Organized (D) Being organized

시 취업 박람회를 조직한 것은 헤이스팅 씨의 올해 주요 업무들 중 하나이다.

해설 동명사 vs. 명사 [동명사 자리] is가 문장의 동사 역할을 하므로 빈칸에는 명사구인 the city job fair와 함께 문장의 주어 역할을 할 수 있는 말이 들어가야 한다. 따라서 동명사 (B) Organizing이 정답이다. 일반 명사인 (A) Organization은 목적어를 취할 수 없기 때문에 빈칸에 들어갈 수 없다. (D) Being organized는 동명사구이긴 하나 수동형이므로 목적어(the city job fair)를 취할 수 없기 때문에 오답이다.

어휘 organize 조직하다, 준비하다 job fair 취업[채용] 박람회 major 주요한 accomplishment 성과, 업적

2.

> In a **report** written in February, Davidson Holdings stated they will stop investing in real estate.
>
> (A) reporter (B) **report**
> (C) reporting (D) reported

2월에 작성된 보고서에서 데이비드슨 홀딩스는 부동산에 투자하는 걸 중단할 거라고 공표했다.

해설 동명사 vs. 명사 [명사 자리] 빈칸 앞에 부정관사 a가 있고 뒤에는 과거분사구 written in February가 있으므로 빈칸은 과거분사구의 수식을 받는 명사 자리이다. 따라서 (B) report가 정답이다. (A) reporter도 명사이지만 과거분사구의 수식을 받으면 의미가 어색해지므로 이 문장에서는 오답이다.

어휘 state (정식으로) 말하다, 공언하다 invest in ~에 투자하다 real estate 부동산, 토지

3.

> **Owners** of homes in Oakdale are required to register any significant home renovation projects.
>
> (A) Owning (B) Owned
> (C) **Owners** (D) Ownership

오크데일에 있는 집들의 소유주들은 중대한 주거 보수 계획이 있을 경우 신고하도록 요구받는다.

해설 동명사 vs. 명사 [명사 자리] 빈칸은 전치사구 of homes in Oakdale의 수식을 받는 명사 자리이다. 또한 주거지 보수 계획이 있다면 주택 소유주들은 관련 기관에 신고하도록 요구받는다는 맥락이 자연스러우므로 '소유주들'이라는 의미의 (C) Owners가 정답이다. 동사 own이 '소유하다'를 의미할 땐 타동사이므로 뒤에 전치사구가 아닌 목적어가 동반되어야 한다. 그러므로 동명사인 (A) Owning은 빈칸에 들어갈 수 없다. (D) Ownership은 '집의 소유를 요구받는다'가 되어 의미가 자연스럽지 않으므로 오답이다.

어휘 require 요구하다, 필요로 하다 register 등록하다, 신고하다 significant 상당한, 중요한, 중대한 ownership 소유(권)

4.

> Mr. Green's method of **training** workers has resulted in higher productivity.
>
> (A) train (B) **training**
> (C) trainer (D) trains

그린 씨가 직원들을 교육하는 방식은 더 높은 생산성을 가져왔다.

해설 동명사 vs. 명사 [동명사 자리] 빈칸 앞에 전치사 of가 있고 뒤에는 명사 workers가 있으므로 빈칸에는 명사를 목적어로 취할 수 있는 동명사가 들어가야 한다. 따라서 (B) training이 정답이다. 일반 명사인 (C) trainer는 목적어를 취할 수 없기 때문에 빈칸에 적절하지 않다.

어휘 method 방식, 기법 train 훈련하다, 교육하다 result in (결과로) ~을 가져오다 productivity 생산성, 생산력

6 동명사 관용 표현

1. (B) 2. (A) 3. (D) 4. (A)

1.

In addition to **arranging** the retirement party, Janet May purchased a gift for Todd Arnold.

(A) arranged (B) arranging
(C) arrange   (D) arranges

퇴직 기념 파티를 주선한 것 외에도 재닛 메이는 토드 아널드를 위한 선물을 구입했다.

해설 동명사 관용 표현 문맥상 파티를 준비하는 것 외에도 선물을 구입했다는 내용이 되는 게 자연스러우므로 '~에 더하여, ~ 외에도'를 뜻하는 in addition to doing 형태가 되어야 한다. 따라서 (B) arranging이 정답이다.

어휘 arrange 주선하다, 준비하다 retirement party 퇴직 기념 파티 purchase 구입하다

2.

Jeff Cartwright stated that he is committed to **donating** half of his fortune to charity.

(A) **donating** (B) donation
(C) donations   (D) donates

제프 카트라이트는 자기 재산의 절반을 자선 사업에 기부할 것을 약속한다고 공언했다.

해설 동명사 관용 표현 문맥상 재산의 절반을 자선 사업에 기부할 것을 약속한다는 내용이 되는 게 자연스러우므로 '~하는 데 전념하다, ~할 것을 약속하다'를 뜻하는 be committed to doing 형태가 되어야 한다. 따라서 (A) donating이 정답이다.

어휘 state (정식으로) 말하다, 공언하다 fortune 재산 charity 자선 (사업) donate 기부하다, 기증하다 donation 기부, 기증

3.

Everyone at Rutherford Tech is looking forward to **attending** Dr. Powell's talk on computer chips.

(A) having attended (B) attendance
(C) attended   (D) **attending**

러더퍼드 테크의 모든 사람들은 컴퓨터 칩에 관한 파월 박사의 강연에 참석하기를 고대하고 있다.

해설 동명사 관용 표현 문맥상 파월 박사의 강연에 참석하는 걸 고대한다는 내용이 되는 게 자연스러우므로 '~하는 것을 고대하다'를 뜻하는 look forward to doing 형태가 되어야 한다. 따라서 (D) attending이 정답이다. (A) having attended는 과거를 나타내는 말이므로 앞으로 일어날 일을 고대한다는 문맥에 어울리지 않기 때문에 오답이다.

어휘 attend 참석하다, 출석하다 talk 강연 attendance 참석, 출석

4.

Upon receiving the package, Ms. Lowell restocked the items that were sold out previously.

(A) **Upon** (B) With
(C) Into   (D) As for

꾸러미를 받자마자 로웰 씨는 예전에 (물건이) 다 팔린 자리에 그 물품들을 채워 넣었다.

해설 동명사 관용 표현 문맥상 상품을 받자마자 진열했다는 내용이 되는 게 자연스러우므로 '~하자마자'를 뜻하는 (up)on doing 형태가 되어야 한다. 따라서 (A) Upon이 정답이다.

어휘 receive 받다 restock (사용하거나 팔린 물건들 자리에 새로운 것들을) 다시 채우다, 보충하다

VOCABULARY

본문 p.174

1. (A) 2. (D) 3. (C) 4. (A) 5. (B) 6. (D) 7. (B) 8. (C)

1.

All reports must be **filed** by the engineer who wrote them.

(A) filed
(B) repeated
(C) positioned
(D) appeared

모든 보고서는 작성한 엔지니어에 의해 **보관되어야** 한다.

(A) 보관되다 (B) 반복되다
(C) 놓이다 (D) 나타나다

해설 | 동사 어휘 All reports를 수동태의 주어로 취해 의미가 가장 자연스러운 과거분사를 골라야 한다. 따라서 '발송하다; (문서 등을 철하여) 보관하다'를 뜻하는 file의 과거분사인 (A) filed가 정답이다.

어휘 | report 보고서 engineer 엔지니어, 기사 write 쓰다, 작성하다

2.

Mr. Grimes gave the keynote **address** at the IT and security conference last Thursday.

(A) receiver (B) reserve
(C) arrangement (D) address

그라임스 씨는 지난 목요일에 정보 기술과 보안 학회에서 기조**연설**을 했다.

(A) 수령인; 수화기 (B) 비축(물)
(C) 준비; 배치 (D) 연설; 주소

해설 | 명사 어휘 빈칸 앞의 keynote와 어울려 의미가 가장 자연스러운 명사를 골라야 한다. 따라서 '연설'을 뜻하는 (D) address가 정답이다.

어휘 | keynote 기조 security 보안

3.

The company's **finances** are suffering due to a lack of funding.

(A) souvenirs (B) appeals
(C) finances (D) questions

그 회사의 **재정**은 투자 부족 때문에 악화되고 있다.

(A) 기념품 (B) 항소
(C) 재정, 금융 (D) 질문, 문제

해설 | 명사 어휘 빈칸 뒤의 are suffering과 어울려 가장 자연스럽게 의미가 통하는 명사를 골라야 한다. 문맥상 투자 부족 때문에 재정이 악화되고 있다는 내용이 되는 게 자연스러우므로 '재정, 금융'을 뜻하는 (C) finances가 정답이다.

어휘 | suffer 악화되다; 겪다, 시달리다 lack 부족, 결핍 funding 투자, 자금 지원

4.

Ms. Lewis could **extract** the necessary information from the data on customer preferences.

(A) extract (B) deserve
(C) function (D) reverse

루이스 씨는 고객 선호도에 대한 데이터에서 필요한 정보를 **추출할** 수 있었다.

(A) 추출하다 (B) 자격이 있다
(C) 기능하다, 작동하다 (D) 뒤집다

해설 | 동사 어휘 빈칸 뒤의 the necessary information을 목적어로 취해 의미가 가장 자연스러운 동사를 골라야 한다. 따라서 '추출하다, 뽑아내다'를 뜻하는 (A) extract가 정답이다.

어휘 | necessary 필요한 preference 선호(도), 취향

5.

Solid Mech needs some workers to **staff** its booth at the job fair.

(A) produce (B) **staff**
(C) load (D) combine

솔리드 메크는 취업 박람회의 자사 부스에서 **근무할** 직원들이 필요하다.

(A) 생산하다 (B) **직원으로 일하다**
(C) 짐을 싣다 (D) 결합하다

> **해설** 동사 어휘 빈칸 뒤의 its booth를 목적어로 취해 의미가 가장 자연스러운 동사를 골라야 한다. 따라서 '~에서 직원으로 일하다'를 뜻하는 (B) staff가 정답이다.

> **어휘** staff ~에서 직원으로 일하다, ~에 인력을 공급하다 booth 부스, (칸막이를 한) 전시 공간 job fair 취업[채용] 박람회

6.

Mr. Ito required thirty minutes to **detail** the planned renovations to the building manager.

(A) result (B) contact
(C) appear (D) **detail**

이토 씨는 계획된 리모델링을 건물 관리자에게 **상세히 알리는** 데 30분이 필요했다.

(A) (~의 결과로) 생기다 (B) 연락하다
(C) 나타나다 (D) **상세히 알리다**

> **해설** 동사 어휘 빈칸 뒤의 the planned renovations를 목적어로 취해 의미가 가장 자연스러운 동사를 골라야 한다. 따라서 '상세히 알리다'를 뜻하는 (D) detail이 정답이다.

> **어휘** require 필요로 하다, 요구하다 plan 계획하다 renovation 개조, 리모델링

7.

The employee **benefits** at Boone Furniture will be improved for full-time workers.

(A) respect (B) **benefits**
(C) features (D) styles

분 가구의 직원 **혜택**이 정규직 사원들을 대상으로 개선될 것이다.

(A) 존중 (B) **혜택**
(C) 특징 (D) 스타일

> **해설** 명사 어휘 빈칸 앞의 명사 employee와 복합 명사를 이루어 의미가 가장 자연스러운 명사를 골라야 한다. 따라서 '혜택, 이득'을 뜻하는 (B) benefits가 정답이다.

> **어휘** employee 직원 furniture 가구 improve 개선하다, 향상되다 full-time 전임의, 정규직의

8.

Ms. Worthy will receive temporary **access** to the company warehouse in Medford.

(A) permit (B) compliment
(C) **access** (D) favor

워디 씨는 메드퍼드의 회사 물류 창고에 대한 임시 **출입 권한**을 받게 될 것이다.

(A) 허가증 (B) 칭찬
(C) **접근(권), 입장** (D) 호의

> **해설** 명사 어휘 빈칸 앞의 형용사 temporary의 수식을 받아 의미가 가장 자연스러운 명사를 골라야 한다. 따라서 '접근(권)'을 뜻하는 (C) access가 정답이다. (A) permit은 의미상으로는 빈칸에 적절할 수 있으나 셀 수 있는 명사이기 때문에 이 문장에서는 답이 될 수 없다. permit가 빈칸에 들어갈 수 있으려면 a permit나 permits로 써야 한다.

> **어휘** receive 받다 temporary 일시적인, 임시의 warehouse 물류 창고

ACTUAL TEST

본문 p.176

1. (B) 2. (A) 3. (B) 4. (C) 5. (B) 6. (A)
7. (C) 8. (B) 9. (C) 10. (A) 11. (D) 12. (D)

1.
> Several stores reported a large **increase** in the number of customers on Mondays.
>
> (A) increases
> **(B) increase**
> (C) increasingly
> (D) increasing

> 몇몇 매장은 월요일마다 고객 수의 증가를 보고했다.

해설 동명사 vs. 명사 [명사 자리] 빈칸은 형용사 large의 수식을 받는 명사 자리이다. 앞에 부정관사 a가 있으므로 단수 명사인 (B) increase가 정답이다. 동명사인 (D) increasing은 부정관사나 형용사의 수식을 받을 수 없기 때문에 오답이다.

어휘 report 보고하다   increase 증가; 증가하다   number 수, 인원수   increasingly 점점[갈수록] 더

2.
> Golden Light stops **making** survey calls to customers at 4:00 P.M. every day.
>
> **(A) making**
> (B) made
> (C) makes
> (D) to make

> 골든 라이트는 매일 오후 4시에 고객들에게 설문 조사 전화를 거는 걸 중단한다.

해설 동명사 자리 [목적어] 빈칸은 동사 stops의 목적어가 들어갈 자리이다. stop은 동명사를 목적어로 취하므로 (A) making이 정답이다. stop 뒤에 to부정사가 올 수도 있지만 이때는 '~하기 위해 멈추다'라는 의미가 되어 문맥상 맞지 않다.

어휘 make a call 전화하다

3.
> Cindy Holmes paid for her schooling by **working** part-time every evening.
>
> (A) works
> **(B) working**
> (C) worked
> (D) work

> 신디 홈스는 매일 저녁 파트타임으로 일해서 학비를 냈다.

해설 동명사 자리 [전치사의 목적어] 빈칸 앞에 전치사 by가 있고 뒤에는 부사구 part-time every evening이 이어지므로 빈칸에는 전치사의 목적어 역할을 할 수 있는 말이 들어가야 한다. 따라서 동명사 (B) working이 정답이다.

어휘 pay for ~을 지급하다, ~을 내다   schooling 학비, 수업료   work part-time 파트타임으로 일하다

4.
> Customers are urged to **contact** the customer service team with their complaints or suggestions.
>
> (A) avoid
> (B) announce
> **(C) contact**
> (D) reserve

> 고객들은 불만이나 제안이 있으면 고객 서비스 팀에 **연락하도록** 거듭 권유받는다.
>
> (A) 피하다   (B) 발표하다
> **(C) 연락하다**   (D) 예약하다

해설 동사 어휘 빈칸 뒤의 the customer service team을 목적어로 취해 의미가 가장 자연스러운 동사를 골라야 한다. 따라서 '~에게 연락하다'를 뜻하는 (C) contact가 정답이다.

어휘 urge 촉구하다, 거듭 권유하다   complaint 불만, 불평   suggestion 제안

5.

Ms. Vela will consider **approving** the plans to open a branch office in Tokyo.

(A) approve			(B) approving
(C) to approve		(D) has approved

벨라 씨는 도쿄에 지점을 개설하는 계획을 승인하는 걸 고려할 것이다.

해설 동명사 자리 [목적어] 빈칸은 동사 consider의 목적어가 들어갈 자리이다. consider는 동명사를 목적어로 취하므로 (B) approving이 정답이다.

어휘 consider 고려하다   approve 승인하다   plan 계획, 방안   branch office 지점, 지사

6.

All homes in Delmont Park **feature** two floors and a spacious backyard.

(A) feature			(B) compliment
(C) involve			(D) construct

델몬트 공원의 모든 집들은 2개 층과 넓은 뒷마당을 **특징으로 한다**.

(A) 특징으로 하다		(B) 칭찬하다
(C) 관련시키다		(D) 건설하다

해설 동사 어휘 빈칸 뒤의 two floors and a spacious backyard를 목적어로 취해 의미가 가장 자연스러운 동사를 골라야 한다. 따라서 '특징으로 하다, 특별히 선보이다'를 뜻하는 (A) feature가 정답이다.

어휘 floor (건물의) 층   spacious 넓은   backyard 뒤뜰, 뒷마당

7.

The mayor **plans** to initiate a volunteer program for youths in the city.

(A) objects			(B) describes
(C) plans			(D) stops

그 시장은 시의 청소년을 위한 자원봉사 프로그램을 시작할 계획이다.

해설 to부정사를 목적어로 쓰는 동사 [plan to do] 빈칸 앞에 주어 The mayor가 있고 뒤에는 to부정사구(to initiate ~ city)가 이어지므로 빈칸에는 to부정사를 목적어로 취하는 동사가 들어가야 한다. 따라서 (C) plans가 정답이다. (A) objects는 to부정사가 아닌 전치사 to가 이어지므로 빈칸에 적절하지 않다. (B) describes는 to부정사를 목적어로 취하지 않을뿐더러 문맥상으로도 어색하며, (D) stops는 동명사를 목적어로 취하는 동사이므로 오답이다. 〈stop + to부정사〉로 쓰기도 하지만 이때는 '~하기 위해서 멈추다'를 뜻하므로 이 문장에는 어울리지 않는 의미이다.

어휘 plan to do ~할 계획이다   initiate 착수시키다, 시작하다   volunteer 자원봉사   youth 젊은이, 청소년

8.

Prior to working at Marlin Fisheries, Eric Lewis was employed by Stoddard, Inc.

(A) If				(B) Prior to
(C) Even though		(D) For

말린 수산에 근무하기 전에 에릭 루이스는 스토다드 사에 고용되어 있었다.

해설 전치사 자리 [동명사 앞] 빈칸 뒤에 동명사구 working at Marlin Fisheries가 있으므로 빈칸에는 동명사를 목적어로 취할 수 있는 전치사가 들어가야 한다. 따라서 (B) Prior to가 정답이다. (D) For는 전치사이지만 문맥상 어색하기 때문에 빈칸에 적절하지 않다. (A) If와 (C) Even though는 접속사이므로 뒤에 주어와 동사를 갖춘 절이 이어져야 하기 때문에 오답이다.

어휘 prior to ~ 이전에   fisheries 수산 회사; 수산업   be employed 고용되다, 취업하다   even though 비록 ~일지라도

To: All Employees, Hastings, Inc.
From: Chelsea Fitzgerald
Subject: Parking Lot
Date: April 28

You should all be happy to know that work on the employee parking lot is nearly finished. The lot will be **9 accessible** no later than this Friday.

The parking lot will have a capacity of 200 standard-sized vehicles. **10 This is 50 more spots than the old lot featured.** So there should be more than enough space for every employee.

New parking passes will be required to park there. To acquire one, download an application from our Web site. **11 Then**, submit the completed form to Jeb Walker in room 201. Mr. Walker is in charge of **12 distributing** parking passes and is also available to answer questions about the lot.

수신: 헤이스팅스 사 전 직원
발신: 첼시 피츠제럴드
제목: 주차장
날짜: 4월 28일

직원 주차장 공사가 거의 마무리되었다는 것을 아시면 여러분 모두가 기뻐하실 것입니다. 늦어도 이번 금요일까지는 주차장에 **9 출입할 수 있게** 될 것입니다.

그 주차장은 보통 크기 차량 200대의 수용 능력을 갖게 될 것입니다. **10 이는 예전 주차장이 제공한 것보다 50자리가 더 많은 것입니다.** 그래서 모든 직원을 위한 공간이 충분하고도 남을 것입니다.

그곳에 주차하려면 새로운 주차증이 필요할 것입니다. 주차증을 받으시려면 우리 웹사이트에서 신청서를 내려받으십시오. **11 그 다음에** 작성한 양식을 201호에 있는 제브 워커 씨에게 제출하십시오. 워커 씨는 주차증 **12 배부**를 담당하고 있으며 주차장에 관한 질문들에 답변해 드릴 수도 있습니다.

어휘 parking lot 주차장 no later than 늦어도 ~까지는 capacity 수용 능력, 용량 standard-sized 보통 크기의 vehicle 차량 parking pass 주차증, 주차권 require 요구하다, 필요로 하다 acquire 얻다, 취득하다 application 신청서, 지원서 complete (서식 등을) 빠짐없이 작성하다 (=fill in) in charge of ~을 담당하고 있는

---

9. (A) approachable (B) viable (C) **accessible** (D) portable

(A) 가까이하기 쉬운 (B) 실행 가능한 (C) 출입할 수 있는 (D) 휴대하기 쉬운

해설 형용사 어휘 주어 The lot의 보어로 가장 자연스럽게 의미가 통하는 형용사를 골라야 한다. 따라서 '접근할[출입할] 수 있는'을 뜻하는 (C) accessible이 정답이다.

---

10. (A) **This is 50 more spots than the old lot featured.**
(B) The work has taken two months to complete.
(C) There are signs showing the lot's location.
(D) Richard Barrow is responsible for the project.

(A) 이는 예전 주차장이 제공한 것보다 50자리가 더 많은 것입니다.
(B) 그 작업은 완료하는 데 2개월이 걸렸습니다.
(C) 주차장의 위치를 알려 주는 표지들이 있습니다.
(D) 리처드 배로 씨가 그 프로젝트를 책임지고 있습니다.

해설 알맞은 문장 고르기 빈칸 앞 문장에서 새 주차장은 보통 크기 차량 200대를 수용할 수 있다고 했으며, 뒤에서는 모든 직원을 위한 공간이 충분하고도 남을 것이라고 했으므로 주차할 자리가 예전보다 더 많다는 내용의 (A)가 정답이다.

어휘 feature 특징으로 하다 complete 완료하다, 끝내다 be responsible for ~을 책임지고 있다; ~에 책임이 있다

---

11. (A) Therefore (B) Nevertheless (C) If so (D) **Then**

(A) 그러므로 (B) 그럼에도 불구하고 (C) 그렇다면 (D) 그 다음에

해설 접속부사 빈칸 앞 문장에서 주차증을 받으려면 회사 웹사이트에서 신청서를 내려받으라고 했고, 뒤에서는 작성한 양식을 제브 워커 씨에게 제출하라고 했으므로 '그 다음에, 그러고 나서'를 뜻하는 (D) Then이 정답이다.

---

12. (A) distributes (B) distributed (C) distribution (D) **distributing**

해설 동명사 자리 빈칸 앞에 전치사 of가 있고 뒤에는 명사구 parking passes가 이어지므로 빈칸에는 명사구를 목적어로 취할 수 있는 동명사가 들어가야 한다. 따라서 (D) distributing이 정답이다.

UNIT 11 분사

1 분사 자리

본문 p.182

1. (C)   2. (B)   3. (A)   4. (D)

1.

Renovations are scheduled for the customs checkpoint **dividing** San Diego and Tijuana.

(A) divide   (B) divides
(C) dividing   (D) division

샌디에이고와 티후아나를 나누는 세관 검문소에 수리 보수가 예정되어 있다.

해설 분사 자리 [명사 뒤] 빈칸 앞에 명사구 the customs checkpoint가 있고 뒤에는 또 다른 명사구 San Diego and Tijuana가 이어지므로, 빈칸에는 앞에 있는 명사를 수식하는 동시에 뒤에 있는 명사를 목적어로 취할 수 있는 말이 들어가야 한다. 선택지 중 이와 같은 역할을 할 수 있는 것은 현재분사인 (C) dividing이다.

어휘 renovation 개조, 보수   be scheduled for ~가 예정되어 있다   customs ((항상 복수형)) 세관   checkpoint 검문소   divide 나누다

2.

The shipping company we use hasn't kept us **informed** of their new shipping schedule.

(A) to inform   (B) informed
(C) informs   (D) informative

우리가 이용하는 그 운송 회사는 그들의 새로운 운송 일정을 우리에게 알려 주지 않았다.

해설 분사 자리 [목적격 보어] 빈칸은 kept의 목적격 보어 자리이므로 형용사가 들어가야 한다. 선택지 중 형용사 역할을 할 수 있는 것은 과거분사인 (B) informed와 일반 형용사인 (D) informative인데, 문맥상 우리가 정보를 받는 입장이므로 과거분사인 (B) informed가 정답이다. 참고로 keep A informed는 'A에게 정보를 계속 알려 주다'라는 의미의 토익 빈출 표현이다.

어휘 shipping (해상) 운송   inform 알리다, 통지하다   informative (도움이 되는) 정보를 주는

3.

To become a member of Fit Gym, please complete the **attached** form.

(A) attached   (B) attach
(C) attachment   (D) attachable

피트 짐의 회원이 되려면 첨부된 양식을 작성해 주세요.

해설 분사 자리 [명사 앞] 빈칸 앞에 관사 the가 있고 뒤에는 명사 form이 있으므로 빈칸은 명사를 수식하는 자리이다. 선택지 중 형용사 역할을 할 수 있는 과거분사인 (A) attached가 정답이다. (D) attachable은 '붙일 수 있는'을 뜻하는 형용사이긴 하나 여기서는 문맥상 어울리지 않으므로 오답이다. (B) attach는 동사, (C) attachment는 명사이므로 빈칸에 적절하지 않다.

어휘 complete (양식, 서식 등을 빠짐없이) 작성하다   attached 첨부된   form 양식

4.

The labor union accepted the new benefits package **offered** by the company.

(A) had offered   (B) is offering
(C) to offer   (D) offered

노동조합은 회사에 의해 제공되는 새로운 복지 혜택을 받아들였다.

해설 분사 자리 [명사 뒤] 빈칸 앞에 명사구 the new benefits package가 있고 뒤에는 전치사구 by the company가 이어지므로, 빈칸에는 앞에 있는 명사를 수식하는 동시에 전치사구를 이끌 수 있는 말이 들어가야 한다. 선택지 중 이와 같은 역할을 할 수 있는 것은 과거분사인 (D) offered이다.

어휘 labor union 노동조합   accept 받아들이다   benefits package 복지 혜택   offer 제공하다

2 현재분사와 과거분사

1. (A)   2. (C)   3. (B)   4. (B)

1.

Guard Corp., an agency **providing** private security services to celebrities, is hiring qualified candidates.

(A) providing   (B) provision
(C) provides   (D) provided

유명 인사들에게 민간 경비 서비스를 제공하는 대행사인 가드 사는 자격을 갖춘 후보자들을 채용하고 있다.

해설 **현재분사** 빈칸 앞에 명사 an agency가 있고 뒤에는 또 다른 명사구(private ~ celebrities)가 이어지므로, 빈칸에는 앞에 있는 명사를 수식하는 동시에 뒤에 있는 명사를 목적어로 취할 수 있는 말이 들어가야 한다. 선택지 중 이와 같은 역할을 할 수 있는 것은 현재분사인 (A) providing이다. (B) provision은 명사, (C) provides는 동사, (D) provided는 동사 또는 과거분사이므로 오답이다.

어휘 agency 대행사, 대리점   provide A to B A를 B에게 제공하다 (=provide B with A)   private 개인 소유의, 민간의   qualified 자격을 갖춘   provision 공급, 제공; 대비; 조항

2.

The **recommended** changes are specified in the checklist that Ms. O'Hare filled out.

(A) recommending   (B) recommendation
(C) recommended   (D) recommends

권고된 변경 사항들은 오헤어 씨가 작성한 체크리스트에 명시되어 있다.

해설 **과거분사** 빈칸 앞에 관사 The가 있고 뒤에는 명사 changes가 있으므로 빈칸은 명사를 수식하는 자리이다. 선택지 중 형용사 역할을 할 수 있는 것은 현재분사 (A) recommending과 과거분사 (C) recommended인데, 이때 수식 대상과의 관계가 능동인지 수동인지 파악해야 한다. 수식 대상인 '변경 사항(changes)'은 행위자에 의해 권고되는 것이기 때문에 빈칸과 수동 관계임을 알 수 있다. 따라서 과거분사인 (C) recommended가 정답이다.

어휘 recommend 권고하다, 추천하다   specify 명시하다   fill out ~을 작성하다

3.

Thanks to **rushed** repairs, the shuttle was able to return to operation quickly.

(A) rush   (B) rushed
(C) rushing   (D) had rushed

서두른 수리 덕분에 셔틀버스는 운영이 빠르게 재개될 수 있었다.

해설 **과거분사** 빈칸 앞에 전치사구 Thanks to가 있고 뒤에는 명사 repairs가 있으므로 빈칸은 명사를 수식하는 자리이다. 선택지 중 형용사 역할을 할 수 있는 것은 과거분사 (B) rushed와 현재분사 (C) rushing인데, 이때 수식 대상과의 관계가 능동인지 수동인지 파악해야 한다. 수식 대상인 '수리(repairs)'는 행위자에 의해 서둘러지는 것이기 때문에 빈칸과 수동 관계임을 알 수 있다. 따라서 과거분사인 (B) rushed가 정답이다.

어휘 repair 수리, 수선   be able to *do* ~할 수 있다   operation 운영; 작업

4.

Commuting staff members are asked to use street parking until further notice.

(A) To commute   (B) Commuting
(C) Commuted   (D) Commute

출퇴근하는 직원들은 추후 공지가 있을 때까지 길가에 주차할 것을 요청받는다.

해설 **현재분사** 빈칸 뒤에 명사 staff members가 있고 그 뒤에 동사구 are asked가 있는 것으로 보아 빈칸은 명사를 수식하는 자리이다. 선택지 중 형용사 역할을 할 수 있는 것은 현재분사 (B) Commuting과 과거분사 (C) Commuted인데, 수식 대상인 '직원들(staff members)'은 능동적으로 출퇴근하는 주체이므로 현재분사인 (B) Commuting이 정답이다. to부정사인 (A) To commute는 명사를 앞에서 수식할 수 없기 때문에 오답이다.

어휘 commute 출퇴근하다, 통근하다   be asked to *do* ~할 것을 요청받다   until further notice 추후 공지가 있을 때까지

3 감정을 나타내는 분사

1. (D)   2. (B)   3. (C)   4. (B)

1.

Stephanie McQueen is the author of dozens of **thrilling** books on the best-sellers list.

(A) thrill (B) thrilled
(C) thrills **(D) thrilling**

스테파니 맥퀸은 베스트셀러 목록에 있는 수십 권의 재미있는 책들을 쓴 작가이다.

해설 감정을 나타내는 분사 빈칸 앞에 전치사 of가 있고 뒤에는 명사 books가 있으므로 빈칸은 명사를 수식하는 자리이다. 선택지 중 형용사 역할을 할 수 있는 것은 과거분사 (B) thrilled와 현재분사 (D) thrilling인데, 감정을 나타내는 분사는 수식 대상이 감정을 느끼게 하는 주체면 현재분사로 쓰기 때문에 (D) thrilling이 정답이다.

어휘 author 저자, 작가 dozens of 많은, 수십의 thrilling 아주 신나는 thrilled 아주 신난

2.

Beacon Athletics **is pleased** to open its first international retail location in Toronto.

(A) is pleasing   **(B) is pleased**
(C) will please   (D) pleases

비콘 애슬레틱스는 토론토에 첫 해외 소매점을 열게 되어 기쁩니다.

해설 감정을 나타내는 분사 수식 대상인 Beacon Athletics가 감정을 느끼는 대상이므로 감정을 나타내는 분사는 과거분사로 써야 한다. 따라서 (B) is pleased가 정답이다.

어휘 pleased 기쁜, 기뻐하는 international 국제적인 retail location 소매점 pleasing 즐거운, 만족을 주는

3.

Despite positive reviews from critics, actor Billy Brandt's latest film's box office numbers were **disappointing**.

(A) disappoints   (B) disappointed
(C) disappointing   (D) disappointment

비평가들의 긍정적인 평가에도 불구하고 배우 빌리 브란트의 최신작 박스 오피스 수익은 실망스러웠다.

해설 감정을 나타내는 분사 빈칸 앞에 be동사 were가 있으므로 빈칸은 주격 보어 자리이다. 문맥상 이 문장의 주어(actor ~ numbers)는 감정을 느끼는 대상이 아니라 감정을 느끼게 하는 주체이기 때문에 (C) disappointing이 정답이다.

어휘 despite ~에도 불구하고 latest 최신의 box office numbers 영화의 매출, 박스 오피스 수익 disappointing 실망스러운 disappointed 실망한

4.

Our software firm would be **delighted** to have you work in our training division.

(A) delighting   **(B) delighted**
(C) to delight   (D) delights

우리 소프트웨어 회사는 귀하를 우리 회사의 교육팀에 모실 수 있다면 기쁠 것입니다.

해설 감정을 나타내는 분사 빈칸 앞에 be동사가 있고 뒤에는 to부정사구(to have ~ division)가 이어지므로 빈칸은 주격 보어 자리이다. 문맥상 이 문장의 주어인 Our software firm이 기쁜 감정을 느끼는 대상이기 때문에 과거분사로 써야 한다. 따라서 (B) delighted가 정답이다.

어휘 firm 회사 delighted 기뻐하는 division 부서, 팀 delighting 기쁨을 주는

4 분사구문

1. (A) 2. (C) 3. (A) 4. (D)

1.

Our startup business' stock value was up again, **marking** another company record.

(A) marking (B) marked
(C) is marking (D) had marked

우리 스타트업 사업의 주식 가치가 다시 오르면서 회사의 또 다른 기록을 세웠다.

해설 | 분사구문 [현재분사] 빈칸 앞에 완전한 절이 있고 콤마로 빈칸 이하가 연결된 것을 보아 〈------- another company record〉는 분사구문임을 알 수 있다. 선택지 중 분사는 (A) marking과 (B) marked인데, 명사구 another company record를 목적어로 취할 수 있는 것은 현재분사이므로 정답은 (A) marking이다.

어휘 | stock 주식 value 가치 mark a record 기록하다, 기록을 세우다

2.

When recently **tested**, Atilla Auto's latest engine proved to be highly energy-efficient.

(A) test (B) tester
(C) tested (D) testing

최근에 검사를 받았을 때, 아틸라 오토의 최신 엔진은 매우 에너지 효율적이라는 것이 입증되었다.

해설 | 분사구문 [과거분사] 빈칸 앞에 접속사 When이 있으며 콤마로 완전한 절이 연결된 것을 보아 〈When recently -------〉은 분사구문임을 알 수 있다. 선택지 중 분사는 (C) tested와 (D) testing인데, 분사구문의 생략된 주어인 Atilla Auto's latest engine은 검사를 받는 대상이기 때문에 빈칸에 들어갈 말과 수동 관계이다. 따라서 과거분사인 (C) tested가 정답이다.

어휘 | recently 최근에 latest 최신의 prove 입증하다 highly 매우 energy-efficient 에너지 효율적인

3.

The fundraising event raised $11,000, **exceeding** its initial goal by 10 percent.

(A) exceeding (B) exceedingly
(C) is exceeding (D) exceeded

그 자금 모금 행사에 11,000달러가 모금되어 초기 목표를 10퍼센트까지 초과하게 되었다.

해설 | 분사구문 [현재분사] 빈칸 앞에 완전한 절이 있고 콤마로 빈칸 이하가 연결된 것을 보아 〈------- its initial goal by 10 percent〉는 분사구문임을 알 수 있다. 선택지 중 분사는 (A) exceeding과 (D) exceeded인데, 명사구(its ~ percent)를 목적어로 취할 수 있는 것은 현재분사이므로 정답은 (A) exceeding이다.

어휘 | fundraising 자금 모금 raise (자금 등을) 모으다; 들어 올리다 initial 처음의, 초기의 exceedingly 대단히, 몹시

4.

Defending his company's reputation, Brian Mars promised compensation to customers for the product recall.

(A) Defense (B) Defender
(C) Defended **(D) Defending**

회사의 명성을 지켜야 하기 때문에 브라이언 마스는 고객들에게 제품 회수에 대한 보상을 약속했다.

해설 | 분사구문 [현재분사] 빈칸 뒤에 명사구 his company's reputation이 있으며, 콤마로 완전한 절이 연결된 것을 보아 〈------- his company's reputation〉은 이유를 나타내는 분사구문임을 알 수 있다. 선택지 중 분사는 (C) Defended와 (D) Defending인데, 명사구 his company's reputation을 목적어로 취할 수 있는 것은 현재분사이므로 정답은 (D) Defending이다.

어휘 | defend 지키다, 방어하다; 옹호하다 reputation 명성 compensation 보상 recall 회수

VOCABULARY

본문 p.188

1. (C)   2. (B)   3. (C)   4. (D)   5. (A)   6. (D)   7. (C)   8. (B)

1.

Increased temperatures in the Golden Coast will have **lasting** harmful effects on the environment.

(A) descending (B) existing
(C) lasting (D) parting

골든 코스트에서 상승되는 온도는 환경에 **지속적인** 해로운 영향을 줄 것이다.

(A) 내려가는 (B) 기존의
(C) 지속적인 (D) 갈라진

> 해설 | 형용사 어휘 명사구 harmful effects를 수식해 가장 자연스럽게 의미가 통하는 형용사를 골라야 한다. 따라서 '지속적인'이라는 의미의 (C) lasting이 정답이다.

> 어휘 | temperature 온도   have an effect on ~에 영향을 미치다   harmful 해로운   environment 환경

2.

The **rising** demand for organic fruits and vegetables is changing the agricultural industry.

(A) profiting **(B) rising**
(C) converting (D) surrounding

유기농 과일과 채소의 **증가하는** 수요가 농업을 변화시키고 있다.

(A) 이익을 주는 **(B) 증가하는, 상승하는**
(C) 전환하는 (D) 인근의, 주위의

> 해설 | 형용사 어휘 명사 demand를 수식해 가장 자연스럽게 의미가 통하는 형용사를 골라야 한다. 따라서 '증가하는, 상승하는'이라는 의미의 (B) rising이 정답이다.

> 어휘 | demand for ~의 수요   organic 유기농의   vegetable 채소   agricultural industry 농업

3.

The marketing firm's application procedure is **challenging**, so applicants are encouraged to submit impressive résumés.

(A) missing (B) including
(C) challenging (D) reacting

그 마케팅 회사의 지원 절차는 **만만치 않으므로** 지원자들은 인상적인 이력서를 제출할 것을 권장받는다.

(A) 없어진, 분실한 (B) ~을 포함하여
(C) 도전적인 (D) 반응하는

> 해설 | 형용사 어휘 빈칸은 주격 보어 자리이므로 주어(The marketing ~ procedure)의 상태나 상황을 표현하는 말이 들어가야 한다. 문맥상 지원 절차가 쉽지는 않지만 해 볼 만하다는 내용이 되는 게 자연스러우므로 '(어렵지만) 도전적인'이라는 의미의 (C) challenging이 정답이다.

> 어휘 | application 지원(서)   procedure 절차   applicant 지원자   submit 제출하다   impressive 인상적인   résumé 이력서

4.

Tech Brite is a **leading** firm in renewable energy technology.

(A) rewarding (B) graduating
(C) saving **(D) leading**

테크 브라이트는 재생 가능한 에너지 기술 분야의 **선두** 기업이다.

(A) 가치 있는 (B) 졸업하는
(C) 절약하는 **(D) 선두의**

> 해설 | 형용사 어휘 명사 firm을 수식해 가장 자연스럽게 의미가 통하는 형용사를 골라야 한다. 따라서 '선두의, 주요한'이라는 의미의 (D) leading이 정답이다.

> 어휘 | leading 선두의, 앞서가는   renewable 재생 가능한   technology 기술

5.

Due to **repeated** noise complaints, pets will no longer be allowed in the apartment building.

(A) repeated (B) conducted
(C) dedicated (D) respected

반복되는 소음 불만 때문에 그 아파트에서는 반려동물이 더 이상 허락되지 않을 것이다.

(A) 반복되는 (B) 실시된
(C) 헌신적인 (D) 존경받는

> **해설** 형용사 어휘 명사구 noise complaints를 수식해 가장 자연스럽게 의미가 통하는 형용사를 골라야 한다. 따라서 '반복되는'이라는 의미의 (A) repeated가 정답이다.

> **어휘** due to ~ 때문에 complaint 불평, 불만 no longer 더 이상 ~않는

6.

Only highly **experienced** leaders get promoted to upper management at most companies.

(A) customized (B) compensated
(C) introduced (D) experienced

대부분의 회사에서 매우 **경험이 풍부한** 리더만이 더 높은 경영진으로 승진된다.

(A) 주문 제작된 (B) 보상되는
(C) 소개된 (D) 경험이 풍부한

> **해설** 형용사 어휘 명사 leaders를 수식해 가장 자연스럽게 의미가 통하는 형용사를 골라야 한다. 따라서 '경험이 풍부한'이라는 의미의 (D) experienced가 정답이다.

> **어휘** highly 매우 get promoted 승진하다 upper 더 높은 management 경영(진)

7.

The **accomplished** product designer was awarded with the industry's top honors.

(A) assisted (B) extended
(C) accomplished (D) refunded

그 **뛰어난** 제품 디자이너는 그 업계에서 가장 큰 상을 수상했다.

(A) 도움을 받는 (B) 연장된
(C) (기량이) 뛰어난 (D) 환불되는

> **해설** 형용사 어휘 명사구 product designer를 수식해 가장 자연스럽게 의미가 통하는 형용사를 골라야 한다. 따라서 '(기량이) 뛰어난'이라는 의미의 (C) accomplished가 정답이다.

> **어휘** accomplished 뛰어난, 걸출한, 성공한 be awarded with ~을 수상하다, ~을 받다 top honors 대상, 최우수상

8.

McCain Pharmaceuticals' main lab only employs scientists with **advanced** degrees in their fields.

(A) accrued (B) advanced
(C) complicated (D) educated

맥케인 제약 회사의 주 연구실은 그 분야의 **고**학력 과학자들만 고용한다.

(A) 누적된, 축적된 (B) 고급[상급]의
(C) 복잡한 (D) 교육을 받은

> **해설** 형용사 어휘 명사 degrees를 수식해 가장 자연스럽게 의미가 통하는 형용사를 골라야 한다. 따라서 '고급[상급]의'라는 의미의 (B) advanced가 정답이다. advanced degree는 석박사 등의 학위를 일컫는 말로 자주 쓰인다. (D) educated는 사람을 수식할 때 쓰는 게 적절하므로 이 문맥에는 어울리지 않는다.

> **어휘** pharmaceuticals 제약 회사 employ 고용하다 degree 학위 field 분야

111

ACTUAL TEST

본문 p.190

| 1. (B) | 2. (D) | 3. (C) | 4. (D) | 5. (C) | 6. (B) |
| 7. (B) | 8. (D) | 9. (D) | 10. (A) | 11. (C) | 12. (B) |

1.

To learn more about insurance plans from Prime State, speak with one of our **certified** representatives.

(A) certify   (B) **certified**
(C) certifying   (D) certification

프라임 스테이트로부터 보험 계획에 대해 더 알고 싶으시다면 공식 판매 대리인과 이야기를 나누십시오.

[해설] **분사 자리 [과거분사]** 빈칸 앞에 소유격 our가 있고 뒤에는 명사 representatives가 있으므로 빈칸은 명사를 수식하는 자리이다. 선택지 중 형용사 역할을 할 수 있는 것은 과거분사 (B) certified와 현재분사 (C) certifying인데, 수식 대상인 '판매 대리인(representatives)'은 인증을 받은 대상이므로 과거분사인 (B) certified가 정답이다.

[어휘] insurance 보험   representative (판매) 대리인   certify 증명하다   certification 증명

2.

Anyone **interested** in joining the charity run should register online by this Friday.

(A) to interest   (B) interesting
(C) interests   (D) **interested**

자선 달리기에 참여하는 데 관심 있는 분은 이번 주 금요일까지 온라인으로 등록해야 합니다.

[해설] **감정을 나타내는 분사** 빈칸 앞에 명사 Anyone이 있고 뒤에는 전치사구 in joining the charity run이 이어지므로, 빈칸에는 앞에 있는 명사를 수식하는 동시에 전치사구를 이끌 수 있는 말이 들어가야 한다. 또한 주어 Anyone은 자선 달리기 행사에 관심을 갖는 대상이기 때문에 감정을 나타내는 분사는 과거분사로 써야 한다. 따라서 (D) interested가 정답이다.

[어휘] interested 흥미 있는   join 합류하다; 가입하다   charity 자선 (단체)   register 등록하다

3.

The receptionist apologized for the delay, **explaining** that there had been a problem with their online system.

(A) explained   (B) will explain
(C) **explaining** (D) explains

접수원은 온라인 시스템에 문제가 있었다고 설명하며 지연에 대해 사과했다.

[해설] **분사구문 [현재분사]** 빈칸 앞에 완전한 절이 있고 콤마로 빈칸 이하가 연결된 것으로 보아 분사구문임을 알 수 있다. 선택지 중 분사는 과거분사 (A) explained와 (C) explaining인데, 설명하는 주체가 The receptionist이므로 현재분사인 (C) explaining이 정답이다.

[어휘] receptionist 접수원   apologize for ~에 대해 사과하다   delay 지연

4.

All guests planning an **extended** vacation at our hotel will be gifted free room upgrades and dining coupons.

(A) accomplished   (B) objective
(C) equal   (D) **extended**

우리 호텔에서 **장기** 휴가를 계획하는 모든 투숙객에게는 무료 객실 업그레이드와 식사 쿠폰이 주어집니다.

(A) (기량이) 뛰어난   (B) 객관적인
(C) 동일한, 동등한   (D) 연장된

[해설] **형용사 어휘** 명사 vacation을 수식해 가장 자연스럽게 의미가 통하는 형용사를 골라야 한다. 따라서 '연장된'이라는 의미의 (D) extended가 정답이다.

[어휘] plan 계획하다   gift (선물 따위를) 주다   upgrade (등급 등의) 상향, 격상; 업그레이드하다, 개선하다   dining 식사

112

5.

Whitehall Library is asking for **experienced** speakers to volunteer as guest lecturers.

(A) regarded (B) imposed
(C) experienced (D) customized

화이트홀 도서관은 초청 강연자로 자원봉사를 할 **경험이 풍부한** 연설자들을 찾고 있다.

(A) 여겨지는, 간주되는 (B) 부과된
(C) 숙련된, 경험이 풍부한 (D) 주문 제작된

해설 형용사 어휘 명사 speakers를 수식해 가장 자연스럽게 의미가 통하는 형용사를 골라야 한다. 따라서 '숙련된, 경험이 풍부한'이라는 의미의 (C) experienced가 정답이다.

어휘 ask for ~을 찾다, ~을 요청하다 volunteer 자원봉사를 하다 lecturer 강연자

6.

Dentists recommend extra **cleansing** process which includes using floss or mouthwash after brushing teeth.

(A) cleanses **(B) cleansing**
(C) cleansed (D) to cleanse

치과 의사들은 양치 후에 치실이나 구강 청결제 사용을 포함한 추가 세척 과정을 추천한다.

해설 분사 자리 [현재분사] 빈칸 앞에 형용사 extra가 있고 뒤에는 명사 process가 있으므로 빈칸은 명사를 수식하는 자리이다. 선택지 중 형용사 역할을 할 수 있는 것은 현재분사 (B) cleansing과 과거분사 (C) cleansed인데, 수식 대상인 '과정(process)'은 '세척되는' 것이 아니라 '세척하는' 것이기 때문에 빈칸과 능동 관계이다. 따라서 현재분사인 (B) cleansing이 정답이다.

어휘 extra 추가의 floss 치실 mouthwash 구강 청결제 cleanse (피부, 상처 등을) 세척하다

7.

Refer to the **enclosed** packet for information on your first day's orientation session.

(A) enclosing **(B) enclosed**
(C) enclosure (D) enclose

오리엔테이션 과정 첫날에 대한 정보는 동봉된 꾸러미에서 확인하십시오.

해설 분사 자리 [과거분사] 빈칸은 관사 the와 명사 packet 사이에 위치해 있으므로 형용사 자리이다. 선택지 중 형용사 역할을 할 수 있는 것은 현재분사 (A) enclosing과 과거분사 (B) enclosed인데, 수식 대상인 '꾸러미(packet)'는 행위자에 의해 동봉되는 대상이므로 빈칸과 수동 관계이다. 따라서 정답은 (B) enclosed이다.

어휘 refer to ~을 참조하다 packet 꾸러미 enclosure 동봉된 것 enclose 동봉하다; 에워싸다

8.

At the product launch, Mr. Hilton gave an **exciting** presentation that everyone enjoyed.

(A) excitingly (B) excitement
(C) excited **(D) exciting**

제품 출시회에서 힐튼 씨는 모두가 즐거워하는 흥미진진한 발표를 했다.

해설 감정을 나타내는 분사 빈칸은 부정관사 an과 명사 presentation 사이에 위치해 있으므로 형용사 자리이다. 수식 대상인 presentation은 감정을 느끼게 하는 주체이기 때문에 현재분사인 (D) exciting이 정답이다. (A) excitingly는 부사, (B) excitement는 명사이므로 빈칸에 적절하지 않다.

어휘 launch 출시 excitingly 흥미진진하게, 신나게 excitement 신남, 즐거움

To: r.ford@smithtowndental.com
From: i.kelsey@digione.com
Date: 12 June
Subject: Re: Database Services

Dear Mr. Ford,

I am glad you contacted me about setting up a secure database for your dental clinic. Digi One offers a wide array of services, ⁹**optimizing** your business' digital operations.

After reviewing the attached service plan options, please ¹⁰**select** the one that would best fit your needs. A service representative can help you with that if you need assistance. ¹¹**In addition**, your specific plan can be customized if necessary.

With our most popular plan, one of our computer technicians will visit your office weekly to perform maintenance and updates. ¹²**This can also be done remotely if you prefer.**

I look forward to hearing back from you soon.

Sincerely,

Ian Kelsey
Service Representative, Digi One

수신: r.ford@smithtowndental.com
발신: i.kelsey@digione.com
날짜: 6월 12일
제목: 회신: 데이터베이스 서비스

포드 씨께,

귀하의 치과에 안전한 데이터베이스를 구축하는 것에 대해 저희에게 연락을 주셔서 기쁩니다. 디지 원은 다양한 서비스를 제공하여 귀하 사업의 디지털 운영을 ⁹**최적화합니다**.

첨부된 서비스 플랜 옵션들을 검토한 후에, 귀하의 필요에 가장 잘 맞는 것을 ¹⁰**선택해** 주십시오. 도움이 필요하시다면 서비스 담당자가 그것을 도와 드릴 수 있습니다. ¹¹**또한**, 필요하다면 귀하의 특정 플랜은 맞춤 변경될 수 있습니다.

저희의 가장 인기 있는 플랜을 선택하시면 저희 컴퓨터 기술자 중 한 명이 유지 보수 및 업데이트를 해 드리기 위해 매주 귀하의 사무실에 방문할 것입니다. ¹²**이 또한 원하신다면 원격으로 진행될 수 있습니다.**

답변 기다리겠습니다.

이안 켈시
디지 원 서비스 담당자

어휘 set up ~을 설치하다 secure 안전한 a wide array of 다양한, 많은 operation 운영 attached 첨부된 fit 맞다
representative 대표자, 담당자 specific 구체적인 necessary 필요한, 필수적인 maintenance 유지 보수

---

9. (A) optimize   (B) optimizes   (C) optimizer   **(D) optimizing**

> **해설** 분사구문 빈칸 앞에 완전한 절이 있고 콤마로 빈칸 이하가 연결된 것을 보아 〈------- your business' digital operations〉는 분사구문임을 알 수 있다. 따라서 현재분사인 (D) optimizing이 정답이다.

---

10. **(A) select**   (B) remove   (C) depend   (D) refer

> **해설** 동사 어휘 문맥상 필요에 가장 잘 맞는 것을 선택하라는 내용이 되는 게 자연스러우므로 '선택하다'라는 의미의 (A) select가 정답이다. (C) depend는 depend on(~에 의지하다), (D) refer는 refer to(~을 참고하다)의 형태로 주로 전치사와 함께 쓴다.

---

11. (A) As in   (B) Although   (A) ~의 경우와 같이   (B) 비록 ~일지라도
    (C) In addition   (D) Likewise   **(C) 또한, 게다가**   (D) 마찬가지로

> **해설** 접속부사 빈칸 앞에서 필요에 맞는 서비스 플랜을 선택할 수 있다고 했고, 뒤에서는 필요에 따라 맞춤 변경도 가능하다는 추가 서비스를 언급했다. 따라서 '또한, 게다가'를 뜻하는 (C) In addition이 정답이다.

---

12. (A) Our databases are simple to browse and update.
    (B) This can also be done remotely if you prefer.
    (C) Digi One is updated bi-weekly for system improvements.
    (D) You can read client testimonials on our homepage.

(A) 저희 데이터베이스는 열람하고 업데이트하는 것이 간단합니다.
(B) 이 또한 원하신다면 원격으로 진행될 수 있습니다.
(C) 디지 원은 시스템 개선을 위해 격주로 업데이트됩니다.
(D) 저희 홈페이지에서 고객의 추천 글을 읽어 보실 수 있습니다.

> **해설** 알맞은 문장 고르기 빈칸 앞에서 기술자가 직접 방문하여 서비스를 유지 보수하고 업데이트해 준다고 했으므로, 빈칸에는 기술자가 방문하지 않더라도 서비스를 받을 수 있는 방법에 대한 내용이 이어지는 게 문맥상 자연스럽다. 따라서 정답은 (B)이다.

UNIT 12　등위 접속사와 부사절 접속사

1 등위 접속사
본문 p.196

1. (A)　　2. (A)　　3. (D)　　4. (B)

1.

> The Duncan Roughrider is the safest **and** most powerful pickup truck on the market.
>
> 덩컨 러프라이더는 시중에서 가장 안전하고 가장 힘이 좋은 픽업트럭이다.
>
> **(A) and**　　(B) but
> (C) either　　(D) both

해설　**등위 접속사 and** 빈칸 앞뒤로 형용사의 최상급인 the safest와 most powerful이 연결되어 있으므로 빈칸은 두 형용사를 연결하는 등위 접속사 자리이다. '가장 안전하고 가장 강력한'이라는 내용이 되는 게 문맥상 자연스러우므로 '그리고'를 뜻하는 등위 접속사인 (A) and가 정답이다. (B) but도 등위 접속사이지만 서로 대립되는 것을 연결하고, (C) either와 (D) both는 각각 or, and와 짝을 이루어 쓰므로 빈칸에 적절하지 않다.

어휘　powerful 힘이 좋은, 강력한　pickup truck 픽업트럭, 소형 오픈 트럭

2.

> The new recliner design is focused on **comfort** and overall size.
>
> 그 새로운 리클라이너 디자인은 편안함과 전반적인 크기에 중점을 두고 있다.
>
> **(A) comfort**　　(B) comfortable
> (C) comfortably　　(D) comforted

해설　**명사 자리** 빈칸 뒤에 접속사 and로 명사 size가 연결되어 있다. 등위 접속사는 품사가 같은 단어를 연결하기 때문에 빈칸에는 size와 같은 품사인 명사가 들어가야 한다. 따라서 (A) comfort가 정답이다.

어휘　be focused on ~에 중점을 두다　comfort 편안함, 안락함　overall 전반적인　comfortable 편안한

3.

> Several items in the package were broken, **so** the customer requested a refund.
>
> 포장 상자 안의 몇 가지 물품들이 깨져서 그 고객은 환불을 요청했다.
>
> (A) or　　(B) while
> (C) yet　　**(D) so**

해설　**등위 접속사 so** 빈칸은 절과 절을 연결하는 접속사 자리이다. 빈칸을 기준으로 앞 문장은 원인을 나타내고, 뒤 문장은 결과를 나타내므로 '그래서'를 뜻하는 등위 접속사 (D) so가 정답이다. (A) or(또는, 혹은)와 (C) yet(그렇지만, 그런데도)은 등위 접속사이지만 의미상 알맞지 않고, (B) while(~하는 동안; ~한 반면)은 부사절 접속사이므로 빈칸에 적절하지 않다.

어휘　item 물품, 품목　package (포장용) 상자, 포장물　request a refund 환불을 요청하다

4.

> Mr. Boothe applied for the open position **but** hasn't heard back from them yet.
>
> 부스 씨는 공석에 지원했지만 아직 그들로부터 결과를 전해 듣지 못했다.
>
> (A) both　　**(B) but**
> (C) so　　(D) for

해설　**등위 접속사 but** 빈칸을 기준으로 동사구 applied for와 hasn't heard back이 연결된 것으로 보아 빈칸은 등위 접속사 자리이다. 문맥상 빈칸 앞뒤 내용이 서로 대립되므로 '그러나'를 뜻하는 (B) but이 정답이다. (A) both는 and와 짝을 이루어 쓰고, (C) so는 인과 관계를 나타내는 접속사이며, (D) for는 전치사 또는 이유를 나타내는 접속사이므로 빈칸에 적절하지 않다.

어휘　apply for ~을 신청하다, ~에 지원하다　position (일)자리, 직위

2 상관 접속사

본문 p.197

1. (C) 2. (B) 3. (B) 4. (C)

1.

> Waitstaff should work **either** the morning shift or the evening shift each week.
>
> (A) both (B) neither
> **(C) either** (D) not only

식당 종업원들은 매주 아침 근무나 저녁 근무 중 하나를 해야 한다.

해설 상관 접속사 either A or B 빈칸 뒤에 〈명사(the morning shift) or 명사(the evening shift)〉 구조가 이어지므로 빈칸에는 접속사 or와 짝을 이루는 상관 접속사가 들어가야 한다. 따라서 (C) either가 정답이다. (A) both와 (B) neither, 그리고 (D) not only는 각각 and, nor, but also와 짝을 이루므로 빈칸에 적절하지 않다.

어휘 waitstaff 식당 종업원들 shift 교대 근무, 교대조; 옮기다

2.

> Not only the diners but also the famous critic, John Hemmings, **comments** food at Joy's Bistro is exceptional.
>
> (A) comment **(B) comments**
> (C) commentary (D) commenting

손님들뿐만 아니라 유명한 비평가인 존 헤밍스도 조이스 비스트로의 음식이 특출하다고 평가한다.

해설 동사 자리+수 일치 빈칸 앞에 있는 〈Not only 명사(the diners) but also 명사(the famous critic, John Hemmings)〉 구조가 문장의 주어 역할을 하므로 빈칸에는 동사가 들어가야 한다. 주어가 상관 접속사로 연결되어 있을 때는 뒤에 있는 명사에 수 일치를 하는데, 이 문장에서는 단수 명사인 the famous critic에 수 일치를 해야 하므로 (B) comments가 정답이다.

어휘 diner 식사하는 사람 critic 비평가, 평론가 exceptional 우수한, 특출한

3.

> After lunch, neither the conference room **nor** the auditorium will be available to use.
>
> (A) but **(B) nor**
> (C) and (D) so

점심시간 이후에는 회의실과 강당 둘 다 사용할 수 없을 것이다.

해설 상관 접속사 neither A nor B 빈칸은 앞에 있는 neither와 짝을 이루는 말이 들어갈 자리이므로 (B) nor가 정답이다. (A) but은 not A but B(A가 아니라 B), (C) and는 both A and B(A와 B 둘 다) 형태의 상관 접속사로 쓰이고, (D) so는 절과 절을 연결하는 등위 접속사이므로 빈칸에 적절하지 않다.

어휘 conference room 회의실 auditorium 강당 available 이용할 수 있는

4.

> The menu at the Western Steakhouse includes regular dishes **as well as** seasonal specialties.
>
> (A) nor (B) either
> **(C) as well as** (D) but also

웨스턴 스테이크하우스의 메뉴에는 계절 특선뿐만 아니라 정식도 포함되어 있다.

해설 상관 접속사 as well as 빈칸 앞뒤로 명사구 regular dishes와 seasonal specialties가 대등하게 연결되어 있으므로 'A뿐만 아니라 B도'를 뜻하는 상관 접속사인 (C) as well as가 정답이다. 참고로 B as well as A는 not only A but also B로 바꿔 쓸 수 있다. (A) nor는 neither와 짝을 이루며, (B) either는 either A or B(A나 B 둘 중 하나) 형태의 상관 접속사로 쓰이므로 오답이다.

어휘 include 포함하다 regular dish 정식 seasonal 계절적인, 계절에 따라 다른 specialty 특제품; 전문, 전공

3 부사절 접속사: 시간, 조건

본문 p.198

1. (B)   2. (A)   3. (B)   4. (B)

1.

Restaurant owners should apply for a permit **before** they start serving customers.

(A) since   (B) before
(C) as well as   (D) while

식당 주인들은 영업을 시작하기 전에 허가증을 신청해야 한다.

해설 부사절 접속사 before 빈칸은 절과 절을 연결하는 접속사 자리이다. 문맥상 영업을 시작하기 전에 허가증을 신청해야 한다는 내용이 되는 게 자연스러우므로 '~ 전에'를 뜻하는 (B) before가 정답이다. (A) since(~ 때문에)와 (C) as well as(~뿐만 아니라), 그리고 (D) while(~하는 동안; ~한 반면)은 모두 의미상 빈칸에 적절하지 않다.

어휘 owner 주인, 소유주   apply for ~을 신청하다, ~에 지원하다   permit 허가증; 허가하다

2.

As soon as Ms. Montpelier got off the plane, she went to the baggage claim area.

(A) As soon as   (B) While
(C) Until   (D) Although

몬트필리어 씨는 비행기에서 내리자마자 수하물 찾는 곳에 갔다.

해설 부사절 접속사 as soon as 빈칸 뒤에 완전한 절이 있으므로 빈칸은 절을 이끌 수 있는 접속사 자리이다. 문맥상 비행기에서 내리자마자 짐을 찾으러 갔다는 내용이 되는 게 자연스러우므로 '~하자마자'를 뜻하는 (A) As soon as가 정답이다. (B) While(~하는 동안; ~한 반면), (C) Until(~할 때까지), (D) Although(비록 ~일지라도) 모두 의미상 빈칸에 적절하지 않다.

어휘 get off (타고 있던 것에서) 내리다   baggage claim area (공항의) 수하물 찾는 곳

3.

The opening ceremony will proceed as scheduled **unless** it rains tomorrow morning.

(A) whereas   **(B) unless**
(C) while   (D) as long as

내일 아침에 비가 내리지 않는다면 개회식이 예정대로 진행될 것이다.

해설 부사절 접속사 unless 빈칸은 절과 절을 연결하는 접속사 자리이다. 문맥상 비가 내리지 않는다면 개업식을 진행할 것이라는 내용이 되는 게 자연스러우므로 '만약 ~가 아니라면'을 뜻하는 (B) unless가 정답이다. (A) whereas(~한 반면)와 (C) while(~하는 동안; ~한 반면), 그리고 (D) as long as(~하는 한) 모두 의미상 빈칸에 적절하지 않다.

어휘 opening ceremony 개회식   proceed 진행하다, 진행되다   as scheduled 예정대로

4.

When you **encounter** any issue on your computer, contact Jay at extension 56.

(A) encountered   **(B) encounter**
(C) will encounter   (D) encountering

컴퓨터에 문제가 생기면 내선 번호 56으로 제이에게 연락하세요.

해설 동사 자리 + 현재 시제 빈칸 앞에 주어 you가 있고 뒤에는 목적어 any issue가 있으므로 빈칸은 동사 자리이다. 또한 빈칸이 있는 절은 접속사 when이 이끄는 시간 부사절인데, 시간이나 조건을 나타내는 부사절에서는 현재 시제가 미래 시제를 대신하므로 현재 시제인 (B) encounter가 정답이다.

어휘 encounter 맞닥뜨리다, 마주치다   contact 연락하다, 접촉하다   extension 내선 번호

4 부사절 접속사: 이유, 양보/대조

본문 p.199

1. (D)　　　2. (C)　　　3. (A)　　　4. (A)

1.

Whereas the Milton Hotel had no vacancies, rooms were available at the Greenbrier Resort.

(A) Because　　　(B) Instead
(C) Since　　　**(D) Whereas**

밀턴 호텔에는 빈방이 없었던 반면, 그린브라이어 리조트에는 방이 있었다.

해설　부사절 접속사 whereas 빈칸 뒤에 완전한 절이 있으므로 빈칸은 절을 이끌 수 있는 접속사 자리이다. 콤마 앞뒤로 대조되는 내용이 이어지므로 '~한 반면'을 뜻하는 (D) Whereas가 정답이다. (A) Because(~하기 때문에)와 (C) Since(~하기 때문에)는 의미상 빈칸에 적절하지 않으며, (B) Instead(대신에)는 부사이므로 오답이다.

어휘　vacancy (호텔 등의) 빈방, 빈 객실　available 이용 가능한, 이용할 수 있는

2.

Even though the attorney reviewed the contract thoroughly, Mr. Wakefield was hesitant to sign it.

(A) As soon as　　　(B) Now that
(C) Even though　　　(D) Once

변호사가 계약서를 철저하게 검토했음에도 불구하고 웨이크필드 씨는 계약서에 서명하기를 망설였다.

해설　부사절 접속사 even though 문맥상 변호사가 계약서를 검토했지만 서명하기를 주저했다는 내용이 되는 게 자연스러우므로 '비록 ~일지라도'를 뜻하는 (C) Even though가 정답이다. (A) As soon as(~하자마자)와 (B) Now that((이제) ~이므로), 그리고 (D) Once(일단 ~하면) 모두 의미상 빈칸에 적절하지 않다.

어휘　attorney 변호사, 법률가　contract 계약(서)　be hesitant to do ~하는 것을 주저하다

3.

Although a gym membership was free, few employees are taking advantage of it.

(A) Although　　　(B) If
(C) Since　　　(D) In order that

헬스장 회원권이 무료였는데도 직원들은 그곳을 거의 이용하지 않는다.

해설　부사절 접속사 although 문맥상 헬스장 회원권은 무료지만 이용하는 사람이 거의 없다는 내용이 되는 게 자연스러우므로 '비록 ~일지라도'를 뜻하는 (A) Although가 정답이다. (B) If(만약 ~라면)와 (C) Since(~ 때문에), 그리고 (D) In order that(~하기 위해서) 모두 의미상 빈칸에 적절하지 않다.

어휘　gym 헬스장, 체육관　membership 회원권　take advantage of ~을 이용하다

4.

Dayton Moore surpassed his monthly quota **while** Kevin Harold was unable to sell any vehicles.

(A) while　　　(B) nor
(C) provided that　　　(D) as

케빈 해럴드는 차를 한 대도 팔지 못한 반면, 데이턴 무어는 자신의 월별 할당량을 초과 달성했다.

해설　부사절 접속사 while 빈칸은 절과 절을 연결하는 접속사 자리이다. 앞뒤로 대조되는 내용이 이어지므로 '~한 반면'을 뜻하는 (A) while이 정답이다. (B) nor는 neither A nor B(A와 B 둘 다 아닌) 형태로 쓰는 상관 접속사이며, (C) provided that(만약 ~라면)과 (D) as(~하기 때문에)는 의미상 빈칸에 적절하지 않다.

어휘　surpass 초과하다, 뛰어넘다　monthly 매월의　quota 할당량, 몫　be unable to do ~할 수 없다　vehicle 차량, 탈것

5 부사절 접속사: 목적, 결과

본문 p.200

1. (C) 2. (D) 3. (B) 4. (A)

1.

Ms. Denton postponed her trip to France **so that** she could attend Dr. Pollard's speech.

(A) that (B) as
(C) so that (D) when

덴튼 씨는 폴러드 박사의 연설에 참석할 수 있도록 프랑스 여행을 연기했다.

해설 부사절 접속사 so that 빈칸은 절과 절을 연결하는 접속사 자리이다. 문맥상 연설에 참석하기 위해 여행을 연기했다는 내용이 되는 게 자연스러우므로 '~하기 위해서'를 뜻하는 (C) so that이 정답이다. (B) as(~하기 때문에)와 (D) when(~ 할 때)은 의미상 빈칸에 적절하지 않다.

어휘 postpone 연기하다   attend 참석하다, 출석하다   speech 연설, 담화

2.

Mr. Marino, the head trainer, was sent to the Toledo factory **in order that** the workers could work efficiently.

(A) because (B) that
(C) as well as **(D) in order that**

직원들이 효율적으로 일할 수 있도록 하기 위해서 수석 교육 담당자인 마리노 씨가 톨레도 공장으로 보내졌다.

해설 부사절 접속사 in order that 빈칸은 절과 절을 연결하는 접속사 자리이다. 문맥상 직원들이 효율적으로 일할 수 있도록 하기 위해서 교육 담당자가 톨레도 공장으로 파견되었다는 내용이 되는 게 자연스러우므로 '~하기 위해서'를 뜻하는 (D) in order that이 정답이다. (A) because(~하기 때문에)와 (C) as well as(~뿐만 아니라)는 의미상 빈칸에 적절하지 않다.

어휘 head trainer 수석 교육 담당자   efficiently 효율적으로

3.

The revolutionary laptop was so **successful** that more than 300 people invested in it.

(A) succession **(B) successful**
(C) successfully (D) success

그 획기적인 노트북은 300명 이상의 사람들이 투자할 정도로 성공적이었다.

해설 형용사 자리 빈칸은 be동사 was의 주격 보어 자리이자 부사 so의 수식을 받는 자리이므로 형용사 (B) successful이 정답이다. (A) succession과 (D) success는 명사이므로 부사의 수식을 받을 수 없고, (C) successfully는 부사이므로 주격 보어 자리에 들어갈 수 없다.

어휘 revolutionary 획기적인, 혁신적인   successful 성공적인   invest 투자하다   succession 연속, 연쇄   success 성공

4.

The interior design by Fredrick Lee was **so** innovative that it won several awards.

(A) so (B) in order
(C) very (D) such

프레드릭 리의 인테리어 디자인은 여러 상을 받을 정도로 혁신적이었다.

해설 so 형용사 that 빈칸 앞에 be동사 was가 있고 뒤에는 형용사 innovative와 that절이 이어지므로 빈칸은 형용사를 수식하는 부사 자리이다. 따라서 (A) so가 정답이다. (D) such는 명사를 수식하기 때문에 오답이다.

어휘 innovative 혁신적인   win an award 상을 받다

6 접속사 vs. 전치사

본문 p.201

1. (D) 2. (C) 3. (D) 4. (A)

1.

The Mobile Towers construction project is behind schedule **because of** government regulations.

(A) because
(B) while
(C) although
(D) because of

정부 규정 때문에 모바일 타워즈 건설 프로젝트는 예정보다 늦어지고 있다.

해설 전치사 자리 빈칸 뒤에 명사구 government regulations가 있으므로 빈칸은 전치사 자리이다. 따라서 (D) because of가 정답이다. (A) because와 (B) while, 그리고 (C) although 모두 접속사이므로 빈칸에 들어갈 수 없다.

어휘 construction 건설, 공사 behind schedule 예정보다 늦게 government 정부 regulation 규정

2.

Jared feels that **when** companies have membership programs, shoppers make regular purchases.

(A) before
(B) in spite of
(C) when
(D) owing to

자레드 씨는 기업들이 회원제 프로그램을 시행할 때 구매자들이 정기 구매를 한다고 생각한다.

해설 접속사 자리 빈칸 뒤에 완전한 절이 있으므로 빈칸은 절을 이끌 수 있는 접속사 자리이다. 문맥상 회원제 프로그램이 있을 때 소비자들이 정기적으로 구매한다는 내용이 되는 게 자연스러우므로 '~할 때'를 뜻하는 (C) when이 정답이다. (A) before는 접속사이지만 문맥상 적절하지 않고, (B) in spite of(~에도 불구하고)와 (D) owing to(~ 때문에)는 전치사구이기 때문에 오답이다.

어휘 shopper 물건을 사는 사람, 쇼핑객 make a purchase 구매하다 regular 규칙적인, 정기적인

3.

The new video game is popular with players **despite** its minor design flaws.

(A) by the time
(B) due to
(C) until
(D) despite

그 새로운 비디오 게임은 사소한 디자인 결함에도 불구하고 사용자들에게 인기가 있다.

해설 전치사 자리 빈칸 뒤에 명사구 its minor design flaws가 있으므로 빈칸은 전치사 자리이다. 문맥상 디자인 결함이 있지만 인기가 많다는 내용이 되는 게 자연스러우므로 '~에도 불구하고'를 뜻하는 전치사 (D) despite가 정답이다. (B) due to와 (C) until은 전치사이지만 문맥상 적절하지 않고, (A) by the time은 접속사이기 때문에 빈칸에 들어갈 수 없다.

어휘 be popular with ~에게 인기가 있다 minor 작은, 가벼운 flaw 결함, 흠

4.

Mr. Rodgers will lead the Personnel Department **while** Ms. Rodriguez attends the seminar abroad.

(A) while
(B) during
(C) so that
(D) prior to

로드리게스 씨가 해외 세미나에 참석하는 동안 로저스 씨가 인사팀을 이끌 것이다.

해설 접속사 자리 빈칸은 절과 절을 연결하는 접속사 자리이다. 문맥상 로드리게스 씨가 해외 세미나에 참석하는 동안 다른 사람이 인사팀을 이끌 거라는 내용이 되는 게 자연스러우므로 '~하는 동안'을 뜻하는 접속사 (A) while이 정답이다. (C) so that은 접속사이지만 문맥상 적절하지 않고, (B) during(~ 동안)과 (D) prior to(~ 전에)는 전치사이기 때문에 절을 연결할 수 없다.

어휘 lead 이끌다, 안내하다 Personnel Department 인사팀 attend 참석하다, 출석하다 abroad 해외에, 해외로

VOCABULARY

본문 p.204

1. (C) 2. (A) 3. (A) 4. (C) 5. (B) 6. (A) 7. (B) 8. (B)

1.

Ms. Badger **recently** offered Terry Haas a promotion to senior vice president.

(A) partially
(B) visually
(C) recently
(D) entirely

배저 씨는 **최근** 테리 하스에게 상무 승진을 제의했다.

(A) 부분적으로
(B) 시각적으로
(C) 최근에
(D) 전적으로, 완전히

해설 부사 어휘 동사 offered를 수식해 가장 자연스럽게 의미가 통하는 부사를 골라야 한다. 따라서 '최근에'라는 의미의 (C) recently가 정답이다.

어휘 offer 제안하다 promotion 승진, 진급; 홍보 senior vice president 상무, 전무

2.

Deliveries from Delmont Logistics **occasionally** arrive two or three days ahead of schedule.

(A) occasionally
(B) fairly
(C) temporarily
(D) approximately

델몬트 로지스틱스의 배달물은 **가끔** 예정보다 이삼일 일찍 도착한다.

(A) 가끔, 때때로
(B) 상당히
(C) 일시적으로
(D) 대략, 약

해설 부사 어휘 동사 arrive를 수식해 가장 자연스럽게 의미가 통하는 부사를 골라야 한다. 따라서 '가끔, 때때로'라는 의미의 (A) occasionally가 정답이다. (D) approximately(대략, 약)는 주로 숫자 표현을 수식할 때 쓰므로 이 문장에는 적절하지 않다.

어휘 delivery 배달(물) ahead of schedule 예정보다 일찍

3.

When the software is installed **properly**, the computer will work better than ever.

(A) properly
(B) apparently
(C) especially
(D) randomly

소프트웨어가 **제대로** 설치되면 컴퓨터가 이전보다 더 잘 작동될 것이다.

(A) 제대로
(B) 보아하니
(C) 특히
(D) 무작위로

해설 부사 어휘 동사구 is installed를 수식해 가장 자연스럽게 의미가 통하는 부사를 골라야 한다. 따라서 '제대로'라는 의미의 (A) properly가 정답이다.

어휘 install 설치하다 work (기계 등이) 작동되다, 기능하다 better than ever 이전보다 더 나은

4.

Pierre Argent studied **diligently** for weeks to be accredited as an accountant.

(A) unanimously
(B) readily
(C) diligently
(D) approvingly

피에르 아전트는 회계사로 공인받기 위해서 몇 주간 **열심히** 공부했다.

(A) 만장일치로
(B) 기꺼이
(C) 부지런히, 애써
(D) 찬성하여

해설 부사 어휘 동사 studied를 수식해 가장 자연스럽게 의미가 통하는 부사를 골라야 한다. 따라서 '부지런히'라는 의미의 (C) diligently가 정답이다.

어휘 accredited 공식 인정을 받은 accountant 회계원, 회계사

5.

Lionel Parker is unable to **adequately** describe the problem with the machinery.

(A) highly (B) **adequately**
(C) previously (D) brightly

라이오넬 파커는 그 기계의 문제를 **적절하게** 설명하지 못한다.

(A) 매우, 많이 (B) **적절하게**
(C) 이전에 (D) 밝게

> 해설 부사 어휘 describe를 수식해 가장 자연스럽게 의미가 통하는 부사를 골라야 한다. 따라서 '적절하게'라는 의미의 (B) adequately가 정답이다.

> 어휘 be unable to *do* ~할 수 없다 describe 말하다, 서술하다 machinery ((집합적)) 기계(류)

6.

Roland Motors executives expect the Norfolk factory to employ **approximately** 1,200 workers next year.

(A) **approximately** (B) sincerely
(C) helpfully (D) repeatedly

롤랜드 모터스 경영진은 노퍽 공장이 내년에 **대략** 1,200명의 직원을 고용할 것이라고 예상한다.

(A) **대략** (B) 진심으로
(C) 도움이 되게 (D) 되풀이해서

> 해설 부사 어휘 뒤에 나오는 숫자를 수식해 가장 자연스럽게 의미가 통하는 부사를 골라야 한다. 따라서 '대략'이라는 의미의 (A) approximately가 정답이다.

> 어휘 executive 경영진, 운영진 expect 예상하다, 기대하다 employ 고용하다

7.

Workplaces should be cleaned **thoroughly** at the end of each workday.

(A) vitally (B) **thoroughly**
(C) evenly (D) busily

업무 현장은 매일 업무가 끝날 때 **철저하게** 청소되어야 한다.

(A) 치명적으로 (B) **완전히, 철저히**
(C) 공평하게; 고르게 (D) 바쁘게

> 해설 부사 어휘 동사구 should be cleaned를 수식해 가장 자연스럽게 의미가 통하는 부사를 골라야 한다. 따라서 '완전히, 철저히'라는 의미의 (B) thoroughly가 정답이다. (C) evenly는 표면이 평평하여 고르거나, 무언가를 골고루 분배한다는 의미가 내포되어 있기 때문에 이 문장에는 적절하지 않다.

> 어휘 workplace 업무 현장, 직장 workday 근무일, 평일

8.

The new Garmacore laptop fits **exactly** into its newly designed packing box.

(A) decisively (B) **exactly**
(C) originally (D) promptly

새로운 가마코어 노트북은 최근에 디자인된 포장 상자에 **정확하게** 맞는다.

(A) 결정적으로 (B) **정확하게**
(C) 원래 (D) 지체 없이

> 해설 부사 어휘 구동사 fits into를 수식해 가장 자연스럽게 의미가 통하는 부사를 골라야 한다. 따라서 '정확하게'라는 의미의 (B) exactly가 정답이다.

> 어휘 fit into ~에 맞다, ~에 들어맞다 newly 최근에; 새롭게 packing 포장

ACTUAL TEST

본문 p.206

1. (B) 2. (D) 3. (A) 4. (B) 5. (D) 6. (B)
7. (C) 8. (B) 9. (D) 10. (D) 11. (C) 12. (A)

1.

All commemorative T-shirts are sold out, **but** postcards may still be purchased.

(A) so
(B) but
(C) because
(D) nor

모든 기념 티셔츠가 매진되었지만 엽서는 아직 구매할 수 있을 것이다.

해설 등위 접속사 but 빈칸은 절과 절을 연결하는 접속사 자리이다. 빈칸 앞뒤로 대조되는 내용이 이어지므로 '그러나'를 뜻하는 (B) but이 정답이다. (A) so는 인과 관계를 나타내는 등위 접속사이고, (C) because는 이유를 나타내는 접속사이므로 빈칸에 적절하지 않다. (D) nor는 neither A nor B(A와 B 둘 다 아닌) 형태로 쓰는 상관 접속사이므로 오답이다.

어휘 commemorative 기념하는 sold out 매진된, 다 팔린 purchase 구매하다; 구매

2.

It is **entirely** safe to repair the machine if the batteries are removed.

(A) unanimously
(B) exactly
(C) repeatedly
(D) entirely

배터리가 제거되면 그 기계를 수리하는 것은 **완전히** 안전하다.

(A) 만장일치로
(B) 정확하게
(C) 되풀이해서
(D) 전적으로, 완전히

해설 부사 어휘 형용사 safe를 수식해 가장 자연스럽게 의미가 통하는 부사를 골라야 한다. 따라서 '전적으로, 완전히'라는 의미의 (D) entirely가 정답이다.

어휘 repair 수리하다; 수리 machine 기계 remove 제거하다

3.

Until Mr. Howard resigns, he will remain the head of the Mumbai office.

(A) Until
(B) As long as
(C) Yet
(D) Prior to

하워드 씨는 사임할 때까지 뭄바이 사무소의 책임자 자리를 유지할 것이다.

해설 부사절 접속사 until 빈칸 뒤에 완전한 절이 있으므로 빈칸은 절을 이끌 수 있는 접속사 자리이다. 문맥상 사임할 때까지 책임자 자리를 유지할 것이라는 내용이 되는 게 자연스러우므로 '~할 때까지'를 뜻하는 (A) Until이 정답이다. (B) As long as(~하는 한)는 의미상 적절하지 않다. (C) Yet(그렇지만, 그런데도)은 등위 접속사이고, (D) Prior to(~ 전에)는 전치사이기 때문에 오답이다.

어휘 resign 사직하다, 물러나다 remain 계속 ~이다, 남아 있다 head 우두머리, 책임자

4.

After the anticipated improvements were made, customer satisfaction at Demarche greatly improved.

(A) While
(B) After
(C) In spite of
(D) So that

기대하던 개선이 이루어진 후에 디마셰의 고객 만족도가 크게 향상되었다.

해설 부사절 접속사 after 빈칸 뒤에 완전한 절이 있으므로 빈칸은 절을 이끌 수 있는 접속사 자리이다. 문맥상 개선이 있고 나서 고객 만족도가 상당히 향상되었다는 내용이 되는 게 자연스러우므로 '~ 후에'를 뜻하는 (B) After가 정답이다. (A) While(~하는 동안; ~한 반면)은 의미상 적절하지 않고, (D) So that(~하기 위해서)은 문장 앞에 쓸 수 없다. 또한 (C) In spite of(~에도 불구하고)는 전치사구이기 때문에 절을 연결할 수 없다.

어휘 anticipated 기대하던, 대망의 improvement 개선, 향상 customer satisfaction 고객 만족(도) greatly 대단히, 크게 improve 개선되다, 나아지다; 개선하다, 향상시키다

123

5.
> Mr. Nealon possesses not only a law degree **but also** a degree in business.
>
> (A) unless (B) in order that
> (C) as well as (D) **but also**

닐론 씨는 법학 학위뿐만 아니라 경영학 학위도 보유하고 있다.

해설 상관 접속사 not only A but also B 빈칸은 앞에 있는 not only와 짝을 이루는 말이 들어갈 자리이므로 (D) but also가 정답이다. (C) as well as(~뿐만 아니라)는 not only와 어울리지 않고, (A) unless(만약 ~가 아니라면)와 (B) in order that(~하기 위해서)은 부사절 접속사이므로 빈칸에 들어갈 수 없다.

어휘 possess 소유하다, 보유하다   degree 학위; 정도

6.
> Ms. Sanderson will calculate the money left in the budget before she **approves** the expense request.
>
> (A) will approve (B) **approves**
> (C) had approved (D) approving

샌더슨 씨는 지출 요청서를 승인하기 전에 예산에 남은 돈을 계산할 것이다.

해설 동사 자리+현재 시제 빈칸 앞에 주어 she가 있고 뒤에는 목적어 the expense request가 있으므로 빈칸은 동사 자리이다. 빈칸이 있는 절은 접속사 before가 이끄는 시간 부사절인데, 시간이나 조건을 나타내는 부사절에서는 현재 시제가 미래 시제를 대신하므로 현재 시제인 (B) approves가 정답이다.

어휘 calculate 계산하다   budget 예산   approve 승인하다, 인가하다   expense request 지출 요청(서)

7.
> **Either** the night manager or the custodian should have the keys to the office.
>
> (A) Both (B) Even though
> (C) **Either** (D) As

야간 매니저 또는 관리인 중 한 사람이 사무실 열쇠를 가지고 있어야 한다.

해설 상관 접속사 either A or B 빈칸 뒤에 〈명사(the night manager) or 명사(the custodian)〉 구조가 이어지므로 빈칸에는 접속사 or와 짝을 이루는 상관 접속사가 들어가야 한다. 따라서 (C) Either가 정답이다. (A) Both는 and와 짝을 이루고, (B) Even though(비록 ~일지라도)와 (D) As(~하기 때문에)는 부사절 접속사이므로 오답이다.

어휘 custodian 관리인

8.
> The company picnic will be scheduled **once** the weather forecast is reviewed.
>
> (A) not only (B) **once**
> (C) whereas (D) owing to

일단 일기 예보를 검토하면 회사 야유회 일정이 잡힐 것이다.

해설 부사절 접속사 once 빈칸은 절과 절을 연결하는 접속사 자리이다. 문맥상 일기 예보가 확인되면 야유회 일정이 잡힐 거라는 내용이 되는 게 자연스러우므로 (B) once(일단 ~하면)가 정답이다. (C) whereas(~한 반면)는 의미상 빈칸에 적절하지 않고, (A) not only는 not only A but also B 형태로 쓰는 상관 접속사이며, (D) owing to(~ 때문에)는 전치사구이기 때문에 오답이다.

어휘 schedule 일정을 잡다; 일정   weather forecast 일기 예보   review 검토하다, 평가하다; 검토, 평가

SAN FREDO (July 14)—Tycho, Inc. recently released its newest software, called Alpha Tech. Alpha Tech **9 enables** users to organize their budgets for both personal and professional purposes. **10 When** users download the software, it starts with a comprehensive tutorial, which makes it very user-friendly. This permits users to understand every **11 service** that the software provides. The software is currently available at a discounted price of $99. **12 Those interested should order it at once.**

샌 프레도 (7월 14일)—티코 사는 최근 알파 테크라는 최신 소프트웨어를 출시했다. 알파 테크는 사용자가 개인적인 목적과 전문적인 목적 모두를 위해 예산을 짤 **9 수 있게 해 준다**. 사용자가 그 소프트웨어를 다운받을 **10 때**, 종합적인 사용 설명이 시작되는데, 그것은 소프트웨어를 매우 사용하기 쉽게 만들어 준다. 이것은 사용자가 소프트웨어가 제공하는 모든 **11 서비스**를 이해할 수 있게 해 준다. 그 소프트웨어는 현재 할인가 99달러에 이용할 수 있다. **12 관심 있는 사람들은 즉시 주문해야 한다.**

어휘 release 출시하다, 공개하다   enable A to do A가 ~할 수 있게 하다   organize 조직하다, 체계화하다   budget 예산
personal 개인적인   professional 직업의, 전문적인   comprehensive 포괄적인, 종합적인   tutorial 사용 지침 프로그램; 개별 지도
user-friendly 사용자 친화적인   permit A to do A가 ~하는 것을 가능하게 하다[허락하다]   provide 제공하다   currently 현재, 지금
available 이용할 수 있는   at a discounted price 할인된 가격으로

9. (A) enabling   (B) to enable
    (C) will have enabled **(D) enables**

해설 동사 자리+현재 시제 빈칸 앞에 주어 Alpha Tech가 있고 뒤에는 목적어 users가 있으므로 빈칸은 동사 자리이다. 문맥상 최근 출시된 소프트웨어를 설명하고 있으므로 현재 시제인 (D) enables가 정답이다. (A) enabling은 동명사 또는 현재분사, (B) to enable은 to부정사로 동사 자리에 올 수 없고, (C) will have enabled는 미래완료 시제이므로 부적절하다.

10. (A) Instead of   (B) Although
     (C) Despite   **(D) When**

해설 접속사 자리 빈칸 뒤에 완전한 절이 있으므로 빈칸은 절을 이끌 수 있는 접속사 자리이다. 문맥상 소프트웨어를 다운받을 때 사용 설명이 시작된다는 내용이 되는 게 자연스러우므로 '~할 때'를 뜻하는 (D) When이 정답이다. (B) Although(비록 ~일지라도)는 의미상 빈칸에 적절하지 않고, (A) Instead of(~ 대신에)와 (C) Despite(~에도 불구하고)는 전치사이기 때문에 오답이다.

11. (A) price   (B) award   (A) 가격   (B) 상
     (C) service   (D) utilization   **(C) 서비스** (D) 이용, 활용

해설 명사 어휘 to부정사인 to understand의 목적어로 가장 자연스럽게 의미가 통하는 명사를 골라야 한다. 문맥상 튜토리얼이 사용자로 하여금 모든 서비스를 이해할 수 있게 해 준다는 내용이 되는 게 자연스러우므로 (C) service가 정답이다. (D) utilization은 무언가를 활용하는 행위 자체를 의미하기 때문에 '소프트웨어가 제공하는 모든 이용을 이해할 수 있게 해 준다'라는 뜻이 되어 어색한 쓰임이 된다.

12. **(A) Those interested should order it at once.**
     (B) The new budgeting seminar is expected to be a success.
     (C) Thank you very much for your recent purchase.
     (D) The software should be available in two months.

(A) 관심 있는 사람들은 즉시 주문해야 한다.
(B) 그 새로운 예산 편성 세미나는 성공을 거둘 것으로 예상된다.
(C) 귀하의 최근 구매에 매우 감사드립니다.
(D) 그 소프트웨어는 두 달 후에 이용할 수 있을 것이다.

해설 알맞은 문장 고르기 빈칸 앞에서 소프트웨어의 특징을 나열한 후 현재 할인가에 제공되고 있다고 했다. 따라서 관심 있는 사람들은 즉시 주문하여 할인 혜택을 누리라는 의미가 담긴 (A)가 이어지는 것이 가장 자연스럽다.

어휘 interested 관심이 있는   at once 즉시   be expected to do ~할 것으로 예상되다   recent 최근의

UNIT 13 명사절 접속사

1 명사절 자리

본문 p.214

1. (C)   2. (D)   3. (A)   4. (A)

1.

Ms. Corbett argued **that** increasing the perks of the company could attract better qualified employees.

(A) for (B) about
(C) that (D) towards

코빗 씨는 회사의 복지 혜택을 늘리면 더 자격 있는 직원들을 끌어들일 수 있을 것이라고 주장했다.

해설 명사절 접속사 that 빈칸 앞에 동사 argued가 있고 뒤에는 〈주어(increasing ~ company)+동사(could attract)+목적어(better ~ employees)〉 구조로 절이 이어지므로 빈칸에는 동사 argued의 목적어인 명사절을 이끄는 접속사가 들어가야 한다. 따라서 (C) that이 정답이다. (A) for와 (B) about, (D) towards 모두 전치사이므로 빈칸에 적절하지 않다.

어휘 argue 주장하다, 논쟁하다 perk 복지 혜택, 수당 attract 끌어들이다, 유인하다 qualified 자격 있는, 적임의

2.

Please let the agent at check-in know **whether** you would like an aisle or window seat.

(A) which (B) but
(C) about **(D) whether**

탑승 수속대에 있는 직원에게 귀하가 통로 쪽 좌석을 원하는지 창가 쪽 좌석을 원하는지 알려 주세요.

해설 명사절 접속사 whether 빈칸 앞에 동사 know가 있고 뒤에는 〈주어(you)+동사(would like)+목적어(an aisle ~ seat)〉 구조로 절이 이어지므로 빈칸에는 동사 know의 목적어인 명사절을 이끄는 접속사가 들어가야 한다. 따라서 (D) whether가 정답이다. (A) which는 불완전한 절을 이끄는 의문 대명사, (B) but은 등위 접속사, (C) about은 전치사이므로 모두 빈칸에 적절하지 않다.

어휘 agent 직원 check-in 탑승 수속대 aisle[window] seat 통로[창가] 쪽 좌석

3.

Ahmed Abadi conducted a survey to determine **how** JNG Motors can reach younger generations.

(A) how (B) unless
(C) among (D) with

아메드 아바디는 어떻게 JNG 자동차가 더 젊은 세대에게 다가갈 수 있는지를 알아내기 위한 설문 조사를 실시했다.

해설 명사절을 이끄는 의문사 how 빈칸 앞에 to determine이 있고 뒤에는 〈주어(JNG Motors)+동사(can reach)+목적어(younger generations)〉 구조로 절이 이어지므로 빈칸에는 to determine의 목적어인 명사절을 이끄는 접속사가 들어가야 한다. 따라서 의문 부사인 (A) how가 정답이다. (B) unless는 부사절 접속사이고, (C) among과 (D) with는 전치사이므로 빈칸에 적절하지 않다.

어휘 conduct 실시하다, 진행하다 survey 설문 조사 determine 판단하다, 알아내다 generation 세대

4.

The problem with the project plan is **that** the deadlines are not realistic.

(A) that (B) whether
(C) due to (D) of

그 프로젝트 계획의 문제점은 마감 기한이 현실적이지 않다는 것이다.

해설 명사절 접속사 that 빈칸 앞에 be동사 is가 있고 뒤에는 〈주어(the deadlines)+동사(are not)+주격 보어(realistic)〉 구조로 절이 이어지므로 빈칸에는 is의 보어인 명사절을 이끄는 접속사가 들어가야 한다. 따라서 (A) that이 정답이다. (B) whether는 명사절 접속사이지만 문맥상 어울리지 않고, (C) due to와 (D) of는 전치사이므로 오답이다.

어휘 deadline 마감 기한 realistic 현실적인

2 명사절을 이끄는 의문사

본문 p.215

1. (A)   2. (D)   3. (B)   4. (D)

1.

Check the software company's Web site to find out **when** the next update will be out.

(A) when   (B) which
(C) who   (D) whether

다음 업데이트가 언제 나올지 알려면 그 소프트웨어 회사의 웹사이트를 확인하세요.

해설 명사절을 이끄는 의문사 when 빈칸에는 to find out의 목적어인 명사절을 이끄는 접속사가 들어가야 한다. 빈칸 뒤에 완전한 문장이 이어지고 문맥상 '다음 업데이트가 언제 나올지'라는 의미가 되어야 하므로 명사절을 이끄는 의문 부사 (A) when이 정답이다.

어휘 check 확인하다   find out ~을 알아내다

2.

The mentors will explain **what** the trainees will be doing each day.

(A) how   (B) that
(C) where   (D) what

그 멘토들은 교육생들이 날마다 무엇을 하게 될지 설명해 줄 것이다.

해설 명사절을 이끄는 의문사 what 빈칸에는 동사 explain의 목적어인 명사절을 이끄는 접속사가 들어가야 한다. 빈칸 뒤에 동사 be doing의 목적어가 없는 불완전한 문장이 나오므로 명사절을 이끄는 의문 대명사인 (D) what이 정답이다.

어휘 mentor 멘토, 스승   explain 설명하다   trainee 교육 받는 사람, 교육생

3.

The advertisement successfully portrayed **how** life can change with Goodwill's new dishwasher.

(A) where   (B) how
(C) what   (D) who

그 광고는 굿윌의 새로운 식기세척기로 삶이 어떻게 변할 수 있는지를 성공적으로 나타냈다.

해설 명사절을 이끄는 의문사 how 빈칸에는 동사 portrayed의 목적어인 명사절을 이끄는 접속사가 들어가야 한다. 빈칸 뒤에 완전한 문장이 이어지고 문맥상 '삶이 어떻게 달라질 수 있는지'라는 의미가 되어야 하므로 명사절을 이끄는 의문 부사인 (B) how가 정답이다.

어휘 advertisement 광고   successfully 성공적으로   portray 나타내다, 보여 주다; 묘사하다

4.

The security guards at the entrance know **who** is on the guest list.

(A) where   (B) when
(C) whether   (D) who

입구의 경비원들은 손님 명단에 누가 있는지 알고 있다.

해설 명사절을 이끄는 의문사 who 빈칸에는 동사 know의 목적어인 명사절을 이끄는 접속사가 들어가야 한다. 빈칸 뒤에 주어가 없는 불완전한 문장이 나오므로 명사절을 이끄는 의문 대명사인 (D) who가 정답이다.

어휘 security guard 경비원, 보안 요원   entrance 입구

3 명사절 접속사 that

1. (B)   2. (A)   3. (A)   4. (C)

1.

Park regulations **state** that visitors are not allowed to eat on the grass.

공원 규칙은 방문객들이 잔디밭 위에서 취식하는 것이 허용되지 않는다고 명시한다.

(A) restrict   **(B) state**
(C) authorize   (D) forbid

해설 **that절을 목적어로 취하는 동사 state** 빈칸 뒤에 that이 이끄는 명사절이 있으므로, that절을 목적어로 취해 가장 자연스럽게 의미가 통하는 동사를 골라야 한다. 따라서 '명시하다'라는 의미의 (B) state가 정답이다.

어휘 be allowed to *do* ~하는 것이 허용되다   restrict 제한하다   authorize 인가하다   forbid 금지하다

2.

Hanik Electronics has announced **that** Howard Cross will take over the position of CFO.

하닉 전자는 하워드 크로스 씨가 최고 재무 책임자 자리를 넘겨받을 것이라고 발표했다.

(A) that   (B) who
(C) while   (D) though

해설 **명사절 접속사 that** 빈칸 앞에 동사 has announced가 있고 뒤에는 〈주어(Howard Cross)+구동사(will take over)+목적어(the position of CFO)〉 구조로 절이 이어지므로 빈칸에는 동사 has announced의 목적어인 명사절을 이끄는 접속사가 들어가야 한다. 따라서 (A) that이 정답이다. (B) who는 뒤에 불완전한 문장이 이어져야 하므로 빈칸에 적절하지 않다.

어휘 electronics 전자 공학[기술]   take over ~을 넘겨받다, ~을 인수하다   CFO 최고 재무 책임자(=chief financial officer)

3.

Ms. Denzel requests that a limousine **wait** for Denton Inc.'s CEO at the airport.

덴젤 씨는 공항에서 리무진 한 대가 덴튼 사의 대표 이사를 기다려 줄 것을 요청한다.

(A) wait   (B) is waiting
(C) waits   (D) will wait

해설 **request+that+주어+(should) 동사원형** 〈명사절 접속사(that)+주어(a limousine)+-------+전치사구(for ~ airport)〉 구조이므로 빈칸은 동사 자리이다. 이 문장에서는 that이 동사 requests의 목적어 역할을 하는데, request가 '요청하다'를 의미할 때는 that절의 동사를 〈(should) 동사원형〉으로 써야 하므로 (A) wait가 정답이다.

어휘 request 요청하다   wait for ~을 기다리다

4.

The technician **recommended** that an anti-virus software be installed on the computer.

그 기술자는 컴퓨터에 바이러스 퇴치용 소프트웨어를 설치할 것을 권했다.

(A) downloaded   (B) registered
(C) recommended   (D) transferred

해설 **that절을 목적어로 취하는 동사 recommend** 빈칸 뒤에 that이 이끄는 명사절이 있으므로, that절을 목적어로 취해 가장 자연스럽게 의미가 통하는 동사를 골라야 한다. 따라서 '권고하다, 권장하다'라는 의미의 (C) recommended가 정답이다. 참고로 recommend에 제안이나 권고 등의 의미가 있을 때는 that절의 동사를 〈(should) 동사원형〉으로 써야 하기 때문에 that절의 동사 자리에 be동사의 원형인 be가 있다는 것을 알아 두자.

어휘 technician 기술자   install 설치하다   download 내려받다   register 등록하다   transfer 전송하다

4 명사절 접속사: if, whether

본문 p.217

1. (D) 2. (D) 3. (B) 4. (D)

1.

Whether the meeting is in the morning or afternoon, the project manager will be there.

(A) If (B) However
(C) Only (D) **Whether**

회의가 오전에 있든 오후에 있든 그 프로젝트 책임자는 그 자리에 있을 것이다.

해설 부사절 접속사 whether 빈칸 뒤에 주어와 동사를 갖춘 완전한 절이 있고, 콤마로 새로운 절이 연결되어 있으므로 빈칸에는 부사절 접속사가 들어가야 한다. 문맥상 회의가 오전이든 오후이든 담당자가 자리에 있을 거라는 내용이 되는 게 자연스러우므로 (D) Whether가 정답이다. 참고로 whether가 부사절 접속사일 때는 'A이든 B이든'을 뜻하고, 명사절 접속사일 때는 '~인지 아닌지'를 의미한다는 점에 유의해야 한다.

어휘 project 프로젝트, 사업 (계획) manager 관리자, 책임자

2.

Mr. Gartner asked the designers if **they** could work on a new logo design.

(A) them (B) themselves
(C) theirs (D) **they**

가트너 씨는 디자이너들에게 새 로고 디자인 작업을 할 수 있는지 물었다.

해설 명사절의 주어 자리 빈칸은 접속사 if가 이끄는 명사절의 주어 자리이므로 주격 인칭대명사인 (D) they가 정답이다. 참고로 이 문장에서 if절은 동사 asked의 직접목적어 역할을 하며, if가 명사절을 이끌 때는 '~인지 아닌지'로 해석한다.

어휘 work on ~에 시간[노력]을 들이다 logo (회사의) 로고, 상징 (=logotype)

3.

The hotel receptionist checked to see **if** there were any free rooms left.

(A) though (B) **if**
(C) however (D) for

호텔 접수 직원은 이용 가능한 객실이 남아 있는지 확인했다.

해설 명사절 접속사 if 빈칸은 to see의 목적어인 명사절을 이끄는 접속사가 들어갈 자리이므로 '~인지 아닌지'를 뜻하는 (B) if가 정답이다. (A) though는 부사절 접속사, (C) however는 접속부사, (D) for는 전치사이므로 모두 빈칸에 적절하지 않다.

어휘 receptionist 접수 직원 see if ~인지 알아보다 free (사용 중이지 않아서) 이용 가능한

4.

The HR manager wanted to know **whether** or not the workshop materials were ready.

(A) if (B) that
(C) how (D) **whether**

인사팀 매니저는 워크숍 자료들이 준비됐는지 알고 싶어 했다.

해설 명사절 접속사 whether 빈칸은 to know의 목적어인 명사절을 이끄는 접속사가 들어갈 자리이며, 문맥상 '워크숍 자료들이 준비되었는지 아닌지'를 의미하는 게 자연스럽다. 선택지 중 '~인지 아닌지'를 나타내는 말은 (A) if와 (D) whether인데, if는 뒤에 or not을 쓸 수 없으므로 정답은 (D) whether이다.

어휘 material 자료; 재료

VOCABULARY

본문 p.220

1. (B) 2. (D) 3. (A) 4. (A) 5. (D) 6. (B) 7. (D) 8. (B)

1.

Timi Cosmetics processed the order **rapidly** and shipped it the same day.

(A) conveniently (B) rapidly
(C) strongly (D) temporarily

티미 화장품은 그 주문을 **신속하게** 처리하여 당일에 그것을 발송했다.

(A) 편리하게 (B) 빠르게
(C) 강력하게 (D) 임시로

> 해설 부사 어휘 빈칸 앞의 동사 processed를 수식해 가장 자연스럽게 의미가 통하는 부사를 골라야 한다. 빈칸 뒤에서 당일에 주문품을 발송했다고 했으므로 '빠르게, 급속히'라는 의미의 (B) rapidly가 정답이다.

> 어휘 cosmetics ((항상 복수형)) 화장품 process 처리하다 order 주문(품) ship 발송하다

2.

The orchestra **expertly** executed the symphony at last night's concert.

(A) efficiently (B) slightly
(C) likewise (D) expertly

그 관현악단은 지난밤의 연주회에서 교향곡을 **능숙하게** 연주했다.

(A) 능률적으로 (B) 약간
(C) 마찬가지로 (D) 능숙하게

> 해설 부사 어휘 빈칸 뒤의 동사 executed를 수식해 가장 자연스럽게 의미가 통하는 부사를 골라야 한다. 따라서 '능숙하게, 전문적으로'라는 의미의 (D) expertly가 정답이다.

> 어휘 execute 연주하다; 실행하다, 수행하다 symphony 교향곡, 심포니

3.

Most survey respondents selected the option to submit their answers **anonymously**.

(A) anonymously (B) constantly
(C) readily (D) analytically

대부분의 설문 조사 응답자들은 **익명으로** 답변을 제출하는 옵션을 선택했다.

(A) 익명으로 (B) 끊임없이
(C) 손쉽게 (D) 분석적으로

> 해설 부사 어휘 빈칸 앞의 to submit를 수식해 가장 자연스럽게 의미가 통하는 부사를 골라야 한다. 따라서 '익명으로'라는 의미의 (A) anonymously가 정답이다.

> 어휘 respondent 응답자 select 선택하다, 고르다 submit 제출하다

4.

The winner of the PBX Radio concert tickets will be chosen **randomly** among the callers.

(A) randomly (B) neatly
(C) thoroughly (D) briefly

PBX 라디오 콘서트의 입장권 당첨자는 전화하신 분들 중에서 **무작위로** 선정될 것입니다.

(A) 무작위로 (B) 깔끔하게
(C) 철저하게 (D) 간략하게

> 해설 부사 어휘 빈칸 앞의 동사 be chosen을 수식해 가장 자연스럽게 의미가 통하는 부사를 골라야 한다. 따라서 '무작위로'라는 의미의 (A) randomly가 정답이다.

> 어휘 winner 당첨자; 우승자 be chosen 선정되다 caller 전화하는 사람

5.

After a four-hour delay, the plane **finally** took off from O'Hara Airport.	4시간의 지연 후에 그 항공기는 **마침내** 오하라 공항에서 이륙했다.
(A) frequently (B) preferably (C) especially (D) finally	(A) 자주, 빈번히 (B) 가급적이면 (C) 특히 (D) 마침내

해설 **부사 어휘** 빈칸 뒤의 구동사 took off를 수식해 가장 자연스럽게 의미가 통하는 부사를 골라야 한다. 빈칸 앞에서 '4시간의 지연 후에'라고 했으므로 '마침내; 마지막으로'라는 의미의 (D) finally가 정답이다.

어휘 delay 지연, 지체 plane 항공기 take off 이륙하다

6.

The committee will review your proposal and give you their feedback **shortly**.	위원회에서 당신의 제안서를 검토해 **곧** 피드백을 드릴 겁니다.
(A) completely (B) shortly (C) essentially (D) wrongly	(A) 완전히 (B) 곧 (C) 본질적으로 (D) 잘못되게

해설 **부사 어휘** 빈칸 앞의 동사 give를 수식해 가장 자연스럽게 의미가 통하는 부사를 골라야 한다. 따라서 '곧, 얼마 안 되어'라는 의미의 (B) shortly가 정답이다.

어휘 committee 위원회 review 검토하다 proposal 제안(서)

7.

Vocanix Academy is **generally** considered the most prestigious music school in the region.	보캐닉스 아카데미는 **일반적으로** 그 지역 최고의 명문 음악 학교로 여겨진다.
(A) precisely (B) promptly (C) sharply (D) generally	(A) 정확히 (B) 즉시 (C) 날카롭게 (D) 일반적으로

해설 **부사 어휘** 빈칸 뒤의 과거분사 considered를 수식해 가장 자연스럽게 의미가 통하는 부사를 골라야 한다. 따라서 '일반적으로, 대개; 개괄적으로'라는 의미의 (D) generally가 정답이다.

어휘 consider 여기다, 간주하다 prestigious 명망 있는, 일류의 region 지역, 지방

8.

Nina Abbas runs a restaurant that **exclusively** serves vegetarian dishes.	니나 아바스는 **오로지** 채식 요리만 제공하는 식당을 운영한다.
(A) punctually (B) exclusively (C) lately (D) significantly	(A) 정각에 (B) 오로지 (C) 최근에 (D) 상당히

해설 **부사 어휘** 빈칸 뒤의 동사 serves를 수식해 가장 자연스럽게 의미가 통하는 부사를 골라야 한다. 따라서 '독점적으로, 오로지'라는 의미의 (B) exclusively가 정답이다.

어휘 run 운영하다 serve (음식을) 제공하다 vegetarian dish 채식 요리

ACTUAL TEST

본문 p.222

| 1. (A) | 2. (A) | 3. (C) | 4. (B) | 5. (B) | 6. (B) |
| 7. (B) | 8. (C) | 9. (D) | 10. (D) | 11. (A) | 12. (C) |

1.

The event organizer will decide **who** will speak first at the ceremony.

(A) who (B) when
(C) what (D) which

행사 주최자가 그 행사에서 누가 맨 처음 연설할지 결정할 것이다.

해설 명사절을 이끄는 의문사 who 빈칸에는 동사 decide의 목적어인 명사절을 이끄는 접속사가 들어가야 한다. 빈칸 뒤에 주어가 없는 불완전한 문장이 나오므로 명사절을 이끄는 의문 대명사인 (A) who가 정답이다.

어휘 organizer 조직자, 주최자   decide 결정하다   speak 연설하다

2.

The Pim Pro software helps companies manage their human resources data more **efficiently**.

(A) efficiently (B) randomly
(C) commonly (D) repeatedly

핌 프로 소프트웨어는 회사들이 인력 데이터를 더 **효율적으로** 관리하는 걸 돕는다.

(A) 효율적으로 (B) 무작위로
(C) 통상적으로 (D) 반복적으로

해설 부사 어휘 빈칸 앞의 동사 manage를 수식해 가장 자연스럽게 의미가 통하는 부사를 골라야 한다. 따라서 '능률적으로, 효율적으로'라는 의미의 (A) efficiently가 정답이다.

어휘 manage 관리하다   human resources 인적 자원, 인력

3.

The director asked that Mr. Thibault **be** present at the weekly board meeting.

(A) was (B) had been
(C) be (D) will be

그 이사는 티보 씨에게 주간 이사회 회의에 출석할 것을 요청했다.

해설 ask+that+주어+(should) 동사원형 〈명사절 접속사(that)+주어(Mr. Thibault)+-------+주격 보어(present)〉 구조이므로 빈칸은 동사 자리이다. 이 문장에서는 that절이 동사 asked의 목적어 역할을 하는데, ask가 '요청하다'를 의미할 때는 that절의 동사를 《(should) 동사원형》으로 써야 하므로 (C) be가 정답이다.

어휘 director 이사   present 출석한, 참석한   weekly 매주의, 주간의   board meeting 이사회 회의

4.

Ms. Kino is analyzing the data to find out how consumers **choose** their cosmetics.

(A) chosen (B) choose
(C) to choose (D) are chosen

키노 씨는 소비자들이 화장품을 선택하는 방식을 알아내기 위해 데이터를 분석하고 있다.

해설 동사 자리 〈명사절 접속사(how)+주어(consumers)+-------+목적어(their cosmetics)〉 구조이므로 빈칸은 동사 자리이다. 따라서 (B) choose가 정답이다. (A) chosen과 (C) to choose는 동사 역할을 할 수 없으며, 수동형인 (D) are chosen은 빈칸 뒤에 목적어가 있으므로 오답이다.

어휘 choose 고르다, 선택하다   cosmetics ((항상 복수형)) 화장품

5.

Please keep your seat belt fastened until the plane has **completely** stopped.

(A) frequently (B) **completely**
(C) quickly (D) neatly

비행기가 **완전히** 정지할 때까지 안전벨트를 계속 매 주시기 바랍니다.

(A) 자주, 빈번히 (B) **완전히**
(C) 빨리 (D) 깔끔하게

해설 부사 어휘 빈칸 뒤의 과거분사 stopped를 수식해 가장 자연스럽게 의미가 통하는 부사를 골라야 한다. 따라서 '완전히, 전적으로'라는 의미의 (B) completely가 정답이다.

어휘 seat belt 안전벨트 fasten 매다, 채우다 plane 항공기

6.

The quarterly report indicates **that** sales increased by 14 percent compared to last year.

(A) what (B) **that**
(C) much (D) since

분기별 보고서는 지난해에 비해 매출이 14퍼센트 증가했다는 걸 보여 준다.

해설 명사절 접속사 that 빈칸 앞에 동사 indicates가 있고 뒤에는 〈주어(sales)+동사(increased)+전치사구(by 14 percent ~ year)〉 구조로 절이 이어지므로 빈칸에는 동사 indicates의 목적어인 명사절을 이끄는 접속사가 들어가야 한다. 따라서 (B) that이 정답이다.

어휘 quarterly 연 4회의, 분기별의 indicate 나타내다, 보여 주다 sales 매출 compared to ~에 비해

7.

At the convention, Limbda Corp.'s spokesperson described **what** their new tablet will look like.

(A) which (B) **what**
(C) that (D) when

그 컨벤션에서 림다 사의 대변인은 새 태블릿이 어떤 모양일지 설명했다.

해설 명사절을 이끄는 의문사 what 빈칸에는 동사 described의 목적어인 명사절을 이끄는 접속사가 들어가야 한다. 빈칸 뒤에 전치사 like의 목적어가 없는 불완전한 문장이 나오므로 명사절을 이끄는 의문 대명사인 (B) what이 정답이다.

어휘 spokesperson 대변인 describe 묘사하다, 설명하다 look like ~처럼 생기다

8.

Ms. Mitsuni called the museum to ask **whether** it gives guided tours.

(A) in order to (B) that
(C) **whether** (D) what

미츠니 씨는 가이드 동반 관람을 제공하는지 물어보기 위해 박물관에 전화했다.

해설 명사절 접속사 whether 빈칸 앞에 to ask가 있고 뒤에는 〈주어(it)+동사(gives)+목적어(guided tours)〉 구조로 절이 이어지므로 빈칸에는 to ask의 목적어인 명사절을 이끄는 접속사가 들어가야 한다. 또한 문맥상 '그 박물관이 가이드 동반 관람을 제공하는지 아닌지'라는 의미가 되는 게 자연스러우므로 (C) whether가 정답이다. (B) that은 명사절 접속사이지만, 문맥상 빈칸 뒤의 절이 불확실한 상황을 나타내므로 빈칸에 적절하지 않다.

어휘 guided tour 가이드 동반 관람

Is your company planning on expanding overseas? ⁹**Breaking into the international market can be difficult.** However, with the right preparation, it can bring about exceptional ¹⁰**opportunities** for your business. Broad Horizons can help you with that. Just tell us where you want to go. We will provide you with an exhaustive country profile, and guide you through the necessary paperwork. Our experts will then show you ¹¹**how** your marketing techniques should be adapted to reach the local culture. ¹²**Above all**, we'll be assisting you in every step of accomplishing your sales goal. Thanks to our services, your company will become an international success in no time.

귀사는 해외 확장을 계획하고 있습니까? ⁹ **국제 시장에 진입하는 것은 어려울 수 있습니다.** 그러나 적절한 준비를 하면 해외 진출은 귀사에 특별한 ¹⁰ **기회들**을 가져올 수 있습니다. 브로드 호라이즌스가 그 일을 도울 수 있습니다. 귀사가 어디로 가기 원하는지 우리에게 알려만 주십시오. 우리는 귀사에 총망라한 국가 개요서를 제공하고 필요한 서류 작업을 단계별로 안내할 것입니다. 그 다음에 우리 전문가들이 귀사의 마케팅 기법들이 현지 문화에 통하게 하기 위해 ¹¹ **어떻게** 조정되어야 하는지 알려 줄 것입니다. ¹² **무엇보다도** 귀사가 매출 목표를 달성하기까지 모든 단계에 도움을 드리겠습니다. 우리 서비스 덕분에 귀사는 즉시 국제적으로 성공한 업체가 될 것입니다.

어휘 plan on ~할 계획이다 expand 확장하다, 성장하다 overseas 해외로 right 올바른, 적절한 preparation 준비, 대비 bring about ~을 가져오다, ~을 초래하다 exceptional 예외적인, 특별한 provide A with B A에게 B를 제공하다 exhaustive 철저한, 총망라한 profile 개요(서), 프로필 guide A through B A에게 B(복잡한 것)를 단계별로 안내하다 adapt 각색하다, 조정하다 reach 도달하다, 닿다 in no time 즉시

---

9. (A) There are many wonderful touristic sites to visit.
(B) This product is finally available in your country.
(C) You may have to pay an additional delivery fee.
(D) Breaking into the international market can be difficult.

(A) 가 볼 만한 멋진 관광지들이 많이 있습니다.
(B) 이 제품을 마침내 여러분의 나라에서 구할 수 있습니다.
(C) 추가 배송료를 내셔야 할 수도 있습니다.
(D) 국제 시장에 진입하는 것은 어려울 수 있습니다.

해설 알맞은 문장 고르기 빈칸 앞 문장에서 회사가 해외로 확장할 계획인지 묻고 있으며, 뒤에서는 적절한 준비를 하면 그것이 회사에 특별한 기회들을 가져올 수 있다고 했으므로 국제 시장에 진입하는 것은 어려울 수 있다고 말하는 (D)가 정답이다.

어휘 touristic site 관광지 available 이용 가능한 delivery fee 배송료 break into ~에 진입하다

---

10. (A) similarities   (B) consequences
(C) negotiations   **(D) opportunities**

(A) 유사점   (B) 결과
(C) 협상   **(D) 기회**

해설 명사 어휘 빈칸 앞의 형용사 exceptional의 수식을 받아 가장 자연스럽게 의미가 통하는 명사를 골라야 한다. 빈칸에는 회사가 국제 시장에 진입함으로써 얻을 수 있는 것으로 가장 적합한 명사가 들어가야 하므로 '기회들'이라는 의미의 (D) opportunities가 정답이다.

---

11. **(A) how**   (B) why
(C) for   (D) because

해설 명사절을 이끄는 의문사 how 빈칸에는 동사 show의 직접목적어인 명사절을 이끄는 접속사가 들어가야 한다. 문맥상 '마케팅 기법들이 어떻게 조정되어야 하는지'라는 의미가 되어야 하므로 방법을 나타내는 의문 부사인 (A) how가 정답이다.

---

12. (A) However   (B) Apparently
(C) Above all   (D) Instead

(A) 하지만   (B) 보아하니, 듣자 하니
(C) 무엇보다도   (D) 대신에

해설 접속부사 빈칸 앞에서 마케팅 기법을 조정해 주겠다고 했으며, 뒤에서는 브로드 호라이즌스의 도움을 받으면 얻을 수 있는 더 큰 이점을 말하고 있으므로 '무엇보다도'라는 의미의 접속부사 (C) Above all이 정답이다.

UNIT 14 가정법

1 가정법 현재

본문 p.228

1. (B) 2. (A) 3. (D) 4. (A)

1.

If the printer **is maintained** well, it will make clearer copies of documents.	프린터가 잘 유지되면 문서들을 더 선명하게 복사하게 될 것이다.

(A) maintains (B) **is maintained**
(C) will maintain (D) will be maintaining

해설 **가정법 현재** 주절의 동사(will make)가 〈will+동사원형〉인 것으로 보아 가정법 현재나 미래 문장임을 알 수 있다. 가정법 현재는 if절에 동사의 현재형이 들어가고 가정법 미래는 〈should+동사원형〉이므로, 선택지 중 동사의 현재형인 (A) maintains와 (B) is maintained가 정답 후보가 된다. 이제는 빈칸에 들어갈 말이 능동형인지 수동형인지 판단해야 하는데, maintain은 타동사이므로 목적어를 취해야 한다. 하지만 빈칸 뒤에 부사 well이 있으므로 수동형인 (B) is maintained가 정답이다.

어휘 maintain 유지하다, 정비하다 make a copy of ~을 복사하다 clear 명확한, 선명한

2.

If you **do not** receive the reservation e-mail by today, call Mr. Sandro.	오늘까지 예약 확인 메일을 받지 못했다면 산드로 씨에게 연락하세요.

(A) **do not** (B) had not been
(C) were not (D) did not

해설 **가정법 현재** 콤마 이하의 주절에 주어와 조동사 없이 동사(call)가 바로 이어지는 것으로 보아 가정법 현재나 미래 문장임을 알 수 있다. 가정법 현재는 if절에 동사의 현재형이 들어가고 가정법 미래는 〈should+동사원형〉이므로, 선택지 중 동사의 현재형인 (A) do not이 정답이다.

어휘 receive 받다 reservation 예약

3.

If Mr. Arnold arrives on time, he **will give** the presentation to the clients.	아널드 씨가 정시에 도착하면 그가 고객들에게 프레젠테이션을 하게 될 것이다.

(A) gives (B) to give
(C) gave (D) **will give**

해설 **가정법 현재** if절의 동사(arrives)가 동사의 현재형인 것으로 보아 가정법 현재 문장임을 알 수 있다. 따라서 주절의 동사는 〈will/can/may+동사원형〉이 되어야 하므로 (D) will give가 정답이다.

어휘 arrive 도착하다 on time 정시에, 시간에 맞추어 client (업체의) 고객, 의뢰인

4.

If the alarm **goes off**, look at the monitor to check for problems.	경보기가 울리면 문제를 파악하기 위해 모니터를 살펴보십시오.

(A) **goes off** (B) going off
(C) will go off (D) had gone off

해설 **가정법 현재** 콤마 이하의 주절에 주어와 조동사 없이 동사(look)가 바로 이어지는 것으로 보아 가정법 현재나 미래 문장임을 알 수 있다. 가정법 현재는 if절에 동사의 현재형이 들어가고 가정법 미래는 〈should+동사원형〉이므로, 선택지 중 동사의 현재형인 (A) goes off가 정답이다.

어휘 go off (경보기 등이) 울리다 look at ~을 살펴보다 check for ~을 확인하다, ~을 조사하다

2 가정법 과거와 과거완료

1. (A)　　2. (C)　　3. (C)　　4. (C)

1.

> If the order had been placed on Monday, it **would have arrived** by Thursday.
>
> (A) would have arrived　(B) has arrived
> (C) is being arrived　(D) would have been arrived
>
> 주문을 월요일에 했다면 목요일에는 도착했을 것이다.

해설 가정법 과거완료 if절의 동사(had been placed)가 〈had p.p.〉인 것으로 보아 가정법 과거완료 문장임을 알 수 있다. 따라서 주절의 동사는 〈would/could/might+have p.p.〉가 되어야 하므로 (A) would have arrived와 (D) would have been arrived가 정답 후보이다. 이제는 빈칸에 들어갈 말이 능동형인지 수동형인지 판단해야 하는데, arrive는 자동사이므로 목적어를 취할 수 없다. 따라서 능동형인 (A) would have arrived가 정답이다.

어휘 place an order 주문을 하다　arrive 도착하다

2.

> They **would have received** a 20% discount if they had ordered a day earlier.
>
> (A) received　(B) have received
> (C) would have received　(D) will have received
>
> 그들이 하루 더 일찍 주문을 했더라면 그들은 20%의 할인을 받았을 것이다.

해설 가정법 과거완료 if절의 동사(had ordered)가 〈had p.p.〉인 것으로 보아 가정법 과거완료 문장임을 알 수 있다. 따라서 주절의 동사는 〈would/could/might+have p.p.〉가 되어야 하므로 정답은 (C)이다.

어휘 receive 받다　discount 할인　a day earlier 하루 일찍

3.

> If Mark **hadn't caught** the error, we would have had a huge complaint from the customer.
>
> (A) didn't catch　(B) hadn't been caught
> (C) hadn't caught　(D) caught
>
> 마크 씨가 오류를 잡지 못했다면 우리는 고객에게 엄청난 항의를 받았을 거예요.

해설 가정법 과거완료 주절의 동사(would have had)가 〈would+have p.p.〉인 것으로 보아 가정법 과거완료 문장임을 알 수 있다. 따라서 if절의 동사는 〈had p.p.〉가 되어야 하므로 (B) hadn't been caught와 (C) hadn't caught가 정답 후보이다. 이제는 빈칸에 들어갈 말이 능동형인지 수동형인지 판단해야 하는데, catch가 '(오류 등을) 잡아내다'를 뜻할 때는 타동사이므로 목적어를 취해야 한다. 빈칸 뒤에 명사 the error가 있으므로 능동형인 (C) hadn't caught가 정답이다.

어휘 error 실수, 오류　huge 거대한, 엄청난　complaint 불평, 항의

4.

> If the weather had been nicer, the groundbreaking ceremony **would have taken place** outdoors.
>
> (A) has taken place　(B) had taken place
> (C) would have taken place　(D) will have taken place
>
> 날씨가 더 좋았다면 기공식이 야외에서 열렸을 것이다.

해설 가정법 과거완료 if절의 동사(had been)가 〈had p.p.〉인 것으로 보아 가정법 과거완료 문장임을 알 수 있다. 따라서 주절의 동사는 〈would/could/might+have p.p.〉가 되어야 하므로 (C) would have taken place가 정답이다.

어휘 groundbreaking ceremony 기공식, 착공식　take place 열리다, 개최되다　outdoors 야외[실외]에서

3 가정법 미래

본문 p.230

1. (B) 2. (A) 3. (D) 4. (A)

1.

If Mr. Simmons **should** have any questions, you can tell him to call me.

(A) would (B) should
(C) will (D) could

혹시라도 시먼스 씨가 질문이 있다면 내게 전화하라고 그에게 이야기해도 됩니다.

해설 가정법 미래 주절의 동사(can tell)가 〈can+동사원형〉인 것으로 보아 가정법 현재나 미래 문장임을 알 수 있다. 가정법 현재는 if절에 동사의 현재형이 들어가고, 가정법 미래는 〈should+동사원형〉이므로, 선택지 중 조동사인 (B) should가 정답이다.

어휘 question 질문, 문의 사항 call 전화하다

2.

If the train should arrive late, Ms. Kerry **will inform** the person meeting her.

(A) **will inform** (B) informs
(C) have informed (D) would have informed

혹시라도 기차가 늦게 도착한다면 케리 씨는 자신이 만날 사람에게 알려 줄 것이다.

해설 가정법 미래 if절의 동사(should arrive)가 〈should+동사원형〉인 것으로 보아 가정법 미래 문장임을 알 수 있다. 따라서 주절의 동사는 〈will/can/may+동사원형〉이 되어야 하므로 (A) will inform이 정답이다.

어휘 arrive 도착하다 inform 알리다, 통지하다

3.

If company revenues should increase, all employees **will receive** a cash bonus.

(A) receive (B) will be received
(C) received (D) **will receive**

혹시라도 회사 총수입이 증가한다면 모든 직원이 현금 보너스를 받게 될 것이다.

해설 가정법 미래 if절의 동사(should increase)가 〈should+동사원형〉인 것으로 보아 가정법 미래 문장임을 알 수 있다. 따라서 주절의 동사는 〈will/can/may+동사원형〉이 되어야 하므로 선택지 중 (B) will be received와 (D) will receive가 정답 후보이다. 이제는 빈칸에 들어갈 말이 수동형인지 능동형인지 판단해야 하는데, receive는 타동사이므로 목적어를 취해야 한다. 빈칸 뒤에 명사 a cash bonus가 있으므로 능동형인 (D) will receive가 정답이다.

어휘 revenue 총수입, 소득 총액 increase 증가하다 receive 받다

4.

If the demonstration were successful, the marketing team **would create** new advertisements.

(A) **would create** (B) creates
(C) has created (D) will create

그 시연회가 성공한다면 마케팅팀에서 새로운 광고들을 만들어 낼 것이다.

해설 가정법 과거 if절의 동사(were)가 동사의 과거형인 것으로 보아 가정법 과거 문장임을 알 수 있다. 따라서 주절의 동사는 〈would/could/might+동사원형〉이 되어야 하므로 (A) would create가 정답이다.

어휘 demonstration 시연, 사용 시범 create 창작하다, 만들어 내다 advertisement 광고, 선전

4 if 생략

1. (C)   2. (C)   3. (A)   4. (A)

1.

> Had Fletcher explained the problem clearly, the repairman **would have fixed** the freezer quickly.
>
> (A) might fix (B) will fix
> **(C) would have fixed** (D) has fixed

플레처 씨가 문제를 명확히 설명했다면 수리공이 냉장고를 빨리 고쳤을 것이다.

해설 if 생략 [가정법 과거완료] Had가 문장 앞으로 도치된 것으로 보아 원래는 'If Fletcher had explained ~'였던 가정법 과거완료 문장임을 알 수 있다. 따라서 주절의 동사는 〈would/could/might+have p.p.〉가 되어야 하므로 (C) would have fixed가 정답이다.

어휘 explain 설명하다 clearly 명확히 repairman 수리공 freezer 냉장고

2.

> **Had** the results of the customer survey been sent earlier, we could have shown the CEO.
>
> (A) Except (B) Should
> **(C) Had** (D) Instead of

고객 설문 조사 결과가 더 일찍 전달되었다면 우리는 대표 이사에게 보여 줄 수 있었을 것이다.

해설 if 생략 [조동사 자리] 콤마 뒤에 있는 주절의 동사(could have shown)가 〈could have+p.p.〉인 것으로 보아 가정법 과거완료 문장임을 알 수 있다. 따라서 if절의 동사는 〈had p.p.〉가 되어야 하므로 (C) Had가 정답이다. 원래는 'If the results of the customer survey had been sent earlier'지만 if가 생략되면서 주어 the results of the customer survey와 조동사 had가 도치된 것이다.

어휘 result ((보통 복수형)) 결과, 성적 customer 고객, 손님 survey 설문 조사

3.

> **Should** your ID card fail to work properly, someone from maintenance will reset it.
>
> **(A) Should** (B) Had
> (C) What (D) Were

혹시라도 신분증 카드가 제대로 작동하지 않는다면 유지 관리부의 누군가가 초기화할 것입니다.

해설 if 생략 [조동사 자리] 콤마 뒤에 있는 주절의 동사(will reset)가 〈will+동사원형〉인 것으로 보아 가정법 현재나 미래 문장임을 알 수 있다. 가정법 현재는 if절에 동사의 현재형이 들어가고, 가정법 미래는 〈should+동사원형〉이므로, (A) Should가 정답이다. 원래는 'If your ID card should fail to work properly'지만 if가 생략되면서 주어 your ID card와 조동사 should가 도치된 것이다.

어휘 fail to do ~하지 못하다 properly 적절히, 제대로 maintenance 유지 (관리), 정비

4.

> Were the applicants hired, the Sales Department **would have** more than thirty employees.
>
> **(A) would have** (B) will have
> (C) having (D) have

그 지원자들이 채용된다면 영업팀은 30명이 넘는 직원을 갖게 될 것이다.

해설 if 생략 [가정법 과거] Were가 문장 앞으로 도치된 것으로 보아 원래는 'If the applicants were hired'였던 가정법 과거 문장임을 알 수 있다. 따라서 주절의 동사는 〈would/could/might+동사원형〉이 되어야 하므로 (A) would have가 정답이다.

어휘 applicant 지원자, 신청자 hire 채용하다 Sales Department 영업팀

VOCABULARY

본문 p.234

1. (A) 2. (B) 3. (C) 4. (C) 5. (A) 6. (D) 7. (A) 8. (B)

1.

Heather Fashion waited **patiently** to unveil their limited edition series for this winter.	헤더 패션은 이번 겨울에 나올 그들의 한정판 시리즈를 공개하기 위해 **참을성 있게** 기다렸다.
(A) patiently (B) severely (C) equally (D) apparently	(A) 참을성 있게 (B) 혹독하게 (C) 똑같이, 동일하게 (D) 보아하니

해설 부사 어휘 빈칸 앞의 동사 waited를 수식해 가장 자연스럽게 의미가 통하는 부사를 골라야 한다. 따라서 '참을성 있게, 끈기 있게'라는 의미의 (A) patiently가 정답이다.

어휘 unveil (새로운 상품 등을) 발표하다   limited edition 한정판

2.

Once the new cosmetics went on sale, revenues at JT Bradford increased **sharply**.	새 화장품이 판매에 들어가자마자 JT 브래드퍼드의 총수입이 **급격히** 증가했다.
(A) proficiently (B) sharply (C) reportedly (D) very	(A) 숙련되게, 능숙하게 (B) 급격히 (C) 소문에 의하면 (D) 매우

해설 부사 어휘 빈칸 앞의 동사 increased를 수식해 가장 자연스럽게 의미가 통하는 부사를 골라야 한다. 따라서 '급격히; 날카롭게, 신랄하게'라는 의미의 (B) sharply가 정답이다.

어휘 once 일단 ~하면, ~하자마자   go on sale 판매에 들어가다, 시판되다   revenue 총수입, 소득 총액

3.

Milton Furniture will **officially** open for business this coming Friday.	밀턴 가구는 이번 금요일에 **공식적으로** 개업할 것이다.
(A) commonly (B) practically (C) officially (D) accidentally	(A) 흔히, 보통 (B) 실제로는 (C) 공식적으로 (D) 우연히

해설 부사 어휘 빈칸 뒤의 동사 open을 수식해 가장 자연스럽게 의미가 통하는 부사를 골라야 한다. 따라서 '공식적으로, 정식으로'라는 의미의 (C) officially가 정답이다.

어휘 open for business 개업하다

4.

Most messages between colleagues at Dillon, Inc. are sent **electronically**.	딜론 사에서 직장 동료들 간의 메시지 대부분은 **전자식으로** 발송된다.
(A) curiously (B) busily (C) electronically (D) fairly	(A) 호기심에; 이상하게 (B) 분주하게 (C) 전자식으로 (D) 공평하게

해설 부사 어휘 빈칸 앞의 동사 are sent를 수식해 가장 자연스럽게 의미가 통하는 부사를 골라야 한다. 문장의 주어가 Most messages이므로 '전자식으로, 컴퓨터로'라는 의미의 (C) electronically가 정답이다.

어휘 colleague 직장 동료   Inc. 주식회사 (=Incorporated)   be sent 발송되다

5.

This program teaches clients how to invest **wisely** so as to avoid losing any money.	이 프로그램은 손실을 보는 걸 막기 위해 고객들에게 **현명하게** 투자하는 방법을 가르쳐 준다.
(A) wisely (B) steadily (C) tightly (D) randomly	**(A) 현명하게** (B) 꾸준히 (C) 단단히 (D) 무작위로

> **해설** 부사 어휘 빈칸 앞의 동사 invest를 수식해 가장 자연스럽게 의미가 통하는 부사를 골라야 한다. 손실을 피하려면 현명하게 투자해야 한다는 흐름이 자연스러우므로 '현명하게'라는 의미의 (A) wisely가 정답이다.

> **어휘** client 고객 invest 투자하다 so as to do ~하기 위해서, ~하려고

6.

Eric Watson **successfully** organized his company's summer picnic for the third straight year.	에릭 왓슨은 3년 연속으로 회사의 여름 야유회를 **성공적으로** 준비했다.
(A) viciously (B) purposely (C) slightly **(D) successfully**	(A) 지독하게 (B) 고의로, 일부러 (C) 약간 **(D) 성공적으로**

> **해설** 부사 어휘 빈칸 뒤의 동사 organized를 수식해 가장 자연스럽게 의미가 통하는 부사를 골라야 한다. 따라서 '성공적으로'라는 의미의 (D) successfully가 정답이다.

> **어휘** organize (행사를) 조직하다, 주최하다 for the third straight year 3년 연속으로

7.

While Ms. Klein **normally** interviews job candidates, Mr. Popper handled them this week.	**보통은** 클라인 씨가 입사 지원자들을 면접하지만 이번 주에는 포퍼 씨가 그들을 상대했다.
(A) normally (B) peacefully (C) safely (D) unanimously	**(A) 보통** (B) 평화롭게 (C) 안전하게 (D) 만장일치로

> **해설** 부사 어휘 빈칸 뒤의 동사 interviews를 수식해 가장 자연스럽게 의미가 통하는 부사를 골라야 한다. 따라서 '보통; 정상적으로'라는 의미의 (A) normally가 정답이다.

> **어휘** while ~이긴 하지만 job candidate 구직자, 입사 지원자 handle 다루다, 상대하다

8.

The keynote speech by Dr. Reaver was considered **particularly** influential by attendees.	리버 박사의 기조연설이 참석자들에게 **특히** 영향력이 컸던 것으로 여겨졌다.
(A) coherently **(B) particularly** (C) prettily (D) locally	(A) 일관되게 **(B) 특히** (C) 귀엽게 (D) 근방에서

> **해설** 부사 어휘 빈칸 뒤의 형용사 influential을 수식해 가장 자연스럽게 의미가 통하는 부사를 골라야 한다. 따라서 '특히'라는 의미의 (B) particularly가 정답이다.

> **어휘** keynote speech 기조연설 consider 여기다, 생각하다 influential 영향력 있는 attendee 참석자, 출석자

ACTUAL TEST

본문 p.236

1. (B)	2. (A)	3. (B)	4. (A)	5. (C)	6. (C)
7. (C)	8. (A)	9. (A)	10. (D)	11. (C)	12. (D)

1.

If Mr. Gill had not attended the AI conference, he **would** not have gotten a chance to get funding.

(A) can (B) would
(C) must (D) will

길 씨가 그 AI 콘퍼런스에 참석하지 않았더라면 그는 투자받을 기회를 얻지 못했을 것이다.

해설 가정법 과거완료 if절의 동사(had not attended)가 〈had p.p.〉인 것으로 보아 가정법 과거완료 문장임을 알 수 있다. 따라서 주절의 동사는 〈would/could/might+have p.p.〉가 되어야 하므로 (B) would가 정답이다.

어휘 attend 참석하다 get a chance to *do* ~할 기회를 얻다

2.

Some manufacturing companies **purposely** locate their warehouses near their factories.

(A) purposely (B) proficiently
(C) variously (D) partially

일부 제조업체들은 물류 창고를 공장 근처에 **일부러** 위치시킨다.

(A) 고의로, 일부러 (B) 숙련되게, 능숙하게
(C) 다양하게 (D) 부분적으로

해설 부사 어휘 빈칸 뒤의 동사 locate를 수식해 가장 자연스럽게 의미가 통하는 부사를 골라야 한다. 따라서 '고의로, 일부러'라는 의미의 (A) purposely가 정답이다.

어휘 manufacturing company 제조업체 locate 위치시키다, 두다 warehouse 물류 창고

3.

Had Ms. Baker not reviewed the hotel invoice closely, she might have been overcharged.

(A) Have (B) Had
(C) Has (D) Having

베이커 씨가 그 호텔 청구서를 면밀히 보지 않았다면 그녀에게 요금이 과다 청구되었을지도 모른다.

해설 if 생략 [가정법 과거완료] 주절의 동사(might have been)가 〈might+have p.p.〉인 것으로 보아 가정법 과거완료 문장임을 알 수 있다. 따라서 if절의 동사는 〈had p.p.〉가 되어야 하므로 (B) Had가 정답이다. 원래는 'If Ms. Baker had not reviewed the hotel invoice closely'지만 if가 생략되면서 주어 Ms. Baker와 조동사 had가 도치된 것이다.

어휘 review 검토하다 overcharge 과다 청구하다

4.

If Ms. Kenneth **had applied** for the job earlier, she could have been the new secretary.

(A) had applied (B) applied
(C) apply (D) should apply

케네스 씨가 그 직무에 더 일찍 지원했다면 그녀가 새로운 비서가 될 수 있었을 것이다.

해설 가정법 과거완료 주절의 동사(could have been)가 〈could+have p.p.〉인 것으로 보아 가정법 과거완료 문장임을 알 수 있다. 따라서 if절의 동사는 〈had p.p.〉가 되어야 하므로 (A) had applied가 정답이다.

어휘 apply for ~에 지원하다 secretary 비서

141

5.

If Eric **had reviewed** the material, he could have caught the mistakes.

(A) reviewed (B) will review
(C) had reviewed (D) have reviewed

에릭이 그 자료를 검토했다면 그 실수들을 잡아낼 수 있었을 것이다.

해설 가정법 과거완료 주절의 동사(could have caught)가 〈could+have p.p.〉인 것으로 보아 가정법 과거완료 문장임을 알 수 있다. 따라서 if절의 동사는 〈had p.p.〉가 되어야 하므로 (C) had reviewed가 정답이다.

어휘 review 검토하다   material 자료   catch 잡아내다, 발견하다(-caught-caught)

6.

Power Books will provide a 10% discount **if** you use the following coupon code.

(A) neither (B) therefore
(C) if (D) whereas

다음의 쿠폰 코드를 사용하시면 파워 북스에서 10퍼센트 할인을 제공할 것입니다.

해설 부사절 접속사 if 빈칸 앞뒤로 주어와 동사, 그리고 목적어를 갖춘 완전한 절이 위치해 있다. 따라서 빈칸은 동등한 절을 연결하는 접속사 자리이다. 또한 문맥상 쿠폰 코드를 사용하면 할인을 제공할 거라는 내용이 되는 게 자연스러우므로 '만약'을 뜻하는 (C) if가 정답이다.

어휘 provide 제공하다, 공급하다   discount 할인   following 다음의

7.

Mr. Parker **would complete** his project report if his supervisor requested he do so.

(A) completes (B) will complete
(C) would complete (D) has completed

부서장이 그렇게 하라고 요청한다면 파커 씨는 사업 계획 보고서를 완료할 것이다.

해설 가정법 과거 if절의 동사(requested)가 동사의 과거형인 것으로 보아 가정법 과거 문장임을 알 수 있다. 따라서 주절의 동사는 〈would/could/might+동사원형〉이 되어야 하므로 (C) would complete가 정답이다.

어휘 complete 완료하다, 완성하다   supervisor 감독, 부서장   request 요청하다

8.

Denton Industries prefers to acquire supplies **locally** to support companies in Rockport.

(A) locally (B) seriously
(C) sharply (D) variably

덴턴 산업은 락포트의 기업들을 지원하기 위해 **근방에서** 공급품을 입수하기를 원한다.

(A) 근방에서 (B) 심각하게
(C) 날카롭게; 급격히 (D) 변하기 쉽게

해설 부사 어휘 빈칸 앞의 to acquire를 수식해 가장 자연스럽게 의미가 통하는 부사를 골라야 한다. 따라서 '(특정 지역) 근방에서; 국지적으로'라는 의미의 (A) locally가 정답이다.

어휘 industry 산업, 공업   acquire 얻다, 입수하다   supplies ((항상 복수형)) 공급품

Spring Flower Festival 〉〉 Home 〉〉 Forum Page

What a great festival!

by David Harper

This year's Cumberland Spring Flower Festival was the best ever. As the ⁹**organizer** of the event, I know exactly how well everything went. Things couldn't have been better. I'd especially like to thank all of our volunteers. If we hadn't gotten so many of them, the festival ¹⁰**would not have been** so successful. Thanks to all of you for the help you provided. ¹¹**I hope you enjoyed yourselves, too.** I was also impressed by the musical performers. I saw the performances ¹²**both** on Friday and the following day. The fans loved those shows almost as much as I did. I'd say it was an amazing festival overall.

봄 꽃 축제 〉〉 홈 〉〉 포럼 페이지

정말 멋진 축제였습니다!

데이비드 하퍼

금년의 컴버랜드 봄 꽃 축제는 역대 최고였습니다. 행사 ⁹**주최자**로서 저는 모든 것이 얼마나 잘 되었는지를 정확히 알고 있습니다. 상황이 더할 나위 없이 좋았습니다. 저는 특히 우리 자원봉사자 여러분 모두에게 감사하고 싶습니다. 우리에게 그렇게 많은 분들이 없었다면 축제가 그토록 성공적이지 ¹⁰**않았을 것입니다.** 여러분이 주신 도움에 대해 여러분 모두에게 감사드립니다. ¹¹**여러분도 즐거운 시간이었기를 바랍니다.** 저는 또한 음악 공연자들에게 깊은 인상을 받았습니다. 저는 금요일과 그 다음 날 ¹²**모두** 공연들을 봤습니다. 팬들은 거의 저만큼이나 그 쇼들을 매우 좋아했습니다. 전체적으로 대단히 훌륭한 축제였다고 말하고 싶습니다.

어휘 forum 포럼, 공개 토론방 the best ever 역대 최고의 것 organizer 조직자, 주최자 exactly 정확히 things 상황, 형편 couldn't have been better 더할 나위 없이 좋았다 especially 특히 volunteer 자원봉사자 successful 성공적인 provide 제공하다, 주다 enjoy oneself 즐거운 시간을 보내다 performer 공연자, 연주자 performance 공연, 연주회 the following day 그 다음 날 amazing (놀랄 만큼) 훌륭한 overall 전체적으로

9. (A) organizer (B) performer (A) 주최자 (B) 공연자
 (C) speaker (D) designer (C) 강연자 (D) 디자이너

해설 명사 어휘 빈칸 뒤의 전치사구 of the event의 수식을 받아 가장 자연스럽게 의미가 통하는 명사를 골라야 한다. 따라서 '(행사의) 조직자, 주최자'라는 의미의 (A) organizer가 정답이다.

10. (A) is not (B) will not be
 (C) has not been (D) would not have been

해설 가정법 과거완료 if절의 동사(hadn't gotten)가 〈had p.p.〉인 것으로 보아 가정법 과거완료 문장임을 알 수 있다. 따라서 주절의 동사는 〈would/could/might + have p.p.〉가 되어야 하므로 (D) would not have been이 정답이다.

11. (A) You'll be paid for your time soon.
 (B) Schedules will be posted online.
 (C) I hope you enjoyed yourselves, too.
 (D) We've got a great show coming up.

(A) 곧 여러분이 일한 시간에 대한 보수를 받을 겁니다.
(B) 일정들이 온라인에 게시될 것입니다.
(C) 여러분도 즐거운 시간이었기를 바랍니다.
(D) 멋진 쇼가 곧 있을 겁니다.

해설 알맞은 문장 고르기 빈칸 앞의 문장들에서 자원봉사자들이 행사가 성공할 수 있도록 도와준 것에 대해 감사하고 있으므로 그들도 즐거운 시간을 보냈기를 바란다고 말하는 (C)가 정답이다.

어휘 be paid 보수를 받다 post (웹사이트에 글을) 올리다, 게시하다 come up (행사나 때가) 곧 다가오다

12. (A) little (B) each
 (C) none (D) both

해설 상관 접속사 [both A and B] 빈칸 뒤에 연결어 and가 있으므로 'A와 B 모두'라는 의미의 상관 접속사 both A and B가 사용된 문장임을 알 수 있다. 따라서 (D) both가 정답이다.

UNIT 15 관계사

1 주격 관계대명사

본문 p.242

1. (C)   2. (A)   3. (D)   4. (C)

1.

R&D staff members **who** can work next weekend should contact Ms. Gordon immediately.

다음 주말에 일할 수 있는 연구 개발 직원들은 고든 씨에게 즉시 연락해야 한다.

(A) what   (B) which
(C) who   (D) they

해설 주격 관계대명사 who 빈칸 뒤의 관계사절에 주어가 없으므로 빈칸에는 주격 관계대명사가 들어가야 한다. 또한 선행사 R&D staff members는 사람이므로 (C) who가 정답이다. (B) which는 선행사가 사물일 때 쓰는 관계대명사이므로 오답이다. (A) what은 선행사를 포함하는 관계대명사, (D) they는 대명사이므로 정답이 될 수 없다.

어휘 R&D 연구 개발 (=research and development) staff member 직원 contact 연락하다 immediately 즉시, 바로

2.

Mr. Collins takes the train **which** departs from Central Station at 7:00 A.M.

콜린스 씨는 오전 7시에 센트럴 역에서 출발하는 기차를 탄다.

(A) which   (B) who
(C) it   (D) but

해설 주격 관계대명사 which 빈칸 뒤의 관계사절에 주어가 없으므로 빈칸에는 주격 관계대명사가 들어가야 한다. 또한 선행사 the train은 사물이므로 (A) which가 정답이다. (B) who는 선행사가 사람일 때 쓰는 관계대명사이므로 이 문장에서는 답이 될 수 없다.

어휘 take (탈것에) 타다 depart 떠나다, 출발하다 station 역, 정류장

3.

Owning an apartment **that** is located downtown is important to Mr. Wendell.

시내에 위치한 아파트를 소유하는 것이 웬델 씨에게는 중요하다.

(A) what   (B) this
(C) who   (D) that

해설 주격 관계대명사 that 빈칸 뒤의 관계사절에 주어가 없으므로 빈칸에는 주격 관계대명사가 들어가야 한다. 또한 선행사 an apartment는 사물이므로 관계대명사 which를 대신해 사용할 수 있는 (D) that이 정답이다.

어휘 own 소유하다 apartment 아파트(의 한 세대) be located 위치하다 downtown 시내에 important 중요한

4.

A free T-shirt is available to anybody who **volunteers** at Carter Park next weekend.

다음 주말에 카터 공원에서 자원봉사를 하는 사람은 누구나 무료 티셔츠를 받을 수 있다.

(A) volunteer   (B) volunteering
(C) volunteers   (D) volunteered

해설 주격 관계대명사절의 동사 자리 빈칸 뒤에 주어가 없으므로 빈칸은 주격 관계대명사 who가 이끄는 관계사절의 동사 자리이다. 선행사인 anybody가 단수이므로 (C) volunteers가 정답이다. (D) volunteered는 동사 또는 과거분사로 볼 수 있는데, 동사라고 하더라도 과거 시제이므로 미래를 나타내는 부사구 next weekend와 함께 쓸 수 없기 때문에 오답이다.

어휘 free 무료의 available 구할[얻을] 수 있는 volunteer 자원하다, 자원봉사를 하다

2 목적격 관계대명사

본문 p.243

1. (B)   2. (C)   3. (D)   4. (C)

1.

Mr. Erikson recovered one of the suitcases **that** he had lost at the airport.

(A) it
(B) that
(C) who
(D) whom

에릭슨 씨는 공항에서 잃어버린 가방 중 하나를 되찾았다.

해설 목적격 관계대명사 that 빈칸 뒤의 문장에 had lost의 목적어가 없으므로 빈칸은 목적격 관계대명사 자리다. 빈칸 앞의 the suitcases가 had lost의 목적어에 해당하며, 선행사가 사물이므로 빈칸에는 that이나 which가 들어가야 한다.

어휘 recover 되찾다   suitcase 여행 가방

2.

The doubtful customers were pleased to know that the appliances **they** purchased work properly.

(A) that
(B) which
(C) they
(D) themselves

의심을 품은 고객들은 자신들이 구입한 가전제품들이 제대로 작동하는 것을 알고 만족해했다.

해설 목적격 관계대명사절의 주어 자리 빈칸 앞에 명사 the appliances가 있고 뒤에는 동사 purchased와 work가 연달아 나온 것으로 보아 〈명사절 접속사(that)+주어(the appliances)+[-------+동사(purchased)]+동사구(work properly)〉 구조임을 알 수 있다. 또한 동사 purchased의 목적어가 없으므로 the appliances와 빈칸 사이에 목적격 관계대명사가 생략된 문장이다. 따라서 빈칸에는 동사 purchased의 주어 역할을 할 수 있는 명사가 들어가야 하므로 주격 인칭대명사인 (C) they가 정답이다.

어휘 doubtful 의심을 품은, 확신이 없는   be pleased to do ~해서 만족해하다   appliance 가전제품   purchase 구입하다   work 작동하다   properly 제대로, 적절히

3.

Mr. Montpelier contacted the woman **whom** he wanted to offer a marketing position to.

(A) herself
(B) which
(C) what
(D) whom

몬트필리어 씨는 마케팅 직책을 제안하고 싶은 여성에게 연락했다.

해설 목적격 관계대명사 whom 빈칸 뒤에 이어지는 관계사절의 전치사 to에 목적어가 없으므로 빈칸에는 목적격 관계대명사가 들어가야 한다. 선행사인 the woman이 사람이므로 (D) whom이 정답이다.

어휘 contact 연락하다   offer 제안하다, 제의하다   marketing 마케팅, 시장 관리   position 직책, 직위

4.

Please review the employee evaluation **that** I have attached to this message.

(A) whom
(B) how
(C) that
(D) who

이 메시지에 첨부해 드린 직원 평가서를 검토해 주십시오.

해설 목적격 관계대명사 that 빈칸 앞에 선행사 the employee evaluation이 있고 뒤에는 have attached의 목적어가 없는 절이 이어지므로 빈칸에는 목적격 관계대명사가 들어가야 한다. 따라서 (C) that이 정답이다. (A) whom과 (D) who는 선행사가 사람일 때 쓰는 관계대명사이므로 오답이다.

어휘 review 검토하다   employee evaluation 직원 평가서, 인사 고과   attach 첨부하다

3 소유격 관계대명사

1. (A)   2. (D)   3. (C)   4. (B)

1.

The curator will meet the donors **whose** financial support keeps the museum operating.

전시 책임자는 재정 지원으로 박물관이 계속 운영되게 해 주는 기부자들을 만날 것이다.

(A) whose   (B) what
(C) which   (D) why

해설 소유격 관계대명사 빈칸 뒤에 〈주어(financial support)+동사(keeps)+목적어(the museum)+목적격 보어(operating)〉 구조로 완전한 문장이 있으며, 주어인 financial support 앞에 관사가 없다. 또한 선행사 the donors와 관계사절의 주어 financial support는 the donors' financial support로 소유 관계가 성립한다. 따라서 소유격 관계대명사인 (A) whose가 정답이다.

어휘 curator (박물관이나 미술관 등의) 전시 책임자, 큐레이터   donor 기부자, 기증자   financial 재정적인   support 지원, 후원   keep A doing A가 계속 ~하게 하다   operate 가동되다, 운용되다

2.

After lunch, Beth Armstrong will demonstrate the new product **whose** computing capabilities are impressive.

점심 식사 후에 베스 암스트롱이 연산 능력이 인상적인 신제품을 시연할 것이다.

(A) which   (B) who
(C) whom   (D) whose

해설 소유격 관계대명사 빈칸 뒤에 〈주어(computing capabilities)+동사(are)+주격 보어(impressive)〉 구조로 완전한 문장이 있으며, 주어인 computing capabilities 앞에 관사가 없다. 또한 선행사 the new product와 관계사절의 주어 computing capabilities는 the new product's computing capabilities로 소유 관계가 성립한다. 따라서 소유격 관계대명사인 (D) whose가 정답이다.

어휘 demonstrate 시연하다   product 제품   computing capabilities ((보통 복수형)) 연산 능력   impressive 인상적인

3.

The award was given to the contestant whose **performance** was loved by the audience.

그 상은 청중의 사랑을 받은 연주를 한 참가자에게 주어졌다.

(A) perform   (B) the performance
(C) performance   (D) performers

해설 소유격 관계대명사절의 주어 자리 빈칸은 소유격 관계대명사 whose가 이끄는 관계사절의 주어 자리이다. whose 뒤에 위치하는 주어는 소유격이나 관사를 쓰지 않고, 빈칸 뒤에 단수 동사 was가 있으므로 관사 없는 단수 명사인 (C) performance가 정답이다.

어휘 award 상, 상금   be given to ~에게 주어지다   contestant (대회, 시합의) 참가자, 출연자   performance 공연, 연주

4.

All owners **whose** property must be inspected should contact the relevant government agency.

부동산을 조사받아야 하는 모든 소유주들은 관련 정부 기관에 연락해야 한다.

(A) which   (B) whose
(C) who   (D) that

해설 소유격 관계대명사 빈칸 뒤에 〈주어(property)+동사구(must be inspected)〉 구조로 완전한 문장이 있으며, 주어인 property 앞에 관사가 없다. 또한 선행사 All owners와 관계사절의 주어 property는 All owners' property로 소유 관계가 성립한다. 따라서 소유격 관계대명사인 (B) whose가 정답이다. 소유격 관계대명사는 that으로 바꿔 쓸 수 없으므로 (D) that은 오답이다.

어휘 owner 소유주, 주인   property 재산, 부동산   inspect 검사하다, 조사하다   contact 연락하다   relevant 관련된, 연관된   government agency 정부 기관

4 관계대명사 what

1. (D) 2. (B) 3. (C) 4. (D)

1.

Ms. Stallings read the product reviews **which** included complaints and attempted to solve the problems.

(A) who   (B) whose
(C) what   **(D) which**

스톨링스 씨는 불만들이 포함된 상품평을 읽고 그 문제들을 해결하려고 시도했다.

해설 주격 관계대명사 which 빈칸 뒤의 관계사절에 주어가 없으므로 빈칸에는 주격 관계대명사가 들어가야 한다. 또한 선행사 the product reviews는 사물이므로 (D) which가 정답이다.

어휘 product review 제품 리뷰, 상품평   include 포함하다   complaint 불만, 불평   attempt to do ~하려고 시도하다   solve 해결하다   problem 문제

2.

What impressed the overseas clients the most was Mr. Reardon's attention to detail.

(A) Who   **(B) What**
(C) This   (D) These

해외 고객에게 가장 깊은 인상을 준 것은 리어든 씨의 세심함이었다.

해설 관계대명사 what 빈칸에는 be동사 was의 주어 역할을 하면서 불완전한 절(impressed ~ the most)을 이끌 수 있는 말이 들어가야 한다. 따라서 선행사를 포함하는 관계대명사인 (B) What이 정답이다.

어휘 impress 깊은 인상을 주다   overseas 해외의   client (업체의) 고객, 의뢰인   attention to detail 세심함, 꼼꼼함

3.

The supervisor decided to ask about **what** Mr. Leonard wanted for his next assignment.

(A) whom   (B) that
(C) what   (D) when

부서장은 레너드 씨가 다음 업무로 원하는 것에 관해 물어보기로 결정했다.

해설 관계대명사 what 빈칸 앞에 전치사 about이 있고 뒤에는 〈주어(Mr. Leonard)+동사(wanted)+전치사구(for ~ assignment)〉 구조로 동사 wanted의 목적어가 없는 불완전한 절이 이어져 있다. 따라서 빈칸에는 전치사의 목적어 역할을 하면서 목적어가 없는 불완전한 절을 이끌 수 있는 말이 들어가야 하므로 선행사를 포함하는 관계대명사인 (C) what이 정답이다.

어휘 supervisor 관리자, 부서장   decide to do ~하기로 결정하다   assignment 과제, 할당 업무

4.

The user manual for the order processing system is **what** Mr. Hand requested last week.

(A) it   (B) that
(C) whose   **(D) what**

그 주문 처리 시스템에 대한 사용자 매뉴얼은 핸드 씨가 지난주에 요청했던 것이다.

해설 관계대명사 what 빈칸 앞에 be동사 is가 있고 뒤에는 〈주어(Mr. Hand)+동사(requested)+부사구(last week)〉 구조로 동사 requested의 목적어가 없는 불완전한 절이 이어져 있다. 따라서 빈칸에는 be동사의 보어 역할을 하면서 목적어가 없는 불완전한 절을 이끌 수 있는 말이 들어가야 하므로 선행사를 포함하는 관계대명사인 (D) what이 정답이다.

어휘 user manual 사용자 매뉴얼, 사용 설명서   request 요청하다

5 관계부사: where, when

본문 p.246

1. (D)   2. (C)   3. (A)   4. (C)

1.

The weekend is the time **when** the amusement park has the most visitors.

주말은 그 놀이공원이 가장 많은 방문객을 받는 때이다.

(A) where   (B) what
(C) why   **(D) when**

해설 관계부사 when 〈주어(the amusement park)+동사(has)+목적어(the most visitors)〉 구조로 빈칸 뒤에 완전한 문장이 있다. 따라서 빈칸에는 부사와 접속사 역할을 겸하는 관계부사가 들어가야 하며, 선행사가 시간을 나타내는 the time이므로 (D) when이 정답이다.

어휘 amusement park 놀이공원   visitor 방문객

2.

The basement laboratory is the place **where** most cutting-edge research is done.

지하 실험실은 대부분의 최첨단 연구가 이루어지는 장소이다.

(A) how   (B) which
(C) where (D) when

해설 관계부사 where 〈주어(most cutting-edge research)+동사구(is done)〉 구조로 빈칸 뒤에 완전한 문장이 있다. 따라서 빈칸에는 부사와 접속사 역할을 겸하는 관계부사가 들어가야 하며, 선행사가 장소를 나타내는 the place이므로 (C) where가 정답이다.

어휘 basement 지하층, 지하실   laboratory 실험실   cutting-edge 최첨단의   research 연구, 조사

3.

Dr. Sandoval will announce the names of the nurses **who** are working the night shift.

샌도벌 선생이 야간 근무조로 일할 간호사들의 명단을 발표할 것이다.

(A) who   (B) which
(C) where   (D) when

해설 주격 관계대명사 who 빈칸 뒤의 관계사절에 주어가 없으므로 빈칸에는 주격 관계대명사가 들어가야 한다. 선행사인 the nurses가 사람이므로 (A) who가 정답이다. (B) which는 선행사가 사물일 때 쓰기 때문에 오답이다.

어휘 announce 발표하다   nurse 간호사   work the night shift 야간 근무조로 일하다

4.

Mr. Filmore will receive a box in **which** product samples have been packed.

필모어 씨는 제품 견본들이 포장된 상자를 받을 것이다.

(A) when   (B) where
(C) which (D) what

해설 전치사+관계대명사 빈칸 앞에 전치사 in이 있으므로 전치사의 목적어 역할을 할 수 있는 목적격 관계대명사 (C) which가 정답이다. 원래는 'a box **which** product samples have been packed **in**'이었으나 관계사절 끝에 남은 전치사가 관계대명사 앞으로 와서 지금의 문장이 된 것이다. 또한 선행사가 제품 견본이 포장된 장소를 나타내는 a box이기 때문에 in which는 관계부사 where로 바꿔 쓸 수 있다.

어휘 product 제품, 상품   sample 견본, 샘플   pack 포장하다, 채워 넣다

6 관계부사: why, how

본문 p.247

1. (A)　　　2. (A)　　　3. (D)　　　4. (C)

1.

> Mr. Bonaventure is planning **how** he can expand his textile business.
>
> (A) how　　　(B) that
> (C) which　　(D) why

보나벤처 씨는 자신의 직물 사업을 확장할 수 있는 방법을 구상하고 있다.

해설 관계부사 how 〈주어(he)+동사(can expand)+목적어(his textile business)〉 구조로 빈칸 뒤에 완전한 문장이 있다. 따라서 빈칸에는 부사와 접속사 역할을 겸하는 관계부사가 들어가야 하며, 문맥상 사업을 확장할 '방법'을 구상한다는 내용이 되는 게 자연스러우므로 (A) how가 정답이다.

어휘 plan 계획하다, 구상하다　expand 확대하다, 확장하다　textile 직물, 옷감　business 사업(체)

2.

> Dylan West explained the reason for **which** he wanted to transfer to the Madrid office.
>
> (A) which　　(B) where
> (C) how　　　(D) why

딜런 웨스트는 마드리드 사무소로 전근하기를 원하는 이유를 설명했다.

해설 전치사+관계대명사 빈칸 앞에 전치사 for가 있으므로 전치사의 목적어 역할을 할 수 있는 목적격 관계대명사 (A) which가 정답이다. 원래는 'the reason **which** he wanted to transfer to the Madrid office **for**'였으나 관계사절 끝에 남은 전치사가 관계대명사 앞으로 와서 지금의 문장이 된 것이다. 또한 for which는 관계부사 why와 같은 역할을 한다.

어휘 explain 설명하다　reason 이유　transfer 이동하다, 전근하다

3.

> **What** can cause a delay for a flight is a mechanical problem.
>
> (A) Which　　(B) How
> (C) Why　　　(D) What

항공편 지연을 야기할 수 있는 것은 기계적인 결함이다.

해설 관계대명사 what 빈칸에는 be동사 is의 주어 역할을 하면서 불완전한 절(can cause ~ a flight)을 이끌 수 있는 말이 들어가야 한다. 따라서 선행사를 포함하는 관계대명사인 (D) What이 정답이다.

어휘 cause 초래하다, ~의 원인이 되다　delay 지연, 지체　flight 비행, 항공편　mechanical 기계(상)의, 기계적인　problem 문제, 결함

4.

> The mayor wants to understand **how** the money in the budget will be spent.
>
> (A) whose　　(B) what
> (C) how　　　(D) whom

시장은 예산의 돈이 쓰이게 될 방식을 알고 있기를 원한다.

해설 관계부사 how 〈주어(the money)+전치사구(in the budget)+동사구(will be spent)〉 구조로 빈칸 뒤에 완전한 문장이 있다. 따라서 빈칸에는 부사와 접속사 역할을 겸하는 관계부사가 들어가야 하며, 문맥상 돈이 쓰이게 될 '방식'을 알고 싶어 한다는 내용이 되는 게 자연스러우므로 (C) how가 정답이다.

어휘 mayor 시장　understand 이해하다, 알고 있다　budget 예산　spend 쓰다, 소비하다

VOCABULARY

본문 p.250

1. (A) 2. (D) 3. (B) 4. (A) 5. (B) 6. (D) 7. (B) 8. (A)

1.

Many electronic exports related to computing are **strictly** regulated by the government.

(A) **strictly** (B) arguably
(C) mutually   (D) brightly

전산과 관련된 많은 전자 제품 수출이 정부에 의해 **엄격하게** 규제되고 있다.

(A) **엄격하게** (B) 주장하건대
(C) 서로, 상호 간에 (D) 밝게

해설 부사 어휘 과거분사 regulated를 수식해 가장 자연스럽게 의미가 통하는 부사를 골라야 한다. 따라서 '엄격하게'라는 의미의 (A) strictly가 정답이다.

어휘 electronic 전자 제품 export 수출 related to ~와 관련된 computing 전산, 컴퓨터 사용 regulate 규제하다

2.

All staff members **currently** on business trips are exempt from the budget committee meeting.

(A) consistently (B) instantly
(C) fairly   (D) **currently**

현재 출장 중인 모든 직원들은 예산 위원회 회의 참석을 면제받는다.

(A) 지속적으로 (B) 즉시
(C) 공정하게   (D) **현재**

해설 부사 어휘 전치사구 on business trips와 어울려 가장 자연스럽게 의미가 통하는 부사를 골라야 한다. 따라서 '현재, 지금'이라는 의미의 (D) currently가 정답이다.

어휘 on business trip 출장 중인 be exempt from ~에서 면제되다 budget 예산 committee 위원회

3.

The keynote speech is scheduled to begin **promptly** at 9:15 A.M.

(A) cautiously (B) **promptly**
(C) seriously   (D) accurately

기조연설은 오전 9시 15분 **정각에** 시작되기로 예정되어 있다.

(A) 조심스럽게   (B) **정확히 제시간에**
(C) 진지하게   (D) 정확하게

해설 부사 어휘 동사 begin을 수식해 가장 자연스럽게 의미가 통하는 부사를 골라야 한다. 빈칸 뒤에 시간 부사구 at 9:15 A.M.이 있으므로 '정확히 제시간에; 지체 없이'라는 의미의 (B) promptly가 정답이다. (D) accurately는 기록이나 정보, 계산 등이 실수나 오류가 없고 확실하다는 표현을 할 때 쓰기 때문에 이 문장에서는 적절하지 않다.

어휘 keynote speech 기조연설 be scheduled to do ~하기로 예정되어 있다

4.

The CEO expects this quarter's profits to improve **significantly** thanks to the booming economy.

(A) **significantly** (B) increasingly
(C) reportedly   (D) approvingly

대표 이사는 이번 분기의 수익이 경기 호황 덕분에 **상당히** 향상될 것으로 예상한다.

(A) **상당히**   (B) 점점, 더욱 더
(C) 전하는 바에 의하면 (D) 찬성하여

해설 부사 어휘 동사 improve를 수식해 가장 자연스럽게 의미가 통하는 부사를 골라야 한다. 따라서 '상당히, 크게'라는 의미의 (A) significantly가 정답이다. (B) increasingly는 시간이 갈수록 상황이나 상태 등이 이전보다 더하거나 덜해진다는 걸 표현할 때 쓰기 때문에 시간의 연속성이나 흐름을 나타내는 문맥에서 쓰는 것이 알맞다. 그러므로 this quarter(이번 분기)로 기간을 한정한 이 문장에서 (B) increasingly를 쓰는 건 적절하지 않다.

어휘 expect 예상하다, 기대하다 quarter 분기, 1년의 4분의 1 profit 수익, 이익 improve 향상되다, 개선되다 booming economy 경기 호황

5.

The lawyer read the contract **closely** to ensure there were no problems.

(A) naturally (B) closely
(C) jointly (D) moderately

변호사는 확실히 문제가 없게 하려고 계약서를 **면밀히** 읽었다.

(A) 자연스럽게 (B) 면밀히
(C) 공동으로 (D) 적당히

해설 부사 어휘 동사 read를 수식해 가장 자연스럽게 의미가 통하는 부사를 골라야 한다. 문제의 소지가 없도록 하기 위해 계약서를 읽는 것이므로 '면밀히; 밀접하게'라는 의미의 (B) closely가 정답이다.

어휘 contract 계약(서) ensure 확실하게 하다, 보장하다

6.

The **highly** anticipated release of the software was a success for Data Pro.

(A) purposely (B) definitely
(C) apparently (D) highly

많이 기대를 모았던 그 소프트웨어의 출시는 데이터 프로에게 성공작이었다.

(A) 고의로 (B) 분명히
(C) 보아하니 (D) 많이

해설 부사 어휘 과거분사 anticipated를 수식해 가장 자연스럽게 의미가 통하는 부사를 골라야 한다. 따라서 '매우, 많이'라는 의미의 (D) highly가 정답이다.

어휘 anticipate 기대하다, 고대하다 release 출시, 발매 success 성공작, 성공한 것; 성공

7.

The parking lot on Waverly Street was **temporarily** closed during the holiday.

(A) sincerely (B) temporarily
(C) importantly (D) evenly

웨이벌리 가의 주차장은 공휴일 동안 **일시적으로** 문을 닫았다.

(A) 진심으로 (B) 일시적으로
(C) 중요하게는 (D) 공평하게; 고르게

해설 부사 어휘 과거분사 closed를 수식해 가장 자연스럽게 의미가 통하는 부사를 골라야 한다. 따라서 '일시적으로, 임시로'라는 의미의 (B) temporarily가 정답이다.

어휘 parking lot 주차장 holiday 공휴일

8.

Ms. Dillon is **widely** respected as an expert in the field of civil engineering.

(A) widely (B) effectively
(C) urgently (D) daily

딜론 씨는 토목 공학 분야의 전문가로 **널리** 인정받고 있다.

(A) 널리, 폭넓게 (B) 효과적으로
(C) 급히, 긴급히 (D) 매일

해설 부사 어휘 과거분사 respected를 수식해 가장 자연스럽게 의미가 통하는 부사를 골라야 한다. 따라서 '널리, 폭넓게; 대단히, 크게'라는 의미의 (A) widely가 정답이다.

어휘 expert 전문가 field 분야 civil engineering 토목 공학

ACTUAL TEST

본문 p.252

| 1. (D) | 2. (A) | 3. (C) | 4. (A) | 5. (D) | 6. (D) |
| 7. (D) | 8. (A) | 9. (C) | 10. (D) | 11. (A) | 12. (A) |

1.

Mr. Montrose shops at a grocery store that **imports** delicacies from Europe.

(A) import
(B) to import
(C) importing
(D) imports

몬트로스 씨는 유럽에서 별미들을 수입하는 식료품점에서 쇼핑한다.

[해설] **주격 관계대명사절의 동사 자리** 빈칸 뒤에 주어가 없으므로 빈칸은 주격 관계대명사 that이 이끄는 관계사절의 동사 자리이다. 선행사인 a grocery store가 단수이므로 (D) imports가 정답이다.

[어휘] shop 쇼핑하다   grocery store 식료품점   import 수입하다   delicacy 진미, 별미

2.

Ms. Ball booked a room at the hotel **where** she had previously stayed.

(A) where
(B) who
(C) when
(D) what

볼 씨는 이전에 묵었던 호텔 방을 예약했다.

[해설] **관계부사 where** 〈주어(she)+동사구(had previously stayed)〉 구조로 빈칸 뒤에 완전한 문장이 있다. 따라서 빈칸에는 부사와 접속사 역할을 겸하는 관계부사가 들어가야 하며, 선행사가 장소를 나타내는 the hotel이므로 (A) where가 정답이다. 동사 stay가 '(손님, 방문객으로) 묵다, 머무르다'를 뜻할 때는 자동사이기 때문에 목적어를 취하지 않는다는 점에 유의해야 한다.

[어휘] book 예약하다   previously 이전에, 그에 앞서   stay 묵다, 숙박하다

3.

Mr. Truss takes graduate classes in the city in which **he** lives.

(A) himself
(B) his
(C) he
(D) him

트러스 씨는 자기가 사는 도시에서 대학원 수업을 듣는다.

[해설] **〈전치사+관계대명사〉절의 주어 자리** 빈칸 앞에 in which가 있고 뒤에는 동사 lives가 있으므로 빈칸에는 동사의 주어 역할을 할 수 있는 말이 들어가야 한다. 따라서 주격 인칭대명사인 (C) he가 정답이다. 참고로 이 문장에서 in which는 관계부사 where로 바꿔 쓸 수 있다.

[어휘] take (과목을) 듣다, 수강하다   graduate class 대학원 수업

4.

Jasmine Polymers has **mutually** beneficial contracts with several suppliers.

(A) mutually
(B) temporarily
(C) hopefully
(D) virtually

재스민 폴리머스는 공급업체 몇 곳과 **상호 간에** 유익한 계약을 맺고 있다.

(A) 서로, 상호 간에
(B) 일시적으로
(C) 바라건대
(D) 사실상; 가상으로

[해설] **부사 어휘** 형용사 beneficial을 수식해 가장 자연스럽게 의미가 통하는 부사를 골라야 한다. 따라서 '서로, 상호 간에'라는 의미의 (A) mutually가 정답이다.

[어휘] beneficial 유익한, 유리한   contract 계약, 협약   supplier 공급자, 공급업체

5.

Individuals **who** plan to travel abroad must make sure their passports are valid for the duration of their trip.

(A) how (B) whose
(C) whom **(D) who**

해외로 여행할 계획인 사람들은 자신의 여권이 여행 기간 동안 유효한지 확인해야 한다.

해설 주격 관계대명사 who 빈칸 뒤의 관계사절에 주어가 없으므로 빈칸에는 주격 관계대명사가 들어가야 한다. 따라서 (D) who가 정답이다. (A) how는 관계부사, (B) whose는 소유격 관계대명사, (C) whom은 목적격 관계대명사이기 때문에 오답이다.

어휘 individual 개인 plan to do ~할 계획이다 travel abroad 해외로 여행하다 make sure 확인하다, 확실히 하다 valid (법적으로) 유효한

6.

All timesheets, **which** are available in Mr. Green's office, should be submitted to Carol Roth.

(A) whose (B) they
(C) these **(D) which**

모든 근무 시간 기록표는 그린 씨의 사무실에서 받을 수 있으며 캐럴 로스에게 제출되어야 합니다.

해설 주격 관계대명사 which 빈칸 뒤의 관계사절에 주어가 없으므로 빈칸에는 주격 관계대명사가 들어가야 한다. 따라서 (D) which가 정답이다. 빈칸 앞에 선행사 All timesheets가 있으므로 대명사인 (B) they와 (C) these는 오답이다.

어휘 timesheet 근무 시간 기록표 available 구할[얻을] 수 있는 submit 제출하다

7.

The Galley is a restaurant **at which** diners enjoy top-flight service and food.

(A) for whom (B) which
(C) what **(D) at which**

더 갤리는 손님들이 최고의 서비스와 음식을 즐기는 레스토랑이다.

해설 전치사+관계대명사 빈칸 앞에 선행사 a restaurant이 있고 뒤에는 〈주어(diners)+동사(enjoy)+목적어(top-flight ~ food)〉 구조로 완전한 절이 있다. 따라서 빈칸에는 관계부사나 〈전치사+관계대명사〉가 들어가야 하는데, 선행사(a restaurant)가 사물이므로 (D) at which가 정답이다. 여기서 at which는 관계부사 where로 바꿔 쓸 수 있다. (B) which는 관계대명사이므로 뒤에 불완전한 절이 이어져야 하며, (C) what은 선행사를 포함한 관계대명사이기 때문에 답이 될 수 없다.

어휘 diner 식사하는 사람[손님] top-flight 최고의, 일류의

8.

We are preparing for the conference **which** many local businesspeople are planning to attend.

(A) which (B) who
(C) whose (D) what

우리는 많은 지역 사업가들이 참석할 계획인 콘퍼런스를 준비하고 있다.

해설 목적격 관계대명사 which 빈칸 뒤에 이어지는 관계사절의 to attend에 목적어가 없으므로 빈칸에는 목적격 관계대명사가 들어가야 한다. 선행사인 the conference가 사물이므로 (A) which가 정답이다. (B) who는 목적격 관계대명사로 쓸 수 있지만 선행사가 사람이어야 하므로 오답이다. (C) whose는 소유격 관계대명사, (D) what은 선행사를 포함한 관계대명사이므로 답이 될 수 없다.

어휘 prepare for ~을 준비하다, ~에 대비하다 conference 콘퍼런스, 대규모 회의 local 지역의, 현지의 businesspeople 사업가들 plan to do ~할 계획이다 attend 참석하다

Cynthia Watts, our vice president, has just published the book *Be Yourself at Work*. Ms. Watts mentioned that she decided to write it because she saw too many workers hiding their real selves from their colleagues. "I sometimes pretended to be someone I wasn't. But I realized that I needed to show my actual ⁹**personality** all the time," said Ms. Watts. The book provides information that ¹⁰**can be used** by people to improve their relationships at work. They can also find tips on how to become better workers. ¹¹**There is something for everyone inside this book.**

Next week, all Bertrom employees will be given signed copies of the book, courtesy of Ms. Watts. She hopes everyone ¹²**finds** the confidence to be themselves after reading this book.

우리 회사의 부사장인 신시아 와츠가 '직장에서 나답게 행동하라'라는 책을 출간했다. 와츠 씨는 너무 많은 직장인이 동료들에게 자신의 본모습을 숨기고 있는 것을 보았기 때문에 그 책을 쓰기로 결심했다고 말했다. "나는 때때로 내가 아닌 다른 사람인 척했어요. 하지만 언제나 내 실제 ⁹**인성**을 보여 주어야 한다는 것을 깨달았습니다." 와츠 씨의 말이다. 이 책은 사람들이 직장에서의 관계를 개선하는 데 ¹⁰**사용될 수 있는** 정보를 제공한다. 그들은 또한 더 나은 직장인이 되는 방법에 관한 요령들을 발견할 수 있다.
¹¹ 이 책 안에는 모든 사람을 위한 것이 있다.

다음 주에 모든 버트롬 직원들은 와츠 씨가 제공하는 그 책의 친필 사인본을 받게 될 것이다. 그녀는 모든 사람이 이 책을 읽고 난 후 자기답게 사는 자신감을 ¹²**발견하기를** 바란다.

어휘 vice president 부사장 publish 출판하다 be oneself 자연스럽게 행동하다 at work 직장에서, 근무 중에 mention 언급하다, (간단히) 말하다 decide to *do* ~하기로 결정하다 hide 숨기다, 감추다 real self 실제 자기, 본모습 colleague 직장 동료 pretend to *do* ~인 척하다 realize 깨닫다 actual 실제의 all the time 언제나, 항상 provide 제공하다 improve 개선하다 relationship 관계 tip (간단한) 조언, 요령 be given 받다 signed copy 사인본, 서명본 courtesy of (무료로) ~가 제공한 confidence 자신(감)

9. (A) performance (B) standard (C) personality (D) opportunity

(A) 성과 (B) 표준 (C) 인성 (D) 기회

해설 명사 어휘 동사 show의 목적어로 가장 자연스럽게 의미가 통하는 명사를 골라야 한다. 빈칸 앞 문장에서 자신이 아닌 다른 사람인 척했다고 했으므로 '인성, 인격'이라는 의미의 (C) personality가 정답이다.

10. (A) it was using (B) will use (C) were used (D) can be used

해설 주격 관계대명사절의 동사 자리 빈칸 뒤에 주어가 없으므로 빈칸은 주격 관계대명사 that이 이끄는 관계사절의 동사 자리이다. 또한 빈칸 뒤에 목적어가 없으므로 빈칸에는 수동형 동사가 들어가야 하며, 선행사 information은 단수이므로 (D) can be used가 정답이다.

11. (A) There is something for everyone inside this book.
  (B) Ms. Watts has worked here for ten years.
  (C) A book signing was held last weekend.
  (D) The book's cover was designed by a Bertrom employee.

(A) 이 책 안에는 모든 사람을 위한 것이 있다.
(B) 와츠 씨는 10년째 이곳에서 근무하고 있다.
(C) 지난 주말에 도서 사인회가 열렸다.
(D) 책의 표지는 버트롬 직원에 의해 디자인되었다.

해설 알맞은 문장 고르기 빈칸 앞에서 와츠 씨의 책에는 직장 내 관계 개선에 사용될 정보와 더 나은 직장인이 될 수 있는 요령들이 있다고 했다. 따라서 와츠 씨의 책에는 모두를 위한 정보와 요령이 있다는 내용이 이어지는 게 자연스러우므로 (A)가 정답이다.

어휘 book signing 도서 사인회 be held 열리다, 개최되다

12. (A) finds (B) writes (C) receives (D) appears

(A) 발견하다 (B) 쓰다 (C) 받다 (D) 나타나다

해설 동사 어휘 the confidence를 목적어로 취해 가장 자연스럽게 의미가 통하는 동사를 골라야 한다. 와츠 씨는 사람들이 자신의 책을 읽고 나서 자신감을 발견하길 바란다는 내용이 되는 게 자연스러우므로 (A) finds가 빈칸에 가장 적절하다.

UNIT 16 비교 구문

1 원급 비교
본문 p.258

1. (B) 2. (A) 3. (B) 4. (C)

1.

People traveling on unpaved roads should drive as **cautiously** as possible.

(A) cautious
(B) **cautiously**
(C) caution
(D) cautioning

비포장 도로를 지나가는 사람들은 가능한 한 조심스럽게 운전해야 합니다.

> 해설 원급 비교 [as 부사 as] as와 as 사이에는 형용사나 부사의 원급이 들어가야 한다. 여기서는 동사 drive를 수식하는 부사가 들어가야 하므로 (B) cautiously가 정답이다.

> 어휘 travel 이동하다 unpaved road 비포장 도로 as 형용사/부사 as possible 가능한 한 ~한/~하게 cautiously 조심스럽게

2.

Some items at retail stores cost twice as **much** as those sold online.

(A) **much**
(B) often
(C) still
(D) quite

소매점에 있는 몇몇 물품은 온라인에서 판매되는 물품보다 두 배 더 가격이 나간다.

> 해설 원급 비교 [배수+as much as] 빈칸 앞에 배수 twice와 as가 있고 빈칸 뒤에도 as가 있으므로 〈배수+as much as〉 구조임을 알 수 있다. 따라서 (A) much가 정답이다.

> 어휘 retail store 소매점 cost (값, 비용이) 들다 twice 두 배로 online 온라인으로 often 종종 still 아직도, 여전히; 그럼에도

3.

The hiring committee believes Mr. Roberts's qualifications are **as impressive as** those of Tina Johnson.

(A) impressively
(B) **as impressive as**
(C) more impressive
(D) the most impressive

채용 위원회는 로버트 씨의 자격증들이 티나 존슨의 자격증들만큼 인상적이라고 생각한다.

> 해설 원급 비교 [as 형용사 as] 빈칸은 be동사 are의 주격 보어 자리이므로 형용사가 들어가야 한다. 문맥상 티나 존슨만큼 로버트의 자격증이 인상적이라는 내용이 되는 게 자연스러우므로 원급 비교 형태인 (B) as impressive as가 정답이다. (C) more impressive는 빈칸 뒤에 비교 대상을 나타내는 전치사 than이 없기 때문에 답이 될 수 없다.

> 어휘 hiring committee 채용 위원회 qualification 자격(증); 자질, 능력 impressive 인상적인 impressively 인상적으로, 놀랄 정도로

4.

Trains can travel to Baltimore from New York as **swiftly** as cars or buses.

(A) swift
(B) swifter
(C) **swiftly**
(D) swiftness

기차는 자동차나 버스만큼 뉴욕에서 볼티모어로 빠르게 갈 수 있다.

> 해설 원급 비교 [as 부사 as] as와 as 사이에는 형용사나 부사의 원급이 들어가야 한다. 여기서는 동사 travel을 수식하는 부사가 들어가야 하므로 (C) swiftly가 정답이다. (A) swift는 형용사, (B) swifter는 swift의 비교급, (D) swiftness는 명사이므로 빈칸에 적절하지 않다.

> 어휘 swiftly 빠르게, 신속하게 swift 빠른, 신속한

2 비교급 비교

본문 p.259

1. (C) 2. (C) 3. (C) 4. (C)

1.

Heath Catering claims that their revised menus are **healthier** than the previous menus.

(A) healthy (B) healthily
(C) **healthier** (D) healthiest

히스 케이터링은 바뀐 메뉴들이 이전 메뉴들보다 더 건강에 좋다고 말한다.

해설 비교급 비교 [형용사의 비교급] 빈칸은 be동사 are의 주격 보어 자리이므로 형용사가 들어가야 한다. 또한 빈칸 뒤에 비교 대상을 나타내는 전치사 than이 있으므로 healthy의 비교급인 (C) healthier가 정답이다. (A) healthy는 형용사, (B) healthily는 부사이므로 오답이다.

어휘 claim (사실이라고) 말하다, 주장하다 revise 변경하다, 수정하다 previous 이전의

2.

Repeated surveys prove that regular customers make purchasing decisions **faster** than new ones.

(A) fastest (B) fast
(C) **faster** (D) the fastest

거듭된 설문 조사는 단골 고객이 신규 고객보다 더 빠르게 구매 결정을 한다는 걸 입증한다.

해설 비교급 비교 [형용사의 비교급] 빈칸 뒤에 비교 대상을 나타내는 전치사 than이 있으므로 fast의 비교급인 (C) faster가 정답이다. (A) fastest는 fast의 최상급, (B) fast는 부사 또는 형용사, (D) the fastest는 최상급이므로 오답이다.

어휘 repeated 반복된, 거듭된 survey 설문 조사 prove 입증하다, 증명하다 regular customer 단골 고객 make a decision 결정하다

3.

The chief reporter at the magazine is more **responsible** than any of the reporters.

(A) response (B) responses
(C) **responsible** (D) responsively

그 잡지의 수석 기자는 어떤 기자들보다 더 책임감이 있다.

해설 비교급 비교 [more 형용사 than] 빈칸은 be동사 is의 주격 보어 자리이므로 명사나 형용사가 들어가야 한다. 명사인 (A) response와 형용사인 (C) responsible 중에서 비교급 부사 more의 수식을 받을 수 있는 것은 형용사이므로 (C) responsible이 정답이다.

어휘 responsible 책임감 있는; 책임지고 있는 response 대답; 반응 responsively 대답하여, 응답하여

4.

At Robinson's, cashiers say that the upgraded system makes assisting customers **more convenient** than ever before.

(A) so convenient (B) as convenient
(C) **more convenient** (D) convenient

로빈슨에서 계산원들은 업그레이드된 시스템이 고객들을 지원하는 걸 그 어느 때보다 더 편리하게 한다고 말한다.

해설 비교급 비교 [more 형용사 than] 빈칸은 동사 makes의 목적격 보어 자리이므로 형용사가 들어가야 한다. 또한 빈칸 뒤에 비교 대상을 나타내는 전치사 than이 있으므로 convenient의 비교급인 (C) more convenient가 정답이다. (A) so convenient와 (B) as convenient의 so와 as는 than과 어울려 쓰이지 않으므로 오답이다.

어휘 cashier 계산원 upgrade (컴퓨터, 기계 등을) 개선하다, 업그레이드하다 assist 지원하다, 돕다, 도움이 되다 convenient 편리한 than ever before 그 어느 때보다

3 최상급 비교

본문 p.260

1. (A) 2. (A) 3. (B) 4. (D)

1.

Dietrich Pro has many fun games, and the **most popular** one is called Dynamo.

(A) most popular
(B) more popular
(C) popularly
(D) popularity

디트리히 프로에는 재밌는 게임이 많은데 가장 인기 있는 게임은 다이나모라고 불린다.

해설 최상급 비교 [the most + 형용사] 빈칸 앞에 정관사 the가 있고 뒤에는 부정대명사 one이 있으므로 빈칸은 부정대명사 one을 수식하는 형용사 자리이다. 문맥상 '가장 인기 있는 것'이라는 내용이 되는 게 자연스러우며, 이때 최상급 표현을 위해 정관사 the와 함께 쓸 수 있어야 하므로 (A) most popular가 정답이다. (B) more popular는 비교급, (C) popularly는 부사, (D) popularity는 명사이므로 오답이다.

어휘 popular 인기 있는, 유명한; 대중적인   popularly 대중적으로, 일반적으로   popularity 인기

2.

The most **successful** salesman in PJ Electronics is Jacob Mercer.

(A) successful
(B) successfully
(C) success
(D) successes

PJ 일렉트로닉스에서 가장 성공한 세일즈맨은 제이콥 머서이다.

해설 최상급 비교 [the most + 형용사] 빈칸 앞에 The most가 있고 뒤에는 명사 salesman이 있으므로 빈칸은 명사를 수식하는 형용사 자리이다. 따라서 (A) successful이 정답이다.

어휘 successful 성공적인, 성공한   salesman 영업 사원   successfully 성공적으로   success 성공, 성과

3.

Of the offices in Garner Towers, the basement units are the **cheapest** to rent.

(A) more cheaply
(B) cheapest
(C) most cheaply
(D) cheaper

가너 타워즈에 있는 사무실 중에서 지하 사무실이 임차하기에 가장 저렴하다.

해설 최상급 비교 [the + 형용사의 최상급] 빈칸은 be동사 are의 주격 보어 자리이므로 형용사가 들어가야 한다. 또한 빈칸 앞에 정관사 the가 있으므로 형용사 cheap의 최상급인 (B) cheapest가 정답이다. cheap의 비교급인 (D) cheaper는 비교 대상을 나타내는 전치사 than과 함께 써야 하기 때문에 빈칸에 적절하지 않다. 참고로 빈칸 뒤에는 offices가 생략되어 있는데, 이와 같이 최상급 표현에서 비교 대상이 명확할 때는 수식받는 명사를 생략하기도 한다.

어휘 basement 지하층   unit (건물의) 한 공간; 구성 단위; 한 개   cheap 저렴한   rent 임차[임대]하다; 임차료

4.

Griswold, Inc., one of the region's **steadiest** manufacturers, will be constructing three new factories.

(A) stead
(B) more steadily
(C) steadily
(D) steadiest

그 지역에서 가장 안정적인 제조사 중 하나인 그리스울드 사는 새로운 공장 세 개를 지을 것이다.

해설 최상급 비교 [the + 형용사의 최상급] 빈칸 앞에 정관사 the가 있고 뒤에는 명사 manufacturers가 있으므로 빈칸은 명사를 수식하는 형용사 자리이다. 따라서 형용사 steady의 최상급인 (D) steadiest가 정답이다. (A) stead는 명사, (B) more steadily는 steadily의 비교급, (C) steadily는 부사이므로 오답이다.

어휘 region 지역   construct 건설하다   steadily 안정적으로, 한결같이; 꾸준하게

4 비교급과 최상급 강조

본문 p.261

1. (C)   2. (C)   3. (C)   4. (A)

1.

The factory manager noticed Kevin Thomas was **much** more productive than other employees.

(A) very   (B) quite
(C) much   (D) by far

그 공장 매니저는 케빈 토마스가 다른 직원들보다 훨씬 더 생산적이라는 걸 알아차렸다.

해설 비교급 강조 부사 빈칸 뒤에 비교급(more productive than)이 있으므로 빈칸에는 비교급을 수식하는 부사가 들어가야 한다. 따라서 비교급을 강조하여 '훨씬'의 뜻을 나타내는 (C) much가 정답이다. (A) very와 (B) quite, (D) by far는 모두 최상급을 강조하는 부사이므로 오답이다.

어휘 notice 알아차리다, 주목하다   productive 생산적인

2.

The entry submitted by Sabrina Duncan was **by far** the most outstanding one.

(A) less   (B) very
(C) by far   (D) a lot

사브리나 던칸에 의해 제출된 출품작은 단연코 가장 뛰어난 작품이었다.

해설 최상급 강조 부사 빈칸 앞에 동사 was가 있고 뒤에는 최상급(the most outstanding)이 있으므로 빈칸에는 최상급을 수식하는 부사가 들어가야 한다. 따라서 최상급을 강조하여 '단연코'의 뜻을 나타내는 (C) by far가 정답이다. (B) very는 〈the+very+형용사/부사의 최상급〉 구조로 쓰기 때문에 빈칸에 적절하지 않다.

어휘 entry 출품작; 출입; 가입   submit 제출하다   outstanding 뛰어난; 두드러진, 중요한; 미지불된

3.

Mr. Kay's speech was a lot **more impressive** than the keynote speech at the conference.

(A) impressive   (B) impressively
(C) more impressive (D) most impressively

케이 씨의 연설은 그 학회의 기조연설보다 훨씬 더 인상적이었다.

해설 비교급 비교 빈칸 앞에 비교급 강조 부사 a lot이 있고 뒤에는 비교 대상을 나타내는 전치사 than이 있으므로 빈칸에는 비교급이 들어가야 한다. 따라서 impressive의 비교급인 (C) more impressive가 정답이다.

어휘 impressive 인상적인   keynote speech 기조연설

4.

Imported foreign items are much **more** expensive than domestic goods these days.

(A) more   (B) far
(C) many   (D) most

요즘에 수입된 외국 제품들은 국내 상품들보다 훨씬 더 비싸다.

해설 비교급 부사 빈칸 앞에 비교급 강조 부사 much가 있고 뒤에는 형용사 expensive와 비교 대상을 나타내는 전치사 than이 있다. 따라서 빈칸에는 형용사 expensive를 수식하는 동시에 than과 어울려 쓰이는 부사가 들어가야 하므로 비교급 부사인 (A) more가 정답이다.

어휘 import 수입하다; 수입(품)   foreign 외국의   domestic 국내의; 가정의   goods ((항상 복수형)) 상품

VOCABULARY

본문 p.264

1. (B) 2. (D) 3. (B) 4. (C) 5. (A) 6. (C) 7. (A) 8. (B)

1.

Thomas Carter's **superior** people skills make him an ideal salesperson.

(A) surrounding (B) superior
(C) eventual   (D) accessible

토마스 카터의 **우수한** 사교술은 그를 완벽한 판매원으로 만든다.

(A) 인근의, 주위의   (B) 우수한, 우월한
(C) 궁극적인, 최후의 (D) 접근[이용] 가능한

해설 형용사 어휘 복합 명사 people skills를 수식해 가장 자연스럽게 의미가 통하는 형용사를 골라야 한다. 따라서 '우수한, 우월한'이라는 의미의 (B) superior가 정답이다.

어휘 people skills ((항상 복수형)) 사교술   ideal 이상적인

2.

The new lotion provides **adequate** protection from the sun's rays.

(A) cheerful   (B) constructive
(C) instinctive (D) adequate

새로운 로션은 햇빛으로부터 **적절한** 보호를 제공한다.

(A) 발랄한, 쾌활한   (B) 건설적인
(C) 본능적인, 직관적인 (D) 충분한, 적절한

해설 형용사 어휘 명사 protection을 수식해 가장 자연스럽게 의미가 통하는 형용사를 골라야 한다. 따라서 '충분한, 적절한'이라는 의미의 (D) adequate가 정답이다.

어휘 protection 보호; 보장   sun's ray 햇빛

3.

The **typical** employee at J.T Bosworth has a graduate degree in engineering.

(A) joint   (B) typical
(C) sufficient (D) confidential

제이티 보스워스의 **일반** 직원은 공학 분야의 석사 학위가 있다.

(A) 공동의, 합동의   (B) 보통의; 전형적인
(C) 충분한, 적절한   (D) 기밀의

해설 형용사 어휘 명사 employee를 수식해 가장 자연스럽게 의미가 통하는 형용사를 골라야 한다. 따라서 '보통의'라는 의미의 (B) typical이 정답이다.

어휘 graduate degree 석사 학위   engineering 공학

4.

Property in the suburban region of Milton is **affordable** to many young couples.

(A) meaningful (B) approved
(C) affordable (D) decisive

밀튼 교외 지역의 땅은 많은 젊은 부부들에게 **가격이 적절**하다.

(A) 의미 있는   (B) 승인된, 인가된
(C) (가격 등이) 알맞은 (D) 결정적인

해설 형용사 어휘 빈칸은 주격 보어 자리이므로 주어(Property ~ Milton)의 상태나 상황을 표현하는 말이 들어가야 한다. 문맥상 밀튼 교외 지역의 땅값이 적절하다는 내용이 되는 게 자연스러우므로 '(가격 등이) 알맞은'이라는 의미의 (C) affordable이 정답이다.

어휘 property 부동산; 재산, 소유물   suburban (도시) 교외의

5.

Martin Textiles remains **dependent** on the sales of cotton fibers for its profits.	마틴 텍스타일즈는 수익을 위해 면섬유 판매에 여전히 **의존적**이다.
(A) dependent (B) certain (C) clear (D) tentative	(A) 의존[의지]하는 (B) 확신하는 (C) 분명한, 확실한 (D) 잠정적인

해설 형용사 어휘 빈칸은 주격 보어 자리이므로 주어(Martin Textiles)의 상태나 상황을 표현하는 말이 들어가야 한다. 문맥상 마틴 텍스타일즈가 면섬유 판매에 어떤 입장인지 묘사하는 말이 들어가는 게 자연스러우므로 '의존하는'이라는 의미의 (A) dependent가 정답이다. 특히 dependent는 전치사 on과 자주 쓰인다는 점에 유의해야 한다.

어휘 cotton fibers 면섬유　profit 수익, 이익

6.

Completing the budget report on time is of **utmost** importance to Ms. Washington.	예산 보고서를 제때 작성하는 것이 워싱턴 씨에게 **가장** 중요하다.
(A) considerate (B) efficient (C) utmost (D) partial	(A) 사려 깊은 (B) 능률적인, 효율적인 (C) 최고의, 최대한 (D) 부분적인; 편파적인

해설 형용사 어휘 명사 importance를 수식해 가장 자연스럽게 의미가 통하는 형용사를 골라야 한다. 따라서 '최고의, 최대한'이라는 의미의 (C) utmost가 정답이다.

어휘 complete 완성하다, 완료하다　budget report 예산 보고서　be of importance 중요하다

7.

Mitch Stallings set the **ambitious** goal of increasing revenues by 40% this year.	미치 스톨링스는 올해 수익을 40%까지 증가시킨다는 **야심 찬** 목표를 세웠다.
(A) ambitious (B) cooperative (C) repealed (D) prosperous	(A) 야심 있는, 야심 찬 (B) 협력하는, 협조하는 (C) (법 등이) 폐지된 (D) 번창한, 부유한

해설 형용사 어휘 명사 goal을 수식해 가장 자연스럽게 의미가 통하는 형용사를 골라야 한다. 따라서 '야심 있는, 야심 찬'이라는 의미의 (A) ambitious가 정답이다.

어휘 set a goal 목표를 세우다　increase 증가시키다, 늘리다　revenue 수입, 수익

8.

Customer service agents were taught to provide **prompt** responses to customer inquiries.	고객 서비스 직원들은 고객 문의에 **즉각적인** 반응을 하라고 배웠다.
(A) severe (B) prompt (C) durable (D) impractical	(A) 심각한 (B) 즉각적인 (C) 내구성이 있는 (D) 비현실적인

해설 형용사 어휘 명사 responses를 수식해 가장 자연스럽게 의미가 통하는 형용사를 골라야 한다. 따라서 '즉각적인'이라는 의미의 (B) prompt가 정답이다.

어휘 agent (특히 판매하거나 고객을 응대하는) 직원　be taught 배우다　provide a response 응답하다, 반응하다　inquiry 문의, 질문

ACTUAL TEST

본문 p.266

1. (D) 2. (A) 3. (C) 4. (D) 5. (B) 6. (D)
7. (C) 8. (D) 9. (A) 10. (D) 11. (A) 12. (C)

1.

If the sale takes place, DataQuest will acquire one of the **newest** firms in the industry.

(A) newer than (B) as new as
(C) newly (D) newest

그 매각이 발생하면 데이터퀘스트는 그 업계에서 가장 새로운 회사들 중 하나를 얻게 될 것이다.

해설 최상급 비교 [the+형용사의 최상급] 빈칸 앞에 정관사 the가 있고 뒤에는 명사 firms가 있으므로 빈칸은 명사를 수식하는 형용사 자리이다. 따라서 형용사 new의 최상급인 (D) newest가 정답이다. 원급 비교인 (B) as new as는 관사의 수식을 받을 수 없기 때문에 오답이다.

어휘 take place 일어나다, 발생하다   acquire 얻다, 획득하다   industry 산업   newly 최근에, 새로

2.

Being transferred abroad is less appealing to Mr. Argus **than** accepting a pay cut.

(A) than (B) for
(C) so (D) still

아르고스 씨에게 있어 해외로 발령받는 것은 임금 삭감을 받아들이는 것보다 덜 매력적이다.

해설 비교 대상을 나타내는 전치사 than 빈칸 앞에 비교급 부사 less가 있고 뒤에 비교 대상인 accepting a pay cut이 있으므로 빈칸에는 비교급과 어울려 쓰일 수 있는 말이 들어가야 한다. 따라서 비교 대상을 나타내는 전치사 (A) than이 정답이다.

어휘 transfer 옮기다, 이동하다   abroad 해외로   appeal to ~의 관심을 끌다   pay cut 임금 삭감

3.

The survey shows that the new copier causes paper jams **more frequently** than the previous one did.

(A) frequent (B) frequently
(C) more frequently (D) the most frequently

설문 조사에 따르면 새 복사기가 이전 복사기보다 더 자주 종이가 끼이는 문제를 일으킨다.

해설 비교급 비교 [more 부사 than] 빈칸은 동사 causes를 수식하는 부사 자리이며, 빈칸 뒤에 비교 대상을 나타내는 전치사 than이 있으므로 frequently의 비교급인 (C) more frequently가 정답이다.

어휘 copier 복사기   previous 이전의

4.

The two scientists made a **joint** presentation about their cancer research.

(A) commercial (B) durable
(C) reported (D) joint

두 과학자는 암 연구에 대해 **합동** 발표를 했다.

(A) 상업의 (B) 내구성이 있는
(C) 보도된 (D) 공동의, 합동의

해설 형용사 어휘 명사 presentation을 수식해 가장 자연스럽게 의미가 통하는 형용사를 골라야 한다. 따라서 '공동의, 합동의'라는 의미의 (D) joint가 정답이다.

어휘 make a presentation 발표하다   research 연구

5.

While **heavier** than expected, the Forest Ranger SUV from Damon Motors handles well.

(A) heavy (B) **heavier**
(C) heaviest (D) heavily

예상보다 더 무겁긴 하지만 데이먼 모터스의 포레스트 레인저 SUV는 조향이 잘 된다.

해설 비교급 비교 [형용사의 비교급] 빈칸 뒤에 than이 있으므로 빈칸에는 비교급이 들어가야 한다. 따라서 heavy의 비교급인 (B) heavier가 정답이다. (A) heavy는 형용사, (C) heaviest는 최상급, (D) heavily는 부사이므로 오답이다.

어휘 expect 예상하다, 기대하다 handle well (차량 등이) 잘 조향되다, 방향 컨트롤이 잘 되다

6.

Employees at Chandler, Inc. are encouraged to provide **meaningful** suggestions regarding workplace improvements.

(A) level (B) prosperous
(C) customary (D) **meaningful**

챈들러 사의 직원들은 직장의 개선점에 관해 **의미 있는** 제안을 하도록 권장받는다.
(A) (표면이) 평평한 (B) 번창한, 부유한
(C) 관례적인 (D) 의미 있는, 중요한

해설 형용사 어휘 명사 suggestions를 수식해 가장 자연스럽게 의미가 통하는 형용사를 골라야 한다. 따라서 '의미 있는'이라는 의미의 (D) meaningful이 정답이다.

어휘 be encouraged to do ~하도록 권장받다 suggestion 제안, 제의 regarding ~에 관해 improvement 향상, 개선

7.

Since Mr. Halls is expecting a lot from this survey, we should analyze the data as **accurately** as possible.

(A) accuracy (B) accurate
(C) **accurately** (D) more accurate

홀스 씨가 이 설문 조사에 기대하는 바가 크니, 가능한 한 정확하게 데이터를 분석해야 합니다.

해설 원급 비교 [as 부사 as] as와 as 사이에는 형용사나 부사의 원급이 들어가야 한다. 여기서는 동사 analyze를 수식하는 부사가 들어가야 하므로 (C) accurately가 정답이다. (A) accuracy는 명사, (B) accurate는 형용사, (D) more accurate는 accurate의 비교급이므로 빈칸에 적절하지 않다.

어휘 expect 예상하다, 기대하다 analyze 분석하다 accurately 정확하게 accuracy 정확(도) accurate 정확한

8.

While work experience is important, Ms. Cole says that personality is the **most vital** feature.

(A) vitality (B) more vitally
(C) vitally (D) **most vital**

경력이 중요하긴 하지만 콜 씨는 인성이 가장 중요한 점이라고 말한다.

해설 최상급 비교 [the most + 형용사] 빈칸 앞에 정관사 the가 있고 뒤에는 명사 feature가 있으므로 빈칸은 명사를 수식하는 형용사 자리이다. 문맥상 '가장 중요한'이라는 내용이 되는 게 자연스러우며, 이때 최상급 표현을 위해 정관사 the와 함께 쓸 수 있어야 하므로 (D) most vital이 정답이다.

어휘 work experience 경력 personality 인성, 성격 vital 필수적인, 중요한 feature 특징, 특성 vitality 활력 vitally 매우 중대하게

Big Change by Local Restaurant

RICHMOND—The Hilltop, a local restaurant, just announced it is making a big change. After receiving numerous ⁹**requests** from customers, the restaurant is finally introducing outdoor dining. The restaurant is currently in the process of adding a dining area behind the restaurant. There will be enough room for approximately ten tables. The purpose is to encourage diners to spend ¹⁰**less** time indoors and to let them enjoy the warm spring and summer evenings in Richmond. The Hilltop will also be open later at night as long as the weather stays nice. ¹¹**Owner Tina Blair hopes customers will respond positively.** Other restaurants in the same region ¹²**are thinking** of adding their own outdoor dining areas in response.

지역 식당의 큰 변화

리치먼드—지역 식당인 힐탑은 큰 변화가 있을 것이라고 발표했다. 고객들로부터 많은 ⁹요청을 받은 후에 그 식당은 마침내 야외 식사를 도입할 것이다. 그 식당은 현재 식당 뒤에 식사 공간을 추가하는 과정에 있다. 약 열 개의 테이블을 둘 충분한 공간이 있을 것이다. 목적은 식사하는 사람들이 실내에서 시간을 ¹⁰덜 보내고 리치먼드의 따뜻한 봄과 여름의 저녁을 즐기게 하려는 것이다. 힐탑은 또한 날씨만 괜찮다면 밤 늦게까지 운영할 것이다. ¹¹**티나 블레어 사장은 고객들이 긍정적으로 반응하기를 희망한다.** 같은 지역의 다른 식당들도 그에 따라 그 식당들만의 야외 식사 공간을 추가하는 걸 ¹²고려하고 있다.

어휘 make a change 변화하다 numerous 많은 outdoor 야외의 dining 식사, 정찬 currently 현재 in the process of ~의 과정에 있는, ~을 진행 중인 approximately 거의, 대략 encourage A to do A가 ~하도록 장려[권장]하다 let ~하게 해 주다 as long as ~하는 한 think of ~을 고려하다 in response (to) (~에) 대응하여

9. (A) requests (B) orders (C) deliveries (D) reservations

(A) 요청 (B) 주문 (C) 배달(품) (D) 예약

해설 명사 어휘 receiving의 목적어로 가장 자연스럽게 의미가 통하는 명사를 골라야 한다. 빈칸 앞 문장에서 힐탑 측이 큰 변화가 있을 거라고 발표했으며, 고객에게 많은 요청이 있었기 때문에 변화, 즉 야외 식사 공간을 도입한다는 흐름으로 이어지는 것이 자연스러우므로 '요청들'이라는 의미의 (A) requests가 정답이다.

10. (A) some (B) more (C) few (D) less

해설 수량을 나타내는 형용사 식당 뒤에 야외 식사 공간을 만들었기 때문에 손님들로 하여금 실내보다는 야외 테이블에서 시간을 보내게 하려 한다는 문맥이 되어야 한다. 그러므로 실내에서 시간을 덜 쓴다는 맥락을 완성하려면 (D) less가 빈칸에 가장 적절하다.

11. (A) Owner Tina Blair hopes customers will respond positively.
    (B) The Hilltop is one of the premier dining locations in the city.
    (C) Customers are already enjoying meals while sitting outdoors.
    (D) The menu at the Hilltop will be expanding soon.

(A) 티나 블레어 사장은 고객들이 긍정적으로 반응하기를 희망한다.
(B) 힐탑은 그 도시에서 최고의 식사 장소 중 하나이다.
(C) 고객들은 이미 야외에 앉아 식사를 즐기고 있다.
(D) 힐탑의 메뉴는 곧 늘어날 것이다.

해설 알맞은 문장 고르기 빈칸 뒤에 이어지는 문장에서 다른 식당들도 힐탑 손님들의 반응에 따라 야외 식사 공간을 추가하는 걸 고려하고 있다고 했다. 따라서 빈칸은 힐탑을 방문하는 손님들이 긍정적으로 반응하길 바란다는 내용이 되는 게 가장 적절하므로 정답은 (A)이다.

어휘 premier 최고의 location 장소 outdoors 야외에서 expand 늘리다, 확장하다, 확대하다

12. (A) thinks (B) to think (C) **are thinking** (D) being thought

해설 동사 자리+수 일치 빈칸 앞에 주어(Other restaurants)가 있고 뒤에는 전치사구가 이어지므로 빈칸은 동사 자리이다. 또한 주어가 복수 명사이므로 (C) are thinking이 정답이다.

PART 7

UNIT 17 문제 유형별 (1)

1 주제/목적 문제

● 문제 풀이 전략   본문 p.272

To: Management Team ⟨managers@v-tech.com⟩
From: Frank Klein ⟨f_klein@v-tech.com⟩
Date: December 2
Subject: Employee Evaluations

Dear Managers,

I would like to remind you that you must finish your employee evaluation forms by December 6. You should complete a separate form for each employee. Detailed notes about employees help us to improve our staff training events. The evaluation form can be downloaded from the company Web site. Please submit the completed evaluation forms to the HR department.

Sincerely,

Frank Klein
Human Resources Manager, V-Tech

수신: 관리팀
발신: 프랭크 클라인
날짜: 12월 2일
제목: 직원 평가

부장 여러분께,

여러분들께 12월 6일까지 직원 평가서를 완료하셔야 한다는 것을 다시 한번 상기시켜 드리고 싶습니다. 여러분은 각 직원별로 각각의 서식을 작성해야 합니다. 직원들에 대한 자세한 설명은 저희 직원 교육 행사를 개선하는 데 도움이 됩니다. 평가 서식은 회사 웹사이트에서 다운받으실 수 있습니다. 작성된 평가지는 인사팀에 제출해 주십시오.

프랭크 클라인
브이 테크, 인사부장

Q. What is the purpose of the e-mail?

(A) To introduce a new employee
(B) To adjust a schedule
(C) To emphasize a deadline
(D) To announce a training session

이메일의 목적은 무엇인가?

(A) 신입 직원을 소개하기 위해
(B) 일정을 조정하기 위해
(C) 마감일을 강조하기 위해
(D) 교육 과정을 알리기 위해

패러프레이징   1. (A)   2. (B)   본문 p.273

1.

Dear Employees,

The staff cafeteria will be closed for renovations from June 3. **The upgrade to the facilities** will take approximately three weeks.

직원들께,

직원 구내식당이 6월 3일부터 보수로 문을 닫습니다. **시설의 업그레이드**는 대략 3주가 걸릴 것입니다.

What is the e-mail mainly about?

(A) To notify employees of workplace improvements
(B) To promote meal options in a cafeteria

이메일은 주로 무엇에 관한 것인가?

(A) 작업장 개선을 직원들에게 알리기 위해
(B) 구내식당의 식사 옵션들을 홍보하기 위해

해설 The upgrade to the facilities가 workplace improvements로 바꿔 표현된 (A)가 정답이다.

어휘 renovation 보수 facility 시설 approximately 대략 notify A of B A에게 B에 대해 알리다 improvement 개선 promote 홍보하다

2.

Cookex, Canada's leading kitchenware retailer, has opened its first store abroad in Milan, Italy. Cookex has built a reputation for style and quality.

캐나다의 선도적인 주방용품 업체인 쿡엑스가 이탈리아 밀라노에 첫 해외 지점을 열었다. 쿡엑스는 스타일과 품질로 명성을 쌓아 왔다.

What is the purpose of the article?

(A) To seek job applicants in Milan
(B) **To highlight an overseas expansion**

기사의 목적은 무엇인가?

(A) 밀라노에 일자리 지원자를 찾기 위해
(B) **해외 사업 확장을 강조하기 위해**

해설 캐나다 회사가 이탈리아에 지점을 열었다는 내용이므로 its first store abroad(해외의 첫 지점)를 an overseas expansion(해외 사업 확장)으로 바꿔 표현한 (B)가 정답이다.

어휘 leading 선도적인 retailer 소매업 abroad 해외에서, 해외로 reputation 명성 seek 찾다, 구하다 applicant 지원자 highlight 강조하다 overseas 해외의 expansion 확장

미니 테스트 1. (D) 본문 p.273

Dear visitors,

Here at the Aurora National Park, **we do not allow dogs in certain areas**, even if they are on a leash. **We aim to provide** an enjoyable experience for all of our visitors. Unfortunately, the noise and mess created by dogs can be an inconvenience to our staff as well as other visitors. This is particularly necessary in our picnic areas. Dog-free zones are clearly marked with signs, so please watch for those if you have a dog with you.

Thank you for your understanding.

Sincerely,

Aurora National Park Management

방문객들께,

이곳 오로라 국립 공원에서, 개 목줄을 한다고 해도 **특정 지역에서는 반려견이 허가되지 않습니다.** 저희는 모든 방문객들께 즐거운 경험을 드리는 것을 **목표로 합니다.** 안타깝게도, 반려견들에 의한 소음과 소란이 다른 방문객들뿐만 아니라 저희 직원들에게도 불편을 끼칠 수 있습니다. 이는 특히 야유회 지역에 필수적입니다. 반려견 금지 구역이 간판으로 명확히 표시되어 있으므로 반려견과 함께라면 이 간판들을 살펴 주십시오.

이해해 주셔서 감사합니다.

오로라 국립 공원 관리팀

어휘 allow 허가하다 even if 비록 ~에도 불구하고 leash 개 목줄 enjoyable 즐거운 unfortunately 안타깝게도 mess 지저분함

1. Why was the notice written?

   (A) To promote a new picnic area
   (B) To apologize for a park closure
   (C) To announce a park improvement project
   (D) **To explain a policy decision**

공지문이 작성된 이유는 무엇인가?

(A) 새로운 야유회 지역을 홍보하기 위해
(B) 공원 폐쇄에 대해 사과하기 위해
(C) 공원 개선 프로젝트를 발표하기 위해
(D) **정책 결정을 설명하기 위해**

해설 글의 초반에 있는 we do not allow, we aim to provide라는 단서를 종합해 보면 반려견과 관련된 정책 결정에 대해 알리는 글임을 알 수 있다. 따라서 정답은 (D)이다.

2 세부 사항 문제

● 문제 풀이 전략

본문 p.274

If an event at Marigold Outdoor Theater is canceled because of bad weather, you are entitled to a full refund of the ticket price. **To claim your refund, bring your ticket to the box office** and present it to one of our staff members. **We require an in-person visit for our refund process.** We do not accept tickets by mail. Additionally, we cannot assist with a refund request over the phone. We apologize for any inconvenience.	악천후 때문에 마리골드 야외극장에서의 행사가 취소된다면, 귀하께서는 표 가격의 전액을 환불 받을 수 있습니다. **환불을 받으시기 위해서는 매표소로 표를 가져오셔서 저희 직원 중 한 명에게 제시해 주십시오. 환불 절차를 위해서는 직접 방문해 주실 것을 요구드립니다.** 저희는 우편으로는 표를 받지 않습니다. 또한, 전화로 환불 요청을 하시는 것은 도와 드릴 수가 없습니다. 불편에 대해 사과드립니다.

Q. How can customers receive a refund?

(A) By completing an online form
(B) By visiting the theater
(C) By mailing a ticket
(D) By calling the box office

고객들이 환불을 받을 수 있는 방법은?

(A) 온라인 서식을 작성함으로써
(B) 극장에 방문함으로써
(C) 표를 우편으로 보냄으로써
(D) 매표소에 전화를 함으로써

패러프레이징 1. (B)   2. (B)

본문 p.275

1.

Before the new features of the security system are used companywide, **the security department has selected ten staff members to perform system tests on September 4.**	보안 시스템의 새로운 기능들이 전사적으로 사용되기 전에, **보안 부서에서는 9월 4일에 시스템 테스트를 수행하기 위해 10명의 직원을 선정하였습니다.**

What will happen on September 4?

(A) The security team will install equipment.
(B) Appointed employees will take part in some testing.

9월 4일에 일어날 일은 무엇인가?

(A) 보안팀이 장비를 설치할 것이다.
(B) 선정된 직원들이 테스트에 참여할 것이다.

[해설] ten staff members(10명의 직원들)가 Appointed employees(선정된 직원들)로, perform system tests(테스트를 수행하다)가 take part in some testing(일부 테스트에 참여하다)으로 바꿔 표현된 (B)가 정답이다.

[어휘] feature 특징, 특색   security 보안, 안전   department 부서   select 선택하다   perform 수행하다   install 설치하다   equipment 장비   take part in ~에 참여하다

2.

Due to routine repairs on a support beam, Ellis Bridge will be closed from today for approximately two weeks. Alternative routes for commuters can be found online.	지지대의 정기 수리 때문에, 엘리스 대교는 오늘부터 대략 2주간 **폐쇄될 것입니다.** 통근객들의 우회 도로는 온라인에서 찾아보실 수 있습니다.

Why is a bridge being closed?

(A) Commuters have complained about traffic.
(B) Maintenance work will be carried out.

대교가 폐쇄되는 이유는 무엇인가?

(A) 통근객들이 교통량에 불평해 왔다.
(B) 유지 보수 작업이 실행될 것이다.

[해설] routine repairs(정기 수리)가 Maintenance work로 바꿔 표현된 (B)가 정답이다.

[어휘] due to ~ 때문에   routine 정기적인   repair 수리   support 지지, 지원   alternative 대안의   route 길, 도로   commuter 통근객   complain about ~에 대해 불평하다   maintenance 유지 보수   carry out ~을 실행하다

미니 테스트   1. (C)   본문 p.275

Notice to Duncan Airlines Passengers:

We do our best to ensure the safe and timely transport of your luggage. Do not pack fragile items in checked luggage, as bags may be handled roughly or stacked while in our care. Scratches and dirt marks are not compensated, as these are normal wear and tear. In addition, ripped pockets or exterior fabric also cannot be included in damage claims. If your bag has damage to major components such as the handles, **wheels**, or zippers, please let us know. **If a Duncan Airlines employee has caused damage to one of these areas, you will be compensated.** For more information, visit www.duncanairlines.com.

던컨 항공사 승객 공지

저희는 귀하의 수하물을 안전하게, 그리고 제시간에 운송하기 위해 최선을 다하고 있습니다. 저희가 보관하는 동안 가방들이 거칠게 다뤄지거나 쌓여 있을 수 있으므로 부치는 수하물에는 깨지기 쉬운 물건들은 넣지 마십시오. 긁힌 자국이나 더러운 자국은 정상적인 마모이므로 보상이 안 됩니다. 게다가, 주머니나 표면의 천이 찢어진 것 또한 손해 배상 청구에 포함되지 않습니다. 만약 귀하의 가방이 손잡이나 **바퀴** 또는 지퍼와 같은 주요 부품에 손상을 입었다면 저희에게 알려 주십시오. **던컨 항공사 직원이 이런 부분 중 하나에 손상을 일으켰다면 보상을 받게 되실 겁니다.** 추가 정보는 www.duncanairlines.com을 방문하세요.

어휘 ensure 보장하다   timely 시간에 맞는   transport 운송   luggage 수하물, 짐   handle 다루다   roughly 거칠게   stack 쌓다   dirt 먼지, 흙   compensate 보상하다   wear and tear 마모, 닳음   rip 찢다   exterior 외부의   fabric 천   component 부품

1. What type of damage can passengers receive compensation for?

(A) Torn pockets
(B) Dirt marks
(C) A broken wheel
(D) Scratches

승객들이 보상을 받을 수 있는 손상의 종류는 무엇인가?

(A) 찢어진 주머니
(B) 더러운 자국
(C) 고장 난 바퀴
(D) 긁힌 자국

해설 보상에 대해 언급된 부분을 찾아 앞뒤를 살펴보면 one of these areas(이런 부분 중 하나)에 wheels가 있음을 알 수 있다.

어휘 passenger 승객   broken 고장 난

3 True/NOT 문제

● 문제 풀이 전략

본문 p.276

Bank Teller Position at Avila Bank

Avila Bank has job openings for a full-time bank teller at its Warren Avenue branch. We are currently seeking a friendly and professional individual for this role.

Duties include **receiving cash deposits and processing withdrawals**, **answering customers' questions** both in person and over the phone. In addition, **bank tellers will suggest other bank services**, such as loans and business banking, as needed.

We offer a competitive hourly wage along with paid vacation time. Visit our Web site for further details.

아빌라 은행의 은행원 직책

아빌라 은행은 워런 가 지점에 정규직 은행원 일자리 공석이 있습니다. 현재 저희는 이 자리에 친절하고 전문적인 사람을 찾고 있습니다.

업무에는 **현금 예금을 받는 것과 출금을 처리하는 것**, 면대면 및 전화로 **고객 문의에 응대하는 것**이 포함되어 있습니다. 또한, **은행원은** 필요에 따라 대출이나 기업 은행 업무와 같은 **다른 은행 서비스들을 제안해 줄 것입니다**.

저희는 유급 휴가와 함께 경쟁력 있는 시급을 제공합니다. 보다 자세한 사항은 저희 웹사이트를 방문하세요.

Q. What is NOT indicated as a job duty of the position?

(A) Responding to inquiries
(B) Recommending other services
(C) Handling cash transactions
(D) Approving loan applications

직책의 업무로 나타나 있지 않은 것은 무엇인가?

(A) 문의 사항에 답하기
(B) 다른 서비스 추천하기
(C) 현금 거래 처리하기
(D) 대출 신청서 승인하기

패러프레이징   1. (B)   2. (A)

본문 p.277

1.

Each meeting room features:
- Comfortable chairs   - A large whiteboard
- Wireless Internet   - **Complimentary tea and coffee**

각 회의실은 다음을 특징으로 합니다.
− 편안한 의자   − 넓은 화이트보드
− 무선 인터넷   − **무료 차와 커피**

What do the meeting rooms NOT offer?

(A) Free beverages
(B) Printing equipment

회의실에서 제공하지 않는 것은 무엇인가?

(A) 무료 음료
(B) 인쇄 장비

해설 Complimentary를 Free로, tea and coffee를 beverages로 바꿔 표현한 (A)는 언급되어 있으므로 언급되지 않은 (B)가 정답이다.

어휘 feature 특징으로 하다   comfortable 편안한   wireless 무선의   complimentary 무료의   beverage 음료   equipment 장비

2.

> Raymond Jordan will replace Caroline Ladner as the lead anchor for **Channel 7's Saturday morning news broadcast**, *Round-Up*. Mr. Jordan brings twenty years of experience to the role.

레이몬드 조던은 **7번 채널의 토요일 아침 뉴스 방송**인 라운드업의 메인 앵커로서 캐롤라인 래드너의 후임이 될 것이다. 조던 씨는 20년의 경력을 가지고 이 자리에 온다.

What is true about *Round-Up*?

(A) It is a weekly broadcast.
(B) It has been on TV for twenty years.

라운드업에 대해 사실인 것은?

(A) 주간 방송이다.
(B) 20년간 방송되었다.

해설 뉴스 방송인 라운드업은 Saturday morning(토요일 아침)에 방송되는 것이므로 매주 토요일, 즉 일주일에 한 번 방송되는 것임을 알 수 있다. 정답은 (A).

어휘 replace 교체하다, 대체하다 broadcast 방송 experience 경력, 경험 role 역할, 자리

미니 테스트 1. (B) 본문 p.277

> To: Ted Emerson 〈ted.emerson@tedsgardening.com〉
> From: Rosa Ocasio 〈rocasio@elmsford1.com〉
> Subject: Web site
> Date: July 10
>
> Dear Mr. Emerson,
>
> I was delighted to discover your gardening Web site when (C) **I was trying to identify a weed in my garden.** (C) **Your online tool** made it easy to figure out what it was.
>
> I now visit your site frequently. I have even used ideas from your (D) **Design of the Week** in my own garden. I also love how you provide (A) **a directory of companies** that sell gardening supplies.
>
> I do have one suggestion, however. It would be great if you could include information about garden pests. I'm sure a lot of your readers are dealing with snails, bugs, and so on.
>
> Many thanks,
> Rosa Ocasio

수신: 테드 에머슨
발신: 로사 오카시오
제목: 웹사이트
날짜: 7월 10일

에머슨 씨께,

(C) 저의 정원에 있는 잡초를 확인해 보려고 하다가 귀하의 원예 웹사이트를 발견하게 되어 기뻤습니다. (C) 귀하의 온라인에 있는 도구 덕분에 잡초를 확인하는 게 수월했습니다.

저는 이제 귀하의 사이트에 자주 방문합니다. 저는 귀하의 (D) '금주의 디자인' 아이디어들을 제 정원에 사용하기도 했습니다. 저는 또한 원예 물품들을 판매하는 (A) 회사들의 명단을 제공해 주시는 방식이 너무 좋습니다.

그런데, 한 가지 제안 사항이 있습니다. 정원 해충에 대한 정보를 다뤄 주시면 좋을 것 같습니다. 귀하의 많은 독자들이 달팽이나 벌레 등에 문제를 겪고 있을 것이라고 확신합니다.

감사합니다.
로사 오카시오

어휘 gardening 원예 weed 잡초 pest 해충

1. What is NOT mentioned about the Web site in the e-mail?

(A) It includes a list of businesses.
(B) It has a chat section for gardeners.
(C) It offers a plant identification tool.
(D) It provides a weekly design suggestion.

이메일에서 웹사이트에 대해 언급되지 않은 것은 무엇인가?

(A) 회사들의 목록이 포함되어 있다.
(B) 정원을 가꾸는 사람들이 대화하는 공간이 있다.
(C) 식물을 확인하는 도구가 제공된다.
(D) 주간 디자인 제안 사항을 제공한다.

해설 언급되지 않은 것을 묻는 문제는 반대로 언급된 것들을 지문에서 찾아 표시한 후 선택지에서 이들을 소거해 정답을 찾아야 한다. 지문에서 언급되지 않은 것은 (B)이다.

어휘 section 부분 identification 확인 suggestion 제안

4 추론/암시 문제

● 문제 풀이 전략 본문 p.278

Join us for an evening to remember!

Harron Publishing is pleased to announce the launch of

The Whispering Winds

January 19, 3 P.M. ~ 6 P.M.

Braxton Bookstore, 2020 Washburn Street

Author Arnold Edmunds will be reading excerpts from his debut novel. He will also discuss **his friend, whose life story provided the main plot for the novel**. Mr. Edmunds will sign copies of the book at the end.

Light refreshments will be served. Please confirm your attendance by e-mailing lauch@harronpublishing.com.

기억될 만한 저녁에 저희와 함께 하세요!
해론 출판사는 '**속삭이는 바람**'의 출시를 발표하게 되어 기쁩니다.
1월 19일 오후 3시~6시
워시번 가 2020에 있는 브랙스톤 서점
저자 아놀드 에드먼즈는 그의 데뷔 소설의 발췌 부분을 낭독할 것입니다. 또한 그는 그의 친구에 대해 이야기할 것이며, **그 친구의 인생 이야기는 소설의 주요 줄거리를 제공했습니다**. 마지막에, 에드먼즈 씨는 책에 사인을 해 줄 것입니다.
가벼운 다과가 제공됩니다.
lauch@harronpublishing.com으로 이메일을 보내 귀하의 참석 여부를 확인해 주십시오.

Q. What is suggested about *The Whispering Winds*?

(A) It is the author's second novel.
(B) It was published on January 19.
(C) It is based on a true story.
(D) It is a best-selling book.

'속삭이는 바람'에 대해 암시된 것은?

(A) 저자의 두 번째 소설이다.
(B) 1월 19일에 출판되었다.
(C) 실제 이야기를 바탕으로 했다.
(D) 가장 잘 팔리는 책이다.

패러프레이징 1. (B) 2. (B) 본문 p.279

1.

Fortunately, Ms. Brandt's uncle, **Norm Fleming, has received many business loans over the years**, so he was able to advise her.

다행히도, 브란트 씨의 삼촌인 **놈 플레밍은 수년간 많은 사업 대출을 받아 보아서** 그녀에게 조언을 해 줄 수 있었다.

What is suggested about Mr. Fleming?

(A) He invested in Ms. Brandt's business.
(B) He is familiar with the loan process.

플레밍 씨에 대해 암시된 것은?

(A) 그는 브란트 씨의 사업에 투자를 했다.
(B) 그는 대출 절차에 익숙하다.

해설 플레밍 씨는 대출을 많이 받아 보았다고 했으므로 대출에 익숙하다는 것을 추론할 수 있다. 따라서 정답은 (B).

어휘 fortunately 다행히 loan 대출 be able to do ~할 수 있다 advise 조언하다 invest in ~에 투자하다 be familiar with ~에 익숙하다 process 절차

2.

Dear Mr. Sherman,

I have checked our database for the books **you said you needed for a medical assistant certification program**. Unfortunately, we are completely sold out, so I recommend contacting other businesses.

셔먼 씨께,

저는 **당신이 의학 보조 자격증 프로그램을 위해 필요하다고 말했던** 책들의 데이터베이스를 확인해 보았습니다. 안타깝게도 저희는 완전히 매진이 되어서 다른 업체에 연락하실 것을 추천합니다.

What is implied about Mr. Sherman?

(A) He made changes to a database.
(B) He is training to work in medicine.

셔먼 씨에 대해 암시된 것은?

(A) 그는 데이터베이스를 변경했다.
(B) 그는 의학 분야에서 일하려고 교육을 받는 중이다.

해설 셔먼 씨가 구하고자 하는 책의 종류를 바탕으로 의학 분야에서 일을 하기 위해 책이 필요하다는 것을 추론할 수 있다. 정답은 (B).

어휘 medical 의학의 assistant 보조, 조수 certification 자격증 completely 완전히 sold out 매진된

미니 테스트   1. (A)   본문 p.279

Canterbury Dairy Farm

Milk ◆ Cheese ◆ Ice Cream
The freshest milk in the region!
Get a free sample of ice cream at our visitor center.
Just 2 miles ahead!

Exit 42, 806 Durham Road

캔터베리 유제품 농장

우유 ◆ 치즈 ◆ 아이스크림
지역에서 가장 신선한 우유!
저희 방문자 센터에서 무료 아이스크림 샘플을 얻어 가세요.
2마일 앞에 있습니다!

더럼 가 806, 42번 출구

어휘 dairy 유제품 region 지역 ahead 앞에

1. Where would people most likely see this advertisement?

(A) On a roadside billboard
(B) In a travel magazine
(C) At a supermarket
(D) On a Web site

사람들이 이 광고를 볼 것 같은 곳은 어디인가?

(A) 도로변 광고판
(B) 여행 잡지
(C) 슈퍼마켓
(D) 웹사이트

해설 광고하는 것은 유제품 농장이며 2마일 앞에 있다고 했으므로 도로에 설치된 광고판임을 알 수 있다. 따라서 정답은 (A)이다. Dairy (유제품)만 보고 슈퍼마켓이라고 생각하지 않도록 주의하자.

ACTUAL TEST

본문 p.280

1. (C) 2. (A) 3. (D) 4. (C) 5. (C) 6. (D)
7. (B) 8. (D) 9. (B)

Camptime Winter Sale

¹**Get a 50% discount on all camping clothing**

Coupon valid at any Camptime branch. No minimum purchase required. ²**Expires January 10.**

캠프타임 겨울 세일

¹ 모든 캠핑 의류에 50퍼센트 할인을 받으세요.

쿠폰은 캠프타임의 모든 지점에서 유효합니다. 최소 구매액은 요구되지 않습니다.

² 1월 10일에 만료됩니다.

어휘 valid 유효한 branch 지점, 지사 purchase 구입 require 요구하다 expire 만기가 되다

1. What item is offered at a lower price?

(A) A flashlight
(B) A tent
(C) A sweatshirt
(D) A sleeping bag

할인된 가격으로 제공되는 제품은 무엇인가?

(A) 손전등
(B) 텐트
(C) 트레이닝복 상의
(D) 침낭

해설 질문의 lower price(할인된 가격)는 지문의 discount(할인)와 같은 의미이다. 캠핑 의류에 할인이 적용된다고 했으므로 의류 종류인 (C)가 정답이다.

어휘 item 제품   offer 제공하다

2. What will happen after January 10?

(A) An offer will not be valid.
(B) A new branch will open.
(C) A price will decrease.
(D) A shipment will arrive.

1월 10일 이후에 일어날 일은 무엇인가?

(A) 할인이 유효하지 않을 것이다.
(B) 새로운 지점이 문을 열 것이다.
(C) 가격이 내릴 것이다.
(D) 배송품이 도착할 것이다.

해설 January 10(1월 10일)이라는 세부 정보를 묻고 있으므로 지문에서 날짜 부분을 확인한다. 1월 10일에 만료된다고 했으므로 Expires를 not be valid(유효하지 않은)라고 표현한 (A)가 정답이다.

어휘 offer 할인   valid 유효한   branch 지점, 지사   decrease 감소하다   shipment 배송품

Dayton Hotel Shuttle Bus (7 A.M. to 9 P.M.)

Dayton Hotel offers a free shuttle bus service between our site and the city center. 3-1 **From June 1, the bus will run more frequently than before.** Every Saturday and Sunday, the bus will depart from the hotel every 15 minutes instead of every 30 minutes. Weekday departures will remain the same. The shuttle will leave the hotel every 90 minutes Monday through Thursday and 4 **every 60 minutes on Fridays.** 3-2 **We have made these adjustments for our guests' convenience.** For a complete schedule, visit www.daytonhotel.com/services.

데이튼 호텔 셔틀버스 (오전 7시부터 오후 9시까지)

데이튼 호텔은 호텔과 도심지 간 무료 셔틀버스 서비스를 제공합니다. 3-1 6월 1일부터 버스는 이전보다 더 자주 운영될 것입니다. 매주 토요일과 일요일에, 버스는 30분 대신 15분마다 호텔에서 출발할 것입니다. 주중 출발은 같습니다. 셔틀은 월요일부터 목요일까지는 90분마다, 4 금요일에는 60분마다 출발합니다. 3-2 저희는 고객들의 편의를 위해 이러한 조정을 하게 되었습니다. 모든 일정을 보시려면 www.daytonhotel.com/services에 방문하세요.

어휘　run 운영하다　frequently 자주　depart from ~에서 출발하다　instead of ~ 대신에　departure 출발　adjustment 조정, 수정　convenience 편리, 편의　complete 완전한

3. Why was the information written?

   (A) To recommend a shorter bus route
   (B) To notify bus passengers of safety rules
   (C) To apologize for shuttle bus delays
   (D) To explain changes to a schedule

정보문이 쓰인 이유는?

(A) 더 짧은 버스 노선을 추천하기 위해
(B) 버스 승객들에게 안전 규정을 알려 주기 위해
(C) 셔틀버스 지연에 사과하기 위해
(D) 일정 변경에 대해 설명하기 위해

해설　글의 목적을 묻는 문제. 제목을 통해 호텔 셔틀버스에 관한 것임을 알 수 있으며, 단서 3-1과 3-2에서 운행 스케줄의 조정을 언급하고 있으므로 (D)가 정답이다.

어휘　route 길, 노선　notify A of B A에게 B를 알리다　passenger 승객　apologize for ~을 사과하다

4. How often does the shuttle bus run on Fridays?

   (A) Every 15 minutes
   (B) Every 30 minutes
   (C) Every 60 minutes
   (D) Every 90 minutes

금요일마다 셔틀버스는 얼마나 자주 운영되는가?

(A) 15분마다
(B) 30분마다
(C) 60분마다
(D) 90분마다

해설　질문에서 on Fridays(금요일마다)라고 했으므로 지문에서 금요일이 언급된 부분을 찾아보면 60분마다 운영됨을 알 수 있다. 정답은 (C). 이러한 문제는 요일과 시간이 나타난 부분을 빠르게 찾아 먼저 풀어도 된다.

To: All Mayorga Inc. Employees
From: Corey Jensen, Office Manager
Date: February 11
Subject: Encouraging teamwork

From March 1, ⁵ **Mayorga Inc. will launch the Mayorga Teamwork Prize (MTP).** The MTP aims to formally recognize employees for their cooperation with their coworkers. ^{6B} **One winner will be announced on the first of each month.** ^{6C} **The person will be allowed to leave work one hour early on each Friday in that month.** We hope that this benefit will be enjoyable to the winner.

^{6A} **All employees are eligible for the MTP**, and anyone can submit a nomination. However, the same person cannot win the MTP twice within six months. If you would like to make a nomination, please pick up a form from the HR office.

수신: 마요르가 사 전 직원들
발신: 코리 젠슨, 사무 담당자
날짜: 2월 11일
제목: 팀워크 장려

3월 1일부터, ⁵ 마요르가 사는 마요르가 팀워크 상(MTP)을 시작합니다. 팀워크 상은 동료들과 협력한 직원들을 공식적으로 인정하는 것을 목표로 합니다. ^{6B} 한 명의 수상자가 매월 첫째 날 발표됩니다. ^{6C} 수상자는 그 달에 매주 금요일마다 한 시간 먼저 퇴근하는 것이 허가됩니다. 이 혜택이 수상자에게 즐거움이 되길 바랍니다.

^{6A} 전 직원들은 팀워크 상을 받을 자격이 주어지며 누구든 후보 추천서를 제출할 수 있습니다. 하지만, 6개월 이내에 같은 사람이 팀워크 상을 두 번 받을 수는 없습니다. 후보 지명을 하고 싶다면 인사팀에서 서식을 가져가시면 됩니다.

어휘 encourage 장려하다, 격려하다 launch 시작하다, 출시하다 aim to do ~하는 것을 목표로 하다 formally 정식으로, 공식적으로 recognize 인정하다 cooperation 협력 benefit 혜택 be eligible for ~의 자격이 있다 submit 제출하다 nomination 임명 pick up ~을 가져가다

---

5. What is the purpose of the memo?

(A) To announce new job duties
(B) To congratulate employees
(C) To introduce a new award system
(D) To explain a vacation policy

이 회람의 목적은 무엇인가?

(A) 새로운 직무를 알리기 위해
(B) 직원들을 축하해 주기 위해
(C) 새로운 포상 제도를 소개하기 위해
(D) 휴가 정책을 설명하기 위해

해설 첫 번째 문장의 launch를 introduce로, Prize를 award로 바꿔 표현한 (C)가 정답이다.

어휘 duty 업무 congratulate 축하하다 introduce 도입하다, 소개하다 policy 정책

---

6. What is NOT mentioned about the MTP?

(A) It can be received by any employee.
(B) It will be announced once a month.
(C) It includes a shorter work schedule.
(D) Its nominations are valid for six months.

MTP에 대해 언급되지 않은 것은 무엇인가?

(A) 어떤 직원도 받을 수 있다.
(B) 한 달에 한 번 발표될 것이다.
(C) 더 짧은 업무 일정이 포함된다.
(D) 후보 지명은 6개월 동안 유효하다.

해설 MTP라는 상에 대해 언급되지 않은 것을 묻는 문제. 반대로 언급된 것을 찾아 소거한다. (D)의 경우, 상을 받은 사람이 6개월 이내에 두 번 연속 상을 받을 수 없다는 내용과는 무관하다.

어휘 nomination 임명, 지명 valid 유효한

To: Samuel Valdez <svaldez@freesemail.com>
From: Westline Railway <contact@westlinerailway.com>
Date: June 19
Subject: A special offer!

Dear Mr. Valdez,

7-1 **I would like to inform you about a survey** we are currently conducting. 7-2 **Sharing your opinions** about Westline Railway's new online booking process can help us to make further improvements. You will be rewarded with a discount on your next ticket purchase. To participate, please follow the steps below.

1. Visit www.westlinerailway.com/survey and complete the survey.
2. Enter your e-mail address at the end of the survey.
3. 8 **You will receive a voucher code in your inbox. You can use it to get 25% off your next Westline Railway journey.**

9-1 **If you have any questions, please feel free to e-mail me at this address.**
Thank you!

9-2 **Diane Harper**
Customer Care Center, Westline Railway

어휘 offer 할인   conduct a survey 설문 조사를 하다   reward 보상하다   voucher 상품권, 할인권

7. Why did Ms. Harper write to Mr. Valdez?

   (A) To thank him for a purchase
   (B) To request some feedback
   (C) To introduce a new product
   (D) To apologize for an error

   해설 Sharing your opinions가 request some feedback으로 바꿔 표현된 (B)가 정답이다.

8. What should Mr. Valdez provide to get a discount on his next journey?

   (A) An account number   (B) A photo ID
   (C) An original receipt   **(D) A coupon code**

   해설 본문에서 할인에 대해 언급된 부분을 찾는다. 단서 8에서 할인권 코드를 사용하여 25% 할인을 받을 수 있다고 했으므로 voucher code와 바꿔 쓸 수 있는 (D) a coupon code가 정답이다.

9. What is suggested about Ms. Harper?

   (A) She has designed a Web site.
   (B) She will answer questions directly.
   (C) She will send a sample to Mr. Valdez.
   (D) She is a new Westline Railway employee.

   해설 하퍼 씨는 이메일을 쓴 사람이며 단서 9-1에서 e-mail me라고 했으므로 하퍼 씨가 직접 답을 해 준다는 것을 추측할 수 있다.

UNIT 18 문제 유형별 (2)

1 문장 삽입 문제

● 문제 풀이 전략

본문 p.286

To: All Redmond Financial Employees
From: Adeline Bates
Date: March 9
Subject: Approved changes

Dear Staff,

I am pleased to announce that Redmond Financial will expand its compensation package for employees from next quarter. —[1]—. Our number of paid vacation days for employees is already well above average compared to other businesses across the country. However, we will still add three more. Performance bonuses will also be increased by 10%. —[2]—.

Redmond Financial is considered the most trustworthy company in the industry. **This trust** is made possible through the dedication of our staff. —[4]—. We hope these changes will make you feel valued.

Warmest regards,
Adeline Bates, HR Director

수신: 레드몬드 파이낸셜 전 직원들
발신: 아델린 베이츠
날짜: 3월 9일
제목: 승인된 변경 사항

직원분들께,

레드몬드 파이낸셜은 다음 분기부터 직원을 위한 복리 후생을 확대할 것임을 알리게 되어 기쁩니다. 직원들의 유급 휴가 일수는 전국의 다른 회사들과 비교했을 때 이미 평균을 훨씬 넘어섭니다. 하지만 저희는 3일을 더 추가할 것입니다. 성과 보너스 또한 10퍼센트까지 인상될 것입니다.

레드몬드 파이낸셜은 업계에서 가장 신뢰할 수 있는 회사로 여겨지고 있습니다. **이러한 신뢰**는 저희 직원들의 헌신을 통해 가능하게 되었습니다. 저희는 이러한 변경 사항으로 여러분이 가치 있게 느껴지길 바랍니다.

인사팀장 아델린 베이츠

미니 테스트 1   1. (B)   2. (B)   본문 p.287

1.
—[1]—. Conference participants can attend talks given by a variety of speakers. Also, they can register for **a workshop on leadership**. This session is limited to the first thirty people who sign up.

학회 참여자들은 다양한 발표자들이 하는 연설에 참석할 수 있다. 또한, **리더십에 관한 워크숍**에 등록할 수 있다. 이 과정은 등록하는 첫 30명까지로 제한이 되어 있다.

해설 주어진 문장에서 This session이 가리키는 것은 a workshop이므로 [2]번 뒤에 들어가야 한다.

어휘 participant 참여자 attend 참석하다 a variety of 다양한 register for ~에 등록하다 session 과정 limited 제한된 sign up 등록하다

2.

Your membership will expire on July 31. —[1]—. Please reply to **this e-mail** before the date to renew your membership. Alternatively, you can use the address to cancel your membership.

귀하의 멤버십은 7월 31일에 만기가 될 것입니다. 귀하의 멤버십을 갱신하시려면 그 날짜 전에 **이 이메일**로 답을 해 주십시오. 혹은 그 (이메일) 주소를 사용하여 (답장하여) 멤버십을 취소하실 수도 있습니다.

해설 Alternatively는 앞의 내용에 추가적으로 다른 대안을 제시할 때 쓰인다. 또한 the address(그 주소)가 가리키는 것이 this e-mail의 주소라는 것을 파악하면 [2]가 정답임을 알 수 있다. 문장을 넣는 문제는 그 문장 속의 특정 단어, 특히 the/this/these/those 등이 들어간 단어가 가리키는 대상을 지문에서 찾아내는 것이 핵심이다.

어휘 expire 만료되다 reply to ~에 답하다 renew 갱신하다 alternatively 대안으로, 그 대신에, 혹은 address 주소 cancel 취소하다

미니 테스트 2   1. (C)   본문 p.287

VANCOUVER, 24 Feb.—Kerr Sports has announced that it has taken over MV Footwear for $18.5 million. —[1]—. Kerr Sports is known for its basketball and baseball equipment. —[2]—. The company's CEO wants to start selling shoes as well. **The acquisition will help Kerr Sports expand its product line. In addition, the move is expected to bring in new customers.** That's because MV Footwear is popular with young consumers. Ann Engel, a spokesperson for Kerr Sports, said that negotiations took several weeks. —[4]—. The company will work to keep all MV Footwear employees on staff.

2월 24일, 밴쿠버—커 스포츠는 1,850만 달러에 MV 풋웨어를 인수한 것을 발표했다. 커 스포츠는 농구와 야구 장비로 유명하다. 회사의 대표 이사는 신발 판매도 시작하길 원한다. **이번 인수는 커 스포츠가 제품 라인을 확장하는 데 도움이 될 것이다. 또한, 이 움직임은 신규 고객들을 유치할 것으로 예상된다.** 왜냐하면 MV 풋웨어는 젊은 소비자들에게 인기가 있기 때문이다. 커 스포츠의 대변인인 앤 엥겔은 협상이 몇 주 정도 걸렸다고 말했다. 회사는 모든 MV 풋웨어 직원들의 고용을 유지하기 위해 노력할 것이다.

어휘 take over 인수하다 be known for ~로 유명하다 as well 또한 acquisition 인수 expand 확장하다 consumer 소비자 spokesperson 대변인 negotiation 협상 on staff (직원으로) 근무하는

1. In which of the positions marked [1], [2], [3] and [4] does the following sentence best belong?

"In addition, the move is expected to bring in new customers."

(A) [1]
(B) [2]
(C) [3]
(D) [4]

[1], [2], [3], [4]로 표시된 곳 중에서 다음 문장이 들어가기에 가장 적절한 곳은?

"또한, 이 움직임은 신규 고객들을 유치할 것으로 예상된다."

(A) [1]
(B) [2]
(C) [3]
(D) [4]

해설 주어진 문장에서 연결어인 In addition(게다가, 또한)은 추가적인 내용을 나타낼 때 쓰이며, the move(움직임)가 가리키는 것은 [3]번 앞의 The acquisition(인수)이다. 따라서 (C)가 정답.

어휘 in addition 또한, 게다가 move 움직임 customer 고객

2 의도 파악 문제

● 문제 풀이 전략

본문 p.288

Gabriel Ruiz (9:48 A.M.)
Hello, Vanessa. **Have you started painting the stairway railings yet?**

Vanessa Sheehan (9:51 A.M.)
Hi, Gabriel. I'll be on it shortly. I just need to hang up some signs first to warn people about the wet paint.

Gabriel Ruiz (9:52 A.M.)
All right. Do you think the smell will bother people in the building?

Vanessa Sheehan (9:54 A.M.)
Most of the building's windows are open, so it shouldn't be a problem.

Gabriel Ruiz (9:55 A.M.)
I'm glad to hear that!

가브리엘 루이즈 (오전 9시 48분)
안녕하세요, 바네사. **계단 난간 페인트 칠은 시작했나요?**

바네사 시핸 (오전 9시 51분)
안녕하세요, 가브리엘. 제가 곧 시작할 거예요. 덜 마른 페인트에 대해 사람들에게 알리는 표시들을 먼저 걸어 놓아야 해요.

가브리엘 루이즈 (오전 9시 52분)
알았어요. 냄새가 건물에 있는 사람들에게 방해가 될 것 같나요?

바네사 시핸 (오전 9시 54분)
건물 창문 대부분이 열려 있어서 문제가 될 것 같지 않아요.

가브리엘 루이즈 (오전 9시 55분)
그렇다니 다행이네요!

Q. At 9:51 A.M., what does Ms. Sheehan mean when she writes, "I'll be on it shortly"?

(A) She will explain a new project.
(B) She will start some work soon.
(C) She will print some signs.
(D) She will meet Mr. Ruiz quickly.

오전 9시 51분에, 시핸 씨가 "제가 곧 시작할 거예요"라고 한 의도는 무엇인가?

(A) 그녀는 새로운 프로젝트를 설명할 것이다.
(B) 그녀는 곧 일을 시작할 것이다.
(C) 그녀는 표시들을 인쇄할 것이다.
(D) 그녀는 루이즈 씨를 빨리 만날 것이다.

미니 테스트 1   1. (B)   2. (A)

본문 p.289

1.

Daniel Hampton (11:19 A.M.)
We still cannot get the copy machine to work, so **a technician will need to fix it.**

Grand Office Inc. (11:21 A.M.)
No problem. **One of our technicians can go there now.**

대니얼 햄턴 (오전 11시 19분)
저희는 아직도 복사기가 작동이 안 돼서 **기술자가 고쳐 줘야 할 것 같아요.**

그랜드 오피스 사 (오전 11시 21분)
문제 없습니다. **저희 기술자 한 명이 지금 그곳으로 갈 수 있습니다.**

(A) He can replace Mr. Hampton's copy machine.
(B) He will send someone to make a repair.

(A) 그는 햄턴 씨의 복사기를 교체할 수 있다.
(B) 그는 수리해 줄 사람을 보낼 것이다.

해설 앞에서 기술자가 필요하다고 하고 이에 긍정적으로 대답했으므로 기술자(technician)를 someone to make a repair(수리를 해 줄 사람)로 바꿔 표현한 (B)가 정답이다.

어휘 replace 교체하다   make a repair 수리하다

2.

Bruno Marchesi (1:25 P.M.)
Would you mind hooking up the projector and laptop?
We'll need them for the meeting.

Emily Rourke (1:30 P.M.)
Done. Is that all?

(A) She has set up some equipment.
(B) She has contacted some employees.

브루노 마르케시 (오후 1시 25분)
영사기와 노트북을 연결해 줄 수 있어요? 회의에 필요해서요.

에밀리 루크 (오후 1시 30분)
다 됐습니다. 더 필요한 거는요?

(A) 그녀는 일부 장비를 설치했다.
(B) 그녀는 일부 직원들에게 연락을 했다.

해설   표시된 표현의 앞뒤 문맥을 살펴보면 바로 앞에서 영사기와 노트북 설치를 도와 달라고 했고, 이를 완료했다는 의미로 'Done.'이 사용되었음을 알 수 있다. 따라서 hooking up을 set up으로, the projector and laptop을 equipment로 바꿔 표현한 (A)가 정답이다.

어휘   hook up ~을 설치하다, ~을 연결하다

미니 테스트 2   1. (B)   본문 p.289

Linda Harrison (2:43 P.M.)
Matthew, I've emailed you the first draft of the catalog. Have you had time to look at it?

Matthew Kemp (2:46 P.M.)
I've just opened the file. It looks like the photos are very small. They will be difficult for customers to see.

Linda Harrison (2:47 P.M.)
I thought I needed to fit a lot onto each page. **I guess I will do it all again.**

Matthew Kemp (2:48 P.M.)
Not necessarily. The colors and text look great. You can just change the picture size and have more pages.

Linda Harrison (2:50 P.M.)
What a relief. That won't take me long.

린다 해리슨 (오후 2시 43분)
매튜, 당신에게 카탈로그 초안을 이메일로 보냈어요. 그걸 볼 시간이 있었나요?

매튜 켐프 (오후 2시 46분)
이제 막 파일을 열었어요. 사진들이 너무 작아 보이네요. 고객들이 알아보기 어려울 거예요.

린다 해리슨 (오후 2시 47분)
저는 각 페이지에 많은 내용을 다 맞춰야 한다고 생각했어요. **전부 다시 해야 할 것 같네요.**

매튜 켐프 (오후 2시 48분)
그럴 필요 없어요. 색감과 본문은 훌륭해요. 사진 크기만 바꾸고 페이지를 좀 더 늘려요.

린다 해리슨 (오후 2시 50분)
다행이네요. 그건 그렇게 오래 걸리지 않을 거예요.

어휘   customer 고객   fit 딱 맞추다

1. At 2:48 P.M., what does Mr. Kemp mean when he writes, "Not necessarily"?

(A) Ms. Harrison should not get help with a task.
(B) Ms. Harrison will not have to start a project over.
(C) Ms. Harrison should not delete some photos.
(D) Ms. Harrison will not have to send an e-mail.

오후 2시 48분에, 켐프 씨가 "그럴 필요 없어요"라고 한 의도는 무엇인가?

(A) 해리슨 씨는 업무에 도움을 받으면 안 된다.
(B) 해리슨 씨는 프로젝트를 다시 시작하지 않아도 된다.
(C) 해리슨 씨는 몇몇 사진들을 삭제하면 안 된다.
(D) 해리슨 씨는 이메일을 보낼 필요가 없다.

해설   주어진 표현의 바로 앞에서 일을 다시 해야 할 것 같다고 한 말에 그럴 필요 없다고 부정하고 있으므로 일을 다시 하지 않아도 됨을 알 수 있다. 따라서 (B)가 정답이다.

3 동의어 찾기 문제

● 문제 풀이 전략
본문 p.290

From: Patricia Lee 〈leepatricia@kentrock.com〉
To: Jerry Callahan 〈j.callahan@greenwood.gov〉
Date: April 14
Subject: Meeting

Dear Ms. Callahan,

I am writing to express my appreciation to the city council. I attended the feedback session for residents on April 10. The participants shared ideas about improvements for the City Hall building and its **immediate** surroundings. The council members carefully listened to everyone's suggestions. I look forward to seeing the new changes to the area.

Sincerely,

Patricia Lee

발신: 패트리샤 리
수신: 제리 켈러핸
날짜: 4월 14일
제목: 회의

켈러핸 씨께,

시 의회에 감사를 표하기 위해 글을 씁니다. 저는 4월 10일 주민들을 위한 피드백 과정에 참석했습니다. 참석자들은 시청 건물과 **근처** 주변 환경의 개선점에 대한 생각을 공유했습니다. 의회 구성원들은 모두의 제안 사항을 주의 깊게 들었습니다. 지역에 새로운 변화를 기대해 봅니다.

패트리샤 리

Q. In the e-mail, the word "immediate" in paragraph 1, line 5 is closest in meaning to

(A) next
(B) current
(C) nearby
(D) prompt

이메일에서 첫 번째 단락 다섯 번째 줄의 "immediate"와 의미상 가장 가까운 것은?

(A) 다음의
(B) 현재의
(C) 근처의
(D) 즉각적인

미니 테스트 1　　1. (A)　　　2. (A)　　　　　　　　　본문 p.291

1.

We understand that you are very busy. Even so, could you please **spare** a few minutes to give us your feedback?

당신이 매우 바쁘다는 것을 이해합니다. 그렇다 하더라도 저희에게 당신의 의견을 주실 시간을 좀 **내어 주시겠습니까**?

(A) give　　　　(B) ask　　　　　　**(A) 주다**　　(B) 묻다, 요청하다

해설　spare는 이 문장에서 시간을 '할애하다', 즉 '주다'란 의미로 쓰였다. 동의어 문제는 단어의 원래 의미도 중요하지만 문장 내에서의 의미를 찾아야 한다. 정답은 (A).

어휘　even so 그렇다고 해도　a few 조금, 약간 있는

2.

| If you have any further **issues** with your computer, please contact the IT team. They can be reached at IT@brisbandsales.net. | 귀하의 컴퓨터에 추후 **문제**가 있다면, IT팀에 연락하세요. IT@brisbandsales.net으로 연락하시면 됩니다. |

(A) problems (B) versions (A) 문제 (B) 버전, 판

해설 문제가 발생하면 연락하라는 내용의 문장에 쓰였으므로 (A) problems와 동의어이다.

어휘 further 더 이상의 reach 연락하다

미니 테스트 2   1. (B)   본문 p.291

To: Josephine Frazier
From: Eric Stanfield
Date: July 19
Subject: Digital Marketing

Dear Ms. Frazier,

I am the vice president of the Salisbury Small Business Association (SSBA). I recently saw your talk on digital marketing at the Essex Center. I found it to be very informative. I am wondering if you could teach one of our monthly workshops **on the same topic**. Our members would love to learn new skills in your **area of expertise**.

The SSBA was founded fifteen years ago to support small businesses. Members can get help obtaining a business loan, access up-to-date information about the current market, and get discounts from suppliers.

If you are available, please let me know the most convenient dates.

Sincerely,

Eric Stanfield

수신: 조세핀 프레이저
발신: 에릭 스탠필드
날짜: 7월 19일
제목: 디지털 마케팅

프레이저 씨께,

저는 살리스베리 소상공인 연합회(SSBA)의 부회장입니다. 저는 최근에 귀하께서 에식스 센터에서 디지털 마케팅에 관해 연설하시는 것을 봤습니다. 저는 그게 매우 유익했습니다. **같은 주제에 대해** 저희 월간 워크숍 중 하나에서 가르쳐 주실 수 있는지 궁금합니다. 저희 회원들은 귀하의 **전문 지식 분야**에서의 새로운 기술들을 배우고 싶어 합니다.

SSBA는 소상공인을 지원하기 위해 15년 전에 설립되었습니다. 회원들은 사업 대출을 받는 데 도움을 받을 수 있고, 현재 시장의 최신 정보를 얻을 수 있으며, 공급업체들에게 할인을 받을 수 있습니다.

시간이 되신다면 가장 편리한 날짜를 알려 주십시오.

에릭 스탠필드

어휘 vice president 부회장, 부사장 association 협회 recently 최근에 informative 유익한 expertise 전문 분야 found 설립하다 support 지원하다, 지지하다 obtain 얻다, 획득하다 loan 대출 access 접근하다 up-to-date 최신의 current 현재의 supplier 공급업체 available 시간이 있는 convenient 편리한

1. In the e-mail, the word "area" in paragraph 1, line 4, is closest in meaning to

(A) distance   (B) **subject**
(C) level   (D) portion

이메일에서 첫 번째 단락 네 번째 줄의 "area"와 의미상 가장 가까운 것은?

(A) 거리   (B) **주제**
(C) 수준   (D) 부분

해설 주어진 단어 area는 '지역, 구역'이라는 의미가 있으나, 뒤에 expertise(전문 지식)가 있으므로 '주제, 분야' 정도의 의미로 쓰였음을 알 수 있다.

ACTUAL TEST

본문 p.292

| 1. (D) | 2. (C) | 3. (C) | 4. (B) | 5. (A) | 6. (D) |
| 7. (C) | 8. (C) | 9. (B) | 10. (C) | 11. (C) | |

From: Travis Baxley
To: Movie Pass Customer Service
Date: August 6
Subject: Account #59250

I am writing about my Movie Pass subscription. —[1]—. I signed up for the video-streaming service in June and selected an annual subscription. ¹⁻¹ **I was surprised to see a charge on my credit card for $12.95 from your company.** A payment of $139.95 for the entire one-year subscription was made up front, so there should be no additional fees until next year. —[2]—.

² **I logged into my account on your Web site this morning to see what previous payments were listed.** Only the original $139.95 transaction was there. However, I don't know whether any information was missing. ³ Would you mind letting me know how often the site is updated? ¹⁻² I would also like a refund of $12.95 issued as soon as possible. —[4]—.

Sincerely,
Travis Baxley

발신: 트레비스 백슬리
수신: 무비 패스 고객 서비스
날짜: 8월 6일
제목: 계정 번호 59250

저는 제 무비 패스 구독에 대해 글을 씁니다. 저는 6월에 비디오 스트리밍 서비스를 신청했고 연간 구독을 선택했습니다. ¹⁻¹ 저는 귀사로부터 12.95달러가 제 신용 카드에 부과된 것을 보고 놀랐습니다. 저는 1년 구독료 139.95달러를 선불로 지불했으므로 내년까지는 추가 비용이 없어야 합니다.

² 오늘 아침에 기존에 지불한 내역을 보기 위해 귀사의 웹사이트의 제 계정에 로그인을 했었습니다. 원래의 139.95달러 거래만 그곳에 나타나 있었습니다. 하지만, 빠진 정보라도 있는 건지 모르겠습니다. ³ 얼마나 자주 웹사이트를 업데이트 하시는지 제게 알려 주실 수 있을까요? ¹⁻² 또한, 지불된 12.95달러를 가능한 한 빨리 환불받고 싶습니다.

트레비스 백슬리

어휘 subscription 구독 sign up for ~을 신청하다 charge 요금 credit card 신용 카드 payment 지급, 지불 entire 전체의 up front 선불로 previous 이전의 transaction 거래 issue 지급하다, 발행하다

---

1. What is the purpose of the e-mail?

(A) To take advantage of an offer
(B) To cancel an online service
(C) To upgrade an account
(D) To report a payment issue

이메일의 목적은 무엇인가?

(A) 할인을 이용하기 위해
(B) 온라인 서비스를 취소하기 위해
(C) 계정을 업그레이드하기 위해
(D) 지불 문제를 보고하기 위해

해설 글의 주제를 묻는 문제. 단서 1-1에서 부과된 요금에 대해 말하고 있으며, 단서 1-2에서 잘못 부과된 요금을 환불해 달라고 했으므로 이를 payment issue(지불 문제)라고 표현한 (D)가 정답이다.

어휘 take advantage of ~을 이용하다, ~을 활용하다 offer 할인 cancel 취소하다

---

2. Why did Mr. Baxley visit the Web site this morning?

(A) To change his contact information
(B) To sign up for a subscription
(C) To check an account history
(D) To watch some movies

백슬리 씨가 오늘 아침에 웹사이트를 방문한 이유는 무엇인가?

(A) 그의 연락처 정보를 변경하기 위해
(B) 구독을 신청하기 위해
(C) 계정 내역을 확인하기 위해
(D) 영화를 보기 위해

해설 세부 내용을 묻는 문제. 질문에서 웹사이트를 언급하고 있으므로 지문에서 이에 해당하는 내용을 찾는다. 단서 2에서 previous payments(이전에 지불한 것)를 보았다고 했으므로 이를 account history(계정 내역)로 표현한 (C)가 정답이다.

3. In which of the positions marked [1], [2], [3], and [4] does the following sentence best belong?

"However, I don't know whether any information was missing."

(A) [1]
(B) [2]
(C) [3]
(D) [4]

[1], [2], [3], [4]로 표시된 곳 중에서 다음 문장이 들어가기에 가장 적절한 곳은?

"하지만, 빠진 정보라도 있는 건지 모르겠습니다."

(A) [1]
(B) [2]
(C) [3]
(D) [4]

> 해설 | 주어진 문장의 적절한 위치를 묻는 문제. 문장에서 any information(어떤 정보)이라고 언급한 부분은 지불된 금액에 관한 것이며, 정보가 정확한지 확인하기 위해 사이트 업데이트 주기를 묻고 있으므로 주어진 문장은 [3]번에 들어가는 게 가장 적절하다.

Pamela Boyer, 11:31 A.M.
Hi, Andre. Are you busy right now?

Andre Hyland, 11:35 A.M.
I'm working on an expense report. What's going on?

Pamela Boyer, 11:36 A.M.
My inspection at the Veltri Building ran later than I expected. It would be really helpful if you could ⁴**set up the chairs and tables in the training room for me.**

Andre Hyland, 11:37 A.M.
⁵Sure. Do you have a layout in mind?

Pamela Boyer, 11:38 A.M.
Yes, I'll take a picture of the layout and send it to you by phone. Fortunately, I picked up the handouts from the printer yesterday.

파멜라 보이어, 오전 11시 31분
안녕, 안드레. 지금 바빠요?

안드레 하이랜드, 오전 11시 35분
지금 비용 보고서를 작성 중이에요. 무슨 일 있으세요?

파멜라 보이어, 오전 11시 36분
벨트리 빌딩에서의 점검이 예상했던 것보다 더 늦어졌어요. ⁴교육실의 의자와 테이블을 제 대신 준비해 주시면 정말 도움이 될 것 같아요.

안드레 하이랜드, 오전 11시 37분
⁵그럼요. 생각해 놓으신 배치가 있으신가요?

파멜라 보이어, 오전 11시 38분
네, 제 휴대폰으로 찍어서 보내 줄게요. 다행히 어제 출력한 걸 가져왔어요.

> 어휘 | work on ~을 작업하다　inspection 검사, 점검　set up ~을 설치하다　layout 배치　fortunately 다행히　handout 유인물

4. What is Mr. Hyland asked to do?

(A) Proofread a handout
(B) Arrange some furniture
(C) Print some materials
(D) Reserve a meeting room

하이랜드 씨가 요청받은 것은 무엇인가?

(A) 유인물을 교정하는 것
(B) 몇몇 가구를 배치하는 것
(C) 자료를 인쇄하는 것
(D) 회의실을 예약하는 것

> 해설 | 오전 11시 36분에 보이어 씨가 부탁을 하고 있는 내용이 단서가 된다. 단서 4의 set up을 Arrange로, the chairs and tables를 some furniture로 바꿔 표현한 (B)가 정답이다.

5. At 11:37 A.M., what does Mr. Hyland mean when he writes, "Sure"?

(A) He is available to assist Ms. Boyer.
(B) He will explain a process to Ms. Boyer.
(C) He agrees with Ms. Boyer's complaint.
(D) He has found Ms. Boyer's belongings.

오전 11시 37분에, 하이랜드 씨가 "그럼요"라고 한 의도는 무엇인가?

(A) 그는 보이어 씨를 도울 시간이 있다.
(B) 그는 보이어 씨에게 절차를 설명할 것이다.
(C) 그는 보이어 씨의 불만 사항에 동의한다.
(D) 그는 보이어 씨의 소지품을 찾았다.

> 해설 | 제시된 표현의 앞 문장에서 helpful(도움이 되는)이라고 했으므로 이를 assist(도와주다)로 바꿔 표현한 (A)가 정답이다.

Northwest Rail Going Strong

PHILADELPHIA (April 6)—Northwest Rail has announced that it will begin offering several express train routes **6-1 from next month.** —[1]—. **6-2 The company expects that the new service will boost the number of passengers by approximately fifteen percent.** Commuters between Philadelphia and New York are expected to make up the majority of the new business. —[2]—.

"We have listened to feedback from passengers and worked to make more convenient options available," said Jessie Cohn, Northwest Rail's vice president.

The change is part of a larger plan to improve services overall. For example, **7 in January, a complimentary Wi-Fi network was added to all Northwest Rail trains.** **8 In addition, passengers will no longer have to visit the ticket window to buy tickets.** They can instead use the automated machines near the platform. The company also plans to invest in new trains with more space for luggage. —[4]—.

노스웨스트 철도의 강력 성장

4월 6일 필라델피아 – 노스웨스트 철도는 6-1 다음 달부터 몇몇 고속 열차 노선을 제공하기 시작할 것이라고 발표했다. 6-2 회사는 그 새로운 서비스가 승객들의 수를 대략 15퍼센트까지 증가시킬 것이라고 예상한다. 필라델피아와 뉴욕 사이를 오가는 통근객들이 신규 사업의 주고객이 될 것으로 예상된다.

"저희는 승객들로부터 의견을 듣고 보다 편리한 서비스들을 제공하도록 노력해 왔습니다."라고 노스웨스트 철도 부사장인 제시 콘이 말했다.

그러한 변화는 전반적으로 서비스 향상을 하려는 큰 계획의 일부이다. 예를 들어, 7 1월에는 모든 노스웨스트 철도 열차에 무료 와이파이 연결이 추가되었다. 8 또한, 승객들은 승차권을 구입하기 위해 더 이상 매표소에 방문하지 않아도 될 것이다. 대신 그들은 승강장 근처의 자동화 기계를 사용할 수 있다. 회사는 또한 수하물용 추가 공간이 있는 새로운 열차에 투자를 할 계획이다.

어휘 express 고속의, 빠른 boost 증진시키다, 북돋우다 passenger 승객 commuter 통근객 make up ~을 차지하다 majority 다수 convenient 편리한 available 이용 가능한 vice president 부사장 improve 개선하다 complimentary 무료의 no longer 더 이상 ~ 않는 luggage 수하물

6. What is mentioned about Northwest Rail?

(A) It will start charging passengers for excess luggage.
(B) It recently began offering an express service.
(C) It will relocate its head office to New York.
(D) It is likely to serve more travelers from May.

노스웨스트 철도에 대해 언급된 것은?

(A) 승객들에게 추가 수하물에 대한 요금을 부과하기 시작할 것이다.
(B) 최근에 고속 서비스를 제공하기 시작했다.
(C) 본사를 뉴욕으로 이전할 것이다.
(D) 5월부터 더 많은 승객들을 태우게 될 것이다.

해설 글의 세부 내용을 묻는 문제. 단서 6-2의 boost the number of passengers를 serve more travelers라고 표현한 (D)가 정답이다. 기사는 4월에 쓰였으며 다음 달부터라고 했으므로 5월이 된다.

어휘 charge 요금을 부과하다 relocate A to B A를 B로 이전하다 be likely to do ~할 듯하다

7. What happened in January?

(A) Northwest Rail hired more staff members.
(B) Ms. Cohn was promoted to vice president.
(C) Passengers were given free Internet access.
(D) A ticket exchange policy changed.

1월에 무슨 일이 있었는가?

(A) 노스웨스트 철도는 더 많은 직원들을 고용했다.
(B) 콘 씨가 부사장으로 승진했다.
(C) 승객들에게 무료 인터넷이 제공되었다.
(D) 승차권 교환 정책이 바뀌었다.

해설 지문에서 1월이 언급된 부분을 찾는다. 단서 7의 complimentary(무료의)란 표현을 free로 표현한 (C)가 정답이다.

어휘 hire 고용하다, 채용하다 be promoted to ~로 승진하다 exchange 교환 policy 정책

8. In which of the positions marked [1], [2], [3], and [4] does the following sentence best belong?

"They can instead use the automated machines near the platform."

(A) [1]
(B) [2]
(C) [3]
(D) [4]

해설 문장이 들어갈 적절한 위치를 고르는 문제. 단서 8을 바탕으로 They는 passengers(승객들)임을 알 수 있으므로 주어진 문장은 [3]번에 들어가는 것이 적절하다.

[1], [2], [3], [4]로 표시된 곳 중에서 다음 문장이 들어가기에 가장 적절한 곳은?

"대신 그들은 승강장 근처의 자동화 기계를 사용할 수 있다."

(A) [1]
(B) [2]
(C) [3]
(D) [4]

9-1 **Modern transportation companies** face unique challenges in an ever-changing industry. Fluctuations in demand, unpredictable fuel prices, evolving customer expectations, and increased competition are 11 **just** a few aspects of the industry that businesses must respond to.

Summit Enterprises is here to help! Thanks to our large team of consultants, 10 **you can be sure to find an expert with experience that meets your particular needs**. For example:

- Training staff members
- Following environmental regulations
- Maximizing automation
- Growing your customer base

Call us at 555-8181 today to discuss how we can help you take 9-2 **your transportation business** to the next level. There is no charge for the initial consultation.

9-1 최근 운송 회사들은 늘 변화하는 업계에서 독특한 도전 과제에 직면하고 있습니다. 수요의 변동과 예측 불가능한 연료 가격, 진화하는 고객들의 기대, 그리고 늘어나는 경쟁은 사업체들이 대응해야만 하는 업계의 몇몇 단면일 11 **뿐**입니다.

서밋 엔터프라이즈가 여러분을 돕기 위해 여기 있습니다! 저희의 대규모 컨설턴트들 덕분에, 10 **귀하의 특정한 필요에 맞는 경험 있는 전문가를 반드시 찾을 수 있습니다**. 예를 들면:

- 직원 교육
- 환경 규정 준수
- 자동화의 최대화
- 고객 기반의 증대

9-2 **귀하의 운송 사업**이 다음 단계로 가도록 저희가 도울 수 있는 방법에 대해 논의하고 싶으시면 오늘 555-8181로 저희에게 전화 주세요. 첫 상담은 요금을 부과하지 않습니다.

어휘 modern 현대의, 최근의 transportation 운송 face 직면하다 unique 독특한 challenge 도전 과제 ever-changing 늘 변화하는 fluctuation 변동 unpredictable 예측할 수 없는 evolve 진화하다 expectation 기대 competition 경쟁 aspect 면, 양상 expert 전문가 environmental 환경의 regulation 규정 consultation 상담

9. For whom is the Web page written?

(A) Professors teaching finance
(B) Owners of transportation businesses
(C) Students studying business
(D) Employees in HR team

웹페이지는 누구를 위해 작성되었는가?

(A) 재정학을 가르치는 교수들
(B) 운송 회사 사업주들
(C) 경영을 공부하는 학생들
(D) 인사팀 직원들

해설 이 글을 읽는 대상을 묻는 문제. 단서 9-1과 9-2를 통해 운송 사업을 하는 사람들을 위한 컨설팅 광고임을 알 수 있다. 따라서 정답은 (B). 굳이 운송 분야라는 것을 언급하지 않고 간단하게 business owners(사업주)라고 해도 답이 될 수 있다.

10. What is suggested about Summit Enterprises?

(A) It has branches in many locations.
(B) It mainly works with large corporations.
(C) It has specialists in a variety of areas.
(D) It will merge with a competitor.

서밋 엔터프라이즈에 대해 암시된 것은?

(A) 많은 곳에 지점들이 있다.
(B) 주로 대기업과 일을 한다.
(C) 다양한 분야에 전문가들을 보유하고 있다.
(D) 경쟁사와 합병할 것이다.

> 해설 위에 언급된 회사에 대해 추론하는 문제. 단서 10의 expert with experience(경험을 갖춘 전문가)를 specialist로, 그 아래 나열된 전문 분야를 a variety of areas(다양한 분야)로 바꿔 표현한 (C)가 정답이다.

> 어휘 branch 지점, 지사 mainly 주로 corporation 회사 specialist 전문가 merge with ~와 합병하다

11. In the Web page, the word "just" in paragraph 1, line 3, is closest in meaning to

(A) correct
(B) lately
(C) only
(D) fair

웹페이지에서 첫 번째 단락 세 번째 줄의 "just"와 의미상 가장 가까운 것은?

(A) 옳은
(B) 최근에
(C) 오직, ~ 뿐
(D) 공정한

> 해설 just는 '단지', '이제 막', '오직' 등 다양한 의미를 지니고 있으나 해당 문장에서는 '단지'의 의미로 쓰였으므로 only가 가장 적절하다.

UNIT 19 지문 유형별 (1)

1 이메일/편지

● 지문의 기본 구조

본문 p.300

To: Malcolm Haynes 〈haynesm@auto-world.net〉
From: Serena Dolan 〈serena@stahrtires.com〉
Subject: Your order
Date: June 20

Dear Mr. Haynes,

I am writing to inform you that your order of 35-inch tires will be late.

Unfortunately, some of our factory's equipment has broken down. We are making repairs as quickly as possible. The order can be sent by June 26.

Please let us know whether you would like to cancel your order. There would be no fee in this case, as outlined in our cancellation policy, which is attached. We apologize for any inconvenience.

Sincerely,

Serena Dolan
Shipping Manager, Auto World

수신: 말콤 헤인즈
발신: 세레나 돌란
제목: 귀하의 주문
날짜: 6월 20일

헤인즈 씨께,

저는 귀하의 35인치 타이어 주문이 늦어질 것을 알려 드리려고 글을 씁니다.

안타깝게도, 저희 공장의 장비 일부가 고장이 났습니다. 저희는 가능한 한 빨리 수리를 하고 있는 중입니다. 주문품은 6월 26일까지 배송될 수 있습니다.

귀하의 주문을 취소하시고 싶으신지 저희에게 알려 주십시오. 첨부되어 있는 저희 취소 정책에 설명되어 있는 것처럼 이런 경우에는 비용이 없습니다. 불편을 끼쳐 죄송합니다.

세레나 돌란
오토 월드, 배송 담당자

미니 테스트   1. (B)   본문 p.301

Gretchen Anderson
1190 Tyson Road
Tucson, AZ 85709

Dear Ms. Anderson,

This letter is provided to alert you to a potential issue. Our records show that your electricity usage has recently increased significantly. Specifically, the usage for May was nearly double the usage for April. It is also much higher than other households of your size.

If you cannot identify the reason for this increase, there may be an issue with your electricity meter. **Should you like a technician to visit your home for an inspection, please fill out the enclosed form and return it to us.**

Sincerely,

The Southwest Electricity Team

Enclosure

그레첸 앤더슨
타이슨 가 1190
애리조나주 투손 85709

앤더슨 씨께,

이 편지는 잠재적인 문제를 귀하께 알리기 위해 제공되는 것입니다. 저희 기록에는 귀하의 전기 사용량이 최근에 상당히 증가했다고 나타나 있습니다. 특히, 5월달 사용량은 4월 사용량의 거의 두 배였습니다. 또한 귀댁의 면적과 유사한 다른 가정들에 비해 훨씬 높습니다.

이번 증가의 이유를 찾지 못하시겠다면 귀하의 전기 계량기에 문제가 있을지도 모릅니다. **점검을 위해 기술자가 댁에 방문하길 원하시면, 동봉된 서식을 작성하셔서 저희에게 보내 주십시오.**

남서부 전기팀

동봉

어휘   alert (위험을) 알리다, 경고하다   potential 잠재적인   recently 최근에   significantly 상당히   specifically 특히   household 가정, 가계   identify 확인하다, 발견하다   technician 기술자   inspection 검사, 점검   fill out ~을 작성하다   enclosed 동봉된, 첨부된

1. What is attached in the letter?

(A) An overdue bill
(B) A request form
(C) A confirmation letter
(D) A discount voucher

편지에 첨부된 것은 무엇인가?

(A) 기한이 지난 청구서
(B) 요청서
(C) 확인 서신
(D) 할인권

해설 이메일이나 편지의 경우 글의 마지막 부분에 첨부 파일에 관련된 내용이 언급된다. enclosed form(동봉된 서식)이 request form(요청서)으로 바꿔 표현된 (B)가 정답.

어휘   overdue 기한이 지난   confirmation 확인   voucher 상품권

2 광고

● 지문의 기본 구조

LUXURY APARTMENT FOR RENT

Located in the Cambridge Building at 703 Kovar Road. Three bedrooms, two bathrooms, spacious kitchen with modern appliances, and balcony with coastal views.

Tenants can use the on-site pool and fitness center. The monthly rent is $3,500. Available from July 1.

To book a tour of the apartment unit and building, call Rhapsody Realty at 555-7930.

고급 아파트 임대

코바 가 703번지 케임브리지 빌딩에 위치되어 있음. 3개의 침실, 2개의 욕실, 최신 가전제품을 갖춘 넓은 주방과 해안가 경치를 가진 발코니가 있음.

세입자들은 아파트 내의 수영장과 헬스장을 이용할 수 있습니다. 월 임대료는 3,500달러입니다. 7월 1일부터 이용 가능합니다.

아파트나 건물의 방문을 예약하시려면 랩소디 부동산 555-7930으로 전화 주세요.

미니 테스트   1. (C)

REDROCK CITY RECRUITMENT CENTER

Administrative Assistant, Helston Architecture

Helston Architecture is seeking a full-time administrative assistant for an immediate start. Duties include scheduling meetings and making travel arrangements for employees, answering calls and general e-mail correspondence, and maintaining office supply levels. The successful applicant must be well organized and ready to work in a fast-paced office. A bachelor's degree is preferred but not required. A friendly attitude and **excellent written and verbal skills are a must**.

The application deadline is August 31.

레드록 시 채용 센터

행정 보조, 헬스턴 건축

헬스턴 건축은 즉시 시작할 수 있는 정규직 행정 보조를 찾고 있습니다. 업무에는 회의 일정 잡기, 직원들의 출장 준비, 전화나 일반 이메일에 답하기, 그리고 사무용품 수준 유지하기가 포함됩니다. 합격자는 정리를 잘하고 빠르게 돌아가는 사무실에서 일할 준비가 되어 있어야 합니다. 학사 학위가 선호되지만 필수는 아닙니다. 친절한 태도와 **뛰어난 쓰기 및 말하기 실력은 필수입니다**.

지원 마감일은 8월 31일입니다.

어휘 administrative 행정의   assistant 보조   immediate 즉각적인   make arrangements 준비하다   correspondence 서신   maintain 유지하다   successful applicant 합격자   fast-paced 빨리 진행되는   bachelor's degree 학사 학위   prefer 선호하다   require 요구하다   attitude 태도   verbal 언어의, 말로 된

1. What qualification is required for the position?

(A) A driver's license
(B) Experience managing a team
(C) Strong writing skills
(D) A bachelor's degree

직책에 요구되는 자격 요건은 무엇인가?

(A) 운전면허증
(B) 팀 관리 경력
(C) 뛰어난 글쓰기 실력
(D) 학사 학위

해설 구인 광고의 핵심인 자격 요건을 묻는 문제. 글의 후반부에 요건들이 나열되어 있다. 그중 쓰기 능력이 필수(a must)라고 했으므로 (C)가 정답이다. (D)는 선호되지만 필수는 아니라고 했으므로 오답이다.

어휘 qualification 자격 요건

3 공고/회람

● 지문의 기본 구조

본문 p.304

Notice to Arlington City Residents: Planned Road Closure

The express lanes of Highway 129 from Exit 16 to Exit 21 will be closed from July 2. The other two lanes in both directions will remain open. The closure will take place so that work crews can repair sections of the road.

Drivers are encouraged to allow for extra travel time through the area. Alternatively, they may take other routes to avoid using Highway 129. The work will take approximately three weeks. For the latest details on the reopening date, visit the city's Web site.

알링턴 시 주민들께 알림: 도로 폐쇄 예정

129번 고속 도로의 16번 출구부터 21번 출구까지의 추월 차선들이 7월 2일부터 폐쇄될 것입니다. 다른 두 개의 양쪽 방향 차선들은 개방된 채로 있을 것입니다. 인부들이 도로 일부를 수리할 수 있도록 도로를 폐쇄합니다.

운전자들은 이 지역을 지나갈 때 시간을 여유롭게 잡을 것을 당부드립니다. 그렇지 않으면, 129번 고속 도로를 피하는 다른 길들로 가셔도 됩니다. 작업은 대략 3주 정도 걸립니다. 재개방 날짜에 대한 최신 세부 사항을 위해, 시 웹사이트를 방문하세요.

미니 테스트 1. (D)

본문 p.305

From: Heather Colbert
To: All staff
Date: Tuesday, December 8
Subject: For your information

The office Internet connection will be unavailable this Thursday, December 10, from 11:30 A.M. to approximately 1:30 P.M. **The system will undergo an upgrade** during this time, which will result in faster speeds for all users. Your supervisors will notify you when the system is working again.

Please plan ahead in order to minimize the disruption to your workflow. If you need to use the Internet urgently during this time, the IT team can set up a temporary mobile hotspot. Please call extension 31 in that case.

Thank you for your cooperation.

발신: 헤더 콜버트
수신: 전 직원들
날짜: 12월 8일 화요일
제목: 참조용

사무실 인터넷 연결이 이번 주 목요일인 12월 10일 오전 11시 30분부터 대략 오후 1시 30분까지 이용이 불가능하게 됩니다. 이 시간에 **시스템이 업그레이드가 될 것이며**, 이로 인해 모든 사용자들이 보다 빠른 인터넷을 이용하게 될 것입니다. 여러분의 상관들이 시스템이 다시 작동하게 되는 때를 알려 줄 것입니다.

작업 흐름의 방해를 최소화하기 위해서 미리 계획을 짜 두십시오. 이 시간 중에 인터넷 사용이 긴급하다면 IT팀이 임시 모바일 핫스폿을 설치해 줄 수 있습니다. 그런 경우 내선 번호 31번으로 전화 주십시오.

협조에 감사드립니다.

어휘 unavailable 이용할 수 없는 approximately 대략, 거의 undergo 겪다 result in ~한 결과를 가져오다 supervisor 상사, 상관 notify 알려 주다 in order to do ~하기 위하여 minimize 최소화하다 disruption 중단, 혼란

1. What does Ms. Colbert indicate in the memo?

   (A) Some security cameras will undergo testing.
   (B) Employees should not visit certain Web sites.
   (C) The office will be temporarily closed on Thursday.
   (D) An Internet connection will be upgraded.

회람에서 콜버트 씨가 언급한 것은 무엇인가?

(A) 몇몇 보안 카메라를 시험할 것이다.
(B) 직원들은 특정 웹사이트들을 방문하면 안 된다.
(C) 목요일에 사무실이 임시적으로 폐쇄될 것이다.
(D) 인터넷 연결이 업그레이드될 것이다.

해설 회람을 쓴 사람이 콜버트 씨이며 전 직원에게 인터넷 시스템이 업그레이드되는 것을 공지하는 것이므로 (D)가 가장 적절하다.

4 기사

● 지문의 기본 구조

본문 p.306

Pierce Sports Sees Changes Ahead

BOSTON (February 7)—Pierce Sports has announced the acquisition of Larson Apparel for $3.4 million. Taking over the clothing company is the next step in Pierce's plans to expand its product lines.

"Larson Apparel is famous for its modern style in sportswear," explained Paul Goodwin, a spokesperson for Pierce Sports. "We are excited about offering our customers high-quality clothes for their workouts."

Pierce Sports is based in Boston and mainly serves domestic customers. However, next year it will open its first branch abroad in London. This is expected to create at least 80 new jobs.

피어스 스포츠 변화를 앞서 보다

보스턴 (2월 7일)—피어스 스포츠는 340만 달러에 라슨 어패럴의 인수를 발표했다. 의류 회사 인수는 피어슨 사의 제품 라인을 확장하려는 계획의 다음 단계이다.

"라슨 어패럴은 스포츠 의류의 최신 스타일로 유명합니다."라고 피어스 스포츠의 대변인인 폴 굿윈이 설명했다. "저희는 고객들에게 운동을 위한 고품질 의류를 제공하는 것에 마음이 들떠 있습니다."

피어스 스포츠는 보스턴에 본사를 두고 있으며 주로 국내 고객들을 대상으로 한다. 하지만, 내년에는 런던에 첫 해외 지사를 열 것이다. 이로써 최소 80개의 새로운 일자리가 만들어질 예정이다.

미니 테스트   1. (B)

본문 p.307

NAIP Conference to Be Postponed

The National Association of Insurance Providers (NAIP) has postponed its annual conference for industry professionals. The event, which was originally scheduled for November 9, will now take place on November 16.

NAIP President Marjorie McGuire cited **emergency repairs at the conference venue, Evergreen Hall, as the reason behind the date change**. Ticketholders are able to get a full refund if they cannot attend the event on the new date.

The conference will include a talk from Natalie Parsons entitled "Making Public-Private Partnerships Work". There will also be opportunities to network with other professionals in the insurance industry. More information can be found at www.naipevents.com.

NAIP 학회 연기되다

전국 보험 협회(NAIP)는 업계 전문가들을 위한 연례 학회를 연기했다. 그 행사는 원래 11월 9일로 예정되어 있었으나 현재는 11월 16일에 개최될 것이다.

NAIP의 협회장인 마저리 맥과이어는 **학회 장소인 에버그린 홀에서의 비상 보수 작업을 날짜 변경의 이유**로 언급했다. 표를 구매한 사람들은 새로운 날짜에 행사에 참석할 수 없다면 전액 환불 받을 수 있다.

학회에는 "공공-민간 협력 증진"이라는 제목의 나탈리 파슨스의 연설이 포함될 것이다. 또한, 보험 업계의 다른 전문가들과 인적 정보망을 만들 기회가 될 것이다. 추가 정보는 www.naipevents.com에서 찾아볼 수 있다.

어휘 postpone 연기하다, 미루다   association 협회   insurance 보험   annual 연례의   professional 전문가   be scheduled for ~로 예정되다   take place 발생하다   venue 장소   get a full refund 전액 환불받다   entitled ~라는 제목의

1. Why was NAIP's conference rescheduled?

   (A) A presenter could not attend the event.
   (B) Building repairs were needed unexpectedly.
   (C) Not enough tickets had been sold.
   (D) There was a booking error at the venue.

NAIP의 학회 일정이 다시 잡힌 이유는 무엇인가?

(A) 발표자가 행사에 참석할 수 없었다.
(B) 건물 보수가 예상치 않게 필요했다.
(C) 표가 충분히 판매되지 않았다.
(D) 현장에서 예약 오류가 있었다.

해설 두 번째 단락에서 학회가 연기된 이유를 emergency repairs(비상 보수 작업)라고 했다. 이를 repairs, unexpectedly라고 표현한 (B)가 정답이다.

ACTUAL TEST

본문 p.308

| 1. (B) | 2. (C) | 3. (D) | 4. (B) | 5. (B) | 6. (B) | 7. (C) |
| 8. (A) | 9. (C) | 10. (C) | 11. (C) | 12. (C) | 13. (D) | |

Help **1-1 your business** look great!

You've researched the market, found the right employees, and provided a high-quality service. But are you making a good first impression? Make sure your workplace is sparkling clean from the moment your customers walk through the door!

For a limited time, **1-2 business owners** in Worthington can get a discount on cleaning services from Enhance Cleaning. **2 Schedule your first visit before October 1 and get 50% off the regular fees.**

We can handle any cleaning job, big or small, and our experienced employees will ensure that a thorough cleaning job is done. Call us today to find out more!

Enhance Cleaning
(879) 555-6477

1-1 당신의 사업이 멋져 보이게 도와 드립니다!

당신은 시장 조사를 했고, 적합한 직원들을 찾았고, 고품질 서비스를 제공했습니다. 하지만 좋은 첫인상을 주고 있나요? 고객들이 문을 들어서는 순간부터 당신의 사업장을 눈부시도록 깨끗한 곳이 되게 하십시오!

제한된 시간 동안만, 워딩턴 지역의 1-2 사업주들은 인핸스 클리닝에서 청소 서비스 할인을 받을 수 있습니다. 2 10월 1일 전에 첫 방문 일정을 잡고 정가 요금에서 50퍼센트 할인을 받으세요.

저희는 크고 작은 어떠한 청소 작업도 처리할 수 있으며, 숙련된 직원들이 꼼꼼한 마무리를 보장합니다. 더 알고 싶으시다면 오늘 전화 주세요!

인핸스 클리닝
(879) 555-6477

어휘 impression 인상 make sure 확실히 하다 workplace 직장 sparkling 반짝이는 owner 소유주 schedule 일정을 잡다 regular fee 정가 handle 다루다, 처리하다 ensure that ~을 보장하다 thorough 꼼꼼한, 철저한

---

1. For whom is the advertisement intended?

(A) Property developers
(B) People who own a business
(C) Cleaning supplies merchants
(D) Job seekers in Worthington

광고의 대상은 누구인가?

(A) 부동산 개발자들
(B) 사업체를 소유한 사람들
(C) 청소용품 상인들
(D) 워딩턴 지역의 구직자들

해설 광고의 대상을 묻는 문제. 단서 1-1의 your business와 단서 1-2의 business owners라는 표현을 통해 사업체를 운영하는 사람들임을 알 수 있다. 정답은 (B).

어휘 property 부동산, 재산 own 소유하다 supplies 용품 merchant 상인

---

2. How can customers be eligible for an offer?

(A) By posting a review on a Web site
(B) By recommending the business to a friend
(C) By booking a service by September 30
(D) By spending at least $50

고객들은 어떻게 할인받을 자격이 될 수 있는가?

(A) 웹사이트에 후기를 게시함으로써
(B) 업체를 친구에게 추천함으로써
(C) 9월 30일까지 서비스를 예약함으로써
(D) 최소한 50달러를 소비함으로써

해설 할인을 받는 방법을 묻고 있으므로 단서 2의 get 50% off the regular fees가 언급된 문장을 확인한다. 10월 1일 전까지 방문 일정을 잡아야 할인받을 수 있다고 했으므로 before October 1을 by September 30로 바꿔 표현한 (C)가 정답이다.

어휘 be eligible for ~할 자격이 있다 offer 할인 post 게시하다 review 평가, 후기 book 예약하다 spend 소비하다 at least 최소한, 적어도

³ **Friday, February 4, from 10 A.M. to 4 P.M., a food festival will be held at Diamond Hotel to showcase local restaurants.**

Visitors can sample a variety of cuisines for free or purchase full meals at a discounted rate. There will be something for everyone, from elaborate seafood dishes to simple deli sandwiches.

⁴⁻¹ **Lori Boehm**, general manager of the Diamond Hotel, said she was delighted to have the hotel host the festival. ⁴⁻² **Thanks to her previous work as a cook at the Beam Café**, she is confident that the festival will help to boost interest in local businesses.

"Restaurants in the area need to show diners what they have to offer," Ms. Boehm said. "This festival is a great way for people to try something new."

³ 2월 4일 금요일 오전 10시부터 오후 4시까지, 지역 음식점들을 소개하기 위해 다이아몬드 호텔에서 음식 축제가 개최가 될 것이다.

방문객들은 다양한 종류의 요리들을 무료로 시식할 수 있고 할인된 가격에 식사를 할 수 있다. 정성 가득한 해산물 요리부터 간단한 델리 샌드위치까지 모두를 위한 음식이 있을 것이다.

다이아몬드 호텔의 총지배인 ⁴⁻¹ **로리 뵘**은 호텔이 축제를 주최하게 되어 기쁘다고 말했다. ⁴⁻² **뵘 카페에서 요리사로 일한 이전 경력 덕분에**, 그녀는 축제가 지역 사업체들의 흥미를 북돋는데 도움이 될 것이라고 자신한다.

"이 지역의 음식점들은 식사를 하고자 하는 사람들에게 그들이 제공할 것들을 보여 줄 필요가 있다."고 뵘 씨는 말했다. "이 축제는 사람들이 새로운 것을 시도해 볼 좋은 방법이다."

어휘 hold 개최하다 showcase 보여 주다 sample 시식하다, 시음하다 a variety of 다양한 종류의 cuisine 요리 elaborate 정성을 들인, 정교한 be delighted to do ~해서 기쁘다 host 주최하다 thanks to ~ 덕분에 previous 이전의 be confident that ~하는 것을 자신하다 boost 북돋다, 증진시키다 diner 식사하는 사람

3. Why was the article written?

(A) To announce a training session
(B) To highlight a manager's achievements
(C) To advertise an investment opportunity
(D) To promote an upcoming event

기사가 작성된 이유는 무엇인가?

(A) 교육 과정을 알리기 위해
(B) 매니저의 성과를 강조하기 위해
(C) 투자 기회를 홍보하기 위해
(D) 곧 있을 행사를 홍보하기 위해

해설 기사의 주제를 묻는 문제는 주로 맨 앞에 그 사실이 언급된다. 첫 문장에서 food festival(음식 축제)의 세부 사항을 언급하므로 이를 upcoming event(곧 있을 행사)로 바꿔 표현한 (D)가 정답이다.

어휘 highlight 강조하다 achievement 성과, 성취 investment 투자 opportunity 기회 promote 홍보하다 upcoming 곧 있을

4. What is indicated about Ms. Boehm?

(A) She is looking for a temporary job.
(B) She has experience in the restaurant business.
(C) She will prepare some food on February 4.
(D) She made a business environmentally friendly.

뵘 씨에 대해 명시된 것은 무엇인가?

(A) 그녀는 임시직을 구하고 있는 중이다.
(B) 그녀는 요식 업계에서 경력을 가지고 있다.
(C) 그녀는 2월 4일에 일부 음식을 준비할 것이다.
(D) 그녀는 사업을 친환경적으로 만들었다.

해설 기사에서 Ms. Boehm이 언급된 부분을 찾으면 단서 4-2에서 요리사로 일했음을 알 수 있다.

어휘 look for ~을 찾다 temporary 임시의 environmentally friendly 친환경적인

18 September

Dayoung Lee
873 Waterview Lane
TORONTO, ON M5B 2L3

Dear Ms. Lee,

5-1 **Thank you for choosing a Pulaski wall-mounted air conditioner.**

5-2 **Your purchase** includes a six-month warranty, which is set to expire on October 31. It's not too late to enroll in our extended warranty program. Enjoy the peace of mind that comes from protecting your appliance. You'll be able to take advantage of the following benefits:

- 6A **As many in-person repairs as needed**
- 6D **Online chat support 24 hours a day, 7 days a week**
- 6C **New air filters** sent every three months (the recommended changing period)
- Free download of our energy-saving tips smartphone application

We offer a two-, five-, and ten-year warranty. 7 **Register for the warranty length that best meets your needs using the enclosed form.** Please feel free to check out our Frequently Asked Questions page at www.pulaski.com/warranty/FAQ.

Sincerely,

Luis Costa

Enclosure

9월 18일

이다영
워터뷰 가 873
온타리오주 토론토 M5B 2L3

이 씨께,

5-1 풀라스키의 벽걸이형 에어컨을 선택해 주셔서 감사합니다.

5-2 귀하의 구입품에는 6개월 간의 품질 보증이 포함되어 있으며, 이는 10월 31일에 만기가 될 예정입니다. 저희의 장기 품질 보증 프로그램에 등록하시기에 늦지 않았습니다. 귀하의 가전제품을 보호함으로써 오는 마음의 평화를 즐기십시오. 귀하께서는 다음과 같은 혜택을 이용하실 수 있습니다.

- 6A 무제한 방문 수리
- 6D 일주일 내내 24시간 온라인 채팅 지원
- 3개월(권장 교체 시기)마다 제공되는 6C 새로운 공기 여과 필터
- 에너지 절약 팁 스마트폰 어플 무료 다운로드

저희는 2년, 5년, 10년 품질 보증을 제공합니다. 7 동봉된 서식을 사용하여 귀하의 필요를 가장 잘 충족시켜 주는 보증 기간으로 신청하세요. www.pulaski.com/warranty/FAQ에서 자주 묻는 질문 페이지를 언제든지 확인해 보십시오.

루이스 코스타

동봉

어휘 wall-mounted 벽에 고정된 warranty 품질 보증 expire 만기가 되다 enroll in ~에 등록하다 protect 보호하다 appliance 가전제품 be able to do ~할 수 있다 take advantage of ~을 이용[활용]하다 benefit 혜택 in-person 직접 period 기간

---

5. Why is Mr. Costa writing to Ms. Lee?

(A) Because she discovered some missing parts
(B) Because she bought a Pulaski product
(C) Because she contacted a customer service team
(D) Because she made a request online

코스타 씨가 이 씨에게 글을 쓰는 이유는 무엇인가?

(A) 그녀가 몇몇 잃어버린 부품을 발견했기 때문에
(B) 그녀가 풀라스키 제품을 구입했기 때문에
(C) 그녀가 고객 서비스팀에 연락했기 때문에
(D) 그녀가 온라인으로 요청을 했기 때문에

해설 단서 문장에서 choosing과 purchase가 bought로 바꿔 표현되었으므로 (B)가 정답이다.

6. What is NOT mentioned as a benefit of the extended warranty?

(A) Unlimited repairs
(B) Free shipping on returned items
(C) Air filter replacements
(D) Access to assistance anytime

장기 품질 보증의 혜택으로 언급되지 않은 것은 무엇인가?

(A) 무제한 수리
(B) 무료 반품
(C) 공기 여과 장치 교체품
(D) 언제든지 도움 받을 수 있음

해설 언급되지 않은 것을 묻는 문제는 언급된 것들을 찾아 선택지를 소거해 가야 한다. 혜택으로 나열된 부분에서 배송에 대한 것은 언급되지 않았으므로 (B)가 정답이다.

어휘 extended 연장된 replacement 교체품 access to ~에의 접근[이용] assistance 도움, 원조

7. What is included with the letter?

    (A) An instruction manual
    (B) A product catalog
    (C) A registration document
    (D) A discount voucher

편지에 포함된 것은 무엇인가?

    (A) 사용 설명서
    (B) 제품 카탈로그
    (C) 등록 서류
    (D) 할인권

해설 이메일이나 편지의 경우 첨부 파일에 대한 문제가 자주 출제된다. 주로 글의 후반부에 언급되는데, 단서 7에서 enclosed form(동봉된 서식)을 작성하여 등록하라고 했으므로 form(서식)을 document(서류)로 표현한 (C)가 정답이다.

Salvidar Inc.

Job Title: IT Support Technician

Description: Salvidar Inc. is a well-respected IT firm with a fast-growing client base using our helpdesk service. We are seeking an experienced IT professional with excellent communication skills and extensive knowledge of business-related software programs.

Key Duties: **8 Answer customer inquiries at our call center to find a solution to technical problems.** Record details of customer issues. Schedule follow-up assistance if needed.

An online skills test is required as part of the application. **9 To request a practice version of the test, e-mail HR Director Aaron Bryson at abryson@salvidarinc.com.** To apply for the position, upload your résumé at salvidarinc.com/HR.

살비다 주식회사

직책명: IT 지원 기술자

설명: 살비다 주식회사는 업무 지원 서비스를 이용하여 빠르게 성장하는 고객 기반을 가진 높이 평가되는 IT 회사입니다. 저희는 뛰어난 의사소통 기술과 사업 관련 소프트웨어 프로그램에 대한 폭넓은 지식을 가진 숙련된 IT 전문가를 구하고 있습니다.

주요 업무: **8 콜 센터로 오는 고객 문의에 응답하고 기술적 문제에 대한 해결책을 찾아 주어야 합니다.** 고객의 문제의 세부 사항을 기록해야 합니다. 필요시에는 후속 지원 일정을 잡아야 합니다.

지원 과정의 일부로 온라인 기술 테스트가 필수적입니다. **9 테스트의 연습 버전을 요청하시려면, 인사팀장인 아론 브라이슨 씨에게 abryson@salvidarinc.com으로 이메일을 보내십시오.** 직책에 지원하기 위해서는, salvidarinc.com/HR에 이력서를 업로드해 주십시오.

어휘 well-respected 존경을 받는, 높이 평가되는   base 기반   helpdesk 업무 지원   seek 찾다, 구하다   experienced 경험 있는   extensive 폭넓은   related 관련된   inquiry 문의 사항   solution to ~의 해결책   issue 문제   follow-up 후속의, 추후의   application 신청, 지원   practice 연습

8. What is a responsibility of the role?

    (A) Resolving technical issues over the phone
    (B) Writing new versions of software programs
    (C) Training coworkers in IT skills
    (D) Visiting customers' homes in person

책임 업무는 무엇인가?

    (A) 기술적 문제를 전화로 해결해 주는 것
    (B) 소프트웨어 프로그램의 새로운 버전을 작성하는 것
    (C) 동료들의 IT 기술을 교육시키는 것
    (D) 고객의 가정에 직접 방문하는 것

해설 구인 광고에서 가장 핵심적인 업무에 관한 질문. 단서 8의 find a solution to technical problems가 (A)의 Resolving technical issues로 바꿔 표현되었다.

어휘 responsibility 책임, 업무   role 역할, 직책   resolve 해결하다   coworker 동료   in person 직접

9. How can applicants receive a sample test?

    (A) By visiting a Web site
    (B) By calling Mr. Bryson
    (C) By sending an e-mail
    (D) By attending an event

지원자들이 샘플 테스트를 받을 수 있는 방법은 무엇인가?

    (A) 웹사이트에 방문함으로써
    (B) 브라이슨 씨에게 전화를 함으로써
    (C) 이메일을 보냄으로써
    (D) 행사에 참석함으로써

해설 구인 광고에서 지원자들이 해야 하는 일에 대한 부분은 주로 후반부에 나타난다. 단서 9에서 연습 버전을 요청하는 방법에 대해 나타나 있으므로 (C)가 정답이다.

어휘 applicant 지원자   attend 참석하다

NOTICE TO ELLISON BANK CUSTOMERS

Please be aware that **10-1 we will be remodeling the first floor** of our bank, including the waiting area. The hours of operation will not change during the work. They will still be Monday to Friday from 8 A.M. to 6 P.M. and Saturday from 10 A.M. to 3 P.M. **11 The project will begin this Monday, October 5, and it is supposed to be completed by the end of the month.** All banking services will still be available during this time. The work crew will try to minimize disruption. **10-2 However, there may be supplies or wires in some areas, so please take care when walking around the first floor.**

Thank you for your understanding.

Timothy Sotelo, Branch Manager

엘리슨 은행 고객께 드리는 공지

저희 은행의 대기 구역을 포함하여 **10-1 1층을 개조할 예정임**을 알려 드립니다. 작업 중에 운영 시간은 변경되지 않을 것입니다. 운영 시간은 여전히 월요일부터 금요일까지는 오전 8시부터 오후 6시까지이며 토요일에는 오전 10시부터 오후 3시까지입니다. **11 프로젝트는 10월 5일 월요일에 시작하여 그 달의 말까지 완료될 예정입니다.** 모든 은행 서비스는 이 기간 동안 여전히 이용 가능합니다. 작업반은 방해가 되는 것을 최소화하도록 노력할 것입니다. **10-2 하지만, 일부 구역에 공사 자재와 철사가 있을 수도 있으므로 1층 주변을 지나가실 때 조심해 주십시오.**

이해해 주셔서 감사합니다.

지점장 티모시 소텔로

어휘 be aware that ~을 알다   operation 운영   be supposed to *do* ~하기로 되어 있다   available 이용 가능한   disruption 방해
supplies 물품, 용품   wire 철사, 전선   take care 조심하다

10. What is the purpose of the notice?

(A) To explain the reason for a building closure
(B) To warn customers about a reduction in services
(C) To ask customers to be careful during renovations
(D) To introduce a bank's new hours of operation

공지문의 목적은 무엇인가?

(A) 건물 폐쇄의 이유를 설명하기 위해
(B) 고객들에게 서비스 축소에 대해 경고하기 위해
(C) 고객들에게 보수 중에 조심할 것을 요청하기 위해
(D) 은행의 새로운 운영 시간을 소개하기 위해

해설 공지문의 목적은 주로 글의 초반에 나타나 있다. 단서 10-1에서 은행 1층을 개조할 거라고(will be remodeling) 했으며, 10-2에서 고객들에게 주의를 당부하고 있음을(please take care) 알 수 있다. (C)에서 remodeling은 renovations로, please take care는 be careful로 바꿔 표현되었다.

어휘 closure 폐쇄   warn 경고하다   reduction 축소   careful 조심하는   operation 운영

11. When will the notice most likely be removed?

(A) October 1
(B) October 5
(C) October 31
(D) November 5

공지문이 제거되는 것은 언제일 것 같은가?

(A) 10월 1일
(B) 10월 5일
(C) 10월 31일
(D) 11월 5일

해설 단서 11에 작업 기간이 언급되어 있으며 이를 통해 추론해야 한다. 10월 5일에 시작하여 그 달 말에 완료될 예정이라고 했으므로 선택지 중 10월 31일인 (C)가 가장 적절하다.

To: Tonya Sparling
From: Frederick Pearson
Date: December 8
Subject: Change in schedule

Dear Tonya,

The management team meeting has been changed to Friday, December 10, at 9 A.M. Eastern Standard Time. Joel, our new administrative assistant, had previously scheduled the meeting for 3 P.M. However, **13 because of the different time zones, the branches in Europe would already be closed at that time.**

I explained to Joel during his orientation that it is important to keep our international branches in mind. **12 Would you please review this again with him and answer any questions he may have?** I want to make sure he is able to do scheduling tasks without support.

Thank you,

Frederick

수신: 토냐 스팔링
발신: 프레데릭 피어슨
날짜: 12월 8일
제목: 일정 변경

토냐 씨께,

관리팀 회의가 동부 표준시 기준으로 12월 10일 금요일 오전 9시로 변경되었습니다. 새로운 행정 보조인 조엘이 이전에 회의를 오후 3시로 잡았었습니다. 하지만 **13 다른 표준 시간 때문에 유럽 지사들은 그때는 이미 문을 닫을 것입니다.**

제가 오리엔테이션 중에 조엘에게 해외 지점들을 신경 쓰는 것이 중요하다고 설명을 했습니다. **12 이에 대해 그와 함께 다시 검토해 주시고 그가 궁금해할 수 있는 점에 답을 해 주실 수 있을까요?** 저는 그가 도움 없이도 일정 관련 업무를 확실히 해낼 수 있기를 바랍니다.

감사합니다.

프레데릭

어휘 administrative 행정의 assistant 보조, 조수 previously 이전에 time zone 시간대 branch 지점, 지사 at that time 그때 explain 설명하다 keep ~ in mind ~을 명심하다 be able to do ~할 수 있다 task 업무

12. Why did Mr. Pearson send the e-mail?

(A) To introduce an employee to a manager
(B) To provide an agenda for a meeting
(C) To request additional training for an employee
(D) To schedule an interview with a job candidate

피어슨 씨가 이메일을 보낸 이유는 무엇인가?

(A) 매니저에게 직원을 소개하기 위해
(B) 회의 안건을 제공하기 위해
(C) 직원의 추가 교육을 요청하기 위해
(D) 일자리 후보자와 면접을 잡기 위해

해설 이 글은 부탁을 하는 글로, 후반부에 이메일을 보낸 이유가 언급되어 있다. 앞에서 상황을 설명하고 단서 12에서 조엘에게 다시 설명을 해 줄 것을 부탁하고 있으므로 (C)가 정답이다.

어휘 agenda 안건 job candidate 일자리 후보자

13. What problem with the original meeting does Mr. Pearson mention?

(A) Some equipment was not ready for use.
(B) Mr. Pearson had another schedule at that time.
(C) It was arranged for a national holiday.
(D) It was after working hours for some branches.

피어슨 씨가 언급한 원래 회의의 문제점은 무엇인가?

(A) 일부 장비가 사용할 준비가 되지 않았다.
(B) 피어슨 씨는 그때 다른 일정이 있었다.
(C) 국경일에 일정이 잡혔다.
(D) 일부 지사의 근무 시간이 끝난 후였다.

해설 회의가 변경된 이유를 묻는 문제이다. 단서 13에서 시차 문제를 언급하고 있으며, be closed(문을 닫다)를 after working hours(근무 시간이 지난 후)로 바꿔 표현한 (D)가 정답이다.

어휘 equipment 기계, 장비 arrange 일정을 잡다

UNIT 20 지문 유형별 (2)

1 양식(form)

● 지문의 기본 구조

본문 p.316

10th Annual Design Innovation Conference
Woodby Center, Toronto ◆ April 28–30

Day 1 Schedule

9:00 A.M.	Registration and refreshments
10:00 A.M.	Presentation: "Boosting Your Design Creativity" by Isabella Hovis
11:00 A.M.	Presentation: "Managing Client Expectations" by Tiffany Bartlett
12:30 P.M.	Lunch break
1:30 P.M.	Workshop: "Software Programs That Improve Efficiency" by Simon Belmore
3:00 P.M.	Presentation: "Trends in Graphic Design" by Diane Atkins
5:00 P.M.	Question-and-Answer Session with small business owners in the field

NOTE: A buffet lunch is included in the registration fee.

제10회 연례 디자인 혁신 학회
토론토 우드비 센터, 4월 28일-30일

첫날 일정

오전 9시	등록 및 다과
오전 10시	발표: 이자벨라 호비스의 "디자인 창의력 증진하기"
오전 11시	발표: 티파니 바틀릿의 "고객 기대 사항 관리하기"
오후 12시 30분	점심 휴식
오후 1시 30분	워크숍: 사이먼 벨모어의 "효율성을 높이는 소프트웨어 프로그램"
오후 3시	발표: 다이앤 애킨스의 "그래픽 디자인 트렌드"
오후 5시	업계 소기업 경영자들과 함께 하는 질의응답 시간

참고: 등록비에는 점심 뷔페가 포함되어 있습니다.

미니 테스트   1. (C)

본문 p.317

Howard and Mitchell Inc. Customer Reviews

Please complete the form below to submit your review.

Name: Marvin Patterson
Date: May 4

I am fully satisfied with the work you carried out at my property. **My garden looks so much better now with the new flowers you planted.** I was also pleased with how thoroughly your crew cleaned up **after trimming the bushes**. I plan to use your regular maintenance services for **lawn mowing** to keep everything looking great. Thanks to your reasonable prices and a friendly crew, I highly recommend you.

Marvin

하워드 앤 미첼 사 고객 평가

아래 서식을 작성하여 귀하의 평가를 제출하세요.

이름: 마빈 패터슨
날짜: 5월 4일

저희 집에서 귀사가 해 주신 작업에 대해 전적으로 만족합니다. **저희 정원은 귀사가 심어 주신 새로운 꽃들로 이제 훨씬 더 멋져 보입니다.** 저는 귀사의 작업반이 **관목을 다듬은 후에** 꼼꼼하게 치워 주신 점도 기뻤습니다. 계속해서 전체적으로 좋아 보이도록 귀사의 **잔디 깎기** 정기 유지 보수 서비스를 이용할 계획입니다. 귀사의 합리적인 가격과 친절한 작업반 덕분에, 저는 귀사를 강력 추천합니다.

마빈

어휘 review 평가   carry out ~을 수행하다   property 부동산, 건물   plant 식물을 심다   thoroughly 꼼꼼히, 철저히   crew 작업반   trim 다듬다   bush 관목   regular 정기적인   maintenance 유지 보수   lawn mowing 잔디 깎기   reasonable 합리적인   highly recommend 강력히 추천하다

1. What type of business is Howard and Mitchell Inc.?

  (A) An inspection service
  (B) A moving company
  (C) A landscaping firm
  (D) A real estate agency

하워드 앤 미첼 사의 업종은 무엇인가?

  (A) 검사 서비스
  (B) 이사 업체
  (C) 조경 회사
  (D) 부동산 중개업

[해설] 고객 평가서를 바탕으로 회사의 업종을 파악하는 문제이다. 평가서에서 전반적으로 사용되는 어휘들이 정원을 가꾸는 일에 대한 것임을 알 수 있다. 이에 따라 하워드 앤 미첼 사는 조경 회사임을 알 수 있다. 정답은 (C).

2 메시지 대화문

● 지문의 기본 구조

본문 p.318

Erwin, Katherine [10:45 A.M.]
Levi, I need you to come to the Danby Bank construction site.

Rossi, Levi [10:47 A.M.]
What's going on?

Erwin, Katherine [10:48 A.M.]
The cement mixer has broken down. It needs to be fixed right away so we don't fall behind schedule.

Rossi, Levi [10:49 A.M.]
You've got to be kidding. I inspected it yesterday.

Erwin, Katherine [10:51 A.M.]
I know.

Rossi, Levi [10:52 A.M.]
All right. I'll be there as soon as I can.

캐서린 어윈 [오전 10시 45분]
레비, 당신이 댄비 은행 공사 현장에 좀 가야겠어요.

레비 로시 [오전 10시 47분]
무슨 일이 있나요?

캐서린 어윈 [오전 10시 48분]
시멘트 혼합기가 고장이 났어요. 우리가 일정에 늦어지지 않으려면 즉시 수리해야 해요.

레비 로시 [오전 10시 49분]
말도 안 돼요. 제가 어제 점검했는데요.

캐서린 어윈 [오전 10시 51분]
그러게요.

레비 로시 [오전 10시 52분]
알았어요. 가능한 한 빨리 가 볼게요.

미니 테스트 1. (D)

본문 p.319

Clara Bellucci (2:09 P.M.)
Mr. MacNeil, I have already received three offers for **the purchase of your home**. The people who have toured it were really impressed.

Nicholas MacNeil (2:12 P.M.)
That's wonderful! I'd like to sell it quickly, but I want to make sure I also get a good price for it. Do you expect more offers to come in?

Clara Bellucci (2:14 P.M.)
Possibly. There is one more person who wants to view the home this week. How about I call you next week so we can discuss your options?

Nicholas MacNeil (2:15 P.M.)
That sounds great. Thanks!

클라라 벨루치 (오후 2시 9분)
맥닐 씨, **당신 집 구입**에 대한 제안을 벌써 세 건이나 받았어요. 집을 둘러보고 온 사람들이 아주 깊은 인상을 받았어요.

니콜라스 맥닐 (오후 2시 12분)
잘됐네요! 저는 집을 빨리 팔고는 싶지만 좋은 가격을 받는 것도 확실히 하고 싶어요. 제안이 더 올 거라 예상하세요?

클라라 벨루치 (오후 2시 14분)
아마도요. 이번 주에 집을 보고 싶어 하는 분이 한 분 더 있어요. 당신의 선택권에 대해 논의할 수 있도록 제가 다음 주쯤 전화하는 거 어때요?

니콜라스 맥닐 (오후 2시 15분)
좋습니다. 감사해요!

[어휘] receive 받다 offer 제안 purchase 구입 impressed 깊은 인상을 받은 view 보다

1. What are the writers mainly discussing?

(A) A business loan
(B) A renovation project
(C) A travel schedule
(D) A property sale

화자들이 주로 논의하는 것은 무엇인가?

(A) 사업 대출
(B) 보수 작업
(C) 여행 일정
(D) 부동산 판매

> 해설 문자 메시지 대화의 주제를 묻는 문제이다. 대화를 나누는 두 사람은 집 매매에 대해 이야기하고 있으므로 부동산 중개인과 집주인임을 알 수 있다. 따라서 정답은 (D).

3 연계 지문_이중 지문

● 문제 풀이 전략   본문 p.320

Ace Flooring Specialists Cost Estimate	
Client: Brentwood Community Center	
DESCRIPTION OF WORK	ESTIMATED COST
Removal of 5,000 sq. ft. of old carpet	$3,750
Disposal of carpet	$800
5,000 sq. ft. of hardwood flooring (materials and labor)	$54,250
Estimated Total	$58,800
Prepared by Vince Ramos on November 8, (697) 555-8140	

에이스 플로어링 스페셜리스트 비용 견적서	
고객: 브렌트우드 커뮤니티 센터	
작업 설명	견적 비용
오래된 카펫 5,000 평방피트 제거	3,750달러
카펫 처리	800달러
원목 바닥 5,000평방피트 (재료 및 인건비)	54,250달러
견적 총액	58,800달러
11월 8일에 빈스 라모스 작성, (697) 555-8140	

To: Ruth Clark, Brentwood Community Center Director
From: Joseph Landrum, Maintenance Manager
Subject: Budget
Date: November 10

Dear Ruth,

I'd like to reserve $58,800 in next year's budget to replace the lobby's carpet with hardwood flooring. The carpet is badly worn because of our 2,000 visitors monthly, so it's time for a change anyway.

Thanks,

Joseph

수신: 루스 클락, 브렌트우드 커뮤니티 센터 관장
발신: 조셉 랜드럼, 유지 보수 부장
제목: 예산
날짜: 11월 10일

루스 씨께,

로비 카펫을 원목 바닥으로 교체하기 위해 내년 예산에서 58,800달러를 따로 빼놓고자 합니다. 매달 2,000명의 방문객들로 카펫이 몹시 마모되어 있으므로 어쨌든 교체해야 할 시기입니다.

감사합니다.

조셉

미니 테스트 1. (A)

본문 p.321

Colonial Lumber Company
630 Berkeley Street
Philadelphia, PA 19103

Colonial Lumber Company supplies high-quality wood products to individuals for woodworking projects. We offer a wide range of sizes in the following options:

Pine: A soft wood that is popular with **woodworkers at the basic level**.	Cedar: A beautiful wood known for its red tones and pleasant scent.
Oak: A sturdy wood with distinct patterns in the wood grain.	Engineered Wood: A manufactured wood made from recycled wood pieces.

We offer free delivery on orders exceeding $100. To place an order, or for inquiries, please call 267-555-9663.

콜로니얼 럼버 사
버클리 가 630
펜실베이니아주 필라델피아 19103

콜로니얼 럼버 사는 목공 작업을 하는 개인들을 위해 고품질의 원목 제품들을 공급합니다. 저희는 아래 선택 사항들을 다양한 종류의 크기로 제공합니다.

소나무: 기초 수준의 **목공 작업자**에게 인기가 많은 부드러운 목재.	삼나무: 붉은색과 기분 좋은 향기로 잘 알려진 아름다운 목재.
오크: 선명한 무늬의 나뭇결이 있는 견고한 목재.	가공 목재: 재활용된 나무 조각으로 만들어진 제조된 목재.

저희는 100달러를 초과하는 주문에 대해 무료 배송을 제공합니다. 주문을 원하시거나 문의 사항이 있으시면 267-555-9663으로 전화 주세요.

어휘 supply 공급하다 individual 개인 a wide range of 다양한 종류의 be popular with ~에게 인기가 있다 known for ~로 알려져 있다 tone 색조 pleasant 기분 좋은 scent 향기 distinct 선명한 grain 결 manufacture 제조하다 exceed 초과하다 inquiry 문의

Colonial Lumber Company: Sales Summary for March and April

Units Sold:

Wood Type	March	April
Pine	**8,965**	**9,177**
Oak	6,287	6,501
Cedar	4,884	4,960
Engineered Wood	3,133	3,279
Total	23,269	23,917

콜로니얼 럼버 사: 3, 4월 매출 요약

판매된 개수:

원목 종류	3월	4월
소나무	8,965	9,177
오크	6,287	6,501
삼나무	4,884	4,960
가공 목재	3,133	3,279
총	23,269	23,917

---

1. What is indicated about Colonial Lumber Company's top-selling product?

(A) It is used by beginners.
(B) It has a nice smell.
(C) It has noticeable patterns.
(D) It is made from recycled materials.

콜로니얼 럼버 사의 가장 잘 팔리는 제품에 대해 언급된 것은 무엇인가?

(A) 초보자들에 의해 사용된다.
(B) 좋은 향기를 가지고 있다.
(C) 뚜렷한 무늬를 가지고 있다.
(D) 재활용된 재료로 만들어진다.

해설 질문에서 가장 잘 팔리는 제품에 대해 묻고 있으므로 두 번째 지문의 표에서 가장 잘 팔리는 제품을 찾는다. 매출 수치가 소나무가 가장 높으므로 이에 표시를 해 두고 첫 번째 지문에서 소나무에 대한 설명을 확인한다. 기초 수준의 작업자에게 인기가 있다고 했으므로 이를 beginners로 표현한 (A)가 정답이다.

어휘 beginner 초보자 noticeable 뚜렷한, 선명한

4 연계 지문_삼중 지문

● 문제 풀이 전략

본문 p.322

Garden in the Sky

The Verona Community Center has just opened its new rooftop garden. It features flower gardens designed by Joshua Duarte as well as metal sculptures created by artist Loretta Cole.

하늘 정원

베로나 커뮤니티 센터는 새로운 옥상 정원을 이제 막 개방했습니다. 그곳은 예술가 로레타 콜에 의해 만들어진 금속 조각상뿐만 아니라 조슈아 두아르테에 의해 설계된 화원들로 특색을 이룹니다.

To:	Violet Piper 〈vpiper@waukeshainc.com〉
From:	Jackson Higgins 〈jhiggins@waukeshainc.com〉
Date:	August 1
Subject:	Verona trip

Dear Violet,

The travel arrangements have been made for your trip to Verona. You will be staying at the Rubin Hotel. I hope you enjoy touring the community center's new garden. I found out that Loretta Cole will be there to answer your questions on August 5.

Sincerely,

Jackson

수신: 바이올렛 파이퍼
발신: 잭슨 히긴스
날짜: 8월 1일
제목: 베로나 출장

바이올렛 씨께,

당신의 베로나 출장 준비가 되었습니다. 당신은 루빈 호텔에 체류하실 것입니다. 커뮤니티 센터의 새로운 정원 관람을 즐기셨으면 합니다. 8월 5일에 당신의 질문에 답을 하기 위해 그곳에 로레타 콜 씨도 온다는 것을 알게 되었습니다.

잭슨

http://rubinhotel.com/home

At Rubin Hotel, we aim to provide guests with a relaxing and comfortable atmosphere. We have just completed construction on our building and we are excited to share it with you. Visit our Booking page to make a reservation.

http://rubinhotel.com/home

저희 루빈 호텔에서는 투숙객들에게 편안한 분위기를 제공하는 것을 목표로 하고 있습니다. 저희는 건물 공사를 이제 막 완료하였으며 이곳을 귀하게 제공해 드리게 되어 기쁩니다. 예약을 하시려면 예약 페이지를 방문해 주세요.

미니 테스트　　1. (D)　　2. (B)

본문 p.323

VITORIA (February 17)—Salvim Laboratories has confirmed that the company has nearly completed the development of a new variety of soybean called Formosa. The plant needs much less water compared to other soybeans. Upon the completion of this project, **1-2 the next generation of Formosa will begin to be developed. It will have a much shorter growing time than previous varieties**.

비토리아 (2월 17일)–살빔 연구소는 포모사라고 불리는 새로운 품종의 대두 개발을 거의 완료했다고 밝혔다. 이 식물은 다른 대두에 비해 물이 훨씬 덜 필요하다. 이 프로젝트가 완료되자마자, **1-2 포모사의 다음 세대가 개발되기 시작할 것이다. 그것은 이전 품종들보다 성장 기간이 훨씬 더 짧을 것이다.**

어휘 development 개발　variety 품종　soybean 대두　compared to ~와 비교하여　completion 완료　generation 세대　previous 이전의

Salvim Laboratories is Hiring!

We have openings in Information Technology, Research and Development, Human Resources, and Sales as we begin the development of **1-1 Damasio, the next generation of the popular Formosa soybean plant.** Previous experience is required for all positions. **2-2 In addition, Research and Development applicants must have a degree in a scientific field.** Apply online at salvimlabs.com.

살빔 연구소는 채용 중입니다!

저희는 **1-1 인기 있는 포모사 대두 식물의 다음 세대인 다마시오**의 개발을 시작하며 정보 기술부, 연구 개발부, 인사부, 그리고 영업부에 직원을 채용하고 있습니다. 모든 직책에 이전 경력이 요구됩니다. **2-2 또한, 연구 개발부의 지원자들은 과학 분야에 학위를 가지고 있어야만 합니다.** salvimlabs.com으로 온라인 지원하세요.

어휘 hire 고용하다, 채용하다   popular 인기 있는   degree 학위   field 분야

To: Yasmin Santos
From: Matheus Costa
Date: July 31
Subject: Document

Dear Ms. Santos,

I would like to thank you once again for the job offer. I am excited about joining the Salvim Laboratories staff. **2-1 Please find attached proof of my degree, which is required for the position.** If you need anything else, please let me know.

Warmest regards,

Matheus Costa

수신: 야스민 산토스
발신: 마테우스 코스타
날짜: 7월 31일
제목: 서류

산토스 씨께,

저는 당신께 일자리 제안에 대해 다시 한번 감사를 드리고 싶습니다. 저는 살빔 연구소 직원으로 합류하게 되어 기쁩니다. **2-1 직책에 요구되는 학위 증명을 첨부하였습니다.** 다른 것이 필요하다면 알려 주십시오.

마테우스 코스타

어휘 job offer 일자리 제안   attached 첨부된   proof 증명, 입증

1. What is a feature of Damasio?

(A) It will produce more beans.
(B) It will use less water.
(C) It will have a better flavor.
(D) It will grow more quickly.

다마시오의 특징은 무엇인가?

(A) 더 많은 콩을 생산할 것이다.
(B) 물을 덜 사용할 것이다.
(C) 더 좋은 맛을 낼 것이다.
(D) 더 빨리 자랄 것이다.

해설 다마시오가 언급된 부분을 찾는다. 두 번째 지문의 단서 1-1에서 포모사의 다음 세대 식물임을 알 수 있으며, 첫 번째 지문에서 다음 세대 식물의 장점을 언급하고 있다. 따라서, 단서 1-2를 바꿔 표현한 (D)가 정답이다.

어휘 feature 특징   produce 생산하다   bean 콩   flavor 맛, 풍미

2. In which department will Mr. Costa work?

(A) Information Technology
(B) Research and Development
(C) Sales
(D) Human Resources

코스타 씨는 어떤 부서에서 일을 할 것인가?

(A) 정보 기술부
(B) 연구 개발부
(C) 영업부
(D) 인사부

해설 코스타 씨는 이메일을 쓴 사람으로 단서 2-1에서 학위 증명을 보낸다고 했으며, 두 번째 지문에서 학위가 필요한 직책으로 연구 개발부를 언급하고 있다. 이 두 가지 단서를 종합하면 (B)가 정답임을 알 수 있다.

ACTUAL TEST

본문 p.324

| 1. (D) | 2. (C) | 3. (B) | 4. (B) | 5. (A) | 6. (D) | 7. (D) |
| 8. (C) | 9. (B) | 10. (C) | 11. (B) | 12. (B) | 13. (C) | 14. (D) |

Dobson Resort
1317 Columbia Road
Denver, CO 80231
Telephone: 720-555-3216

Dear Brett Lewis,

We would like to remind you that **1-1 your membership** will expire on August 31. Be sure to renew it **1-2 so that you can continue playing golf at our site**. In addition to giving you unlimited time on the course, membership also allows you to get 10 percent off all equipment at the Dobson Resort clubhouse and **2 15 percent off meals at our restaurant**.

To make a renewal, visit www.dobsonresort.com.

돕슨 리조트
컬럼비아 가 1317
콜로라도 덴버 80231
전화번호: 720-555-3216

브렛 루이스 씨께,

1-1 귀하의 멤버십이 8월 31일에 만기가 될 것임을 상기시켜 드리고자 합니다. **1-2 저희 구역에서 골프를 계속 치기 위해서는** 반드시 갱신을 하셔야 합니다. 멤버십은 코스에서 무제한 시간을 드릴 뿐만 아니라, 돕슨 리조트 클럽하우스에서 모든 장비에 10퍼센트 할인과 **2 저희 식당에서 15퍼센트의 식사 할인**을 받을 수 있게 해드립니다.

갱신하시려면 www.dobsonresort.com에 방문하세요.

어휘 remind 상기시키다 expire 만기되다 be sure to do 반드시 ~하다 renew 갱신하다 site 장소, 현장 in addition to ~ 외에도, ~뿐만 아니라 unlimited 무제한의 equipment 장비 meal 식사 renewal 갱신

---

1. Who most likely is Mr. Lewis?

(A) A business investor
(B) A resort owner
(C) A golf instructor
(D) A golf club member

루이스 씨는 누구인 것 같은가?

(A) 사업 투자자
(B) 리조트 소유주
(C) 골프 강사
(D) 골프 클럽 회원

해설 이 엽서를 받는 사람이 누구인지 묻는 문제이다. 단서 1-1과 1-2를 바탕으로 골프 클럽 회원임을 알 수 있다. 정답은 (D).

어휘 investor 투자자 instructor 강사

---

2. What is indicated about Dobson Resort?

(A) It provides customers with free equipment.
(B) Its prices will increase after August 31.
(C) It has an on-site dining facility.
(D) It will open a new location soon.

돕슨 리조트에 대해 언급된 것은 무엇인가?

(A) 고객들에게 장비를 무료로 제공한다.
(B) 8월 31일 이후에 가격이 인상될 것이다.
(C) 현장에 식사 시설이 있다.
(D) 곧 새로운 지점을 열 것이다.

해설 단서 2에서 골프 클럽이 소유한 식당에서 할인을 받을 수 있다고 했으므로 (C)가 정답이다.

어휘 provide A with B A에게 B를 제공하다 on-site 현장의 facility 시설

Eva Peralta [11:03 A.M.]
³**What was the magazine you needed for the training workshop?** I'm at a newsstand. I could look for it now.

Spencer Gresham [11:07 A.M.]
It's called World Finance, and I need the June edition. There's an interesting article in it that I wanted to share.

Eva Peralta [11:08 A.M.]
All right. I'll check for you.

Eva Peralta [11:12 A.M.]
They have it! I'll pay cash for it and get ⁴⁻¹ **a receipt.** ⁴⁻² **Please submit that** so I can get reimbursed. It's a small amount, but it's still a business expense.

Spencer Gresham [11:13 A.M.]
I'll do that. Thanks!

어휘 newsstand 신문 잡지 판매대 look for ~을 찾다 share 공유하다 receipt 영수증 submit 제출하다 reimburse 환급하다 expense 비용

에바 페랄타 [오전 11시 3분]
³ 교육 워크숍에 필요하다고 했던 잡지가 뭐였죠? 제가 신문 잡지 판매대에 있는데요. 지금 그걸 찾아보려고요.

스펜서 그레셤 [오전 11시 7분]
'월드 파이낸스'라고 불리는 건데요, 6월호가 필요해요. 거기에 제가 공유하고 싶은 흥미로운 기사가 있어요.

에바 페랄타 [오전 11시 8분]
알았어요. 확인해 드릴게요.

에바 페랄타 [오전 11시 12분]
있다고 해요! 제가 현금으로 그걸 사고 ⁴⁻¹ **영수증**을 받을게요. 제가 환급을 받을 수 있도록 ⁴⁻² **그것을 제출해 주세요.** 적은 금액이지만 여전히 업무 비용이니까요.

스펜서 그레셤 [오전 11시 13분]
그렇게 할게요. 고마워요!

---

3. What is probably true about the magazine?

(A) It is not sold at most newsstands.
(B) It will be used in a training session.
(C) It has an article about Ms. Peralta.
(D) It is published once a week.

그 잡지에 대해 아마도 사실인 것은 무엇인가?

(A) 대부분의 신문 잡지 판매대에서 판매하지 않는다.
(B) 교육 과정에 사용될 것이다.
(C) 페랄타 씨에 대한 기사가 있다.
(D) 일주일에 한 번씩 출간된다.

해설 대화문에서 잡지가 언급된 단서 3을 바탕으로 (B)가 정답임을 알 수 있다.

어휘 probably 아마도 publish 출간하다

4. At 11:13 A.M., what does Mr. Gresham mean when he writes, "I'll do that"?

(A) He will meet Ms. Peralta.
(B) He will submit a receipt.
(C) He will withdraw some cash.
(D) He will check a policy.

오전 11시 13분에, 그레셤 씨가 "그렇게 할게요"라고 말한 의도는 무엇인가?

(A) 그는 페랄타 씨를 만날 것이다.
(B) 그는 영수증을 제출할 것이다.
(C) 그는 약간의 현금을 인출할 것이다.
(D) 그는 정책을 확인할 것이다.

해설 대화문에 반드시 출제되는 의도 파악 문제는 바로 앞뒤 문장의 상황을 살펴보아야 한다. 앞에 있는 문장의 단서 4에서 that이 가리키는 것이 a receipt임을 알면 (B)가 정답임을 알 수 있다.

어휘 withdraw 인출하다 policy 정책

7-2 To: Timothy Hensley
From: Zaida Dawson
Subject: Reimbursement request
Date: June 18
Attachment: business expenses form, Dawson receipts

Hi Mr. Hensley,

[6] **I started working at Medina Enterprises a couple of weeks ago**, and I've already completed my first business trip. My manager told me that [5] **I should send the receipts for my business expenses** [7-1] **to the finance team**, along with a completed form. As I understand it, the cost of the airline tickets, hotel, and taxi fares are [8] **covered**. In addition, [9-1] **I can receive reimbursement for up to $45 per day for my meals**.

Please find the necessary details on the attached form. Scans of the relevant receipts are also attached. I used taxis to travel between the airport and the hotel as well as between the hotel and the convention center. If you need further details, please let me know.

Sincerely,

Zaida Dawson

어휘 reimbursement 환급 receipt 영수증 complete 완료하다 fare 요금 up to ~까지 meal 식사 necessary 필요한 attached 첨부된 relevant 관련된 as well as ~뿐만 아니라

Medina Enterprises Business Expenses Form

To receive reimbursement, please complete this form and submit it to the finance team. Receipts should be provided. The reimbursement will be processed within five business days.

Employee Name: Zaida Dawson
Reason for Expenses: Business trip to attend annual sales convention in Dallas, Texas

Category	Dates			
	June 12	June 13	June 14	June 15
Airline Tickets	$235.00	—	—	$235.00
Taxi Fares	$56.00	$14.80	$15.90	$53.00
Hotel	$129.00	$129.00	$129.00	$129.00
[9-2] Meals	$28.50	**$52.00**	$43.50	$18.00

어휘 submit 제출하다 process 처리하다 within ~ 이내에 annual 연례의

5. What is the purpose of the e-mail?

(A) To comply with a process
(B) To sign up for an event
(C) To schedule a meeting
(D) To recommend a job opportunity

이메일의 목적은 무엇인가?

(A) 절차를 준수하기 위해
(B) 행사에 등록하기 위해
(C) 회의 일정을 잡기 위해
(D) 일자리 기회를 추천하기 위해

> 해설) 첫 번째 이메일 지문의 목적을 묻는 문제. 단서 5에서 부장이 알려 준 비용 처리 절차에 대해 언급하고 있으므로 이를 포괄적으로 표현한 (A)가 정답이다.

> 어휘) comply with ~을 준수하다   sign up for ~에 등록하다, ~을 신청하다   opportunity 기회

6. What does Ms. Dawson mention about herself?

(A) She gave a talk at a conference.
(B) She has lost a receipt.
(C) She used to live in Texas.
(D) She is a new employee.

도슨 씨가 자신에 대해 언급한 것은 무엇인가?

(A) 그녀는 학회에서 연설을 했다.
(B) 그녀는 영수증을 잃어버렸다.
(C) 그녀는 텍사스에 살았었다.
(D) 그녀는 신입 직원이다.

> 해설) 단서 6에서 몇 주 전부터 일을 시작했다고 했으므로 신입임을 알 수 있다. 정답은 (D).

> 어휘) give a talk 연설하다   receipt 영수증   used to do ~하곤 했다

7. What is suggested about Mr. Hensley?

(A) He works at a different branch from Ms. Dawson.
(B) He is Ms. Dawson's manager.
(C) He is in charge of scheduling business trips.
(D) He is a member of the finance team.

헨슬리 씨에 대해 암시되는 것은 무엇인가?

(A) 그는 도슨 씨와 다른 지점에서 일한다.
(B) 그는 도슨 씨의 부장이다.
(C) 그는 출장 일정을 잡는 일을 담당한다.
(D) 그는 재무팀원이다.

> 해설) 먼저 헨슬리 씨가 언급된 부분을 찾아보면, 이메일 수신자에 해당 이름이 나타나 있다. 단서 7-1에서 재무팀에 영수증과 서식을 보낸다고 했으므로 수신자인 헨슬리 씨가 이 팀에 있음을 알 수 있다. 따라서 정답은 (D). 이메일의 경우 수신자, 발신자 등의 정보도 잘 살펴야 한다.

> 어휘) branch 지점, 지사   in charge of ~을 담당하는

8. In the e-mail, the word "covered" in paragraph 1, line 4, is closest in meaning to

(A) wrapped up
(B) kept safe
(C) paid for
(D) stored away

이메일에서 첫 번째 단락 네 번째 줄의 "covered"와 의미상 가장 가까운 것은?

(A) 마무리된
(B) 안전하게 보관된
(C) 지불된
(D) 비축된

> 해설) 동의어 찾기 문제는 해당 단어가 그 문장에서 어떠한 의미로 쓰였는지를 파악해야 한다. '덮다'라는 의미의 cover는 '보상하다, 돈을 대다'라는 의미도 가지고 있다. 문장 내에서 출장 비용이 지불되는 것을 언급하고 있으므로 (C)가 정답이다.

9. For which day's expenses will Ms. Dawson not receive full reimbursement?

(A) June 12
(B) June 13
(C) June 14
(D) June 15

도슨 씨는 어떤 날의 비용을 전액 환급받지 못하게 될 것인가?

(A) 6월 12일
(B) 6월 13일
(C) 6월 14일
(D) 6월 15일

> 해설) 두 지문의 내용을 종합해서 풀어야 하는 연계 문제. 도슨 씨는 단서 9-1에서 식비에 대해 언급하고 있고, 아래 서식에 그 내역이 표로 정리되어 있다. 식비는 하루에 45달러까지 환급받을 수 있는데, 두 번째 지문에 6월 13일 식비가 52달러라고 써 있으므로 해당 날짜의 식비는 일부만 환급받게 됨을 알 수 있다.

From: Christina Irving, General Manager
To: All Charleston branch employees
Date: April 3
Subject: Building closure

10 **The Hodge Building will be closed from 4 P.M. on Friday, April 7, to both employees and visitors so that a new air conditioning system can be installed.** 11 **The new system will be more energy efficient than the current one. It will consume much less electricity each month.**

Employees can leave work at 4 P.M. without using any vacation time. Please note that the building will also be closed for part of Saturday, as the 13-1 **work is expected to be completed by Saturday morning around 11 A.M.** 14-1 **To prevent dust from getting into your work computers, please cover them with plastic sheets before you leave on Friday.** Materials are provided in the Human Resources office.

발신: 크리스티나 어빙, 총괄 매니저
수신: 찰스톤 지점 전 직원들
날짜: 4월 3일
제목: 건물 폐쇄

10 4월 7일 금요일 오후 4시부터 새로운 에어컨 시스템이 설치될 수 있도록 직원들과 방문자들 모두에게 호지 빌딩이 폐쇄됩니다. 11 새로운 시스템은 현재의 시스템보다 에너지 효율이 더 좋을 것입니다. 그것은 매달 전기를 훨씬 덜 소비할 것입니다.

직원들은 휴가를 사용하지 않고 4시에 퇴근을 하실 수 있습니다. 13-1 작업은 토요일 아침 11시 정도까지 완료될 예정이므로 토요일에도 일부 시간 건물이 폐쇄될 것임을 유념해 주십시오. 14-1 업무 컴퓨터에 먼지가 들어가는 것을 막기 위해, 금요일 퇴근 전에 컴퓨터를 비닐로 덮어 주십시오. 재료는 인사부 사무실에서 제공됩니다.

어휘 closure 폐쇄 | install 설치하다 | efficient 효율적인 | current 현재의 | consume 소비하다 | electricity 전기 | around 대략 | prevent A from B A가 B하는 것을 막다 | dust 먼지 | cover 덮다 | plastic sheet 비닐 | material 재료

TELEPHONE MESSAGE

For: Christina Irving
Caller (Company): 12-1 **Samuel Cordova** (Nelson Inc.)
Date: Thursday, April 6
Time: 10:52 A.M.

☑ New call
☐ Returning your call
☐ Please call back
☑ Caller left a message (see below)

Message:
12-2 **Some of the components needed for the installation will not be delivered until Friday evening.** Because of this, we cannot begin the work as planned. That also means 13-2 **the work will be completed about three hours later than we had originally promised.**

Message taken by: Aaron Trin

전화 메시지

수신인: 크리스티나 어빙
발신인 (회사): 12-1 **사무엘 코도바** (넬슨 사)
날짜: 4월 6일 목요일
시각: 오전 10시 52분

☑ 새로운 전화
☐ 회답 전화
☐ 전화를 주세요
☑ 발신인이 메시지 남김 (아래 참고)

메시지:
12-2 설치에 필요한 일부 부품들이 금요일 저녁이 되어서야 배송될 것입니다. 이 때문에 저희는 계획대로 작업을 시작할 수 없습니다. 이는 또한 13-2 저희가 원래 약속했던 것보다 3시간 정도 늦게 작업이 완료될 것이라는 걸 의미합니다.

메시지 수신: 아론 트린

어휘 installation 설치 | deliver 배송하다 | as planned 계획대로 | originally 원래

From:	Dean Boyd
To:	Finance Team
Date:	April 6
Subject:	Closure

Dear Team,

I have just been informed that tomorrow's installation work will begin later than planned. If you have any work projects to finish up, you do not need to leave the building at four o'clock. Whether you leave early or on time, ¹⁴⁻² **please remember to carry out the necessary preparations requested by Ms. Irving in her memo.**

Thanks!

Dean

발신: 딘 보이드
수신: 재무팀
날짜: 4월 6일
제목: 폐쇄

팀원들께,

내일 설치 작업이 계획보다 늦게 시작될 것이라는 걸 방금 알게 되었습니다. 끝내야 할 프로젝트가 있다면 4시에 건물을 떠나지 않아도 됩니다. 일찍 퇴근을 하든 정시 퇴근을 하든 상관없이 ¹⁴⁻² **어빙 씨가 회람에서 요청했던 필요한 준비를 수행할 것을 기억해 주십시오.**

감사합니다!

딘

어휘 inform 알리다　whether A or B A이든 B이든　carry out ~을 수행하다, ~을 실행하다　necessary 필요한

10. According to the memo, why will the Hodge Building be temporarily closed?

(A) A potential buyer will take a tour.
(B) Safety inspections will be conducted.
(C) A cooling system will be installed.
(D) Some walls will be painted.

회람에 따르면, 호지 빌딩이 임시 폐쇄되는 이유는 무엇인가?

(A) 잠재 구매자가 건물을 둘러볼 것이다.
(B) 안전 검사가 실시될 것이다.
(C) 냉방 시스템이 설치될 것이다.
(D) 일부 벽에 페인트칠이 될 것이다.

해설 단서 10의 a new air conditioning system(새로운 에어컨 시스템)이 A cooling system으로 바꿔 표현된 (C)가 정답이다.

어휘 temporarily 임시로　potential 잠재적인　inspection 검사, 점검　conduct 실시하다

11. What benefit of the change does Ms. Irving mention?

(A) Increasing security
(B) Using less energy
(C) Saving time
(D) Attracting new clients

어빙 씨가 언급한 변경의 이점은 무엇인가?

(A) 보안을 높이는 것
(B) 에너지를 덜 쓰는 것
(C) 시간을 절약하는 것
(D) 신규 고객을 유치하는 것

해설 단서 11에서 에어컨 시스템 변경에 대해 언급하고 있으며, 에너지 효율이 좋아 전기를 덜 소비할 것이라고 했으므로 (B)가 정답이다.

어휘 benefit 혜택, 이점　security 보안　attract 끌어들이다, 유치하다

12. Why did Mr. Cordova call Ms. Irving?

(A) To ask how to access a building
(B) To explain a problem with some parts
(C) To report an issue with a regulation
(D) To get approval on a budget increase

코도바 씨가 어빙 씨에게 전화를 한 이유는 무엇인가?

(A) 건물 출입 방법을 물어보기 위해
(B) 일부 부품의 문제를 설명하기 위해
(C) 규정에 대한 문제를 보고하기 위해
(D) 예산 증가에 대해 승인을 받기 위해

해설 두 번째 지문의 주제를 묻는 문제. 단서 12-2에서 일부 부품의 배송이 늦어진다는 메시지를 남겼으며 components를 parts로 바꿔 표현한 (B)가 정답이다.

어휘 access 접근하다　part 부품　regulation 규정　approval 승인　budget 예산

13. What is the new expected time for the project to be completed?

(A) Friday evening
(B) Saturday morning
(C) Saturday afternoon
(D) Sunday morning

프로젝트가 완료되는 새로운 예상 시간은 언제인가?
(A) 금요일 저녁
(B) 토요일 아침
(C) 토요일 오후
(D) 일요일 아침

해설 첫 번째 지문과 두 번째 지문의 연계 문제이다. 단서 13-1에서 작업이 토요일 아침 11시에 완료될 것이라고 했으나, 단서 13-2에서 3시간 정도 늦어진다고 했으므로 대략 오후 2시 정도에 마무리될 것임을 알 수 있다. 이를 토요일 오후라고 표현한 (C)가 정답이다.

14. What does Mr. Boyd remind his team to do?

(A) Use a different entrance
(B) Move some office furniture
(C) Take personal items home
(D) Cover some equipment

보이드 씨가 그의 팀에게 상기시키는 것은 무엇인가?
(A) 다른 출입구를 사용하는 것
(B) 일부 사무 가구를 옮기는 것
(C) 개인 물품을 집으로 가져가는 것
(D) 일부 장비를 덮는 것

해설 첫 번째 지문과 세 번째 지문의 연계 문제이다. 단서 14-2에서 보이드 씨가 팀원들에게 어빙 씨가 요청했던 단서 14-1의 내용을 상기시키고 있다. 단서의 computers를 equipment로 바꿔 표현한 (D)가 정답이다.

어휘 remind 상기시키다 entrance 출입구 furniture 가구 equipment 장비

실전 모의고사

본문 p.332

101. (B)	102. (D)	103. (A)	104. (A)	105. (D)	106. (A)	107. (D)	108. (B)	109. (A)	110. (C)
111. (B)	112. (A)	113. (A)	114. (C)	115. (A)	116. (C)	117. (C)	118. (A)	119. (C)	120. (A)
121. (B)	122. (C)	123. (C)	124. (B)	125. (C)	126. (D)	127. (D)	128. (C)	129. (D)	130. (C)
131. (C)	132. (A)	133. (D)	134. (D)	135. (C)	136. (A)	137. (C)	138. (A)	139. (A)	140. (B)
141. (C)	142. (B)	143. (C)	144. (C)	145. (A)	146. (B)	147. (B)	148. (B)	149. (B)	150. (D)
151. (D)	152. (C)	153. (B)	154. (B)	155. (A)	156. (C)	157. (A)	158. (C)	159. (B)	160. (D)
161. (B)	162. (D)	163. (C)	164. (D)	165. (D)	166. (B)	167. (A)	168. (D)	169. (D)	170. (C)
171. (A)	172. (D)	173. (C)	174. (B)	175. (D)	176. (D)	177. (C)	178. (C)	179. (A)	180. (C)
181. (C)	182. (D)	183. (A)	184. (C)	185. (D)	186. (A)	187. (B)	188. (B)	189. (D)	190. (C)
191. (B)	192. (C)	193. (A)	194. (A)	195. (D)	196. (C)	197. (A)	198. (B)	199. (B)	200. (C)

101.

All valuables are stored **securely** in the hotel's safe.

(A) secures
(B) **securely**
(C) security
(D) secure

모든 귀중품은 호텔 금고에 안전하게 보관된다.

해설 부사 자리 [동사 수식] 빈칸은 동사구 are stored를 수식하는 부사 자리이므로 (B) securely가 정답이다.

어휘 valuable ((보통 복수형)) 귀중품; 귀중한 securely 안전하게 safe 금고; 안전한 secure 확보하다; 안전한

102.

Following an intense **negotiation**, the Alvarado Inc. managers were able to finalize the contract's terms.

(A) negotiate
(B) negotiated
(C) negotiating
(D) **negotiation**

치열한 협상 끝에 알바라도 사의 운영자들은 계약 조건을 마무리 지을 수 있었다.

해설 명사 자리 [전치사의 목적어] 빈칸은 전치사 following의 목적어 자리이며, 부정관사 an과 형용사 intense의 수식을 받는 명사 자리이므로 (D) negotiation이 정답이다.

어휘 following ~ 후에; 그 다음의 intense 치열한, 극심한 terms ((항상 복수형)) (합의, 계약 등의) 조건

103.

A reception was held to welcome Ms. Dennis and **her** team.

(A) **her**
(B) hers
(C) she
(D) herself

데니스 씨와 그녀의 팀을 환영하기 위해 환영회가 열렸다.

해설 소유격 자리 빈칸은 명사 team을 수식하는 자리이므로 명사를 수식할 수 있는 소유격인 (A) her가 정답이다.

어휘 reception 환영회 hold (모임, 식 등을) 열다, 개최하다

104.

The human resources department **maintains** the compliance records required by the federal government.

(A) **maintains**
(B) cultivates
(C) persuades
(D) associates

인사부는 연방 정부에 의해 요구되는 (규정) 준수 기록을 **유지한다**.

(A) 유지하다
(B) 경작하다
(C) 설득하다
(D) 관련시키다

해설 동사 어휘 명사구 the compliance records를 목적어로 취해 가장 자연스럽게 의미가 통하는 동사를 골라야 한다. 문맥상 연방 정부에서 요구하는 규정 등에 대한 준수 기록을 유지한다는 내용이 되는 게 자연스러우므로 '(수준 등을 동일하게) 지키다, 유지하다'라는 의미의 (A) maintains가 정답이다.

어휘 human resources department 인사부 compliance (법, 명령 등의) 준수 federal government 연방 정부

210

105.

Fairway Shipping cannot issue refunds for delays caused by circumstances **beyond** its control.

(A) below (B) before
(C) behind **(D) beyond**

페어웨이 통운은 통제를 **넘어선** 상황으로 인한 지연에 대해서는 환불금을 지급하지 못한다.

(A) ~ 아래에 (B) ~ 전에
(C) ~ 뒤에 **(D) ~ 너머에**

> **해설** 전치사 어휘 명사구 its control을 목적어로 취해 가장 자연스럽게 의미가 통하는 전치사를 골라야 한다. 문맥상 회사가 통제할 수 있는 범위를 벗어난 일 등으로 인해 배송이 지연됐을 때는 환불해 줄 수 없다는 내용이 되는 게 적절하므로 '~ 너머에'라는 의미의 (D) beyond가 정답이다. beyond (one's) control은 '불가항력적인, 제어할 수 없는'이라는 뜻으로, 어떻게도 할 수 없는 상황을 묘사할 때 잘 쓰인다.
>
> **어휘** issue 발부하다, 지급하다 refund 환불(금) delay 지연, 지체; 미루다 circumstance ((보통 복수형)) 환경, 상황

106.

Nothing can be spent on repairs without the written consent of the building manager.

(A) Nothing (B) Never
(C) Somebody (D) Another

건물 관리자의 서면 동의 없이는 아무것도 수리에 쓰일 수 없다.

> **해설** 부정대명사 빈칸은 수동태 문장의 주어 자리이며, 문맥상 건물 관리자의 동의 없이는 아무것도 수리에 쓰일 수 없다는 내용이 되는 게 자연스러우므로 (A) Nothing이 정답이다. (B) Never는 부사이고, (C) Somebody는 사람을 가리키는 부정대명사이므로 빈칸에 적절하지 않다. (D) Another는 '또 하나, 또 다른 것[사람]'을 의미하므로 오답이다.
>
> **어휘** spend 시간/돈 on ~에 [시간/돈]을 쓰다 repair 수리, 보수; 수리하다 consent 동의, 허락; 동의[허락]하다

107.

Under the new policy, salespeople are responsible for **finding** their own clients.

(A) to find (B) find
(C) found **(D) finding**

새로운 정책 하에 판매원들은 그들만의 고객을 찾을 책임이 있다.

> **해설** 동명사 자리 [전치사의 목적어] 빈칸은 전치사 for의 목적어 역할을 하는 명사 자리이므로 동명사 (D) finding이 정답이다.
>
> **어휘** policy 정책, 방침 salespeople 판매원 be responsible for ~에 책임이 있다; ~을 책임지고 있다

108.

The shuttle bus was running behind schedule due to getting **stuck** in rush-hour traffic.

(A) forced **(B) stuck**
(C) rejected (D) stood

셔틀버스가 혼잡 시간대의 교통 체증에 **갇혀 꼼짝 못 하게 되어** 일정보다 늦게 운행하고 있었다.

(A) 강요된 **(B) 꼼짝 못 하게 된**
(C) 거절된 (D) 세워진

> **해설** 형용사 어휘 빈칸 앞의 getting과 어울려 가장 자연스럽게 의미가 통하는 형용사를 골라야 한다. 문맥상 셔틀버스가 교통 체증에 갇혀서 일정보다 늦게 운행했다는 내용이 되는 게 자연스러우므로 '꼼짝 못 하게 된'이라는 의미의 (B) stuck이 정답이다. get stuck은 '꼼짝 못 하게 되다'라는 뜻으로, 무언가에 갇히거나 끼여 난처한 상황을 묘사할 때 자주 쓰인다.
>
> **어휘** run (버스, 기차 등이) 운행하다 behind schedule 일정[예정]보다 늦게 due to ~ 때문에

109.

The theater's parking lot fills up quickly, so we **recommend** arriving early to find a spot.

(A) recommend (B) recommendation
(C) to recommend (D) recommending

극장의 주차장은 빨리 만차가 되므로 자리를 찾기 위해 일찍 도착할 것을 권장합니다.

> **해설** 동사 자리 빈칸 앞에 주어 we가 있고 뒤에는 동명사 arriving이 있으므로 빈칸은 동사 자리이다. 따라서 (A) recommend가 정답이다. recommend는 동명사를 목적어로 취해 '~하는 것을 권하다'라는 의미로 쓰인다.
>
> **어휘** fill up 가득 채워지다; ~을 가득 채우다 spot (특정한) 장소, 자리 recommendation 권고, 추천

110.

Banquet guests received a bag of party **favors** when they arrived.

(A) favored	(B) to favor
(C) favors	(D) favorably

연회 손님들은 그들이 도착했을 때 파티 선물 가방을 받았다.

해설 명사 자리 [복합 명사] 빈칸은 명사 party와 복합 명사를 이루어 전치사 of의 목적어 역할을 할 명사 자리이다. 따라서 (C) favors가 정답이다. party favor는 파티 등에 참석한 손님에게 주는 기념품 같은 작은 선물을 가리킨다.

어휘 banquet 연회, 만찬

111.

New safety measures will be implemented at the factory **later** this month.

(A) soon	**(B) later**
(C) often	(D) almost

공장에서의 새로운 안전 대책이 이번 달 **말에** 시행될 것이다.

(A) 곧	**(B) 나중에, 후에**
(C) 자주	(D) 거의

해설 부사 어휘 빈칸 뒤의 this month와 어울려 가장 자연스럽게 의미가 통하는 부사를 골라야 한다. '나중에, 후에'라는 의미의 later는 today, this month, this year 같은 표현 앞에 위치하여 '오늘 늦게', '이번 달 말에', '올해 말에'를 의미하므로 (B) later가 정답이다.

어휘 safety measures 안전 대책 implement 시행하다

112.

The hotel's lobby will be repainted because the current color is too **bright**.

(A) bright	(B) brightly
(C) brighter	(D) brightest

그 호텔의 로비는 현재 색상이 너무 밝아서 다시 칠해질 것이다.

해설 형용사 자리 [주격 보어] 빈칸은 be동사 is 뒤의 주격 보어 자리이자 부사 too의 수식을 받는 형용사 자리이므로 (A) bright가 정답이다.

어휘 repaint 다시 칠하다 bright 밝은

113.

The Harrison Gym invited all its members **to** a class on proper weightlifting techniques.

(A) to	(B) out
(C) of	(D) about

해리슨 체육관은 적절한 웨이트 트레이닝 기술에 관한 수업**에** 모든 회원을 초대했다.

(A) ~로, ~에	(B) ~ 밖에
(C) ~의	(D) ~에 대해

해설 전치사 어휘 동사 invite와 어울려 가장 자연스럽게 의미가 통하는 전치사를 골라야 한다. 문맥상 수업에 모든 회원을 초대했다는 내용이 되는 게 자연스러우므로 방향을 나타내는 전치사인 (A) to가 정답이다.

어휘 proper 적절한 weightlifting (역도, 바벨 따위의) 무거운 기구를 써서 하는 운동 technique 기술, 기법

114.

While other talks at the journalism conference were **comparatively** brief, the keynote speech lasted two hours.

(A) comparison	(B) comparing
(C) comparatively	(D) compare

저널리즘 콘퍼런스의 다른 강연들이 비교적 짧았던 반면, 기조연설은 2시간 동안 계속되었다.

해설 부사 자리 [형용사 수식] 빈칸은 형용사 brief를 수식하는 부사 자리이므로 (C) comparatively가 정답이다. (A) comparison은 명사, (B) comparing은 동명사 또는 현재분사, (D) compare는 동사 또는 명사이므로 형용사를 수식하는 자리에 올 수 없다.

어휘 talk 강연, 연설 comparatively 비교적 brief 짧은, 간단한 keynote speech 기조연설 last 계속되다, 지속되다

115.

This file cabinet contains health insurance certificates along with other confidential **documents**.

(A) **documents** (B) treatments
(C) structures (D) events

이 파일 캐비닛에는 다른 기밀**문서**와 함께 건강 보험 증서가 들어 있다.

(A) **문서** (B) 치료
(C) 구조 (D) 행사

> **해설** 명사 어휘 형용사 confidential의 수식을 받아 가장 자연스럽게 의미가 통하는 명사를 골라야 한다. 문맥상 다른 기밀 문서와 함께 건강 보험 증서가 들어 있다는 내용이 되는 게 자연스러우므로 '문서'라는 의미의 (A) documents가 정답이다. confidential document는 '기밀 문서'라는 뜻이다.

> **어휘** contain ~가 들어 있다, ~을 포함하다   along with ~와 함께   confidential 비밀의, 기밀의

116.

The **cooperating** partner should provide help such as administrative support when needed.

(A) cooperates (B) cooperate
(C) **cooperating** (D) cooperatively

협력 파트너는 필요할 때 행정적 지원과 같은 도움을 제공해야 한다.

> **해설** 형용사 자리 [명사 수식] 빈칸은 명사 partner를 수식하는 형용사 자리이므로 현재분사 (C) cooperating이 정답이다. (A) cooperates와 (B) cooperate는 동사, (D) cooperatively는 부사이므로 명사를 수식하는 자리에 올 수 없다.

> **어휘** cooperate 협력하다, 협조하다   administrative 행정상의, 관리의   support 지원, 지지; 지원하다, 지지하다

117.

Although Mr. Jenkins received a better offer from the competitor, she decided to stay at her current company.

(A) Rather (B) Whether
(C) **Although** (D) As well as

젠킨스 씨는 경쟁업체로부터 더 좋은 제안을 받았을지라도 자신의 현재 회사에 머물기로 결정했다.

> **해설** 부사절 접속사 빈칸 뒤에 완전한 절이 있으므로 빈칸은 절을 이끌 수 있는 부사절 접속사 자리이다. 문맥상 경쟁업체로부터 더 좋은 제안을 받았지만 지금 회사에 머물기로 결정했다는 내용이 되는 게 자연스러우므로 '비록 ~일지라도'라는 의미의 (C) Although가 정답이다. (B) Whether(A이든 B이든; ~인지 아닌지)와 (D) As well as(~뿐만 아니라)는 접속사이지만 의미상 적절하지 않고, (A) Rather(꽤, 상당히)는 부사이므로 오답이다.

> **어휘** competitor 경쟁업체, 경쟁자   current 현재의

118.

There are several projects that need attention, but the sales pitch for Purnell Enterprises is the **most urgent**.

(A) **most urgent** (B) urgent
(C) more urgently (D) urgently

관심이 필요한 몇 가지 프로젝트가 있지만 퍼넬 사의 구매를 유도하는 게 가장 긴급하다.

> **해설** 형용사 자리 [최상급] 빈칸은 be동사 뒤의 주격 보어 자리이자 정관사 the의 수식을 받는 자리이므로 최상급 형용사인 (A) most urgent가 정답이다. (B) urgent는 원급이므로 정관사 the의 수식을 받을 수 없고, (C) more urgently와 (D) urgently는 부사이므로 형용사 자리에 올 수 없다.

> **어휘** attention 주의 (집중), 주목   sales pitch 구매를 유도하는 설득   urgent 긴급한

119.

Participants are expected to write down their questions instead of asking them **during** the workshop.	참가자들은 워크숍 **동안** 질문을 하는 대신 질문을 적어 놓기로 되어 있다.
(A) directly (B) in case **(C) during** (D) while	(A) 곧장, 똑바로 (B) ~에 대비해서 **(C) ~ 동안** (D) ~하는 동안

해설　전치사 자리　빈칸 뒤에 명사 the workshop이 있으므로 빈칸은 전치사 자리이다. 문맥상 워크숍 동안 질문을 하는 대신 질문을 적어 놓기로 했다는 내용이 되는 게 자연스러우므로 '~ 동안'이라는 의미의 (C) during이 정답이다. (A) directly(곧장, 똑바로)는 부사이고, (B) in case(~할 경우에 대비해서)와 (D) while(~하는 동안; ~한 반면)은 접속사이므로 뒤에 절이 이어져야 하기 때문에 오답이다.

어휘　be expected to do ~하기로 되어 있다, ~할 예정이다; 마땅히 ~을 해야 하다　write down ~을 적어 놓다

120.

Stimson Automotive is **completely** changing the sales commission plan for its full-time employees.	스팀슨 오토모티브는 자사의 정직원들을 위한 판매 수수료 방침을 완전히 바꿀 것이다.
(A) completely (B) completeness (C) complete (D) completed	

해설　부사 자리 [be동사+부사+현재분사]　빈칸은 be동사 is와 현재분사 changing 사이의 부사 자리이므로 (A) completely가 정답이다. (B) completeness는 명사, (C) complete는 동사 또는 형용사, (D) completed는 동사 또는 과거분사이므로 오답이다.

어휘　sales commission 판매 수수료　plan 방침, 방안, 계획　complete 완료하다, 끝마치다; 완벽한, 완전한

121.

Low-income patients are **eligible** to receive free medication through the patient support program.	저소득 환자들은 환자 지원 프로그램을 통해서 무료 약물 치료를 받을 **자격이 있다**.
(A) typical **(B) eligible** (C) accurate (D) unfair	(A) 전형적인 **(B) 적격의, 적임의** (C) 정확한 (D) 불공평한

해설　형용사 어휘　빈칸 앞에 be동사 are가 있고 뒤에는 to부정사가 있으므로 빈칸에는 to부정사와 어울려 쓰이는 형용사가 들어가야 한다. be eligible to do는 '~할 자격이 있다'는 뜻이며, '무료 약물 치료를 받을 자격이 있다'는 의미가 되어 문맥에도 알맞으므로 (B) eligible이 정답이다.

어휘　low-income 저소득의　medication 약, 약물 (치료)

122.

The total number of bike **messengers** in the city has nearly doubled in the past decade.	그 도시에서 오토바이 배달을 하는 총 인원은 지난 10년간 거의 두 배가 되었다.
(A) message (B) messaging **(C) messengers** (D) messaged	

해설　명사 자리 [전치사 뒤]　빈칸 앞에 있는 명사 bike와 복합 명사를 이루어 전치사 of의 목적어 역할을 하는 명사 자리이므로 (C) messengers가 정답이다. (A) message는 명사이지만 '오토바이 메시지의 총계'라는 어색한 문맥이 되므로 오답이다. (B) messaging은 동명사 또는 현재분사이고, (D) messaged는 동사 또는 과거분사이므로 답이 될 수 없다.

어휘　messenger 배달원　nearly 거의　decade 10년　message 메시지; 메시지를 보내다

123.

Because the department has a small budget, purchases of **over** $50 must be approved by a manager.

(A) except (B) than
(C) over (D) toward

그 부서는 예산이 적기 때문에 50달러가 **넘는** 구입은 관리자의 승인을 받아야 한다.

(A) ~을 제외하고 (B) ~보다
(C) ~을 넘는, ~ 이상의 (D) ~을 향하여

해설 전치사 어휘 빈칸 뒤의 $50를 목적어로 취해 가장 자연스럽게 의미가 통하는 전치사를 골라야 한다. 문맥상 50달러를 넘는 구입은 관리자의 승인을 받아야 한다는 내용이 되는 게 자연스러우므로 '~을 넘는, ~ 이상의'라는 의미의 (C) over가 정답이다.

어휘 budget 예산 purchase 구입(한 것); 구입하다 approve 승인하다

124.

At the moment, Morgan Industries **is hesitant** to renew its contract with the supplier.

(A) hesitant **(B) is hesitant**
(C) was hesitant (D) to be hesitant

현재 모건 인더스트리 사는 그 공급업체와 계약을 갱신하는 걸 망설이고 있다.

해설 동사 자리 + 현재 시제 빈칸 앞에 주어 Morgan Industries가 있고 뒤에는 to부정사인 to renew가 있으므로 빈칸은 동사 자리이다. (B) is hesitant와 (C) was hesitant 중에서 '현재'를 의미하는 전치사구 at the moment와 어울려 쓰일 수 있는 것은 현재 시제이므로 (B) is hesitant가 정답이다.

어휘 at the moment 현재 renew 갱신하다, 재개하다 supplier 공급업체

125.

You will not be reimbursed for company expenses **unless** you provide a receipt.

(A) since (B) whereas
(C) unless (D) while

만약 영수증을 제공하지 **않는다면** 회사 경비를 상환받을 수 없을 것입니다.

(A) ~ 이후로; ~ 때문에 (B) ~한 반면
(C) 만약 ~가 아니라면 (D) ~하는 동안

해설 접속사 어휘 빈칸은 절과 절을 연결하는 접속사 자리이다. 문맥상 영수증을 제공하지 않으면 경비를 상환받을 수 없다는 내용이 되는 게 자연스러우므로 '만약 ~가 아니라면'이라는 의미의 (C) unless가 정답이다.

어휘 reimburse 상환하다, 변제하다 expense ((보통 복수형)) 경비, 비용

126.

Using his **past** experience, the real estate agent was able to provide an accurate estimate of the home's value.

(A) apart (B) once
(C) either **(D) past**

그의 과거 경험을 이용하여 부동산 중개인은 그 주택 가치의 정확한 견적을 제공할 수 있었다.

해설 형용사 자리 [명사 수식] 빈칸 앞에 소유격 his가 있고 뒤에는 명사 experience가 있으므로 빈칸은 명사를 수식하는 형용사 자리이다. 따라서 (D) past가 정답이다. (A) apart(떨어진; 떨어져서)는 형용사 또는 부사인데, 형용사로 쓸 땐 명사 뒤에 위치하므로 답이 될 수 없다. (B) once(한 번; 일단 ~하면)는 부사 또는 접속사이고, (C) either가 '둘 중 어느 하나'를 뜻할 때는 명사를 수식할 수 있지만 소유격 뒤에 올 수 없으므로 오답이다.

어휘 real estate agent 부동산 중개인 accurate 정확한 estimate 추정(치), 추산, 견적서

127.

By this time tomorrow, the hiring committee **will have finalized** its decision on who will replace Ms. Gibbs.

(A) finalizes
(B) had finalized
(C) is finalizing
(D) will have finalized

내일 이맘때쯤이면 고용 위원회는 누가 깁스 씨를 대신할지에 대한 결정을 마무리 지을 것이다.

해설 동사 자리+미래완료 미래의 특정 시점까지(By this time tomorrow) 완료되는 일에 대해 서술하고 있으므로 미래완료 시제인 (D) will have finalized가 정답이다. 미래완료 시제는 〈by+미래 시점〉과 자주 쓰인다는 것을 알아 두자.

어휘 hiring committee 고용 위원회 finalize 마무리 짓다, 완결하다 replace 대신하다, 대체하다

128.

Answers to the most **frequently** asked questions will be posted on the company Web site.

(A) actively
(B) finally
(C) frequently
(D) absolutely

가장 **자주** 묻는 질문들에 대한 답변들이 회사 웹사이트에 게시될 것이다.

(A) 활발하게
(B) 마침내
(C) 자주
(D) 절대적으로

해설 부사 어휘 빈칸 뒤의 과거분사 asked를 수식해 가장 자연스럽게 의미가 통하는 부사를 골라야 한다. 문맥상 가장 자주 묻는 질문들이 회사 웹사이트에 게시될 거라는 내용이 되는 게 자연스러우므로 '자주'라는 의미의 (C) frequently가 정답이다. frequently asked questions는 '자주 묻는 질문'이라는 의미로, 줄여서 FAQ로 자주 쓰는 표현이다.

어휘 post (안내문 등을) 게시하다, 공고하다

129.

Boar County will oversee the installation of the jogging trails, the purpose of **which** is to fulfill the demand for outdoor exercise.

(A) any
(B) whom
(C) one
(D) which

보어 카운티는 조깅 코스 시공을 감독할 것인데, 그 공사의 목적은 야외 운동에 대한 수요를 충족하기 위한 것이다.

해설 관계대명사 [계속적 용법] 두 개의 절이 접속사 없이 연결되어 있으므로 빈칸은 접속사 역할을 하면서 두 문장을 연결해 주는 관계대명사 자리이다. 또한 the installation of the jogging trails가 선행사 역할을 하므로 (D) which가 정답이다. (B) whom은 선행사가 사람일 때 쓰는 관계대명사이므로 오답이다. (A) any와 (C) one은 대명사이므로 접속사 역할을 할 수 없다.

어휘 oversee 감독하다 installation 설치 trail 루트, 코스; 오솔길

130.

The **primary** reason for the newly imposed regulations is to improve the factory's safety rating.

(A) intensive
(B) creative
(C) primary
(D) dependable

최근에 도입된 규정의 **주된** 이유는 공장의 안전 등급을 향상시키기 위함이다.

(A) 집중적인
(B) 창의적인
(C) 주된
(D) 믿을 수 있는

해설 형용사 어휘 명사 reason을 수식하여 가장 자연스럽게 의미가 통하는 형용사를 골라야 한다. 문맥상 '최근에 규정을 도입한 주된 이유'라는 뜻이 되는 게 자연스러우므로 (C) primary가 정답이다.

어휘 impose 도입[시행]하다; 부과하다 regulation ((보통 복수형)) 규정 rating 등급, 평가

BEAUMONT, TX (April 20)—As part of the celebration of our city's history, Centennial Hall **131 will host** an orchestra concert featuring the work of local composer Emilia Oyola. Tickets go on sale at the box office and online tomorrow. The show is set for June 3 at 7:30 P.M.

While Ms. Oyola will be the conductor, some of the pieces will not be **132 hers**. Two songs written by other local composers are also part of the lineup. **133 It is these composers' official debut.**

The concert will mark the first performance of the Beaumont City Orchestra since the concert hall was renovated. **134 Regular** attendees to Centennial Hall will certainly notice a vast improvement in sound quality thanks to sound reflectors added to the ceiling.

텍사스 주, 보몬트 (4월 20일)—우리 도시의 역사를 기념하는 행사의 일환으로, 센테니얼 홀에서 우리 지역 작곡가인 에밀리아 오욜라의 작품을 선보이는 오케스트라 연주회를 **131 주최할 것이다**. 티켓은 매표소와 온라인에서 내일 판매된다. 공연은 6월 3일 저녁 7시 30분으로 정해졌다.

오욜라 씨가 지휘자이긴 하지만 작품들 중 일부는 **132 그녀의 것**이 아닐 것이다. 다른 지역 작곡가들이 쓴 두 곡 역시 연주 예정 곡들의 일부다. **133 이것은 이 작곡가들의 공식 데뷔이다.**

연주회는 콘서트 홀이 보수된 이후 보몬트 시립 오케스트라의 첫 공연을 기념하게 될 것이다. 천장에 추가된 음향 반사 장치 덕분에 센테니얼 홀을 **134 자주 찾는** 관객들은 음질이 크게 개선된 것을 분명히 알아차릴 것이다.

어휘 as part of ~의 일환으로   celebration 기념[축하] 행사   host (행사를) 주최하다   feature (특별히) 선보이다, 포함하다; 특색, 특징   composer 작곡가   go on sale 시판되다   set 정하다, 결정하다   conductor 지휘자   piece 작품, (작품) 한 점   lineup (방송 프로, 행사 따위의) 예정표   mark 기념하다, 축하하다   regular 정기적인   attendee 참석자   certainly 틀림없이, 분명히   vast 어마어마한   improvement 개선, 향상   thanks to ~ 덕분에   reflector 반사 장치

131. (A) host   (B) hosted   **(C) will host**   (D) has hosted

해설 동사 자리 + 미래 시제 빈칸에 알맞은 동사 형태를 고르는 문제로, 빈칸이 포함된 문장뿐만 아니라 이후의 문장까지 파악해야 정답을 찾을 수 있다. 오케스트라 연주회는 6월 3일로 예정되어 있는데 이 기사가 작성된 시점인 4월 20일을 기준으로 미래에 일어날 일이다. 따라서 미래 시제인 (C) will host가 정답이다.

132. **(A) hers**   (B) ours   (C) theirs   (D) its

해설 소유대명사 문맥상 오욜라 씨가 지휘를 하지만 작품들 중 일부는 그녀의 것이 아닐 거라는 내용이 되는 게 자연스러우므로 '그녀의 것'을 뜻하는 (A) hers가 정답이다. (B) ours와 (C) theirs도 소유대명사이지만 Ms. Oyola를 지칭하는 말로 쓸 수 없고, (D) its는 소유격이므로 빈칸에 올 수 없다.

133. (A) Ms. Oyola grew up just outside of Beaumont.
(B) The orchestra is looking for new members.
(C) Ms. Oyola plays the piano and violin.
(D) It is these composers' official debut.

(A) 오욜라 씨는 보몬트 밖에서 성장했다.
(B) 오케스트라는 새로운 구성원을 찾고 있다.
(C) 오욜라 씨는 피아노와 바이올린을 연주한다.
(D) 이것은 이 작곡가들의 공식 데뷔이다.

해설 알맞은 문장 고르기 빈칸 앞 문장에서 다른 지역의 작곡가들이 쓴 두 곡이 연주될 예정이라고 했다. 따라서 빈칸에는 해당 작곡가들에 대해 부연 설명하는 내용이 이어지는 것이 적절하므로 (D)가 알맞다.

어휘 grow up 성장하다, 자라다   look for ~을 찾다   official 공식적인

134. (A) Authorized   (B) Sensible   (C) Preceding   **(D) Regular**

(A) 인정받은   (B) 분별 있는, 합리적인   (C) 앞서는   **(D) 정기적인**

해설 형용사 어휘 빈칸 뒤에 있는 attendees를 수식해 가장 자연스럽게 의미가 통하는 형용사를 골라야 한다. 문맥상 콘서트 홀을 자주 찾는 사람들은 음질이 크게 개선된 걸 알아차릴 것이라는 내용이 되는 게 자연스러우므로 '정기적인'이라는 의미의 (D) Regular가 정답이다.

To: Ivan Bryson 〈ivanb@brysonart.com〉
From: Heather Wallace 〈heather@zamora-gallery.com〉
Date: June 10
Subject: Zamora Gallery plans

Dear Mr. Bryson,

On behalf of the Zamora Gallery, I would like to say how pleased we are to be featuring some of your work at our upcoming exhibit. Our marketing team uses a variety of ¹³⁵ **strategies** to highlight new artists such as yourself. For instance, we ¹³⁶ **will promote** you on our homepage so that visitors can learn more about your work. ¹³⁷ **This is most effective when we have more information about your background.** Therefore, we would like you to write a brief biography of yourself, around two hundred words. You can see examples of other artists' biographies on our Web site if you are not sure what should be included. Upon completion, please send ¹³⁸ **it** to me as soon as possible.

Should you have any questions, I would be more than happy to answer them. I can be reached at this e-mail address.

Warmest regards,

Heather Wallace

수신: 이반 브라이슨
발신: 헤더 월리스
날짜: 6월 10일
제목: 사모라 갤러리 정책

브라이슨 씨께,

사모라 갤러리를 대표하여 다가오는 전시에서 당신의 작품 중 일부를 선보이게 되어 얼마나 기쁜지 말씀드리고 싶습니다. 저희의 마케팅 팀은 당신과 같은 새로운 예술가들을 돋보이게 하기 위해서 다양한 135 **전략들**을 활용합니다. 예를 들어, 방문자들이 당신의 작품에 대해 더 많이 알 수 있도록 저희 홈페이지에 당신을 136 **홍보할 것입니다**. 137 **이것은 저희가 당신의 배경에 관해 더 많은 정보를 가지고 있을 때 가장 효과적입니다.** 따라서 당신의 간단한 이력을 약 200단어 정도로 적어 주셨으면 합니다. 무엇이 포함되어야 할지 잘 모르시겠다면 저희 웹사이트에서 다른 예술가들의 이력 예시들을 보실 수 있습니다. 완성하시는 대로 가능한 한 빨리 138 **그것을** 제게 보내 주시기 바랍니다.

혹시라도 질문이 있으면 제가 기꺼이 답변해 드리겠습니다. 저에게 이 이메일 주소로 연락하시면 됩니다.

헤더 월리스

어휘 on behalf of ~을 대신하여, ~을 대표하여   feature (특별히) 선보이다, 포함하다; 특색, 특징   effective 효과적인   biography 일대기, 전기

---

135. (A) strategies   (B) investigations   (C) assets   (D) competitions

> **해설** 명사 어휘 문맥상 새로운 예술가들을 돋보이게 하기 위해서 다양한 전략을 활용한다는 내용이 되는 게 자연스러우므로 '전략들'이라는 의미의 (A) strategies가 정답이다.

136. (A) will promote   (B) promoting   (C) had promoted   (D) promotes

> **해설** 동사 자리 + 미래 시제 빈칸 앞부분에서 편지의 수신자인 브라이슨 씨의 전시가 예정되어 있음을 알 수 있고, 빈칸이 포함된 문장을 비롯하여 이후 내용이 그 전시를 홍보하기 위한 방법들이므로 미래 시제인 (A) will promote가 정답이다.

137. (A) Over time, it is very common for the artwork to increase in value.
(B) A senior marketer oversees all parts of the campaign from start to finish.
(C) This is most effective when we have more information about your background.
(D) Each painting is carefully wrapped and labeled before being transported.

(A) 시간이 지나면서 미술품 가치가 상승하는 것은 아주 흔합니다.
(B) 선임 마케터가 처음부터 끝까지 캠페인의 모든 부분들을 감독합니다.
(C) 이것은 저희가 당신의 배경에 관해 더 많은 정보를 가지고 있을 때 가장 효과적입니다.
(D) 각 그림은 운송되기 전에 조심스럽게 포장되고 라벨이 붙을 것입니다.

> **해설** 알맞은 문장 고르기 빈칸 뒤에 결과를 나타내는 접속부사 therefore가 있으므로 빈칸에는 뒤 문장의 원인이나 이유에 해당하는 내용이 나와야 한다. 따라서 작품을 전시할 예술가에 대한 정보가 필요하기 때문에 200자 분량으로 이력을 적어 달라고 하는 흐름이 자연스러우므로 (C)가 정답이다.

138. (A) it   (B) them   (C) your   (D) some

> **해설** 대명사 [목적격] 빈칸은 동사 send의 목적어 자리이며, 문맥상 빈칸에 들어갈 말은 브라이슨 씨에게 써 달라고 요청한 a brief biography of yourself를 가리키므로 단수 대명사인 (A) it이 정답이다.

Reiko Refrigerated Transportation Services

Do you need to ship goods that must be refrigerated while in transit? **139 We can ensure your items stay at the right temperature.** Reiko has been in the shipping industry for decades, and we can help you whether you are transporting medications, perishable food, or more.

We have a variety of vehicle sizes to suit your shipment. **140 These** include small vans, mid-sized trucks, and large trailers. We only work with refrigerated items, and we have done so throughout our company's history. This **141 specialization** means our employees are highly experienced in keeping a controlled environment for your goods.

We want potential customers **142 to feel** confident in our services. That's why we insure all items and offer a money-back guarantee.

레이코 냉장 운송 서비스

수송하는 동안 냉장 보관되어야 하는 제품을 운송해야 하시나요? 139 저희가 당신의 물품들이 적정 온도에서 유지되도록 보장해 드릴 수 있습니다. 레이코는 수십 년간 운송업계에 있었고, 여러분이 의약품, 잘 상하는 식품, 혹은 그 이상의 어떤 제품을 운송하시든 저희가 여러분을 도와드릴 수 있습니다.

저희는 여러분의 수송품에 맞는 다양한 크기의 차량을 보유하고 있습니다. 140 이것들에는 소형 밴과 중형 트럭, 그리고 대형 트레일러가 포함됩니다. 저희는 냉장된 물품만을 작업 대상으로 하며, 저희 회사 역사 내내 그렇게 해 왔습니다. 이러한 141 전문화는 저희 직원들이 여러분의 제품을 위해 통제된 환경을 유지하는 데 매우 능숙하다는 것을 의미합니다.

저희는 잠재 고객들이 저희 서비스에 대한 확신을 142 느끼시기를 원합니다. 그것이 저희가 모든 물품에 보험을 가입하고 환불 보장을 해 드리는 이유입니다.

어휘 refrigerate 냉장하다 transportation 수송, 운송 ship 수송하다, 운송하다 goods ((항상 복수형)) 상품, 제품 in transit 수송 중에 ensure 반드시 ~하게 하다, 보장하다 temperature 온도 for decades 수십 년간 perishable 잘 상하는 suit ~에게 맞다 shipment 수송(품) work with ~을 작업 대상으로 하다 insure 보험에 들다 money-back guarantee 환불 보장

139. (A) We can ensure your items stay at the right temperature.
(B) The thermometer can detect even the smallest changes.
(C) Reiko may be under new ownership soon.
(D) An insulating layer in the packaging would be better.

(A) 저희가 당신의 물품들이 적정 온도에서 유지되도록 보장해 드릴 수 있습니다.
(B) 온도계는 심지어 아주 작은 변화도 감지할 수 있습니다.
(C) 레이코는 곧 새로운 소유주 하에 있게 될 수도 있습니다.
(D) 포장재 안의 절연층이 더 좋아질 것입니다.

해설 알맞은 문장 고르기 빈칸 앞 문장에서 냉장 보관된 상태로 제품을 수송해야 하는지 물었고, 뒤에서 자사가 수십 년간 운송업계에 있어 왔기에 어떤 물품의 운송이든 도와줄 수 있다고 했다. 따라서 빈칸에는 이 회사가 제공하는 냉장 운송 서비스와 관련한 내용이 이어지는 게 문맥상 가장 자연스러우므로 (A)가 정답이다.

어휘 thermometer 온도계 detect 감지하다, 발견하다 ownership 소유(권) insulating layer 절연층 packaging 포장(재)

140. (A) Anything (B) These (C) Everyone (D) Both

해설 지시대명사 빈칸은 복수 동사 include의 주어 자리이므로 복수 지시대명사인 (B) These가 정답이다. (D) Both는 복수 대명사이지만 앞에서 both(둘 다)로 받을 만한 두 가지 대상이 제시되지 않았으므로 오답이다.

141. (A) manuscript (B) incentive (C) specialization (D) routine

(A) 원고 (B) 장려책 (C) 전문화 (D) 판에 박힌 일

해설 명사 어휘 다양한 크기의 차량을 확보하고 있다는 것이나 회사 창립 이래로 냉장 보관 물품만 취급해 왔다는 것은 '전문화'라는 말로 압축할 수 있으므로 (C) specialization이 정답이다.

142. (A) have felt (B) to feel (C) and felt (D) who feels

해설 to부정사 [명사적 용법] 빈칸은 동사 want의 목적격 보어 자리이므로 to부정사인 (B) to feel이 정답이다.

Duane Shepherd
215 Fairfield Road
Cambridge, MA 02142

September 3

Dear Valued Patient,

The Patterson Dental Clinic **143 will relocate** to 1575 Kerry Way on November 1. From that date, **144 all** appointments will take place at the new location. We are excited to offer our patients more modern facilities, a larger waiting area, and better parking options at our new site. We are also considering expanding our business hours to make it easier for people working full-time to find an appointment after work or on weekends. **145 However**, the final schedule has not been determined yet.

We are excited to serve you at our new office. **146 If you have difficulty finding the building, please feel free to call us.** One of our staff members would be happy to give you directions.

Sincerely,
The Patterson Dental Clinic Team

두에인 셰퍼드
215 페어필드 가
케임브리지, 매사추세츠 주 02142

9월 3일

소중한 환자 여러분께

패터슨 치과가 11월 1일에 케리 웨이 1575번지로 143 이전할 것입니다. 그 날짜부터 144 모든 예약은 새로운 장소에서 이루질 것입니다. 저희는 새로운 장소에서 환자 여러분들에게 더욱 현대적인 시설과 더 넓은 대기실, 그리고 더 나은 주차 선택권을 제공하게 되어 들떠 있습니다. 저희는 또한 전일제로 일하는 분들이 퇴근 후나 주말에 예약을 더 쉽게 잡을 수 있도록 운영 시간을 확장하는 걸 고려하고 있습니다. 145 하지만, 최종적인 일정은 아직 결정되지 않았습니다.

저희는 새로운 장소에 여러분을 모시게 되어 기쁩니다. 146 만약 건물을 찾는 데 어려움이 있으시면, 언제든 저희에게 전화하시기 바랍니다. 저희 직원들 중 한 명이 기꺼이 길을 안내해 드릴 겁니다.

패터슨 치과팀

어휘 relocate 이전하다　take place 개최되다, 일어나다　facility ((보통 복수형)) 시설　consider doing ~하는 것을 고려하다
expand 확장하다　determine 결정하다, 확정하다　feel free to do (부담 없이) 마음대로 ~하다　give ~ directions ~에게 길을 안내하다[알려 주다]

143. (A) relocated　　(B) relocate　　**(C) will relocate**　　(D) relocating

해설 동사 자리 + 미래 시제 빈칸이 포함된 문장은 11월 1일에 일어날 일을 서술하고 있는데, 편지를 쓴 시점인 9월 3일 이후이므로 미래 시제인 (C) will relocate가 정답이다.

144. (A) other　　(B) those　　**(C) all**　　(D) they

해설 수량형용사 all 빈칸 뒤에 나오는 복수 명사 appointments를 수식하기에 가장 적절한 것을 골라야 한다. 문맥상 11월 1일부터 모든 예약은 새 장소에서 이뤄진다는 내용이 되는 게 자연스러우므로 (C) all이 정답이다. (A) other와 (B) those도 복수 명사를 수식할 수 있지만, '다른 예약들'이나 '그 예약들'이라고 표현하려면 앞에서 특정 예약에 대해 언급했어야 하므로 답이 될 수 없다. (D) they는 주격 대명사이므로 오답이다.

145. **(A) However**　　(B) Similarly　　(C) Above all　　(D) For example

해설 접속부사 앞뒤 내용을 자연스럽게 이어 줄 접속부사를 골라야 한다. 빈칸 앞에서 운영 시간 연장을 고려한다고 한 반면에, 뒤에서는 일정이 아직 결정되지 않았다고 했으므로 '하지만, 그러나'라는 의미의 (A) However가 정답이다.

146. (A) A new dentist will be joining our practice soon.
(B) If you have difficulty finding the building, please feel free to call us.
(C) Your personal dental records will be kept confidential at all times.
(D) The variety of services offered by our clinic remain the same as before.

(A) 새로운 치과 의사가 저희 병원에 곧 합류할 것입니다.
(B) 만약 건물을 찾는 데 어려움이 있으시면, 언제든 저희에게 전화하시기 바랍니다.
(C) 당신의 개인적인 치과 기록은 항상 비밀로 유지될 것입니다.
(D) 저희 병원에서 제공되는 다양한 서비스는 이전과 똑같이 유지됩니다.

해설 알맞은 문장 고르기 빈칸 앞에서는 새로운 장소에서 서비스를 제공하게 되어 기쁘다고 했고, 뒤에서는 기꺼이 길 안내를 해 주겠다고 했다. 따라서 빈칸에는 새롭게 이전하게 될 장소로 찾아오는 것과 관련된 내용이 들어가는 게 자연스러우므로 (B)가 정답이다.

어휘 practice (의사, 변호사 등의) 업무, 영업　keep ~ confidential ~을 비밀로 지키다　variety 여러 가지, 다양성

MEMO

To: Prolance Customer Service Team
From: Olivia Cronin
Re: Customer complaints
148 Date: September 2

147 The August electricity bills were calculated incorrectly, so customers received bills that were too high. We're issuing new bills this week, so please explain this to customers if needed.

Additionally, we are receiving a lot of positive feedback from customers. **148** Therefore, starting next month, we will make printouts of what customers are saying and hang them up in the break room to help motivate the staff.

메모

수신: 프롤란스 고객 서비스팀
발신: 올리비아 크로닌
주제: 고객 불만
148 날짜: 9월 2일

147 8월 전기 요금이 부정확하게 계산되어서 고객들이 요금이 너무 많이 나온 청구서를 받았습니다. 우리가 이번 주에 새로운 청구서를 발부할 것이니 필요하면 이것을 고객들에게 설명해 주시기 바랍니다.

덧붙여 우리는 고객들로부터 많은 긍정적인 의견을 받고 있습니다. **148** 그래서 다음 달부터 직원들을 동기 부여하는 데 도움이 되도록 고객들이 하는 말을 인쇄하여 휴게실에 걸어 둘 것입니다.

어휘 complaint 불평, 항의   electricity bill 전기 요금   calculate 계산하다   incorrectly 맞지 않게, 부정확하게   issue 발부[발행]하다; 발행; 쟁점   additionally 추가적으로   positive 긍정적인   make a printout 인쇄하다   hang up ~을 걸다   break room 휴게실   motivate 동기를 부여하다

147. Why did Ms. Cronin send the message?

(A) To describe a policy
(B) To explain a problem
(C) To introduce new equipment
(D) To announce a staff change

크로닌 씨가 메시지를 보낸 이유는 무엇인가?

(A) 정책을 설명하기 위해서
(B) 문제를 설명하기 위해서
(C) 새로운 장비를 소개하기 위해서
(D) 직원 교체를 알리기 위해서

해설 주제/목적 문제 글의 주제나 목적은 대개 지문 도입부에 제시된다. 이 지문은 8월 전기 요금이 부정확하게 계산되어서(The August electricity bills were calculated incorrectly) 고객들에게 요금이 과도하게 청구되었다(customers received bills that were too high)는 문제를 지적하며, 이를 해결하기 위한 방안을 제시하고 있다. 따라서 크로닌 씨가 문제를 설명하기 위해 메시지를 보낸 것을 알 수 있으므로 (B)가 정답이다.

어휘 describe 서술하다, 묘사하다   policy 정책, 방침   equipment ((집합적)) 장비

148. When can employees start to see comments from customers?

(A) In September
(B) In October
(C) In November
(D) In December

직원들은 언제 고객들의 의견을 보기 시작할 수 있는가?

(A) 9월에
(B) 10월에
(C) 11월에
(D) 12월에

해설 세부 사항 문제 다음 달부터(starting next month) 고객들이 보내 준 의견을 인쇄하여(we will make printouts of what customers are saying) 휴게실에 걸어 두겠다(hang them up in the break room)고 했는데, 이 메시지를 쓴 날짜가 9월 2일이므로 직원들이 고객들의 의견을 볼 수 있는 시기는 10월임을 알 수 있다. 따라서 (B)가 정답이다.

패러프레이징 what customers are saying → comments from customers

NOTICE

On Wednesday, August 4, Ocala Electricity Services will repair the main breaker here at Avalon Suites. This requires shutting off the electricity to all units. ¹⁴⁹ **Those living in the building will not have electricity during the maintenance work**, which will start at 10 A.M. Prior to this time, we recommend that you power down computers and other electrical devices to avoid damage. Refrigerators can remain without electricity for up to four hours without affecting the food, as long as the door is kept closed. ¹⁵⁰ **The work will be completed by 11 A.M.** We apologize for any inconvenience this may cause.

공지

8월 4일 수요일에 오캘러 전기 서비스 사가 이곳 아발론 스위트에서 주 차단기를 수리할 예정입니다. 이것은 모든 세대에 전력을 차단하는 것을 요구합니다. ¹⁴⁹ 이 건물에 거주하는 분들은 정비 작업 동안 전기를 이용하지 못하게 될 것이며, 작업은 오전 10시에 시작될 것입니다. 이 시간에 앞서, 피해를 막기 위하여 컴퓨터와 다른 전자 기기의 전원을 끄실 것을 권합니다. 냉장고는 문이 닫혀 있는 한 음식물에 영향을 주지 않고 최대 4시간 동안 전기 없이 유지될 수 있습니다. ¹⁵⁰ 작업은 오전 11시에 끝날 것입니다. 이로 인해 야기될 불편에 사과드립니다.

어휘 electricity 전기, 전력 main breaker 주 차단기 require 요구하다, 필요로 하다 shut off ~을 차단하다, ~을 정지시키다 unit (공동 주택 내의) 한 가구; 구성 단위 prior to ~ 전에 power down (컴퓨터 등의) 전원을 끄다 avoid 방지하다, 막다 damage 손상, 피해 affect 영향을 미치다 as long as ~하는 한 complete 완료하다, 끝마치다 apologize for ~에 대해 사과하다 inconvenience 불편 cause 야기하다, 초래하다

149. Who is the intended audience of this notice?

(A) Electricians
(B) Tenants
(C) Building owners
(D) Maintenance workers

이 공지가 의도하는 대상은 누구인가?

(A) 전기 기사들
(B) 세입자들
(C) 건물주들
(D) 관리 직원들

해설 세부 사항 문제 지문 초반부에서 아발론 스위트에 주 차단기 수리가 진행될 거라고(Ocala Electricity Services will repair the main breaker here at Avalon Suites) 했으며, 정비 작업이 진행되는 동안에는 건물 거주자들이 전기를 이용할 수 없다(Those living in the building will not have electricity during the maintenance work)고 했다. 따라서 이 공지는 아발론 스위트에 거주하는 사람들을 대상으로 한 것임을 알 수 있으므로 (B)가 정답이다.

패러프레이징 those living in the building → tenants

150. What most likely will happen at Avalon Suites at 11 A.M. on August 4?

(A) New computers will be set up.
(B) An entrance will be off limits.
(C) Some units will be inspected.
(D) People can use the electricity again.

8월 4일 오전 11시에 아발론 스위트에서 어떤 일이 있겠는가?

(A) 새 컴퓨터들이 설치될 것이다.
(B) 입구가 출입 제한될 것이다.
(C) 일부 세대가 점검될 것이다.
(D) 사람들이 다시 전기를 사용할 수 있다.

해설 추론/암시 문제 질문의 키워드인 8월 4일 오전 11시에 집중하여 지문을 파악한다. 지문 후반부에서 오전 11시에 작업이 끝날 거라고(The work will be completed by 11 A.M.) 한 것으로 보아 그 시간부터는 전기 사용이 다시 정상화될 것임을 알 수 있으므로 (D)가 정답이다.

어휘 set up ~을 설치하다 entrance (출)입구 off limits 출입 금지의 inspect 점검하다, 검사하다

Charles Griffith (9:58 A.M.)
Hi, Penelope. I'm here at the factory, and I just found out that the delivery from Treetop Textiles is late. We were supposed to get the leather for the front-pocket handbags yesterday.

Penelope Lapierre (10:01 A.M.)
Not again! 151 **I think we need to start looking for another supplier for our leather.** This is the third late delivery from Treetop Textiles this month.

Charles Griffith (10:04 A.M.)
I agree, but 151 **wouldn't there be a penalty for canceling the contract?**

Penelope Lapierre (10:06 A.M.)
151 **The current one is coming to an end in just a few weeks.**

Charles Griffith (10:07 A.M.)
Oh, really? Then let's get on with it.

Penelope Lapierre (10:10 A.M.)
Sounds good to me. But as for today, does that mean there is nothing for the production floor workers to do?

Charles Griffith (10:12 A.M.)
152 **I'll assign the handbag workers to something else now.** That way, we won't lose any working hours while we wait for the delivery from Treetop.

찰스 그리피스 (오전 9시 58분)
안녕하세요, 페넬로페 씨. 제가 이곳 공장에 있는데요, 트리톱 텍스타일 사로부터 배송이 늦는다는 걸 방금 알았어요. 앞주머니가 있는 핸드백에 쓸 가죽을 어제 받기로 되어 있었는데 말이죠.

페넬로페 라피에르 (오전 10시 01분)
또요! 151 또 다른 가죽 공급업체를 찾기 시작해야 할 것 같네요. 트리톱 텍스타일 사에서 배송이 늦은 게 이번 달에만 세 번째예요.

찰스 그리피스 (오전 10시 04분)
저도 동의하지만, 151 계약 취소에 대한 위약금이 있지 않을까요?

페넬로페 라피에르 (오전 10시 06분)
151 현재의 계약은 몇 주만 지나면 종료돼요.

찰스 그리피스 (오전 10시 07분)
아, 정말요? 그러면 그렇게 합시다.

페넬로페 라피에르 (오전 10시 10분)
난 좋아요. 그런데 오늘은 그렇게 되면 생산 현장 직원들이 할 일이 없는 건가요?

찰스 그리피스 (오전 10시 12분)
152 제가 지금 핸드백 작업자들에게 다른 일을 배정할게요. 그렇게 하면 우리가 트리톱으로부터 배송을 기다리는 동안 근무 시간을 낭비하지 않을 거예요.

어휘 find out ~임을 알아내다, ~을 발견하다 be supposed to *do* ~하기로 되어 있다 supplier 공급업체 penalty 벌금, 위약금 come to an end 끝나다 as for ~에 관해 말하자면 production floor 생산 현장 assign A to B A를 B에 배정하다

151. At 10:07 A.M., what does Mr. Griffith mean when he writes, "Then let's get on with it"?

(A) They should pay a fee for rush delivery.
(B) They should start working on the handbags.
(C) They should update some contract terms.
(D) They should try to find a new supplier.

오전 10시 07분에, 그리피스 씨가 "그러면 그렇게 합시다"라고 한 의도는 무엇인가?

(A) 긴급 배달에 대해 수수료를 지불해야 한다.
(B) 핸드백 작업을 시작해야 한다.
(C) 계약 조건을 업데이트해야 한다.
(D) 새로운 공급업체를 찾아야 한다.

해설 의도 파악 문제 의도 파악 문제는 제시된 문장 주변에서 단서를 찾아야 한다. 10시 01분에 라피에르 씨가 다른 가죽 공급업체를 찾자고 하자 10시 04분에 그리피스 씨가 계약 취소 위약금에 대해 우려했다. 이어서 라피에르 씨가 계약이 몇 주만 지나면 종료된다는 사실을 알려 주자 안심하며 새로운 공급업체를 찾는 데 동의하는 의도로 한 말이므로 (D)가 정답이다.

어휘 fee 수수료, 요금 rush delivery 긴급 배달 contract term 계약 조건

152. What will Mr. Griffith probably do next?

(A) Inspect some finished handbags
(B) Check a delivery address
(C) Reassign employees to other tasks
(D) Order leather from another business

그리피스 씨는 아마도 다음에 무엇을 할 것인가?

(A) 완성된 핸드백 검사하기
(B) 배송 주소 확인하기
(C) 직원들을 다른 업무에 다시 배정하기
(D) 또 다른 업체로부터 가죽 주문하기

해설 세부 사항 문제 앞으로 일어날 일은 대개 지문 후반부에 제시된다. 그리피스 씨가 마지막 메시지에서 지금 핸드백 작업자들에게 다른 일을 배정하겠다(I'll assign the handbag workers to something else now)고 했으므로 (C)가 정답이다.

어휘 inspect 검사하다, 점검하다 reassign (임무, 직책 등을) 다시 맡기다 order 주문하다

Preston Swim Center

The days are getting colder, but that doesn't mean you have to give up swimming. You can swim indoors with Preston Swim Center. We offer two Olympic-size swimming pools and one shallow junior pool. **153 And from October 10, we will stay open one hour later on weekdays and two hours later on weekends.**

Special Offer: Purchase a 30-day pass and get a free towel. **154 The pass can be used by the purchaser or their family. It is valid for all Preston Swim Center activities, including group classes, and it will save you 60% compared to the daily rate.**

프레스턴 수영 센터

날이 점점 추워지고 있지만 그렇다고 당신이 수영을 포기해야 한다는 것을 의미하지는 않습니다. 당신은 프레스턴 수영 센터와 함께 실내에서 수영할 수 있습니다. 저희는 두 개의 올림픽 규격 수영장과 얕은 어린이용 수영장 하나를 제공합니다. 153 그리고 10월 10일부터 주중에는 1시간 더 늦게, 그리고 주말에는 2시간 더 늦게까지 운영할 것입니다.

특가 제공: 30일 이용권을 구매하시고 무료 수건을 받으세요. 154 이용권은 구매자 또는 구매자의 가족이 사용할 수 있습니다. 이용권은 단체 수업을 포함하여 모든 프레스턴 수영 센터 활동에 유효하고, 일일 요금에 비해 60% 절약됩니다.

어휘 indoors 실내에서, 실내로 shallow 얕은 purchase 구입하다; 구입 pass 출입증, 통행증 valid 유효한 activity (특별한 목적을 위한) 활동 including ~을 포함하여 save ~가 …을 아끼게 해 주다 compared to ~와 비교하여 rate 요금; 속도; 비율

153. What is true about Preston Swim Center?

(A) It has four indoor swimming pools.
(B) It will extend its hours of operation.
(C) It sells swimming accessories on site.
(D) It was not open on weekends previously.

프레스턴 수영 센터에 관해 사실인 것은?

(A) 네 개의 실내 수영장이 있다.
(B) 운영 시간을 연장할 것이다.
(C) 현장에서 수영 용품을 판매한다.
(D) 이전에는 주말에 문을 열지 않았다.

해설 TRUE 문제 첫 번째 단락 마지막 부분에서 운영 시간이 변경될 예정임(we will stay open one hour later on weekdays and two hours later on weekends)을 알리고 있다. 주중에는 1시간, 주말에는 2시간 더 늦게까지 운영한다고 했으므로 (B)가 정답이다. (A)는 올림픽 규격 수영장 두 개와 어린이용 수영장 한 개(two Olympic-size swimming pools and one shallow junior pool)가 있다고 했으므로 오답이다. (C)는 언급된 바가 없으며, (D)는 주말 운영 시간을 2시간 연장한다(two hours later on weekends)는 것으로 보아 이전에도 주말에 문을 열었다는 걸 알 수 있으므로 오답이다.

패러프레이징 stay open ~ on weekends → extend its hours of operation

어휘 extend 연장하다, 확대하다 operation 운영, 영업 on site 현장에서 previously 이전에

---

154. What is NOT mentioned about the 30-day pass?

(A) It is cheaper than paying the daily rate.
(B) It is replaced for free if lost.
(C) It can be transferred to another person.
(D) It includes group activities.

30일 이용권에 대해서 언급되지 않은 것은?

(A) 일일 요금을 지불하는 것보다 더 싸다.
(B) 분실하면 무료로 교환된다.
(C) 다른 사람에게 양도될 수 있다.
(D) 단체 활동을 포함한다.

해설 세부 사항 문제 이용권을 분실했을 때 무료로 교환해 주는지에 대해서는 언급되지 않았으므로 (B)가 정답이다.
(A) 일일 요금에 비해 60% 절약된다(it will save you 60% compared to the daily rate)고 했다.
(C) 구매자나 그들의 가족이 사용할 수 있다(The pass can be used by the purchaser or their family)고 한 것으로 보아 이용권이 양도 가능하다는 걸 알 수 있다.
(D) 단체 수업을 포함한 모든 활동에 유효하다(It is valid for all Preston Swim Center activities, including group classes)고 언급되어 있다.

패러프레이징 can be used by the purchaser or their family → can be transferred to another person

어휘 replace 교체하다, 대신하다 transfer (재산, 권리 등을) 넘겨주다, 양도하다

True to the Fruit
May 1–14
Available at participating supermarkets nationwide!

At TC Beverage Co., we don't add any artificial flavors to our line of Refresh juice. That means each bottle of Refresh is both healthy and delicious, and it tastes the same as if you squeezed fresh fruit yourself at home.

155 **No other juice on the market can compete with Refresh's natural taste.** But don't take our word for it—in our nationwide "True to the Fruit" event, 155 **you can do a blind taste-test of Refresh and another brand to see how they compare**. Look for the "True to the Fruit" kiosk at your local supermarket.

156 **Anyone who participates in the store taste-test will be given a code to use on our Web site to get 50% off any Refresh product.**

157 **For further details about the event, visit www.tcbevco.com, call our help line at 1-800-555-6600, or talk to a customer service agent at your local supermarket.**

과일 그대로
5월 1일~14일
전국의 참여 슈퍼마켓에서 이용할 수 있습니다!

저희 TC 베버리지 사는 리프레시 주스 제품 라인에 어떤 인공적인 맛도 첨가하지 않습니다. 그것은 리프레시 한 병 한 병이 모두 건강하고 맛있으며, 마치 여러분이 집에서 직접 짠 싱싱한 과일 같은 맛이 난다는 것을 의미합니다.

155 시판되는 어떤 주스도 리프레시의 천연의 맛에 견줄 수 없습니다. 하지만 저희 말만 믿지 마세요. 저희의 전국적인 "과일 그대로" 행사에서 155 그것들이 어떻게 비교되는지 확인하기 위하여 여러분은 리프레시와 다른 브랜드의 블라인드 맛 테스트를 할 수 있습니다. 여러분이 사는 지역의 슈퍼마켓에서 "과일 그대로" 가판을 찾아보세요. 156 매장 시음 행사에 참여하는 분들은 웹사이트에서 리프레시 제품을 50% 할인가에 구매할 수 있는 코드를 받게 될 것입니다.

157 행사에 관해 더 자세한 정보를 원하시면 www.tcbevco.com을 방문하시거나 고객 상담 전화 1-800-555-6600으로 전화하시거나 여러분이 가시는 슈퍼마켓의 고객 서비스 직원에게 말씀하세요.

어휘 true to ~에 충실한 artificial 인공적인 line 제품군 squeeze 짜다 compete with ~와 겨루다[경쟁하다] take one's word for it ~의 말을 곧이곧대로 받아들이다 kiosk (신문, 음료 등을 파는) 작은 가판

155. Why is TC Beverage Co. holding the event?

(A) To compare its products to those of its competitors
(B) To promote recipes made with its products
(C) To thank customers for their business
(D) To introduce a new product line

TC 베버리지 사는 왜 행사를 개최하는가?

(A) 자사의 제품과 경쟁사의 제품을 비교하기 위해서
(B) 자사의 제품으로 만든 조리법을 홍보하기 위해서
(C) 거래해 준 고객들에게 감사하기 위해서
(D) 신제품 라인을 소개하기 위해서

해설 세부 사항 문제 시판되는 어떤 주스도 자사의 주스에 견줄 수 없다(No other juice on the market can compete with Refresh's natural taste)고 한 후, 행사에서 리프레시와 다른 브랜드의 제품을 블라인드 테스트로 비교해 볼 수 있다(you can do a blind taste-test of Refresh and another brand)고 했으므로 (A)가 정답이다.

156. What will participants in the event be given?

(A) A TC Beverage Co. T-shirt
(B) A prize drawing entry
(C) A discount code
(D) Samples to take home

참가자들은 행사에서 무엇을 받을 것인가?

(A) TC 베버리지 사의 티셔츠
(B) 경품 추첨 응모권
(C) 할인 코드
(D) 집에 가져갈 샘플

해설 세부 사항 문제 매장에서 주스를 시음하면 웹사이트에서 리프레시 제품을 50% 할인가에 구매할 수 있는 코드(a code to use on our Web site to get 50% off any Refresh product)를 받게 될 거라고 했으므로 (C)가 정답이다.

157. What is NOT mentioned as a way to get more information about the event?

(A) Signing up for a newsletter
(B) Visiting a Web site
(C) Making a phone call
(D) Speaking to a supermarket employee

행사에 대해 더 많은 정보를 얻기 위한 방법으로 언급되지 않은 것은?

(A) 소식지 신청하기
(B) 웹사이트 방문하기
(C) 전화하기
(D) 슈퍼마켓 직원에게 말하기

해설 세부 사항 문제 더 자세한 행사 정보를 원하면 (B) 웹사이트에 방문하거나(visit www.tcbevco.com), (C) 고객 상담 번호로 전화를 걸거나(call our help line), (D) 슈퍼마켓의 고객 서비스 직원에게 얘기하라고(talk to a customer service agent at your local supermarket) 했다. 소식지 신청에 대해서는 언급하지 않았으므로 (A)가 정답이다.

Centennial Stadium Strikes Out

November 22, SARASOTA — **158 Centennial Stadium, owned by Arcadia Corp., submitted plans for a second stadium, but permission to start construction was denied by the city's planning commission.**

The proposed plan would have used 6 acres of non-developed land in 159 **the Hampton neighborhood**, directly across the street from the current stadium. Arcadia Corp. purchased the land three years ago with the intention of creating a second stadium. However, as 159 **the land is classified as a wetland and is the natural habitat of many birds and reptiles**, environmental groups are pushing to protect the area, and they have worked to block the proposal.

The head of Arcadia Corp., Craig Amos, argues that Sarasota needs a second stadium. "We need a site for the stadium, and this is the best neighborhood for attracting visitors and keeping heavy traffic out of the city center," Amos said in a recent statement.

Amos says the new sports facility would create hundreds of jobs for the city and give a boost to the tourism sector. 160 **He has scheduled a meeting with Sarasota city council members for next Tuesday** in hopes of reviving the proposal.

어휘 strike out 실패하다   deny 거부하다; 부인하다   commission 위원회   intention 의도, 목적   classify A as A를 ~로 분류하다
wetland 습지(대)   natural habitat 자연 서식지   block 막다, 차단하다   keep A out of A를 ~의 안에 들이지 않다
give a boost to ~에 활력을 불어넣다   in hopes of (=in the hope of) ~할 거라는 희망으로   revive 소생시키다, 되살리다

---

158. What is the topic of the article?

(A) The closure of a stadium
(B) The announcement of a sports tournament
(C) The rejection of a building project
(D) The opening of an environmental park

기사의 주제는 무엇인가?

(A) 경기장 폐쇄
(B) 스포츠 토너먼트 발표
(C) 건설 계획 불승인
(D) 환경 공원 개장

해설 주제/목적 문제 글의 주제나 목적은 대개 지문 도입부에 제시된다. 첫 번째 단락에서 센테니얼 스타디움이 두 번째 경기장을 건설하기 위해 계획안을 제출했지만(submitted plans for a second stadium) 허가를 받지 못했다(permission to start construction was denied)고 했으므로 (C)가 정답이다.

---

159. What is suggested about the Hampton neighborhood?

(A) It enforces strict traffic regulations.
(B) It is the home of some wildlife.
(C) It includes several tourist attractions.
(D) It has changed a lot in three years.

햄프턴 인근에 대해 암시된 것은?

(A) 엄격한 교통 규정을 시행한다.
(B) 일부 야생 생물의 서식지이다.
(C) 여러 관광 명소가 포함되어 있다.
(D) 3년간 많이 변했다.

해설 추론/암시 문제 질문의 키워드인 Hampton neighborhood는 두 번째 단락에 언급되어 있다. 햄프턴 인근의 미개발지는 많은 조류와 파충류의 자연 서식지(the natural habitat of many birds and reptiles)인 탓에 환경 단체들이 경기장 건설 계획을 막고 있다고 했으므로 (B)가 정답이다.

패러프레이징 the natural habitat of many birds and reptiles → the home of some wildlife

어휘 enforce 시행하다, 실시하다   strict 엄격한   tourist attraction 관광 명소

160. What does Mr. Amos plan to do next week?

(A) Propose a city tour
(B) Start a new job
(C) Take part in a competition
(D) Meet with local officials

아모스 씨는 다음 주에 무엇을 할 계획인가?

(A) 도시 관광 제안하기
(B) 새로운 일 시작하기
(C) 대회에 참가하기
(D) 지역 공무원들과 만나기

> **해설** 세부 사항 문제 마지막 단락에서 아모스 씨가 다음 주 화요일에 사라소타 시 의회 의원들과 회의(a meeting with Sarasota city council members)를 한다고 했으므로 (D)가 정답이다.
>
> **패러프레이징** a meeting with Sarasota city council members → Meet with local officials
>
> **어휘** take part in ~에 참가하다 competition (경연) 대회, 시합 official 공무원, 관리; 공식의

Attention: Wadena LTD Employees

—[1]—. The Wadena LTD management team is thrilled to inform everyone that **161 we have been nominated for the Innovative Workplace Award**. The winner will be announced on July 10. —[2]—. As you know, this is a highly prestigious award. **161 Great job, everyone!** **163 Over the past years, we have restructured our management system and provided intensive training to employees.** These measures have clearly been effective.

We plan to continue to strive for improvement at all levels of the company, and **162 the HR department would love to hear your ideas on how to do so**. Please e-mail Helen Callaway at h.callaway@wadenaltd.com if you have anything to share. —[4]—.

와데나 LTD 직원들은 주목해 주세요.

와데나 LTD 경영팀은 모두에게 **161 우리가 혁신적인 회사상 후보로 지명되었다**는 것을 알리게 되어 흥분됩니다. 수상자는 7월 10일에 발표될 것입니다. 여러분도 아시다시피 이것은 매우 권위 있는 상입니다. **161 모두 수고하셨습니다!** **163 지난 몇 해간 우리는 경영 체제를 개편하고, 직원들에게 집중 교육을 제공했습니다.** 이러한 조치는 분명히 효과가 있었습니다.

우리는 회사의 모든 역량을 동원하여 개선을 위해 계속해서 노력할 계획이며, **162 인사부는 그렇게 하는 방법에 관한 여러분의 의견을 듣고 싶습니다.** 무엇이든 공유할 게 있으면 헬렌 캘러웨이에게 h.callaway@wadenaltd.com으로 이메일을 보내 주시기 바랍니다.

> **어휘** attention 주의 (집중), 주목 management 경영, 운영, 관리 be thrilled to do ~해서 흥분되다 inform 알리다, 통지하다 be nominated for ~의 후보로 지명되다 innovative 혁신적인 workplace 직장, 업무 현장 highly 매우, 대단히 prestigious 명성 있는, 권위 있는 restructure 개편하다, 구조를 조정하다 intensive 집중적인 strive for ~을 얻으려고 노력하다 improvement 향상, 개선

161. What is the purpose of the announcement?

(A) To introduce a new management structure
(B) To congratulate employees on an achievement
(C) To encourage staff to attend a training session
(D) To confirm an award winner

공지의 목적은 무엇인가?

(A) 새로운 경영 구조를 소개하기 위해서
(B) 성취에 대해 직원들을 축하해 주기 위해서
(C) 직원들이 교육 시간에 참석하도록 독려하기 위해서
(D) 수상자를 확인하기 위해서

> **해설** 주제/목적 문제 글의 주제나 목적은 대개 지문 도입부에 제시된다. 첫 문장에서 자사가 혁신적인 회사상의 후보로 지명되었다(we have been nominated for the Innovative Workplace Award)는 것을 알린 다음 직원들에게 수고했다(Great job, everyone)고 격려했다. 따라서 직원들이 거둔 성과를 축하하기 위한 글임을 알 수 있으므로 (B)가 정답이다.
>
> **어휘** congratulate on ~에 대해 축하하다 achievement 업적, 성취 encourage A to do A가 ~하도록 권장하다

162. What is true about the HR department?

(A) Its manager will be promoted soon.
(B) It will assess employees' performance.
(C) Its newest employee is Helen Callaway.
(D) It is seeking feedback from employees.

인사부에 대해서 사실인 것은?

(A) 인사부장이 곧 승진될 것이다.
(B) 직원들의 실적을 평가할 것이다.
(C) 가장 최근에 들어온 직원이 헬렌 캘러웨이다.
(D) 직원들로부터 의견을 구하고 있다.

해설 TRUE 문제 질문의 키워드인 the HR department가 언급된 부분에 집중해야 한다. 지문 후반부에서 개선을 위해 노력할 계획(We plan to continue to strive for improvement)이라고 언급하며, 인사부에서는 직원들의 의견을 듣고 싶다(the HR department would love to hear your ideas)고 했으므로 (D)가 정답이다.

패러프레이징 hear your ideas on how to do so → is seeking feedback from employees

어휘 promote 승진시키다; 홍보하다   assess 평가하다   performance 실적, 성과; 공연, 연주   seek 구하다, 찾다

163. In which of the positions marked [1], [2], [3], and [4] does the following sentence best belong?

"These measures have clearly been effective."

(A) [1]   (B) [2]   **(C) [3]**   (D) [4]

[1], [2], [3], [4]로 표시된 곳 중에서 다음 문장이 들어가기에 가장 적절한 곳은?

"이러한 조치는 분명히 효과가 있었습니다."

(A) [1]   (B) [2]   **(C) [3]**   (D) [4]

해설 문장 삽입 문제 주어진 문장의 These measures가 가리키는 대상이 무엇인지 찾아야 한다. 보통 '조치'라 함은 특정 상황에 필요한 대책을 말하므로 이와 관련한 내용 뒤에 위치하는 것이 적절하다. 첫 번째 단락 후반부에서 경영 체제를 개편했으며(we have restructured our management system) 직원 교육을 실시했다(provided intensive training to employees)고 했으므로 (C)가 정답이다.

어휘 measure 조치; 척도; 측정하다   clearly 분명하게   effective 효과적인

Turn your garden into a new income stream!

Fairmont Skills Center Course #5892: Growing Herbs for Profit

Fresh herbs are a popular product all year round, including in winter. With just a few skills, you can operate your own business growing and selling herbs.

The ongoing work for an herb garden is minimal, meaning **164 you won't have to spend endless hours tending to your plants**.

Fairmont Skills Center offers:
- Experienced instructors who can personalize class materials to the students' needs
- A range of class structures to suit the schedules of busy people
  Course A: Mondays 6 P.M.–8 P.M.
  Course B: Wednesdays 1 P.M.–3 P.M.
  Course C: Saturdays 9 A.M.–11 A.M.
- **165 Lower course fee with proof of residence in Fairmont**
- A complete explanation on the process from start to finish, including **166 teaching you the best ways to market your herbs** to local restaurants and individuals
- Upon completing the course, **167 you will be given a password that gives you access to our exclusive online forum**, where you can ask questions and get help from other herb growers.

당신의 정원을 새로운 수익 창출원으로 바꿔 보세요!

페어몬트 기술 센터 강좌 5892번: 수익을 위한 허브 기르기

신선한 허브는 겨울을 포함해서 일 년 내내 인기 있는 상품입니다. 단 몇 가지 기술만 있으면 허브를 길러서 판매하는 당신만의 사업을 운영할 수 있습니다.

허브 정원을 위해 하는 작업은 아주 미미한데, 이는 곧 **164 식물에 신경 쓰느라 무한정 시간을 보내지 않아도 된다**는 것을 의미합니다.

페어몬트 기술 센터는 다음을 제공합니다:
• 수업 자료를 학생들의 요구에 맞출 수 있는 경험 많은 강사들
• 바쁜 분들의 일정에 맞는 다양한 수업 체계
  A강좌: 월요일 오후 6시–8시
  B강좌: 수요일 오후 1시–3시
  C강좌: 토요일 오전 9시–11시
• **165 페어몬트 거주 증명서가 있으면 수강료 인하**
• 지역 식당이나 개인에게 **166 당신의 허브를 선보이기 위한 가장 좋은 방법을 가르치는 걸** 포함하여, 하나부터 열까지 꼼꼼한 과정 설명
• 강좌를 끝내자마자 **167 당신은 저희의 전용 온라인 포럼에 접속하는 비밀번호를 받게 되며**, 그곳에서 질문을 하고 다른 허브 재배자들로부터 도움을 받을 수 있습니다.

How much can you make by selling herbs? Here are the prices currently paid by local restaurants.

| Basil | $14.00/lb. | Chives | $13.50/lb. |
| Oregano | $13.75/lb. | Coriander | $17.00/lb. |

Enroll by March 1 at www.fairmontsc.com!

허브를 판매해서 얼마나 벌 수 있을까요? 다음은 지역 식당들이 현재 지급하는 가격입니다.

| 바질 | 14.00달러/파운드 | 차이브 | 13.50달러/파운드 |
| 오레가노 | 13.75달러/파운드 | 고수 | 17.00달러/파운드 |

3월 1일까지 www.fairmontsc.com에서 등록하세요!

어휘 turn A into B A를 B로 바꾸다   income stream 지속적으로 창출되는 수익   profit 이익, 수익   all year round 일 년 내내
ongoing 진행 중인   tend to ~에 신경을 쓰다   personalize (개인의 필요에) 맞추다   proof 증명(서)   residence 거주; 거주지
market (상품을) 내놓다, 선보이다   upon doing ~하자마자   exclusive 전용의; 독점적인   enroll 등록하다

---

164. What benefit of growing herbs as a business is mentioned in the brochure?

(A) Small space needed
(B) Guaranteed large profits
(C) Ease of using equipment
(D) Short time commitment

사업으로 허브를 재배하는 어떤 이점이 브로슈어에 언급되어 있는가?

(A) 작은 공간 필요
(B) 상당한 이익 보장
(C) 장비 이용의 용이함
(D) 짧은 시간 투입

해설 세부 사항 문제 두 번째 단락에서 허브 정원을 가꾸는 작업은 많지 않기 때문에(The ongoing work for an herb garden is minimal) 시간을 많이 투자하지 않아도 된다고 했으므로 (D)가 정답이다.

---

165. Who can get a discount on the course?

(A) Advanced gardeners
(B) Restaurant owners
(C) Students with high grades
(D) People who live in Fairmont

누가 강좌에 대해 할인을 받을 수 있는가?

(A) 수준급 정원사들
(B) 식당 주인들
(C) 점수가 좋은 학생들
(D) 페어몬트에 사는 사람들

해설 세부 사항 문제 리스트의 세 번째 항목에서 페어몬트 거주 증명서(proof of residence in Fairmont)가 있으면 수강료가 저렴하다고 했으므로 (D)가 정답이다.

---

166. What is true about the course?

(A) It will have ten total hours of training.
(B) It offers information about marketing.
(C) It will be taught outdoors.
(D) It is offered only in winter.

강좌에 대해 사실인 것은?

(A) 총 10시간의 교육이 있을 것이다.
(B) 마케팅에 관한 정보를 제공한다.
(C) 야외에서 수업을 받을 것이다.
(D) 강좌는 겨울에만 열린다.

해설 TRUE 문제 리스트의 네 번째 항목에서 지역 식당이나 개인들에게 허브를 선보이는(to market your herbs) 최고의 방법을 가르친다고 한 것을 마케팅에 관한 정보를 제공한다고 바꿔 표현한 (B)가 정답이다.

---

167. What will course participants receive?

(A) Ongoing online support
(B) Some gardening supplies
(C) A certificate of completion
(D) A contract with a local restaurant

강좌 참가자들은 무엇을 받을 것인가?

(A) 진행 중인 온라인 지원
(B) 몇몇 정원 용품
(C) 수료증
(D) 지역 식당과의 계약

해설 세부 사항 문제 리스트의 다섯 번째 항목에서 강좌를 마치면 전용 온라인 포럼(exclusive online forum)에 접속하는 비밀번호를 받게 되는데, 그곳에서 질문을 하거나(you can ask questions) 다른 허브 재배자들로부터 도움을 받을 수 있다(get help from other herb growers)고 했다. 따라서 강좌를 수료하면 현재 진행되고 있는 온라인 지원 서비스를 받을 수 있는 것이므로 (A)가 정답이다.

Kayla Lambert (9:05 A.M.): Hi, Tara and Sven. **168 Is the due date for the spring catalog still March 6?**

Tara Hull (9:07 A.M.): It needs to be sent to the printer on March 3.

Kayla Lambert (9:08 A.M.): I hadn't heard about that change.

Tara Hull (9:09 A.M.): Sorry, Kayla! We discussed it at Monday's meeting, but **169 I forgot that you took that day off.**

Kayla Lambert (9:10 A.M.): I should still be able to make that work.

Tara Hull (9:11 A.M.): I'm glad to hear that.

Kayla Lambert (9:12 A.M.): How are you two doing with your catalog assignments?

Tara Hull (9:14 A.M.): Actually, I've finished preparing the cover and the layout. **170 If either of you need some help, I'm available.**

Kayla Lambert (9:16 A.M.): I'm fine.

Sven Ebersbach (9:17 A.M.): Would you mind helping me write some of the product descriptions? They're taking a lot longer than I expected.

Tara Hull (9:19 A.M.): Sure! I'll head over to your office. **171 But first, let me stop by the warehouse to get some samples. It will be easier to do if we can see and touch the clothes in person.**

Sven Ebersbach (9:21 A.M.): That sounds perfect. Thanks!

Tara Hull (9:22 A.M.): My pleasure.

케일라 램버트 (오전 9시 05분): 안녕하세요, 타라, 스벤. **168 봄 카탈로그 마감일은 여전히 3월 6일인가요?**

타라 헐 (오전 9시 07분): 그것은 3월 3일에 인쇄소에 보내져야 해요.

케일라 램버트 (오전 9시 08분): 그런 변경에 대해서는 듣지 못했어요.

타라 헐 (오전 9시 09분): 미안해요, 케일라! 우리가 월요일 회의에서 그것을 논의했는데, **169 당신이 그날 휴가를 냈다는 걸 잊었어요.**

케일라 램버트 (오전 9시 10분): 그래도 해낼 수 있을 것 같네요.

타라 헐 (오전 9시 11분): 그렇다니 다행이에요.

케일라 램버트 (오전 9시 12분): 두 분은 카탈로그 업무가 어떻게 되어 가고 있나요?

타라 헐 (오전 9시 14분): 저는 표지와 레이아웃 준비를 끝냈어요. **170 여러분 중 누구든 도움이 필요하면 제가 시간이 돼요.**

케일라 램버트 (오전 9시 16분): 난 괜찮아요.

스벤 에버스바흐 (오전 9시 17분): 상품 설명 일부를 쓰는 걸 도와주시겠어요? 예상했던 것보다 시간이 훨씬 더 오래 걸리네요.

타라 헐 (오전 9시 19분): 물론이죠! 제가 당신의 사무실로 갈게요. **171 하지만 우선 샘플을 좀 얻으러 창고에 잠시 들를게요. 우리가 직접 옷을 보고 만질 수 있으면 하기가 더 쉬울 거예요.**

스벤 에버스바흐 (오전 9시 21분): 그거 좋네요. 고마워요!

타라 헐 (오전 9시 22분): 천만에요.

어휘 due date 마감일, 만기일 take a day off 하루 휴가를 내다 assignment 할당된 일, 담당 업무 layout (책 등의) 레이아웃, 배치 product description 제품 설명 head over to ~로 가다, ~로 향하다 stop by (~에) 잠시 들르다 in person 직접

168. What does Ms. Lambert want to know about?

(A) A project deadline
(B) A workshop date
(C) A printer function
(D) A meeting schedule

램버트 씨는 무엇에 대해 알고 싶어 하는가?

(A) 프로젝트 마감일
(B) 워크숍 날짜
(C) 프린터 기능
(D) 회의 일정

해설 세부 사항 문제 첫 번째 메시지에서 램버트 씨가 봄 카탈로그의 기한이 여전히 3월 6일인지 물었으므로 (A)가 정답이다.

패러프레이징 due date → project deadline

어휘 deadline 마감일 function 기능; 기능하다

169. What is indicated about Ms. Lambert?

(A) She recently joined Ms. Hull and Mr. Ebersbach's team.
(B) She is unable to work additional hours.
(C) She supervised the catalog last time.
(D) She was not in the office on Monday.

램버트 씨에 대해 명시된 것은 무엇인가?
(A) 최근에 헐 씨와 에버스바흐 씨 팀에 합류했다.
(B) 추가 근무를 할 수 없다.
(C) 지난번에 카탈로그 작업을 지휘했다.
(D) 월요일에 사무실에 없었다.

해설 **TRUE 문제** 헐 씨의 9시 09분 메시지에 정답 단서가 있다. 월요일 회의에서 카탈로그 마감 기한 변경을 논의했는데, 그날이 램버트 씨의 휴가일이라는 걸 깜빡했다(I forgot that you took that day off)고 했다. 따라서 램버트 씨가 월요일에 사무실에 없었다는 걸 알 수 있으므로 (D)가 정답이다.

어휘 recently 최근에 join 합류하다 additional 추가의 supervise 지휘하다, 감독하다

---

170. At 9:16 A.M., what does Ms. Lambert mean when she writes, "I'm fine"?

(A) She is enjoying her part of the assignment.
(B) She is not upset about a miscommunication.
(C) She does not need any help from Ms. Hull.
(D) She would like to work with Mr. Ebersbach.

오전 9시 16분에, 램버트 씨가 "난 괜찮아요"라고 한 의도는 무엇인가?
(A) 그녀에게 할당된 업무를 즐겁게 하고 있다.
(B) 의사소통 오류에 대해 기분 나쁘지 않다.
(C) 헐 씨의 도움이 전혀 필요하지 않다.
(D) 에버스바흐 씨와 함께 일하고 싶다.

해설 **의도 파악 문제** 헐 씨의 9시 14분 메시지 마지막 문장에서 도움이 필요하면 자기가 시간이 된다고 했고, 제시된 문장은 램버트 씨가 이에 대한 응답으로 한 말이다. 따라서 도와주지 않아도 괜찮다는 의도이므로 (C)가 정답이다.

어휘 upset 화가 난, 마음이 상한 miscommunication 의사소통 오류

---

171. What will Ms. Hull most likely do next?

(A) Pick up some clothing items
(B) Meet some clients at her office
(C) Carry out a warehouse inspection
(D) Print descriptions of some products

헐 씨는 다음에 무엇을 하겠는가?
(A) 일부 의류 품목 가져오기
(B) 그녀의 사무실에서 몇몇 고객 만나기
(C) 창고 점검 수행하기
(D) 일부 상품의 설명서 출력하기

해설 **추론/암시 문제** 에버스바흐 씨가 도움을 요청하자 헐 씨는 자신이 에버스바흐 씨의 사무실로 가겠다(I'll head over to your office)면서, 그 전에 창고에 들러 샘플을 가져오겠다(stop by the warehouse to get some samples)고 했다. 뒤이어 옷을 직접 보고 만지면(see and touch the clothes in person) 작업이 더 쉬울 거라고 한 것으로 보아 헐 씨가 창고에서 가져올 샘플이 의류임을 알 수 있으므로 (A)가 정답이다.

패러프레이징 get some samples → pick up some clothing items

어휘 carry out ~을 수행하다 inspection 점검, 검사

Reviewed by Christina L.

When I renovated my kitchen, I was excited about getting a new oven. **172 After seeing the Zesta 115 being demonstrated at my local department store, I decided to buy it.** —[1]—.

The Zesta 115 has very thick walls, so **173 it takes much less energy to operate** than most ovens. —[2]—. The interior is 115 liters, **173 leaving plenty of space** for a large cooking tray, yet **173 it can still get up to the desired temperature rapidly.** I thought the various settings were straightforward, and I especially love that it is easy to clean. **174 You can use the steam-cleaning function** to loosen the stuck-on substances inside and wipe them off. —[3]—. **174 Alternatively, you can use the extreme-heat function**, which burns food and grease down to ash. The oven is locked during that setting for safety reasons.

Overall, I am pleased with this appliance, but I was not impressed by the interior shelves. **175 It is very difficult to remove the shelves to place them higher or lower.** This is a major issue if you have a wide variety in the sizes of foods you cook. I think that part of the design could have been improved.

크리스티나 L.의 평가

제 주방을 보수했을 때, 저는 새 오븐을 살 생각에 신났습니다. 172 저희 지역 백화점에서 제스타 115가 시연된 것을 본 후, 저는 그것을 구입하기로 결정했습니다.

제스타 115는 내벽이 매우 두꺼워서 대부분의 오븐보다 173 작동하는 데 훨씬 적은 에너지를 소모합니다. 내부는 115리터이며 대형 요리용 쟁반이 들어갈 정도로 173 공간이 충분합니다. 그런데도 173 희망 온도까지 신속하게 올라갈 수 있습니다. 저는 다양한 설정들이 직관적이라고 생각했고, 특히 세척하기 쉽다는 점이 매우 마음에 듭니다. 내부에 달라붙은 물질을 불려서 씻어내는 174 스팀 세척 기능을 사용할 수 있습니다. 174 아니면 극열 기능을 사용할 수 있는데, 이것은 음식물과 기름기를 모두 태워 재가 되게 합니다. 안전상의 이유로 이 설정 중에는 오븐이 잠깁니다.

전반적으로 저는 이 가전제품에 만족하지만, 내부 선반들은 인상적이지 않았습니다. 175 위치를 높이거나 낮추기 위해 선반을 떼어 내기가 아주 어렵습니다. 만약 당신이 요리하는 음식의 크기가 아주 다양하다면 이것은 중요한 문제입니다. 그 부분의 디자인이 개선될 수 있었을 것이라고 생각합니다.

어휘 renovate 개조하다, 보수하다 demonstrate (용법을) 보여 주다, 설명하다 operate 작동되다; 가동시키다 interior 내부(의) plenty of 많은, 충분한 desired 희망하는, 바라는 temperature 온도 rapidly 빨리, 신속히 setting 설정 straightforward 간단한, 쉬운 function 기능; 기능하다 loosen 느슨하게 하다 stuck-on 달라붙은 substance 물질 wipe off ~을 닦아 내다 alternatively (~가 아니면) 그 대신에 extreme 극도의, 극심한 grease 기름, 지방 burn down ~을 다 태우다 overall 전반적으로; 전반적인

172. Why most likely did the reviewer purchase the Zesta 115?

(A) It is well known for its low price.
(B) It had the most positive reviews.
(C) It was recommended by her friend.
(D) It was presented in a demonstration.

평가자는 왜 제스타 115를 구입했겠는가?

(A) 저렴한 가격으로 유명하다.
(B) 가장 긍정적인 리뷰들이 있었다.
(C) 친구에게 추천을 받았다.
(D) 제품 시연에서 선보여졌다.

해설 추론/암시 문제 첫 번째 단락의 마지막 문장에서 제품 시연을 보고 난 후(After seeing the Zesta 115 being demonstrated) 구입하기로 결정했다고 했으므로 (D)가 정답이다.

어휘 be known for ~ 때문에 유명하다 present 보여 주다, 나타내다

173. What is NOT a benefit of the Zesta 115 mentioned by the reviewer?

(A) It has multiple shelves.
(B) It is energy efficient.
(C) It is an ample size.
(D) It can heat up quickly.

평가자가 언급하지 않은 제스타 115의 이점은?

(A) 선반이 많이 있다.
(B) 에너지 효율이 좋다.
(C) 크기가 넉넉하다.
(D) 빨리 뜨거워질 수 있다.

해설 세부 사항 문제 두 번째 단락에 제스타 115의 장점이 열거되어 있는데, 선반의 수에 대해서는 언급되지 않았으므로 (A)가 정답이다. (B)는 훨씬 적은 에너지가 든다(it takes much less energy to operate)고 했으며, (C)는 공간이 충분하다(leaving plenty of space)고 언급했고, (D)는 희망 온도에 빨리 다다른다(get up to the desired temperature rapidly)고 나와 있다.

패러프레이징 takes much less energy to operate → energy efficient
plenty of space → an ample size (= a good / fair / nice size = fairly big)
get up to the desired temperature rapidly → heat up quickly

어휘 benefit 혜택, 이득 multiple 다수의, 많은 energy efficient 에너지 효율이 좋은 ample 충분한

---

174. What is true about the Zesta 115?

(A) It is the company's newest model.
(B) It offers two options for cleaning.
(C) It is endorsed by professional chefs.
(D) It comes with a free cooking tray.

제스타 115에 대해 사실인 것은?

(A) 회사의 최신 모델이다.
(B) 두 가지 세척 옵션을 제공한다.
(C) 전문 요리사에 의해 광고된다.
(D) 무료 요리용 쟁반이 딸려 있다.

해설 TRUE 문제 두 번째 단락 후반부에서 스팀 세척 기능을 사용할 수 있다(You can use the steam-cleaning function)고 했으며, 그게 아니면 극열 기능도 있다(you can use the extreme-heat function)고 했으므로 (B)가 정답이다.

어휘 option 선택(권), 옵션 endorse (유명인이 광고에 나와서) 홍보하다 come with ~가 딸려 있다

---

175. In which of the positions marked [1], [2], [3], and [4] does the following sentence best belong?

"This is a major issue if you have a wide variety in the sizes of foods you cook."

(A) [1]
(B) [2]
(C) [3]
(D) [4]

[1], [2], [3], [4]로 표시된 곳 중에서 다음 문장이 들어가기에 가장 적절한 곳은?

"만약 당신이 요리하는 음식의 크기가 아주 다양하다면 이것은 중요한 문제입니다."

(A) [1]
(B) [2]
(C) [3]
(D) [4]

해설 문장 삽입 문제 주어진 문장에 지시대명사 This가 있고, 이를 major issue라고 한 것으로 보아 제품의 단점과 관련한 내용 뒤에 위치하는 것이 적절하다. 마지막 단락에서 내부 선반을 떼어 내기가 아주 어렵다(It is very difficult to remove the shelves)고 했는데, This는 바로 이 문장, 즉 선반을 분리하기 어려운 점을 가리킨다. 따라서 선반 높이 조절이 어렵기 때문에 음식 크기가 다양하다면 제품을 사용하기가 힘들 거라는 문맥이 되어 자연스럽게 연결되므로 (D)가 정답이다.

From: Chun Liu 〈liuc@raverdevelopment.com〉
To: Matheus Jones 〈jonesm@raverdevelopment.com〉
Subject: Staff meeting
Date: January 18

Hi Matheus,

¹⁷⁶ **Thanks again for agreeing to conduct Thursday's staff meeting since I've changed my travel plans and won't be back in the office until next week.** I know you're currently working on the notice for the new parking policy. If you need someone to look it over, please send it to Troy Saldana. I'd do it myself, but I didn't bring my laptop with me on vacation, and ¹⁷⁷ **my phone does not have the encryption software needed to open confidential company files.**

¹⁷⁸ **The monthly fee for on-site parking will be $160.** The lot will open on February 1, and we are expecting a lot of people to be interested in getting a parking space.

Thanks!

Chun

발신: 천 리우
수신: 마테우스 존스
제목: 직원 회의
날짜: 1월 18일

안녕하세요, 마테우스 씨.

¹⁷⁶ 목요일 직원 회의 진행에 동의해 주셔서 다시 한번 감사드려요. 제가 여행 계획을 변경하는 바람에 다음 주까지 사무실에 없을 거라서요. 당신이 현재 새로운 주차 정책을 위한 공지 작업을 하고 있다는 걸 알아요. 만약 그것을 검토할 누군가가 필요하면 트로이 살다나 씨에게 보내시기 바랍니다. 제가 직접 하고 싶지만 휴가지에 노트북을 가져오지 않았고, ¹⁷⁷ 제 전화기에는 회사 기밀 파일을 여는 데 필요한 암호화 소프트웨어가 없어요.

¹⁷⁸ 현장 주차 월 요금은 160달러가 될 거예요. 주차장은 2월 1일에 개방할 것이고, 우리는 많은 사람들이 주차 공간을 확보하는 데 관심 갖기를 기대하고 있습니다.

감사합니다!

천

어휘 conduct 이끌다, 지휘하다   work on ~에 착수하다, ~에 노력을 들이다   look over ~을 검토하다   encryption 암호화
confidential 기밀의, 비밀의   on-site 현장의   lot (특정 용도의) 부지

Notice to Raver Development Staff

The new policy for our on-site lot will go into effect on February 1. ¹⁷⁹ **Employees who wish to have a designated parking space should visit the administration department and complete the paperwork as below.**

¹⁷⁹ **Terms and Conditions Agreement**	¹⁷⁹ **Employees must sign this document to demonstrate that they will follow all parking rules and maintain the parking space.** (no littering, no repair work on-site, responsible driving, etc.)
Banking Instructions	¹⁷⁸ **A fee of $125 will be charged automatically every month.** This will be collected on the 25th of the month for use of the parking space the following month.
Vehicle Information	Employees should provide information about the make and model of their vehicle along with the license plate number. A parking pass with the plate number will be issued if you are selected for a space.

레이버 개발 공사 직원들에게 알립니다

우리의 현장 주차장을 위한 새 정책이 2월 1일부터 발효될 것입니다. ¹⁷⁹ 지정 주차 공간을 갖길 바라는 직원들은 관리부에 방문하여 아래와 같은 서류를 작성해야 합니다.

¹⁷⁹ 약관 동의	¹⁷⁹ 직원들은 모든 주차 규정을 따르고 주차 공간을 잘 유지할 것임을 보여 주기 위해 이 서류에 서명해야 합니다. (쓰레기 투기 금지, 주차장에서 수리 작업 금지, 책임감 있는 운전 등)
뱅킹 관련 설명	¹⁷⁸ 매달 125달러의 요금이 자동으로 빠져나갈 것입니다. 이것은 익월 주차 공간 사용을 위해 당월 25일에 징수될 것입니다.
차량 정보	직원들은 차량 번호와 함께 차량의 제조사 및 모델에 관한 정보를 제공해야 합니다. 지정 주차 공간 대상자로 선정되면 차량 번호가 있는 주차권이 발부될 것입니다.

Employee Profile	As the demand is expected to exceed the availability, the spaces will be allocated in the following order: disabled employees, senior full-time employees, junior full-time employees, part-time employees. ¹⁸⁰ **We may also leave five spaces for visitor use, but this has not been decided yet.**	직원 신상 명세	수요가 이용 가능 정도를 초과할 것으로 예상되므로, 주차 공간은 다음과 같은 순서, 즉 장애가 있는 직원들, 직급이 높은 정규 직원들, 직급이 낮은 정규 직원들, 시간제 직원들 순으로 할당될 것입니다. ¹⁸⁰ 우리는 또한 방문객이 이용할 수 있도록 다섯 자리를 남겨 둘 수도 있지만 이것은 아직 결정되지 않았습니다.

어휘 go into effect (정책 등이) 발효되다, 실시되다   designated 지정된   administration 관리, 행정   complete (빠짐없이) 기입하다, 작성하다; 완료하다   paperwork 서류 작업   terms and conditions 약관   agreement 합의, 동의   litter 쓰레기를 버리다; 쓰레기   charge (요금을) 청구하다; 요금   collect 징수하다; 모으다   make (특정 회사에서 만든) 제품   along with ~와 함께   license plate number 차량 번호   parking pass 주차권   issue 발부하다, 교부하다   exceed 초과하다   availability 이용 가능성   allocate 할당하다   disabled 장애가 있는   senior 상급의; 상급자, 연장자   junior 하급의; 하급자, 아랫사람

176. What does Ms. Liu indicate in the e-mail?

(A) Mr. Jones can borrow her work laptop.
(B) Mr. Jones should arrive to the meeting early.
(C) She will send an updated notice to Mr. Jones.
(D) She will not return to the office in time for a meeting.

이메일에서 리우 씨가 명시한 것은 무엇인가?

(A) 존스 씨는 그녀의 작업 노트북을 빌릴 수 있다.
(B) 존스 씨는 회의에 일찍 도착해야 한다.
(C) 그녀가 존스 씨에게 업데이트된 공지를 보낼 것이다.
(D) 그녀가 회의 시간에 맞춰 회사에 돌아오지 못할 것이다.

해설 TRUE 문제 이메일 첫 번째 문장에서 리우 씨는 여행 계획이 변경되어(I've changed my travel plans) 다음 주까지 사무실에 없을 거라고(won't be back in the office until next week) 했다. 따라서 리우 씨가 여행 때문에 목요일 회의에 참석하지 못할 것임을 알 수 있으므로 (D)가 정답이다.

177. Why will Ms. Liu be unable to review a policy document?

(A) She is not familiar with the plans for the policy.
(B) She does not have time to do it during her vacation.
(C) She cannot open sensitive files on her phone.
(D) She did not get permission in advance from Mr. Saldana.

리우 씨는 왜 정책 서류를 검토할 수 없을 것인가?

(A) 정책 기획에 익숙하지 않다.
(B) 휴가 동안 그것을 할 시간이 없다.
(C) 자신의 전화기로 민감한 파일을 열 수 없다.
(D) 살다나 씨로부터 사전에 허락을 받지 않았다.

해설 세부 사항 문제 이메일 첫 번째 문단 마지막 문장에서 자신이 직접 검토하고 싶지만(I'd do it myself) 노트북을 가져오지 않았다(I didn't bring my laptop with me)고 했다. 게다가 전화기에는 회사 기밀 파일을 여는 데 필요한 암호화 소프트웨어가 없다고 했으므로 (C)가 정답이다.

178. What changed about Raver Development's parking policy after Ms. Liu's e-mail?

(A) The person in charge of assigning spaces
(B) The date the policy will take effect
(C) The cost of using a parking space
(D) The day of the month to pay a fee

리우 씨의 이메일 이후에 레이버 개발 공사의 주차 정책에 대해 무엇이 바뀌었는가?

(A) 주차 공간 할당 업무를 하는 사람
(B) 정책이 시행될 날짜
(C) 주차 공간을 이용하는 비용
(D) 요금을 지불할 월의 날짜

해설 연계 문제 [세부 사항] 이메일 두 번째 문단에서 현장 주차 월 요금이 160달러가 될 것(The monthly fee for on-site parking will be $160)이라고 했다. 하지만 공지의 뱅킹 관련 설명(Banking Instructions)에는 매달 125달러가 자동으로 청구된다(A fee of $125 will be charged automatically every month)고 적혀 있다. 따라서 주차 요금이 변경된 것을 알 수 있으므로 (C)가 정답이다.

179. What will employees do in the administration department?

(A) Confirm they agree to set terms
(B) Provide proof of their car insurance
(C) Request reimbursement for vehicle repairs
(D) Indicate the preferred location of a parking space

직원들은 관리부에서 무엇을 할 것인가?

(A) 정해진 조건들에 동의한다고 확인해 주기
(B) 자동차 보험 증서 제공하기
(C) 차량 수리에 대한 변제 요청하기
(D) 선호하는 주차 공간 위치 알려 주기

해설 세부 사항 문제 직원들은 관리부에 방문하여(visit the administration department) 주차 규정을 따르고(follow all parking rules) 주차 공간의 상태를 잘 유지하겠다(maintain the parking space)는 약관에 서명하라고 했으므로 (A)가 정답이다.

어휘 set 정해진   terms (계약 등의) 조건   reimbursement 변제, 상환   indicate 나타내다, 보여 주다

---

180. According to the notice, what is being considered?

(A) Allocating spaces based on a lottery system
(B) Purchasing another parking area
(C) Adding parking for non-employees
(D) Running a workshop on responsible driving

공지에 따르면 무엇이 고려되고 있는가?

(A) 추첨제에 기반해 공간을 할당하는 것
(B) 또 다른 주차 지역을 구입하는 것
(C) 직원이 아닌 사람들을 위해 주차 공간을 추가하는 것
(D) 책임 있는 운전에 관한 워크숍을 운영하는 것

해설 세부 사항 문제 직원 신상 명세(Employee Profile) 마지막 문장에서 방문객이 이용할 수 있도록 다섯 자리를 남겨둘 수도 있지만(leave five spaces for visitor use) 아직 결정되지 않았다(this has not been decided yet)고 했으므로 (C)가 정답이다.

From: Katrina Hume ⟨hume_k@barringtonconsultants.com⟩
To: Barry Roderick ⟨barryroderick@green-world.org⟩
Date: July 9
Subject: Green World Annual Meeting

Dear Mr. Roderick,

I am honored that **181 you have asked me to take part in the upcoming Green World Annual Meeting** on August 20, and **181 I am glad to say that I am able to do so**. I always enjoy sharing my knowledge about improving recycling rates. **183 It's always wonderful to have a reason to return to my hometown for a visit.**

I understand that you have not finalized the start time yet. Due to another speaking engagement that I have on the same day, **185 I would not be able to give the opening speech if you start before 10:00 A.M.** If that is the case, I would be happy to be the closing speaker.

I truly **182 appreciate** the efforts your organization has made to help the environment, and I look forward to promoting recycling and sustainable living with you.

Sincerely,

Katrina Hume

발신: 카트리나 흄
수신: 배리 로데릭
날짜: 7월 9일
제목: 그린 월드 연례 회의

로데릭 씨에게,

181 다가오는 8월 20일 그린 월드 연례 회의에 참여해 달라고 요청해 주셔서 영광이며, 181 그렇게 할 수 있다고 말씀드리게 되어 기쁩니다. 저는 항상 재활용률 향상에 관한 제 지식을 나누는 것을 좋아합니다. 183 방문차 제 고향으로 돌아올 이유가 있다는 건 언제나 기분 좋은 일입니다.

당신이 아직 개회 시간을 확정하지 못한 것을 이해합니다. 같은 날 제가 또 다른 연설 약속이 있기 때문에, 185 만약 오전 10시 전에 시작하신다면 개회사를 할 수 없을 것입니다. 그렇다면 기꺼이 폐회사 연설자가 되겠습니다.

당신의 단체가 환경을 돕기 위해 해 온 노력을 진심으로 182 높게 평가하며, 당신과 함께 재활용과 친환경적인 생활을 촉진하기를 고대합니다.

카트리나 흄

어휘 be honored that ~해서 영광이다   take part in ~에 참가하다   rate 비율, -율; 속도; 요금   engagement (업무상의) 약속   opening speech 개회사   if that is the case 그렇다면, 그런 이유라면   truly 진심으로   appreciate 인정하다; 고마워하다; 감상하다   sustainable (환경에 해를 끼치지 않고) 지속 가능한

Green World Hosts Annual Meeting
by Lisa Grise

The nonprofit environmental organization Green World hosted [184] **its annual meeting on August 20**. [183] **The event took place in Huntsville** on the Brookside University campus. The aim of the event was to raise awareness about environmental issues and provide practical advice. The event included speeches, workshops, and [184] **a session in which policymakers and business owners debated strategies for reducing single-use plastics**.

With [185] **highly respected consultant Katrina Hume as the opening speaker** and Reuse Manufacturing founder Eugene Akins as the closing speaker, there was a high level of expertise on display. Those interested in joining Green World or participating in future events are encouraged to visit www.green-world.org.

어휘 host 주최하다 nonprofit 비영리의 take place 개최되다 aim 목표, 목적 raise awareness 인식을 높이다 issue 문제, 쟁점; 발표하다, 발행하다 practical 실질적인 session (특정한 활동을 위한) 시간 policymaker 정책 입안자 debate 토론하다; 토론, 논의 strategy 전략 highly respected 매우 존경받는 consultant 컨설턴트, 자문 위원 founder 창립자, 설립자 expertise 전문 지식 on display 전시된 interested in ~에 관심이 있는 participate in ~에 참가하다 be encouraged to do ~하도록 장려되다

---

181. What is the purpose of the e-mail?

(A) To recommend an event
(B) To suggest a presentation topic
(C) To accept an invitation
(D) To change a date

이메일의 목적은 무엇인가?

(A) 행사를 추천하기 위해서
(B) 발표 주제를 제안하기 위해서
(C) 초청을 수락하기 위해서
(D) 날짜를 바꾸기 위해서

해설 주제/목적 문제 이메일의 목적은 대개 도입부에 제시된다. 첫 번째 단락에서 그린 월드 연례 회의에 참여해 달라고 요청해 주어서 영광이며, 그렇게 할 수 있다고 말하게 되어 기쁘다(I am glad to say that I am able to do so)고 한 것으로 보아 초청을 수락하기 위해 쓴 이메일임을 알 수 있으므로 (C)가 정답이다.

어휘 recommend 추천하다, 권장하다 suggest 제안하다 accept 받아들이다, 수락하다

---

182. In the e-mail, the word "appreciate" in paragraph 3, line 1, is closest in meaning to

(A) value
(B) realize
(C) enhance
(D) assess

이메일에서 세 번째 단락 첫 번째 줄의 "appreciate"와 의미상 가장 가까운 것은?

(A) 소중하게 생각하다
(B) 깨닫다
(C) 강화하다
(D) 평가하다

해설 동의어 찾기 문제 appreciate는 '가치를 인정하다; 고마워하다; 감상하다' 등 여러 가지 뜻으로 쓰인다. 여기서는 환경을 위해 해 온 노력을 진심으로 '높게 평가한다'는 의미이므로, 이와 의미가 가장 유사한 말은 (A) value이다.

183. What is true about Ms. Hume?

   (A) She grew up in Huntsville.
   (B) She started her own business.
   (C) She graduated from Brookside University.
   (D) She used to work with Mr. Roderick.

   흄 씨에 대해 사실인 것은?
   (A) 헌츠빌에서 자랐다.
   (B) 자신만의 사업을 시작했다.
   (C) 브룩사이드 대학을 졸업했다.
   (D) 로데릭 씨와 함께 일한 적이 있다.

   해설 연계 문제 [세부 사항] 첫 번째 지문의 첫 번째 단락 후반부에서 고향으로 돌아올 이유가 있다는 건 언제나 기분 좋은 일(It's always wonderful to have a reason to return to my hometown)이라고 했다. 두 번째 지문의 두 번째 문장에서는 그린 월드의 연례 회의가 헌츠빌에서 열렸다(The event took place in Huntsville)고 한 것으로 보아 흄 씨의 고향이 헌츠빌임을 알 수 있으므로 (A)가 정답이다.

   어휘 grow up 자라다, 성장하다   used to do 과거에 ~하곤 했었다 (cf. be used to doing ~하는 데 익숙하다)

---

184. According to Ms. Grise, what happened on August 20?

   (A) Environmental awards were presented.
   (B) New Green World members were confirmed.
   (C) A debate on disposable plastics was held.
   (D) A new recycling policy was proposed.

   그리즈 씨에 따르면 8월 20일에 무슨 일이 있었는가?
   (A) 환경 상이 수여되었다.
   (B) 새로운 그린 월드 회원이 확정되었다.
   (C) 일회용 플라스틱에 관한 토론이 열렸다.
   (D) 새로운 재활용 정책이 제안되었다.

   해설 세부 사항 문제 질문의 키워드인 August 20은 그린 월드 연례 회의가 열린 날짜이다. 두 번째 지문의 첫 번째 단락 후반부에서 정책 입안자들과 사업주들이 일회용 플라스틱을 줄이기 위한 전략들을 토론하는 시간(a session in which policymakers and business owners debated strategies for reducing single-use plastics)이 있었다고 했으므로 (C)가 정답이다.

   패러프레이징 debated strategies for reducing single-use plastics → A debate on disposable plastics was held.

   어휘 present 주다, 수여하다   confirm 확정하다, 확인해 주다   disposable 일회용의, 처분할 수 있는   be held (행사 등이) 열리다

---

185. What is implied about the Green World Annual Meeting?

   (A) It started after 10:00 A.M.
   (B) It had a speaker cancel at the last minute.
   (C) It included a meal for attendees.
   (D) It will be in the same location next year.

   그린 월드 연례 회의에 관해 암시된 것은?
   (A) 오전 10시 이후에 시작되었다.
   (B) 마지막 순간에 연사 취소가 있었다.
   (C) 참석자들을 위한 식사가 포함되었다.
   (D) 내년에 같은 장소에서 열릴 것이다.

   해설 연계 문제 [추론/암시] 첫 번째 지문의 두 번째 단락에서 흄 씨는 행사가 오전 10시 전에 시작하면 개회사를 할 수 없다(I would not be able to give the opening speech if you start before 10:00 A.M.)고 했다. 두 번째 지문의 두 번째 단락에서는 흄 씨가 개회사를 했다(Katrina Hume as the opening speaker)고 한 것으로 보아 연례 회의가 오전 10시 이후에 시작되었다는 걸 유추할 수 있으므로 (A)가 정답이다.

   어휘 at the last minute 마지막 순간에, 임박해서   attendee 참석자   location 위치, 장소

Marketing Coordinator Position at Diaz&Associates

Diaz&Associates, a Seattle-based firm dedicated to providing financial planning services, is looking for a new marketing coordinator. We have been in operation for two decades, and, for the first time in our company's history, [186] **we are expanding our business into the insurance industry**. Therefore, effective marketing will be crucial.

Position description: The marketing coordinator is primarily responsible for managing our social media accounts, [187] **writing articles for our online newsletter**, and organizing in-person and virtual events.

Requirements: [188] **A bachelor's or master's degree in marketing, business administration, or advertising is required along with three years of project management experience. Proficiency in GoCreate design software is a plus.**

Interested applicants should send a résumé to hr@diazandassoc.com.

디아즈&어소시에이츠 사 마케팅 진행 직무

디아즈&어소시에이츠 사는 재무 계획 서비스를 제공하는 데 몰두한, 시애틀에 기반을 둔 회사로 새로운 마케팅 진행 담당자를 찾고 있습니다. 우리는 20년간 운영해 왔으며, 우리 회사 역사상 처음으로 [186] **보험 업계로 사업을 확장하려고 합니다**. 따라서 효과적인 마케팅이 중요할 것입니다.

직무 설명: 마케팅 진행 담당자는 주로 우리의 소셜 미디어 계정을 관리하고, [187] **온라인 소식지를 위한 기사를 작성하고**, 대면 및 비대면 행사를 기획하는 일을 책임집니다.

자격 요건: [188] **3년간의 프로젝트 관리 경력과 함께 마케팅, 경영 또는 광고 분야의 학사 또는 석사 학위가 요구됩니다. 고크리에이트 디자인 소프트웨어에 능숙하면 유리합니다.**

관심 있는 지원자는 hr@diazandassoc.com으로 이력서를 보내세요.

어휘 coordinator 코디네이터, 조정자, 진행자 dedicated to *doing* ~하는 데 몰두[전념]한 in operation 운영[가동] 중인 decade 10년 expand 확장하다 insurance 보험 effective 효과적인 crucial 중요한, 결정적인 position description 직무 설명 primarily 주로 be responsible for ~에 책임이 있다; ~을 책임지고 있다 organize 조직하다, 준비하다 in-person 직접의 virtual (컴퓨터를 이용한) 가상의, 네트워크상의 requirement ((보통 복수형)) 필요 조건 bachelor's degree 학사 학위 master's degree 석사 학위 business administration 경영 관리 along with ~와 함께 proficiency 능숙함 plus ((비격식)) 이점, 좋은 점, 우대 applicant 지원자

Marketing Coordinator Interviews		
Applicant	Date&Time	Employment Details
Corina Geiger	October 8, 2:00 P.M.	Bachelor's degree in marketing; 2 years project management; proficient in GoCreate
[188] **Byoungmin Kim**	October 8, 4:00 P.M.	[188] **Master's degree in business administration; 3 years project management; proficient in GoCreate**
Darrell Crawford	October 9, 1:00 P.M.	Bachelor's degree in advertising; operates personal blog; 3 years project management
[190] **Sebastian Trevino**	[190] **October 10, 3:30 P.M.**	Master's degree in advertising; winner of Campaign Creativity Award; proficient in GoCreate
Margaret Echols	October 11, 10:00 A.M.	Master's degree in literature; 4 years project management; proficient in GoCreate

마케팅 진행 담당자 면접		
지원자	날짜 및 시간	채용 세부 정보
코리나 가이거	10월 8일 오후 2시	마케팅학 학사 학위; 프로젝트 관리 2년; 고크리에이트에 능숙함
[188] 병민 김	10월 8일 오후 4시	[188] 경영학 석사 학위; 프로젝트 관리 3년; 고크리에이트에 능숙함
대럴 크로퍼드	10월 9일 오후 1시	광고학 학사 학위; 개인 블로그 운영; 프로젝트 관리 3년
[190] 세바스찬 트레비노	[190] 10월 10일 오후 3시 30분	광고학 석사 학위; 광고 캠페인 창작상 수상; 고크리에이트에 능숙함
마거릿 에컬스	10월 11일 오전 10시	문학 석사 학위; 프로젝트 관리 4년; 고크리에이트에 능숙함

어휘 employment 고용, 채용 details ((항상 복수형)) 세부 정보 proficient 능숙한 personal 개인적인 literature 문학

From: Rhonda Fitch 〈rfitch@diazandassoc.com〉
To: William Austell 〈waustell@diazandassoc.com〉
Subject: Interview
Date: October 3

Hi William,

I would like you to ¹⁸⁹**cover** one of the interviews for the marketing coordinator position, as I don't want to reschedule it. ¹⁹⁰**Please interview Mr. Trevino on my behalf, as I've been invited to give a speech at a small business luncheon in Westerville on that day**, and I think this would be great exposure for our company. We can meet when I get back to discuss what you thought of the candidate.

Thank you so much!

Rhonda

발신: 론다 피치
수신: 윌리엄 오스텔
제목: 면접
날짜: 10월 3일

안녕하세요, 윌리엄 씨.

당신이 마케팅 진행 담당자 직무 면접 중 하나를 ¹⁸⁹**맡아 주셨으면** 해요. 면접 일정을 바꾸고 싶지 않아서요. ¹⁹⁰**저를 대신해서 트레비노 씨를 면접해 주세요. 제가 그날 웨스터빌의 작은 비즈니스 오찬에서 강연해 달라고 초대를 받았거든요.** 그리고 이것이 우리 회사를 알리기에 아주 좋을 거라고 생각해요. 제가 돌아오면 만나서 그 후보자에 대한 당신의 생각을 논의하면 돼요.

정말 고마워요!

론다

어휘 cover (부재중인 사람의 일을) 대신하다 reschedule 일정을 변경하다 on one's behalf ~을 대신하여 luncheon 오찬 exposure 알려짐, 노출

186. What is indicated about Diaz&Associates in the job posting?

(A) It is entering a new field.
(B) It was founded two years ago.
(C) It will open a new branch in Seattle.
(D) It specializes in security.

채용 공고에서 디아즈&어소시에이츠 사에 대해 명시된 것은 무엇인가?

(A) 새로운 분야에 진출할 것이다.
(B) 2년 전에 창립되었다.
(C) 시애틀에 새로운 지사를 열 것이다.
(D) 보안을 전문으로 한다.

해설 세부 사항 문제 첫 번째 지문의 첫 번째 단락에서 보험 업계로 사업을 확장할 것(we are expanding our business into the insurance industry)이라고 했으므로 (A)가 정답이다. (B)는 2년 전이 아니라 20년 전(We have been in operation for two decades)이기 때문에 오답이고, (C)는 시애틀에 기반을 둔 회사(Diaz&Associates, a Seattle-based firm)라고 했으므로 답이 될 수 없다. (D)는 보안이 아니라 재무 계획 서비스를 제공한다(dedicated to providing financial planning services)고 했으므로 오답이다.

패러프레이징 expanding our business into the insurance industry → entering a new field

어휘 enter 진입하다, 들어가다 field 분야; 현장 found 설립하다 specialize in ~을 전문으로 하다 security 보안, 경비

187. What is one responsibility mentioned in the job posting?

(A) Finding new customers
(B) Creating online content
(C) Traveling for events
(D) Conducting staff training

채용 공고에 언급된 한 가지 책무는 무엇인가?

(A) 새로운 고객을 찾는 것
(B) 온라인 콘텐츠를 만드는 것
(C) 행사를 위해 출장을 가는 것
(D) 직원 교육을 하는 것

해설 세부 사항 문제 첫 번째 지문의 두 번째 단락에서 직무를 자세히 설명하고 있다. 그중 하나가 온라인 소식지를 위한 기사를 작성하는 일(writing articles for our online newsletter)이므로 (B)가 정답이다. 나머지 선택지는 모두 언급된 내용이 없다.

패러프레이징 writing articles for our online newsletter → creating online content

어휘 responsibility 책임, 책무 create 만들어 내다, 창작하다 conduct (특정한 활동을) 하다, 수행하다

188. Who best matches the company's stated requirements and preferences?

(A) Ms. Geiger
(B) Mr. Kim
(C) Mr. Trevino
(D) Ms. Echols

누가 회사가 언급한 자격 요건과 선호 사항에 가장 잘 맞는가?

(A) 가이거 씨
(B) 김 씨
(C) 트레비노 씨
(D) 에컬스 씨

> 해설 　연계 문제 [세부 사항] 첫 번째 지문인 채용 공고에서 언급된 자격 요건과 두 번째 지문인 면접 일정표에 있는 지원자 정보를 종합해 정답을 찾아야 하는 연계 문제이다. 첫 번째 지문에서 3년간의 프로젝트 관리 경력(three years of project management experience)과 마케팅, 경영 또는 광고 분야의 학사 또는 석사 학위(A bachelor's or master's degree in marketing, business administration, or advertising)가 요구되며, 고크리에이트 디자인 소프트웨어에 능숙(Proficiency in GoCreate design software)하면 유리하다고 했는데, 이 세 가지 자격 요건을 모두 갖춘 지원자는 김 씨이므로 (B)가 정답이다.

> 어휘 　match 일치하다　preference 선호(하는 것)

189. In the e-mail, the word "cover" in paragraph 1, line 1, is closest in meaning to

(A) protect
(B) include
(C) conceal
(D) handle

이메일에서 첫 번째 단락 첫 번째 줄의 "cover"와 의미상 가장 가까운 것은?

(A) 보호하다
(B) 포함하다
(C) 숨기다
(D) 처리하다

> 해설 　동의어 찾기 문제 cover는 '대신하다; 덮다; 가리다; 다루다' 등 여러 가지 뜻으로 쓰인다. 여기서는 트레비노 씨의 면접을 '대신 맡아서' 진행해 달라는 의미이므로, 이와 가장 유사한 말은 (D) handle이다.

190. When will Ms. Fitch give a talk?

(A) On October 8
(B) On October 9
(C) On October 10
(D) On October 11

피치 씨는 언제 강연할 것인가?

(A) 10월 8일에
(B) 10월 9일에
(C) 10월 10일에
(D) 10월 11일에

> 해설 　연계 문제 [세부 사항] 세 번째 지문에서 피치 씨가 트레비노 씨 면접에 자기 대신 들어가 달라고(Please interview Mr. Trevino on my behalf) 부탁하면서, 자신은 그날 비즈니스 오찬에 강연 초청을 받았다(I've been invited to give a speech at a small business luncheon in Westerville on that day)고 했다. 두 번째 지문에 트레비노 씨의 면접 날짜가 10월 10일로 기재되어 있으므로 피치 씨는 10월 10일에 강연할 것임을 알 수 있다. 따라서 (C)가 정답이다.

> 어휘 　give a talk 강연하다

Home Matters

Does new insulation really make a difference?

An efficient insulation system offers both immediate and long-term benefits. The amount of energy needed to heat your home is greatly reduced when your walls and roof are properly insulated, 191 **making it both eco-friendly and economical. Without insulation, sounds can be easily carried between rooms. This can be corrected with thick insulation.**

193 **Some old types of insulation are hazardous to your health, and these are eligible for free removal and disposal through the government's recently launched Home Protections Program (HPP).**

Watson Insulation Services: In-Home Visit Request

Name: Melinda Varner   Date of request: May 1
Address: 956 Straford Park Drive, Grand Rapids, MI 49503
Phone/E-mail: 948-555-8701/m.varner@santiagopro.com
Preferred form of contact: [ ] phone   [✓] e-mail
Best Date(s)/Time(s) to visit:
Date(s):   May 9 or 10

194 **Time(s): [✓] morning (9–noon)**
           [ ] early afternoon (noon–2)
           [ ] late afternoon (2–4)
Type of request: [✓] provide pricing estimate
                 [ ] inspect previous work
                 [ ] other: _____

192 **All Watson Insulation employees are required to successfully complete a comprehensive hands-on education program to ensure their level of expertise is fit for the job.** This program is twice as long as those provided by our competitors, so you know you're getting the best of the best.

We will contact you within 2 business days of completing this form.

To: Melinda Varner ⟨m.varner@santiagopro.com⟩
From: Watson Insulation Services ⟨reply@watsoninsulation.com⟩
Date: May 9, 4:53 P.M.
Subject: Insulation installation
Attachment: Price quote

Dear Ms. Varner,

194 **I am following up on the home visit made by our technician, Jeremy Regan. I'm pleased that we could accommodate your request for the best time to visit.** Please find attached the official price quote that Mr. Regan has prepared. 193 **You will see that you will not be charged for removing the insulation, as it is eligible for free removal through HPP.** This quote is valid for thirty days, 195 **so please reply to this e-mail or call 555-9961 if you wish to go forward.**

Warmest regards,

Curtis Donahue

수신: 멜린다 바너
발신: 왓슨 단열 서비스
날짜: 5월 9일 오후 4시 53분
제목: 단열재 설치
첨부 파일: 가격 견적서

바너 씨께

194 저희 기술자 제레미 리건의 가정 방문에 대한 후속 조치로 연락을 드립니다. 최적의 방문 시간에 대한 귀하의 요청에 맞출 수 있었던 것을 기쁘게 생각합니다. 리건 씨가 준비한 공식 가격 견적서를 첨부합니다. 193 단열재 철거는 HPP를 통한 무료 철거 대상이기 때문에 이에 대해서는 비용이 청구되지 않을 거란 점을 아실 겁니다. 이 견적서는 30일간 유효하므로 195 작업을 진행하길 원하시면 이메일로 회신 주시거나 555-9961로 전화 주시기 바랍니다.

커티스 도나휴

> **어휘** installation 설치 follow up on ~에 후속 조치를 취하다 technician 기술자 accommodate (요구에) 부응하다 official 공식적인 price quote 가격 견적(서) prepare 준비하다 charge (요금을) 청구하다 remove 제거하다 valid 유효한; 타당한 reply to ~에 답하다 go forward (계획 따위를) 진척시키다

191. What is NOT indicated in the article as a benefit of insulation?

(A) Saving money
(B) Keeping out moisture
(C) Helping the environment
(D) Reducing noise disturbances

기사에서 단열재의 이점으로 명시되지 않은 것은?

(A) 돈을 절약하는 것
(B) 습기가 들어가지 않게 하는 것
(C) 환경에 도움이 되는 것
(D) 소음 공해를 줄여 주는 것

> **해설** 세부 사항 문제 첫 번째 지문의 첫 번째 단락에서 단열 시스템의 이점을 열거했는데, 습기 차단에 대해서는 언급하지 않았으므로 (B)가 정답이다. (A)는 집을 난방하는 데 드는 에너지가 상당히 줄어든다(The amount of energy needed to heat your home is greatly reduced)고 했으며, (C)는 난방 에너지가 줄어들기 때문에 친환경적이며 경제적(making it both eco-friendly and economical)이라고 나와 있다. 마지막으로 (D)는 단열재가 없으면 소리가 방과 방 사이로 쉽게 이동하는데, 두꺼운 단열재가 이 점을 바로잡는다(This can be corrected with thick insulation)고 했다.

> **패러프레이징** eco-friendly → helping the environment

> **어휘** save 아끼다, 절약하다 keep out ~가 들어가지 않게 하다 moisture 수분, 습기 disturbance 방해

192. What is mentioned about Watson Insulation Services?

(A) It only serves customers within Grand Rapids.
(B) It has lower prices than its competitors.
(C) Its staff members undergo extensive training.
(D) It does not offer visits on weekends.

왓슨 단열 서비스 사에 대해 언급된 것은?

(A) 그랜드 래피즈 내의 고객들에게만 서비스한다.
(B) 경쟁업체들보다 가격이 저렴하다.
(C) 직원들이 광범위한 교육을 받는다.
(D) 주말에는 방문을 하지 않는다.

해설 세부 사항 문제 두 번째 지문의 후반부에서 왓슨 단열의 전 직원은 종합적인 현장 교육 프로그램을 이수하라는 요구를 받는다고 했으므로 (C)가 정답이다.

패러프레이징 complete a comprehensive hands-on education program → undergo extensive training

어휘 serve (손님, 고객 등을) 응대하다   undergo 받다, 겪다, 경험하다   extensive 광범위한

193. What is suggested about Ms. Varner's property?

(A) It contains a harmful substance.
(B) It has insurance to cover repair work.
(C) It is owned by the government.
(D) It has some damage to its roof.

바너 씨의 건물에 대해 암시된 것은?

(A) 해로운 물질을 포함하고 있다.
(B) 수리 작업을 보장하는 보험에 가입되어 있다.
(C) 정부가 소유하고 있다.
(D) 지붕이 일부 파손되었다.

해설 연계 문제 [추론/암시] 첫 번째 지문의 마지막 단락에서 일부 구형 단열재는 건강에 유해하기(Some old types of insulation are hazardous to your health) 때문에 정부의 주택 보호 프로그램(HPP)을 통해 무료 철거 및 처리 대상(free removal and disposal)이 된다고 했다. 세 번째 지문의 후반부에서는 바너 씨 집의 단열재가 HPP를 통해 무료 철거 대상(it is eligible for free removal through HPP)이라고 한 것으로 보아 바너 씨의 집에 유해 단열재가 있다는 걸 알 수 있으므로 (A)가 정답이다.

패러프레이징 hazardous → harmful

어휘 property 부동산 (건물), 재산   substance 물질   insurance 보험   cover (보험으로) 보장하다   own 소유하다

194. What is true about Mr. Regan?

(A) He visited Ms. Varner's home in the morning.
(B) He needed two days to prepare a report.
(C) He suggested making an adjustment to an estimate.
(D) He is a founding member of the company.

리건 씨에 대해 사실인 것은?

(A) 오전에 바너 씨의 집에 방문했다.
(B) 보고서를 준비하기 위해 이틀이 필요했다.
(C) 견적을 조정할 것을 제안했다.
(D) 회사의 창립 멤버이다.

해설 연계 문제 [TRUE 문제] 질문의 키워드인 Mr. Regan은 세 번째 지문에 나오는데, 지문의 초반부에서 바너 씨가 원했던 시간에 맞춰 리건 씨가 방문했다(accommodate your request for the best time to visit)고 했다. 두 번째 지문에서 바너 씨가 기입한 방문 최적 시간대(Best Date(s)/Time(s) to visit)는 오전이었으므로, 리건 씨가 오전에 바너 씨의 집에 방문했다는 걸 알 수 있다. 따라서 (A)가 정답이다.

어휘 suggest 제안하다   make an adjustment 조정하다   estimate 견적; 견적을 내다   founding member 창립 멤버

195. What does Mr. Donahue ask Ms. Varner to do?

(A) Call the company to resolve a problem
(B) Provide details about the size of her home
(C) Send a deposit before starting the work
(D) Indicate whether she wants the work completed

도나휴 씨는 바너 씨에게 무엇을 하라고 요청하는가?

(A) 문제를 해결하기 위해 회사에 전화하기
(B) 그녀의 집 크기에 대해 세부 정보 제공하기
(C) 작업을 시작하기 전에 보증금 보내기
(D) 작업이 완료되는 걸 원하는지 알려 주기

해설 세부 사항 문제 질문의 키워드인 Mr. Donahue는 세 번째 지문인 이메일을 작성한 사람이다. 마지막 문장에서 작업 진행을 원하면 이메일이나 전화로 연락을 달라고(please reply to this e-mail or call 555-9961 if you wish to go forward) 했으므로 (D)가 정답이다.

어휘 resolve 해결하다   details ((항상 복수형)) 세부 정보   deposit 보증금, 착수금   indicate 나타내다, 보여 주다

To: inquiries@valley-rentals.net
From: Joseph Dansby <jdansby@avenueinsurance.net>
Date: August 6
Subject: Chair rental inquiry

To Whom It May Concern:

I am planning an awards banquet for my company, Avenue Enterprises, on Saturday, September 18. We will need three hundred chairs to accommodate our guests. I've never rented chairs before, but **196 someone at my office used your business for her friend's retirement party and highly recommended you**. Could you please let me know what options are available for us? **197 We have a budget of three dollars per chair** and can arrange to pick them up if necessary.

Sincerely,

Joseph Dansby

To: Joseph Dansby <jdansby@avenueinsrance.net>
From: inquiries@valley-rentals.net
Date: August 7
Subject: RE: Chair rental inquiry
Attachment: Price list

Dear Mr. Dansby,

Thank you for your interest in using Valley Rentals for your upcoming event. Please find attached our latest price list. You may place your rental order by replying to this e-mail. We are pleased to announce that **198 we have just added a folding chair option**. It is perfect for events in which you may need to clear the seating area quickly to make room for other activities. If you have any questions about the rental process, please let me know.

Warmest regards,

Marla Gonzalez

Valley Rentals: Chair Rentals Price List			
Item #	Description	Color Options	Daily Rate
197 **203**	Plastic Patio Chair	white, green	197 **$2.70**
204	Plastic Patio Chair with Armrests	white, green	$3.20
317	198 **Metal Folding Chair**	silver	198 **$3.80**
487	Hardwood Chair with Slotted Back	light brown, dark brown	$5.40
495	Aluminum and Wood Café-Style Chair	silver/black, silver/brown	$6.00

- Open daily, excluding public holidays.
- Items are cleaned thoroughly before dispatch and 200 **can be used in all weather conditions**.
- Customers may pick up items in person or pay a flat fee of $25.00 for delivery and pickup.
- 199 **Please call 697-555-0014 to inquire about getting up to sixty percent off rentals over extended periods.**

어휘 description 설명, 서술 rate 요금; 속도; 비율 slotted 기다란 구멍이 나 있는 excluding ~을 제외하고 thoroughly 철저하게 dispatch 발송; 파견; 보내다, 파견하다 in person 직접 flat fee 고정 금액 extended 길어진, 늘어난

196. What does Mr. Dansby indicate in the first e-mail?

(A) He has recently started working for Avenue Enterprises.
(B) He plans to use Valley Rentals' services regularly.
(C) He found out about the business through a coworker.
(D) He has been nominated for a company award.

해설 세부 사항 문제 댄스비 씨와 같은 사무실에서 일하는 어떤 사람이 친구의 은퇴 파티를 위해 이 업체를 이용해 본 후 적극 추천했다 (someone at my office used your business for her friend's retirement party and highly recommended you)고 했으므로 (C)가 정답이다.

패러프레이징 someone at my office → a coworker

어휘 recently 최근에 plan to do ~할 계획이다 regularly 정기적으로, 규칙적으로 find out ~을 알게 되다 coworker 함께 일하는 사람, 동료 be nominated for ~의 후보로 지명되다

197. Which item will Mr. Dansby most likely rent?

    (A) Item 203
    (B) Item 204
    (C) Item 487
    (D) Item 495

댄스비 씨는 어떤 제품을 빌릴 것 같은가?

    (A) 203번 제품
    (B) 204번 제품
    (C) 487번 제품
    (D) 495번 제품

> 해설   연계 문제 [추론/암시] 첫 번째 지문의 마지막 문장에서 의자 하나당 예산이 3달러라고(We have a budget of three dollars per chair) 했다. 세 번째 지문의 가격표에서 이 가격에 해당하는 의자는 203번 제품이므로 (A)가 정답이다.

---

198. What is the daily charge for Valley Rentals' newest chair type?

    (A) $2.70
    (B) $3.80
    (C) $5.40
    (D) $6.00

밸리 대여점의 최신 의자는 하루 요금이 얼마인가?

    (A) 2.70달러
    (B) 3.80달러
    (C) 5.40달러
    (D) 6.00달러

> 해설   연계 문제 [세부 사항] 두 번째 지문의 중반부에서 접이식 의자를 선택 사항에 추가한 지 얼마 안 되었다(we have just added a folding chair option)고 했다. 세 번째 지문의 가격표에 접이식 의자의 일일 사용료가 3.80달러라고 나와 있으므로 (B)가 정답이다.

> 어휘   daily charge 하루 요금

---

199. According to the price list, what is true about Valley Rentals?

    (A) It requires a $25 deposit for rental requests.
    (B) It provides discounts for long-term rentals.
    (C) It is open every day of the year.
    (D) It operates at more than one location.

가격표에 따르면 밸리 대여점에 대해 사실인 것은?

    (A) 대여 신청에 대해 보증금 25달러를 요구한다.
    (B) 장기 대여에 할인을 제공한다.
    (C) 일 년 내내 문을 연다.
    (D) 한 장소 이상에서 운영된다.

> 해설   세부 사항 문제 세 번째 지문 하단의 마지막 문장에서 장기 대여 시 60%까지 할인을 받을 수 있다(getting up to sixty percent off rentals over extended periods)며 이와 관련해 문의할 수 있는 전화번호를 제시한 것으로 보아 (B)가 정답이다. 25달러는 배송 및 수거 수수료(a flat fee of $25.00 for delivery and pickup)라고 했으므로 (A)는 오답이다. 또한 공휴일을 제외하고 매일 운영한다(Open daily, excluding public holidays)고 했으므로 (C)도 틀린 설명이다.

> 패러프레이징   rentals over extended periods → long-term rentals

> 어휘   require 요구하다, 필요로 하다   deposit 보증금   long-term 장기적인   operate 영업하다, 운영하다   location 위치, 장소

---

200. What is suggested in the price list about all Valley Rentals chairs?

    (A) They will be delivered at no cost.
    (B) They are inspected for damage before the rental.
    (C) They are suitable to use outdoors.
    (D) They should be cleaned before being returned.

밸리 대여점의 의자 전체에 대해 가격표에 암시되어 있는 것은?

    (A) 무료로 배달될 것이다.
    (B) 대여 전에 파손에 대한 점검을 받을 것이다.
    (C) 야외에서 사용하기에 적절하다.
    (D) 반납되기 전에 세척되어야 한다.

> 해설   추론/암시 문제 세 번째 지문의 하단 설명 중 모든 날씨 상태에서 사용할 수 있다(can be used in all weather conditions)고 한 것으로 보아 날씨의 영향을 받는 야외에서도 사용할 수 있다는 걸 알 수 있으므로 (C)가 정답이다. 25달러의 배송 및 수거 수수료(a flat fee of $25.00 for delivery and pickup)가 있다고 했으므로 (A)는 오답이다. 대여를 보내기 전에 철저하게 세척된다(Items are cleaned thoroughly before dispatch)고 했으므로 파손 점검을 받을 거라고 한 (B)도 틀린 설명이다.

> 어휘   at no cost 무료로   inspect 점검하다, 검사하다   damage 손상, 피해   suitable 알맞은, 적절한   outdoors 야외에서

정답 및 해설

에듀윌 토익 베이직 READING RC
정답 및 해설

고객의 꿈, 직원의 꿈, 지역사회의 꿈을 실현한다

에듀월 도서몰
book.eduwill.net
- 부가학습자료 및 정오표: 에듀월 도서몰 > 도서자료실
- 교재 문의: 에듀월 도서몰 > 문의하기 > 교재(내용, 출간) / 주문 및 배송